McGRAW-HILL PUBLICATIONS IN PSYCHOLOGY
JOHN F. DASHIELL, Ph.D., Consulting Editor

Personality Maladjustments
and
Mental Hygiene

McGraw-Hill Publications in Psychology
JOHN F. DASHIELL
CONSULTING EDITOR

Personality Maladjustments
and
Mental Hygiene

A TEXTBOOK FOR STUDENTS OF MENTAL HYGIENE
PSYCHOLOGY, EDUCATION, SOCIOLOGY, AND COUNSELING

BY

J. E. WALLACE WALLIN, Ph.D.

*Visiting Professor of Clinical Psychology, Upsala College.
Former Director of Psychoeducational Clinics and
Special Education and Mental Hygiene Depart-
ments in the University of Pittsburgh, Miami
University, and the Departments of Edu-
cation in St. Louis, Baltimore,
Wilmington, and Delaware*

SECOND EDITION

NEW YORK   TORONTO   LONDON
McGRAW-HILL BOOK COMPANY, Inc.
1949

PERSONALITY MALADJUSTMENTS AND MENTAL HYGIENE

To

F. T. W., V. S. W., AND G. T. W.

AND THE
PARENTS AND TEACHERS OF AMERICA,
THE PRIMARY ARCHITECTS
OF THE WHOLESOME PERSONALITY DEVELOPMENT
OF THE NATION'S CHILDREN

PREFACE TO THE SECOND EDITION

Before this revision was launched, suggestions were invited by the publishers from a number of university professors, and by the author from graduate and undergraduate students who had used the book as a text, regarding recommended modifications, deletions, and additions. A great number of the suggestions from professors and students alike involved only minor alterations, deletions, or additions. Some suggestions, however, were rather discrepant, and some were irreconcilable. Only one instructor suggested any considerable deletions, additions, and regroupings. The regroupings were designed to provide a more logical, systematic arrangement of some of the materials.

The choice and organization of the topics and the wealth of concrete illustrations and recommendations in the first edition represent the winnowings of extensive classroom experimentation, in the attempt to render mental-hygiene concepts and principles meaningful and vital to the student and mental-hygiene suggestions practically effective in the program for the prevention of maladjustments and the preservation of mental soundness. These being the prime objectives, the main concern has been with the effective presentation of the vital truths of mental hygiene, rather than with implementing a meticulously exact or logical structuralization of the material.

Although by far the larger number of the students felt that certain suggested rearrangements would not greatly improve the vitality of the presentation or greatly modify the over-all effect of the practical message that the book is intended to convey, the material in the new edition has been arranged in 17 chapters, instead of 11, through the splitting of chapters and the regrouping of certain contents. The material on psychotherapeutic methods has been transferred from Chap. I to Chap. VI and greatly expanded. New sections have been added on different forms of expressive and release therapy (nondirective therapy, therapeutic interviewing and counseling, play techniques, the psychodrama, group therapy, hypnotherapy, psychosurgery, electro-shock treatment). A new chapter on the educational elements and implications of the mental-hygiene program contains the material formerly in Sec. 4 of Chap. III, besides additions. The practical suggestions in Chap. VIII and in the Appendix for preventing or overcoming various maladjustments have been combined in Chap. IX. Sections (rather than chapters, because of space limitations) have been added on basic human urges and needs, the endocrine glands, the atomic age, the psychology of the dictators, and projective techniques; and the material on hysteria has been somewhat enlarged. The sections can readily be extended by the resourceful instructor if he so desires.

Under the reorganization, the material on psychoanalysis occupies the last five chapters. My experience has been that students are keenly interested in this subject, and that is why it has been retained in the new edition. These chapters can, of course, be omitted without serious damage to the earlier chapters if such omission is found desirable in brief courses, or if the instructor prefers not to deal with this phase of the problem, or if he deems it more important to devote time to other problems.

Some case histories have been deleted to make room for the new additions referred to above and for "snapshots" from the current scene of personality aberrations of presumably normal persons at large in society. These highly condensed biographical pictures supply more pointed illustrations of the psychological principles and dynamisms discussed in the text than many of the less extreme or less dramatic adjustment problems presented by the normal student population. They should add high lights to the picture of personality distortions and handicaps and adjustment difficulties of the "normal" (noninstitutional) population at large in society.

Extensive topical lists of references have been added throughout the book and the final bibliography has been greatly modified, extended, and brought down to the date when the manuscript went to the publisher. It has not been possible to include all references to contributions to the field that have appeared since the manuscript was turned over to the publishers, although a few last-minute publications have been added.

It is a pleasure to extend my gratitude to the writers of the numerous letters that have come from many parts of the country expressing appreciation for the benefits that have been derived from study of the first edition; also, to the students and instructors for the suggestions offered in connection with this much-delayed revision. Miss Virginia S. Wallin has cooperated in the preparation of the final draft of the manuscript, in proofreading the galleys, in preparing the author index, and in typing certain sections.

J. E. WALLACE WALLIN

LYNDALIA, DEL.
August, 1949

PREFACE TO THE FIRST EDITION

This book is the outcome of the first-hand investigation of numerous cases of mental defects, disabilities, and adjustment difficulties, and of the perusal of a wealth of technical memoirs, monographs, and books in the field of personality defects and mental hygiene. It first appeared in the form of lectures on personality maladjustments and mental hygiene offered both to popular audiences and to students in courses in a number of universities. The casework includes over 13,000 examinations of children and youths subject to all kinds of handicaps and difficulties, referred by schools, courts, social agencies, homes, and other organizations, and the investigation of personality maladjustments in college and university graduate and undergraduate students.

In spite of the many years devoted to the accumulation of the data—the publication has been long postponed in order to afford more time for first-hand investigation and reflection—the author would caution the reader against regarding the book as a finished product and against assuming that finality has been reached in this discussion of personality problems and mental hygiene. So intricate and difficult of analysis and solution are the problems of the development and distortion of personality traits, and so recently, comparatively speaking, have the methods of science been applied to their study, that we are merely in the pioneering stage of the investigation of some of the most baffling and significant problems of the psychic and social life of modern man. It is inevitable that the improved research techniques that the psychology and psychiatry of the next few decades will perfect will contribute a truer and deeper understanding of the mechanisms discussed in this text. Undoubtedly significant modifications and refinements of the fundamental concepts of personality growth and improved methods for the prevention of maladjustments are in the offing.

It has seemed to the author that the best approach to an understanding of the problems of mental health and mental hygiene is to begin with a preliminary exposition of the positive concept of mental health and the wholesome personality, the different objectives and factors of the mental-hygiene program, and the types of cases with which mental hygiene is concerned, and then proceed to a detailed discussion of the symptoms of personality maladjustments as they are revealed in the numerous faulty and unwholesome reaction patterns that unadjusted or poorly adjusted people, and even apparently well-adjusted people, utilize in the effort to solve their problems, indicating the evils and possible virtues of each mode of inadequate response and the remedial measures required to correct it. A discussion of such faulty adjustment mechanisms, made vital and concrete through the introduction of a large number of original autobiographies of maladjustments of numerous types, should enable the student to acquire a vivid recognition of behavior patterns which are indicative of personality disturbances and faulty mental adjustments, and which, if continued, may tend toward the development of serious mental conflicts and mental derailment.

Although the aim has been to canvass all the significant kinds of faulty reaction types and to outline the important remedial, preventive, and preservative aspects of the mental-hygiene program with respect to its physical, psychological, social, and educational factors, it is obvious that there are other methods of approach to the topic and many fields of application of mental-hygiene principles that could not receive consideration in this book without undue expansion of the contents.

The aim of this book is to introduce the student to the problems of mental health and mental hygiene. He should be urged to familiarize himself with the points of view of other writers. For this purpose a fairly complete list of references, topically arranged, is supplied at the end of the book. A few titles marked with an asterisk will, it is believed, prove of most value to teachers or educators, either because of the comprehensiveness of the publication or because of the introductory or nontechnical character of the discussion or because the contents are of peculiar significance for education.

It is the author's belief that the method of treatment of the problems of mental health and mental hygiene followed in this book will prove equally adapted to the needs and interests of teachers, educators, psychologists, social- and mental-hygiene workers, physicians, psychiatrists, and intelligent parents. The case histories, which have been contributed through the generous and invaluable cooperation of the author's graduate and undergraduate students, an excellent cross section of the normal population, are couched in language that can be comprehended by any intelligent parent or high-school student. The theoretical and topical discussions have been made as direct and as free as possible from unnecessary technical terms, and an attempt has been made to explain briefly the technical words that have been introduced.

A certain amount of repetition is inevitable in treating a highly ramified subject with many close interrelations; in fact many aspects are largely phases of the same problem. The consensus among students who have listened to the lectures is that the repetitions are distinctly advantageous rather than disadvantageous. Until the student has become thoroughly conversant with the subject matter, repetition should make the presentation more effective by clearing up ambiguities, by supplying more varied application of principles, and by fixation of the learning process.

J. E. W. W.

WILMINGTON, DELAWARE.,
September, 1935.

CONTENTS

PART I

INTRODUCTION

CHAPTER I

THE CONCEPT OF MENTAL HEALTH AND MENTAL HYGIENE

The Field of Mental Hygiene; Mental Health and Mental Hygiene as Complex Problems of Science. Stated most succinctly, mental hygiene deals with the attainment and preservation of mental health. Such a simple statement may be fraught with unjustifiable implications or interpretations. To many it may suggest that mental health is a simple, all-inclusive, independent quality of mind that can be easily attained by the conscious acceptance of certain beliefs or by the mechanical or wishful repetition of certain potent phrases or formulas of an all-sufficient, all-embracing cult or discipline called mental hygiene. Emile Coué's formula for the attainment of health, assiduously repeated by millions, is still fresh in memory:

Every day in every way,
I am getting better and better.

Thousands have relaxed and meditated upon the mantra:

I am a soul of mighty power;
I am triumphant every hour.

Meditation upon such slogans or maxims may not be without value in instilling desirable, positive mind sets, but the fact is that mental health is not an isolated, independent aspect of life attainable by mere acts of wishing or resolution. Nor is there any discipline, science, or art that can be regarded as a unitary, all-inclusive, independent science or art of mental hygiene. On the contrary, mental health is a highly complex condition that involves many elements and is dependent upon many factors, while mental hygiene, at its best, represents a careful winnowing of the pertinent facts and conclusions from many fields of knowledge, such as psychology, education, psychiatry, sociology, physiology, biology, medicine, and hygiene. Accordingly adequate programs of mental well-being and mental hygiene must be as comprehensive as the complexity of the organism with which they are concerned, and they must grant due consideration to all the factors that affect its growth and development.

The Ancient Mind-Body Controversy. It is obvious that the position you assume on the age-old speculative question of the relation of the "body"

3

and the "mind" to each other will vitally affect your system of mental hygiene. What is the issue involved in this controversy? The issue can be very briefly stated. Can the organism ultimately be reduced to one element or substance? If so, what is the nature of this substance? Is it matter, is it mind, or is it something else? Or, if ultimate reality cannot be reduced to one substance, how many ultimate entities are there?

The doctrine that reduces ultimate reality to one element is known as monism. According to one school of monists, ultimate reality consists of matter, possibly some irreducible chemical or electrical element, while another group of monists holds that the ultimate "thing-in-itself" is mental or spiritual in nature. The doctrine of dualism, as opposed to monism, maintains that there are two irreducible elements—namely, matter and mind—each separate and distinct. The doctrine of interactionism, which accepts the dualistic assumption that reality consists of two separate and independent ultimate entities, maintains that these entities are capable of acting upon each other in some way. In opposition to monism and dualism, the doctrine of pluralism denies that reality can be reduced to one or two elements. Ultimate reality consists of numerous irreducible elements that cannot be converted into one another. Of what practical import are these philosophical questions to the mental hygienist?

The answer the mental hygienist gives to these apparently irrelevant metaphysical speculations regarding the nature of ultimate reality or regarding the relations of the mental and the physical will in a large measure determine what he will include in his program of mental hygiene. To illustrate: Christian Science is a system of metaphysics, treatment, and religious doctrine which denies the existence of matter and affirms the universality of mind, declaring that all sickness is an error of the mind and completely replacing the medical treatment of disease with a system of faith cure or mental treatment. It is, after all, a system of psychotherapy (psychic treatment) based on the doctrine of psychic monism. Sharply contrasting with this system of cure is the practice of a thoroughly materialistic materia medica, which limits the healing art to the drug or surgical treatment of the diseased or malfunctioning organ and which undervalues or completely neglects the treatment of the patient as a whole, as a functional unity. Such an attitude is unconcerned about the adjustment of the patient's more complicated personality disturbances by agencies other than those of physical medication. This crass "materialistic" system of treatment, followed perhaps by only a limited number of the disciples of medicine, is now happily waning.

The Relation of the Mental and the Physical in Mental-health Conservation: The Organism an Inseparable, Interdependent, Interacting Psychophysical Unit. What is the point of view of the author upon this historical, philosophical question? The writer believes that systems of mental hygiene and mental treatment (psychotherapy) will become more scientific and will prove more successful practically if the human organism is conceived as a highly complex ensemble of mental and physical traits and functions that are inextricably intertwined and interdependent; that these factors exert a reciprocal influence upon one another and are mutually affected by numerous environmental and hereditary influences that conduce toward mental soundness or unsoundness. In fact, the Cartesian dichotomy into the mental and the physical, with the assumption that the physical is subject to mechanical laws while the mental is not, was repudiated long ago by the science of psychology. The human organism, at least as we know it here and now phenomenologically, is a psychosomatic unity. The bodily and the mental are merely two aspects of the same unitary organism, subject to a common set of laws, just as the obverse and the reverse are merely two sides of the same shield, the one as indispensable as the other. It would be just as fantastic to attempt to separate the mental and the physical as to attempt to separate the locomotive from its functions. Organic structure and function constitute an indissoluble integration, and no sharp line of demarcation can be drawn between nervous function and mental activity, at least so far as concerns the practical control of the individual's reactions. One can separate the soma and the psyche in thought, but not in reality. The ultimate nature of the processes is unknown and is the problem of metaphysics and religion, not of scientific psychology. The organism functions at all times as a more or less highly integrated unity and must at all times be studied in its totality and not in artificially dissected parts. It should be clearly understood, therefore, that when in this book, as a matter of convenience or as a matter of habit, we employ the terms "mental," "physical," the "mind," and the "body," we are not postulating two separate entities. We are merely referring to two phases of one unitary organism, without attempting to determine the ultimate nature of this organism. We are employing words that have become a part of our linguistic heritage without implying that we are dealing with two disparate substances.

In accordance with this organismic concept, we are, then, dealing with a multiphase organism, an inseparable whole, whose organs and functions exert a reciprocal influence upon one another, and which is influenced by the total environmental situation at all times, and whose behavior patterns represent an ensemble of "bodily" and "mental," social and individual, novel and habitual, constitutional and acquired, conscious and unconscious, emotional, motor, perceptual, and intellectual components. An attempt at refining the definition of these universally employed terms is the function of a text in psychology rather than one in mental hygiene. But any program for the attainment and maintenance of mental health that neglects any vital factors that influence this complex organism is one-sided, incomplete, and unsatisfactory.

But is there any evidence to indicate that "mental" and "physical" factors exert a reciprocal influence upon one another? To present a complete summary of the relevant observational facts and experimental data and expert opinions would take us too far afield. Nevertheless, an adequate comprehension of the problem of how to develop a healthy personality requires at least a cursory acquaintance with the facts, which show that bodily conditions can modify the individual's behavior and that mental states may influence the physical organism.

Facts Suggestive of the Influence of the Physical upon the Mental. Two lines of evidence will be briefly presented.

The first and more important of these deals with evidence that is derived from *the study of bodily diseases, injuries, and defects, which sometimes produce sudden and profound mental disturbances, or subtle, insidiously developing personality distortions or conduct disorders.* Thus, a blow on the head or the bursting of a cerebral blood vessel may produce sudden stupor or unconsciousness, while a blood clot in a blood vessel of the brain may lead to partial loss of memory, loss of speech, or localized motor paralysis. Disturbances in the sense organs may produce hallucinations[1] or illusions.[2] Similarly, a sluggish liver tends to produce a sluggish mind, while irritability and testiness are frequently the product of dyspepsia, rheumatism, headaches, or neurasthenia. Old grouches are often the victims of dyspepsia.

According to T. Wingate Todd, Samuel Johnson's nervous depressions in 1766 were caused by his chronic indigestion. Chronic indigestion, Todd maintains, often goes with brilliance of imagery and creative thought. This thought is conveyed in the expression, "quick wit and queasy stomach." Todd seems to attribute Darwin's imagery to his chronic indigestion.

Persistent insomnia is sometimes responsible for inattention, loss of memory, irritability, apprehension, and emotional instability. Excessive fatigue may produce inattention, muscular incoordination, memory lapses, temper tantrums, and in certain cases momentary hallucinations and delusions. It is known that jaundice does not conduce to generosity or philanthropy. Heart sensations or aortic disease may induce anxiety and apprehension, while advanced nephritis (kidney disease) often results in delirium. A variety of mental disturbances can sometimes be traced to protein poisons and toxemias, while mental activity may be slowly impaired by dental infection (oral sepsis).

Mental normality is most intimately dependent upon normal cortical activity. Serious numerical insufficiency or lack of development of the cortical nerve cells (neurons) may produce varying degrees of mental impairment, from idiocy to backwardness, while brain inflammations sometimes have a

---

[1] A subjective perception of an object in the absence of an objective stimulus.

[2] A perverted or false perception, a mistaken apprehension of an actual objective stimulus.

devastating effect on behavior. The brain disease referred to in newspaper parlance as sleeping sickness, technically called "encephalitis lethargica," often produces the most profound personality distortions. Child victims of the disease who have been previously stable and well-behaved may become restless, irritable, quarrelsome, disobedient, destructive, impudent, or criminally inclined; or they may grow apathetic, dull, or deficient.

An adequate discussion of the effects of the malfunctioning of the glandular system upon mental health and efficiency and upon physical normality would require a volume. In the condensation that follows, illustrative defects are presented from dysfunctioning of four of the most important glands.

Endocrine Gland Disorders. Mental and physical health and efficiency are intimately related to the balanced, integrated action of the glandular and nervous systems. Our knowledge of the endocrine glands (also called "ductless glands" and "glands of internal secretion") still contains many gaps, although it has been greatly enriched by the intensive research of the last few decades. Because of the present limitations of endocrinology, some of the statements here made should be regarded as tentative.

The endocrine glands, which are ductless—that is, without external outlets —pour their secretions (known as "hormones" or "autacoids") directly into the lymph or blood stream, which carries them to all parts of the body. The endocrine system includes the following glands: (1) the thyroid, which weighs about an ounce and which straddles the upper part of the trachea; (2) the four parathyroids, each about the size of a pea, adjacent to the thyroid or embedded in it; (3) the thymus, in the lower neck region beneath the upper part of the sternum; (4) the pineal, a pea-sized, cone-shaped organ near the pituitary; (5) the pituitary (also called "hypophysis"), about the size of a hazelnut, situated at the base of the brain in a protecting, saddle-shaped bony cavity (called *sella turcica*); (6) the two adrenals, one at the upper end of each kidney; and two glands that possess both duct and ductless functions, namely, (7) the pancreas (whose internal secretion, from the islands of Langerhans, is called "insulin") and (8) the gonads, or sex glands (the reproductive cells and the hormone from the interstitial cells).

The secretions of the ductless glands play a central role in the human economy through their effects upon the nervous system and the chemistry of the blood. They vitally affect metabolism; tissue differentiation; mental and physical growth; sex activity; the general energy and efficiency of the circulatory, gastrointestinal, muscular, and nervous systems; and the personality make-up of the individual. Some of the glands—such as the adrenal, thyroid, and sex glands—are very susceptible to emotional disturbances. The best known alterations probably affect the blood sugar and calcium, especially in the direction of deficient secretion. A reduction of blood sugar (hypoglycemia) [3] and calcium (hypocalcemia) impairs or disorganizes the functioning of the nervous system more or less, depending upon the extent of the deficiency. Nervous tissue cannot function without an adequate supply of blood sugar.

The endrocrine glands constitute one unitary system, which is as highly integrated as the nervous system. They are closely related to one another and to the nervous system and react upon one another. The health of each gland affects the functional efficiency of all the others. Some glands reinforce one another, while the influence of others is antagonistic. Thus the thyroid and the adrenal glands increase the basal metabolic rate. The thyroid probably cannot function without the thyrotropic hormone from the pituitary. The thyroid exerts a stimulating effect on the thymus, while the thymus, which slowly atrophies during early adolescence, probably inhibits the activity of the sex glands before puberty.

The effects on the functions of the organism of the malfunctioning of the glands vary greatly with the extent of the deficient or excessive functioning. Although slight deviations doubtless occur more frequently than large ones, they often go unrecognized.

Many adjustment difficulties of children and adults that, no doubt, are caused by endocrine dysfunctioning may not be recognized as such. On the basis of the examination of 1,000 successive cases of child behavior disorders, Louis A. Lurie concluded that 20 per cent showed endocrine disturbance, the glandular disturbance (especially of the pituitary) being the principal cause of the malbehavior.[4] Of 68 behavior cases with endocrine disorders, Allan Rowe classified 57 as pituitary cases.[4] Of 97 glandular cases among delinquents in the Jamesburg, N.J., State Home for Boys, 59 were classed as hyperpituitary cases, 33 as hypopituitary, and 5 as adiposogenital cases. The ratio of inmates classed as endocrine cases is not stated.[5] Severe disturbances of some of these glands are almost always reflected in mental concomitants, direct or indirect. The indirect effects, the result of the subject's attitude toward his defects, are sometimes far more important than is the direct effect (the weakness, the fat accumulation, the girlish voice, etc.). The morbid consciousness of the presence of corpulence or hirsutism (hairiness) may produce timidity, shyness, seclusiveness, introversion, self-pity, or feelings of inadequacy and possibly compensatory aggressiveness or antisocial behavior. Unfortunately, many gaps still exist in the psychology of the different forms of endocrinopathy. Most of our knowledge is based upon uncon-

---

[3] "Hypo" (under) means deficient; "hyper" (over) means excessive.

[4] Louis A. Lurie, "Endocrinology and the Understanding and Treatment of the Exceptional Child," *Proceedings of the Fourth Institute on the Exceptional Child of the Woods Schools,* Langhorne, Pa., 1937, 6–19.

[5] Matthew Molitch and Sam Poliakoff, "Pituitary Disturbances in Behavior Problems," *The American Journal of Orthopsychiatry,* 1936, 125–133.

trolled observational data, the subjective estimates or clinical evaluations of psychologically untrained observers. The literature based on the results of controlled, objective psychological tests is comparatively scant, except for that on certain types, such as the cretin, mongol, and pituitary children.

This review must be limited to the presentation of the most striking physical and mental abnormalities associated with extreme defects of four important endocrine glands: (1) the thyroid gland, which regulates oxygen combustion, metabolism, the rate of respiration and circulation, mental activity, and the activity of the reproductive organs; (2) the pituitary gland (sometimes called the master gland), which secretes a half dozen different hormones that influence the activities of the thyroid, the adrenal gland, the sex glands, and the pancreatic glands, metabolism in general, and body growth; (3) the adrenal glands, the "energy" glands that secrete a hormone, the most powerful of all the hormones, which regulates the circulation and blood pressure and sex activity; and (4) the parathyroids, which secrete parathormone—a hormone that controls calcium metabolism, which in turn regulates neuromuscular excitability, heart contractions, blood clotting, and ossification of the bones.

Hyper- and Hypothyroidism; Goiter. Someone has remarked that a "pinch too little of thyroxine spells idiocy, a pinch too much spells raving delirium." [6] Although a slight dose of thyroid extract may have a sedative influence, large doses produce an exciting effect—nervousness, restlessness, and insomnia— that may last two or three days. The "thyroid personality," produced by a moderate degree of oversecretion, is characterized by vivacity, alertness, initiative, emotional lability, restless energy, and sometimes brilliance. Marked hyperthyroidism produces an acceleration of the heart, increased oxygen consumption, a heightened metabolic rate, loss of weight, excess calcium secretion, muscular tremors, nervousness, insomnia, and emotional instability. Excessive hyperthyroidism is typical of various kinds of goiter, which often result from lack of iodine in the food, water, and soil. They may possibly arise from other causes, such as excess of lime in the water, infection, or a fungus growth (André Crotti). In exophthalmic goiter (or Graves', or Basedow's, or Parry's disease), characterized by protruding eyes ("popeyes"), the excess secretion has become toxic (thyrotoxicosis). The toxic discharge tends to produce restlessness, irritability, throbbing, heightened blood pressure, cardiac weakness, sweating, blushing, tremors, a startled expression, and emotional instability. Extreme cases develop a mental disorder characterized by excitement, anxiety, confusion, delusions, and hallucinations. This condition usually affects adults and occurs in women seven or eight times as often as in men. Treatment, fairly successful in many cases, may consist of surgery

[6] Roy G. Hoskins, *Endocrinology, The Glands and Their Functions*, New York, W. W. Norton & Company, Inc., 1941, 101.

(the most effective form), X-ray irradiation, and sometimes the administration of iodine.

The adolescent form of goiter, which usually develops between the ages of 10 and 17, often tends to disappear spontaneously as adulthood approaches but the thyroid may degenerate and become toxic. As was shown by David C. Kimball, a few grains of iodine salt reduced the percentage of goitrous children in Detroit from 36 per cent in 1924 to 2.1 per cent 7 years later.[7]

Cretinism and Myxedema. The contrasting condition, complete lack of thyroid secretion (athyroidism or hypothyroidism), produces a low grade of mental defectiveness known as "cretinism" when the thyroid deficiency dates from very early life, and as childhood and adult "myxedema" when it begins, respectively, in childhood and in adulthood. Both cretinism and myxedema are characterized by mental torpor, the slowing of the bodily processes because of a low metabolic rate, and the accumulation of fat.

The physical characteristics of the frank, untreated adult cretin of the sporadic (or congenital or aplastic) [8] type include, among other features, dwarfish stature (commonly from about 3 to 4 feet), affecting the trunk and especially the limbs; bent spine and legs; a fat, bloated appearance; a pendulous abdomen; dry, scaly, sallow skin; puffy eyelids, with narrow palpebral fissures; harsh, coarse black hair; a large, long, heavy head; a short neck; a broad face, with thick lips and tongue, a wrinkled forehead, prominent cheekbones, and a dull, unobservant, apathetic expression; large, flexible ears; a broad, flat nose, with depressed bridge and flexible tip; broad hands with short fingers and flabby, wrinkled skin; and infantile genitalia, with delayed puberty and sterility. The ossification of the bones is retarded, with unfilled cartilaginous spaces; the pituitary gland is frequently hypertrophied; the brain, although enlarged, may contain many inert hypoplastic (imperfectly developed) cells. Subnormal temperature and chronic constipation are ever present, while umbilical hernia is a frequent complication. The typical untreated cretin is an apathetic, unobservant imbecile, who is docile, placid, good-natured, inoffensive, rather imperturbable, and somewhat shy. His speech is thick, indistinct, low-pitched, and greatly retarded. His gait is slow and waddling. The continuous administration of thyroid tablets (usually made from the thyroid glands of sheep) in proper dosage often produces a magical physical transformation and may also produce considerable mental improvement, especially if it is begun during the first year or two. The cretin then becomes brighter and more interested, observant, responsive, and

---

[7] Inactive goiters exhibit the symptoms of hypothyroidism.

[8] The sporadic cretin, the prototype, occurs occasionally anywhere outside of goitrous areas. The endemic cretin, who comes from goitrous areas, while presenting certain differences, is also caused by the lack of secretion of the thyroid gland, even though it may be enlarged.

sociable. He may be able to realize his native intellectual potentials, be they low or high.

Lurie's evidence seems to show that milder forms of hypothyroidism in young children often lead to pronounced motor restlessness, destructiveness, and speech defects that can be overcome by "appropriate glandular therapy." [9]

Adult myxedema, commonly developing in middle life and affecting women far more frequently than men, is, in the more severe cases, characterized by chilliness, with cold hands and feet, due to a subnormal temperature of several degrees; growing obesity, with bloated appearance; thickening of the tongue, lips, and vocal cords (which lowers the pitch of the voice); growing forgetfulness, inability to concentrate, indecision, loss of initiative, lack of endurance, dissatisfaction, and distrust. In the most extreme cases the disorder may culminate in a psychosis (mental disease) characterized by confusion; uncontrollable actions; delusions (false judgments or beliefs that are immune to logical or factual evidence); and hallucinations of sight, hearing, smell, and taste.

Hypo- and Hyperpituitarism; Dwarfism. Serious undersecretion of the growth hormone (somatropin) of the anterior lobe of the pituitary gland (hypopituitarism) during the first few years after birth causes symmetrical dwarfism, also referred to as "nanism," "nanosomia," or the "Lorain-Levi" type of infantilism. Such mature midgets are miniature adults, who present a graceful appearance with normal body proportions. All body parts are small, including the face, head, hands, and feet. The fingers are narrow and tapering, and the hair is soft and silky. The genitalia are infantile and the secondary sex characteristics are only partly developed. Sterility in women and impotence in men are common sequelae. Those undersized from birth are sometimes referred to as cases of pituitary infantilism, although this term has usually been reserved for the Fröhlich deviates. Some pituitary dwarfs tend to retain childish personality traits and constitute cases of psychic infantilism. Their immature facial expression (facial juvenilism) assumes a wizened appearance as they undergo premature aging. While some are mentally retarded, the majority are alert, intellectually normal, or bright. They tend to be somewhat aggressive, probably as a protective defense against their diminutive size.

The undersecretion of the growth hormone may be due to congenital hypoplasia (incomplete development) or to a lesion of the gland, produced by an infection or by a tumorous growth. Injection of the missing growth hormone (possibly in combination with the gonadotropic factor) has not proved very efficacious; it increases the height by only from 6 to 9 inches. Many of these midgets tend to die young from some intercurrent disease.

[9] *Op. cit.,* 10f.

A contrasting type of dwarf—many varieties exist—originates in intra-uterine life from some obscure disturbance (perhaps involving one or more glands) that interferes with the development of the cartilage part (*a chondros,* "without cartilage") at the end of the long bones and causes premature union of the epiphyses (bones that are separated from the long bones in early life). This is the strong-man type, of circus fame, known as "achondroplastic" dwarf. The condition is also referred to as "Ollier's disease." The chief physical characteristic is gross asymmetry between the trunk, which is about normal in length, and the limbs. The latter are very short, thickened, enlarged at the joints, and muscular. The skull appears large, with prominent forehead, while the bridge of the nose is saddle-shaped. While many of these dwarfs are normal or above normal in intelligence, energy, and foresight, some are mentally limited in varying degrees and require special educational adjustments in school. Not enough psychological studies have been made to determine the percentage of mental deficients among them. Such pupils should be treated as normal persons and not as curios. No attention should be directed to their physical anomalies and they should not be subjected to invidious comparisons or derisive comments because of their diminutive size. No medical treatment exists for achondroplasia, other than overcoming localized limb deformities, knock-knees, and bowlegs by proper orthopedic procedures.

Gigantism. Excessive secretion of the growth hormone (or of the acid-staining cells, known as "acidophile") of the anterior lobe (hyperpituitarism) in childhood or adolescence, before the calcification of the epiphyses, results in a form of symmetrical overdevelopment known as "gigantism," the opposite of pituitary dwarfism. The height of the pituitary giant varies from 6½ to 8 feet. The limbs, hands, and feet are excessively long, with arm span exceeding the total stature and the lower limbs exceeding the trunk measurement. In about 50 per cent of the cases, the thyroid is enlarged. The early stages are characterized by rapid growth, excessive muscular strength, and hyper-sexuality. The terminal hypofunctional stage, after the disorder has burned itself out, is marked by muscular weakness, obesity, somnolence, genital regression, loss of sex power (gonadal atrophy), or amenorrhea and sterility.

The tallest authentic case of gigantism in medical literature was a Finnish giant who measured 9 feet 4 inches. In this country, one of the tallest giants on record was Robert P. Wadlaw, of Alton, Ill., who died (on July 15, 1940) at the age of 22 from a foot infection caused by the chafing of an ankle brace that he wore to support his weight. His height, according to one press report, was 8 feet 10.3 inches, and his weight was 431 pounds on June 27, 1940, at a St. Louis hospital. According to another report, his height was 8 feet 9 inches. He wore size 39 shoes. His weight at birth had been 9 pounds and, at the age of 6 months, 30 pounds. His abnormal growth acceleration was not noticed until he was a year old.

Acromegaly. When the overactivity of the anterior lobe begins in maturity, after the cartilage (epiphysis) has ossified, a rare and grotesque developmental distortion occurs, known as "acromegaly." Ordinarily, the malady develops slowly and insidiously between 20 and 30 years of age (seldom after 40) and may go through periods of remission, arrest, or exacerbation. The exaggerated growth affects particularly the bones that have remained soft. While the stature is little affected, the feet, hands, ends of the fingers, ears, nose, tongue, and lips undergo marked enlargement. The pawlike hands, broad face, large head, projecting lower jaw (hence "horse disease"), bulbous lips, shaggy eyebrows, profuse hairiness, deep-set eyes, low hairline on the forehead, coarse features, and the low-hanging hands incident to a bent back combine to produce a gorillalike monstrosity. The large tongue often produces labored speech. The early signs include growing fatigability, somnolence, muscular pains, headaches, irritability, and insomnia. Outbursts of temper are not infrequent, probably caused by a tumor in the anterior lobe (eosinophilic adenoma), the usual cause of acromegaly. The thyroid often enlarges and the voice tends to become coarse, while the appetite may become ravenous. In the later hypopituitary stages, the patient tends to become sullen, absent-minded, forgetful, apathetic, and mentally sluggish. After the tumor has burned itself out, muscular atrophy (similar to progressive muscular atrophy) may supervene. Loss of libido and impotency, or amenorrhea, eventually follow. Some acromegalics remain relatively comfortable throughout the course of the disorder.

The treatment of gigantism and acromegaly, not always successful, includes the administration of thyroid extract, sex hormone, or X-ray irradiation of the gland; or the surgical removal of a tumor. The medical literature to 1938 records 1,606 cases of acromegaly. The problems of adjustment that confront these deviates are due largely to their sensitiveness regarding their physical monstrosities and the mental deterioration that sometimes ensues.

Fröhlich's Syndrome or Pituitary Infantilism. Pronounced underfunctioning of the posterior lobe of the pituitary gland (hypopituitarism) before adolescence gives rise to an entirely different kind of disorder of development, known as "Fröhlich's syndrome," [10] or "dystrophia adiposogenitalis," or "pituitary infantilism." In this relatively rare disorder, the stature is diminished somewhat and the hands, feet, and bones are small. There is a marked obesity of the girdle type; that is, over the lower abdomen, hips, and breasts, giving a boy a feminine outline and a "sissy" appearance (pituitary adiposity). A third pronounced characteristic is hypogenitalism, or genital infantilism (underdeveloped genitalia and secondary sex characteristics), ordinarily accompanied by amenorrhea, frigidity, and sterility, and sometimes

---

[10] A syndrome is a group of clinical symptoms characteristic of a disease.

homosexual practices. The skin is usually soft, delicate, and hairless, but it may be dry. Ordinarily, the hands are pudgy and the fingers tapering. The facial and bodily appearance is infantile or juvenile and feminine. The condition is accompanied by increased sugar tolerance and headaches when the gland is tumorous. The condition may be due to a constitutional defect or it may follow an infectious disease, such as encephalitis lethargica. The mental picture is one of sluggishness, phlegmatism, sleepiness, and psychomotor and mental retardation. Children of this type readily fall asleep, even in the classroom. Charles Dickens's description of somnolent Joe applies to some torpid, corpulent school children whose condition may be due to posterior lobe hypopituitarism: "Joe!   Joe!   Damn the boy, he is asleep again." Ordinarily calm, cheerful, and contented, but passive, submissive, and compliant, they may react to their structural defects—*e.g.*, the genital infantilism and feminine type of adiposity on the part of boys—by suffering from feelings of timidity, shyness, distrust, sullenness, and hostility. Their reactions of resentment and frustration not infrequently engender efforts at compensation through exhibitions of aggressiveness or antisocial behavior.

Although some of these cases are mental defectives, usually of the higher levels (sporadic cases are found in the institutions and classes for mental defectives),[11] and although some are mentally and emotionally infantile (hence pituitary infantilism), many appeal duller than they actually are because of their listless, sluggish responses. David M. Levy classified only 5 of 33 Fröhlich boys (functional cases, diagnosed largely on the basis of fat distribution) at the New York Institute for Child Guidance as below average in intelligence, while he classified 17 as above average.[12] The Stanford-Binet I.Q.'s ranged from 70 to 140. The median was from "110 to 119" as compared with a "median quotient of 99" for the entire group of behavior cases examined at the Institute. Twenty-six of the 33 were characterized as constitutionally submissive, 5 as aggressive, and 2 as mixed; whereas, the majority of the other behavior cases were aggressive. Bronstein, Wexler, Brown, and Halpern,[13] on the basis of a battery of psychological tests, classified 48 per cent of 35 obese children (24 boys and 11 girls) as superior, 25 per cent as average, and 25 per cent as below average. The I.Q.'s (based on the Stanford-Binet Form L) varied from 39 to 147, with a median of 109.

---

[11] Whether the mental defect in these and other endocrine cases is primary or secondary to the endocrine defect has not been definitely determined. In some cases the mental defect is probably of combined primary and secondary genesis.

[12] David M. Levy, "Aggressive-Submissive Behavior and the Fröhlich Syndrome," *Archives of Neurology and Psychiatry*, November, 1936, 991–1020.

[13] I. Pat Bronstein, Samuel Wexler, Andrew W. Brown, and Louis J. Halpern, "Obesity in Childhood," Psychologic Studies, *American Journal of Diseases of Children*, February, 1942, 238–251. (References.)

Only 2 out of 24 boys showed a tendency toward femininity. No endocrinological basis was found for their obesity. Molitch and Poliakoff,[14] on the basis of many intelligence tests, classified 3 of their 5 Fröhlich cases as average, one as inferior, and one as subnormal. Incidentally, their anterior-lobe hyper- and hypopituitary cases tended to be brighter (especially the hyper cases) than the nonglandular institutional inmates. Of the anterior-lobe hyperpituitary boys, 18 per cent were classified as immature, 12 per cent as infantile, and 28 per cent as unstable. The corresponding ratings for the anterior-lobe hypopituitary group were 8, 4, and 32 per cent. Although in school progress the pituitary cases were superior to the controls in the institution, they were inferior in general adjustment and behavior. Mental subnormality is the exception and not the rule among the different kinds of pituitary cases.

Many investigators have concluded that the Fröhlich disorder is not caused solely by underfunctioning of the posterior pituitary lobe, but that it involves a lesion of the hypothalamus, a part of the brain which includes the pituitary gland, and that this lesion accounts for the obesity. Moreover, some authorities believe that too many children have been diagnosed as pituitary cases, especially as Fröhlich cases. Thus no endocrine disorders were found by Weiner in 10 alleged Fröhlich cases,[15] and by Bronstein, Wexler, Brown, and Halpern in 35 obese children. They attributed the adiposity to sedentary habits, abnormal appetites, or other factors. Obviously, the diagnosis of pituitary infantilism cannot be based solely on the presence of a mons-mammary-girdle type of adiposity; and functional types of pituitary disorders may not be revealed by present methods of diagnosis.

A number of writers (*e.g.*, L. A. Lurie) report very favorable results from the treatment of young Fröhlich children with the appropriate hormones, such as pituitary and other glandular extracts. Others (*e.g.*, Hoskins) [16] express skepticism regarding any favorable outcome of such treatment. The negative results from administration of pituitary extract to Fröhlich cases reported by Tredgold [17] is corroborated by the author's experience as far as it concerns mentally defective cases, the only kind with which he has dealt.

Hyper- and Hypoadrenalism; Addison's Disease; Virilism. Overactivity of the adrenal medulla (the central part, which secretes adrenalin or epinephrin) sometimes results in a sudden elevation of blood pressure, pallor, tremors, sweating, nausea, headaches, and anxiety feelings. Deficient secretion of cortin from the adrenal cortex (outside layer) may result in low blood pressure, loss of appetite, high fatigability, irritability, insomnia; eventually,

14 *Op. cit.*, 127*f*.
15 Alexander T. Cameron, *Recent Advances in Endocrinology*, Philadelphia, The Blakiston Company, 1945, 352.
16 *Op. cit.*, 181.
17 Alfred F. Tredgold, *A Textbook of Mental Deficiency*, Baltimore, William Wood & Company, 1937, 294.

perhaps, coma, convulsions, and physical collapse. Serious chronic deficiency of cortin produces Addison's disease, chiefly affecting men, which is marked by emotional vacuity, a bronze skin pigmentation, low blood pressure, weakness, loss of appetite, anemia, sensitiveness to cold, and diminished libido. Overfunction of the cortex in childhood may result in precocious puberty in both sexes and in virilism, or masculinism, in girls. Virilism and sex precocity are discussed in Chap. XIII. The complete destruction of the cortex by disease or by surgery results in labored breathing, cardiac failure, paralysis, and death within a few hours or days.

Hypo- and Hyperparathyroidism. Severe underaction of the parathyroids, resulting in deficient calcium and phosphorus secretion, produces nutritional disturbances, rickets, nervous irritability, muscle spasms, tetany, and sometimes convulsions, with occasional fatal results. Partial degrees of parathyroid deficiency may exist for months without detection and may be the cause of the child's restlessness, touchiness, emotional instability, and hypersensitiveness. The calcium-starved individual tends to become excitable, irritable, and cross. According to L. A. Lurie, many conduct disorders in children are connected with calcium deficiency. Striking improvement in disposition and conduct has been recorded from the administration, under medical supervision, of parathyroid extract and calcium—single or in combination—and of vitamin D, with sunshine and high calcium foods (*e.g.*, milk and cheese), with the avoidance of phosphorus-containing foods and drugs (phosphorus depresses calcium and vice versa). Some types of mental defectiveness have been attributed to calcium deficiency; this conclusion still requires experimental confirmation. Overaction of the glands may produce disturbances of the bony structures because of excessive withdrawal of lime salts from the bones, muscular weakness, and apathy, without mental impairment. This condition is known as "Recklinghausen's disease" (osteitis fibrosa).

Many behavior disorders have been traced to pituitary dysfunction. Thus one endocrinologist reports that, among 100 children manifesting behavior abnormalities, such as lying, disobedience, and bullying, 70 showed endocrine disorders, usually involving the pituitary gland; conduct improvement followed the administration of pituitary extract. Such broad generalizations, however, require verification before they can be accepted at face value. Improvement in behavior may have been due to psychic motivation.

The treatment of deficiency endocrine disorders consists essentially of supplying, under medical supervision, some form of the deficient hormone, with or without related hormones, possibly supplemented by various vitamins (such as D vitamin and B complex). In the case of excessive functioning, a portion of the gland (especially a diseased part) and existent tumors or cysts may be surgically removed or the gland may be subjected to X ray irradiation. The outcome of the treatment varies with the severity, type, stage, and complications of the disorder and its mode of origin (*i.e.*, whether it is constitutional or consequent upon infections, accidents, or pathological growths). The results vary from complete ineffectualness to complete restoration.[18] Hypothyroid conditions respond better to glandular extracts than do hypopituitary disorders.[19]

A second line of evidence suggesting the influence of the physical upon the mental concerns *the influence of foods, drugs, narcotics, or other substances, or the lack of nutritional elements, upon psychoneural functioning*. White rats are rendered very irritable when fed on a diet low in calcium and high in phosphorus (E. V. McCollum). Lack of magnesium (supplied in green vegetables) also produces hyperexcitability aand hyperirritability in rats (D. M. Greenberg). Certain foods will inhibit sex activity in rats; other foods will cause them to devour their young. An excess of sugar in the blood in the human organism tends to produce depression and even confusion and disorientation. A marked deficiency of blood sugar, produced by doses of insulin, may produce unconsciousness and convulsive seizures. Serious nutritional deficiency may produce lethargy, mental vacuity, body and brain fag, indecision of movements, and lack of interest and ambition.[20]

It is now well recognized that many persons (perhaps 10,000,000) are hypersensitive (allergic) to one or more substances in their surroundings,

[18] For further references on the endocrine glands and hormones, consult

Frank A. Beach, *Hormones and Behavior,* New York, Paul B. Hoeber, Inc., Medical Book Department of Harper & Brothers, 1948.

Lennox R. Broster, *Endocrine Man,* New York, Grune & Stratton, Inc., 1945.

Alexander T. Cameron, *Recent Advances in Endocrinology,* Philadelphia, The Blakiston Company, 1945.

Edwin C. Hamblen, *Endocrinology of Women,* Springfield, Ill., Charles C Thomas, Publisher, 1945.

Jacob Hoffman, *Female Endocrinology, Including Sections on the Male,* Philadelphia, W. B. Saunders Company, 1944.

Gregory Pincus, ed., *Recent Progress in Hormone Research,* New York, Academic Press, 1948.

C. Donnell Turner, *General Endocrinology,* Philadelphia, W. B. Saunders Company, 1948.

[19] For a more complete treatment of these and other deviant types of humans produced by glandular dysfunctioning and still others produced by metabolic disorders, see the author's *Children with Mental and Physical Handicaps,* New York, Prentice-Hall, Inc., 1949.

[20] On the effects of nutrition, consult

Isaac N. Kugelmass, *Superior Children through Modern Nutrition,* New York, E. P. Dutton & Co., 1942; and *Growing Superior Children,* New York, Appleton-Century-Crofts, Inc., 1946.

"The Role of Nutritional Deficiency in Nervous and Mental Disease," *Proceedings of the Association for Research in Nervous and Mental Disease,* Baltimore, The Williams & Wilkins Company, 1943.

which tend to produce definite allergic reactions. Over 125 offending substances have been identified, including various foods, such as milk, eggs, melons, chocolate, wheat, beef, shellfish, tomatoes, strawberries, and corn; substances that may be inhaled, such as dust, plant pollens (*e.g.*, from ragweed), cosmetics, emanations from animals, and odors of foods and other substances; contact substances, such as furs, feathers, ointments, nail polish, poison dogwood, poison ivy, poison oak, and poison sumac; and drugs (*e.g.*, histamine, aspirin, penicillin, the sulfas, or a laxative). The allergic reactions, varying greatly among individuals, include asthma, hay fever, hives, skin rashes, contact dermatitis, eczema, headaches, migraine (recurrent headaches, usually unilateral, accompanied by nausea, vomiting, and disturbed vision), convulsive disorders, dizziness, colitis, chronic bronchitis, serum sickness, cold sores, mouth ulcers, swellings of the lips or tongue, watery eyes, rhinitis, indigestion, irritability, nervous strain, mental dullness, languor, and confusion. Allergic susceptibility may in some cases be heightened by emotional upheavals, and it may change with the years. The treatment of allergies produced by material agencies is to withdraw the offending substances from the organism and to desensitize the individual by means of allergic extracts or vaccines ("pollen shots"), or to use palliative antidotes or antihistamines, such as benadryl (valuable for hives, eczema, penicillin, sulfa, and hay fever allergies) and pyribenzamine (PBZ), which is especially effective against hay fever. The antidotes give only temporary relief. PBZ ointment stops the irritation from eczema, poison ivy, and allergic dermatitis.[21]

The concept of allergy has more recently been extended to include "psychic allergy" (psychoallergy), or extreme sensitivity to certain words or ideas that have become conditioned symbols for emotional responses. Doubtless, some persons have become allergic to such words as bolshevism, Hitlerism, nazism, fascism, and Japanese war lords because of the atrocities committed by the minions of these groups. Psychoallergies may even produce bodily symptoms, such as increased pulse, temperature, and blood pressure.

The effects of excessive indulgence in alcohol include loss of motor control, thick speech, mental confusion, forgetfulness, excitement, depression, and sometimes auditory or visual hallucinations and delirium tremens. Cocaine first acts as a stimulant and then as a depressant. It may produce a greater degree of moral degradation than the related drug, morphine. Opium, among

[21] Rebecca Eitola, "Adjusting the School Program to the Allergic Child," *Journal of Exceptional Children*, March, 1946, 162, 167, 191. (References.)

Reich Urbach, *Allergy*, New York, Grune & Stratton, Inc., 1946.

Paul de Kruif, "Antidotes for Allergy," *The Reader's Digest*, September, 1947, 79–83.

Hyman Miller and Dorothy W. Baruch, "Psychological Dynamics in Allergic Patients as Shown in Group and Individual Psychotherapy," *Journal of Consulting Psychology*, March–April, 1948, 111–115.

other effects, induces a dream state characterized by vivid and pleasurable hallucinations, followed by deep, dreamless sleep. The victim of this drug may become so enamored with his excursions into the land of imagery that he continues to indulge until he deteriorates mentally, physically, and morally. He may even succumb from malnutrition. According to H. R. C. Rutherford, the slow, insidious effects of excessive smoking may render the individual more susceptible to mental attacks or mental illness because of gastric disturbances, loss of appetite, and lowered physical vitality.

After this rapid recital of facts, our *general conclusions regarding the effects of the physical upon the mental* may be briefly summarized as follows:

1. Every organ of the body projects its influence into the brain, and thereby modifies the psychic life.

2. The chemistry of the endocrine glands, as well as of other glands and organs, affects the chemistry of the brain, and the brain chemistry affects the mental processes. Toxic blood poisons the cells of the nervous system no less than the cells of the muscles.

3. Harmonious, coordinated activity of the bodily organs is an important prerequisite of effective, coordinated mental activity. The physical organism, in order to remain efficient and healthy, requires properly coordinated action between the organs that produce, discharge, distribute, and store energy. The integrity of the nervous system is dependent to a large extent upon the harmonious, coordinated action of these systems of organs; and the integrity of the mental activity is in considerable measure directly dependent upon the integrity of the nervous system.[22]

Facts Showing the Influence of the Mental upon the Physical. Is there comparable evidence in support of the thesis that mental states may similarly influence the brain and other parts of the body? The evidence is indisputable, not only so far as it concerns the widespread somatic reverberations of emotional experiences, but also so far as it concerns the influence of mere emotionless thinking or attentive states upon the circulation of the blood and upon motor innervation.

That mere thoughts or ideas can affect the circulation of the blood through the excitation of the nervous system can be shown by the balance-board experiment. In this experiment the subject, while lying quietly upon a perfectly balanced platform, is asked to read an unemotional passage of prose, or to solve a mathematical problem, or to engage in calm, unemotional thinking. After a brief interval the experimenter will observe that the end of the board on which the head rests gradually begins to descend. Obviously, thinking has affected the circulation; it has caused the blood to flow to the

[22] The practical implications of these conclusions will be discussed in Chap. III. The psychological effects of morbid sensitivity toward one's physical defects will be discussed in Chap. V and in other sections of the book.

head, in consequence of which the head grows heavier and the board begins to tilt. Similarly, if attention is concentrated upon an active muscle, the flow of blood can be increased to that muscle. If attention is fixed upon the feet and the subject thinks of running a race, the balance board will tip in the direction of the feet, although more slowly. The effect of attention upon the circulation can be most convincingly shown in states of hypnosis, in which the subject becomes highly suggestible. In some cases the mere suggestion by the hypnotist that the subject has a scar or a burn on the arm may produce a localized area of hyperemia on the skin.

The so-called muscle-reading experiment shows that the mere idea of a movement or the direction of attention on an anticipated movement tends to produce the movement (sometimes referred to as the law of ideomotor action or dynamogeny). In this experiment a blindfolded subject wagers that he can locate a concealed object by grasping the hand or the arm of the experimenter who knows where the object is hidden. The explanation is that the experimenter is thinking of the place where the object has been concealed; he is directing his attention toward it, and this tends to produce a certain degree of muscular tension and incipient or actual involuntary movements in the direction of the location of the object. A sensitive muscle reader may be able to find the object by perceiving the involuntary motor tendencies of the experimenter.

The following is a verbatim report of a case in point from Amsterdam, Holland, concerning the finding of an 8-year-old girl by a blindfolded "mind reader" (Hilda van Arnem), who volunteered to locate the missing girl but who stipulated, "I must have two persons to go with me, one on each side, to prevent me from falling or being run over." She selected a policeman and a young man from the crowd. She was then blindfolded and started forth, followed by the crowd, which was kept at a distance by several policemen. After having proceeded for about a mile, she suddenly turned and entered a fruit warehouse, ascended the stairs to the attic, and stopped before a banana crate. She removed the bandage from her eyes and said to the policeman on her left, "You will find Sonia there." In the crate they found the girl, murdered. Then the captain of police said to Hilda, "And now, perhaps, you can tell us who committed this fiendish crime." "Certainly," replied Hilda. "Arrest the man who walked on my right side. He is the murderer." Later, at the police station, the man confessed. Assuming that the event is correctly reported (it contains some questionable elements), the phenomenon is one of muscle reading, not mind reading. The number of persons, however, who are sufficiently sensitive to perceive slight muscle movements or changes in muscle tension is relatively small.

The practical conclusions to be drawn from these few illustrative facts may be stated as follows:

1. The nervous system controls the blood supply on which the life of every cell of the body depends.

2. The functioning of the nervous system does not, however, depend exclusively upon the chemical substances in the blood and in the nervous system. On the contrary, it also depends upon mere unemotional thoughts or mere concentration of attention. So highly sensitized is the brain to mere ideas that, as someone has remarked, "every thought or idea that passes through the mind leaves a neural trace." Every neural trace thus produced probably exerts some subtle influence upon the organism, whether for better or for worse.

The most striking illustrations of the influence of the mental upon the physical are not derived from a consideration of processes of calm, logical thinking or of mere perceiving or attending. It is when mental processes consist of emotionalized experiences or when they are closely connected with biological functions and glandular activities that the effects of mental states upon physical conditions become most clearly apparent. To generalize broadly, it may be stated that any mental activity that stimulates the endocrine glands will exert a subtle influence that may pervade the whole organism and sometimes may produce the most profound organic disturbances.

The extreme sensitivity of some of the glandular functions to mere ideas or perceptions is well recognized. In some persons the sex centers in the brain and the cord are so responsive that mere images or thoughts can serve as adequate erogenous stimuli. The mere thought or perception of appetizing or unappetizing foods or of savory or unsavory odors is sufficient to stimulate the salivary or gastric nervous centers in most persons. The mere thought or visual perception of a luscious red watermelon will cause "watering of the mouth" in many persons. Such secretory activity is known as "psychic secretion." Many experiments have shown the effects of agreeable and disagreeable stimuli upon the secretion of gastric juice. In a well-known experiment upon a dog, in which the gastric secretion was diverted into a container instead of into the stomach, an undisturbed, pleasurable 5-minute feeding resulted in the secretion of 66.7 c.c. of gastric juice in from 15 to 30 minutes. On a later occasion, when the dog became excited by being shown a cat just before the feeding, no secretion occurred during the 5-minute feeding period, and the secretion amounted to only 9 c.c. during the following 20 minutes. Emotional excitement thus inhibits the flow of the gastric juice.

In a somewhat similar experiment upon a boy with a closed esophagus who was fed through a gastric tube, it was discovered that the mere chewing of agreeable foods produced gastric secretion before the food was deposited in the stomach, but no secretion occurred when indifferent substances were chewed.

While, therefore, merely ideational or perceptual processes can arouse glandular activities, no intellectual stimuli can compare with violent emotions in their effects upon the glandular organs or in producing bodily disturbances (referred to as psychosomatic disorders). Emotional experiences are the chief source of nervous dyspepsia or acute indigestion, rather than the food that may have been ingested. Many physicians (*e.g.,* George K. Pratt) regard the term "nervous indigestion" as a misnomer. The inability to digest food is attributed to the unwillingness to digest disagreeable experiences. One is reminded of the woman brought to the hospital because of an attack of acute indigestion. It was found the following morning that the evening meal had remained in the stomach all night. Further investigation disclosed the fact that she had been upset in the evening by a quarrel with her husband, who had returned home in a state of intoxication.

Why do emotional upsets halt the activity of the stomach? The investigations by T. Wingate Todd on about 800 Western Reserve students during a period of 11 years in all seasons of the year, with the use of X rays and barium-test meals, revealed that the fluids remained longer in a disquiet stomach because of the closing of the pylorus (the opening from the stomach into the intestine) and the continuance of the closure for some time.[23] The disturbing emotions included examination apprehension (particularly among the freshmen, because of the lurid tales of the upperclassmen regarding the difficult tests and examinations in anatomy), excitement, feeling ill, and hurrying. Physical fatigue or exhaustion and some foods, such as eggs, milk, or strawberries, also closed the pylorus. The subjects were probably allergic to the offending foods. The results of the damming-up process included tenderness in the upper part of the abdomen, acidity, pain, drowsiness, mental inefficiency, irritability, daydreaming, and defensive sneezing. The sneezing probably opened the pylorus and thus served as a corrective. The old treatment of cinnamon and pepper for indigestion may have had the same effect. The investigation showed that when confidence was restored the stomach movements were revived. Todd's statement that the stomach is the "organ of social adjustment" is not a meaningless figure of speech. The stomach is subject to "moods" that greatly influence the psychic reactions of the individual.

The profound organic commotion that can be produced by intense emotional experiences may be illustrated by reference to the effects of one emotion that nearly all people have experienced in more or less violent form, namely, fear. The most patent overt effects of intense fear are trembling, shrinking, raising of the eyebrows, irregular breathing, and movements of escape or of combat. Inner conditions, less obvious to the onlooker, include

---

[23] This would seem to justify the conclusion that there is just as much need for rest and relaxation before meals as afterward.

dryness of the mouth, due to inhibitory action upon the salivary glands; inhibition of the flow of the gastric juice; and acceleration of the heart action. The heightened cardiac activity increases the blood pressure, thereby forcing the blood into the arms and legs, which enables the individual to meet the vigorous demand upon these members for flight or fight.

How are these effects to be explained? Control experiments by Walter B. Cannon and others upon animals, in which various factors have been subjected to rigid control, and observations upon abnormal or pathological human beings have shown that exciting emotions, such as fear, anger, and pain, cause the adrenal glands to discharge excessive amounts of adrenalin, the hormone secreted by these glands. Experiments have shown that adrenalin checks the secretion of gastric juice by stopping the contractions of the smooth muscle along the digestive tract, and that it stimulates the liver to discharge excessive amounts of starch (glycogen) into the blood stream In the blood the glycogen is converted into sugar. The blood sugar in turn is absorbed by the skeletal muscles and is converted into heat or energy. This enables the muscles to contract more vigorously. It is thus apparent that emotional upsets can change the body chemistry by acting on the endocrine glands.

Chemical tests have shown that adrenalin is an amazingly powerful element. One part in a million inhibits the contraction of the intestinal muscle, while one part in three million renders the contractions sluggish. Hearts that have apparently stopped beating have been revived by the injection of this hormone directly into the heart.

Further experiments on animals and on man have shown that strong excitement, worry, or anxiety may produce such a copious secretion of glycogen as to cause it to seep through the kidneys and produce glycosuria (temporary diabetes). Thus four out of nine Harvard students after a hard examination and 50 per cent of the Harvard football squad after an exciting football game showed evidence of glycosuria (W. B. Cannon). Five of the latter, who had not participated in the game, apparently experienced the emotional strain of the game through vicarious participation from the side line. Likewise cats subjected to prolonged excitement have shown sugar in the urine within 30 minutes.

What sorts of physical difficulties and disorders can be produced by such emotional upheavals as fear, anger, rage, grief, worry, and anxiety? The long list of reputed disturbances, based mostly on observational data, may give a somewhat exaggerated picture of the devastating effects of emotional storms and stresses. Certainly, if the victim of emotional upsets can make adequate adjustments to his difficulties, the consequences will be less serious. However, it has been asserted by medical and psychological writers that emotional upheavals may aggravate or produce stomach trouble, indigestion, metabolic disturbances leading to possible emaciation, diabetes or glycosuria (mentally disordered persons subject to fears often suffer from diabetes), jaundice, degeneration of the liver, heart disorders, overaction of the thyroid and adrenal glands, loss of vitality, insomnia, increased susceptibility to colds (perhaps through the dryness of the nose and throat), and dysentery. A defeated army is liable to suffer from dysentery, produced by mental collapse rather than by intestinal infection.

According to D. Yellowlees, "nervous anxiety" may precipitate a vicious circle of disturbances, including hyperacidity, which may lead to duodenal ulcer, and dyspepsia, which, in turn, may lead to "gastric atony (lack of tone) and dilation." These lead to visceroptosis (downward displacement of the visceral organs), to intestinal stasis, to toxic absorption, to endocrine disorder, and back to nervous anxiety. Yellowlees does not hesitate to affirm that psychological states which express themselves in "a lax and drooping posture" may be responsible for "actual bony deformities."

While the effects of emotional disturbances are primarily functional, prolonged emotional upsets may produce such organic changes as peptic or gastric ulcers, which affect from 5 to 15 per cent of the general population. Although these ulcers are organic diseases, the causation is frequently psychogenic. "The chances are that every acute flare-up is the direct result of worry or unhappiness. In prescribing treatment, the physician insists upon three things: rest; the avoidance of psychic upsets; and the taking of some easily digestible food every two hours. The average ulcer can be healed by this treatment, but a new one commonly forms if the patient does not find mental and emotional peace" (Walter C. Alvarez). "Peptic ulcer is, then, a part of the personality of the sufferer, and is determined by the emotional conditions at the time. Violent destructive emotional outbreaks—fear, anger, jealousy, and the like—frequently cause an increase in the symptoms of peptic ulcer" (George Draper). Andrew C. Ivy asserts that the mortality from gastric ulcer increased 25 per cent during the recent depression—an increase that he ascribes to worry. Whether this statement is correct or not, excessive worry has no doubt undermined the health of multitudes of people. According to J. H. Hatton, high blood pressure may be produced, even before the hardening of the arteries, by anxiety, fear, anger, excitement, and hurry, as well as by eating too much salt.

Press reports are replete with accounts of the fatal effects of fear, anger, or excitement upon persons with heart disease. "Excitement over the 'thrill-a-minute' heavyweight fight, in which Max Baer defeated Primo Carnera proved fatal to two Pennsylvanians. At Holidaysburg, Edward Cassiday, 72, an ardent fight fan, slumped over dead from a heart attack last night as he heard how the giant Carnera was knocked down in the first round. At Big Run, Henry Geist, 62, thrilled by the account of the savage battle, suffered a heart attack, and died." A 75-year-old man in Michigan fell dead while listening to a radio recital of the third round of the Louis-Baer heavy-weight fight. Many similar fatalities have terminated the lives of persons who have listened to the vivid radio descriptions of football games. Emotion-arousing descriptions may prove just as exciting, if not more exciting, than the observation of the spectacle itself. "In 33 out of 100 fatal cases of angina pectoris, long journeys had been taken just before the final disaster. Associated with a long journey there is always unusual activity in getting ready, loss of sleep, overeating, emotional stress; and the trip may include overindulgence in smoking and alcohol. . . . Many a business man has had his first attack of angina pectoris after he has suffered severe business re-verses" (Morris Fishbein). Even apparently trivial occurrences may produce too great an emotional strain on a weak heart. A St. Louis contractor, aged 61, who had a weak heart, died, according to the coroner's report, from the emotional shock of having his finger caught in a mousetrap. In "heart neurosis," even when the heart is organically sound, palpitation and rapid heartbeats are easily induced by exciting thoughts or by any kind of emotional stress. It may be not inappropriate to point out in this connection that longevity seems to go with three low physiological levels: low blood pressure, low pulse rate, and low weight.

The exhausting and disturbing effects of emotional upsets upon the nervous, glandular, digestive, and circulatory systems may lead to nervous exhaustion or hyperexcitability, as well as nervous maladies. Nervousness in general is due more frequently to emotional stresses and adaptive difficulties than to physical disease or injury, although physical derangements aggravate the condition. Nervousness is usually a disorder of function rather than a defect of structure. It is more of an emotional than a physical disorder. Emotional agitation may even wreck a body that is organically sound and free from disease.

Cases of psychic blindness or deafness or paralysis (without any organic counterpart) may be produced by severe emotional upheavals.

A young man, 29, complained that during the last few weeks of school his eyes "went wild" and could not be focused. Physical and optometric examinations re-vealed no defects. Investigation showed that he was working under great emo-tional strain, writing a theological thesis containing material repugnant to his in-tellectual integrity. His conscience rebelled and his eyes joined the protest by refusing to function. When the thesis was complete, his eyes returned to normal. A 17-year-old girl became fearful of going blind because her vision blurred sud-denly at times. Investigation showed her mother, separated from her husband, was visited frequently by another man whom the girl hated. The hatred caused her vision to fail so she might not see him. She experienced difficulty only when the man visited her mother (Lewis H. Kraskin).

Temporary psychic blindness is a frequent phenomenon in hysteria (see pages 303*f.*) and war neuroses.

During the First World War many cases of psychic blindness, usually affecting only the sighting eye, were erroneously attributed to shell shock, but proved on closer study to be a species of subconscious malingering, precipitated by emotional conflicts due to the fear of the battle line and the disgrace of cowardly flight. An affliction was developed, perhaps in the marginal field of consciousness, as a protective device, as an escape or a face-saving mechanism. Their feelings of self-respect would not permit them to run away, so a trick of the mind came to their rescue. Such cases of psychic blindness are more than a mere "figment of the imagination." Of course, some of the nervous disorders of the servicemen were deliberately faked.

The term "soldier's heart" in the Civil War is probably the equivalent of "shell shock" in the First World War. "Battle fatigue" or "combat fatigue" seems to be the term most frequently used in connection with similar battle casualties during the Second World War, in which the condition was treated more successfully than was the case during the First World War. Instead of postponing treatment until the victims of exhaustion neurosis could be carried to distant hospitals, they were afforded prompt therapy near the battle line or in the base hospital. They were put to bed, fed well, kept warm, and provided with release or suggestive treatment while in a state of induced narcosis (by a drug, pentothal sodium).

It has been estimated that 90 per cent of the cases of shell shock in the First World War were due not to any physical injury received in battle, but to disturbed emotions and to emotional collapse from fear, anxiety, dread, and the desire to escape from the battle front. According to J. W. Barton's estimate, more than 50 per cent of all patients consulting physicians or seeking hospital treatment have no real organic trouble. Edward A. Strecker believes that fully 50 per cent of the problems of the acute stage of an illness and 75 per cent of the difficulties of convalescence have their primary source in the patient's mind rather than in his body. Somewhat similar is the statement of Maurice Craig that from 50 to 70 per cent of the patient's illness may be due to his attitude toward his disorder. It is notorious that the patient's attitude toward his illness is often harder to treat than is the sickness itself.

In a series of 900 cases of stomach ailments in which an operation seemed to be indicated, it was found that in almost 60 per cent of them the symptoms were due not to any stomach ailment, but to some emotion, such as fear, worry, or anxiety (J. W. Barton). Observations in the Presbyterian Hospital in New York in 1934 showed that emotional factors affected more than half of the patients who had diabetes and heart disorders—diseases that are related to organic impairment. In times of emotional excitement, the diabetes and the heart condition were worse (G. W. Gray). W. C. Alvarez reports that "in 50 per cent of the indigestion cases, the specialist can discover nothing wrong with the digestive tract. He is faced here by the functional type of indigestion. . . . The commonest causes of nervous indigestion are fatigue, worry, hypersensitiveness, and insomnia. . . . One patient in three who comes to a doctor has no real physical reason to account for his symptoms. . . ." Sixty-five per cent of the dispensary patients at Johns Hopkins medical school whose homes are visited by the senior students, have adverse social conditions as a background of their illness, and 35 per cent have emotional conditions mainly responsible for their diseases. A poll of medical-school professors reported by Edward Wise indicated that 35 per cent of all persons seeking medical advice are suffering partly or entirely from some sort of emotional problem. One group of 235 patients from one clinic, who had been diagnosed as suffering only from "chronic nervous exhaustion" but who had had on the average one operation each, showed when they were checked 6 years later that the original diagnosis of nervous exhaustion was correct. One woman had undergone four operations for an imagined illness; [24] her trouble was traced to her chagrin over her sister's being married while she remained a spinster. These citations are typical of growing medical opinion regarding the dynamic role of mental factors in the production of bodily disorders. As has been emphasized by C. A. Martin of McGill University, "every patient is a mental patient."

Mental Maladjustments and Morbidities from Mental Causes. Not only do many somatic abnormalities have a psychogenic origin, but many mental maladies, oddities, and difficulties can be traced to mental causes. Mental factors may produce not only minor but also major mental idiosyncrasies and disorders. One of the chief purposes of this book is to describe in considerable detail various kinds of inadequate or undesirable mental-reaction patterns that result from the individual's experiences and from his attitudes toward his experiences and toward the problems created by his social and physical environment, and to vitalize the presentation by an abundance of pertinent, bona fide illustrative cases. At this point it is sufficient to emphasize the general thesis, that mental states may affect one another and thereby create problems of adjustment.

Collective Behavior as a Manifestation of Group Psychology. Moreover, mental disturbances or abnormalities may also be produced in whole groups of people—in the so-called "collective" or "group" mind—as a result of the mental states and behavior patterns of the crowd. In groups or mobs, people are highly suggestible; they relinquish their own judgments in favor

[24] For opinions and data on unnecessary operations, see Albert Deutsch, "Unnecessary Operations," *The Reader's Digest,* December, 1947, 69–72 (condensed from *Woman's Home Companion,* July, 1947).

of the leader and follow him implicitly, whether he is scrupulous or unscrupulous. They become completely subservient to some striking personality, and share in his impatience, intolerance, vaingloriousness, and lack of personal responsibility. All the blame is attributed to the mob, and the mob is absolutistic and uncompromising and eternally right while everybody else is wrong. In mobs people lose their identities, inhibitions, and critical judgment, revert to primitive forms of behavior, and give way to blind impulses—hence the fury and savagery of the mob. In mobs people are in a state of mind that may be fittingly described as a psychic or behavior epidemic, or mental contagion, or mass hysteria.

Among recent instances of reported behavior epidemics or mass hysterias may be mentioned the labor riots and sit-down strikes in America in 1937; the mass faintings in Lille, France, in 1937; and the mass suicide attempts in Hungary in 1934. Thirty girls, mostly 17 years of age, in a sugar factory in Lille, suddenly began to tremble and fell to the floor in a swoon. In the afternoon 40 others followed suit. A second mass swooning occurred 5 days later when the weather was comparatively cool, as compared with the "sweltering heat" on the first occasion. Experts, in their attempt to investigate the suggested causes, could find no trace of gas or other poisons in the blood. The ventilation and working conditions in the factory were good. What was the explanation of the swooning? It was explained locally as a "faint strike" against unsatisfactory working conditions by some, and also as a "psychopathological phenomenon induced by autosuggestion." In a "wave of mass suicide hysteria" among girls 12 to 18 years old in a Hungarian reformatory, 70 girls "swallowed shoehorns, teaspoons, toothbrushes, hairpins, and other indigestible objects in order to be sent to hospitals where they hoped their boy friends would visit them and bring the traditional flowers." They had been denied the privilege of seeing their boy friends and "threatened to renew the attempt to kill themselves" unless they were granted the privilege.

In the same year in Hungary, 1,200 coal miners remained 5 days underground without food, water, or light, in a "mass suicide attempt to obtain a higher wage scale. They stood up for 150 hours and were driven by the pangs of hunger to eat their leather belts and to gnaw at their shoes." All these group-behavior anomalies possess some of the characteristics of behavior epidemics: high suggestibility, lack of critical judgment, and irresponsibility.

A variety of social phenomena may be explained as behavior contagions. Such are the Crusades epidemics (1095–1270), a migration mania that affected even children at one time; the widespread belief in witchcraft from the sixteenth to the eighteenth century; the rage for tulips in Holland in the seventeenth century, which paralyzed industry; real estate booms, such as the Mississippi Bubble (1717), the California gold rush (1876), and the Florida land boom (1926); and the dancing manias of the Middle Ages. These uncontrollable dancing deliriums, in which the victim often danced until he fell exhausted, which were at times faked and often attended by profligacy, were especially common in Germany, particularly in the crowded cities. They spread rapidly from Aix-la-Chapelle (in July, 1374) to Cologne, Metz, and Strasbourg. The term "St. Vitus's dance," originally applied to these frenzied orgies, is now used as the equivalent of the nervous disorder, chorea. Religious revivals often tend to become a species of behavior epidemic. A more recent manifestation of religious behavior epidemics has taken the form of snake-handling rituals by glory-shouting Holiness Faith Healers at the dedication exercises of their "shrines of divine healing." Disease epidemics sometimes produce hysterical upheavals, resulting in enervating fears. Epidemics of infantile paralysis or of encephalitis lethargica have been known to produce a train of mental contagion. The emotional contagion of war psychology has precipitated war neuroses in thousands of soldiers. Nazi and Japanese mass atrocities in the Second World War were criminal behavior epidemics fanatically instigated and directed by the Nazi and Japanese war criminals, whose war psychology was that "might makes right" and that "the end justifies the means." One of the inevitable consequences of such a philosophy was demonstrated in criminal mob epidemics. Freed from all restraints by such a national ideology, the primitive, sadistic impulses of the irresponsible criminal mobs sank to the lowest depth of brutality in recorded history, in defiance of our vaunted cultural achievements. In conditions of mass psychic contagion there is only one step between civilization and savagery.

These illustrations—to which may be added the everyday phenomenon of the surging spread of fads and fashions—show to how enormous an extent group beliefs and practices are determined by psychic stimuli.

Preservative and Curative Influences of Mental States. Fortunately the effects of mental states are not limited to destructive or injurious influences. They may also exert beneficial or salubrious influences. The whole mental-hygiene program is vitally and directly concerned with this aspect of the problem of mental health.

The favorable influence of mental states is twofold. In the first place, wholesome mental states conduce to good mental and physical health. They tend to promote normal mental and physiological functioning and to prevent mental and physical derailments. This is the positive and preventive aspect of mental-health conservation. In the second place, salubrious psychic states tend to mitigate, correct, or cure bodily and mental disturbances and maladjustments. To a large extent, mental-hygiene treatment consists essentially in inducing wholesome mental states in the individual. Frequently it is a process of supplanting injurious mental states with health-producing ones.

The psychic states that have a health-preservative and curative value are considered in connection with the discussion of the positive concept of mental health (see pages 35–44 and 106–109).

The Springs of Human Behavior, Both Normal and Abnormal. The conservation of mental health is largely a problem of providing satisfactory outlets for the individual's basic urges, providing a balanced or harmonious adjustment of the various urges to one another, and adjusting the individual's egocentric drives to the cultural demands of the family and the community.

Why do people behave as they do? The answer involves a consideration of stimuli, drives, goals, and purposes. All behavior is, essentially, motivational or goal-seeking in nature. It is a purposive response to a great variety of internal and external stimuli. Human reaction tendencies and behavior patterns are the joint product of the dynamic interaction of the interrelated cravings and needs of the total organism in specific environmental and cultural situations.

The basic stimuli that incite, sustain, and direct behavior are variously referred to as strivings, desires, tensions, excitements, drives, urges, needs, propensities, dispositions, impulses, instincts, instinctual cravings, and ego satisfactions. Any reaction pattern may be regarded as basic that results from fundamental organic needs or from persistently recurrent stimulations that require organic adjustments. Motives and goals may be regarded as drives of a more complex nature and are the product of processes of learning. Motives are at the basis of beliefs, attitudes, and habits. Strong habits, both intellectual and emotional, result from strong motivations. Attitudes and habits, in turn, become motives to action.

The individual's springs to action may operate consciously or unconsciously; they may be native or acquired; they may be, in whole or in part, physiological, psychological, or social; but they never operate as isolated entities. Rather, they operate as dynamic, interdependent factors or constituents of the total personality in a total environmental situation. The strength of the different cravings and motivations is determined by the needs of the organism as a whole—in the light of past experiences and in particular environmental settings.

The basic physiological drives, innate in nature, related to states of tension and disequilibrium, include hunger (visceral tension) and thirst, elimination activities, removal of sensory irritants or evading painful stimuli (avoidant reactions), seeking pleasure- or satisfaction-yielding experiences (adient reactions), the drives for self-preservation and for propagation (the sex urge), general random or spontaneous activities (from an excess of kinetic energy), the desire for relaxation, rest, and sleep as means of obtaining relief from fatigue or exhaustion. To these fundamental adjustment needs should be added transient or permanent primary automatic activities—"inherited reflexes," as they are called—such as the movements of the lungs (breathing) and of the heart (circulation), the pupillary reaction to changes in illumination or distance, and various mechanical and nonvoluntary responses to external stimuli, such as the eyewink, the knee jerk, coughing, and sneezing.

The concept of human instinctive activities, in the sense of unlearned or inherited complex, coordinated responses to external stimuli, has been largely abandoned by the psychologists of the present generation. The word "instinct" has been replaced by the words "drive," "urge," and "propensity"; but most of the reaction patterns designated by these terms are the result of conditioning and habit formation rather than of inheritance.

The psychological and social drives to action —for our purpose, it is unnecessary to distinguish sharply between the two—include a great variety of goal-seeking activities, such as the desire for affectional, social, physical, and economic security; the need for recognition, prestige, and social status (a condition denominated by yet other terms, such as "ego satisfaction" and "mastery motive"), with the attendant drives toward successful achievement, self-realization, self-assertiveness, and dominance; the desire for acceptance by the group, with the attendant tendencies toward adaptation, conformity, and submissiveness; the urge for acquiring new experiences or adventures; the passion for accumulating possessions; the drive to rid oneself of the feelings of frustration, conflict, and inadequacy by developing counterbalancing superiorities, or by adopting, consciously or unconsciously, various kinds of escape or defense mechanisms, or by rationalizing behavior responses on fictitious levels of aspiration or in terms of spurious goals.

The satisfactory adjustment and resolution of the individual's basic psychosomatic needs and urges are prime conditions for the attainment and preservation of mental integration and soundness. The failure to achieve inner harmony among the individual's ambivalent (incompatible, antagonistic) tendencies, and to reconcile them with the folkways and mores of society, will tend to produce personality modifications or distortions of varying kinds and degrees, depending upon the nature and severity of the intellectual and especially of the emotional conflicts involved and the degree of success of the individual's pattern of response to the conflicts. For better or for worse, man lives in a ready-made society. His ego satisfactions must be realized in a social order of exacting laws, codes, and conventions that impose rigid controls and restrictions upon his liberty of action in the interest of the common good. The demands for conformity mean inhibition, suppression, repression, or sublimation (elevation, refinement) of egocentric trends. Some of the social barriers to rampant individualism are inescapable and insurmountable and will produce unadjusted behavior if the individual is unable to readjust his needs in conformity with recognized social goals. It is the conflicts with the implacable cultural demands that constitute the real source of the more severe emotional conflicts and maladjustive response patterns. Further consideration will be given to conflict situations and their resolution in later pages, especially in Chap. XIII.

Recapitulation of Conclusions Reached Regarding the Conditions of Mental Health and the Methods of Attaining It. In the preceding pages data have been presented in abundance to justify three basic conclusions regarding the conditions of mental health and the type of hygiene required for its attainment and preservation. These conclusions may be briefly stated as follows:

1. Bodily states and conditions can exert a profound influence, both salutary and destructive, upon mental states. In other words, mental health is partly dependent on physical health. Therefore, mental hygiene is vitally concerned with the improvement of the physical organism as an aid to the establishment and maintenance of mental soundness.

2. Mental processes or experiences can influence profoundly, both favorably and unfavorably, physiological processes, particularly nervous, glandular, and circulatory functions. That is to say, physical health is partly dependent upon mental health. Therefore the hygiene of the mind is an aid to the development of a sound body.

3. One set of mental processes may influence another set of mental processes, for better or worse. Moreover, the mental attitudes and behavior patterns of the "collective mind" can vitally affect the mental processes and behavior characteristics of large crowds of people. Therefore, the problem of mental health requires the development of salubrious mental states and attitudes by educational and psychological procedures, both in the individual (individual mental hygiene) and in the group (community mental hygiene).

By now it should also have become apparent that the complexity of the subject is so great that the provisional definition of mental hygiene given on page 3 is too brief for exactness. To frame a concise definition that will include all the essential components and aims of the mental-hygiene program is no easy matter. Nevertheless, the following definitions may be suggested as fairly comprehensive, yet concise.

Definitions of Mental Hygiene. Mental hygiene represents the application of a body of hygienic information and technique, culled from the sciences of psychology, child study, education, sociology, psychiatry, medicine, and biology, for the purpose of (1) the preservation and improvement of the mental health of the individual and of the community, and (2) for the prevention and cure of minor and major mental diseases and defects and of mental, educational, and social maladjustments. This definition has been so drawn as to include three specific objectives of the mental hygiene pro-gram—namely, the remedial (or curative), the preventive, and the positive—all of which are given detailed consideration in the next chapter. The preventive and positive objectives are emphasized in four of the following contemporary definitions by other authorities, the remedial and preventive by one, the positive by two, and the preventive by one.

The New York State Health Commission: "In its fullest meaning mental hygiene is directed to developing personality to its greatest possibilities, so that every individual gives his best to the world and knows the deep satisfaction of a life richly and fully lived."

Laurence F. Shaffer (1936): [25] "Mental hygiene refers to the prevention of inadequate adjustments and to the processes by which maladjusted persons are restored to normal living."

Harry N. Rivlin (1936): [26] "Mental hygiene is the attempt to reduce the prevalence of mental illness or emotional maladjustment by pointing the way to the development of habits conducive to good mental health. Mental hygiene is not concerned with the treatment of pathological conditions."

Norman Fenton (1943): [27] "The modern definition of the total field of hygiene is the preservation, inculcation, and promotion of those conditions or influences that lead to the most effective development of the personality of the individual and his most interesting, wholesome, and useful life in society."

D. B. Klein (1944): [28] Mental hygiene represents "the investigation and utilization of all factors having a bearing on the attainment and preservation of individual and group morale. The total field may be envisaged as involving both the prevention of mental disease as well as the promotion of mental health."

Thomas V. Moore (1944): [29] Mental hygiene is "a practical science which studies the human personality and its deviations from ideal perfection with a view to their prevention."

Encyclopedia of Modern Education (1943): [30] "Mental hygiene is an approach toward human adjustment and achievement, concerned with pre-

[25] Laurence F. Shaffer, *The Psychology of Adjustment,* Boston, Houghton Mifflin Company, 1936, 435.

[26] Harry N. Rivlin, *Educating for Adjustment,* New York, Appleton-Century-Crofts, Inc., 1936, 2.

[27] Norman Fenton, *Mental Hygiene in School Practice,* Stanford University, Calif., Stanford University Press, 1943, 4.

[28] D. B. Klein, *Mental Hygiene,* New York, Henry Holt and Company, Inc., 1944, 483.

[29] Thomas V. Moore, *Personal Mental Hygiene,* New York, Grune and Stratton, Inc., 1944, 2.

[30] Harry W. Rivlin and Herbert Schueler (eds.), *Encyclopedia of Modern Education,* New York, Philosophical Library, Inc., 1943, 487.

venting emotional maladjustments and enabling individuals to operate at their most efficient levels."

Dictionary of Education (1945): [31] Mental hygiene consists in "the establishment of environmental conditions, emotional attitudes, and habits of thinking that will resist the onset of personality maladjustments." Or it is "the study of principles and practice in the promotion of mental health and the prevention of mental disorder."

Thus far in our discussion the fact has been emphasized that the objective of mental hygiene is, in general, the attainment of mental health or mental soundness. But no attempt has been made so far to indicate what is involved in the positive concept of mental health from the psychological and social point of view. It is not sufficient to describe a sound mind negatively as a mind that is free from defect or disease or maladjustment. In planning programs for the conservation of mental health, we must do more than merely recognize undesirable mental symptoms that we should strive to avoid. It is even more important to have clearly in mind the desirable mental traits that we should attempt to cultivate. Certainly we shall fall short of our goal of developing wholesome personalities if we put the emphasis only upon the development of a healthy body, no matter how desirable such a body may be. A sound body will not in itself guarantee that the individual will possess those positive mental and social traits without which he cannot be considered to have a desirable, efficient personality make-up.

The Positive Concept of Mental Health from the Psychological and Social Points of View. What, then, are the positive mental and social traits that the well-balanced personality should possess? What characteristics must the individual have in order that his thinking, feeling, and doing will be concordant, unified, and efficient? What are the specific character traits that parents and teachers should strive to develop in children, as well as in themselves, in order that all will attain maximum mental health and develop well-adjusted, contented, and efficient personalities? Stated in another way, what are the criteria by which we shall judge or measure a wholesome personality? Our suggestions will involve the consideration of one general criterion and eight specific criteria.

GENERAL CRITERION

Sane, socially efficient conduct is the most decisive pragmatic or common-sense test of mental soundness. That individual may be considered to be mentally sound and efficient who is able to react to his physical and social environment in an effective, consistent, and integrated manner. An individual's mental soundness can be judged by the appropriateness and rationality

[31] Carter V. Good (ed.), *Dictionary of Education*, New York, McGraw-Hill Book Company, Inc., 1945, 208.

of his behavior patterns on the psychological and social levels. This is perhaps the most practical general criterion of sane *versus* insane behavior, and some of the specific criteria could be regarded merely as extensions or refinements of this general standard.[32]

SPECIFIC CRITERIA

To attempt to draw up a comprehensive list of specific qualities that will include every important component of the healthy mind would be a herculean task. Our modest effort will be limited to a brief discussion of certain mental attributes and attitudes that at least are desirable, if not positively essential, in the development of an integrated, harmonious, efficient personality.

1. The Well-adjusted Person Must Possess Proper Insight and Understanding Regarding His Personality Make-up and His Problems of Adjustment.

Ignorance is the taproot of many of our difficulties, conflicts, fears, and superstitions. The sure way to prevent many maladjustments or to cope with those already formed is through proper understanding. He who wishes to become well adjusted will seek self-knowledge and self-evaluation. He will try to gain a rational insight into his personality problems—his talents, interests, motives, handicaps, emotional and intellectual peculiarities, the causes of his weaknesses or failures, and the adaptations required by the various situations confronting him. He will try to evaluate the relative importance of various interconnected factors that bear on his problems. He will attempt to locate the sources of his problems. To conquer difficulties requires the correction of disturbing conditions at their origin.

Among the more important things that the individual must understand is the nature of the motivations of his ambitions, feelings, and actions. Why does he act as he does? What does he expect to gain by his conduct? What is he attempting to avoid by the form of behavior he has adopted? What are the interests and the aims that actuate him?

Motives play a basic role in the determination of character traits. Motives become consolidated into more or less fixed attitudes, and attitudes tend to become guiding principles. They are at the bases of our life philosophy.

[32] The definition of mental health proposed in the report of the Joint Committee of the National Education Association and the American Medical Association on health problems in education, formulated in 1939, several years after the publication of the first edition of this book, may be reproduced by way of comparison: "Mental health in its broadest sense has come to mean the measure of a person's ability to shape his environment, to adjust to life as he has to face it, and to do so with a reasonable amount of satisfaction, success, efficiency, and happiness."

They determine how we will react to life's various exigencies and experiences. Since we can correctly interpret behavior only as we understand its underlying attitudes, it is important for each one to understand his fundamental attitudes, especially how they are formed and how they influence his behavior. It is important to realize that attitudes are acquired and not inherited. They are learned by the individual, sometimes as the result of a single occurrence or episode and sometimes as a result of repeated experiences. In the latter case, attitudes are the result of habit formation and possess some of the characteristics of fixed habits.

The first step in the effort to control or modify attitudes is to discover just how they were acquired. This often proves difficult, because the individual may have forgotten how he acquired a certain disposition toward certain experiences, and the attitudes themselves frequently exert an unconscious sway. Many apparently irrational or odd likes and dislikes may be thus explained. Your dislike for men with black beards may seem irrational. You do not know why you should be subject to such a silly aversion; but the irrationality disappears the moment you discover how the dislike originated. Perhaps as a young child you were greatly frightened by a man with a black beard. Eventually you forgot the incident; but the dominant emotional undertone produced by the fright has continued unconsciously and without interruption to influence your attitude toward all black beards. The following is an interesting case in point, showing how a definite inhibition and amnesia was produced by an occurrence in early life.

A LONG-LIVED AMNESIA AND INHIBITION PRODUCED BY EARLY EMOTIONAL CONDITIONING DUE TO RACIAL ANTAGONISM

A month or so ago when I was in Reynold's buying candy, I realized that a maladjustment of over three decades ago had recurred. I saw a favorite childhood candy, and, although good social usage frowned upon such action, I found myself pointing to it rather than calling its name.

It was the chocolate drop, a candy with a racial association of my childhood days. An old incident leaped up, as if by magic, from some part of consciousness, and the experience was relived as if a day old.

The story centers around a little white girl, a saloonkeeper's daughter and myself. Racial antagonism was great between the two of us. I never went past her father's saloon without hearing her shrill tones and sing-song rhythm:

> Nigger, Nigger never die,
> Black face and shiny eye.

I made faces at her and let it go at that, but one day she changed her epithet to "chocolate drop." For some reason that went to the marrow of my bones, I hated it worse than the jingle, maybe because of its newness and suddenness.

I made up my mind then and there to "get even." When everything was ready, an errand called me around the corner again, but this time I had my "ammunition" with me.

At the first sound "choc," I went up, surprised her by grabbing her by the shoulders, and recited to her my piece of prize poetry that I had struggled over:

> Poor white trash with stringy hair
> Your father sells whiskey and old stale beer.

It is interesting to observe that we weren't enemies any more after this, nor were we friends. There was a truce. It is more curious still that after all these years, I couldn't tell the clerk I wanted chocolate drops, due to the strength of an early conditioning process. A week or so after this occurrence, I went back to the store, asked for chocolate drops, and thought what a simpleton I had been the previous week.

(T.B.N.; F.; Col.; Asst. H.S.P.; M.A.; Age 45)

This is merely an illustration of an acquired peculiarity. Scores of similar ones will appear throughout the book. Idiosyncrasies frequently can be overcome as soon as insight is gained regarding their nature and genesis.

So we conclude that a prime characteristic of a sound mind is that it attempts to discover, understand, and evaluate itself. "Know thyself" in order to control thyself is a sound mental-hygiene precept. "To make oneself known to oneself is the beginning and the end of cure" (Wilhelm Stekel). Objective self-discovery, free from emotional distortions, is valuable not only for the cure but also for the prevention of mental illness. The three maxims, "Know thyself," "Be thyself," "Accept thyself," represent sound mental-hygiene advice. While gaining insight into the nature of one's behavior mechanisms and motivations will not prevent or overcome all adjustment difficulties—it is not offered as a panacea for all kinds of mental disorders—nevertheless, it usually represents the first step and, sometimes, an essential step on the road toward self-control and self-mastery.

The second characteristic is very similar.

2. The Healthy Mind Must Have Achieved a Satisfactory Philosophy of Life.

The healthy mind must have adopted wholesome attitudes toward life's workaday problems. It must manifest a healthy interest in living and must secure satisfaction from the mere process of living. Healthy living is joyous living. The healthy mind will enjoy wrestling with the multitudinous problems that constantly arise in a complicated social order. To such a mind every problem is a challenge to a victorious solution. The sign of a well-adjusted mind is that it recognizes its own difficulties quickly and fearlessly, and attempts to make satisfactory adjustments to its everyday problems. It meets issues squarely and faces the facts of life with frankness and without resorting to dodging, compromises, daydreaming, or other mechanisms for escaping from the stern realities of existence. The willingness to face one's social and vocational problems, the daily ups and downs of life, in an honest, straightforward manner makes for mental adaptability and soundness. Such an attitude has a health-preservative and -curative value.

A crucial criterion of a sound and efficient mind is the willingness and the ability to make successful adjustments to life's critical situations. This is a more important practical test than the ability to think straight or to feel properly, however important these attributes may be. The ability to act wisely and constructively in difficult life situations is the essence not only of mental soundness but also of high statesmanship and leadership.

The value of this characteristic may be shown from the results of failure to adjust one's thinking and doing to the realities of life. Failure to adjust usually manifests itself in feelings of dissatisfaction, frustration, emotional disturbances, mental maladjustments or disease, unwholesome habits of thought and conduct, excessive daydreaming, fears, worries, development of inferiority feelings and various kinds of defense mechanisms or tricks for dodging difficulties, bad sex habits, or antisocial conduct. Evading the issues of life and attempting to deceive ourselves and others regarding our internal conflicts constitute very important causes of mental disruption. On the other hand, facing the vicissitudes of life openly and courageously conduces to the development of mental virility. We conclude that one's philosophy of life, one's attitude toward life's vital problems, one's code of values, and one's basic ideals, ambitions, and beliefs exert profound molding influences upon one's personality make-up and pattern of living.

The next two traits are essentially corollaries of this philosophy of life.

3. The Healthy, Efficient Mind Is Adaptable and Resilient, and Possesses the Ability to Make the Necessary Adjustments to the Constant Changes and Vicissitudes of Life.

Life is a constant flux; the physical, mental, and social conditions of existence are constantly undergoing change. The individual's needs are constantly altering as he matures and as circumstances change. From a condition of helpless dependence upon the parents in infancy, the individual as he grows older must become self-reliant and independent. He must free himself from the apron strings during the adolescent period, so that he can "stand on his own feet" and solve his own problems. This is the period for achieving complete psychological and social weaning.

The ability to achieve independence and to adjust oneself to all the exigencies of life is an important index of a well-balanced, successful life. Mental health as adaptability means at least two things:

1. It means successful adjustment to the ever-changing physical and social order.

2. It means the adjustment of the individual's thinking, attitudes, feelings, cravings, and impulses to his stages of growth and development. This aspect of adjustment merits special emphasis.

4. The Wholesome Personality Will Have Achieved a Well-balanced Adjustment of Its Ambitions, Impulses, and Desires in Harmony with Approved Social Goals.

The young child is egocentrically inclined; he is interested only in satisfying his own inner cravings. But these often run counter to the social good and must be socialized, as the child cannot live an isolated hermit existence. He is a part of a social order that demands a good measure of social conformity. Unfortunately, the processes of socialization and sublimation of the individual's inner urges often give rise to intense mental conflicts and discord, as will be shown on later pages. There is, of course, implicit in this criterion the social concept of mental health.

5. Mental Health Connotes Social Adequacy and Adaptability.

What is involved in this statement? Primarily, the ability to get along with people—the ability to attain and maintain satisfactory human relationships in the family, community, school, church, shop, or factory. No one can be rated as mentally normal and well adjusted who cannot conform to reasonable social standards, or who is socially ineffective and unacceptable. An individual who is constantly at odds with his associates, querulous, fussing, contending, entering into lawsuits (litigious), or withdrawing from human contacts and becoming a hermit, or recluse, is socially inadequate. As a social creature, born into society, man must exercise social tolerance and adaptability. He must maintain social contacts with other human beings. If he withdraws from such contacts his social sense will eventually atrophy. Social-mindedness and "social intelligence" thus become important indexes of normal-mindedness. The ability properly to adjust socially is an important factor in achieving satisfactory mental adjustment. To avoid deep-rooted conflicts, there must be a satisfactorily balanced adjustment between the individual's egoistic demands and society's social requirements.

6. There Must Be an Adequate and Satisfying Emotional Undertone and Normal Emotional Maturation.

A well-regulated emotional life is of fundamental importance for the conservation of mental health. Indeed some authorities go so far as to assert that mental derangements are fundamentally emotional disturbances that are due to emotional conflicts and maladjustments and to emotional immaturity. Feelings of frustration, conflict, and dissatisfaction are symptoms of maladjustment and morbidity; they are a challenge to seek the cause and the remedy.   Many psychologists and psychiatrists believe that mental soundness is dependent more upon emotional maturity and balance than on any other factor, and that there is little danger of mental breakdown if the emotional life is wholesome.   This may be true so far as the functional type of mental disorders is concerned.   There can be little doubt that proper emotional underpinning will tend to preserve mental normality.

On the feeling side, the normal personality is characterized by emotional tranquility, serenity, and contentment; by feelings of well-being; by attitudes of confidence, hope, optimism, determination, and faith in one's capacity to achieve.

The value of the attitude of self-confidence has been well expressed by Emerson: "To those who believe they are able to conquer, victory is assured." The attitude of confidence is essential for success.   Such confidence is an essential constituent of the psychology of the faith healers.

Joy and satisfaction in work and play are essential for a satisfying emotional background.   Happiness and hopefulness are the normal resultants of successful achievement, while failure brings discouragement and dissatisfaction.   Failure may have a most devastating effect upon the individual's mental harmony unless he can reestablish a condition of emotional poise.   Feelings of unhappiness and dissatisfaction should be regarded as symptoms of maladjustment and discord that call for diagnosis and therapy.

The emotional life must be well ordered.   There must be emotional poise, balance, stability, and control.   Violent emotional outbursts may have a ruinous effect upon mental and physical well-being, as has already been shown.   Perhaps the greatest danger to mental normality is that one may not grow up emotionally, but remain emotionally infantile, or that one may regress to childish or infantile forms of emotional reaction (see Chap. IX).

Essential for the growth of normal emotional maturity and self-trust is a feeling of "at homeness," or a feeling of security—emotional, physical, filial, social, and economic.   No sharp line can be drawn between these different kinds of security.   Basically, the kind of security or insecurity that may profoundly influence the child's personality development is emotional in nature—particularly the emotional security or insecurity engendered by the expressed beliefs, the attitudes, and the behavior patterns of the parents, primarily, and of siblings, playmates, teachers, and others, secondarily.   Emotional security can exist in the child in the midst of dire poverty, provided that the psychic climate of the home is characterized by feelings of acceptance, respect, and affection; while feelings of insecurity may coexist when there is every evidence of affluence in the home if the child's morale is undermined by discord between the parents, by parental favoritism or discrimination with respect to any sibling, or by rejection of the child by the parents or by siblings. The protean source of children's early adjustment problems and feelings of insecurity is anxiety regarding the loss of the love of the parents, or the feeling of being unwanted or of not belonging in the home. The main root of emotional security is embedded in the child-parent relationship. A child who does not possess the emotional security that springs from feeling at home under the parental roof cannot feel at home in the larger world. The feeling of emotional security may be regarded as the keystone of mental health. Emotional security and emotional health are largely synonymous; both are intimately dependent upon the feelings of self-respect and self-esteem that are the natural resultants of the recognition accorded to the child's intrinsic worth and social status by the home and by the community. One of the prime objectives of early education is the development of emotional security; persistent feelings of insecurity are incompatible with wholesome personality unfoldment.

The next criterion constitutes another important factor in the acquisition of a satisfactory emotional undertone.

7. The Well-adjusted Personality Finds a Reasonable Enthusiasm and Satisfaction in the Day's Work and in the Accomplishment of Worthwhile Life Purposes.

It is probable that no one can remain mentally well integrated and efficient unless his life is directed and controlled by definite, socially acceptable life goals, no matter what the goals may be—authorship, teaching, homemaking, agriculture, commerce, statesmanship, or marriage. A definite plan of life in the pursuit of a socially approved objective that holds the attention and the interest of the subject is needed to give purpose, direction, and significance to life. During the period of childhood, the transitional goals that vitalize and give meaning and direction to the child's strivings are ordinarily application to interest-arousing school tasks and absorption in individual or group recreational activities, such as plays, games, and sports. There is some justification for William Burnham's apparently extreme statement: "The essentials, without which a person cannot be quite sound mentally and with which, apart from accident, infection, or heredity, one can have no serious mental disorder, the absolutely essential conditions are these: A task, a plan, and freedom." [33] One value of definite objectives is that they serve to integrate the expenditure of the individual's energy. They prevent its dissipation in fruitless, planless activities, in mere random nervous discharges. Singleness of purpose, with

[33] Quoted with the permission of Appleton-Century-Crofts, Inc., from *The Normal Mind*, 1924, 207.

wholehearted concentration upon the attainment of a definite purpose, tends to prevent the splitting or disintegration of mental life. Rapt concentration of attention is the quintessence of integration. A second distinct value of concentration upon a definite objective task is that this furthers the healthy objectification of interest and attention, and thus tends to prevent unhealthy subjective preoccupations, which often produce morbid sensitiveness, self-consciousness, and emotional upsets. A third advantage is that definite life goals will spur the individual to lead an active existence. The healthy life is the active life. Inactivity spells stagnation, deterioration, and disintegration.

To achieve this objective in satisfactory measure requires the adjustment of occupational pursuits to meet the individual's needs, penchants, mental and physical capacities, and emotional and personality make-up, and the institution of worth-while programs of educational and vocational guidance.

The rich achievement of this objective also entails the liberation of the individual's energies for constructive achievement, for some form of creative self-expression, whether in literary, artistic, or scientific fields, or in the practical pursuits of handicraft, homemaking, etc. This involves the opportunity to plan details and to carry them into execution, as well as freedom from unnecessary external restrictions and from hampering personal limitations, habits, or desires. This kind of constructive achievement, which makes for abundant positive personality fulfillment and enrichment, should be the goal of all our cultural strivings.

One of the stark tragedies of our modern technological world is the fact that our highly mechanized type of industrial civilization leaves little room for initiative, creativeness, and self-enrichment. Deadening, monotonous repetition of the same routinized movements constitutes the daily grind of millions of human factory machines.

8. The Well-adjusted Life Is Buttressed upon a Secure Foundation of Good Habits Acquired in Early Life.

The acquisition of good habits makes for efficiency, economy of effort, and freedom from friction. The reduction of many routine details to automatisms frees the mind for higher constructive achievements.

What kind of habituations will prove an aid to the maintenance of mental health? The repertoire should include at least the following:

1. Orderly physical habits—such as habits of eating, sleeping, and exercise. The physical care of the body should rest upon a foundation of well-regimented habits.

2. The formation of desirable habits of social response and adjustment— such as approved forms of social amenities, courtesies, greetings, acknowledgments, the dependable discharge of responsibilities, and proper social attitudes.

3. The regimentation of various mental activities—such as the formation of habits of emotional control and poise; of emotional expression and sublimation; of intellectual work and study; of concentrating, attending, and memorizing; of controlled, logical thinking; of forming orderly associations; of making thinking correspond to objective facts, instead of to one's wishes or prejudices; of doing, or motor performance; of working, playing, and behaving; of performing promptly and regularly all the little social and occupational duties of life.

The importance of acquiring habits of objective, orderly, unemotional thinking cannot be overstressed. We cannot think very clearly or accurately if we are resistant to change or if we allow our emotional prejudices and personal wishes to determine what we are to believe. One of the greatest menaces to lucid, factual, consistent thinking is the wish to believe. Arguments in support of our personal wishes are often fallacious and must be heavily discounted. In the well-ordered, efficient mind, thinking is objective, factual, accurate, and systematic. One of the outstanding characteristics of many mentally disordered minds is that their intellectual processes are disordered and disorganized. Their associations are incoherent, irrelevant, and false. They are often disoriented as to time or place or personal identity, and they are subject to delusions (false judgments or beliefs that are immune to facts), hallucinations, or illusions.

Accordingly, the early acquisition of desirable habits of feeling, thinking, and doing will prove to be a powerful bulwark against the development of mental unsoundness. The acquisition of good habits, as well as of wholesome attitudes, is more important for mental health and efficiency than is the mere accumulation of knowledge or scholastic accomplishments.

Summary Concept of the Wholesome Personality and of Mental Health. The wholesome personality is well adjusted, well integrated, consistent, adaptable, efficient, and contented. A personality that functions in a balanced, unified manner must be free from intellectual schisms and inconsistencies, emotional and nervous tensions, discords, and conflicts. It must be able to make continuous satisfactory adjustments to the ever-changing social and physical environments. Its behavior must be dependable and congruent with the lessons of experience. The various activities of the sane mind must be consistent and compatible. The sane mind does not comport itself like a series of compartmentalized selves, a series of Doctor Jekylls and Mr. Hydes, honest on Sunday, dishonest on Monday, generous today, crabbed tomorrow, reasonable and logical at times, at other times confused and inconsistent. Inconsistency in thinking, feeling, and doing is an outstanding characteristic of the disordered mind. The wholesome personality will be characterized by optimism; confidence; cooperativeness; frankness; sincerity; intellectual and emotional poise; balanced judgment; wisdom; ability to make judicious self-appraisals and self-criticisms and correct estimates of its motives and accomplishments; freedom from irrational beliefs, conscious or unconscious prejudices, and errors of ignorance, superstition, and bigotry; an inflexible will to achieve; and an output of energy sufficient for every fray of the day.

Finally, satisfactory and complete integration must include the totality of the individual. All factors and aspects of mentation or personality, as well as of the psychophysical organism, must be coordinated and integrated into a balanced, harmonious whole. Harmony must prevail between the individual's physical, psychic, and social activities. A healthy mind is at peace with itself. Mental health is, in a sense, a state of mind—a state of mind that enables the individual to attain his greatest amount of happiness and maximum efficiency with the minimum amount of strain or friction. Such a state of mind is largely the product of the formation of proper habits and attitudes in early life.

Possibility of Attaining the Ideal of Mental Health and Personality Fulfillment. Let us admit at once that this concept of mental health and the wholesome personality is an ideal that should serve as a guide to our objectives of health, normal-mindedness, and happiness. Few persons can be found whose psychophysical processes are so perfectly attuned and who are so perfectly adjusted to their environment that they can fully measure up to our ideal. One is reminded of the words of Aristotle: "No excellent soul is exempt from a mixture of madness." Even the best of men are a little hysterical and schizophrenic at times (Lyman Wells). But this fact should not deter us from "hitching our wagon to a star," if we want to reach the highest goal of mental health and efficiency. It is not very likely that anyone will shoot higher than he aims; most of us aim much lower than the altitude of our possibilities. But striving to attain the ideal of mental wholeness will pay rich dividends in the conservation of brain power and mental soundness.

Scope of Application of Mental-hygiene Work. 1. The problem of the preservation of mental health pertains to all levels, kinds, and classes of human beings: the young and the old; the normal and the abnormal; those apparently healthy and those obviously sick; those who suffer from major mental disorders and those subject to minor or apparently trivial mental disabilities or twists.

2. Mental-hygiene principles are applicable to every situation and relationship in life. There is no aspect of the individual's personal activities and no social agency to which mental-hygiene principles cannot be applied with profit. They are applicable to the management of the home, the school, the campus, the church, the hospital, the correctional institution; to the management of the institutions for mental defectives, for the mentally diseased, and for the dependent; to the management of the orphanage, the retreat, the court, the legislative hall, the social or business club, the office, the store, the factory,

the farm, the municipality, the state, the nation; last, but not least, to the management of the society of nations. While the fundamental principles of mental hygiene are largely the same, irrespective of the particular character of the human relationship involved, nevertheless, it remains true that the mental-hygiene problems of the school differ somewhat from those of home, orphanage, institution, church, or theater; the problems of the counting room differ from those of the farm or the factory; the problems of the home-bound pupil in the elementary or high school differ from those of the student on the campus away from home. There is, therefore, a mental hygiene of the home, the school, the church, the factory, the hospital, and every other social institution.

Courtship, mating, marriage, the rearing and education of children in the home and in the school, and the reciprocal relations of parents, of siblings, of siblings and parents, of teacher and pupil, of pastor and flock, of lawyer and client, of doctor and patient, of warden and convict, of rich man and beggar, of statesman and citizen, and of ruler and the ruled—all these relations will be improved if due consideration is given to the mental-hygiene elements involved. The roles of the teacher and the school and of the parent and the home are so commanding in the execution of the program of mental hygiene that special consideration will be accorded these factors in the next three chapters.

The application of mental-hygiene principles in the ordering of the school is of outstanding significance. The activities of the schools all along the line, from the nursery school to the postgraduate and professional schools of the university, should be administered in conformity with the demands of mental hygiene, not only with regard to the general atmosphere and management of the school and the recitation room, but also with regard to the processes of instruction in general and of the learning procedure in each branch of study.

The Need of Mental Hygiene in the Conservation of Mental and Social Health in Modern Life. Perhaps never before in the history of civilized man has the application of the principles of mental hygiene to every compartment of individual and communal life been more important than today. This is due to the fact, already emphasized, that the hectic tempo of our highly mechanized, industrial type of existence creates greater nervous and mental strain than was characteristic of the simple life of earlier generations, except, perhaps, during the primitive period of intense, savage combat for physical survival. Moreover, the present generation of men, women, and children, combatants and noncombatants alike, have been forced to live through the unprecedented horrors of two of the most colossal and terrifying wars of all time. These wars (particularly the second one) have touched bottom in wanton destruction of whole cities by means of artillery and immensely effective missiles, contrived by modern ingenuity and projected through the air. The conflicts have brought about the subjugation and enslavement of whole nations of peoples, who happened to be in the way of the aggressors; the undermining of the mental and physical health of whole countries by wholesale starvation; the ruthless massacre of millions of people; and the perpetration of frightful atrocities upon the vanquished, with the purpose of destroying morale. That such world-wide holocausts should not be attended by a host of psychosomatic disorders in the decades ahead would be difficult to believe. Healthy survival in this rushing age of intense specialization and competition, international intrigue and rivalry, and global warfare demands a degree of nervous and mental balance and capacity for adjustment never before required.

Civilization has marched ahead in relentless advance; science, discovery, and invention have extended the frontiers of knowledge; and the material agencies of production and destruction have multiplied at an amazing speed during this "Century of Progress." But has man's capacity for adaptation, especially on the psychological and social levels, made equal progress? Has man's control of himself kept pace with increasing control and utilization of the forces of nature? Must we not admit that man has lagged so far behind in the development of nervous and mental poise, in emotional stability, and in self-mastery that it is at least possible he may be destroyed by his own material and cultural creations? Is there not genuine danger that the intriguing but amazingly complicated civilization that man has fashioned may become his Juggernaut and bring about his destruction, unless his powers of personal adaptation become equal to the strain?

In his rather fanciful "Psychiatric Analysis of the Present-day Madness in the World," [34] Samuel H. Kraines, writing in 1937, compared the United States to a person with manic-depressive psychosis. The nation was on the height of the manic phase in 1929 and in the depression phase for some years thereafter. Germany was like a person in the depression phase with paranoid symptoms. Italy was like a feeble-minded person. Japan, like a psychopath, was subject to psychopathic outbursts and ideas of grandeur. China was lazy and philosophical. France was subject to excessive emotionalism and apprehension. England, like a settled businessman, was too set in her ways. The only really normal countries, according to Kraines, were Sweden, Norway, Denmark, Holland, and Switzerland.

Whether or not these mental disorders exist as national characteristics or psychoses—much of the world has been cockeyed to the point of complete irrationality since those words were penned—we must at least admit that every step of advance in civilization means an increase in the complexity of the problems with which the brain must wrestle in the attempt to adapt the

[34] *Science,* Oct. 22, 1937, 372*f.*

organism to the social, civic, psychological, educational, economic, and physical demands of life. Every advance means so many more chances for mental derailment and maladjustment. Has there ever before in the history of civilization been a greater need for mental balance, adaptability, resourcefulness, cooperativeness, tolerance, and good will? Civilizations have crumbled before, but not because Mother Nature failed man. The sun has continued to shine in the skies; vegetation has continued to flourish in lavish abundance; the earth has continued to produce boundless wealth from mine, forest, field, and sea. Surely nature has not defaulted. But man has failed to achieve satisfactory adjustment, particularly to his psychic and social needs.

A large proportion of our social and political distempers can, doubtless, be traced to the disfigured, discordant, dissatisfied personalities that inhabit the earth. Were the earth peopled with more harmonious and better integrated personalities, there would be less political and social conflict and fewer wars and rumors of wars. If the nations of the earth showed more regard for the principles of mental sanity and mental hygiene in their relations with one another, occasions for the exhibition of nationalistic bigotry, violent jingoism, jealousies, hatreds, and international strife would be reduced to a minimum, if not to the vanishing point. Mental health and mental hygiene in international as in personal relations mean facing the facts and issues candidly and dispassionately, without bias, duplicity, hypocritical diplomacy, or subservience to insensate emotional urges.

Mental-hygiene workers believe that in this age of supercivilization mental-hygiene principles have a profound bearing on all these problems of human adjustment that relate to the preservation of the mental welfare and contentment of the individual and of society. Mental hygiene has been referred to as the greatest contribution of this century for the improvement of the mental and social life of the young and the old, the rich and the poor, the sick and the well. It has been rated as "civilization's latest gold-mine district," the "most hopeful event in the history of man" (Ernest R. Groves and Phyllis Blanchard). Certainly, mental hygiene brings an improved technique, based on the methods of science, for the prevention and adjustment of man's personality disturbances. Although many of the elements of mental hygiene are as old as education, religion, medicine, and marriage, as old as civilization itself —for mental hygiene is a mixture of good common sense, common knowledge, science, and art—it remains true that the greatest progress in this field of psychodynamics has been made during the present century. This is due to the great forward stride made by all its underlying sciences, especially psychology and psychiatry. In spite of the great progress and the extravagant assertions of some of the enthusiastic disciples of Hygeia, mental hygiene as a well-documented science or a well-authenticated art has perhaps reached only its adolescent stage of development. There can be little doubt that the discoveries in the future will match those of the past in intrinsic interest and value and that many treatment techniques now regarded as the ne plus ultra of mental-hygiene therapy will be replaced by more effective ones.

The Importance of Mental Hygiene Shown by the Prevalence of Mental and Social Inadequates. The importance of mental hygiene in the program of social reclamation can be shown by the briefest reference to the widespread prevalence throughout the country of mental disease, mental defect, and serious social maladjustments, and of handicapped children of all types in the public schools, all of whom present in varying degree some problem for the mental hygienist.

The number of inmates supported largely at public expense in the institutions throughout the country for the mentally diseased and defective and for delinquents and criminals exceeds 800,000.[35] A much larger number of neurotics,[36] psychoneurotics, and mental and social defectives and dependents are at large in society, imposing a serious financial and social burden upon the homes, welfare organizations, and law-enforcement agencies. According to the *Manufacturer's Record* (as quoted in Royal S. Copeland's speech before the Senate on January 11, 1934), the annual cost of our bill for crime and crime suppression amounted to almost 13 billion dollars, more than a decade ago. It may be larger now. About 3 million of the country's elementary

[35] According to the statistics issued by the U.S. Bureau of the Census, at the end of the year 1946, there were 468,285 resident patients in the state, county, and city hospitals for mental disease (*Current Population Reports,* Mental Institutions, Sept. 10, 1947).

In 1945, there were 113,652 mental defectives and 21,040 epileptics in public and private residential institutions (*Ibid.,* July 17, 1947).

In 1942 there were 157,514 prisoners in state and Federal prisons, penitentiaries, reformatories, penal farms, road camps, correctional institutions, vocational schools, and some institutions for the criminally insane, but exclusive of juvenile offenders, and, with two exceptions, municipal jails and county jails and workhouses (see *Prisoners in State and Federal Prisons and Reformatories,* 1942, U.S. Department of Commerce, Bureau of the Census, 1945, 3).

The public-school classes for the mentally deficient and the retarded enrolled 98,416 pupils in the school year 1940–1941.

The cost of the public institutions for psychotics in 1946 reached the stupendous sum of $187,510,218; for the institutions for mental defectives and epileptics, in 1945, $42,726,769. Nearly all of this huge outlay had to be borne by the taxpayers.

[36] As it is commonly understood, a neurosis is a functional nervous disorder which is not dependent upon any clearly defined structural nervous defect and which is characterized by nervous and emotional instability. A psychoneurosis is a functional disorder of the central nervous system, less pronounced than a psychosis (a form of mental disease, disorder, or insanity), caused by mental factors (psychogenically produced) and restricted by some authorities to the hysterias and compulsion neuroses (see J. E. Wallace Wallin, *Clinical and Abnormal Psychology,* Boston, Houghton Mifflin Company, 1927, Chap. IX, 264–268) ; also, Roy M. Dorcus and G. Wilson Shaffer, *Textbook of Abnormal Psychology,* Baltimore, The Williams & Wilkins Company, 1935, 52–53, 265–292.

school children are so handicapped physically, mentally, or socially as to require special education treatment,[37] while many millions of other school children are subject to an amazingly large number of minor emotional, intellectual, social, or educational disabilities or maladjustments. In the space of a decade, the increase in suicides amounted to 23 per cent; in homicides, to 13.8 per cent.

Marital discord increased about eightfold for the 50-year period from 1890 to 1940, based on the Federal statistics of decrees of divorce and annulments (from 33,461 to 264,000 divorces).[38] From 1940 to 1946 (the all-time high, with an estimated 613,000 divorces and annulments), the increase amounted to almost 233 per cent. The rise during this period was from 2.4 divorces per 1,000 of the total population to 4.3. From 1940 through 1945, the marriage-divorce ratio rose from 16.5 to 30.8 divorces per 100 marriages—an increase of almost 90 per cent. (There was a fall to 26.8 in 1946, based on incomplete statistics.) In 1909 the marriage-divorce ratio was only 8.9. The increase in the divorce rate is doubtless due to a variety of causes, such as changes in the attitude of the individual regarding the sacredness and inviolability of the marriage contract, a more liberal attitude of society toward the granting of divorces, and the willingness of married people to reveal their discords and to take drastic steps to untangle their marital snarls, rather than to a real increase in family discord. Nevertheless, mental-hygiene elements exist in most cases of marital discord. Marital disharmony and divorce often constitute evidences of some kind of personal or sexual maladjustment, or some other type of incompatibility, or character anomalies, such as fickleness or temperamental instability, the inability to adjust personal desires or habits, or the tendency to follow the line of least resistance by severing the bond and fleeing from the solution of a difficult problem. Divorce is essentially an escape mechanism. In many cases, it is to a considerable extent a problem of mental hygiene and a problem for a mental-hygiene clinic. A few marriage and divorce clinics have been established, best known of which is the Los Angeles Institute of Family Relations.

The attitude of youth, the innocent victims of divorce, toward the disruption of family life is shown in an investigation in 1937 by the Institute of Public Opinion. Seventy-three per cent of 100,000 youths between the ages of 21 and 25 voted against liberal divorce laws, while 27 per cent were in favor of such laws.

The inescapable conclusion from all of the foregoing evidences of defects, frictions, and maladjustments is that man is finding it very difficult to adjust

[37] See *Special Education, The Handicapped and the Gifted,* White House Conference on Child Health and Protection, 1931, 5, 6, 554.

[38] *Marriage and Divorce Statistics, United States, 1946,* Federal Security Agency, U.S. Public Health Service, Oct. 24, 1947.

himself satisfactorily to his environment. He is out of step with the social, economic, biological, and physical demands of his surroundings. The annual cost for the maintenance of our vast army of the mentally, socially, educationally, and physically defective and handicapped and of the otherwise maladjusted and discontented amounts every year to several times the four billion dollars that we spent in 1948, according to a recent estimate, for the support of the schools at all levels. Perhaps we would not have to spend as much as four billion on crime control if we diverted half of the crime bill to the support of efficient systems of schools with adequate special education and mental-hygiene provisions for the individual needs of the children.

Of course, the whole army of the mentally, socially, and physically handicapped cannot be wiped out by programs of mental hygiene alone; but mental hygiene has something to contribute to the program of rehabilitation of all these groups of maladjusted and malcontented children and adults. There is little doubt that the total number of such cases could be greatly reduced by the nation-wide application of comprehensive programs of mental hygiene coupled with programs of remedial instruction and special education to meet individual needs, feasible eugenic measures, programs for the early treatment of physical defects and diseases, and programs of community sanitation, slum clearance, the elimination of crime-breeding centers, and the improvement of the physical attractiveness and the morale and esprit de corps of the home.

CHAPTER II

THE REMEDIAL, PREVENTIVE, AND POSITIVE OBJECTIVES OF THE MENTAL-HYGIENE PROGRAM

Triple Objectives of the Mental-hygiene Program. A measurably complete mental-hygiene program will include three fundamental objectives: remedial, preventive, and positive. Although the line of demarcation between these triple objectives must not be too sharply drawn, because they naturally overlap and supplement one another, as will be reemphasized on later pages, clarity in our thinking will be furthered by a separate treatment of each phase.

1. THE REMEDIAL OR CORRECTIVE OBJECTIVE

The remedial phase of mental-hygiene treatment consists in the cure or the amelioration of physical and mental diseases, defects, or maladjustments; the correction of hampering physical, mental, or social habits and attitudes; and the overcoming of specific or general educational disabilities. In some cases the treatment may be primarily surgical or medical; in some cases it may be primarily educational, as, for example, some process of reeducation or of diagnostic or corrective education; in other cases the process may be fundamentally psychological, psychotherapeutic, or social.

The curative treatment of advanced forms of mental disease is the oldest phase of mental-hygiene work. Long before any attempt was made to prevent mental difficulties or to preserve good mental health, efforts were made to cure those who had already become mentally deranged. Generations before hospitals for the mentally disordered were established, mental patients were merely incarcerated in so-called madhouses or asylums or in institutions for delinquents and dependents.

More recently, attention on the curative side is being devoted to the correction of minor mental blemishes and maladjustments. This curative or negative phase of mental hygiene will always occupy a prominent place in any adequate mental-hygiene program, so long as children and adults exist who have already acquired mental, social, or educational defects or abnormalities. One of the chief concerns of the state should be, and for some time will continue to be, to provide the best physical and mental care for its unfortunate mental defectives, psychotics, neurotics, psychoneurotics, and epileptics, besides all those who tend to develop social, mental, or educational maladjustments because of specific physical or mental defects. But, essential as is the remedial objective, it cannot be regarded as the most important aspect of mental hygiene. Of still greater urgency is the second objective.

2. The Preventive Objective

It is more important to prevent mental disease and personality disorders than to try to overcome them after they have been acquired. The needless acquisition of abnormal traits and handicaps is very uneconomical. It reduces the social and economic efficiency of the individual concerned, and the processes of cure are frequently very tedious and expensive and sometimes futile. Moreover, most minor mental maladjustments and many of the major ones could have been prevented by the application of appropriate preventive measures in the home, school, church, factory, or playground.

Emphasis upon the preventive objective has come largely as a result of the discovery of the causes of mental disorders and maladjustments—which has made it possible to devise more effective methods of prophylaxis—and also as a result of the growing recognition of the importance of treating mental difficulties in the incipient stages before they become ingrained. One authority has estimated that the percentage of cures of many mental diseases is twice as large during the first year as during the second year. As a result of emphasis upon the preventive aim, observation wards and mental-hygiene clinics have been established all over the country for the examination and treatment of early cases. Increasing efforts are being made to discover and remove the causes of incipient mental disorders, as well as of minor mental inadequacies and conflicts.

Threefold Nature of the Preventive Program. The preventive program must include a consideration of all the basic causative factors of mental abnormalities. These may be reduced to three groups:

1. *The Eugenic Aspect.* Positive eugenics consists in encouraging the mating of biologically normal and healthy stock. The importance of inheriting a sound nervous system is universally conceded. The individual's native endowment is to a considerable extent responsible for his general capacity and for some of his trends and talents. Heredity determines innate structure and the limits of development, while environment determines the particular direction of the individual's development within the bounds of hereditary limitations. But heredity is dependent upon experience for its opportunity for development. It cannot develop in a vacuum. Apart from experience and training, it is impossible to determine the hereditary limitations of any individual. It is no easy task to determine accurately what proportion of the infant's endowment comes from heredity in the narrow sense, how much comes from his prenatal environment, and how much from external environmental stimulation.

Negative eugenics, on the other hand, consists in the prevention of the reproduction of defective or dysgenic stocks by such methods as sterilization, colonization, and prevention of marriage among the unfit.

The theory on which negative eugenics is based is that a neuropathic heredity and the resulting unstable nervous system constitute favorable predisposing conditions for the development of mental abnormalities. Few doubt the influence of the hereditary factor in the production of certain grave nervous disorders, such as feeble-mindedness (defective inheritance is its most important cause) and some types of epilepsy and mental disorder. But the role of cacogenic (defective) heredity in the production of minor mental twists and anomalies is a different problem. We know from innumerable case studies that personality maladjustments of all kinds may develop in persons whose nervous systems apparently are essentially sound and relatively free from hereditary taint. In fact, the best soil for the development of a great variety of mental disturbances to which humans fall heir would seem to be found in those whose nervous systems are very responsive and highly sensitized.

Brief Excursus on the Role of Heredity in the Acquisition of Behavior and Personality Traits as Shown by Genetic Investigations. Since the radical antiheredity pronouncement of the prince of behaviorists, John B. Watson, in the mid-twenties, it has been a vogue on the part of some social psychologists, sociologists, cultural anthropologists, and educationists to apotheosize the influence of the environment and to deny almost *in toto* the influence of heredity, except so far as it relates to the inheritance of the anatomical structures, the simple reflexes (such as the wink reflex and sucking in infants), and simple emotions. In 1924 Watson completely rejected the instinct concept: "there are then for us no instincts—we no longer need the term in psychology." The behavior patterns called instincts are the results of "learned behavior." "There is no such thing as an inheritance of capacity, talent, temperament, mental constitution and characteristics." [1]

We have no real evidence of the inheritance of traits. I would feel perfectly confident in the ultimately favorable outcome of careful upbringing of a healthy, well-formed baby born of a long line of crooks, murderers, thieves, and prostitutes. . . . I would like to go one step further tonight and say, give me a dozen healthy infants, well-formed, and my own specified world to bring them up in and I'll guarantee to take any one at random and train him to become any type of specialist I might select—a doctor, lawyer, artist, merchant-chief, and yes, even into beggar-man and thief, regardless of his talents, penchants, tendencies, abilities, [the] vocations and the race of his ancestors.[2]

[1] John B. Watson, *Behaviorism,* New York, W. W. Norton & Company, Inc., 1924, 94.
[2] *Ibid.,* "What the Nursery Has to Say about Instincts," *Pedagogical Seminary and Journal of Genetic Psychology,* June, 1925, 301f.

Even as late as 1928, Watson categorically affirmed that "there is nothing from within to develop." [3]

Watson's extreme statements probably served a useful purpose in instigating many of the numerous observations and experiments carried out during the last quarter century on the genesis of many stereotyped behavior patterns in many orders of mammals, the results of which have led an outstanding biologist, George H. Parker, to conclude "that we are perhaps about nine-tenths inborn and one-tenth acquired. . . . What education gives us counts tremendously in everyday life." Nevertheless, "what we get by education is a small acquisition planted on a very large inborn background." [4] An outstanding comparative psychologist, Leonard Carmichael, also adopts the same view from his own experiments and from an analysis of the literature: "there is nothing that I know of in the recent quantitative study of the early growth of behavior which tends to deny the possibility of the truth of the statement quoted at the beginning of this paper that human nature is nine-tenths inborn." [5]

The return to sanity and a factual appraisal of the relative influence of nature and nurture—heredity and environment—in the acquisition of behavior responses is the inevitable consequence of the fuller knowledge of the problem that has been bequeathed by the extensive objective observations and experiments of the last quarter of a century. For a brief summary of the experimental contributions and references, consult the "Symposium on Heredity and Environment" in *Psychological Review* for November, 1947, pages 297 to 352. The major types of investigations carried out, usually on subprimates (rodents, guinea pigs, cats, dogs) but also on primates, may be classified briefly as follows:

1. The relation of mating (the oestrus) and sex behavior to the secretion of the endocrine glands (which, of course, are inherited structures), such as the secretions from the gonads, ovaries, and the pituitary—gonadotropic hormones, androgens, and estrogen (see pages 7*ff*. and Chap. XIII).

2. The effects of cortical excisions on sex behavior.

3. Studies of the embryology of behavior: the response of the fetus prior to experience, imitation, learning, or practice (especially in guinea pigs) to stimuli—such as pressure, thermal, light, and electrical stimuli—and the observation of anesthetized fetuses (*e.g.*, of salamanders, which feed on the yolk of the egg from which they develop).

[3] *Ibid., Psychological Care of the Infant and Child,* New York, W. W. Norton & Company, Inc., 1928.

[4] George H. Parker, *The World Expands,* Cambridge, Mass., Harvard University Press, 1946 (quoted from Carmichael).

[5] Leonard Carmichael, "The Growth of the Sensory Control of Behavior before Birth," *Psychological Review,* 1947, 323.

4. The relation of specific and general behavior responses to processes of maturation, shown most strikingly in the field of sex.

5. The study of the relations of behavior to innate perceptual organization of the brain and to small and large (pathological) variations in nervous tissue.

6. The studies of the effects of a uniform habitat on varied heredity (such as Stockard's experiments on pure breeds of dogs [6] and Schoolland's experiments on chicks and ducks [7]) and of varied environments on uniform heredity (such as Kuo's experiments on cats' rat responses [8]).

7. The study of complicated unlearned activities usually classified as instincts, such as web building by spiders, nest building by birds, swimming by ducks, and hoarding by rats.

8. The modification of behavior in various stages of animal life by experience, practice, conditioning, and learning.

While the results differ greatly, according to the evolutionary complexity of the organism, the conclusions most pertinent to the subject matter of this volume, justified by these many-sided investigations, may be stated as follows:

a. Innate functional specificity exists in the brain cells and in the perceptual organization of the brain. Innate differences exist in the size and form of the cells, in their structural and chemical (metabolic) constitution, in their responsiveness to stimuli, and in the electrical brain waves. All these differences influence behavior more or less. The neonatus (newborn) begins independent existence with pronounced variations in the cerebral neuron potentialities and responsiveness, although the general brain architecture is similar throughout the mammalian series.

b. In terms of Stockard (as conveyed in a personal communication of October 3, 1934), "The genetic constitution of the tissue governs its response to internal secretions." The qualities of the baby's "tissue constitution" primarily govern its responses to the secretion of the endocrine glands, such as the thyroid or the pituitary. These tissue qualities are the results of inheritance. Different babies have inherited different qualities of "tissue constitution," and so they respond differently in their "tissue reactions" to the same glandular secretions. Moreover, differences in body type or build

[6] Charles R. Stockard, Oscar D. Anderson, and William T. James, *Genetic and Endocrine Bases for Differences in Form and Behavior as Elucidated by Studies of Contrasted Pure-line Dog Breeds and Their Hybrids,* Philadelphia, Wistar Institute of Anatomy and Biology, 1941.

[7] John B. Schoolland, *Are There Any Innate Behavior Tendencies,* Genetic Psychology Monographs, May, 1942, 219–287 (106 references).

[8] Zing Y. Kuo, "The Genesis of the Cat's Response to the Rat," *Journal of Comparative Psychology,* 1930, 11, 1–35.

(morphology),[9] as well as tissue constitution, probably also determine to a large extent the character of the child's responses to external stimuli and his basic temperamental, motivational, and dispositional trends.

c. The general behavior patterns of the organism and sometimes also certain specific behavior patterns are dependent upon the stage of maturation of its inherent anatomical structures.

d. Embryologic behavior and immediate postnatal behavior are adaptive and purposive, prior to any possible experience or learning, depending upon the innate structure, the blood chemistry resulting from its metabolic processes, and its predetermined patterns of response to external stimulations. For example, when the hair esthesiometer is pressed just below the ear of the fetal guinea pig, an ear twitch is evoked. If the pressure is continued or repeated, the paw on the same side is raised toward the irritant, in the apparent effort to brush it away. If the stimulus is continued longer, the whole head and trunk and eventually most of the muscles of the body may be called into action (Carmichael). Such unlearned, complicated, coordinated responses to external stimuli are, evidently, purposive. A varied assortment of goal-directed activities is present in the guinea pig, at least a week before birth.

e. The process of birth does not alter suddenly the basic response patterns of the nervous system. Hereditary trends continue beyond birth. Many complicated, coordinated behavior patterns (instincts) do not emerge until certain stages of maturity have been reached, irrespective of experience or learning. Such are web weaving, nest building, and food hoarding.

f. Constant reaction patterns are found in a given species (species constants) and constant differences between certain species (interspecies constants), irrespective of environmental variables, obviously dependent upon inherent structures.

g. Experimental induction of precocious puberty and of sex activity in asexualized males (castrated) and females (ovariectomized) is possible merely from the administration of certain hormones (e.g., androgen and estrogen).

h. The native response patterns, however, are subject to modification by environmental factors (experience, education, conditioning, culture). The modifiability is far greater in the primates, especially man, than in the sub-primates. The human neopallium, which is the cerebral cortex, exclusive of the olfactory area (the phylogenetically most recent part of the brain), is

[9] For evidence on the relation of morphology to temperamental and emotional characteristics and "constitutional psychology," consult

William H. Sheldon, Stanley S. Stevens, and William B. Tucker, *The Varieties of Human Physique, An Introduction to Constitutional Psychology,* New York, Harper & Brothers, 1940; and Sheldon and Stevens, *Varieties of Temperament; A Psychology of Constitutional Differences,* Harper & Brothers, 1942.

essentially an organ of adjustment or learning, and is subject to amazing development in the lifetime of the individual.

i. Individual differences are apparent in the psychological response patterns of children very early in life, dependent to some extent at least on structural and functional differences in the inherited glandular and neuromuscular systems. Obviously, the younger the infant, the more likely is it that the behavior differences are of genetic origin. The experiment of H. Zoepffel [10] on twenty infants during the first year of life is suggestive. She carefully observed the reactions of these infants as they were lying in their cribs, using a variety of stimuli, such as moving a gold watch back and forth before the child's eyes, pricking and stroking the skin, giving the infant sweet and salt solutions, playing a tune on the mouth harmonica, and speaking to the child in tones and words of censure (such as "Shame on you. Now will you behave and be a good babe?") or of praise ("You are a nice, beautiful child; we like such children"). The striking outcome of the experiment was the marked individual differences that these infants showed in their responses. Some reacted sluggishly and phlegmatically, others quickly and vivaciously. Some evidenced pleasurable reactions, others discomfort. Some responded by laughing, others by crying. These individual differences in response patterns were sufficiently constant to indicate definite personality trends. Since they occurred so early in life, the conclusion seems to be that they were mainly dependent upon innate constitutional trends.

j. It is no easy task to determine accurately what proportion of the human infant's endowment comes from heredity in the narrow sense, how much comes from his prenatal environment, and how much from external environmental impacts. Biological heredity obviously accounts for all the tendencies, traits, and characteristics that the child possesses at the beginning of life in the embryo (after insemination). But the maternal environment begins to operate in the embryonic stage and makes an indeterminate contribution to the sum total. The child at birth starts his life voyage with a congenital heritage of assets and liabilities, largely determined by the transmitted nature of the genes (the hereditary germinal factor) and partly by the effects of the maternal environment on the somatic (body) cells. The balance of the transmitted and the acquired influences, however, alters enormously as the child begins to undergo conscious experiences with his physical and social environment. Just as soon as he begins to have experiences, native trends are subjected to a process of development and modification.[11] What may be

[10] H. Zoepffel, "Ein Versuch zur experimentellen Feststellung der Persönlichkeit in Saulingsalter," *Zeitschrift für Psychologie,* 1929, 273–306.

[11] It is possible to elicit reactions from the fetus to external stimulations of various kinds applied to the mother's soma (body). That such antenatal experiences exert any influence upon the "personality" of the child has not been shown. Such putative psychic

referred to comprehensively as social heredity begins to supplement and modify biological heredity.

As the child grows older, the element of personal experience becomes increasingly important in determining his detailed reactions. The theory of biological heredity is inadequate to explain the great variety of ways in which different people respond to identical physical, social, or psychological stimuli after experience has begun to modify behavior. Few mental reaction patterns have been transmitted to the human individual ready-made by heredity. The study of the formation of specific traits, especially maladjustments, in thousands of cases forces us to the conclusion that most of the behavior patterns of children, youths, and adults have been acquired through the individual's impacts against his physical and social environments. The essential basis for the specificity of the individual's behavior patterns is the series of experiences he has lived through since the day of birth. As we shall see later, behavior patterns are often the product of processes of conditioning.

It may, therefore, be concluded that defective heredity may furnish a fertile soil for the development of mental and nervous diseases, but that, so far as minor personality maladjustments are concerned, it supplies only a predisposing condition, just as do the stresses and strains that accompany the processes of maturation. Certain crises of development, particularly the onset of puberty and the adolescent stage, may also supply a fertile soil for the production of personality maladjustments. But many of the personality difficulties incident to the processes of psychophysical development are probably created by the restrictions imposed by the customs and laws of society upon the free, uninhibited expression of the child's impulses and cravings, such as desires to dominate others, to appropriate others' property, and to give expression to the promptings of sex.

The eugenic aspect of the mental-hygiene program is important in both its positive and negative phases, but it is very difficult to carry out and it cannot be depended upon as the mainstay in any constructive program of mental hygiene.

2. *The Prevention of Injury to the Nervous System of Persons Already in Existence.* The mental ravages produced by the diseases, passions, stresses, shocks, and injuries suffered by the individual from the time of birth until the time of death are well known. Most of these injuries to the nervous system could have been prevented through the exercise of proper prophylactic care, and thus many mental maladies could have been avoided.

3. *The Protection of the Individual from Injurious Mental Experiences.* Perhaps the greatest contribution made by the modern mental-hygiene move-

---

effects from the maternal environment would be congenital (and constitutional, in the larger sense), but not hereditary.

ment is the demonstration of the dependence of the individual's mental health upon his own previous experiences and the importance of forestalling or preventing experiences that may lead to mental maladjustment or disintegration. The evidence is conclusive that many mental difficulties have been acquired by the individual in his contact with his physical and social environment— with things, natural phenomena, animals, and especially other people. In consequence, the emphasis is being placed more and more on the influence of human relationships in the production of mental maladjustments, especially the minor ones. Many of these, if not most of them, as we shall see, are socially produced.

All of the individual's experiences may be of importance in producing mental discord, but especially significant are the experiences that produce emotional upsets, such as frights, fears, anxieties, worries, repressions, emotional conflicts, inhibitions, superstitions, false beliefs, and cutting remarks. It is also being increasingly recognized that the experiences of early life are those which are most important in shaping the individual's destiny, in determining his fundamental attitudes toward the problems of life, and in laying the basis for his mental soundness or unsoundness. In early childhood, the nervous system is very receptive and plastic. Because of this and because of his lack of experience and his natural credulity, the child can be very easily influenced. In point of fact, as we trace back the genesis of mental disorders in the adult, we frequently find the premonitory symptoms in early childhood. The outstanding pathological traits in the psychotic are often merely exaggerated forms of the same peculiarities that were already apparent in the early life of the individual. And as we investigate more fully the nature of the process of trait formation, we find again and again that a great number of the individual's idiosyncrasies and attitudes, instead of being inherited, were acquired from his contacts with his parents, siblings, playmates, and others.

How, then, is the process of formation of these acquired characteristics to be explained? The explanation involves a consideration of the doctrine of the conditioned response.

Conditioning in Early Childhood as the Cause of Mental Maladjustments. According to this doctrine, the mental traits that the child acquires are essentially conditioned reflexes or responses. To many authorities the conditioned type of response represents par excellence the method of learning or of habit formation. What, then, is a conditioned response or reflex? Perhaps the best way to approach the question is to contrast conditioned reflexes with the unconditioned or ordinary kind of reflexes, which are usually referred to simply as reflexes. Unconditioned reflexes, such as the eyewink, the knee jerk, or the sucking reflex in the infant, are inherited, ready-made, coordinated, mechanical, adaptive responses to appropriate stimuli. Owing to hereditarily preformed connections between certain sensory and motor neurons in the spinal cord or medulla, the eyelids of the newborn child close automatically when the eye or the skin nearby is touched; later a similar effect is produced by the rapid approach of a missile. The leg of the child or of the adult kicks automatically in direct response to a sharp tap upon the patellar tendon (patellar reflex). Such responses are simple, direct reactions to so-called biologically adequate or natural stimuli that are inherited or unlearned.

Conditioned responses or reflexes, on the other hand, have been learned by the individual. They have been acquired by a process of associating artificial stimuli with the biologically adequate stimuli, in consequence of which the same responses may be produced by the associated stimuli as by the original ones. This result is based upon the general psychological principle of association: when two stimuli or events have occurred together, they tend to become so linked together that either one of them may produce the same response, even though the relationship between the stimuli is purely arbitrary or fortuitous. By a process of association, then, or "conditioning" as it is technically called, the individual becomes conditioned to or by a new stimulus. The conditioned responses, once established, in general acquire the characteristics of the inherited reflexes: directness and automaticity of response to the conditioned stimulus and strength of connection. These characteristics can be readily discerned in many of the illustrative cases scattered throughout the pages of this book.

Illustrations of the Two Types of Responses. The difference between the conditioned and unconditioned reflexes can be made clear by contrasting the two types in the case of simple and more complex reaction patterns.

1. *Simple Reflexes.* The secretion of the saliva is normally an inherited reflex. The salivary glands automatically secrete saliva when they are stimulated by a natural stimulus, such as the perception of food by the visual, gustatory, or olfactory sense organ. Now, let us suppose that a bell is sounded every time a dog is fed—the experiment performed by Ivan P. Pavlov, the Russian physiologist and pioneer investigator of the conditioned reflex. What will eventually happen when the bell is rung without the presentation of the food stimulus? After a certain number of repetitions of the simultaneous presentations of these two stimuli, it will be observed that the salivary glands will discharge when the bell alone is sounded (without feeding). In other words, a conditioned response has been established. By a process of conditioning, the dog's salivary glands will now be excited by an indifferent, "inadequate" stimulus. An artificial, substitute stimulus has been conditioned to arouse the same response as the natural one. To put the matter in another way, the salivary glands have learned to respond properly to an artificial stimulus that was intentionally associated with the natural

one; thus by a process of learning, the substitute stimulus has acquired the attributes originally possessed only by the natural stimulus. That such conditioning or association may occur purely accidentally (and a surprising number of conditioned responses are accidentally established) will be shown by the following examples of complex behavior responses.

2. *Complex Behavior Responses.* Let us take, as a fairly common reaction pattern, the fear of thunder and lightning. The fear of thunder is explained as an inherited reflex, based on the fear of noise. The fear of noises is one of John B. Watson's three inherited modes of response. The fear of the flash of lightning, on Watson's theory, is not an inherited response but a conditioned response. After the child has associated the flash with the thunder, the lightning alone may induce terror. Similarly, when loud noises become linked to gasoline engines (an instance will be cited later), locomotives, or barking dogs, these originally neutral stimuli may produce conditioned fear responses.

Watson, in his classic experiment on early conditioning, cites the case of an 11-month-old baby who had never been outside the hospital, who had never seen an animal prior to the experiment, and who evinced only approaching responses to the animals shown him—rats, rabbits, cats, and dogs. The only tested stimulations that produced fear responses were loud noises and loss of support. On the first presentation of a white rat, suddenly withdrawn from a basket, the child's left hand reached for the rat. The moment the hand touched the rat an iron bar behind the infant's head was struck with a hammer. "The infant jumped violently and fell forward, burying his face in the mattress." The same reaction, with the addition of whimpering, occurred when the experiment was repeated. While it required about seven combined stimulations to condition a strong fear of rats with this particular infant (characterized as "phlegmatic"), only one or two stimulations were needed with others who were more sensitively organized. The conditioning was retained in its original intensity over a period of 5 days and eventually spread to the rabbit, the dog, a fur coat, a bundle of cotton wool, and the whiskers of a mask of Santa Claus.[12]

---

[12] John B. Watson, *Psychology from the Standpoint of a Behaviorist,* Philadelphia, J. B. Lippincott Company, 1924, 232–233.

The conclusions reached by Watson regarding the original emotional nature of infants have been brought into question by later researches. See Amalie K. Nelson and K. H. Sun, *The Behavior of the Newborn Infant,* Columbus, The Ohio State University Press, 1930.

Mandel Sherman, "The Differential of Emotional Responses in Infants": I., "Judgments of Emotional Response from Motion Picture Views and from Actual Observation," *Journal of Comparative Psychology,* Vol. 7, 1927, 265–284; II., "The Ability of Observers to Judge the Emotional Characteristics of the Crying of Infants and of the Voice of the Adult," *Journal of Comparative Psychology,* Vol. 7, 1927, 335–351.

Another typical complex reaction pattern, anger, often results from similar processes of conditioning. The rage that the young infant shows when its limbs are held is an inherited reflex: the adequate or original stimulus to anger in the infant is physical restraint (J. B. Watson). But the child who has temper tantrums when not noticed sufficiently or when refused some request is showing a conditioned response. He has learned by a process of conditioning (popularly called "spoiling") that the way to secure attention or acquiescence to his whims is to throw a fit or to shout or cry.

The concept of the conditioned response has enabled the psychologist to explain rationally the development in children (as well as in adults) of a vast number of hitherto inexplicable idiosyncrasies; mental snarls and quirks; peculiar attitudes; habits; likes and dislikes; persistent and apparently irrational emotional trends; and particular reactive tendencies, such as aggressiveness, domination, submissiveness, or resignation. Such phenomena are often due to some process of early conditioning, whether intentional or accidental. While the mechanism of conditioning does not account for the origin of all normal or abnormal personality traits, it occupies a position of central significance, especially in early life.

How readily can conditioned responses be established? Ordinarily a number of associations must have occurred between the artificial and the natural stimulus before the artificial stimulus will function independently. In general, the more satisfying the results of the association, the fewer are the repetitions needed to establish the linkage (Edward L. Thorndike's "law of effect").[13] But this does not exhaust the possibilities. Frequently a conditioned response can be firmly established by a single episode. One intense or dramatic occurrence that is very painful or unpleasant may be more effective than many satisfying repetitions. Moreover, a mere fortuitous concurrence of apparently neutral stimuli; a commonplace event; a casual, innocent remark, may result in an emotional conditioning that may persist for years and lead to most tragic consequences. The potency of such isolated experiences probably is due to the intensity of the emotional response produced, although the feeling may be successfully concealed. So far as the more intense and persistent conditioned responses are concerned, the process of conditioning is

---

[13] On the controversial question of the psychological effects of punishment and rewards, consult

Leo Postman, "The History and Present Status of the Law of Effect," *Psychological Bulletin*, November, 1947, 489–563 (332 references).

G. Raymond Stone, "A Note on Postman's Review of the Literature on the Law of Effect," *Psychological Bulletin*, March, 1948, 151–160 (31 references).

Edward L. Thorndike, "The Law of Effect: A Round Table Discussion, III," *Psychological Review*, Vol. 45, 1938, 204–205; also *Man and His Works*, Cambridge, Mass., Harvard University Press, 1943.

fundamentally emotional in character. The associated experiences are welded together by emotional bonds.

ILLUSTRATIONS FROM THE AUTHOR'S CASE STUDIES OF NORMAL PEOPLE, OF TRAIT FORMATION, AND OF THE ACQUISITION OF PERSONALITY MALADJUST-MENTS BY THE PROCESS OF ARTIFICIAL CONDITIONING

The role of early conditioning in the formation of character traits can be most effectively shown by a study of actual cases. Because of the fact that a large number of original autobiographies of maladjustment will be introduced at various stages in this book to illustrate various processes and principles, it is desirable to pause at this point to explain why and how these personal data were obtained.

Nature of the Author's Autobiographies of Mental, Educational, and Social Maladjustments. The preponderance of case data on mental deviations and maladjustments hitherto accessible to the mental hygienist, psychologist, educationist, and sociologist has been based on distinctly pathological material, such as psychotics, mental defectives, pronounced neurotics, misdemeanants, and criminals. Data from such sources are not lacking in dramatic appeal or in basic significance, but the vast army of betterment workers (parents, teachers, ministers, and the like) who devote themselves to the service of the normal population tend to regard such data as extreme, pathological, inapplicable to their problems, and therefore lacking in convincingness so far as work with normal groups is concerned. In addition, the study of mental abnormalities in the distinctly pathological classes is sometimes fraught with the danger that the student may become so enamored of the study of the pathological as to exaggerate the gravity of minor mental deviations in normal persons (admittedly important as they are) and to regard such deviations as convincing evidence of mental disease, thereby becoming unduly concerned about the sanity of such persons or of himself. Such a state of mind is distinctly inimical to the maintenance of good mental health. While autobiographies of derangements and difficulties obtained from normal groups, described without attempt at embellishment or exaggeration, will be less thrilling than the fantastic and grotesque aberrations of the mentally diseased, they will be more "true to life" and more valuable to students interested primarily in the mental hygiene of normal people, who constitute perhaps about 90 per cent of the total population.

Data secured from normal people possess further merit in that they supply irrefutable evidence that normal folk, so called, are not free from personality blemishes, but are subject to the same kinds of mental deviation that characterize the pathological groups, although, naturally, the involvements are less extensive and less severe. One learns from the study of such data that mental normality is a relative term, that intellectually normal persons may be subject to an amazing variety of transient or lasting mental disturbances, conflicts, or idiosyncrasies; and that mental maladjustments and upsets may be produced by all sorts of occurrences, even the most trivial.

With a view to obtaining first-hand data on personality maladjustments in normal people, the writer for years has secured from his graduate and undergraduate students (in the University of Virginia, University of Chicago, Johns Hopkins University, New York University, and University of Delaware, State Teachers College at Buffalo, and other institutions in which he has lectured) written reports on "early difficulties of adjustment." The students were requested to describe the nature of their personal maladjustments or idiosyncrasies as accurately as possible and without exaggeration, to trace them to their source, if possible, indicating when and how they originated and when they disappeared, and to sketch the method of resolution that may have been worked out by their parents, teachers, or guardians, or by themselves. In case the difficulties continued uncorrected, they were also asked to describe the nature of the problems that affected them at the time of the report.

These inventories constituted a part of the regular requirements of courses in clinical, abnormal, systematic, and educational psychology and courses on mentally retarded, psychopathic, and deficient children in which occasional references were made to mental-hygiene problems. The reports were submitted as term papers in the graduate courses.

The students submitting the reports varied in academic status from sophomores to graduate students working on their doctorate dissertations. The large majority were professional educators—namely, special-class teachers, teachers in the elementary and secondary schools, principals, supervisors, superintendents, and instructors of psychology or education in colleges and teacher-training schools. Most of them were graduates of normal schools, teachers colleges, or liberal-arts colleges. While most of them had pursued many courses in psychology and education, only a relatively small number had taken systematic courses in mental hygiene or psychoanalysis. (Only a relatively limited number of biographies later secured from students in mental-hygiene courses have been included in this volume.) The material is thus supplied by relatively mature students without technical training in mental hygiene.

Reports from 95 students are included in this volume. The reports differ greatly in length, complexity, and thoroughness of description and analysis. Some are merely sketchy descriptions, while others are detailed and discriminating analyses. Some students submitted brief reports of one or two hampering traits or peculiarities, while others described in more or less detail from a half dozen to a dozen or more minor and major maladjustments, abnormalities, or deviations, some of which have continued for many decades without diminution or abatement. An insignificant number have stated that they have no known personal problems to report, although many at the outset of the self-analysis declared that they were unable to recall any personality problems of any consequence. Although the students were asked to be perfectly frank in unburdening themselves and although they were assured that the reports would be treated with absolute confidence and that they would be published only under protective *noms de plume,* doubtless some respondents were unable to free themselves from their resistances. One student remarked:

> When I began thinking about a personality inventory of myself, I simply balked at the idea. The difficulty of the psychoanalytic technique is the resistance of the individual. He will talk about every subject under the sun, but will neglect his most intimate self. This, too, has been my difficulty. I wanted to get rid of the idea of discovering and discussing my problems and their causes. However, after long hours of introspection and reminiscence, I am going to express my thoughts with the utmost freedom, and already have grown confident and expansive.
>
> (T.A.M.; F.; E.S.T.; B.A.) [14]

Most of the reports were submitted in topical form, in conformity with the suggested topics. The list of supplied "representative personal adjustment problems," which, it was explained, was merely intended to be suggestive, included food fads and antipathies and fears or phobias concerning

darkness	noise	examinations
snakes	strangers	tests
animals	high places	audiences
thunder	open places	people in general
	dirt	

The other topics included

frights	hampering habits hard	sex experiences and diffi-
superstitions	to overcome	culties
peculiar ideas	procrastination	daydreaming
obsessions	rationalization	anxieties
inferiority feelings	humoring	worries
lack of charm or defects	seclusiveness	sleepwalking
compulsive acts	self-consciousness	absent-mindedness
infantile fixations	timidities	amnesias
inhibitions or repressions	tantrums	overfastidiousness

In some instances, however, the problems were so intimately interlinked that a more or less genetic or narrative account was substituted for the topical

---

[14] The abbreviations should be interpreted as follows: the first letters are the respondent's initials; F., female; M., male; T., teacher; S., school; C., college; E., elementary; H., high; S.C., special class; P., principal; Supv., supervisor; U.S., undergraduate student; Col., colored. The ages are as of the time of the report. The complete data cannot always be published because the reports failed to supply them.

treatment. Sometimes the respondents returned once or even several times to the consideration of a common problem in the discussion of different topics. Occasionally they have treated a number of topics under a common rubric, doubtless because they have felt, rightly or wrongly, that these topics have sprung from the same source, or that they have become intimately related in the course of time, or that they are more or less closely connected by a common bond although genetically distinct. It is obvious that mental problems do not unfold in isolation or independently but often constitute a complicated, interrelated network. An apparently independent problem will sometimes prove, on more complete analysis, to be merely a phase of another problem or a cluster of related problems.

Nature of the Editorial Preparation of the Case Histories for Publication. The headings for all the reports have been supplied by the author. They furnish a brief summary of the more significant features of the reports and, sometimes, interpretative suggestions. The author has also condensed many of the reports, corrected some of the more obvious instances of weak or faulty sentence structure, and sometimes transferred material from one topic to another topic, to which it appeared more properly to pertain. Where the problems have seemed to be intimately interrelated, genetically and causally, the material has sometimes been arranged by the writer under inclusive rubrics. In the work of condensation or rearrangement, considerable pains have been taken not to modify the thoughts of the contributors. The constant aim has been to allow the respondents to express their thoughts in their own words. Changes in phraseology have been made only in order to avoid obvious grammatical or lexical errors. Ambiguous statements have not been altered except in cases in which they could be cleared up through personal communications with the respondents.

Because of the fact that a topical plan of presentation is followed in this book, only very brief reports are presented in their entirety under one heading. Those parts which are germane to the particular problem under discussion are reproduced. But this is not invariably true. To have split some sketches into fragments would have been tantamount to robbing them of much of their interest and essential unity and to substituting an artificial simplicity for a complex ramification of the same problem. A child who is afraid of darkness may also be afraid of snakes, ghosts, and water, and all these fears may be related to a pathological timidity and a tendency toward withdrawal. The inadvisability of segregating related phases of the same problem into detached reports will explain why some of the reports contain material apparently irrelevant to the question under consideration. More will be gained from retaining material apparently irrelevant to the limited aspect of the topic under discussion than from marring essential integrations by rigid deletions. From what has been said, it is obvious that many reports can be used to illustrate various problems and principles.

It is scarcely necessary to emphasize that, from the point of view of the clinical study of the problems besetting each respondent, it would be necessary to reproduce each biography in its entirety and to study the individual's problems in all their interrelations and in their situational totality, just as it is necessary in the psychological and mental-hygiene clinics to study the living patients from many points of view in order to obtain a complete picture before arriving at a diagnosis. But we are not here concerned with comprehensive clinical investigations of the authors of these reports, however desirable such a synoptic picture may be from other points of view. Our task in this book is merely to present true factual stories from the experiences of normal persons which illustrate different kinds of difficulties of adjustment and mental antics and which shed light upon the origin and the methods of resolution of personal difficulties.

Owing to the fact that the reports were not submitted until the end of the terms, clinical use could not be made of them for consultation purposes with the students concerning their personal problems, except when advance copies were submitted (oral or written) and the students requested therapy interviews. Of course, little or no time is available for conferences on personal problems in off-campus extension courses or during the crowded summer-school sessions—most of the courses were extension and summer-school offerings. Obviously, it is not safe to carry interpretative analysis very far without a many-sided clinical study of the respondents, such as was out of the question in these investigations. Fortunately, many of the suggestions offered in sundry places in the text can be applied by the intelligent reader to many of the disturbances that pass under review.

The Respondent's Responsibilities for the Proffered Explanations of Their Maladjustments. Each respondent is responsible for the descriptions, analyses, interpretations, and explanations offered regarding the mode of origin of his problems. The explanations suggested may be correct and adequate or wrong and inadequate. Causes that seem obviously fundamental to the subject may be merely superficial, contributory, or exciting factors. The basic causes may have been suppressed and forgotten, or they may never have been recognized in their true relation to the subject's peculiarities.

Although the writer has introduced the personality inventories for the purpose of illustrating certain facts or theories, it should not be inferred that he has uncritically accepted all the explanations advanced by the biographers. He is convinced that the explanations offered are not always the correct ones. To have attempted to criticize in detail the respondent's interpretation would have required more space than is available and would have defeated one of the values of the case reports in their present form. The reports will prove doubly valuable if they stimulate critical reflection, if they lead the student and the instructor to make a careful analysis of all the data submitted and to reach their own interpretations in the light of known psychological and mental-hygiene principles, and if they arouse a determination to reexamine theories in the light of the facts obtained from sources that are largely unspoiled by the type of sophistication and dogmatic presupposition that often are the end result of having read too much about a subject.

Certainly two of the important lessons learned from a study of these reports are that the process of formation of character traits is sometimes a relatively simple matter, not the obscure mysterious process that some would have us believe; and that the origin of many attitudes, predilections, aversions, or aberrations can be readily discovered by the ordinary methods of sustained scientific study, without resort to esoteric theories or procedures. This statement must not, however, be construed to imply that all processes of trait formation are obvious, simple, and direct. This is by no means the case. Some processes are exceedingly intricate and difficult to unravel, even by highly refined psychoanalytic techniques.

No amount of abstract discussion or theorizing or dogmatic preaching will take the place of these case histories. The simplicity, naturalness, and realism of these reports tell a more effective and convincing tale than do embellished imaginary cases, made to fit a theory. These reports tell their own story. They are pregnant with suggestions to the mental hygienist regarding the social and educational treatment of children. The practical implications are in many cases so obvious that to attempt to elaborate upon them would seem superfluous. It would perhaps be difficult to overstress the unique contribution that these autobiographies of personal maladjustments and difficulties make to the literature of personality maladjustment and mental hygiene. They represent, almost without exception, conditions that obtain among people who would unquestionably be classified as normal. They are not based on unnatural, freakish, abnormal, or pathological specimens of the genus homo.

The value of the case data to the student has been amply demonstrated by actual trial in many groups. In lecture courses in which extensive use has been made of the material, the students have been requested to answer frankly and anonymously various queries regarding the relative value of the case reports. Although occasionally two double periods have been devoted to the presentation of the biographies (often with interpretative comments that do not appear in connection with the histories in this book), the students have stated, with only a few exceptions, that even more time could profitably be given to this illustrative material.[15]

[15] The value accorded this case-history material is indicated by the estimates received from a group of nineteen students who pursued a lecture course on personality malad-

In spite of their demonstrated value, however, limitations of space render it necessary to restrict the number of biographies of maladjustments that can be included in this text. Even so, 164 concrete illustrations are included.

The following reports show the great variety of factors that may produce early transitory or permanent conditioning, the surprising variety of the resulting effects of such conditioning, and the corrective measures that have been followed in the case of food antipathies and dietary caprices, fears, and early spoiling.

Instances of Food Antipathies and Dietary Caprices Due to Early Conditioning. Fussiness or fastidiousness about dietary matters is one of the most prevalent annoyances of early childhood. It is often the result of accidental or unwise conditioning. The conditioning may be based on some aspect of the food itself—its visual appearance, taste, odor, or consistency; the knowledge of its source; some apparently innocent remark, jest, accidental association, or imagined relationship; overindulgence, humoring, nagging, and the like. Food aversions may produce intense repugnance to a certain dish, nausea, paleness, or illness.

AVERSION TO CARROTS, PARSNIPS, AND CABBAGE, OVERCOME, BUT NOT TO TURNIPS; ATTEMPT TO OVERCOME AVERSION TO TURNIPS BY UNSUCCESSFUL DECEPTION; TURNING PALE FROM ODOR OF COOKING TURNIPS

My earliest recollection of a personal adjustment problem relates itself to food antipathies and reluctance to take an afternoon nap. My particular antipathies were turnips, boiled cabbage, parsnips, and carrots. My mother had strong ideas about children learning to eat what was set before them and used all manner of methods to persuade me that these things were all good. She succeeded very well indeed with the carrots and parsnips and got me to taste boiled cabbage, but to this day I have not overcome my aversion to turnips. I had always said that I could not bear to smell either of these latter vegetables cooking, and mother once saw me turn white when I appeared in the kitchen where there was a strong odor of some turnips we were to have for dinner. That day she decided to prove clearly that it was my imagination and obstinacy which caused my hatred of these vegetables, and so, without my knowledge, she carefully mashed in a few turnips with my potatoes, intending to have a good laugh on me when I ate them, to cure me

justments and mental hygiene in which a much larger number of case histories were presented than have been incorporated in this book. In anonymous written answers to the question as to whether the large amount of time devoted to the presentation and discussion of the illustrative material was justified, all answered in the affirmative; nine indicated that the time given to the concrete material was about right, while seven said that even more histories could profitably be introduced. For additional similar case histories, see the author's *Minor Mental Maladjustments in Normal People,* Durham, N.C., Duke University Press, 1946 (third printing).

once and for all. But I took one bite and again turned pale. Mother did not force the issue and that was her last effort to persuade me to eat turnips. I think I was about seven at the time. I do not know whether there may have been a physical reason then, or if it was something akin to obstinacy, but it was long before I overcame my aversion to the odor of cooking turnips, and now, although I can stand that, I do not like the taste. My stomach seems to revolt against taking them in.   (W.C.H.; F.; Ph.B.; Age 37)

NAUSEA PRODUCED BY OKRA APPARENTLY DUE TO ITS SLIMINESS, BUT OVERCOME DURING ADULTHOOD; UNCONQUERABLE ANTIPATHY TO CHITTERLINGS ATTRIBUTED TO NAUSEATING ODOR AND KNOWLEDGE OF THEIR SOURCE

As a child I disliked intensely even the presence of boiled okra on the table. I can remember when visiting other homes that the children, knowing my dislike for it, would place it on their tongues and taunt me by saying, "Look at it slide down," or by making some other rude remark. Finally the okra so nauseated me that I dreaded the washing of the dish which had contained it. The slimy residue did not break up readily in soap and water. To me it seemed like a repulsive mass of mucus-like substance. I have overcome my dislike for okra and it is now regularly on my table. I do not like boiled okra but eat it fried (the stickiness of it is decreased in the browning process), combined with corn and tomatoes, and also in okra gumbo. This adjustment has been made since my maturity, perhaps because I have become imbued with the idea that one should learn to eat the things that furnish the necessary substance for proper growth.

My dislike for chitterlings continues to the present time. The very odor connected with them led me to shun the table which contained them. My knowledge of what and where they had previously been often led me to tell those who ate them that I thought it was nasty even to think of eating such things. I have attempted to eat the horrid things since I became older but I am unable to succeed. The odor makes one mouthful of them get larger and larger until I must run and eject them and subject my mouth to a listerine rinsing. I suppose I shall never overcome this dislike since I seem unable to convince myself that they will contribute anything needed for growth.

                        (A.H.T.; F.; Col.; Univ. Instr. of Psychology; M.S.; Age 26)

AVERSION TO EATING SOFT EGGS, APPARENTLY BECAUSE OF VISUAL APPEARANCE OF RUNNING EGGS (ACCIDENTAL CONDITIONING); CURED BY DETERMINATION TO EAT EGGS IN ANY FORM, OWING TO SHOCK PRODUCED BY EMBARRASSING SITUATION IN A HOTEL

One of my earliest recollections was seeing my oldest sister and brother eating eggs at breakfast. These eggs were half done and I did not like the way they ran. My mother gave me one that did not run. From then on I would not eat an egg that was not hard cooked, however prepared. I remember that on one occasion only a guest and my mother prevented my father from forcing me to eat a half-done egg. I was crafty enough to avoid another possibility by asking her to let the cook give me my egg on a special plate. All through my high-school and college days I would refuse to eat any egg that wasn't well done. This often caused trouble and inconvenience, but I thought I could not eat it.

I had just finished college and was a member of a party which was spending a few days at a very expensive hotel in one of the southern states. A specially good-looking, popular man in the party asked me to take breakfast with him. I let him do the ordering, and never dreamed what was going to happen.

When the eggs were served, to my horror they were soft. The outcome of it was that they were sent back three times to be re-cooked and, when finally they were to my taste, they were almost as hard as rocks and I was mortified almost to tears.

Then and there I made up my mind I'd eat them raw rather than repeat that experience and that was the last time I was ever silly about how my eggs were cooked.   (C.L.E.; F.; F.S.T.; Ph.B.; Age 40)

DISLIKE FOR A SILVER CUP AS A CONDITIONED REFLEX

The subject has a very vivid recollection of his dislike for a certain silver cup from which he was made to drink coffee after having taken a dose of castor oil, even though the cup was his prized possession previously. The cup always tasted of castor oil after that experience.   (B.O.I.; M.; C. Instr. of Psy.; M.A.)

The above dislike is strictly a case of conditioning in its narrowest sense. Similar is the unreasonable aversion to orange juice exhibited by some people as a result of artificial conditioning in early life, when castor oil was administered in orange juice. The writer recently observed an instance of similar conditioning to oranges in a girl of twelve who suffered from an attack of influenza and happened to vomit after she had eaten an orange. Thereafter she betrayed a dislike for oranges and for some time refused to eat them.

OBDURACY IN REFUSING TO EAT SEEDED FOODS, UNVANQUISHED BY THREATS OF PUNISHMENT, COAXING, OR RIDICULE, CAUSED BY LISTENING TO A HORRIFYING DESCRIPTION OF AN APPENDICITIS OPERATION WHICH WAS BELIEVED TO RESULT FROM SEEDS WORKING INTO THE STOMACH AND POISONING IT; OTHER EATING PECULIARITIES THROUGH CONDITIONING

From earliest childhood I have had an antipathy for seeds in foods. This has engendered a particular dislike for berries and grapes, although it does not include cherries and stoned fruits. I have always declined seeded foods, wherever and whenever they have been offered. During childhood, coaxing, threats, and punishments on the part of my parents were ineffective in overcoming my refusal to eat these foods, and frequently created turbulent scenes from which it took me days to recover. In later life this peculiarity has caused me many an embarrassing moment when dining with friends. Other manifestations probably traceable to this source are these: I can eat seedless grapes, but only after I have opened each one and examined it for stray seeds; I dislike any kind of fish which contains small bones; while eating my food I habitually feel about for small, hard particles, and, upon noticing even the tiniest of such particles, I must eject the mouthful, either abandoning the dish or finishing it without relish.

I ascribe this antipathy to an incident that occurred when I was about seven years of age. A lady, visiting at my home, discussed with my mother, in my hearing, the grave condition of a young girl in the neighborhood, resulting from appendicitis. The details of the operation, horrifying to me, were related and talked over. The "appendiceetis" was caused, according to our visitor, from eating too many grapes, the seeds of which went into the stomach and poisoned it. That was my interpretation, at any rate, and, since my mother apparently agreed with the "diagnosis," there remained with me the vivid picture of seeds creeping into the stomach to work their poisonous destruction.

The fact that the girl died and that I was taken to the wake undoubtedly helped to fix the impression. Furthermore, I recall questioning my mother about operations and learning that they consisted of cutting people open to let the poison out. Thereafter, no scoffing on the part of my family, no promises of rewards or punishments were strong enough to erase the grim picture that had impressed itself upon my imagination. It came to be accepted that I disliked seeds.

I do not recall that I ever made a conscious effort to overcome this antipathy. During army service I forced myself to eat berries on a few occasions, but never with relish and always with a distinct uneasiness as to the gastronomic consequences.

(C.J.P.; M.; E.S.P.; B.A.)

Instances of Fears Induced by Emotional Conditioning. Doubtless the preponderance of fears is the result of early artificial, accidental, or intentional conditioning, although very frequently the circumstances producing the fear reactions cannot be discovered. The reports that follow furnish fairly clear-cut cases of emotional conditioning due to specific accidental associations or occurrences or to the remarks, suggestions, or emotional reaction patterns of the subject's associates. The most violent physical and mental commotions, often productive of ineradicable aftereffects, may be caused by contacts with animals, natural phenomena, and human beings.

Animal Fears. Animal fears, sometimes amounting to actual phobias [16] often result from encounters with all kinds of animals, frightful tales, acci-

[16] Phobias are intense, persistent, irrational, and uncontrollable fears that attach to specific stimuli or situations (*e.g.,* cats or caterpillars). They often tend to spread to related objects by processes of association or reconditioning. Ordinarily the cause of these morbid fears is some fear-conditioning episode (emotional conditioning) in childhood. They often appear inexplicable because the fear-producing incident has been repressed from consciousness, owing to its distressing or shame-producing characteristics. Although the exciting incident cannot be recalled, the original fear reaction may con-

dental occurrences, warnings regarding animals, or pranks perpetrated by playmates. The results of the conditioning include emotional upsets, morbid dreads, timidities, escape movements, reckless or precipitate motor discharges, pantomimic writhing movements, physical weakness, illness, shivers, nervous sensations, insomnia, terrifying dreams, etc.

PERSISTENT DREAD OF SNAKES CAUSED BY RUNNING INTO A RIVER WHEN CHASED BY A BOY WITH A SNAKE; PECULIAR FEELINGS, TWITCHINGS, AND JERKINGS IN HAND AFTER HAVING ACCIDENTALLY TOUCHED AN UNSEEN NEST OF SNAKES IN A PILE OF STONES; WRITHING FEET AND LEGS WHEN HAVING REALISTIC DREAMS OF SNAKES; VISITING A SNAKE HOUSE VOLUNTARILY IN SPITE OF THE FEAR

Most distinct among my early difficulties of adjustment was an excessive fear of snakes, dread of being in enclosed places (claustrophobia) and probably smothering to death, and fear of thunderstorms. I frequently played with older children (some of whom were my own brothers and sisters) in hayfields where small non-poisonous snakes were prevalent. They took great pleasure in telling me that such snakes would sting and poison men, and in observing my reactions to such remarks, usually flight. On one occasion a boy produced one from his pocket and chased me. Regardless of what lay ahead of me, I ran, and soon found myself in a river. I realized as I grew a little older that there was no reason for such fear and yet it was always present when walking through long grass or weeds.

On one occasion I assisted in removing a small pile of stones from a very conspicuous place in the schoolyard. No thought of snakes was in my mind but on removing a rather large stone in the lower layer of the pile I was horrified to feel something cold and to see a nest of snakes. I suppressed a cry as I didn't want to appear a coward before my fellow-pupils and especially before my teacher, but I suffered intensely both physically and mentally. Some brave pupils killed the snakes, but that experience wasn't forgotten. I had peculiar feelings in the hand that had touched the snake whenever I thought about it. I found myself twitching my hand and jerking it back quickly. It was not unusual for me to dream of snakes and I frequently disturbed my bed companion by the writhing of my feet and legs. The presence of snakes was so real that it took a short time after awakening to realize fully it was a dream. I remember some of my schoolmates' having dream books, and the predictions contained therein were generally

---

tinue and may attach itself to some other objects, in consequence of which the phobia becomes symbolical in character. Trembling at the sight of a boat may not be a fear of the boat itself but of some forgotten shame-producing escapade that occurred in a boat. The fear of open spaces (agoraphobia) may typify the fear of death, from the fact that heaven is envisaged as an open space. The recognition of the absurdity of a phobia does not extinguish it until the victim has discovered its true meaning, until he has assimilated it and unconditioned it through repeated reenvisagement by means of verbalization. Further discussion of the causation, significance, and treatment of phobias and allied mental morbidities occurs in various subsequent sections of the book.

believed. My parents taught us that to be superstitious revealed ignorance, and therefore the prediction that to dream of snakes meant a death in the family did not really influence me.

During my training at normal school, I studied nature study under a brilliant instructor who conscientiously believed it was our duty to overcome any horror of snakes. He kept some live specimens in the classroom and frequently asked members of the class to assist him in feeding them some finely chopped meat. The operation was most repulsive to me and I always tried to get a seat near the back of the room during his lecture period. The most uncomfortable hour I ever spent in his class was when he brought some new specimens to the school and put them away for class purposes on the following day. I was in his first class and he announced that he was unable to find them. My common sense told me that they couldn't be in my desk and yet my excessive fear triumphed over my judgment. I felt I couldn't go into that classroom on the following day. Before the day was ended I heard from a member of another class that the snakes had been found and would be put in safe keeping.

It is a strange thing that with this excessive fear of snakes I should of my own accord visit the snake house at the London Zoo, especially when my time was limited and I was unable to see other things which would have given me pleasure. My childhood fear was still present, although it had ameliorated a little. This fear, by occupying attention, had become a fascinating obsession that brought me under subjection to the very thing I was trying to avoid. Before a group of spectators a keeper removed a large snake from a case and allowed it to coil around his arm. I shuddered and evidently he noticed it, as he requested anyone to leave who was afraid. I didn't leave, but that night my sleep was disturbed by a horrible dream of snakes. At the present time if I find a child being frightened by a snake, I may appear calm and undisturbed but my organism does not function normally. My mother had a similar dread of snakes and no doubt this had some influence on my behavior. Education and training have succeeded in eliminating some of my childish fears but I cannot behold snakes without experiencing the emotion of fear.   (M.V.J.; F.; E.S.P.; B.A.; Age 32)

PERSISTENT FEAR OF SNAKES ORIGINATING IN AN IMAGINED SNAKE BITE AND AGGRAVATED BY AN INSTRUCTOR WHO THREW SNAKES AMONG THE STUDENTS IN THE NATURE-STUDY CLASS

I have always been afraid of snakes. When in college, I took a course in nature study, in which the teacher explained how harmless most snakes were. He used to pick them up and throw them down among the students and enjoyed hearing the cries of horror from the girls. It frightened me terribly. I do not know what I would have done, if one had ever touched me. I think that my inability to overcome this fear may be connected with an experience I had while in the country one summer when I was about eight years old. My three cousins, who were boys, and I used to wade in the ponds on the farm and kill frogs for frying. On one of these trips I was bitten by a snake, I thought. Both of my feet became very sore, especially between my toes. I could not put on my shoes and could not walk. My aunts did not think that it was serious and waited until it was almost at the point of blood poisoning before they took me home. On arriving home, streaks of black were shooting up my legs and, when the doctor came, he asked my mother what she was thinking of to wait so long before calling a doctor. It was a long time before the ailment healed and every summer since then I have had a minor attack of the same thing until last summer. A doctor then told me it was not a snake bite but a vegetable growth of some kind and gave me some very strong salve to use. This healed it very soon. But I always thought that that trouble came from a snake bite until last summer. I do not think that I shall ever get rid of my fear of snakes.   (M.E.; F.; Counselor; Ph.B.; Age 40)

INTENSE INERADICABLE DETESTATION OF CATS DUE TO SEEING TWO DEAD CATS IN EARLY CHILDHOOD, AND LATER TO SEEING THE GHASTLY LOOK IN THE EYES OF A MENACING CAT; PERMANENT EMOTIONAL HANG-OVER

Cats are absolutely the bane of my existence. Although I am extremely fond of most other domesticated animals, cats have always been a revolting sore spot in my life. No matter how lovely or appealing these creatures seem to other eyes, they never fail to produce in me a feeling of disgust, fear, revulsion, or absolute hatred. If everyone has the "killer instinct" hidden somewhere in him, a cat will surely call forth mine some day.

At the impressionable age of four, I lived very close to the water. One morning, while playing down on the shore, I saw the body of a dead cat floating on top of the water. It was a horrible-looking sight to me. For days after that, I would not go near the water. Nearly a week later, while out driving in an automobile, I saw another dead cat, presumably run over by some vehicle. This sight not only intensified my loathing of cats; it actually made me ill.

When I was twelve years old, I visited my uncle's farm. He had all sorts of domesticated animals, including a cat. I just fell in love with the farm, but I raised so much devilment about the cat that he had to get rid of it. One day a good friend of my uncle's came out to visit him. When he heard about my aversion to cats, he laughed at my silliness and said he would send me a cat that I would be bound to like. Soon after his departure, I received a huge white angora. I must admit that this one was truly remarkable looking with its magnificent fur. I tried mighty hard to like that cat, and perhaps I would have succeeded, in some manner or other, but for an unfortunate incident. One day the cat killed quite a number of small chickens, so I chased him into the house. As I followed him through the door, he turned and sprang directly at my throat. I successfully warded him off, but to this day I can see that ghastly look in his eyes and those horribly menacing paws.

The other evening while having dinner in the dining hall, I felt something touch my foot. I knew in an instant that it was a cat, and I could not suppress the squawk that arose in my throat, much to my embarrassment and the amusement of the others.

My loathing for cats is just as strong as it ever was. The feeling that I have borders on the indescribable. It is a queer mixture of fear, hatred, and detestation. While I haven't obstinately made up my mind always to dislike cats, I firmly believe I always will. (B.J.; F.; U.S.)

INTENSE FEAR OF FLYING CREATURES CAUSED BY THE UNEXPECTED
FLYING OF A CHICKEN AGAINST HER FACE WHILE LOOKING INTO A
BARREL

Miss S. C. W., age twenty-seven, a school teacher, has a great fear of birds and all flying things. This phobia was caused by a chicken which flew unexpectedly against her face while she was looking into a barrel. She never sees a bird without experiencing the fear that it is going to strike her in the face. On several occasions the presence of a bat in her room has almost caused her to go into convulsions.
(From B.R.M.; M.; H.S.P.; B.A.)

Fear of Natural Phenomena Such as Darkness, Thunder, Lightning, and Storms. The process of emotional conditioning to natural phenomena is often traceable to some fright-inducing characteristic of the phenomena themselves, to surprise scares, ghost stories, gruesome tales, mystery films, the warnings or emotional manifestations of adults, etc.

The consequences of emotional upsets may include quaking, sweating, nervousness, illness, covering the eyes or head, running, hiding, shrieking, crying, dread of being alone or sleeping without a light, refusal to do outside errands at night, seeing apparitions, and experiencing haunting images, frightening dreams, obsessions, compulsions, or agonizing dreads.

WHAT ONE NIGHT OF TRIVIAL NOISES AND DARKNESS AWAY FROM
HOME MAY DO TO A SIX-YEAR-OLD GIRL: THE INITIATION OF A FIVE-
YEAR-OLD TERROR OF SLEEPING IN A DARK ROOM ONLY COUNTER-
ACTED BY THE USE OF A NIGHT LIGHT

When I was about six years old, my sister was taken very ill with scarlet fever. It was necessary that my brother and I stay somewhere else during the quarantine period, so my aunt took us to her home in Richmond. Because her home was very small, my small brother and I were put in the same room to sleep. The first three days we were in Richmond we had a lovely time. We played out of doors all day and at night we were so tired we almost slept at the supper table. During our fourth night I was awakened by a weird sound. Instantly I sat up and listened with every nerve taut. I was too frightened to cry out and for several seconds I sat tense, listening, listening. All at once it occurred to me that it was my baby brother snoring. I lay back on my pillow laughing softly to myself. How relieved I was! I thought, of course, that I would go to sleep again immediately. Had I known the mental agony I was to go through that night, I'm sure I should have screamed out in terror. After I had lain awake for about five minutes that seemed to me ages, I heard a scratching on the back porch. I immediately sat up again to discover that it was only the cat. I tried to sleep again, but the longer I lay there the more wide awake I became. If I had been at home, I should have called out for mother to turn on the light and tell me that I was quite safe. This would have made me sleep again. But I was a long way from home and I hated to admit to my aunt that I was afraid. There really wasn't anything to be afraid of, I kept telling myself. Hadn't mother always said I was her brave little girl? I was sure she would die of mortification if she knew that her bravest little daughter had cried out that she was afraid of the dark. I tried covering up my head, but it was even darker under the covers, and when I stuck my head out again the silence seemed threatening. I remembered tales of terrible things that happened in the night when everything was quiet. I rolled, I tossed, I perspired until all my clothes were wringing wet, all the while letting my imagination run away with me. It was the first time I had ever been awake when everyone else was asleep. Finally, not being able to stand the strain longer, I burst into tears, sobbing into my pillow and shaking like a leaf on a tree. My aunt heard me and came and put her hand on my shoulder. I shrieked, terrified, certain that some dreadful monster had pounced upon me out of the awful black stillness. She held me in her arms until I slept from exhaustion.

The next day she told me that she would put brother in her room to sleep so that he wouldn't disturb me. I agreed that that would be fine, but secretly I was overcome with fear at the prospect of sleeping in that dark room all by myself. Suppose I should wake up again in the dead of the night? I was sure I could never survive it. With this in mind I went to bed that night. I lay there half an hour—an hour—I could hear my aunt in the next room talking to her guest. Then I heard them leave. In another hour I heard her preparing for bed. All the lights were put out and still I lay awake, dreading the time when even the sounds in the street would cease. I don't know how long it was before I slept. Every night thereafter seemed worse to me than the one before, but I wouldn't admit to my aunt that I was afraid. Since I have grown older I realize that there is where I made a great mistake. If I had told her, she would have understood and helped me overcome my fear, but childish pride made me keep my secret.

Finally it was time to go home and I was overjoyed. I would sleep in my own bed and call mother if I were frightened. The first night I was home, mother gave me my bath and put me to bed. No sooner had the covers been tucked in than I became wide awake. I was nervous and fidgety, and wondering if I was going to spend another sleepless night.

I heard mother and dad in their room talking, then the lights went out and all was quiet. Now I shall sleep, I thought, but I didn't. I tortured my mind with imaginary creatures in the corners of my room, waiting till I closed my eyes to pounce upon me. I couldn't stand it another minute, and called mother. She came and lay down beside me for a few minutes, and instantly I fell asleep.

Instead of becoming less afraid of the dark, however, my terror grew into an obsession. Even during the day I would sometimes think of the hours to be spent between the dusk and the dawn and would, figuratively speaking, quake in my boots.

Finally mother bought a bedside lamp for my room. She put a very small bulb in it and left it burning all night. This helped some, but it took me five years sufficiently to overcome my terror of the dark to sleep in a dark room. Even now if I awake in the still of the night and realize that I am the only one awake I become restless, reach for my lamp and read for a short while before I feel sleepy again.   (R.M.N.; F.; U.S.)

PARALYZING FEAR OF DARKNESS AND OF GHOSTS AND GROTESQUE MONSTERS, ESPECIALLY ON MOONLIGHT NIGHTS, LASTING INTO EARLY ADOLESCENCE, ATTRIBUTED TO REPEATED VIVID DESCRIPTIONS OF GRUESOME ENCOUNTERS WITH GHOSTS TOLD BY ILLITERATE FAMILY; EMOTIONAL TRANSFER TO PERCEPTION OF WEIRD FORMS

In my recollection one of the worst early experiences that could have befallen a child of four or five years was having rather intimate association with a rather illiterate family that had almost a "mania" for seeing ghosts and telling ghost stories. To make bad matters worse, they seemed to have such a firm belief in their stories that they told them with a vividness almost beyond one's power to describe. Besides, they were always looking for ghosts and always seeing them, particularly around our yard and in various places around our home. Almost each night they came with some new story of what they had seen the night before on their way home, how the ghosts were chased, what voices they heard, and what awful experiences they had had. In case they had not seen anything themselves, they always had much to relate about some other neighbor or friend of theirs who had some thrilling encounter, hairbreadth escape, or some terrible experience a short time previously. My father, as well as other members of our family, would take a great deal of interest in these stories. To my mind, all of the older children (one boy and three girls) in our family firmly believed in ghosts, and they, too, frequently had strange experiences when out at night. Of course, it is easy now to see that they may only have aimed to have a little amusement in an apparently unharmful way, but it was a very serious belief with me in those early days, for I became dreadfully afraid of the dark. No one could get me out of the house when darkness came unless mother or father closely accompanied me or unless I had some close friends, in whom I reposed great confidence, very near at hand. Even at that I could clearly see all sorts of goblins, ghosts, and apparitions. Almost everything I could see in the dark took the form of some grotesque monster of which I had heard so many times in the days gone by. On moonlight nights it was very much worse than on darker nights, as I recall it, for when the moon was shining I could see many more shadows or darker spots, and, since these were the source of my troubles, the latter very greatly increased numerically on moonlight evenings. Every stone, post, cow, or other animal became a more or less real ghost to me and it really took more courage than I possessed to approach them alone.

Even after I had reached the age of ten or eleven years I could not be depended upon to go anywhere after night by myself. After nightfall someone else had to do the outside errands for I simply was paralyzed with fear of the darkness. As well as my recollection serves me, it was during my fourteenth or fifteenth year before I was able to go out alone and then it took all of the courage at my command. I still saw, not exactly ghosts, but many weird forms of various kinds that tended to bring back my earlier childhood experiences. When I did go out alone it was only with great effort and I always wanted to carry a gun with me for protection. And I might add that to this good hour I "prefer" to take my walks before the evening shades of night come on, although perhaps not because I am afraid of the darkness particularly.   (L.I.S.; M.; Instr. in T.C.; M.A.)

FEAR OF LIGHTNING AND THUNDER INDUCED BY A MOTHER'S BE-HAVIOR AND TEACHINGS; METHODS OF CURE

As far back as I can remember I have always been afraid of lightning and thunder.

My mother has always been very uneasy during storms owing to the fact that at one time lightning struck a barn directly behind the house in which we lived. Since this fear was outwardly manifested by her during storms, the fear was automatically transferred to the children. At the approach of a storm mother would call the children into the house and would warn them not to sit near a window and by no means to go out upon any of the porches. If the clouds were particularly threatening we would be told to go in our rooms and lie down upon a feather mattress. Under no circumstances were we to hold any metallic substance in our hands for it would attract lightning. If the storm came during the night-time, the children would be awakened from their sleep, and be required to dress and assemble in a room downstairs.

As I grew older this fear still continued but it was not quite so great as in my childhood days for many occasions came when I could not be under my mother's protective care. While in my first year in high school I found out that other boys were not afraid of lightning. In my general-science class I learned about the cause of storms and the meaning of the phenomena which accompanied storms. We studied electrical machines and appliances and had contact with a small machine that would send electric sparks a short distance through the air. I made up my mind that I would not hide from storms but instead would look at them. I even began to enjoy, in a way, the beautiful designs that flash lightning made in the skies.

I have overcome my fear of lightning by the following methods:

1. By understanding that other individuals did not have this same fear. Thus, why should I continue having the fear? Later in my life I was not with people who were afraid of lightning and thunder.

2. By making a study during my freshman year in high school of the object which caused the fear.

3. By actually coming in contact with a machine which could produce small sparks of lightning. This enabled me to understand more clearly the nature of the object which caused my fear.   (P.L.W.; M.; Jr. C. T.; M.A.; Age 35)

Miscellaneous Fears. Fear of examinations and tests is one of the tortures that make schoolwork a nightmare to some children and even to adults who have not been able to resolve this phobia. Among conditioning causes are threats to give hard examinations or warnings that all depends on the examination result, the feeling that failure would be a disgrace, ridicule by playmates or others, parental displeasure, and the attitude of worry.

The results of the examination dread include confusion, inability to remember or to think clearly, preoccupation with the idea of failure, paroxysms of fear, the feeling of numbness, physical weakness, dropping out of the course, and dislike for schoolwork.

PRONOUNCED EXAMINATION PHOBIA ATTRIBUTED TO TEACHER'S THREATS TO GIVE HARD EXAMINATIONS AND TO THREATS OF FAILURE

As a child in the public school I developed a most pronounced fear of examinations and tests. I am sure this fear was instilled into me by a teacher who always threatened her pupils with the hard examinations she was going to give, and with the fact that if we did not pass we would not be promoted. During all my four years at normal school my mother was continually telling me I must work hard, for it would be very disgraceful if I should fail in examination.

I must confess I have never been able to overcome the fear of tests. To this day examinations and tests almost make me ill.   (H.E.M.; F.; S.C.T.)

LIFE-LONG DREAD OF EXAMINATIONS; NO COURSE EVER THOROUGHLY ENJOYED BECAUSE OF EXAMINATION AT THE END

I went to private schools where no examinations were given, and was in the high school before I faced a real examination. The pupils made a mountain out of a molehill, and gave me the idea that failure and disgrace were synonymous. I felt that if I failed I would bring reproach not only to myself but also on the rest of the family.

When examination time came, I thought only of the possibility of failure and not of the subject matter. My teachers, having found out how I feared an examination and also how I shrank from any public appearance, such as reciting in class, made things easy for me. When I went to college, fortunately for me, the examination counted only one-third of the grade and I made a good record.

I have taught high-school girls and college girls and I know that this fear of examinations is not due to lack of knowledge of the subject matter, or to lack of preparation.

When I take an examination, I am conscious only of the fact that I might fail and not of how much I know. All during the course I am thinking about the examination at the end. I never remember making a voluntary recitation. I have never, in all my life, thoroughly enjoyed any course I have ever taken on account of the examinations at the end. When I have been excused from examinations on account of good daily grades, I have not known of this until the end of the term.

The only examination that I ever took that did not fill me with despair was for a scholarship offered to the state. I won one of the seven, but this victory has in no way lessened my fear. Why I should dread an examination, I do not know, for I never have failed to pass any course I have ever taken.

(C.L.E.; F.; E.S.T.; Ph.B.; Age 40)

DREAD OF WRITTEN TESTS PRODUCED BY A SPECIES OF WRITER'S
CRAMP, OF UNDETERMINED ORIGIN, DATING FROM EARLY CHILDHOOD

In recalling my early difficulties of adjustment a picture comes before me of a frail, timid child of about six years, seated, writing stiffly in a very unattractive old-fashioned schoolroom, making a desperate effort to learn to write. The more I tried, the tighter I clutched the long, thin pencil in my frail fingers. Unmolested I struggled on, each day holding the pencil tighter in my hand.

As I passed from year to year there was always a feeling of worry and anxiety because I never could write so quickly as the other children. Finally I just gave up in despair and tried to hide my feelings. No one at home knew, because they had troubles enough of their own. This led to an aversion to writing and a dislike to answering letters.

However, because of my strong interest in children, I decided to become a teacher, and determined not to let my handicap get the better of me. Although I struggled hard to overcome it, I could not take notes quickly with my hand in its clenched position. So I began practicing the arm movement at home, and succeeded fairly well when alone. But in school the old fear possessed me and in the stress of the daily tests I would fall back on the old clenched method. Even though I struggled like a Trojan to push the pencil along rapidly to keep pace with my thoughts, I would be the last to finish.

The writing impediment eventually produced great dislike for examinations, so I decided to leave the teachers' training school. The psychology teacher, who was full of warmth and kindness, had always appealed to me, and I therefore made up my mind to face her bravely and tell her about my predicament. She smiled and told me she had noticed it. She said that almost every one has a short and long side, that this was my short side, and that she was convinced that I was better in oral work. I soon began to feel that she had faith in me, and, owing to her influence, I stuck it out.

Nobody was happier than I was in my first classroom. Strange as it may seem all the old fears had vanished. I was able to write on the board with ease by using the arm movement. In the end, however, I discovered that my worry had not been uprooted; it was only sleeping.

A few years ago I attempted to take Miss G.'s course. In the very first test the writer's cramp again seized me, and I could scarcely push the pencil along. The muscles were almost rigid. When I finished the last question I was cold and clammy. Well, I never went back again, losing my money and my credits. This old bugbear had come upon the scene again coupled with an awful dread of examinations.

This summer is the first time for several years that I have attempted to master written tests. I did fairly well until one day, when I was overfatigued, the writer's cramp returned. I became very much confused and bewildered at my predicament, was unable to take notes from the lectures fast enough, and all the old fears came trooping back.

I must confess I do not know what to do about my difficulty unless I take a course in penmanship—that is, if my muscles are not too stiff now.

[The victim was unable to trace the origin of this affliction, probably a phobia or an obsession dating from early life.]   (K.H.; F.; S.C.T.)

The following instances of fears are of special interest from the standpoint of the specificity of the emotional conditioning.

KNOWN ACCIDENTAL CAUSE OF AN UNCONQUERED FEAR: FEAR OF WATER FROM EARLY EXPERIENCE

The writer is filled with fear when crossing large bodies of water on high bridges. When she realizes she is above the water she has a feeling of being pulled down beneath the water. It seems to pull her down until she becomes dizzy and has the sensation of being beneath the water.

This sensation has not been overcome by the writer and she doesn't know how to overcome it. She is not bothered when driving across such places.

The origin of this fear occurred when the author was a child. She was bathing in a mill dam and was caught in a whirlpool. The water dragged her down several times and when she was rescued she was unconscious for several hours. The experience was so dreadful that it has stayed with her.

(M.R.; F.; H.S. Supv.; B.A.)

DREAD OF WATER DUE TO FRIGHT FROM GOING UNDER; OVERCOME BY BEING THROWN INTO SEVEN FEET OF WATER

When I was a boy, eight or ten years old, I used to go in bathing in a river near home. My uncle taught me to swim by using a rail to help support me. One day I let the rail float from under me and I became frightened and went under the water. I was unnerved because I got strangled, and someone had to help me out. The remainder of the summer I found other places in which to spend my leisure hours, but the next summer the temptation grew stronger and stronger to go in bathing until one day I decided to try it again. A neighbor took me with him. I was nervous at first, so he took me on his back and swam to a rock some distance from the bank. While sitting on the rock he tried to persuade me to jump off the rock and swim out. Because the water was about seven feet deep I wasn't in any frame of mind to do this, although he argued that I could swim and that this would be the only way to rid myself of the dread. Finally, after he saw I wasn't going to listen to his argument, he picked me up and threw me out into the deep water. I went under, but, failing to strike the bottom, I readily came up, and believe me I swam out. This cured me of the dread and from that time on I could swim without any fear of going under. (H.A.; M.; H.S.T.; B.A.)

FEAR OF FIRES PRODUCING NERVOUS CHILLS AND SHAKINGS, ASCRIBED
TO FATHER'S TALE OF A GIRL WHO BURNED TO DEATH AND TO HEARING
THE SHRIEKS OF HORSES INCINERATED IN A LIVERY STABLE; DREAMS
PRODUCED BY THE TALE OF THE BURNED GIRL; NERVOUS CHILLS
FROM HEARING BELLS, A CONDITIONED RESPONSE TO A SUBSTITUTE
STIMULUS

My fear of fire was instilled by my parents, I believe. We had large trees in our yard, and made many bonfires in the fall to dispose of the leaves. Father always kept us at a distance away from the fires, saying that we could get burned easily. He told us about a little girl whose dress caught on fire when she stood too near the fire. She was burned to death. Because she ran, no one could put out the fire. For nights, I had dreams of that little girl running, her dress on fire. The fires fascinated me but I nearly became frantic when some one would go near. I did not make any commotion but experienced an inner feeling as if I had to scream but couldn't. I can remember very well when all the bells in town rang in the night for a fire in a large livery stable. All the men hurriedly ran to help. We could hear the horses in the stable and could see the fire from all parts of the town. Mother did not let us go, but I can remember the odor, the yelling, and the falling of lumber. When father came home, he told about the number of horses burned. When we grew older, all the family would dress and go to the fires, nearly all of which were in the night. But I would never go. As soon as the bells began to ring, I began to shake and would have a nervous chill, although mother always stayed at home with me. One time our school burned in the night. Every one went. Mother wanted to go, so she persuaded me to dress and go along. When I was nearly dressed, my nose began bleeding. Mother couldn't stop it with her remedies, and called all the doctors in town but they were all at the fire. She finally succeeded in stopping it, but did not take me to the fire. I now hate to hear many bells ring. It gives me an uneasy feeling. I hate to hear the whistles blow and the bells ring on New Year's Eve. However, I have not experienced the nervous chills during big fires for about eight years. (R.E.; F.; E.S.T.; Age 35)

A SEVERE FRIGHT CAUSED IN A GIRL AT THE AGE OF SIX BY A GRUE-
SOME OBJECT REACHING IN THE DARK TO GRAB HER, PRODUCING
TREMBLING WHENEVER REFERENCE WAS MADE TO THE EVENT LATER
UNTIL THE AGE OF THIRTEEN: RESIDUAL EFFECTS FELT MANY YEARS
AFTER ACCIDENTAL DEATH OF HUSBAND

When I was about six years old, I had a terrible fright. My mother let my brothers go out on Halloween night. I could not go because I was a little girl. I was so disappointed that at last she said that I could go to a little girl a block away. She could see me all the way, so it seemed safe. As I passed a small lane between a grocery store and a house, a gruesome object reached out to grab me. He had on a false face with black tears streaming down and leaving white streaks on his face. I gave a terrifying scream and running to my mother threw myself in her arms. My terrible goblin, an older boy in the neighborhood, followed to explain. My brother had squirted a water pistol in his face, hence his tears. The people in the neighborhood came to see why I screamed. Whenever my mother would refer to it later I would tremble and hide in the corner to keep my brothers from knowing it. My life wouldn't have been worth living had they discovered it. Even my mother never knew. Great was my relief when I was thirteen to discover that I no longer trembled when she told the story. I had no recurrence of it until my husband was killed in an automobile accident sixteen years ago. Since then, if I am suddenly frightened, I tremble and find it hard to talk.

(R.M.; F.; S.C.T.)

LIFELONG IDIOSYNCRASY ACQUIRED FROM HORROR CAUSED BY AN UNFORGETTABLE INCIDENT (PEEPING UNDER A SHADE ON A CHARIVARI NIGHT AND BEHOLDING AN UGLY FACE), LEAVING AS A RESIDUAL EFFECT THE INABILITY TO LOOK UNDER SHADES, AND AN UNCOMFORTABLE FEELING WHEN IT GETS DARK IF THE SHADES ARE NOT UP OR DRAWN ALL THE WAY DOWN

A decade ago it was quite a common practice to have a charivari for a newly married couple. The more grotesque the members of the party could make themselves, the better it pleased them. Armed with everything that might be used to make a noise, from horns to old tin pans, they approached the premises of the bride's parents. One of the earliest experiences that I remember was the charivari at my eldest sister's wedding. We heard noises in the distance which increased in volume as they came up our street. Soon loud noise proclaimed the fact that they were on our veranda. The shades were drawn and my only opportunity to see them was to peek beneath the shade. To my surprise and horror an ugly face was pressed against the pane. I withdrew quickly but was so afraid I could not flee to my father or mother, but my outcry attracted their attention. Their presence near me and their assurance that it was just a neighbor wearing a "funny face" calmed me somewhat. Later I had an opportunity to see two or three of the boys with masks removed and actually to handle a mask. But I never forgot the incident and even to this day I either leave a shade up or else pull it down all the way to the lower window sill. Ridiculous as it may seem that I should be expecting to see an ugly face peeking beneath the shade, I cannot bring myself to look beneath a partially lowered blind. When I am a guest for a short time in a home, I am rather uncomfortable if shades are not pulled right down as soon as it gets dark, or else left up. I am much happier if I can sit with my back to the window.

(M.V.J.; F.; E.S.P.; B.A.; Age 32)

ADOLESCENT AND ADULT FEARS AND TIMIDITIES; LACK OF CONFI-
DENCE, STAGE FRIGHT, FEAR OF EXAMINATIONS, SHRINKING FROM
KEEPING APPOINTMENTS, OBSESSIONAL DOUBTS, AND IDEAS OF PER-
SONAL REFERENCE; ASCRIBED TO MARRIAGE TO A FAULTFINDING OLDER
HUSBAND

As I remember, my fears were few until the time of my marriage at the age of
fifteen. My husband was about twice my age—twenty-nine, a graduate of the
local university, and a trained tenor soloist. I was just out of high school. Because of the difference in our ages, he treated me like a child, criticising everything
that I did. I looked to him more as a parent or teacher than as a husband.

Because of his numerous adverse criticisms, which were not always based on
good judgment, I lost confidence in my real ability. I gave up appearing on programs, except when he insisted upon it, though I had been given special music
training under well-known tutors. When I did appear, I usually failed. The
punishment of having to appear against my will brought beads of perspiration to
my face. Trying to sing and at the same time watch the signs which he was send-
ing me from the end of the hall was tragic.

When I entered into conversation with friends, he listened, not only for grammatical errors, but for things I might discuss which he thought should not be
discussed. I was ever alert for a soft, rapid tap of his toe against the floor, sig-
nalling to me to hush. I finally got the idea that I would go insane if I remained
with him much longer; but the society of that time would not stand for grass
widows. I became morose, and brooded over my lot. Sometimes I would allow
my thoughts to escape. I did this once in church. The preacher was delivering his
sermon. The audience was all attention. All at once, I said in a clear voice, "Yes,
I am going crazy. I know it." The woman next to me stared, then edged away;
others near-by gazed at me, while my husband was plainly disgusted.

Lack of confidence has exhibited itself in later years in many different ways.
I seem to expect adverse criticism where none is meant. Too often compliments
well meant are taken in the light of cheap flattery. A look from a passer-by has
only one meaning—that something is wrong—and I take out my handkerchief to
wipe my face. I have been teaching music in public schools for twenty-four years.
I have conducted very large choruses during all these years. My conducting was
commented on very favorably at the American Conservatory where I was compared with teachers and supervisors throughout the country. Still, although I
am told I do not show outward sign of it, when I am to appear on a program, I
am uncomfortable with stage fright for days before the date of the program. My
heart is in my mouth when I lift the baton.

Examination Phobia

Likewise, I have a horror of examinations. Regardless of how much time I
have spent in preparation for an examination, or how well I may know it, I am
frightened when the time comes to take it. Fear drives the facts from my mind.
As soon as my paper has been given in, I begin to recall the correct answers to

the questions asked. In this, as in other things, it seems that the moment the burden of the task or the fear and anxiety of it is removed, I can think clearly.

Public-school examinations for teachers are timed. The addition of this feature appears to add to my discomfort. I have drilled applicants, who were to take an examination in music; have taken the same examination with them; and, when the final marks are reviewed, have received from ten to twenty points below those whom I had drilled. In each case, they had no preparation other than that I had given them. Five years ago, while taking a promotional examination in music, I developed terrible pains in the abdomen and became very dizzy. From later study, I should say that the pains were probably a result of my fears.

My average as a teacher during the entire time of my teaching has been superior. I feel that this is due primarily to the fact that my work has been supervised and observed when I was not cognizant of it. If I am to receive visitors, I have asked my principal not to notify me. I have explained my situation to her, and she has considered my wishes in this matter.

Dread of Keeping Appointments

I am timid about keeping business appointments. The very fact that I must meet someone on a business appointment upsets me. I am always doubtful that the visit will accomplish what I want it to accomplish. I have often dressed, after planning to see someone—anyone, gone to the office, even reached the entrance, and then changed my mind and turned away. Often I desire information but, rather than face someone and have my questions answered, I prefer to make any number of mistakes.

Perhaps I am wrong in attributing all my weaknesses to my marriage, but I do. I cannot hear any proposals of a second marriage without seeing my husband's face and remembering my experiences with him. Thus I am frightened away from a repetition of that experience.   (W.G.C.; F.; Col.; H.S.T. of Music, B.S.)

Instances of Early Spoiling. It is not necessary to supply at this point instances of spoiling as a result of unfavorable conditioning; many such instances are related in other parts of the book, for example, in Chap. III.

Emphasis in the Programs of Prevention Placed on Children and on Parents and Teachers. The array of definite illustrative data presented on the foregoing pages should have made evident, if the fact was not apparent before, that the emphasis in the preventive program of mental hygiene must be placed on the young children and on those responsible for their nurture and training. These case histories, which have shown explicitly how many personal traits and difficulties originate (and later histories will demonstrate other similarly definite causative factors), strongly indicate that many, if not most, of the child's fundamental attitudes toward the problems of life, his dominant emotional trends, his difficulties of adjustment, and his maladjustments result mainly from processes of conditioning. The conditioning, usually emotional in character, often occurs in early childhood, although the mental disturbances or overt effects may not become prominent until adolescence or adulthood. The inference from this conclusion (and from our histories) is that many mental difficulties need not have been acquired at all. They could have been readily prevented by proper care and conditioning.

As we study these autobiographies of maladjustments (and the others that will follow), the conviction also grows upon us that the child acquires many, if not most, of his reaction patterns, basic conceptions, ideas, and ideals, and many of his abnormalities and maladjustments, from his parents and teachers.[17] In fact, it may not be an exaggeration to say that the problem of the mental hygiene of childhood reduces largely to the problem of efficient parenthood and efficient teacherhood. It becomes a problem of supplying the child with wholesome, well-balanced, sane, and efficient parents and teachers who are free from the evil effects of mental discord and morbidity. The slogan has become almost hackneyed nowadays that the problem of problem children is more a problem of problem parents or problem teachers.

Reasons for the Importance of the Parent's Role. Why is the influence of the parents so overshadowing, especially during the first five or six years of the child's life? First, because of the constant intimate relations that necessarily exist between the young child and his parents, especially his mother. Second, because the influences of the home come into play in maximum degree during the years when the child is most plastic, when he is acquiring the groundwork for all his fundamental life attitudes, and when he is not regularly under the influence of any other social agency. The first five years of life are probably twice as important as any later period of similar length in establishing the child's habit patterns, in molding his attitudes and viewpoints, and in supplying the basic elements of control for a healthy emotional life. Even though the study of child behavior during the first year of life has disclosed evidences of strong native traits and tendencies (H. Zoepffel), many if not most of the child's early attitudes or character traits are probably the outcome of subtle unconscious emotional conditioning by the parents, or of parental indoctrination, or of imitative absorption of parental attitudinal and behavior patterns. Children tend to reflect the reaction patterns of their parents (and also of their siblings, of course) much as the mirror reflects objects. During the early formative years, most of the child's acquired traits are, perhaps, learned through the unconscious process of conditioning and imitative absorption; and it is probable that the most

[17] This statement should not be construed as denying the importance of the child-child and sibling-sibling relationships. Many mental conflicts and personality difficulties spring from sibling jealousy, rivalry, and hostility. The child relationships seem to play a minor role in our autobiographic data, but this may be due to early amnesias. Data garnered from children by the clinical method would doubtless modify the picture somewhat. Nevertheless, the child-child relationships should more or less automatically adjust themselves.

effective and wholesome conditioning is that which occurs more or less unconsciously.

The factors in the parental situation which are productive of adjustment or personality difficulties in the children are multitudinous (as has already been shown and as will be further shown from other biographies of maladjustment). Some of the prolific sources of character distortions in children are the peculiarities or abnormalities from which the parents suffer. These may vary from eccentricities, emotional fixations, emotional immaturity, and emotional and nervous instability to pronounced neuroticism, mental deficiency, mental disease, morbidity, immorality, or criminality. It would prove exceedingly difficult for the average child to avoid absorbing the parental behavior patterns by a subtle process of emotional conditioning or identification (see Chap. X). Parental behavior patterns that may exert a baneful influence upon the child's development include pampering, overprotection, overindulgence; or the opposite, excessive harshness, cruel punishment, excessive condemnation, threats, scares, fear-provoking warnings, harsh criticisms, snubbings, ridicule, sarcasm; exhibitions of anger, impatience, cowardice, fear, emotional upheaval, arbitrariness, domination, autocratic treatment, arrogance, fickleness, vacillation, inconsistency in discipline; incessant quarreling between parents or children; lack of mutual affection and respect between parents and between siblings and parents; lack of sincerity and frankness; making flippant, heedless, careless, thoughtless remarks; playing pranks; telling lurid ghost stories, fairy tales, or vivid accounts of harrowing tragedies; indoctrination of the child's mind with superstitions, false beliefs, and prejudices; blundering, ignorant, or pernicious methods of training; discrimination against the child or outright rejection; and the like. The operation of many of these factors is vividly portrayed in the following: [18]

Illustrations of Pernicious or Undesirable Influences Exerted by Parents upon Children. The reports themselves adequately indicate the nature of the factors and the attitudes they engendered.

MORBID FEAR OF ELECTRICAL STORMS DUE TO GRANDMOTHER'S UNWISE TEACHING AND ATTITUDES

When I was three years old my mother went to a lake in the Adirondacks for the summer, leaving my brothers and me with her mother. During the summer many electrical storms occurred. Whenever a storm arose, grandmother ordered all the windows and doors closed in order to shut out drafts, and warned us to keep

---

[18] Other factors are operative in the case histories supplied in connection with the discussion of the social factors of the mental-hygiene program in the next chapter.

The "Ten Commandments for Parents," by Paul Pitman, in the *Parents' Magazine*, Jan. 13, 1930, give terse expression to some mental-hygiene precepts affecting the parent-child relationship.

away from stoves, sewing machines or anything made of iron because they would draw lightning. She, herself, spent the time pacing up and down a long hall which ran through the middle of the house secure from drafts. She would wring her hands continuously and scream at each sharp crash, while we, wide-eyed and breathless, watched her. Sometimes she would weep.

When mother returned she felt very badly over finding us afraid of thunder and lightning. She had tried to bring us up without a knowledge of fear. Her efforts were all undone. My oldest brother was so affected that he would almost go into hysterics and I am still afraid, though forty years old. No one would ever guess it from my attitude, but down deep in my heart I really am afraid of electrical storms. The only time I ever enjoyed a display was one evening when I was out in the middle of a lake in a canoe and my boy friend assured me that there was no danger whatsoever on the water as we weren't near enough to the shore to be injured if anything should be struck. I believed him and thoroughly enjoyed the sight of trees crashing all around on the shores and islands.

During the remainder of my childhood I was with people who always hailed with delight an electrical storm, going on porches to watch it, exclaiming, ever and anon, "How exquisite!" But this did not undo the mischief already done.

In later years, a girl friend of mine was killed by lightning, but this did not leave the indelible impression upon me that my grandmother's attitude did.

(V.G.C.; F.; S.C.T.)

FREEDOM FROM FEARS EXCEPT THOSE ENGENDERED BY MOTHER'S SHARP REPROOFS AND RUTHLESS SARCASM, WHICH PRODUCED RE- TALIATORY "SNAPPING BACK," THE USE OF SARCASM AS A PROTECTIVE DEFENSE, AND A FEELING OF HELPLESSNESS. FAMILY QUARRELS AS A BASIS FOR VAGUE FEARS AND HELPLESSNESS TO ESCAPE; NERVOUS TENSION DUE TO LACK OF AFFECTION AND EMOTIONAL SUPPRESSION IN THE PARENTAL HOME

My father never allowed us to read fairy tales because of the unreasonable ideas which children sometimes get from them. Never were any of us frightened by the dark or by any living thing. I cannot remember any fear in early childhood except that of my mother's anger and displeasure. My thinking in many directions was affected by her. She was sharp in her reproofs and ruthless sarcasm, and early in life I learned the same art of "snapping back." Even though I understand my mother better now and see reasons for her disposition, I still feel the same fear at her attacks. This same sarcasm has always been used by me as a protective measure. The fear of my mother's disfavor was, I believe, the beginning of other fears. In difficult situations a feeling of helplessness to do anything always comes over me. Disputes, especially heated ones, between two people always produce the same fear in me, even though I am not concerned.

Family quarrels are a part of my feeling of helplessness. My mother has always, since I can remember, nagged and harangued my father for things he did, large or small, of which she did not approve. At such times my father remained silent and never made much attempt to defend his position, but my mother's words did not in any way change his conduct. During these one-sided affairs I felt dreadfully afraid of something that I cannot name. I always wanted to hide. I wanted nothing to do with it, but yet could not escape from it. My only feeling was that, if my mother would stop, the situation would be corrected.

Having been raised in an atmosphere of level emotions, I had to learn to enjoy affection. In our family no one ever kisses or embraces anyone else unless someone is leaving or has returned from a journey. Likewise we have been taught to suppress extremes of joy and sorrow in the same way. When we lost a brother in the war we tried to go on as though nothing had happened and his name was not spoken for so long I wanted to cry out. We cannot understand women who pout and cry to obtain their way. It is unheard of in our family. Many situations would be much less tense if a little natural emotion were shown by us.

(R.R.; F.; Critic T.; B.S.; Age 26)

FEELINGS OF RANKLING INJUSTICE, REPRESSION, INADEQUACY, DE-
PENDENCE, DISSATISFACTION, AND CONCEALMENT ENGENDERED BY
PARENTS' UNJUST, UNSYMPATHETIC, AUTOCRATIC, BELITTLING, AND
INCONSISTENT CRITICISMS, PUNISHMENT, AND TREATMENT; EFFORTS
TO PLEASE PARENTS BAFFLED AND BALKED BY INCONSISTENT TREAT-
MENT, BRUTAL SNUBBINGS, AND INSISTENCE ON DICTATING ALL DE-
TAILS OF RESPONDENT'S LIFE; SHRINKING FROM AND SUBMISSIVE-
NESS TO FATHER, TRANSFERRED TO ALL MEN; DETERRED FROM MAR-
RIAGE BECAUSE OF IMAGE OF FORBIDDING FATHER

Although my parents were unusually strong characters and exerted themselves to provide a good home, they were exceedingly autocratic. They did not act on the theory that children should become obedient through their own process of reasoning. Failure to obey brought punishment swiftly and surely in its trail. When we were small it was likely to be corporal punishment.

My first remembrance of being resentful about a chastising was when I was six years of age. I stopped to visit a little friend whom I idolized and was unceremoniously switched as soon as I entered my home. Since I was not conscious of wrongdoing or of disobeying, I resented this treatment very much. A sense of injustice rankled in my mind, but I knew better than to argue about the matter.

One Fourth of July evening, much later, I went into the house to get matches. To reach them I stepped on the upraised leaf of a table on which were standing dishes left to be put away later. The table tipped and threw me and the dishes with a crash to the floor. Added to my utter dismay and fright was the inevitable scolding and punishment. Again a sense of exasperated injustice rankled within me.

At a later stage in my life, I saw my sister enjoying a ride on an improvised raft on the pond. Naturally I wanted to ride also. My added weight made the raft sit so low in the water that it began to leak. In spite of my sister's frantic efforts the old trunk, nailed to some boards, circled around and around in the middle of the pond. My screams for help brought my mother and the neighbors. Since people had been drowned here, my fright was very real. As usual we were severely scolded and punished. I felt this time that insult had been added to injury and the sense of injustice rankled more than ever in my mind.

I realize now how far-reaching the influence of these feelings was. Try as I might, there seemed to be no way for me to avoid these occasions that always left me baffled and wondering. In my limited experience, I thought my parents were perfect. But as I visited often in the home of my chum where the atmosphere was always calm, I began to compare our lives in order to detect my difficulty. My sense of loyalty to my parents was too strong to permit me to mention my trouble to anyone—in fact it has always been so to this day. I even now have a feeling of violating this loyalty in writing this paper, but these were my long-continued and outstanding difficulties.

In my efforts to solve this situation, I am conscious of having deliberately set to work to seek my mother's approbation. I longed for feelings of satisfaction. One of my first steps was to study secretly how my chum's actions toward her mother differed from mine. Then I would try to imitate them. But it seemed that, no matter how conscientiously I tried, I always did the wrong thing, or at least it always drew criticism. Finally, I made a renewed effort, only to receive the inquiry, "Why didn't you do it this way?" I got the feeling of having met this situation with a decided degree of inadequacy, as I had almost all previous situations. Perseverance is one of my strongest traits and I determined to try again. I was more encouraged than I had been at any other time, because I had for the basis of my action her previous question. You can imagine my utter amazement and despair when my mother immediately inquired why I had not done as I had previously—the very action she had criticized unsparingly. I turned this answer over and over in my mind and chafed at the limitation of my powers for dealing with my problems.

It is difficult to trace what goes on in us and to express definitely states of feeling because some are so vague. When I reached a stage of intellectual development where I could reason, I came to the conclusion that it was impossible for me to please my mother. I felt it was useless for me to continue the effort, as I was convinced that no matter what I did the opposite was what she would want. It was not easy for me to arrive at this decision as I did not want to believe it, but, with the evidence I had, I could come to no other conclusion. I reasoned that the only sensible thing for me to do was to use my judgment as to what actions to pursue and to perform them without any qualms of conscience. This decision relieved me of a great strain, but it was not a panacea for all my problems.

My patience was sorely tried through all stages of my growth. I always had an ambition to try to do anything that I knew others did. But my long-suffering was ever taxed because my mother would insist on regulating the oven, on dictating to me how to mix ingredients for a cake or bread, or on supervising the removal of the pan from the oven. When I wanted to put up fruit, I was permitted to peel it, seed it, or place it in the bottles, but never to cork it or seal it. I remember vividly how I exploded over this detail and finally won my point. However, I felt that the unpleasantness created and my reaction to the intense emotions aroused within me were much too great a price to pay for the privilege of putting up fruit independently. My mother's habit of constant criticism of my manner of practicing my vocal or my instrumental music, of the time I spent in making myself presentable, of practically everything I did had an effect upon me in spite of my decision to ignore it and just go my way. An attitude of impatience at any criticism from her must have been established gradually and subconsciously from these influences. However, this attitude has not extended to criticisms received from others given in a constructive spirit; I have consciously used those as a means of growth.

When I became entirely self-supporting I decided mother must not dictate what clothes I should wear, or when, or where, or what price I should pay for them. I justified my actions on the ground that I was a mature, independent person. This habit of my mother's had this very significant effect—I became even less confidential than I had been before. This was motivated by my desire to escape from unpleasant situations and the attendant emotional upheaval.

My father was as autocratic as my mother and not nearly so companionable; in fact, he was not companionable at all. After two or three outstanding experiences with him, I felt afraid of him and avoided him. His attitude toward me had a different effect: he created and fostered my inferiority complex. I am sure that he did not do it deliberately and has never been conscious of doing it.

My first memory of trying to create a favorable impression on him was to show him that I had memorized the Ten Commandments. When he harshly told me to keep still, I was crushed. He absolutely refused to let us attend dancing school with our friends, and refused in no uncertain terms to let us accept an invitation to our first evening party. The manner of his refusal left as bitter a sting as the refusal itself. From the time I could remember he was constantly impressing us with how little we knew. If I ventured to express an opinion, he usually contradicted me flatly, with the result that the attendant unpleasant feelings impelled me to conceal my opinions from him. As a consequence, I had little to say in his presence.

However, with my ever-widening contacts outside of my home, I gradually realized that I was an individual with the same privilege of forming opinions as he had. With this difficulty solved, I had another one to overcome for I had transferred to all men my opinion of him. For years I would not voice any opinion in the presence of men that conflicted with theirs. In fact, I involuntarily withdrew within myself when they were near, just as I did when my father was near.

The fact that I have reason to think that father is proud of me, although he never compliments me, is some slight consolation to me. He has provided a very nice home, has given us many advantages and many expensive gifts, such as a garage for my car and payment of my property tax for years, but I know he is still imbued with the idea of my insignificance. Very recently he told me he had made me administrator of his estate, but almost in the same breath he said that I knew nothing about business.

He doesn't realize that it requires some business ability to be an administrator of two public elementary schools; to raise funds amounting to at least $1,750 for equipment in a period of seven years, sometimes with the help of the teachers, sometimes alone; to outfit and finance a basketball team in a league for several years; or to serve in an official capacity in a number of organizations and clubs.

These undercurrents have not always come to the surface and, although I have risen above these conditions which have existed for all these years, it seems to me that the loss to me is inestimable. Many happy hours of close companionship might have filled the months and years, in which I was earnestly seeking an adjustment of my perplexities. Since I have adopted a philosophical attitude toward these home maladjustments, they have ceased to worry me. By being persistent and concentrating on my purpose, I have come a long way from a timid, shrinking child to an independent woman. However, I am not so confidential as I probably would have been under different circumstances and under ordinary conditions. I am not aggressive in advancing my opinions. I am not sure that my attitude toward men is not still affected by my association with my father for, with opportunities to marry, a picture of his autocratic and forbidding attitude rose in my consciousness. Although I have the satisfaction of knowing that I have accomplished difficult and worth-while tasks, I think my personality has not developed harmoniously. I am very restrained in expressing my emotions.

My early social difficulties and eye trouble (described elsewhere) may have been productive of some good. In dealing with children, I have tried to profit by my childhood experiences both at home and at school. I have made it a rule to punish no child by wounding his feelings, never to punish without getting the child's viewpoint—it so often differs from an adult's—and never to make a child feel that what he said and did was of no importance. It may be that my perplexities, though painful to me, have had an unforeseen good influence extending over a long teaching career. I am conscious of having handled many problem children with much greater ease than my predecessors or successors through this dearly bought insight into child experiences.   (M.H.; F.; E.S.P.; Age 49)

DOMINATION BY OLDER SIBLINGS; DESPERATE FEAR OF QUARRELING, BRUSQUE, PROFANE AND DRUNKEN FATHER

I have one brother and one sister, four and seven years older than I, respectively. I remember them as dominating me, in the capacity of beings with superior judgment, initiative, and physical prowess. The milieu was a small Texas city, about 15,000 in population, in one of the poor residential sections. I always had a fear of my father which it is no exaggeration to call desperate. There was constant and serious trouble between him and my mother, although I had no comprehension of this. I assumed that all fathers were brusque, profane, given to heavy-handed punishment and intermittent drunkenness—that they were due various services with no obligation in return. My father often laid the weight of his hand on my mother in the presence of the children. Once, when displeased with me, finding no switch at hand, he beat me with a stick of stove wood. Strangely, I felt much more abused and afraid when my mother flew to my defense and sympathized with me. At this time (the preschool stage) and later, I can remember that my father often ridiculed me for wordlessness. His physical presence paralyzed me. From my earliest recollection I was timid and diffident.

(K.D.O.; M.; Univ. Instr. of Psych.; A.M.; Age 32)

ILLUSTRATIONS OF THE BARBAROUS TREATMENT OF CHILDREN BY PARENTS AND OTHERS

Juvenile court records are replete with examples of the brutal or inhuman treatment of children by parents in fits of ungovernable temper. The following cases supply examples of the brutal physical assaults to which children are subjected by irresponsible adults who are unfit to become parents, and of the irreparable damage that may be inflicted upon the personality development of children by such brutalities. Although only a few definite diagnoses are available, the perpetrators of the atrocities here recorded were doubtless victims of various kinds and degrees of mental maladjustments or disorders.

An 8-year-old boy was brought into a New York City court (in June, 1938) with arms and trunk covered with welts and bruises from the beatings inflicted upon him by his father, an unemployed housepainter, "because he came home from school 30 minutes late."

In Lawrence, Mass. (in November, 1938), a father was charged with assault and attempted murder for trying to "freeze a 2-months-old son by unclothing him in cold weather."

A 22-year-old divorcee in Fremont, Ohio (in June, 1939), who had reported her 10-weeks-old son as having been kidnapped, confessed, "after a lie detector had broken the case," that she threw her baby from a bridge into a creek "because she had quarreled with her mother regarding the child's care."

A girl of 10 was treated in the juvenile detention home in Indianapolis (in December, 1934) for burns inflicted on her hands and leg by the mother with a heated curling iron as a form of punishment for eating a "jar of mayonnaise because she was hungry." Her 12-year-old brother "reluctantly admitted that a fresh scar on his temple was the result of his attempt to escape while a stick was being twisted in his hair."

A Los Angeles woman received a sentence of 180 days (in July, 1934) for holding the arm of her 8-year-old daughter over a flame until it was severely burned, in order "to make her a good girl." The child was found by neighbors hiding in a garage. Another mother in Lakewood, N.J., received 30 days for branding "with a red-hot poker" the leg of her 6-year-old daughter, who had won a baby beauty prize 2 years earlier. "When I was a child they did that to me to make me mind, lots of times," explained the mother.

In El Paso, Tex. (in February, 1939), in a fit of temper, a welder turned his flaming blow-torch, with which he was working, on the face of his pretty 16-year-old daughter because she had bought a pair of shoes with some of her overtime money earned in a laundry, although she had handed over her usual $6 wages. "When she told her father that a friend gave her the money for the shoes, he accused her of lying, became very angry, and turned the torch on her face." She was ordered to stay in the house and did not receive medical attention for 2 days.

In Baltimore (in July, 1945), a mother was under arrest for having scalded her son, who had appeared in court the week before with 20 burns on his body. A man was also arrested for having beaten the child on the legs with a rope.

In Washington, D.C. (in December, 1931), the father and the stepmother were given a 2-year sentence for having confined their 13-year-old girl for 4 years in a dark, dirty closet, where she had "suffered from hunger and beatings." She was "so pitiably wasted she could not stand. Her answers were delayed and sometimes she sulkily refused to speak, but when she did, it was rationally and politely. Her voice was low and husky." She had been imprisoned at home "because she was abnormal from birth," said the parents, "and they did not want to send her to an institution." She was reported to be "improving rapidly under treatment in the Gallinger hospital."

In Rochester, N.Y. (in May, 1934), the Society for the Prevention of Cruelty to Children found a 5-year-old girl in a dark attic, "who had been tied, face down, on a bed for three and a half hours." Her mother had frequently tied her in the pitch-dark attic, "in order to scare her. 'I wanted to keep her from turning on the gas in the kitchen,' she said."

In Uniontown, Pa. (in September, 1938) "humane agents" found a 6-year-old emaciated and crippled girl, unable to talk or walk, "wedged into a broken chair with her frail arms tied above her head" in a farmhouse storage room where she had been tied in "long confinement." Eight months after release she had "gained seven pounds, but had the mentality of an 8-months-old baby."

An agent of the Massachusetts Society for the Prevention of Cruelty to Children (in May, 1938) found two brothers and two sisters, from 14 to 25, "hopelessly crippled mentally and physically," who had lived in semidarkness for 14 years in a shabby Roxbury tenement. "They were living in indescribable filth, were unable to speak, unable to walk, and were dragged from place to place by their 53-year-old mentally deficient mother. None of the children had seen daylight except what filtered through the drawn shade during this time." The 14-year-old (a boy) was blind and partly deaf. The 73-year-old father was bedridden.

A 29-year-old man of Altoona, Pa., diagnosed as mentally defective, killed (in 1936) the 3-year-old son of his sweetheart "with a railroad spike while the mother held the child in her arms." "We could not go to any shows because Sonny would go home and tell his dad," said the slayer, who was electrocuted for his crime 3 years later, while the mother was sentenced to prison for 10 to 20 years.

In Detroit (in April, 1937), a 33-year-old mother of eight children beat her 1-year-old daughter to death and threw her body on an ash heap "because she made me mad by crying."

In Clinton, Ky. (in October, 1937), a 45-year-old, "shell-shocked" World War veteran "lost his head," according to his wife, "when I protested his treatment of the children, seized the knife and rushed to the bed and killed all four children and stabbed me."

In Lancaster, S.C. (in May, 1939), a millworker came home "crazy drunk" and "decapitated his 6-months-old baby with a butcher knife."

A 32-year-old motor assembler in Sandusky, Ohio (in November, 1937), decapitated his 7-months-old son with a handsaw as he lay in his crib. The father's explanation was that he "just wanted to. I'd kill anybody." . . . "If I had had time and if my wife would have held still, I'd have killed her, too." He had been receiving medical treatment for a nervous condition.

A woman in Waverly, Iowa (in December, 1937), shot four of her children in their sleep in the family's farm cottage because they "wouldn't mind her." Two were found dead, while the other two were critically injured.

On Staten Island (in January, 1938), a W.P.A. worker was held without bail on a homicide charge for striking his 4-year-old daughter so hard for crying after she fell from a stair that she succumbed from the blows. "He admitted striking the child and then drenched her in the kitchen to revive her."

A 5-months-old child was brought to a hospital in Norwalk, Conn. (in May, 1938), with a broken neck produced by the violent shaking administered by the father, who was annoyed by the infant's crying while the mother was hanging up the clothes. "He picked up the infant by the armpits and shook him so hard that the neck broke."

In Norwood Park, Ill. (in November, 1938), a father slapped his infant son on the head because of his prolonged crying. He gave himself up at the police station with the explanation that he was caring for the child while his wife was at work, he had tried for 2 hours to quiet him, became distracted, and suddenly slapped him, with fatal consequences.

An unemployed chauffeur suffering from arthritis in Paterson, N.J. (in February, 1939), crawled from his bed to the crib of his 3-months-old son, who was "whimpering and crying in his sleep," and gave him such savage blows in the face that both jaws were broken and both eyes blackened. "The mother was threatened with death if she squealed. Because of protracted crying spells the neighbors filed a report with the police twelve days later, when the father was placed under arrest."

The 2-year-old "Rosebud baby" of Juniata County, Pa., died (in March, 1939) from a brutal beating by a former brickyard employee, who said he beat her "at least 50 times" and branded her with a hot stove-lid lifter "because I was jealous of her father." "I was in love with Helen" [her unwed mother], and she made me mad by always talking of the other man." The babe, with a brain injury and half of the body paralyzed, died after 5 days of unconsciousness. Within a week in Mahanoy City, Pa., a 3½-year-old boy was smothered to death by his mother "because he cried too much." She held his "mouth and nose closed for eight or ten minutes," according to her admission.

Reasons for the Strategic Role of the Teacher. Under modern conditions in civilized society the role of the teacher has become more and more important in the execution of the program of mental hygiene. Not only does the child enter school earlier and remain longer than was the case in earlier generations, but he now receives nearly all his formal instruction in the school. Again, the influence of the teacher is pervasive in the life of the child. It vitally affects, first of all, the mental hygiene of the processes of instruction and determines whether the child will acquire efficient, economical, and healthy habits of learning, as well as satisfactory informational and attitudinal outcomes from his scholastic efforts. In the second place, the viewpoints, prejudices, ambitions, attitudes, and personality make-up of the teacher, because of her position of authority, exert upon every pupil a subtle, irresistible molding influence that makes for mental health or mental disharmony. The teacher's methods of discipline; her basic philosophy of life; the opinions she expresses; her prejudices, emotional fixations, or oddities; the insidious influences that radiate from her appearance, manner of speech, comportment, and emotional poise; her calmness or instability; her mental health or mental discord—all these and many other influences leave a profound impress upon many of her pupils for evil or for good. A dyspeptic teacher may quickly dampen the ardor of a roomful of children so that they come to dislike the teacher and become soured on everything pertaining to the school. This is particularly true of younger children, who tend to transfer their dislike for the teacher to the whole educational system, and who may thus form an aversion to study and begin to fail. The dyspeptic teacher is inclined to radiate impatience, irritability, and cantankerousness, even though she may make a desperate effort to be sweet and even tempered and to hide the disagreeable feelings produced by her upset digestive system.

The extent of the mental-health hazards to which pupils may be subjected by impact with seriously maladjusted teachers is suggested by the following studies, none very accurate from the standpoint of diagnosis.

Based on certain studies of New Jersey public-school teachers, M. E. Townsend reached the conclusion that the "chances are almost seven to one that in the course of twelve years of public-school education the child will encounter at least two such maladjusted persons in a teacher's position." [19] The popular

---

[19] M. Ernest Townsend, "Mental Hygiene and Teacher Recruiting," *Mental Hygiene,* 1933, 598–604. See also Townsend's *The Administration of Student Personnel Services in Teacher-training Institutions of the United States,* New York, Bureau of Publications, Teachers College, Columbia University, 1932.

view, he says, regards teachers as irritable, ill-humored, quick to take offense, isolated, aloof, unsympathetic, and given to outbursts of temper. But teachers mostly represent an unselected cross section of the American population. One of his suggested remedies is selective admission to teacher-training institutions, based not only on scholarship but on sound mental health and emotional balance.

Emil Altman in 1934, when he was chief medical examiner in New York City, estimated that almost 4,500 of about 35,000 public-school teachers of the city were in need of psychiatric treatment, of which 1,500 were definitely mental cases. He is, however, of the view that there are no more mental cases among teachers than there are in the general population.[20]

Boynton, Dugger, and Turner, from an investigation in Nashville, Tenn., of the effects of 73 teachers on 1,095 pupils, as revealed by the Woodworth-Mathews personal-data sheet, reached the conclusion that "the pupils of the teachers who had the best mental health were more stable on the average than were the pupils of the most unstable teachers although the student-teacher relationship had existed only about two and a half months prior to the study." "Emotionally unstable teachers tend to have associated with them children who tend toward instability, whereas emotionally stable teachers tend to be associated with more emotionally stable pupils. . . . If a teacher is of a hyper-emotional type, she tends to disturb her pupils emotionally, but if she is emotionally stable, she tends to bring about emotional stability among her pupils."[21]

Bernice Baxter, with the aid of several trained observers, conducted an intensive observational study in the classroom during a period of from 3 to 6 months of the interplay of the classroom personalities and, particularly, of the reaction patterns engendered in the pupils by 42 teachers in action, who presented varying degrees of teaching effectiveness and were of widely differing personality characteristics. The conclusions reached were based on detailed daily records kept of the events in the classrooms and of teacher-pupil behavior reactions to the different classroom situations. The common observation that the teachers' behavior characteristics tend to be reflected in the behavior patterns of the pupils is abundantly substantiated by this investigation.[22] The results indicated that high-strung, tense teachers tend to engender tense pupils. Restless, erratic, nagging teachers tend to have noisy, irritable, and disorderly children. Worried, apprehensive, diffident, confused, insecure

[20] Emil Altman, "Mentally Unbalanced Teachers," *American Mercury,* 1941, 391–401.

[21] Paul L. Boynton, Harriet Dugger, and Masal Turner, "The Emotional Stability of Teachers and Pupils," *Journal of Juvenile Research,* 1934, 223–232.

[22] Bernice Baxter, *Teacher-Pupil Relationships,* New York, The Macmillan Company, 1946. The book contains a characterization of successful and unsuccessful teachers and of desirable pupil behaviors, and a teacher-rating scale.

teachers tend to foster timid, perplexed, and insecure pupils. Wearied, listless, uninterested teachers tend to produce spiritless, unanimated learners. Domineering, autocratic teachers may produce aggressive, domineering children or craven, fearsome, or inhibited ones. On the other hand, free, uninhibited teachers tend to beget free, uninhibited, responsive learners. Considerate, cooperative teachers beget polite, respectful, and cooperative juvenile citizens. Calmness, poise, self-control, confidence, cheerfulness, optimism, industry, enthusiasm, candor, sincerity, fair-mindedness, and friendliness in the teacher tend to elicit similar reaction patterns in her charges. These statements apply particularly to young children, who are very suggestible, impressionable, and imitative.

Anderson and the Brewers recorded the detailed behavior reactions of pupils from the kindergarten level to the sixth grade to teachers who were "dominative" and "integrative," as the reactions were observed in various situational types of teacher contacts. A recording technique was used that permitted the computation of correlations and critical ratios. Dominative behavior methods of classroom contact include the use of commands, force, threats, blaming, and shaming to get pupils to conform to the teacher's purposing. Integrative methods rely on suggestions and requests, rather than on commands; they are flexible and adjustable to individual pupil differences, rather than rigid and proscriptive; they are democratically and scientifically motivated, rather than dictatorially executed.

Very briefly, the results showed that dominating teachers incite conflict among the pupils, produce frustrations, evoke resistance and nonconformity, stifle initiative and spontaneity, and reduce social participation. Integrative teachers, on the other hand, evoke social participation and contribution, increase harmony in the schoolroom, reduce conflict, and stimulate willing compliance and spontaneity of action. Dominative and integrative behavior patterns are "circular" in character among both pupils and teachers; like produces like in a circular chain reaction. The psychological environment reaction is quite different in the classroom of the dominative and of the integrative teacher.[23]

Leigh Peck studied the adjustment problems of 100 teachers and 78 control students (men and women), who were enrolled in the author's classes in the summer school of the University of Texas. The students were asked to check their personality characteristics on Thurstone's Personality Schedule, to rate their degree of adjustment on a five-point scale, and to submit written statements of their adjustment problems. All reports were anonymous. The

[23] Harold H. Anderson and Helen N. Brewer, *Studies of Teachers' Classroom Personalities, I,* Applied Psychology Monographs, No. 6, July, 1945; Harold H. Anderson and Joseph E. Brewer, *Studies of Classroom Personalities, II,* Applied Psychology Monographs, No. 8, June, 1946.

women teachers had more maladjustments than the women students (not teachers) or the men (teachers and prospective teachers). "One-third of the women teachers are definitely maladjusted, and one-sixth need psychiatric advice as judged by the Thurstone Personality Schedule. One-fifth can be classified as well adjusted." [24]   According to their reports, one-fifth of the women teachers were frequently in low spirits, one-fourth were often in a state of excitement, one-fourth were easily upset, one-fourth frequently suffered from indigestion, one-fourth suffered from conflicts between sex and morality, one-third were nervous, one-third were shy, one-fifth were tired most of the time, while one-sixth lost their tempers quickly.

In the questionnaire investigation of the health of teachers conducted by the Yearbook Committee of the Department of Classroom Teachers of the National Education Association, it was concluded that "about 15 or 20 per cent lack the kind of vigorous health needed for successful classroom work," while about 37.5 per cent were subject to persistent worries serious enough to interfere with sleep, efficiency, or health. One-third were subject to nervousness more or less frequently.[25]   The chief causes of the worries were financial difficulties, occupational insecurity, illness, unsatisfactory pupil progress, lack of normal family relationships, and religious qualms. But the investigators believe that personality maladjustments are less prevalent among teachers than they are in the general population. By way of contrast with another professional group, 46 per cent of a class of senior medical students were considered by physicians to have "neurotic handicaps of a major nature." [26]

Studies by the National Committee for Mental Hygiene have shown, according to W. C. Ryan,[27] that from one-third to one-half of the lengthy absences of teachers from duty are attributed to mental difficulties.

Norman Fenton's investigation [28] of 241 teachers from small communities in California by means of personal observations of their classroom behavior patterns and conferences with school administrators indicated that "77.6 per cent were considered to be in reasonably good mental health and at least fairly well adjusted to teaching as an occupation. . . . 22.5 per cent were considered by their superintendents and principals, and also by the writer, to be maladjusted and in need of the assistance which mental hygiene could offer them."

[24] Leigh Peck, "A Study of Adjustment Difficulties of a Group of Women Teachers," *Journal of Educational Psychology,* 1936, 401–416.

[25] *Fit to Teach,* Washington, D.C., Department of Classroom Teachers, National Education Association, Ninth Yearbook, 1938, 77.

[26] S. Alan Challman, "As the Psychiatrist Sees the Teacher," *Understanding the Child,* 1937, 18.

[27] W. Carson Ryan, *Mental Health through Education,* New York, Commonwealth Fund, Division of Publication, 1938, 22. The quotations have the publisher's permission.

[28] Norman Fenton, *Mental Hygiene in School Practice,* Stanford University, Calif., Stanford University Press, 1943, 288f. Quoted with the publisher's approval.

"In 15.4 per cent of the total group the teachers were considered to be definitely handicapped in their professional work by their evidences of maladjustment." In the Agnews State Hospital, serving seven counties in the central part of California, the number of professional teachers was "5.1 per cent of the 666 women inmates gainfully employed before commitment. This is less than the expectation of 7.4 per cent of teachers among the employed female population of the state." [29]

All this attains added significance if we accept the thesis that the teacher's highest function consists in the development of an agreeable, liberated, concordant, dynamic personality, and that the emotional climate of the classroom is largely the product of the teacher's behavior characteristics. This supreme function of the teacher cannot be accomplished in disregard of the principles of mental hygiene. The teacher who fails at this point has missed the highest goal of her calling, no matter how efficient she may be in the technique of imparting instruction or stimulating pupil participation, fine as those objectives concededly are. This is more especially the case when younger children are concerned.

It follows from this that all teachers need to practice the principles of mental hygiene, not only with regard to their teaching and management techniques, but also with regard to the development, control, and regulation of their own lives. Teachers need to understand and practice the teachings of mental hygiene in order that they themselves may become well adjusted, harmonious, and unified personalities, who will radiate good mental health and set the pattern of what the children should become through their own attitudes and behavior. In the field of personality influence, if anywhere, the adages apply, "actions speak louder than words," and "example is more potent than precept." To quote Robert A. Millikan, "Example is the supreme teacher. All our pedagogy and all our educational organization, no matter how many billions we spend, are trivial and impotent in comparison." [30]

The conclusions reached by Ryan after a year spent in visiting schools in many sections of the country under the aegis of the Commonwealth Fund, to determine to what extent mental-hygiene principles were being applied in the conduct of the classroom, show the urgent need for the application of mental

[29] *Ibid.,* 287.

[30] Robert A. Millikan, "The Education of a Scientist," *The Journal of the National Education Association,* 1942, 107–108. For further references on teacher personality traits, see

A. S. Neill, *The Problem Teacher,* New York, International Publishers Co., 1944.

Percival M. Symonds, "Personality of the Teacher," *Journal of Educational Research,* May, 1947, 652–661.

Paul Witty, "An Analysis of the Personality Traits of the Effective Teacher," *Journal of Educational Research,* May, 1947, 662–671.

hygiene in school practice. "Simple friendliness in the schoolroom would seem to be one of those easily attainable and obviously desirable conditions for any human enterprise having to do with mental good health, but the visitor to schools finds it in shockingly few of the places he visits." [31]   Why?   "The school habits of generations are against it. For years the tradition of unsympathetic teachers and fear as the motive for control of children's behavior was so completely accepted that only by radical steps have modern educational workers begun to be able to create a different setting and a different attitude." [32]   The best conditions from the standpoint of mental health were found in nursery schools, kindergartens, special classes, progressive schools, and in the elementary schools as compared with the secondary schools.

Some comments on the special-class adjustment are quoted:

One finds the principle [a wholesome recognition of the individual education principle] well understood and acted upon . . . in the "special classes" of the city public school systems, where not infrequently the visitor will see a thoroughly modern individual program going on for "subnormal" and "difficult" children, while the "regular" classes of "normal" children will be doing very much the same sort of thing they were doing when Burk was denouncing the evils of the class-grade plan.

One of the oddities of the curriculum situation is that a youngster apparently must have something the matter with him or at least deviate seriously from the norm to have the advantage of a better educational program. . . . In many school systems today one will find an antiquated type of subject matter and instruction for the "normal" children, but if a youngster happens to be sufficiently "subnormal" or difficult he will have the benefit of well-planned "activities," a program of lively and significant experiences, adapted to individual interest and directed by well-prepared teachers in very small classes.

For children of low mentality a much better educational program was provided with small classes, individual attention, and a varied and interesting curriculum. . . .

It is worthy of note that in some city school systems today "normal" children and youth would be better served educationally if they had, instead of the artificial "regular" program of studies, the more appealing and valuable curriculum provided for "subnormal" and "difficult" children in special classes.[33]

Illustrations of the Teacher-Pupil Relationships in the Production of Conflicts and Maladjustments in Children.

The following instances of adjustment difficulties ascribed to teachers by respondents, all of whom are now teachers, portray incidents in which teachers have been responsible for the development in children of fears, feelings of numbness, speech timidities, shamming illness as an escape or protective mechanism, feelings of confusion, or of being a dummy, neglect of work or misconduct as a compensatory

[31] Ryan, *op. cit.*, 31.
[32] *Ibid.*, 32*f*.

[33] *Ibid.*, 37, 134*f*, 180, 295.

defense, lasting traces of emotional upheaval, and a horror of teachers. To these reports may be added one in which a vivid contrast is drawn by an elementary-school supervisor between the mental atmosphere of an old-type formal school and a new-type progressive activity school.[34]

FIRST IMPRESSIONS OF SCHOOL UNDER A CROSS AND SOMBER "OLD MAID"; PERSISTENT DREAD OF APPEARING BEFORE PUPILS AND PEOPLE, LEADING TO THE FEIGNING OF ILLNESS IN ORDER TO ESCAPE THE ORDEAL AND THE FORMATION OF THE HABIT OF ABBREVIATED TALKING AND WRITING

When I was a child I looked forward with great anticipation to the time when I would go to school and have books and pencils of my own like my big sisters. I shall never forget my first few weeks of school. My teacher was a typical old maid, wearing a black dress and high lace collar, with her hair done high on her head although not exactly in a corkscrew. She was very cross with the pupils, and punished them in different ways. One of her favorite methods was to have us stand up in front of the room before all the other pupils. This teacher punished us for dropping a pencil or book, for talking, and for other trivialities that worry some teachers. I certainly do not believe that a set old maid should teach first-grade pupils.

My father soon realized that I was unhappy, so he sent me to a private kindergarten and first grade for the remainder of the year.

The next year I entered second grade in the public school I first attended. It was then that my timidity or fear of appearing before people began to manifest itself. I always dreaded to stand in front of the pupils. In those days we had assemblies for the whole school every morning, and pupils were often assigned recitations. It seems to me that my time came very often. Since it was such a dreadful ordeal for me to stand before the pupils, I tried to get excused from reciting, but this failed. To escape from appearing before pupils, I would pray that something would happen to me, or that I would get sick before my turn arrived.

This fear was with me to a great extent during all my school days and perhaps interfered with my progress. We used to have to stand by our seats when answering questions. I could not make my answers short enough. I always answered in just as few words as possible so that I could sit down again. I believe that the habit thus acquired of answering in just as few words as possible in my oral work induced the same characteristic in written work. My mother and sisters tell me that the letters I now write sound like telegrams. If I had any early tendencies toward the raving kind, they were certainly knocked out of me.

I have not overcome this fear or timidity entirely yet. I believe that if I had to appear before an audience to read or make a speech I would have heart failure.

(J.F.; F.; S.C.T.)

---

[34] Scholastic disabilities traced to emotional upsets produced by teachers are considered in Chap. V.

INFERIORITY FEELING DEVELOPED BY FIRST SCHOOL CONTACT WITH
AN AWESOME, TACTLESS TEACHER, WHO EXERTED A DAZZLING AND
DISCONCERTING EFFECT UPON RESPONDENT; MORTIFICATION OVER
LOSS OF CONTROL OVER BODILY PROCESSES DUE TO FEAR OF ASKING
TEACHER TO BE EXCUSED; OTHER FACTORS PRODUCING INFERIORITY
FEELING

With attendance at school began what I consider my major formative influences, from the point of view of personality liabilities. From the outset the teacher struck me as an awesome, remote person whose favor I ought to court, if I only knew how. I came into disfavor with her on the first day of school. She assigned me a place to sit; in order to be near a little boy and girl to whom I was attracted, I, without obtaining permission, moved to their table. The teacher reprimanded me and ordered me to move back at once. I felt as if the world were "upside down" because this motherly looking woman was not allowing me to gratify my wishes. From that point forward I had an awe of teachers, and felt somewhat dazzled by their direct attention to me, as when one looks too straight at the sun. This feeling led me into predicaments that left definite psychic scars. For instance, once after the teacher had been complaining about the pupils' asking too often to be excused from the room, I began to feel a strong desire for micturition, but would not ask to be excused. After a protracted effort to hold back, I was eventually compelled to urinate, wetting myself and the seat. The teacher, upon discovering this fact, upbraided me for not asking to be excused, which attracted the derisive attention of nearly all the pupils in the room. I felt almost numb with the intensity of my mortification. When during recess I was subjected to further teasing on account of my wet trousers, which I tried unsuccessfully to hide by going to an inconspicuous corner and sitting down, I was seized with the conviction that I was inferior to other people; that my ideas and opinions did not carry weight with others; that other people did not take me seriously. Even the intensity of my shame from this occurrence, however, was not enough to enable me to overcome my embarrassment in asking to be excused from the room from that time forward, and I remember being repeatedly affected with attempts to postpone urination, with varying amounts of success, so that I came to be uneasy about being near people on account of the possibility that there might be traces of disagreeable odor about me. The climax came during my first grade. One day I became troubled with a desire to defecate which I tried to control until we should be released for the lunch period. As we filed from the room and out on a little porch I lost control and defecated in my clothes. I sat down and refused to budge until one of the teachers sent my brother to take me home. He was annoyed, but my mother was sympathetic and had nothing disparaging to say. This event established with final certainty in my mind that I was inferior.

Other school comparisons contributed to the inferiority feeling. I felt that I was ugly, or slightly comical looking in facial features. It seemed to me that the more desirable associates I might have had among the boys were not interested in me because I was not clever enough or competent enough in active games. Among the girls I had not the pluck to make advances toward the ones whom I secretly desired as sweethearts (not having the faintest suspicion of what that implied had I secured my desire). I did not have the fresh, pretty clothes, the gay lunch boxes, the bright pencils, neckties, and the like, that I saw almost all the other children about me have, for my family was poor even in a poor section. There were no pennies to be spent in the little store opposite the school grounds. These lacks did not pinch so hard, however, until later, in high-school days.

(K.D.O.; M.; Univ. Instr. of Psy.; A.M.; Age 32)

DEEPLY IMPLANTED INFERIORITY COMPLEX ATTRIBUTED TO A GRADE TEACHER WHO KEPT RESPONDENT THREE YEARS IN THE THIRD GRADE AND MADE HER FEEL SHE WAS A DUMBBELL; NEGLECT OF WORK AND MISCONDUCT BECAUSE OF HATRED OF TEACHER

My friends are always talking about my inferiority complex. I have always considered myself dumb, and had little confidence in my ability to get high grades or to achieve much in school, in spite of the fact that I continue to find my university courses very interesting. I think my inferiority feelings sprang up in my third grade, when I had a teacher whom I hated. She is the one who mocked and made fun of my thumb sucking. . . . I so hated her that I would do nothing that I thought would please her in the least, and went out of my way to cause her all manner of trouble. She said I was naughty, inattentive, and unable to get my work, and kept me in third grade for three years, while my classmates with probably no more ability than I had were advanced. When the fourth-grade teacher got hold of me and became aware of the injustice done me, she shoved me on as fast as she could, so that I made up about a year that way. Although I advanced a grade every year thereafter, as long as I was in that particular school I always felt that I was a dumbbell. When I transferred to another school, where I had no bad record, I worked with real zest and during the last few years of grammar school I was among the first six or seven in the class. But this did not entirely eliminate my deeply implanted inferiority feeling. In my heart I felt that I was dumb but the teachers in this school didn't know it, and I felt I was putting something over on them. My inferiority feeling is still with me, although my later successes have helped some to overcome it. Fortunately I have confidence along the line of handwork, and also in my ability as a teacher. But a rebuke puts me in the dumps and a word of praise, instead of going to my head, makes me want to do better still.

(B.C.V.; F.; E.S.T.; Age 31)

A CONTRAST BETWEEN THE DELIGHTFUL ATMOSPHERE OF A PROGRESSIVE PRIVATE SCHOOL AND THE BORING, REPRESSIVE ATMOSPHERE OF A FORMAL PUBLIC-SCHOOL CLASS WITHOUT AN ACTIVITY PROGRAM, COMPLICATED BY THE RESENTMENT AT BEING CALLED THE TEACHER'S PET

My schooling began in a private school with a very refined elderly teacher. As I recall her she must have had the qualifications of a progressive teacher of today. We had so many interesting things that every day was a delight: music, physical exercise, handwork, and dramatization, as well as the regular school subjects. Every morning we had an interesting opening exercise and the part of it that stands out most clearly in my memory is the group singing with the teacher at the piano. She played beautifully and nearly every day when we finished singing she would play beautiful, soft melodies to which I listened with rapture. I always wanted her to continue playing. I also remember very vividly the sewing cards and the paper cutting, the pictures in my first reader, one or two stories, the time we made candy and had a party, and an entertainment at the "opera house." I attended this school for two years and then, when the teacher moved away, entered the third grade in the public school.

I soon found out that the public school was very different from the "select" school which I had attended. I had to sit still a large part of the time and be very quiet. Everything seemed so much more serious and the days seemed twice as long. We did not have a piano. We seldom sang, there was no paper cutting or card sewing, and the teachers did not show us new games to play. My teacher was young and pretty and I believe she tried her best to help me but the public school was a very formal place and little children had to be very quiet. Because of the distance of the school from home I had to take my lunch with me. Every night I went home so tired that I was usually crying and went to sleep before supper. The family thought that I was tired because I walked so far. We visited this little town last fall and the distance that seemed so far to me as a child is not an unusual walk for a third-grade child. I feel sure it was not the walk but the experience in that formal school that made me so tired. I think I could have walked twice as far from the first little school and come home happy instead of crying.

Another source of unhappiness in that class was the fact that the teacher was engaged to my brother and the children called me her "pet." I can remember yet how I resented it. She was lovely and I liked her, but I was not sufficiently acquainted with the world to know that motives are often questioned by others. I liked her not because she "went with" my brother but because she was young and pretty.   (D.M.; F.; E.S.Supv.; B.S.; Age 41)

Doubtless some pupils exert a similarly injurious influence upon the teacher's personality, although no such reports have been submitted in connection with the inventories.

The third objective of the mental-hygiene program, to which we now turn, also reflects the modern emphasis upon the child in mental-hygiene work.

3. The Positive or Preservative Objective

The outstanding emphasis in mental-health conservation work has no doubt gradually been shifted to the positive objective of the preservation of normal mental health rather than the negative aim of the rehabilitation of shattered mental integrity. The positive program is concerned with the application of the principles and procedures that will ensure the preservation of mental soundness and efficiency rather than restore mental integrity after the mind has become impaired. It represents the constructive effort to surround the individual with all the influences that will tend to promote and maintain good mental-health habits and attitudes; develop the individual's highest potentials and his peculiar penchants and talents; stimulate his initiative, creativeness, resourcefulness, and spontaneity; tend to maintain him at his highest level of efficiency; and prevent aberrations, hampering habits, and crippling attitudes.

This ideal is expressed by the so-called activity school, in which due recognition is accorded the fact that children are preeminently motor creatures; in the child-centered school, in which the attempt is made to adapt and individualize the program of work to meet the growing needs of each child; in the socially oriented school, which provides abundant opportunities for social contacts and cooperative learning; in the special-class type of organization, in which remedial, developmental, and corrective work is provided to meet individual shortcomings; and in the so-called progressive schools, of which the Winnetka and Dalton plans are well-known examples.

The ideal is also represented by the modern educational movement that places the emphasis upon the education of the whole child, physically, intellectually, emotionally, and socially; upon creative education, which affords the child opportunities for self-expression and self-enrichment, which stimulates spontaneity, develops individuality, and tends to supply the soil for the development of a healthy personality, free from the fears and inhibitions that go with the suppression of spontaneity and individuality; and upon personality development in accordance with the most enlightened principles of education, psychology, and mental hygiene as the highest goal of the educational process. The positive ideal also finds expression in the project and unit methods of instruction.

One of the weaknesses of the departmental method of instruction is that the teachers tend to confine their interests to their particular subject-matter fields and take little interest in the child except as a pupil who enters their classrooms one or two periods a day solely for the mastery of certain assignments. Subject-matter specialists may easily lose sight of the wider problems confronting the child as a human being who is more than a pupil, as a person with a unique personality who is confronted with unique personality problems in need of discriminating adjustment. Their dominant, if not exclusive, interest is in John as a learner of Latin, or chemistry, or ancient history. To them, a child is a learner of subject-matter contents and not an inexperienced but aspiring architect of a potentially marvelous, wholesome, and dynamic personality. In departmentalized work the child may be thoroughly compartmentalized, primarily, of course, in the matter of instruction but often also in the matter of general treatment or regimentation.

In contrast to the departmental procedure, the unit method puts the emphasis on giving the child meaningful experiences in social settings that somewhat approximate the natural conditions and complexities of life. When a variety of areas of experience are brought into practical relationship, as is done by the unit method, they become dynamic centers of interest and meaning, and therefore arouse more varied intellectual, emotional, and motor responses on the part of the learner. Accordingly, the unit method affords better opportunities for developing the child as a whole than does the departmentalized method. Moreover, the teacher of units is more inclined to adjust the learning procedures to the varying needs and interests of each child than is the subject-specialist teacher. She frequently spends practically the whole day with the same group and thus has the opportunity to study each child from every angle and to learn to know his peculiarities and needs. From the mental-health point of view, therefore, the virtues of the project and unit methods are that they make for personality integration through the use of correlated, interesting, and meaningful experiences that tend to arouse concentrated and sustained attention, that supply abundant opportunities for self-purposing, and that are more easily learned and retained because the learning procedures are "lived through" in realistic, concrete activities and therefore are better comprehended. The project method also provides abundant opportunities for cooperative learning. Learning experiences such as these should, obviously, further healthy, normal mental integration. Of course, it may be possible so to conduct departmental instruction as to reflect many of the special virtues of the unit and integrational procedures. One elementary school visited in a large city made considerable use of integrated units or projects, although the work above the third or fourth grades was departmentalized. Each teacher placed upon a bulletin board a brief outline of the program of activities in her field for a given period of time. Each teacher was expected to correlate her own work, or some phases of it, with that of the other teachers so far as possible, so that there would be continuity and interrelation between different stages and phases of the same and different subject-matter fields. The success of such a plan requires thorough cooperation between the different teachers. Of course, it is possible, and often desirable, even from the mental-hygiene point of view, to supplement the unit or project method with the traditional procedures of study assignments, reviews, and drills.

In home care and nurture, the positive ideal is exemplified in homes that make an effort to surround the child not only with all the physical comforts needed for the development of a vigorous physical organism, but also with the cultural advantages and mental and social atmosphere essential for the growth and development of a robust, well-rounded, wholesome personality. It cannot be stressed too often that the family milieu is of paramount importance in the attainment of all the objectives of the mental-hygiene program.

The most important consideration in the attainment of the positive program of mental health is to surround the child with parents and teachers who are models of what harmonious, well-adjusted, well-integrated personalities should be.

The Clinical Approach and Individual Equation in Mental-hygiene Work. After this discussion of the objectives of mental-hygiene work it may be opportune to emphasize a very important consideration in all such work, which, indeed, has been implicit in much that has already been said. The point to be stressed is that we must always reckon with the individual equation in all aspects of mental-hygiene work, including the discovery of the causes of mental maladjustments, the cure and prevention of maladjustments, and the positive program for the conservation of mental health. The factor of the individual equation or idiosyncrasy can never be ignored in this type of work. The mental hygienist deals, not with lifeless machines that can respond in only one way, but with living organisms, with sensitive, responsive personalities that differ in their native and acquired tendencies and in the ways they are affected by external stimuli and by their own experiences. One of the ultimate facts the mental hygienist must never forget is that he is always dealing with differing, deviating individuals, and that not all individuals are affected similarly by the same stimuli. The factor of individual peculiarity and adaptability is more important, perhaps, in the field of mental hygiene than in any other field of applied psychology. How an individual will react to the stimuli of his physical or social environment depends not only upon the nature of the external situation but also upon his reaction tendencies, native and acquired, and upon his mind-set and experiences at the moment. There may, of course, be some typical reaction patterns to certain typical social or physical situations or experiences. However, exactly how any given social situation or physical happening will affect any given child cannot be precisely predicted on the basis of general psychological or mental-hygiene principles. The truth of these observations can be readily illustrated by the effects produced by such natural events as lightning or thunder. The autobiographies already presented have shown what profound emotional disturbances can be produced by the perception of these phenomena, the effects sometimes continuing for several decades. But these occurrences do not invariably produce emotional upsets. In some individuals they produce only slight, transitory disturbances or no unfavorable effects at all, or even favorable effects, even in persons of the same social or cultural class or educational level. The following reports are cases in point.

FREEDOM FROM FEAR OF LIGHTNING AND THUNDER IN SPITE OF MOTHER'S EXPRESSION OF INTENSE FEAR

Curiously, although my mother was excessively afraid of storms and lightning and would always take us to an underground cellar when a dark cloud came up, I never developed the fear, but rather enjoyed the experience as something novel to break the monotony of the everyday round. I especially liked, as I still do, to be out when the wind was blowing high. I own that I feel uneasy when lightning is striking close by, but it is not the loudness of the thunderclap, rather it's the shortness of the interval between the flash and the report. My mother felt an exaggerated fear for snakes and worms (note the Freudian symbolism) and a certain amount of that repugnance exists in me, although it is a first-moment flare, and dies away almost at once, leaving me free to look at them and manipulate them unmoved.   (K.D.O.; F.; Univ. Instr. of Psy.; A.M.; Age 32)

ADMIRATION FOR THUNDERSTORMS AND LIGHTNING IN SPITE OF A STROKE NEAR-BY, ATTRIBUTED TO SENSIBLE PARENTAL ADVICE; MAKE-BELIEVE ACTIVITIES INDUCED BY STORMS

Thunderstorms and lightning have always been rather fascinating, provided, of course, the lightning is at a reasonably safe distance. Although the writer was once within 100 feet of a tree split by lightning, he never had any fear of it. As a young child he was told to take ordinary precautions during a storm, which he has always done. But he has no recollections of excitability or fear of a storm as a child even though he recalls the fears of others in the same room. Behind his stoicism as a child in this particular matter seems to be the effect of very sensible advice given to him by his father who taught him safety precautions and by his mother who taught him the folly of fear.

From an early age storms furnished emotional background for make-believe and imaginary activities. He would at times locate himself imaginatively in the woods, with only a hollow tree for protection. As a child he liked to sit in a tent or shack and watch a storm alone, while he enjoyed being an imaginary Robinson Crusoe. He has always enjoyed the feeling of being in close touch with the elements during a storm, the futility of man against God, the music of the rain—always that music, whether inside or out in the storm. He could probably write a page on how beautiful a storm is to him. (B.C.I.; M.; C. Instr. of Psych.; M.A.)

ENJOYMENT OF THUNDERSTORMS AND FREEDOM FROM FEAR OF THUNDER, IN SPITE OF BEING STUNNED TWICE BY LIGHTNING

On two occasions I was stunned with lightning but this has not produced any phobia in any form as far as I can determine and I still enjoy thunderstorms. The two experiences came when I was about eighteen years of age and therefore did not happen during early life. Once I was standing on the back porch at home enjoying the phenomenon when a neighbor's barn was struck. It rather dazed me for a short time and I staggered into the house in a sort of semi-intoxicated condition. Father noted it and became concerned but I soon regained normality and was none the worse off for my experience. A couple of minutes later we found the adjoining barn in flames which indicated that the direct charge had struck a couple of hundred feet away. Shortly after that I received an electrical shock when the lightning struck into the rigging of a drilling machine where I was working. This was another case of getting the shock from a secondary source and not the primary charge. To me it was a most interesting experience; it was not upsetting, and I have suffered no aftersensations from the two experiences. I still enjoy the thunderstorm, especially when it is approaching.

(M.E.M.; Director of Vocational Guidance in a T.C.; M.A.; Age 33)

It is apparent from the numerous case reports in this book that the nature of the individual's attitudes, prepossessions, present mind-set, and prior emotional conditioning is fundamental in determining the character of his responses to social and physical stimuli. One of the most important practical observations in the field of mental hygiene is that, from the standpoint of mental health, the essential thing is not what happens to you in life, but the way you feel about it, the way you take it, the way it affects you; that depends upon all the factors responsible for the peculiarities of your personality make-up, especially upon your prior emotional conditioning and the attitudes engendered by such conditioning. So infinitely complex is the network of factors responsible for the individual's reaction patterns that one can never predict with absolute certainty what the psychic reaction will be to any personal (subjective), social, or physical situation. All psychic processes may be "strictly determined," but the external and internal variables are often so numerous or so obscure as to preclude any attempt at accurate prediction of behavior responses in terms of S-R (stimulus response). In this domain we are dealing with probabilities, not certainties. One person can live through the most harrowing experiences, even to the extent of becoming stunned by a bolt of lightning, without showing any traces of permanent or even temporary psychic maiming, while another person may become a mental or nervous wreck as a result of a trivial episode or an apparently innocuous remark.

It is apparent, therefore, that the approach to the individual's mental-hygiene problems must be clinical. That is, each individual must be individually studied and diagnosed. The causal factors, both immediate and remote, must be determined in each case, whether they are physical, social, or educational, objective or subjective. An attempt must be made to trace the genesis of each maladjustment, the chain of events or experiences that preceded the crisis, and the nature of the social milieu in which it developed. An intimate, adequate understanding of the personality make-up of each individual is essential for successful mental-health work. The mental hygienist must understand the problems with which each individual has to wrestle, the nature of the pitfalls he must avoid or overcome in order to become adjusted, his attitudes, biases, confirmed habits, personality assets and deficits, emotional and intellectual limitations, and the like. The process of orthogenesis also requires the adaptation of the general mental-hygiene principles to meet the conditions found in each case, and much adjustment to meet individual requirements is needed in the application of the program of positive constructive development. Perhaps we may generalize broadly and say that the task of the mental hygienist is to lead each individual to achieve his ideal of a well-adjusted, efficient, resourceful personality through an adequate understanding of his own nature, of his own mental mechanisms, and of his own motivations, through the formation of proper attitudes, ideals, and habit patterns, and through a continuous process of inner adjustment and integration.

Essentially each individual must achieve his own mental adjustment or salvation. The mental hygienist can only help the individual to a proper understanding of his problems. He can assist him to gain insight into the real nature of his conflicts, inhibitions, frustrations, and symptom formations (maladjustments); he can aid him in finding adequate remedial outlets for his dammed-up affects; he can incite him to effort and direct his strivings into proper channels; he can help him to adopt adjustment techniques that will fit his particular requirements. It is this need for individualization that renders mental hygiene a fine art. Mental hygiene, as well as guidance or counseling, is not something that anybody can apply by rule of thumb. Professional efficiency in this type of work requires not only profound understanding, insight, and resourcefulness, but also the ability to handle cases tactfully and sympathetically, a high order of diplomacy, and unfailing patience. Skill in the technique of case work from the psychological and mental-hygiene points of view is required to ferret out successfully the causes of mental conflicts and to apply the needed treatment techniques.

In view of what has been said about the need of individualization, a final word of caution will not be amiss, namely, that unjustifiable implications should not be deduced from the emphasis on the individual approach to mental-hygiene problems. It should not be inferred that the programs must be purely individual. Fortunately, many mental-hygiene principles and treatment techniques possess more or less general application as preventive, preservative, and remedial measures. They can, therefore, be applied as general procedures in the education and management of most children. Moreover, group therapeutic procedures sometimes prove as effective as methods of individual treatment, or even more so. This will be emphasized in Chap. VI.

CHAPTER III

THE PHYSICAL, PSYCHOLOGICAL, AND SOCIAL FACTORS OR ELEMENTS OF THE MENTAL-HYGIENE PROGRAM

Four Basic Elements of the Mental-hygiene Program. A thoroughly comprehensive program of mental hygiene would concern itself with the control and direction of all of the individual's activities that in any way contribute to or affect his well-being. It would provide information of value or practical rules for the balanced, integrated development and management of every trait and function of the personality. But such an elaborate program of mental hygiene is still merely an ambitious dream. A sufficient body of established facts does not now exist for filling in the details of such a comprehensive picture. The far more modest task with which we are concerned in this chapter is confined to the discussion of the fundamental elements or factors of mental-hygiene work. The minimal elements of the program cannot, in our judgment, be reduced to less than four.

1. THE PHYSICAL FACTORS IN THE CONSERVATION OF MENTAL HEALTH

Logically, priority should perhaps be given to the consideration of the improvement of physical health and efficiency. While a sound mind can doubtless exist temporarily in an unsound body, in the long run the maxim holds, *mens sana in corpore sano*. Physical fitness at least supplies an excellent groundwork for an abundant and healthy mental life. In fact, in most persons it should be rated as an indispensable substratum of efficient, normal mentation. Physical vitality makes for mental virility and optimism and greater intellectual alertness, eagerness, curiosity, vocational enthusiasm, and psychic endurance (I. S. Wile). We should, first of all, be concerned with producing people who are physically fit to live, to achieve, and to lead a vital, aggressive existence. A good, robust physique should at least tend to promote and preserve both mental and physical efficiency and health; therefore, any system of mental hygiene that completely ignores or even belittles the demands of physical hygiene will ultimately prove inadequate or abortive, although mental health means far more than physical health.

Mental hygiene is interested in physical hygiene and preventive and curative medicine both as preliminary steps toward the attainment of mental soundness and as preservative measures. All phases of physical care possess a direct or indirect mental-health value: the cure of disease, the prevention of infection, vaccination, immunization, the correction of physical defects, and the building up of vitality and resistance of the body through proper hygienic regimentation with respect to food, drink, air, bathing, elimination, exercise, work, sleep, rest, relaxation, mental and social recreation, and the development of positive health practices and a positive health consciousness. Such programs of physical care should ensure the harmonious, efficient functioning of all the bodily organs and tend to maintain a proper balance between the organs of production, distribution, and expenditure of psychophysical energy.

To become maximally effective, this program of physical orthogenesis should begin at birth (nay, rather with the parents, especially the mother, prior to the child's birth), and should include periodic health examinations at least once a year during the preschool period and throughout the school life of the child. The perfunctory routine inspections now obtaining on a large scale throughout the schools of the country should eventually be superseded by more thorough examinations by experts on physical (as well as mental) health and disease.

Abundant evidence of the urgent need of physical-health improvement has been furnished by innumerable physical inspections of children in the schools, of older adolescents, and of adults in the army. For example, according to Thomas A. C. Rennie, 28.1 per cent of 15 million selectees for the Second World War were rejected as unfit for military services—11.6 per cent because of "nervous and mental disease" and 13.8 per cent because of "mental deficiency."[1] Of 483,119 registrants of various ages in the Second World War, not previously examined, who were given preinduction examinations from August through December, 1944, 195,346—or 40.4 per cent—were rejected for general military service because of physical and mental defects. The number of defects in the two categories was about equal.[2] Some of the defects may not have been very serious from the standpoint of mental health or vocational efficiency. Thus, of 457,000 men discharged from the army between January, 1942, and June, 1945, 320,000 were eliminated because of neuropsychiatric disorders. This constituted 41 per cent of "all medical discharges." The remaining 137,000 presumably were less serious, as they were "discharged for neuropsychiatric disorders under a nonmedical category."[3]

The results of school physical examinations usually show that from 35 to 75 per cent of the children are suffering from hampering physical defects of some kind. Yet, according to the statements of physicians, 80 per cent of children are born perfect. The opinion is general that the vast majority of physical defects have been acquired and that most of these defects can be prevented or overcome by the prophylactic and corrective procedures of

[1] Thomas A. C. Rennie "Needed: 10,000 Psychiatrists," *Mental Hygiene,* 1945, 644–649.

[2] *Induction Examinations,* Bulletin of the U.S. Army Medical Department, Office of the Surgeon General, April, 1945, 54–60.

[3] *Mental Hygiene,* July, 1946, 499*f.*

modern hygiene and medicine. The results of the Fargo (N.D.) Health Demonstration is very suggestive in this respect. During the 5-year period from 1922 to 1927, when school children of Fargo were given proper physical care and treatment and instruction in physical hygiene through the cooperative service of the Commonwealth Fund and Fargo physicians, nurses, and teachers, the health of the pupils increased from a score of 24 before the inauguration of the demonstration to a score of 141 at its close. Five years later, during the years of the depression, the Fifteenth Annual Report of the Commonwealth Fund recites "that children entering school are sturdier and better nourished than their predecessors a decade ago." Unfortunately no measures of improvement are supplied on the basis of comparable scores.

Let us, therefore, make physical health a national ideal, as did the ancient Greeks, something superlatively worth while in itself and not a mere adjunct. Perhaps the intellectual fecundity of the ancient Greeks as compared with the sterility of the people of the Middle Ages was due in no small measure to the emphasis that the former placed on a sound, robust physical organism and the scorn the latter had for matters pertaining to the welfare of the body. The contempt for the human body instilled by some of the church fathers continued to influence thought and practice for many centuries. St. Jerome (died about 420) proclaimed that "baths stimulate the sense and therefore are to be avoided." St. Giles in the seventh century said that "our flesh is the devil's knight, for it resists and fights against all those things that are of God for salvation." St. Paula (died 1507), many centuries later, still embraced the superstition that "a clean body and a clean dress mean an unclean soul." Moreover, the people of the Dark Ages apparently practiced what they preached. Many saints of the church, through the centuries, boasted that they never washed. It is reported that 130 nuns in a convent "shuddered at the mere mention of a bath." The allowance each month for each pupil in one of the most celebrated schools in France (the St. Cyr) for young women of the nobility was one pair of hose, one set of underwear, and two handkerchiefs; one towel a week was allowed, one foot bath a month, and three complete baths a year, in May, June, and July. The hapless nurses were treated still more impecuniously. They received only one towel every 2 weeks and no baths except by special permission of the mother superior. The studied disregard of the most elemental principles of hygiene may have contributed to the vulnerability of the population to the scourge of the Black Death, a bubonic pestilence, which swept through Europe and the Orient during this period with decimating results. According to one "moderate" estimate, the mortality in Europe was 25 million human beings. The average longevity during these Dark Ages, based on one estimate, dropped to about 17 years. John Graunt's estimate of the expectation of life at birth during the first half of the seventeenth century was only 18.2 years. In 1945, according to the Statistical Bulletin of the Metropolitan Life Insurance Company for April,

1947, the average length of life, based on the expectation of life at birth, was 64.44 years for white males and 69.54 for white females.

But after having thus placed merited emphasis upon the physical conditions behind good mental health, let us repeat the observation that the development of physical virility merely lays the foundation for a sound superstructure of mental health. Although it is an aid toward the achieving of mental normality, it by no means guarantees the attainment of that condition. Frequently it plays merely a secondary or contributory role, and sometimes its influence proves to be quite negative. Evidence has conclusively shown that poor mental health not infrequently coexists with excellent physical stamina. In spite of all this, it is not advisable to proceed on the assumption that the physical factors are so negligible that they can be safely disregarded. It is always preferable to give the physical elements the benefit of the doubt, because it is frequently impossible to predict in advance what will be the results of the removal of physical disabilities in the cure of disease. The wise course is to correct the physical defects and improve the physical stamina as rapidly as possible. If this improves or restores mental soundness, so much the better; if no benefits accrue, little if any damage will have been inflicted, in the vast majority of cases. The physical treatment should at least prevent some diseases, later undesirable aftereffects of the physical defects, and the premature deterioration that sometimes results from uncorrected physical abnormalities, although it may not guarantee that the individual will be freed from mental difficulties or that he will not acquire any new ones.

Mental health means more than physical health as that term is ordinarily used. There are other factors of mental health that sometimes are as important as, and sometimes much more important than, the physical factors. We turn now to the consideration of the first of these factors, namely, the psychological elements, which have been inferentially discussed in Chap. I.

2. The Psychological Elements of the Program: The Mental-hygiene Problem and Objective on the Psychological Level

With what is the mental-hygiene program concerned on the psychological level? Briefly, it is concerned with the reactions of the individual as a whole, with the functioning of the entire personality. It is concerned with effecting harmonious inner adjustment of the individual's different traits, urges, ideals, and motives, to the end that the individual will not be at war with himself. The worst battles one is called upon to wage in life are frequently those with one's own ambivalent drives. To be at peace with oneself requires inner harmony. The psychological program is equally concerned with the adjustment of the individual's overt responses to the demands of his physical and social environment, to the end that he may achieve a peaceful, harmonious adjustment to his surroundings. From yet another point of view, we may say that the purpose of mental hygiene on the psychological level is the consolidation from the individual's early life of all his lines of development or growth, physical, intellectual, emotional, social, and moral, into coordinated and unified habit patterns, so that the end result will be an integrated, harmonious personality, capable of attaining maximum efficiency, satisfaction, and self-realization with the least expenditure of energy and the least strain from interfering and conflicting desires and habits, and maximally free from serious inner strife, maladjustment, or other evidence of mental discord.

It is important to reemphasize that many mental conflicts and difficulties originate purely on the psychological level, such as conflicts between feelings, emotions, thoughts, ideals, attitudes, ambitions, beliefs, and prejudices. It is also important to stress the fact that the ideal of sound mental health must be the goal for our entire citizenry, because the realization of some such ideal of mental normality is essential for the attainment of an efficient, harmonious, cooperative democracy, founded on the concept of the brotherhood of man and imbued with the spirit of good will and mutual helpfulness. Progress toward the realization of this national goal will be very slow unless the ideal of mental normality and health becomes a national ideal comparable in importance with the ideal of sound physical health.

Perhaps it is not an exaggeration to affirm that this psychological ideal is even more important than physical soundness, for what shall it profit a nation if its citizens are perfect in physique but unsound in mind and subject to all sorts of mental distempers or anomalies that breed social discord, strife, and war? Twisted, discordant personalities are a prolific source of dissatisfaction, controversy, divorce, murder, and war. Therefore no government has fully discharged its obligations to its subjects if it has failed to make the conservation of the brain power of its constituents one of its supreme objectives.

That the Government of the United States is at last awakening to interest in this problem is attested by the passage of the National Mental Health Act, which became effective on July 3, 1946. This marks the first entry of the Federal government upon a comprehensive program for the improvement of the mental health of the citizenry. The Act provides for research in the field of mental and nervous diseases, the training of psychiatric and psychological personnel, and assistance in the expansion of mental-health services in the states. An appropriation is authorized, not to exceed $7,500,000, for the erection of a National Institute of Mental Health, under the Public Health Service, to be located in or near the District of Columbia, besides an appropriation, not to exceed $30,000,000, for each fiscal year for grants to the states.[4]

A Healthy, Well-balanced Personality Is an Acquisition Rather Than an Inheritance. We have already emphasized the fact that most

---

[4] "The National Mental Health Act," *Mental Hygiene,* October, 1946, 676–681.

Robert H. Felix, "The National Mental Health Act," *Mental Hygiene,* July, 1947, 363–374.

maladjustments are acquired rather than inherited. We now want to stress the parallel fact, namely, an efficient, well-balanced personality is also an acquisition rather than an inheritance. No matter how healthy and wellborn the infant may be, he cannot attain or maintain the ideal of the efficient, wholesome personality, free from disintegrating trends and handicaps, without personal effort. No one is born with a personality so perfect and invulnerable that it will remain flawless irrespective of what may happen to it in life. In point of fact, we are all born with very incomplete psychological patterns. We inherit nothing but rudimentary personalities, which, however, are endowed with enormous possibilities for development. Nature has decreed that each of us must develop and perfect his own peculiar ensemble of personality traits. Each one of us is in no meaningless sense of the term the architect of his own fate. That the acquisition of some form of maladjustment or mental difficulty from the workaday experiences of life is not an exceptional occurrence but the general rule, not only with the ordinary run of mortals, but with those who may be rated as above average in brain power, has been conclusively demonstrated by our case histories of personality difficulties in college and university students. This group of respondents would undoubtedly rank higher in intelligence than the "run-of-the-mine" humans.

Minor Personality Maladjustments Typical Even of Superior Individuals. Our studies have revealed very few students who are perfectly balanced and completely free from personality blemishes or handicaps. One student remarks:

MASQUERADING AS NORMAL IN SPITE OF A WEALTH OF PERSONALITY
MALADJUSTMENTS

When I begin introspectively to examine my past for the purpose of analyzing my peculiarities and personality maladjustments, I am startled by the overwhelming number of bewildering idiosyncrasies that I find, and I am led to exclaim, "Am I really a normal individual or have I only been lucky enough to fool society and masquerade as normal?"

I am surprised at the oddities of my nature which this analysis has revealed to me. Some things which have been unconscious or buried fragments have been excavated, while I have been fully aware of other matters mentioned in this inventory. This self-analysis has led me to see vividly my many peculiarities. Do other people act so foolishly or am I a psychopathic case? I try to persuade myself that I am perhaps a so-called normal individual.

(A.H.T.; F.; Col.; Univ. Instr. of Psy.; M.S.; Age 26)

The number of mental peculiarities and difficulties, usually minor ones, which trouble some people whose intellectual and social status is above average, is little less than amazing.   An analysis of our records reveals almost as great a variety of symptoms as would be disclosed by a similar inventory of an equal number of patients in a hospital for the mentally diseased.   Many of the anomalies are of the same character as those found in advanced mental cases, although they are less pronounced.   In time, some will doubtless become parts of symptom complexes in frank psychoses, but certainly not all of them.   The outlook is not so gloomy.   The records of the psychological, psychiatric, and mental-hygiene clinics, which represent a contribution of the present century to the mental-health conservation movement, have demonstrated that many tendencies toward mental deviation or disorder in children and youth can be stayed or completely overcome by proper medical, mental-hygiene, and educational treatment.   Fortunately, fears, although they are very annoying, do not ordinarily culminate in the disintegration of the personality.   The following list indicates, in a measure, the multiplicity of mental annoyances and troubles that afflict students.

PARTIAL LIST OF MENTAL MALADJUSTMENTS FOUND IN SO-CALLED NORMAL PROFESSIONAL PEOPLE (GRADUATE AND UNDERGRADUATE STUDENTS)

Absent-mindedness, or undue absorption or preoccupation
Abnormalities or idiosyncrasies of attitude toward various problems of life
Acrophobias
Agoraphobias
Amnesias of various kinds
Astrophobias
Bashfulness and timidities of various kinds
Claustrophobias
Compensatory maladjustments
Compulsions and obsessions
Daydreaming tendencies
Dreams, fears, and ideas regarding death
Dreams induced by or producing fears
Emotional conflicts and upsets
Examination anxieties
Fears and phobias of all kinds
Feelings of insecurity
Fixations and regressions to infantile levels
Food antipathies, fads, and idiosyncrasies
Frustrations
Hampering habits
Indecision
Inferiority and inadequacy feelings
Inhibitions and repressions
Introvert feelings and ruminations
Mental dissociations and disintegrations

Misophobias
Morbid sensibility
Nervousness
Nightmares
Overfastidiousness
Overscrupulousness
Parental treatment and the home situation as the source of maladjustments
Peculiar, odd, or fantastic ideas
Procrastination
Pyrophobia
Rationalizing defenses
Schizophrenic tendencies
Seclusiveness
Self-consciousness and sensitiveness
Sex problems and difficulties
Sleepwalking and talking in sleep
Speech inhibitions
Spoiling in early life from unwise management
Stage fright
Superstitious beliefs and practices
Tantrums or outbursts of viciousness
Thumb sucking
Timidities
Worries, anxieties, and dreads
Zoophobias

Some of these difficulties have been described in histories already cited, and others will appear in subsequent reports.

Emphasis in the Development of a Wholesome Personality upon the Preventive and Remedial Phases of Mental Hygiene. Because of the great proneness of human beings to develop maladjustments of all sorts, so that all must plead guilty of being maladjusted to some extent, it is evident that, in the present stage of development of the human race, the positive ideal of mental symmetry and soundness cannot be attained without much remedial or corrective work. This conclusion is obvious from the data presented in earlier pages. Another point already emphasized is that this conclusion is applicable to the higher no less than to the lower levels of society. Before the average individual's energies can be freed for rich, joyous, unimpeded, productive achievement, he must be liberated from forces that obstruct his normal development, whatever they may be: quirks, antics, superstitions, fears, misconceptions, emotional conflicts, compulsions, repressions, rationalizations, unwholesome escape mechanisms, and the like. Probably few persons exist, even among the better endowed, who are not in need of psychotherapeutic treatment of some kind for freeing them from some sort of mental twist or emotional complex.

It is, of course, not sufficient to release the individual from hampering subjective states; it is also important to remove extrinsic conditions, whatever they may be, which interfere with the realization of the individual's highest constructive efforts. Here, too, the ideal is to prevent injurious external influences from becoming operative at all. Under present conditions our positive goal of wholesome personality development can be achieved only by placing increasing emphasis on the prevention of the causes of both the minor and the major forms of mental maladjustments. In the present stage of development, the remedial, preventive, and positive mental-hygiene programs must go hand in hand, reinforcing one another. The remedial and preventive measures will prove excellent positive measures by removing obstacles that interfere with normal adjustment and maximum achievement, while the positive measures will also prove to be the best preventive measures.

The discussion of the psychological elements leads directly to the consideration of the social elements of the mental-hygiene program. In point of fact, no sharp line of demarcation can be drawn between the psychological and the social. Social factors are in large part psychological and psychological factors are largely socially conditioned. Both the psychological and the social represent higher levels of integration and functioning than physiological activities, and perhaps require more intricate and complicated adjustments.

3. The Social Elements of the Mental-hygiene Program

Nature of the Social Aspect of the Problem of Mental Hygiene.
The social problem is concerned with man's social level of functioning—his participation in the social activities of other human beings or groups of people. Of particular interest are the reactions that are produced in the individual by communal life or by any sort of social situation. In other words, we are here concerned with the social dynamics of mental soundness or unsoundness, of mental adaptability or nonadaptability. It will be profitable to devote separate consideration to the negative and positive side of the picture of social conditioning.

The negative aspect relates to the types of social situations and the kinds of human contacts that tend to produce mental warps, abnormalities, or adjustment problems. The biographies presented in connection with the discussion of conditioned responses have already shown in convincing detail that many mental maladjustments are socially produced, although they were not specifically introduced to illustrate social conditioning. In fact, we have found reasons to suspect that social situations are the prime source of mental maladjustments rather than contacts with natural phenomena, and that mental soundness is fundamentally dependent upon the soundness of the social milieu. This thought is fittingly expressed by David Klein's modernization of the Latin aphorism: "A sound mind in a sound body in a sound society." [5]

Illustrations of Personality Problems Produced by Unfortunate Social Conditioning. The following records, which are introduced as illustrations of socially produced adaptive difficulties, will supply impressive evidence of the astonishing number and variety of peculiarities and maladjustments that can be produced by all sorts of social factors in the home, in the school, and in other social agencies. Since success in preventive and remedial work in mental hygiene depends to a large extent upon an accurate understanding of the mechanisms of symptom complex formations (the causation or etiology of anomalies) and an adequate recognition of the great variety of symptoms of mental disturbances (the symptomatology), the ample space allocated to the presentation of concrete cases should constitute a profitable investment. Not the least value of this illustrative material is that it will supply an indispensable background of experience, although vicarious in nature, for the comprehension of the great variety of reaction patterns that will receive detailed consideration in Part II.

Grouping of Cases. The case histories have in the main been grouped according to the similarity of social causation, although many social factors

[5] David B. Klein, *Mental Hygiene, The Psychology of Personal Adjustment,* New York, Henry Holt and Company, Inc., 1944, 17.

have in some cases been instrumental in the production of the behavior patterns, as will become obvious from the perusal of the records.

The Effects of Criticism, Ridicule, Sarcasm, Teasing, Jesting Remarks, Pranks, Threats, Etc.   Such factors as these comprise a veritable Pandora's box of childhood troubles.   As is shown in part by our histories,[5a] the effects include all kinds of fears, horrifying dreams, timidities, compulsive doubts and worries, feelings of inferiority or submissiveness, embarrassment, bashfulness, distrust, stage fright, the blighting of careers, feelings of resentment or revenge, and the like.

HORRIFYING DREAMS ABOUT FIRE AND FEAR OF GYPSIES AND ALL
COVERED WAGONS CAUSED BY THE THREAT OF A NEIGHBOR THAT THE
GYPSIES WOULD GET RESPONDENT AND POSSIBLY BURN HER IF SHE
DID NOT STOP GOING ON "CALLING EXPEDITIONS"; EFFORTS AT CURE;
SOMNAMBULISM AS A POSSIBLE SEQUELA

When I was five years old and my sister was seven we played with a neighbor girl about our age.   That was in the days when women wore long dresses.   So we secured long play dresses.   We eventually decided that grown women went calling and we started to go "calling" and found it so fascinating that we wanted to "call" most of the time.   My mother objected and spanked us but never frightened us.   Our playmate's mother, however, had no scruples about frightening children.   After one of our calling expeditions she became angry and told us that if we didn't stay at home the gypsies would get us and carry us away in a covered wagon and that they might burn us at their campfire.   She said that they would like to get me especially to be their little girl as I had such dark eyes and hair, and I could never get back home.

With my vivid imagination, I could almost see each detail as she filled in the gruesome picture.   I went home and for days I did not leave the house unless I was accompanied by an older person.   She was pleased that her method of making us play in our yard had worked.   In my case it had worked too well.   My playmate was not bothered by the threat as she had heard so many threats that never came true.   Nor was my sister disturbed, probably because she was not dark.

A few nights after the neighbor had told us about the gypsies I awakened screaming.   When my family could get me quiet enough to talk to me I told them about the fire that they were about to put me on.   Every few nights for months I would awake from a dream screaming.   It was not the same dream every time but fire always occupied a prominent place in my dreams.

My father and mother always went to church and my sister and I usually went with them.   We passed a zinc smelter and used to be delighted by the beautiful, multicolored tongues of flames that could be seen through the cracks in the board building.   I usually went to sleep during the church service and my father carried

[5a] See also the case data in the author's *Minor Mental Maladjustments in Normal People,* Durham, N.C., Duke University Press, 1946.

me home until I was six or seven years old as I was small for my age and he was a good-sized man. However, after my fear of fire had started I would scream when I saw the fire at the smelter when we started home. In consequence of this I was kept at home for a long time Sunday evenings.

On many occasions I would run into the house and hide under the bed when I saw a wagon that resembled a covered wagon on our street. It didn't make any difference if it was a huckster hawking, "onions, eggs; onions, eggs," I was afraid of a covered wagon.

My family was very angry at our neighbor for frightening me, as none of them had frightened me about the dark, or bears, or any of the things that serve to frighten some children. The neighbor, on learning how she had frightened me, was very sorry. She had no idea of how badly she had upset me.

Again and again different members of the family told me that there were no gypsies near and that if there were they did not want me because they had little boys and girls of their own. They would also tell me of the life of the gypsies, so as to get me to see that they lived much as the rest of us live, only they were rovers. But it was probably two years before I seemed to completely get over my fear of gypsies, fire, and covered wagons.

During the time that I was recovering from my fear I developed into a sleepwalker. I seemed always to be looking for something. Once in the summertime I was climbing to an upper shelf of a closet. When found and asked what I was doing, I said that I was looking for my winter hat. At another time I was looking in the button box for something I wanted. As I forgot my fear, my sleepwalking decreased and finally was overcome.

Now I am not afraid of fire and always enjoy an outing that includes a campfire. I seldom dream and fire never enters into my dreams. I believe the old fear is more often recalled by covered wagons than by anything else, probably because they are seen so seldom while fire is almost constantly seen. I have always been interested in gypsies and in their ways of living and thoughts of them do not now recall that childish fear. (D.M.; F.; E.S.Supv.; B.S.; Age 41)

PERSISTENT COMPULSIVE DOUBTS AND WORRIES CONCERNING THE PERFORMANCE OF THE DAY'S DUTIES, DUE TO CRITICISMS BECAUSE OF FORGETFULNESS IN TURNING OFF THE GAS IN THE WATER HEATER

An outstanding trait of mine, which I would like very much to overcome because it causes me much loss of time and inconvenience, is the constant fear that I have forgotten some responsibility, such as locking the back door, turning out the gas, etc.

Many mornings, even when I am in a big hurry, something makes me go back into the house after getting outside to see if I have locked the back door. Invariably I'll find it locked but if I hadn't turned back I would have been uneasy, in fact, rather miserable all day. One day last summer I had to go downtown before my dinner had finished cooking. I turned out the gas and went on my way. While on the car I thought of that dinner and could not convince myself that the gas was out. I felt so worried I could not get it off my mind. Of course, when

I reached home, all was well. Often I awake at night wondering whether I put my rings in my jewelry case, and can't get back to sleep until I've investigated. Many similar examples could be cited. The part that I dislike very much is that the more responsibilities I assume the more I am troubled with these silly fears.

Recently I have tried to unravel the past to see if I could discover the beginning of this most annoying characteristic. I can trace it back to an incident, which, at the time, made quite an impression on me. At the breakfast table one morning when I was a child, my father asked who had last used the instantaneous water heater in the bathroom. I was the last to take my bath the night before. It so happened that the gas had not been turned off and the light had blown out. Therefore much gas had escaped. He scolded me for my carelessness and impressed upon me the danger to which I had subjected the whole family. After that whenever I used the heater I would go back to see if the gas was turned entirely off. Sometimes after I was in bed I would get up to make sure.

I have been trying the two following remedies: First, at the time of locking the back door, turning out lights, and the like, I try to impress myself with the fact that the acts are being done. Secondly, when the question arises in my mind I endeavor to pay no attention to it and try to dismiss it. I am beginning not to turn back though the annoyance remains with me.   (W.W.V.; F.; S.C.T.)

CAREER AS A SINGER BLIGHTED BY THE DISPARAGING REMARKS OF AN OLDER JEALOUS, DOMINATING SISTER; THIS LED TO THE DEVELOPMENT OF A SUBMISSIVE ATTITUDE; SOME COMPENSATION IN FINDING OPPORTUNITY FOR SELF-EXPRESSION IN DEBATING

Musical ability was inherent in our family. At an early age and without much training, my name appeared on local concert programs as a juvenile vocal soloist. Jazz was unknown then but I sang "popular songs" as well as sacred ones. I felt no timidity before audiences, which received me kindly and enthusiastically. I don't think this overemphasized my self-assertive instinct, nor do I think it engendered any undue desire for self-praise. However, this recognition did not please a sister a few years my senior. Unknown to other members of the family, she made disparaging remarks about my singing which displeased and worried me considerably. I thought about her remarks and grew doubtful of myself. Before long, because of excessive fixation upon the ideas suggested by her, I became diffident about singing. A vocal teacher was anxious for me to secure special training as she recognized the possibilities of my voice, but I was not sufficiently interested just then. I lacked confidence and ere long didn't want to appear before audiences at all. My parents did not urge me to do so, probably because my schoolwork and singing did not leave much time for play. I missed this means of self-expression and the accompanying recognition it brought me, and I bore resentment toward the one whom I considered responsible for checking my career. It so happened that a debating club was organized among my classmates and I found an opportunity here for self-expression, with the result that I have done much public speaking but no more singing except in school and church choirs. This same sister dominated my life to a greater or less degree until I began teaching and many times I was forced to alter my activities in harmony with her purposes. I believe this has had a noticeable and lasting effect on my life. I often feel that I must submerge my desires and aspirations and conform to the wishes of others. There have been many struggles between my habitual self, which has been constructed to please others, and my original, deeper, instinctive life.

(M.V.J.; F.; E.S.P.; B.A.; Age 32)

LONG-CONTINUED CRIPPLING BASHFULNESS AND SELF-CONSCIOUS-
NESS TRACED TO EMBARRASSMENT PRODUCED IN EARLY CHILDHOOD
BY LAUGHTER OF AUDIENCE AT FORGETTING LINES; PARTLY OVERCOME
THROUGH THE ATTEMPT TO LEARN THE ORIGIN OF THE TROUBLE AND
THE REALIZATION OF ITS FANTASTIC NATURE

I have been the victim of some sort of a bashful complex for many years. In fact, I can't recall any particular period of my life when I was altogether free and easy in the company of others. To have more than two persons focus their attention upon me at the same time caused the utmost mental agony. As this state of affairs dawned on me more forcibly with the passing of time, I began to wonder how it originated. The realization that my bashfulness was most foolish and childish did not help me at all. I resolved time and time again to free myself from this mental monster, but when the occasion presented itself I always found myself in my usual embarrassing predicament. Resolutions proved of no value, and I seemed powerless to help myself.

Not until quite recently when I sat down and tried to recall the time when this thing began, have I been able to gain some kind of control over this phobia.

I am of the opinion that it began when I was about six or seven years of age. I was prevailed upon to memorize short poems to recite at the special gatherings of our neighborhood. After I had filled my mind with many cute and simple lines and had been coached in the way they should be delivered, with the necessary gestures and facial expressions, I was ready to acquaint others with my histrionic powers. Accordingly, at the very next family reunion the little boy with so many dormant possibilities was asked to get up and entertain the home folks.

The little boy arose and instantly became the cynosure of all eyes. As he opened his mouth to speak he caught the tantalizing and amused expression of his elder sister. As the lines faded from his memory he asked his mother to make big sister "stop laughing at me." He was rewarded by unsuppressed laughter on the part of the rest of the company present and grew excited and gave vent to childish tears. He was frightened out of his wits and mortified beyond consolation: another victim of ridicule and misunderstanding.

The bogie grew as the years passed and even to this day I always feel some kind of a restraint when called on at private or small public gatherings. I am quite sure that the fright which I received on that day long ago is the basis for many similar experiences in my later life. This fright grew into a form of self-consciousness which has rendered me almost speechless on numerous occasions.

I think an analysis of this trouble has helped me to overcome it to a very great extent. Realization of the fact that it existed only in my mind and was only a fantastic notion has aided me considerably toward achieving victory over a very unpleasant mental obstacle. Knowing the truth is, to my mind, a big step toward freedom. (G.J.J.; M.; U.S.)

GREAT PERTURBATION AND FEELING OF IMPOTENCY PRODUCED BY TRIVIALITIES APPARENTLY TRACEABLE TO A JESTING REMARK WHEN AWAY VISITING AT THE AGE OF FOUR THAT RESPONDENT WOULD HAVE TO PAY A QUARTER FOR HER MEAL, WHICH MADE HER FEEL SO WEAK AND EMBARRASSED THAT SHE COULD NOT EAT AND WHICH CAUSED A LASTING FEELING OF DISTRUST FOR THE PERPETRATOR OF THE REMARK

One noon, not long ago, I missed meeting my sister for lunch at Ida Noyes Hall and went on in without her. A friend told me she believed my sister had gone in. Realizing that I did not have enough money to pay for my lunch, I felt terror take possession of me and I became so weak that I was forced to rest the tray on the table. At about the height of my panic I spied my sister.

This terrible feeling of panicky exhaustion, which I have felt before on seeing injured men lying unconscious on the street, I now realize can be produced by trivial things and is unreasonable and should be overcome.

When a tiny child, not more than four, I visited an older playmate all day for the first time. She lived across town and I was to be taken home after supper. At the table one of this girl's grown brothers asked me if I had any money. I said "No." He said that I would have to pay a quarter for my meal. I became so weak that it was impossible to overcome the feeling, even when assurances were given that he was only teasing me, and I did not eat another bite. To this day I have a feeling of distrust for that man, even though he still is a friend of the family. Recently I saw him after an interval of at least ten years and was surprised to realize what a thoroughly attractive person he is. During all my childhood I was so resentful of the embarrassment he had caused me that I pictured him as a person not at all likable. This may be the basis of the terror with which helplessness in public strikes me. (R.R.; F.; E.S. Critic T.; B.S.; Age 25)

FEAR OF CATERPILLARS DUE TO A BOY'S PRANK; CURED BY OBTAINING REVENGE

Other early childhood fears were of caterpillars and German police dogs, and of being lost. The first developed in this manner: A cousin of mine visited us when I was almost nine. He was not only a bully, but was always very fond of committing practical jokes, and received particular joy from teasing me. My experiences with caterpillars had up to this time been very pleasant. I had collected several types during the summer and had observed the changes in their life stages. However, I had never felt that I would fancy having them crawl over me. This cousin, after learning that mice and rats failed to intimidate me, secured some exceedingly fat caterpillars. One he proceeded to put on top of my head, and casually remarked that I had some dirt in my hair. After procuring my brush, I proceeded to brush out the dirt, and, of course, mashed the caterpillar. Certainly this was sufficient cause for "murder"—my brush and hair completely dirtied by the "insides" of a caterpillar. His second prank was the famous one of putting one on my neck and having it crawl down my back. The details of that scene can be easily imagined. My fury against my cousin knew no bounds and a growing fear of caterpillars developed because of their ability to make life for me very uncomfortable. I wondered why so many existed in our neighborhood shrubbery but, instead of killing every one I saw, I did my best to get as far away from the shrubbery as possible.

I am quite sure that my fear would have permanently remained with me if I had not secured ample revenge against my cousin by shaving his hair as closely as possible—his most admired attraction and the source of his colossal pride. The fear disappeared along with his hair, and fortunately he soon was sent back to his school. (T.A.M.; F.; E.S.T.; B.A.)

Tales of Ghosts, Spooks, Goblins, the Bogeyman, Negro Folklore, and Superstitions. Closely akin to tales and threats intended to provoke fears are spook and ghost stories and superstitious lore. That superstitions still constitute a not negligible part of our vaunted twentieth-century culture is shown by some of the studies listed by Maller and by a reported cataloguing in 1932 of about 4,000 separate superstitions found in the state of Kentucky at that time. No state is free from the blight of superstitious beliefs and practices. Hexing, witchcraft, and voodooism influence the folkways and beliefs of some people in all sections of the country. To illustrate:

Into the municipal court in Philadelphia (in 1934) a man was brought by the Society to Protect Children from Cruelty for persistent refusal to provide surgical treatment for the 2-year-old leg fracture of his 16-year-old son. The father protested that the crippled leg was an "act of God." "He thumbed through a well-worn Bible and quoted passages concerning the 'visitation of God upon the flesh,' to prove his 'right' to prevent treatment of his son, who was suffering severe pain." "When the boy a week later was ordered sent to the hospital for treatment, the father threatened legal action to stop what he termed an 'insult' to the Deity."

The same year, a 24-year-old taxi driver (later declared mentally disordered) confessed that he shot a 64-year-old woman in Schuylkill County, Pa., because "she had me hexed. She sent a black cat down from the skies. I had to kill her to break the hex. I was hexed eight years ago because I cut across her property to go fishing. One day she caught me with her eyes. I felt as though someone had me by the throat. I ran around and around, trying to shake off the grip. I couldn't do it. I know I'm going to be electrocuted, but I don't care now. Now I have peace."

The following year, a farmer near Abertin, Pa., fired his barn, "to burn up a man hiding there who had cast a spell on his stock." Because one of his mules refused to eat, he said his stock had been hexed.

In 1929, according to report, an entire school in York County closed because of the fear of the "hex."

In New Jersey (in 1936), "three serious-minded, middle-aged housewives who told a wild tale of black magic in court were sternly warned by the Recorder not to molest further the woman they accused of being a 'witch,' and were placed on probation for a month. The women apparently were unshaken in their belief that their neighbor was a 'witch.' They 'saw her change herself into a horse, walk on her hind legs, and change her head into a dog's head as she bent down.' They 'saw her head shrink to the size of a fist, and horns appear on her head.' She would 'walk on all fours like an animal. She was the devil's servant and did the devil's work.' . . . The alleged witch protested that the witch's brew cited by her accusers was a medical preparation she made from herbs and that the weird shapes were flickering shadows on the wall."

Voodooism, a form of superstitious magic or religious worship of snakes attended by debased, secret nocturnal rites and orgies, has its devotees in widely scattered areas in this country, mostly in the form of hocus-pocus charms and fetishes, and shamanistic practices. The "charm" business in New Orleans is estimated at $1,000,000 a year, with a "hoodoo doctor" or a "conjure woman" in almost every district. The hoodoo talisman bag, at a dollar, contains a piece of scorched leather, a piece of charcoal, two small bones, and a snarl of hair. "Samson's oil" is for your muscles; "black wash" for your enemies; "gambler's luck" and "fast luck" for dice shooters. Charms "sell like hot-cakes at busy street corners" in Harlem; "guffer dust, new moon No. 1," "happy dust," "tying down goods," and "chasing away goods," at $50; "buzzard nest," at $100; "black cat's ankle dust," at $500; and "black cat's wishbone," at $1,000.

To counteract belief in superstitions, 13 Chicagoans during the early part of the last decade formed an Antisuperstition Society. "During the first thirteen days of the year, these men are out to flout as many ancient superstitions as they can think of. They will walk under ladders, let black cats cross their paths, light three cigarettes off one match, and so on; and at last, on Friday, January 13, they will have a banquet."

According to a news report, a number of scientists made a study of jungle black magic in Brazil in 1934, because "African jungle magic, scientists say, is responsible for much mental suffering in this country." The role of superstitions, magic, and witchcraft in the production of major and minor forms of mental disorder is deserving of more careful investigation than the casual consideration given the matter by psychopathologists in the past. Undoubtedly, emotionally surcharged superstitious beliefs are a source of maladjustments and malbehavior.[6]

Some of the psychic maladjustments produced by early exposure to superstitious indoctrination are brought out in our case histories: belief in omens, bad luck, witchcraft, black magic, or superstitions; indulgence in the practice of magic, hoodoo, "hexing," or "conjure"; wearing charms or amulets; development of fears, dreads, worries, nervousness, restlessness, creepy feelings, insomnia, nightmares, feelings of panic, terror of death, and a superstitious nature.   The methods used to overcome or counteract the disconcerting effects of the false beliefs are also indicated.   Some of these methods are suggestive.

FEAR OF THE DEAD AND OF FATHER'S CORPSE INDUCED BY SUPERSTITIOUS TALES; SUPERSTITIOUS BELIEF IN MIRACULOUS CURE FROM TOUCHING FATHER'S FACE

When we were quite young, our aunts would tell us tales about student doctors, "voodoo" men, ghosts, and spirits.   Even though most of these tales were told with good intentions, they induced in me an attitude of fear toward the dead.

The dead had a most gruesome effect upon me, and I was unable to look at a dead person.   To do so would undoubtedly bring spirits into the house.   As I grew a little older this fear became less prominent, because I heard less of these fantastic tales.

However, one morning about seven o'clock when I was in my seventeenth year, I was awakened rather suddenly by my sister's voice: "Father won't wake up. Mother has called him but he will not answer.   Try to get a doctor.   Maybe he is dead."

The sound of the word "dead" brought back my early childhood fear.   We did call the doctor and when he came he pronounced him dead.   The coroner was called.   The association of the word "coroner" with the dead brought me more horrid thoughts.   The coroner asked one of us to show him the body.   None of us volunteered.   We were afraid of our father in this new form.   We were afraid that he, like other spirits, would haunt us.   The thought of the terror I would have to endure that night when I went to bed was heart-rending.   As I had anticipated, sleep would not overtake me at all.   Every moment I expected to see my father enter the room.   When I heard the dogs in my neighbor's yard howl, I was certain that they were hailing his arrival.

[6] Among recent references on superstitions, consult
Earle E. Emme, "Supplementary Study of Superstitious Belief among College Students," *The Journal of Psychology,* 1941, 183–184.
J. B. Maller, "Superstition and Education," in *Encyclopedia of Educational Research,* New York, The Macmillan Company, 1941, 1186–1190 (see the excellent bibliography).
Vance Randolph, *Ozark Superstitions,* New York, Columbia University Press, 1947.
Rosalind M. Zapf, "Comparison of Responses to Superstitions on a Written Test and in Actual Situations," *Journal of Educational Research,* 1945, 13–24.

The day before the funeral services the body was brought back to the house. We lined up to see it and, according to instructions, each of us touched his face. This, according to my mother, would prevent us from being afraid of our father or any other dead people.

No sooner had I touched my father's face than a sudden change overtook me. I felt as if I were a different person. I was no longer afraid of him. That evening I was able to sleep soundly as if nothing had happened.

Since then I have not been afraid of the dead, and stories of spirits and ghosts have become merely imaginative tales. I have even earned money assisting an undertaker and am always ready for service when the firm calls me.

(M.A.J.; M.; Col.; Stenog.; Age 24)

BELIEF IN WITCHCRAFT, MAGIC, AND SUPERSTITIONS INSTILLED BY NEGRO FOLKLORE; CHRONIC VICTIM OF SUPERSTITIOUS OBSESSIONS

When I was at the impressionable age of four years, my mother died and my brother, two years my senior, and I were sent to live on a large old Virginia plantation, away from our father. As all the members of the household were grown people whose conversation was largely above my head, I naturally turned to the people nearest my mental level, the darkies on the farm.

The cook and the maids gathered in the kitchen every day and while performing their duties they told direful tales of "conjure" and talked about signs. Some of these superstitions have preyed upon me all my life, and, try as I may, they will crop up unconsciously at all times.

Of course, my governess and other members of the family told me not to believe the silly things that the darkies told me, but I enjoyed far more the weird Negro folklore than I did most of the storybook tales.

Once I received some lovely old jewelry from my grandmother. The darkies assured me if I buried it properly my future husband would step over it. Very promptly I buried the jewelry according to directions and awaited my fate. Soon the jewelry was missed by my governess and reluctantly I explained what I had done with it in order to find out whom I was going to marry. Needless to say the buried treasure was never discovered and my faith was nearly shaken in the art of "conjure" for a while.

One day, on discovering that my right hand was nearly covered with warts, the cook promised to conjure them off if I would do as she said. As no jewelry was involved this time I proceeded once more to indulge in the fascinating art of witchcraft. I was to steal a dishcloth from the kitchen, rub it over my warty hand, and then bury the cloth under a rock. If any one saw me do this the spell would be broken. Evidently no one saw me perform this ritual for in a short time my hand was actually free from those ugly warts that I so hated.

From then on I was reconverted to witchcraft and signs, although as I grew older the idea of "conjure" faded away. Nevertheless to this day I believe in all sorts of superstitions in spite of the fact that they are silly and devoid of logic.

Always I was told that it was unlucky to eat at the table with thirteen people. One person would certainly die before the year was out. About five years ago

I had to eat at the table with thirteen people and before the year was over one of the persons present did die.

I am the daughter of a Presbyterian minister and, of course, believe in predestination. Yet I automatically cross my fingers when a cat of any color crosses my path, or when I see a cross-eyed person. Not for any consideration would I walk under a ladder or sweep anything out of my door after the sun goes down. I never sing before seven in the morning for my nurse told me, "If you sing before seven, you'll cry before eleven." She also told me that "a whistling girl and a crowing hen always come to some bad end." Unconsciously sometimes now when riding along I will tag a white horse as my nurse taught me to do. She also said that to tag a white mule brought ten times better luck than to tag a white horse.

When my left hand itches I expect a gift, and when my right hand itches I'm sure to shake hands with a stranger. For one's nose to itch is a sign that a letter is on the way, and for a rooster to walk up to the door and crow is a sure sign that company is coming. Not for any consideration would I begin a new piece of work on Friday for one never lives to finish the job. Always when fishing I spit on my hook, as an old darky taught me to do when I was a child. Even now when washing dishes, if a knife drops, a hungry man is sure to come to our house, and if a fork drops I expect soon to be the hostess of a hungry woman.

These are only a few of the many superstitions which have carried over since my early childhood. I am still struggling to overcome them by just putting them out of my mind whenever they arise, and they do arise daily. Just at Christmas my husband and I were invited to dinner at the home of my father-in-law. I counted over and over again the number of people in the family who were sure to be there and it always worked out to be thirteen. Knowing my aversion to sitting at a table with thirteen people, the family had arranged two tables so that all thirteen would not be sitting together. In order to overcome this uncomfortable superstition I made fun of myself, encouraged by the ones who were not superstitious and who were teasing me. I still kept thinking which one of us would die before the year ended when the youngest member of the family, who is about eighteen months old, was brought to the table for her dinner, making fourteen present. From then on I enjoyed the dinner.   (G.R.M.; F.; E.S.T.)

CREEPY FEELINGS PRODUCED BY NOISES, TRACEABLE TO SPOOKY STORIES

Oh, what creepy feelings I have when I hear peculiar noises! When I was very small and company would come in, I used to sit before the fireplace and listen to all sorts of spooky stories. My mother told about the noises that were heard and the shadows she had seen at her old homestead. She said that when everything was quiet someone would walk up the stairs and all through the hallway. When she investigated no one would be there. She has also seen peculiar shadows on the wall in the same hall. My father also used to relate that he had heard the same noises and they even now often speak about them to me. The noises were heard at a certain time of the day and night when no wind was blowing and there was nothing to make a noise. When I was sick with the typhoid fever at the age of five in this house, located in Norfolk County, my father called my attention to the noise. The stairs were heavily padded and carpeted, yet that thump, thump, thump was heard.

Another story told by my father that led me to fear peculiar noises was about a happening when he was fourteen years old. His people were moving and he had to spend the night in the house to watch the furniture they had already moved. During the night something would walk across the floor upstairs. It continued coming down the stairs to the door of the room in which he was, and then would walk back upstairs. When he looked all over the house, there was nothing to be found. The windows were all lowered and there was nothing upstairs. But as he walked through the house the doors would come to and lock. The next day when he related the happening the folks told him it was his imagination. However, during the day they had the same experience with the doors, and the next night his grandmother heard the same noises, so they moved immediately.

(W.N.; F.; U.S.)

NIGHTMARE INDUCED BY GHOST STORIES, AND ALSO FEAR OF DARKNESS AND OF GHOSTS; OVERCOME BY MOTHER'S EXPLANATIONS, A FRIENDLY NIGHT LIGHT, AND PLEASANT GAMES BEFORE RETIRING

I never heard the word "ghost" until I was eight. One evening just before bedtime three of my friends introduced me to my first ghost tales. They also thanked their stars that their mothers and fathers were living so that they would never see a ghost, and regretted that my father would have to return at various times to see how well I was getting along. They ardently believed in the existence of ghosts. I was fascinated with the stories and urged the three on to greater exaggerations. That night I experienced my first nightmare. So great was my fright that I jumped out of bed and rushed down the hall to my mother's room. I tripped over her doorsill and fell headlong into her room, awakening, of course, the whole house.

I had the idea that a ghost had made me fall and, since ghosts and the dark were welded so closely together, I feared both by dreading one. My mother understood this fear and helped me get rid of it. A realization that ghosts were mythical creatures like fairies, elves, goblins, and the like eliminated that part of the fear. A friendly light was left burning in the hall outside my room, and many activities of a most pleasant nature were kept going until dark, such as games of hide-and-go-seek. The movies helped to eliminate this fear also, because I had never been allowed to attend them at night up until now.

(T.A.M.; F.; E.S.T.; A.B.)

TERROR OF DEATH LASTING INTO ADULTHOOD, DUE TO BELIEF IN SUPERSTITIOUS TALES AND SIGNS; THE BANSHEE FEAR, OVERCOME BY CONVINCING NIECE OF ITS SILLINESS

The fear of death was one of the first and by far the worst fear of my childhood and adolescent years. I believed in many signs and superstitions in my early years. If a bird flew into the house some member of the family would die within twenty-four hours. A bird really did fly into the house and that night Aunt L. died. I firmly believed in my childish fancy that, if we could have kept the bird out of the room, Aunt L. would have recovered. Another time a bird entered the schoolroom and sat on the window sill above my brother's desk. I was almost hysterical when I came from school that day and it was far in the night by the time my dear patient mother had quieted my fears. For many years I thought that my brother would not live very long. My brother was about nine or ten years old at that time. He is fifty years old now and in excellent health. Dreams were also signs of death. I would tremble and often cry when someone told of dreaming of a black horse, or digging into the dirt. A black cat in the middle of the road was enough to worry me for several days. But of all the signs of the grim old monster, the banshee or old woman was the most terrible. She caused me many a wretched night. I was about seven when I first heard of the banshee through an Irish woman who was visiting my mother. The story was of a little old woman called a banshee who came to warn the family of the approach of death. This banshee would fly to the window in the dead of night and give a plaintive little cry to warn the victim of the approach of death. For many years after hearing this story I was on the alert for the banshee's wail. The whine of a dog or the mew of an owl would cause a real panic. I told no one of my fears and on one occasion when my scream brought my mother to my bed, I dared not tell her because I was sure that the banshee had come to warn my mother. After my mother left me I prayed earnestly to God to spare her. This fear continued long after I was a grown woman. I became so ashamed of it that I determined to rid myself of this silly fear. My favorite niece asked me if this story of the banshee were true. By the time I had convinced her that there was nothing to it, I had also conquered this ridiculous fancy.   (S.B.R.; F.; H.S.T.; B.S.; Age 58)

CONQUERING A FEAR OF GHOSTS

When I was a young boy I used to hear the people around home talking about the old haunted house. This particular house was on the road to my uncle's home, so for several years they were never bothered with me after night. The story went that the last people who lived there had to leave because of the noises. They asserted that you could go there at night and hear somebody dragging chains down the stairs. After I grew up, at least in high school, I used to be out after night and would have to come home alone after I left my uncle's home. I always ran by this place, being afraid to look around. After I began to think I was a grown man I decided that I would stop that foolishness before someone caught me, and naturally I had reached the age that I wanted to appear brave. I finally reached the stage where I could walk by, but I always was uneasy for fear something would happen. The expectation soon happened, for soon afterwards I was passing and I heard something jump down on the porch from the window. I didn't look or wait any longer. The faster I ran the more convinced I became that it was following me. When I ran upon the porch at home a neighbor's dog reached my side. I thought for a few minutes and decided that never again would I run until

I had some real reason. A few nights later, a crowd went hunting and didn't get back until after 1 o'clock in the morning. As I passed this house I saw what appeared to be something, sure enough, but I was determined to find out what it was before I left. At first I thought it was someone trying to frighten me by putting a sheet over his head. The object was up against the house which made the approach even more difficult. I approached it very cautiously; when I was almost against it the thing moved and groaned. I couldn't stand my ground any longer, so I left that place running with all power. As I ran I tried to think until finally I convinced myself that it was a cow. I stopped, debated, and returned to convince myself that it was in reality a cow. This one act meant more to me than any other, because I had conquered the one thing that had been a mountain in my early life and experience. (H.A.; M.; H.S.T.; B.A.)

The fear of acquiring a monster of a stepmother, brought about by fairy-story delineations of this parent substitute, may be conveniently introduced at this point.

TORMENTS, FEELINGS OF INFERIORITY, FEAR OF RECITING, AND SELF-PITY ENGENDERED FROM DREAD OF ACQUIRING A FAIRY-STORY MONSTER OF A STEPMOTHER THROUGH FATHER'S REMARRIAGE; POSSIBLY ALSO DUE TO EXCESSIVE BABYING AND SHIELDING FROM FACING REALITY BECAUSE OF BEING THE YOUNGEST CHILD; METHODS OF CURE

The adjustment problems that have been pronounced in my life relate to fears, self-pity, and an inferiority feeling. These seem to have dovetailed one into another, making a composite picture of the difficulties of my childhood and early life.

I was the youngest of a very large family. Several of my brothers and sisters were married before I was born. I grew up with the remaining group who made much of the baby in the family. My parents, too, lavished much affection upon me, thinking there would be no more babies in the family to fondle and love. Consequently I grew up with elders, who not only were willing to do everything for me, but who seemed to enjoy doing it and exempting me from all unpleasant tasks. Naturally I loved this pleasant home. Although I often made an earnest effort to be a helpful member of this group, I was always persuaded that it was so much easier for them to do it, and that I must just study, practice my music, and play. Unfortunately my mother died when I was still in the primary grades. Then began my torments of fear! Foremost was the fear that my father would remarry and I would have one of those terrible fairy-story stepmothers. Every unmarried woman or widow who came to our house would arouse in me this foolish fear, and following closely in its footsteps would come an overwhelming feeling of self-pity. I would lie awake at night imagining all sorts of dreadful things that would happen to me if my father should bring a new mother into this happy household. How I would pity myself! My childish mind suffered real torments.

I once timidly ventured to ask my father if he ever thought of remarrying. He answered me that he loved his family very deeply and that we seemed to be getting along nicely as things were. This allayed my mind for a time, but again and again I would be tortured by these ever-recurring fears. My family and outside friends showed their pity for me and would say, "poor child! It is too bad you had to lose your wonderful mother." This of course would boost up my self-pity. Scarcely a night passed that I did not cry myself to sleep, all because of self-pity.

During my high-school years this nightmare, which I knew now was purely imaginary, seemed to pass. My father showed no inclination to remarry and introduce this terrible monster into our home. But an inferiority complex seemed to have sprung up from these fears of my early life. I was afraid to recite for fear others would laugh at me, in spite of the fact that in my written examinations I always passed with good grades, due to the fact that I liked to study and was afraid to come to class without my lessons almost letter perfect. My high-school teachers were fond of me and helped me make adjustments by praising my work, so that in time I learned to recite without fear or embarrassment.

But when I entered a state university and had to meet a new situation these fears again assailed me with renewed vigor. The classes were very large and I had to compete with good material from all over the state. At first when called upon I invariably said, "Not prepared"; and had it not been for our written tests I am quite sure I would have been asked to "vacate" at the end of the first semester for the good of the cause! But written lessons saved the day for me.

I began taking courses in psychology under Dr. S. and Dr. J. Then and only then did I learn to talk to myself. I said to myself again and again, "Do your best. Forget about the other fellow. He probably has much more natural endowment than you have, but he must not have more zeal or more eagerness to learn than you have. One is God given, the other you and you alone must take care of. You must have no crutch to lean on, but walk boldly alone and feel satisfied with whatever rating you may be given provided you have done your best." It is an ever-constant struggle to keep oneself fit for the highest things of which one is capable and no one is fit who is assailed with fears and doubts. Life's battles can only be won by maintaining a winning attitude.

Worry and discouragement assail me now at times but I try to meet life's situations rationally. I fight them because I do not enjoy them and realize that they are peculiarly disqualifying and upsetting to mental poise. How can we keep mental poise and health? There are many roads that lead to mental health. I have chosen study as my solution. I am no longer a young student but I hope always to have a deep interest in study. My self-pity is entirely a thing of the past, but unfortunately some remnants of the monsters, Fear, Worry, and Inferiority, ever and anon creep into my life and I have to become the "General" and order them "out of my way."

Through the vital interest of study, I am able at least to keep in the "middle path" of successful living.   (M.F.M.; F.; S.C.T.; B.A.)

Invidious Comparisons. Disparaging comparisons constitute a prolific source of feelings of inadequacy, futility, obsessional doubt, lack of self-confidence, timidity, indifference, indolence, jealousy, desire for solitude, desire for revenge, protective bravado, or compensatory superiority.

EMBARRASSMENT AND LACK OF CONFIDENCE PRODUCED BY FEELINGS OF OBSESSIONAL DOUBT THAT WRITTEN INSTRUCTIONS HAVE BEEN MISREAD OR MISINTERPRETED, ATTRIBUTED TO UNFAVORABLE COMPARISON AND LACK OF APPRECIATION IN HIGH SCHOOL ENGENDERING FEELINGS OF FUTILITY AND LACK OF CONFIDENCE

I am not sure how long I've had this problem to face, but I have been conscious of it for the last two or three years. Whenever I am given any kind of written instructions I discredit my interpretation of them, regardless of their importance; simple, more or less unimportant directions affect me just as do important ones. For example, if I am making a cake and reading the directions, invariably when I begin to measure the ingredients I am never positive of the amount I wanted. If I go back and read the directions again, more often than not I am as dubious as before. The same experience has occurred in examinations in which there are block questions, part of them to be answered differently from the others. When the same process occurs in the laboratory I take the temperature of some substance and never feel sure I've read the directions correctly or recorded the correct results. Another pronounced example of this difficulty is in telephoning. I never feel that I've given central the right number or dialed properly, and once I have gotten the connections I never quite want to credit what I hear.

If the directions are given orally, nine times out of ten I respond correctly. When the instructions are printed I may do perfectly what is demanded but I always have the feeling that I didn't do what the directions required. I don't think my feeling of uncertainty is evident to the onlooker. No one has ever mentioned it to me. But it often causes me embarrassment and a lack of confidence in myself. It seems that I get this feeling of being unable to read what's written most frequently when I'm trying hardest to concentrate. If I forget that I have to carry out the instructions exactly right I read the explanations and proceed without difficulty.

While in high school I was the constant companion of an unusually brilliant girl. We sat together in class and one of us was invariably called upon to recite before the other. Always, her recitation was favorably commented upon, while mine, although it might be satisfactory, never seemed to be spectacular. I still had the feeling that I had the brain to get as much as she did, but gradually began to believe that any achievement on my part would either be wrong or be ignored. This may have helped start this phobia which has become such a bugbear. The trouble is not with my eyes because I read the matter correctly; but after reading it comes the feeling that I might have read it incorrectly. There is, of course, a possibility that in earlier childhood, my mother may have written me something to do, and I read it wrong unknowingly and then, perhaps, was punished for disobedience. However, I have no recollection of such an incident. To overcome this handicap I have tried reading the directions only once, and then proceeding as if I knew I was right. But this seems to make matters worse: I always feel uncertain and helpless. I have also tried the reverse, namely, reading the directions many times before proceeding, but this doesn't seem to help much.

It is very unfortunate as the activities I'm interested in require detailed instructions and I foresee even a greater handicap, unless I can break the hold this obsession has on me. (H.E.; F.; U.S. Age 19)

FEELING OF INFERIORITY AND INABILITY TO MIX, BASED ON RETIRING NATURE INDUCED BY UNFAVORABLE COMPARISON BY MOTHER WITH YOUNGER AND PRETTIER SISTER AND BY LACK OF CONTACT WITH PLAYMATES OWING TO THE EARLY ASSUMPTION OF ADULT RESPONSIBILITIES; ENCOURAGEMENT FROM FATHER'S PRAISE; DETERMINATION TO ACHIEVE IN SPITE OF INFERIORITY COMPLEX

I am a mixture of resolutions and inferiority feelings. If an obstacle stands in the way of my ambitions, I will work hard to overcome it and do not mind the task no matter how hard it is. On the other hand, I am a very poor mixer and find it hard to get acquainted with people. Both sides of my character I can explain to a certain extent.

My inferiority complex was partly developed while I was a child. I was naturally a timid, sensitive child who lived in books more than in reality. My greatest joy was my little sister. She was everything that I was not. My mother constantly told me how attractive she was until I was sure that never had such a wonderful child been born before. She was pretty and I was at the awkward age where I was always doing the wrong thing. She could sing and I could not carry a tune. The first compliment my mother passed on me was after I had cut my eyelashes to make them prettier. Then she told me that I had had beautiful lashes and should not have cut them. I gazed at her in astonishment and said, "Why haven't you told me that before, Mamma?" She was always telling me how dear and sweet my sister was and impressing me with the fact that she was the dearest thing in my life. I realize now that she did this because she knew she would not live long and wanted me prepared to take her place. She idolized her baby girl and wanted her to have everything. When new clothes were bought for her and I had made-overs, I realized it was because K. was so much prettier and sweeter than I. This feeling of always being in the background was not a good one for a retiring nature like mine. More and more, I grew to feel that everyone could do things better than I. Since I've been old enough to teach school, this belittling feeling has affected me when supervisors come into the room. I cannot teach when anyone is present. I merely let the children recite.

I could probably have overcome my childhood complex if my mother had lived. She died when I was seventeen, leaving me with my adored little sister and the house to care for. She made me promise before she died that I would finish high school for she wanted all her children to go at least that far in school. My home duties in addition to my school work took all of my time and I had no time for the pleasures most girls have at that time. By the time I began to teach, my father's health broke down so my salary went to the home. My experiences made me so much older than the girls of my age that I went with mature women. I know that I am a poor mixer and find it hard to make friends. If I had been encouraged as a child to associate more with children, I might be able to meet people more easily. I have never been able to bridge the gap that this lack of association made. Just before he died my father told me that of all his children I was the one he and mother had always depended upon and that I had always been his comfort and blessing. This remark has encouraged me often when I felt blue.

In my teens, I used to say, "If I have to cross a mountain and can't go over, I will tunnel a path." Since the day when I promised my mother that I would finish high school, I have been forging ahead little by little. Through summer schools and extension work I am now in my senior year and expect to get my degree in three more summers. Thus an ideal planted by a high-school teacher of graduating from college will be realized many years after the seed was sown. In the same way, I have struggled on for other things that seemed worth while even though at times they appeared hopeless.   (R.E.M.; F.; S.C.T.)

FEELINGS OF INFERIORITY, TIMIDITY, SENSITIVENESS, JEALOUSY, AND DESIRE FOR SOLITUDE TRACED TO UNFAVORABLE COMPARISONS AND FAILURE TO RECEIVE AFFECTION AND SYMPATHY; CONSTANT BEATINGS BECAUSE MISUNDERSTOOD PRODUCED FURTHER FEELINGS OF INFERIORITY, NERVOUSNESS, AND "DESIRE TO TEAR TO PIECES"

I was age five, my brother age three, and my sister was a baby. The baby was considered pretty, while I was the object of ridicule by friends as well as relatives. I was always measured by someone else and always falling short of their attainments. This annoyed me beyond utterance, and I would feel like getting even with someone and despising everyone. Why I never became deceitful, truant, or criminalistic I cannot see. However, the result was most drastic upon my temper and nervous system. Many times my mother would become vexed at their remarks, but she would only smile. The statements made by friends caused me to feel quite inferior. Moreover, my relatives would never dress me and take me out for walks, but were constantly asking for my sister. They brought her pretty clothes and dressed her nicely, so my mother did not have to worry about her. My sister looked like my mother's people and I was decidedly like my father's. When my sister was three, she died of pneumonia. My brother and I looked very much alike so I did not have to suffer any more because of unfavorable comparisons along that line. However, the inferiority feelings were hard to overcome, so much so that I felt no one liked me. My father, who understood me and whom I adored, had died a short time before. Consequently, I became very timid, shy, selfish, unduly sensitive, unduly fearsome, stubborn, and jealous. Naturally, I developed a love of solitude. These traits were noticed by my mother and she and my grandmother attempted to "break" me, so I would become a lovable girl. No one understood that I was hungering for love, sympathy, affection, and attention like my sister received and like I had received from my father. I was whipped constantly and each whipping aroused in me the desire to tear to pieces. But I was afraid. I knew better than to indulge in temper tantrums, which I would have liked to have done and which would have been a great outlet for my feelings. Instead I became a nervous child. Anything frightened me. I dared not do what I desired for fear that I would be whipped. My grandmother did all the whipping except once. My mother had me on the floor and I rolled over and fastened my teeth in her leg. The harder she would spank, the harder I would bite. Mother would not let me think that she stopped because of the biting, but I was fully determined to bite as long as she continued to whip. That is the last whipping I remember from my mother. Fortunately, no teacher ever attempted to whip me at school. My mother had always said that if we received a whipping at school she would give us another one when the report came to her. This added again to my inferiority complex, for there were many times at school when I should have defended my rights, both with teachers and pupils.

The early traits of sensitiveness, fear, timidity, selfishness, and nervousness still mar my life and I have to work very hard to keep them repressed. The jealousy that arose because of the attention paid my baby sister still exists, but now I am jealous of any girl with whom my brother goes and I hope that he will never marry. I know that this is a mean, selfish trait and I try hard to overcome it. If a girl and I are very friendly and she becomes friendly with my brother, then she and I become strangers. Should he marry, I would soon learn to love the girl, but never beforehand.

(P.K.B.; F.; Col.; Vocational Counselor; A.B.; Age 30)

Early Spoiling. The process of "spoiling," to which reference was made in Chap. II, includes not only excessive humoring, overindulgence, or overprotection, but also such factors as the general atmosphere or the social and economic condition of the home, general treatment or training, specific indoctrination, and parental attitudes, prejudices, and behavior patterns. Of course, spoiling is not limited to the home situation, although the home is doubtless the chief source of personality distortion from this cause. The results of spoiling are very varied and may include the development of stubbornness, a furious temper, indecision, procrastination, worry, fastidiousness, timidity, avoidance of people, speech inhibitions, fear of the parents, panicky fear of audiences, feelings of loneliness, reclusiveness, inferiority, and penuriousness—in fact practically any kind of idiosyncrasy or annoyance. Some of the histories contain suggestions for correcting the difficulties with which the respondents had to contend.

A FURIOUS TEMPER ASCRIBED TO EXCESSIVE HUMORING DURING EIGHT YEARS OF ILLNESS; CURED BY OBSERVING THE MISERY CAUSED BY A TEMPERAMENTAL WOMAN AND BY A PROCESS OF REEDUCATION

From about ten to fourteen the writer had a very uncontrollable temper. Any little injustice, or what she considered wrong treatment, provoked a furious rage of temper which lasted for several hours and sometimes for days, usually in the form of sulkiness.

About this time, the writer had to live with a woman whose temper made her whole life miserable and everyone around her unhappy. She seldom lived a day without being furious about something. The writer soon became disgusted with this woman because she did not control her temper, and therefore began to realize that she should not allow her own temper to run wild. She found a hard problem before her but each time she tried to conquer her temper she found that it was easier to accomplish. She would get away from those with whom she became angry and try to return in a short time in a cheerful and talkative mood. When she did get angry she would analyze the cause and thus come to realize how unnecessary the feeling was. By persistence along this line she has learned to use her temper instead of letting it use her.

In trying to analyze the cause of this temper defect, the writer believes it can be traced to a sickly childhood in which she was humored in everything. She was ill for the first eight years of her life and always allowed to do as she pleased. When conditions changed and she could not be humored, she expressed her revolt in violent outbursts of temper.   (M.R.; F.; H.S. Supv.; B.A.)

HABITS OF INDECISION, PROCRASTINATION, AND RATIONALIZATION TRACED TO MOTHER'S OVERSOLICITOUSNESS AND TENDENCY CONSTANTLY TO INSPECT AND MODIFY CHILD'S PLANS

A hampering habit I have been unable to control is undecidedness in attacking a new problem. My mother after my father's death was so solicitous about me that every move I planned to make had to be discussed and explained before I was allowed to undertake it. Nine out of ten times my original plan was altered or postponed. I was never allowed to do the simplest deed without anxiety on her part. The result now is that I delay every task. If I have visits to make, I wait until the last possible moment before I go. I may even fail to make the calls, always finding some excuse, which I make myself believe is the real cause of my not going. Constant fear of attacking and mastering anything new besets me, but after I actually begin the tasks I usually perform them very satisfactorily. This habit certainly retards and hampers my activities. At this moment, while writing this paper, I am making a great effort against this habit. Ordinarily it would be postponed until the last night of the term.

(T.A.M.; F.; E.S.T.; A.B.)

PSYCHOLOGICAL ANALYSIS OF A HAMPERING HABIT OF PROCRASTINATION; ATTRIBUTED TO HEREDITY AND A MOTHER'S EXAMPLE; METHOD OF ATTEMPTED CORRECTION

The habit of procrastination has persisted in my life since my earliest recollection. The thought of something to be done has set in motion a series of cogitations, impulses, counterimpulses, and anxieties which have become crystallized into a kind of activity (or inactivity) pattern for almost all tasks and duties, save those born of dire emergency.

The pattern has assumed this general form: When a task first presents itself, calculation is made as to the ultimate time needed for its completion.   There follows immediately an initial effort, which usually results in a somewhat hazy general outline of the job to be done, plus the beginnings of actual accomplishment.   Almost invariably, however, this primary impulse is followed by a lapse, during which nothing constructive is attempted, and which commonly lasts until the "deadline" looms uncomfortably near.   During this hiatus of effort, there is frequent obtrusion into consciousness of: (a) alarm at the incomplete condition of the task, (b) self-reproach for the obvious dilatoriness, (c) self-exhortation concerning the need for getting to work, (d) resolution to get started in real earnest at the earliest possible moment, (e) rumination as to when the earliest possible moment can be fixed, (f) decision that the resumption of the task, is, after all, subordinate to other more immediate and more pressing demands, (g) recalculation of the time limit, (h) decision that the thing really cannot be attacked robustly until a certain day or hour (usually the latest possible day or hour), and (i) reassurance that when once under way the matter will be handled with sufficient concentration and enthusiasm to bring it through promptly and satisfactorily.

This interplay of thought and impulse recurs in the above order, occupying, however, considerably less time than is consumed in the reading of it.   Finally, the actual plunge into the work becomes a high-tension performance, demanding a high degree of attention, concentration, and clarity of thought.   Fatigue rarely interrupts the pace.   The current passage of time is unnoted.   Occasional regrets that the work was not begun sooner are brushed aside.   While there is undoubtedly a keen interest in the work itself, as well as pleasure in the doing of it, nevertheless the dominating motive at this stage is the battle against time.

My opinion is that the roots of this habit lie, first, in heredity, and, second, in a change that took place in my early adolescence.   My father was decidedly the more methodical of my parents.   I recall his intense dislike of procrastination and his contempt for those who were guilty of it.   I remember his insistence on my being regular in matters of personal hygiene and in the doing of my various chores, such as mowing the lawn, cleaning the stoves, cutting wood, and sifting the ashes. I recall also that being regular was exceedingly difficult for me; reprimands and withdrawals of privileges for my lack of promptness were frequent.

On the other hand, my mother, while able to get things done, was not nearly so meticulous about regularity or promptness, and was often in difficulty because of having too many things to do at one time.   There come to mind instances of Saturdays on which ironing, baking, dusting, and mending had to be accomplished, and instances of feverish Christmas shopping on Christmas Eve.   I responded to my father's regimen and lived a fairly systematic existence during his lifetime. However, I believe that the trait was acquired and that my mother's mode of living was dominant. My father died when I was thirteen, leaving me to follow my mother's example, and, as I believe, my natural bent.

Another factor that I consider to have played a part in developing this habit was the manner in which I carried on my schoolwork. Throughout my elementary- and secondary-school career, I was rarely forced to exert myself to keep within the upper quartile of the class. Possessed of a good logical memory and capacity for observation, I was usually able to perform creditably without more than a cursory preparation. This led to the practice of alternately drifting and cramming. I am certain that this was my program of action in late high-school and early college years.

During my third year of college a professor of philosophy gave a talk on pro-crastination. At that time I began an attempt to eliminate the habit. Especially since attaining an executive position I have consistently set down well-defined schedules and have made serious efforts to follow them. Despite occasional lapses, I feel that I have improved markedly. But I cannot say that the habit has been conquered.   (C.J.P.; M.; E.S.P.; A.B.)

FUSSINESS ABOUT DIRT POSSIBLY DUE TO EARLY TRAINING IN SCRUB-BING AND TO ATTEMPT TO PLEASE FASTIDIOUS MOTHER

My earliest memory of myself is as a small child of four or five, "scrubbing" the front doorsteps, my mother and our next-door neighbors praising the excellence of the job. I can see myself yet as I puffed up with pride over my achievement.

Being the eldest of five children, it naturally fell to my lot to assist with light jobs around the house, not to say anything about acting as nursemaid to the younger children. When I could dust, sweep, or even wash windows to suit my mother, who was very hard to please, I was overjoyed.

Whether these conditions of my early life produced or only accentuated my aversion for dirt, I do not know. I do know, however, that anxiety about dirt has been my most unrelenting taskmaster.

As I grew older I assumed more and more home responsibilities and I can remember how, when my aunts and grandmother would visit us, my mother would open the dresser drawers and clothes closet in my room and they would all exclaim, "She is a born old maid." Of course they were all wrong about this as I married when very young and just out of school.

When attending high school, my sister, three years younger than I, was my roommate. She was just as careless as I was particular and I was made very miserable by having my room mussed up by her.

After I married and had children of my own I realized that I could make my family very miserable if I did not conquer some of my aversion to dirt. So I just let the children play as they pleased, taught them to put their toys away when they were through playing with them, and no matter how much "dirt" they made, I would say nothing but just go and clean it up.

I remember once, in my early married life, having purchased a beautiful plain green velvet rug for my living-room floor. The rug was a beautiful one, but it showed every footmark. Every time any one walked on that rug I experienced an overwhelming desire the minute they left the room to get the broom and gently stroke those footmarks from that rug. This obsession gave me no peace of mind until I got the broom and went to work. For years I became the joke of my family and friends and I finally gave the rug away and bought a new one—this time, however, one that did not show the footmarks.

When I started to teach, I wanted to keep my home as scrupulously clean as I had always done. But I have learned that one dusting a day does just as well as six, and I have reached the point where I am able to cast a last longing look with a sigh at some task left undone as I leave for school in the morning. When I have reached the stage where I can look back and not see the "dirt," then I will feel that I have truly conquered that bugbear "Dirt."

(B.M.E.; F.; Attendance Officer)

TIMIDITY AND BASHFULNESS IN MEETING PEOPLE, MAKING IT DIFFI-CULT TO EAT WHEN AWAY AND TO RECITE IN CLASS; ASCRIBED TO EARLY TRAINING AND RELUCTANCE OF MOTHER TO MEET PEOPLE

I was always extremely bashful and timid. Reciting in class was always a difficult task. Meeting people also was a hardship. This stayed with me for a long time. It was not until I was actually compelled to meet people that I began to enjoy it. My timidity was so great during my youth that when I visited with other people I found it difficult to eat. Eating was a burden. The food simply would not go down. This timidity was especially pronounced in school. I never dared to raise my hand to ask the teacher for any help or information.

Here, again, training has undoubtedly served as an important influence. My parents very seldom went out, and they always taught us to stand back. When we did visit we were warned beforehand not to be too bold. My mother always resented meeting people. She does not enjoy the company of strangers. It is possible that this timidity was inherited, that my mother's fears were passed on to us. Now that I have become older and have become accustomed to meeting people, I have learned to enjoy it. I have not yet entirely overcome my timidity in class. Reciting in class still makes me feel like wanting to hide my face. It may be that enough experience will help me overcome this difficulty.

(V.A.J.; M.; E.S.P.; Ph.B.; Age 31)

DREAD, NUMBNESS, CONFUSION, AND PANIC PRODUCED BY FACING AUDIENCES, ATTRIBUTED TO THE RESENTMENT AND ANGER CAUSED BY BEING CONSTANTLY FORCED BY MOTHER INTO THE LIMELIGHT AND BY THE TEASING REMARKS OF PLAYMATES; A DEFENSE REACTION TRANSFORMED INTO AN ANTIPATHY; METHOD OF INCOMPLETE RESOLUTION

My fear of audiences dates back to my early school life. Since then, although I have appeared scores of times in public and private gatherings as a singer and speaker, I have never been able to face a group of people, large or small, without experiencing hampering sensations of dread, numbness, and confusion. On two occasions during later adolescence (once during a high-school debate and again during a musicale) this condition resulted in complete panic. The upset may precede my appearance, being felt acutely for several moments and thereafter diminishing gradually in intensity; or it may appear in the midst of a performance, stifling all spontaneity and causing a mechanical, colorless rendition during the remainder of the effort. The seizures have varied considerably in their intensity and in their effects. I have found that the fear is less acute in the presence of persons with whom I am familiar than before a strange audience.

I trace this fear to the many appearances I made in early childhood, unwillingly and often rebelliously, as a violinist, a speaker of pieces, an actor, or a principal in religious ceremonials. My mother took every opportunity to keep me in the forefront of things. Although I entered these affairs obediently, I resented the encroachments on my play time, the dressing up, the references to myself as a "model boy" by relatives and neighbors, and the teasing remarks of my playmates.

In this connection, an incident that I consider an important causative factor occurred when I was eight or nine years old. A certain annual religious ceremony was to take place, in which a small child took the leading part, usually a girl. A few days preceding this particular occasion, I was informed by my mother that I was to have the leading role. I recall that I protested vigorously, saying, among other things, that it was for a girl and not for a boy, that the kids would call me a sissy, and that I wanted to play on Sunday afternoon anyway. My protests were without avail. During the intervening days I lived in misery, silent but rebellious. On the afternoon of the performance I contrived to leave my home immediately after dinner and repaired to a vacant lot where I knew a number of my friends would foregather. I went with a vague determination to stay away from the hated affair entirely.

Some time later my play was interrupted by the breathless arrival of my sister, who reported that the procession was about to begin, mother was frantic, and I was to come home at once to get ready. I went. My mother was obviously very angry but grimly quiet as she prepared me and brought me under her personal escort to the meeting place. Seething with mingled resentment, fear of the task, and fear of maternal wrath to come, I went through the performance. Afterwards I was brought home and put to bed immediately, without supper. Although I afterwards participated in many school exercises, musicales, and similar affairs, the feelings of apprehension, self-consciousness, and momentary panic invariably arose.

Once during my undergraduate college years I confessed my fear of audiences to one of my instructors. He advised that the only way to conquer the fear would be to speak or sing in public as frequently as I could find opportunities to do so. I have followed this course assiduously, at lodge meetings, teachers' meetings, even in political campaigns. I have succeeded in reducing this audience fear greatly, although it is always present in some degree.   (C.J.P.; M.; E.S.P.; A.B.)

Tragic Social Happenings. In addition to seriously disturbing experiences related in other connections, the following two cases are apropos.

SIXTEEN YEARS OF WORRIES, DREADS, HARROWING DREAMS, AND DIRE
ANTICIPATIONS OF MOTHER'S DEATH PRECIPITATED BY FATHER'S SUD-
DEN DEMISE, TERMINATED BY MOTHER'S SUDDEN AND UNEXPECTED
COLLAPSE IN RESPONDENT'S ARMS, WITH RESULT THAT RESPONDENT
RESOLVED NEVER TO WORRY AGAIN

From the day of the sudden death of my father, whom I passionately idolized,
until my mother's even more sudden death, sixteen years later, I never was free
from worry, from dread, from bondage. Every time the Western Union messenger
came down the street, or every time the telephone rang, I anticipated a summons
to come home or word of the death of the one I loved the dearest and the most.
Not one night during this period passed by but what I experienced harrowing
dreams and would often jump out of bed and flash on the electric light to make
sure that I was really dreaming and that things were not as I dreamed. And after
all those years of torture, of fear, of dread, one beautiful August morning, without
any warning or premonition, my dear mother simply keeled over dead in my arms.

Then I resolved never, never to worry again and from that fatal moment I have
never allowed anything to disturb me for a long period of time or to any great
extent. What I can't control must be accepted is my philosophy now.

(F.E.D., F.; Col.; E.S.T.; Ph.B.; Age 28)

HOW THE TRAGIC DEATH FROM BURNS OF AN ADORED YOUNGER SISTER
CREATED AN AGONIZING EMOTIONAL UPHEAVAL IN A YOUNG ADOLES-
CENT, PRODUCING INSOMNIA, INTROVERSION, THOUGHTS OF ANNI-
HILATION, HYPERSENSITIVITY TO THE CRIES OF CHILDREN, A MORE
TENDER UNDERSTANDING OF THE WOES OF MAN AND ANIMALS, AND
A DETERMINATION TO ENTER THE MINISTRY TO SANCTIFY HIS SISTER'S
MEMORY AND TO FIND COMPENSATORY SOLACE IN SERVICE TO THE
LIVING

Another painful experience which drove me further into introversion, occurred
when I was fourteen years old. A little sister five years my junior was dearly
beloved by me. From the meager savings that I laid aside through working after
high school and on Saturday nights, I would buy candy and toys for her. One
year the Fourth of July happened to fall on a Saturday. I asked her to wait up
for me until I would return home from work, and promised that I would have a
surprise for her. That Saturday night I purchased various kinds of fireworks
which I planned to give her as the surprise I had promised her. That night I ran
almost all of the way home from work, eager to make her happy with my little
surprise. When I was about fifty yards from my home, I saw a large crowd and
asked what was the matter. Several persons whom I addressed looked at me, but
none answered. Rushing up the stairs I heard the most excruciating cries I had
ever heard and it was not difficult to recognize that they came from my sister.
Just fifteen minutes before my return her little dress had ignited from a supposedly harmless sparkler. Before my father could reach her, she was a mass of

flames. All through the night her cries of pain continued and three days later she went back to God. I was deeply affected. Knowing my introverted nature, my parents sent me to the home of an uncle and I was unable to attend the funeral. From that day I have been a lost human being, for on that day part of me died. I became even more silent, my sleep became more troubled, and a thousand times I wished that I might die. Often I thought of suicide; this thought seemed a happier release from my loneliness. But my father, sensing the agony that was torturing me, spoke words of wisdom to me. I recall distinctly his words: "Dear boy, the only way to sanctify the dead is to serve the living." He spoke to me of courage and filled me with a new hope. It was at this time that the desire to become a minister took hold of me, and from that day whatever plans I had made for the future were supplanted by this great hunger to become a minister. My father convinced me that the best way to keep beautiful the memory of the dead is to help the living. This became the dominating stimulus to all my thought processes, and it brought me the solace that I needed. Years later, when I was ordained into the ministry, I felt that I had triumphed over my burden of grief, and since that time I have dedicated my services particularly to those who, in life's seething maelstrom, must wear the habiliments of woe.

Even today I am deeply moved when I hear little children crying. I know that this reaction goes back to that fateful Fourth of July when I died in part. Another experience may be mentioned here to illustrate this reaction. When I was a student at the university, I taught late in the evening in order to tide me along. Late one evening, as I was walking toward my home, the crying of a little child sounded through the stillness of the night. I gazed toward the window from which the sound was coming and kept on my journey homeward. I was almost a block away when I suddenly stood still in my tracks and listened. The crying had not ceased. A compulsive force within me made me turn back, and I sat on the steps of that house for fully twenty minutes until the crying stopped.

Another episode, which occurred a year or two earlier, will further illustrate the tenderness of my emotional life. I happened to be spending a few weeks in a mountain resort. One afternoon a group of friends and I were eating what was then known as "syrup suckers." Several bees were attracted by these suckers, and I struck one down as it flew near me. That night I found it difficult to sleep. The thought of the bee that I struck down would not leave my mind. Perhaps I had not killed it, but had left it maimed to suffer. I continued restless for an hour or more. Finally I felt myself pitying the bee to such an extent that I dressed and went back to the spot where I had been. Unable to find the bee, I went back to my cottage and went to sleep.

How this tenderness asserted itself only recently will appear from the following experience. About five months ago I had occasion to go to New York City. As I walked down Broadway I noticed the great number of beggars who asked for alms—blind, crippled, deaf, deformed men and women, and even children begging with their eyes and their pitiful faces. I was unable to pass any of them without responding. At last, this picture of woe became so oppressive and so depressing to me that I had to turn down a side street where I knew I would not meet any of these unfortunates.

And yet, I wish to make clear that all this emotionality has not created any special adjustment problems. Although it is true that after more than a decade in the ministry I am still deeply affected by the sight of suffering and by the sound of weeping, I do not feel that sense of futility and of frustration which might be expected under the circumstances. In spite of my introverted nature, I have not failed to develop a sense of practicality in connection with my duties. On the contrary, I feel that I am all the more adequately prepared to minister to those who are in need of an understanding heart. My internal feelings are seldom, if ever, revealed to those with whom I come in contact. I realize that this involves constant repression and that it will ultimately require a dear cost of emotional stability. But these factors seldom distract me. My ministry is not only a dedication to those whom I am privileged to serve, but it is also a sanctification of my sister's memory. That thought brings enough sunshine into my life to dissipate whatever gloom I feel from time to time.

(S.A.A.; M.; Clergyman; M.A.; Age 37)

So much, then, for the negative side of the picture, the production of mental deviations and difficulties by social experiences and contacts. Let us now turn to the positive side.

The positive aspect is concerned with supplying the types of social situations in the home, school, church, or elsewhere which will conduce to the development and maintenance of desirable mental and social traits and which will aid the individual in becoming socially adjusted, in maintaining satisfactory human relations, and in getting along reasonably well with other persons. Man's highest level of functioning is probably his social level—his ability to play his part in the social order as a self-reliant participating member of a community of similar human beings organized as a social democracy. Man cannot achieve maximum happiness or attain his highest intellectual, emotional, or moral satisfactions or his most satisfying feelings of worthwhileness except through social contacts and through willing participation in the life of the family, the community, the state, and the nation. The keenest satisfactions that most people experience in life are derived from social conquests. Few awards make a higher appeal than those that spring from the recognition accorded the individual by friends, associates, colleagues, and peers. On the other hand, some of the deepest feelings of humiliation and mortification that man can experience come from snubbings, social ostracism, or loss of status.

For these and other reasons one is constrained to accept the social criterion of mental health as one of the primary tests of mental normality (see page 39). The healthy mind must be sufficiently integrated on the social level to be able to adjust itself to the social environment. If the individual is lacking in social adequacy and adaptability, if he is unable to make satisfactory social adjustments, he is shunned or ignored as a social nonentity or a nincompoop, or he is forcibly confined in an institution as a social dependent or derelict who cannot be trusted at large in society. This criterion is valid. for the general run of mortals. Society is, no doubt, willing to tolerate eccentric geniuses and outstanding leaders who may defy accepted conventions and usages with impunity, provided they make contributions of recognized value to the contemporary life of the community or the state. Another observation may be apropos at this point, namely, that the criterion of social conformity is not static and is not universally valid. The behavior patterns demanded by the social milieu vary according to the cultural level and cultural idiosyncrasies of the community in which the individual finds himself. Moreover, the mores and practices of any social group undergo more or less constant and extensive changes. It is apparent, therefore, that the well-adjusted individual must be able to make progressive adaptations to environmental changes. This applies particularly to changes in the socioeconomic order.

Threefold Objectives of the Mental-hygiene Program on the Social Level. These objectives, already anticipated by implication, may be explicitly formulated as follows:

1. The child (as well as the adult) should be definitely inoculated with all those positive attitudes, beliefs, ideals, practices, and habits which will render him socially adequate or efficient as a member of society and which will develop socially desirable qualities, such as companionableness, cooperativeness, geniality, generosity, kindness, fair-mindedness, courteousness, and the like. Major emphasis is placed on the development of desirable social attitudes because of confidence, born of experience, in the effectiveness of proper social conditioning, and because of the belief that man's habits of thought, beliefs, attitudes, and ideals are essentially the result of social processes of conditioning.

2. Our second aim should be to remove or minimize all the social influences tending to produce mental conflicts and maladjustments that may arise in every form of social and industrial institution, such as the home, school, church, factory, and neighborhood streets and parks. The kinds of social situations or social stimuli that tend to warp the individual's life and produce mental difficulties are well-nigh unlimited, as has been already shown by our illustrative cases. The commonest home factors are the only-child situation, poverty, neglect, cruel punishment, arrogance, excessive suppression or dominance, pampering, overprotection, immorality, crime, drunkenness, divorce, quarreling and bickering, and unfavorable comparisons. (The parental factor was discussed in Chap. II, pages 86–97.) The commonest inimical neighborhood conditions, mostly characteristic of the slums, are the influence of bad companions, low social and economic standards, vicious social

practices and forms of social recreation, perverse sexual practices,[7] gang activities, and unsupervised forms of child activity in the streets, alleys, vacant yards, and parks. The school situations that are productive of personality malformations that sometimes last throughout life include the teacher factor, discussed in Chap. II (pages 97–106); repeated scholastic failures; want of emotional satisfaction from lack of successful achievement; rebellion against the school because of lack of adaptation of the processes of instruction to meet individual needs, resulting in truancy, misconduct, or unwholesome defense reactions; conflicts with other pupils; nervousness, jealousies and fears produced by scholastic and other types of contests; fears and other mental difficulties produced by tests and examinations; and various forms of reward and punishment, excessive assignments, and similar factors. The church situation includes, among other factors, unwise, infantile, or superstitious indoctrination; the stimulation of unjustifiable feelings of guilt, fears, dreads, and emotional conflicts and inhibitions; the manifestation of inimical attitudes, such as those of intolerance, fanaticism, pharisaism, hypocrisy, cant, or excessive condemnation; and excessive emotionalism, excitement, shouting, and mass hysteria.

Obviously, the preventive program on the social level must concern itself with the factors enumerated above and similar factors.

3. In the case of those who have already acquired maladjustments and handicaps, attempt should be made to determine whether or not the causative factors are social in nature. If such proves to be the case, effort should be made to remove the social irritants and to modify the social situation or to modify the individual's attitude toward it. Frequently the process of modification must include both the endogenous and the exogenous factors.

The educational elements (a fourth group of basic factors) and implications of the mental-hygiene program are of such central importance as to justify a separate chapter. Chapter IV contains a brief summary of the educational phases of mental hygiene already considered and a discussion of some further mental-hygiene implications of the program of education.

---

[7] According to an estimate by secret police in 1934, 22,000 persons in Berlin, 11,000 in Hamburg, and 3,000 in Munich were sexual perverts.

CHAPTER IV

THE EDUCATIONAL ELEMENTS AND IMPLICATIONS OF THE MENTAL-HYGIENE PROGRAM

Brief Summary of Educational Elements Already Considered. The educational bearings of the problem of mental health and mental hygiene already brought out in the discussions as well as in the case histories are of such fundamental importance that a brief recapitulation may add merited emphasis to the conclusions already reached.

1. As we have already seen, the causes of mental soundness or unsoundness are often educational. Mental stresses often spring from the individual's lack of ability to make proper adjustments to his physical or social environment. But making efficient or faulty adjustments is often merely a matter of learning ability. Some of the data presented have shown that many intellectual, emotional, or social difficulties and conflicts have been produced by the demands in the home and in the school to which the child has not learned to adjust himself properly.

2. We have seen that error and misinformation are the cause of many mental difficulties, and that the latter can often be easily cleared away by proper enlightenment. Truth will not only "make us free," but it will prevent many personality difficulties. Illustrations of the salutary influence of proper understanding, in addition to those already given, will be supplied in Chap. XVII. Proper enlightenment is, of course, an educational problem.

Perhaps it is no exaggeration to declare that the processes of correcting the large majority of mental maladjustments that respond to treatment are essentially educational in nature. This is particularly true of the types of minor maladjustments that are characteristic of children and youths and normal adults. To some extent at least, all forms of treatment consist in conveying information, enlightenment, insight, encouragement, or advice, whether the process is that of instruction by voice or pen, suggestion by means of words or attitude, interpretation of behavior mechanisms or motivations, changing the person's attitude by stimulating new interests, reeducation, occupational therapy, desensitization, or some more technical aid to self-analysis, self-understanding, or self-discovery, such as hypnosis or psychoanalysis. All these devices are in essence educational, no matter by what esoteric name they may be known in the professional jargon, such as analytical psychology, psychoanalysis, child analysis, self-analysis, nondirective therapy, expressive or release therapy, therapeutic interviewing, or play therapy; and no matter by what name the healer or adjuster may be designated, such as psychotherapist, mental healer, faith curist, psychiatrist, psychologist, counselor, or analyst. The conclusion of the psychologist J. J. B. Morgan, in discussing the work of the Child Guidance Clinic, is of interest in this connection:

> The result of this has been that we have learned that most of the mental problems that can be successfully handled are problems of psychology and not of medicine. While the clinics have been headed by medical men, the approach that has yielded results has been the psychological approach. . . . This readjustment has in most cases been found to be a problem of education, and this has in turn directed the center of interest to proper education. Mental hygiene, which began as a medical problem, has now been found to be an educational problem. Instead of clinics for treatment of mental disease we have turned to educational clinics.[1]

Of like tenor is the statement of psychiatrist L. C. Marsh: "The nervous or mental 'case' should be considered as a student, not a patient. He should be reeducated, not 'treated'" This conclusion applies to many neuropsychiatric cases, at least.

If it is conceded that the process of cure is essentially educational in many cases, then we have all the more reason to believe that the process of prevention of maladjustments and the development of mental normalness are also fundamentally educational problems. They are essentially processes of learning and conditioning.

3. The importance with respect to mental health and efficiency of developing proper and wholesome attitudes toward all the issues and problems of life has already been emphasized and will receive added emphasis on later pages. We have particularly emphasized the importance (*a*) of teaching the child early in life to face frankly and squarely all of his social and vocational obligations; (*b*) of his developing acceptable ideas and ideals regarding his function and place in the scheme of things; (*c*) of his developing a philosophy of life that will make for normal, sound, purposeful living and that will afford healthy, satisfying outlets for his emotional, intellectual, and physical energy; and (*d*) of his developing proper attitudes toward his schoolwork. These attitudes are, of course, equally important for adults who never acquired proper attitudes in childhood and youth. The ranks of society are congested with such hapless individuals. All this—the development of proper attitudes and an acceptable philosophy of life—is, of course, a prime function of education. The development of proper attitudes toward studies, the peculiar task of the teacher, is of fundamental importance for learning. Learning does not take place readily in the absence of proper learning attitudes: attitudes of receptivity, curiosity, interest, eagerness to learn, enthusiasm to know facts, and love of truth. This theory of learning is the exact opposite of Mr. Dooley's educational philosophy. Said Mr. Dooley, "It doesn't matter

---

[1] Quoted from J. J. B. Morgan, *The Psychology of Abnormal People*, 1928, 27, with the permission of the publishers, Longmans, Green & Co., Inc., New York.

what you teach a boy, Hennessy, so long as he doesn't like it." This ascetic doctrine of education and discipline is reflected in the facetious comment of the young high-school instructor: "To teach high-school boys, you need to ram it down their throats. It doesn't matter whether they like it or not." But knowledge acquired under the whip of compulsion does not harmonize with the mental-hygiene ideal of economical learning. Knowledge does not affect behavior, except adversely, unless it is accompanied by the proper attitude; without the right feeling tone, learning is difficult of accomplishment.

4. The importance of forming and fixing desirable, useful, and dependable habit patterns, by appropriate methods of stimulation and guidance and economical and efficient methods of implantation, has already been emphasized as one of the most important problems of infancy and early life (see Chap. I, page 42). The significance of correct habit formation for the conservation of efficiency and sound mental health has not been adequately appreciated. All of us inevitably become bundles of good or bad habits, depending largely on the character of the behavior patterns acquired in early life. We all become fettered to chains of habits that often are as unbreakable as chains of iron. Habits soon become consolidated into trends, inclinations, sentiments, and prejudices, which determine the individual's course of thought and action and often constitute the basis of his personality and character traits, such as honesty or dishonesty, tolerance or intolerance, sincerity or insincerity, freedom from bias or narrow-mindedness.

Let us emphasize that good mental health must, in a measure, become a matter of good habit formation—the formation in early life of good habits of feeling, doing, and thinking. It is difficult to conceive that bad habits could be compatible with good mental health. Good habit formation is not only desirable; it must be rated as one of the essential elements of good mental hygiene. All this, again, is primarily an educational problem—one of the major educational problems of both the home and the school.

5. Lastly, the importance of the teacher's attitudes and personality make-up for the effective execution of the mental-hygiene program of the schools has already been given so much attention that no elaboration is required for the purpose of reemphasizing this factor, probably the most important element from every point of view for ensuring the success of programs of public education.

Due consideration of all the above facts justifies the conclusion that the educational elements of the mental-hygiene program are of cardinal moment. It now remains to present a few additional considerations regarding the school's mental-hygiene service.

Seven Additional Facts and Suggestions Concerning the Mental-hygiene Elements of the School Program. A few suggestions will be made concerning the orderly implementation of certain school procedures, in order that the varied activities of the school may be conducted in harmony with the best principles of mental hygiene and in such a way as to tend to prevent or to correct maladjustments and to contribute toward the development of mental normality.

1. Of cardinal importance is the consideration that all the activities of the school should be administered in compliance with the demands of mental health and mental hygiene. Mental-hygiene considerations should, first of all, govern the general atmosphere, processes, and procedures of the school and the recitation room with respect to the reciprocal relations of pupils, teachers, school administrators, and parents. An educational institution represents a very complicated form of congregate social activity, in which three groups are vitally concerned: the pupils, the teachers, and the parents. Innumerable problems of human relationship and adjustment of all degrees of complexity and difficulty—human relationships create the most difficult types of adjustment problems—must be so handled as to conserve the mental-health interests of all groups and to prevent unnecessary conflicts, dissensions, tensions, and dissatisfactions.

Mental hygiene must grapple with the serious mental-health hazards, particularly as they affect pupils and teachers, that are implicit in a human institution which requires the most delicate integration and coordination of many diverse interests in the school community if it is to function harmoniously and efficiently. The larger the school, the more intricate and difficult are these problems and hazards. The adjustment of these larger, ramified problems of the school and community personnel cannot occur in contravention of the principles of mental hygiene if the mental health of the school and the community is to be developed and conserved.

In the second place, mental-hygiene implications are involved in all learning motivations and in all instructional situations. Mental-hygiene considerations affect the particular learning procedures and aims of each branch of study.[2] Mental-hygiene objectives should find their pertinent application no less in the teaching of history or literature or science or art than in the development of student and staff morale and school esprit de corps.

In the third place, the facts of mental hygiene are of peculiar significance for the cultivation of efficient, wholesome personality traits in the child as a learner. These traits include resourcefulness, initiative, independence, creativeness, social-mindedness, cooperativeness, concentration of attention,

---

[2] For a good discussion of the mental-hygiene phases of the different branches of instruction, see Lawrence A. Averill, *The Hygiene of Instruction,* Boston, Houghton Mifflin Company, 1928, 218–276. For a more general discussion of teaching methods that retard and facilitate adjustment, see Harry N. Rivlin, *Education for Adjustment,* New York, Appleton-Century-Crofts, Inc., 1936, 337–394. Consult also Karl C. Garrison, "Learning the Fundamental School Subjects," Chap. XIII, in *Educational Psychology,* rev. ed., Charles E. Skinner, ed., New York, Prentice-Hall, Inc., 1945.

persistence, objective-mindedness, scientific-mindedness, open-mindedness or freedom from emotional bias, mental integrity, proper study habits, and other desirable characteristics.

Finally, the observance of the principles of mental hygiene is not limited to special classes for handicapped or maladjusted children or to the kindergarten or primary schools. Mental-hygiene principles find fertile application at every level of the educational ladder from the nursery school to the postgraduate and professional schools of the university, although, obviously, the mental-hygiene problems differ somewhat at different levels and for different kinds of classes and schools. It is doubtless true that, up to the present time, mental hygienists have devoted most of their time to the consideration of the mental-hygiene problems of the nursery school, the kindergarten, the primary grades, and the special classes. Least attention has been devoted to the application of mental-hygiene principles in the high schools, universities, medical schools, and divinity schools. The study and application of the principles of mental hygiene may not be neglected in any kind of educational institution. Moreover, courses in mental hygiene should be made available to students of any phase of human engineering. It is gratifying to note that many teacher's colleges and universities now offer courses in mental hygiene, usually as electives, in both the regular and the summer sessions.

2. The instructional activities should be individualized to meet the needs of the pupil material. Both the contents and the methods of instruction should be adapted to meet pupil interests and abilities (see pages 106, 256*f.*). The satisfactory consummation of this aim involves the provision of more individual attention and remedial instruction; the establishment of special classes for the extreme deviates (see Chap. V); sectioning or classification according to ability and interest (such sectioning should always be provisional and flexible—never watertight—and might be limited to the basic tool subjects, such as reading and arithmetic); adaptation of instruction in the regular grades through increased flexibility of classroom procedures by means of such devices as activity programs, socialized recitation procedures, and class-individual recitation techniques; modification of curricular requirements to meet individual talents; the use of materials of greater social significance to the learners at the time they are acquiring knowledge; the provision of worthwhile, actual experiences rather than reported or imaginal experiences; and many other similar expedients that make for instructional adaptation and individualization.

3. The successful prosecution of programs of individualized instruction and differential treatment of pupils—in fact, the whole program of educational, psychological, psychiatric, and social therapy—requires a careful study of the personality make-up of each child. It necessitates a determination of each child's abilities and limitations; his special interests and aptitudes; his atti-

tudes; his mental, educational, emotional, and social maladjustments, etc. Such a study requires the use of various investigation techniques, such as intelligence and achievement tests, interest questionnaires, personality inventories, rating scales, individual physical and psychological. examinations, observation of reaction traits as manifested in the classroom and on school premises, counseling, interviews with pupils, parents, and teachers—in a word, the skillful employment of the case-study technique. He who would undertake such studies must possess at least some proficiency in collating and interpreting findings and in drawing valid conclusions from a correct evaluation of all the relevant facts.

A Brief Excursus on the Use of Objective Standardized Tests as a Basis for Adjustment and Therapy. Literally, many hundreds of standardized educational (achievement), intelligence, psychomotor (performance), pictorial, specific aptitude, trade, vocational, and personality tests have been devised for the more accurate discovery (diagnosis) of the nature of the individual's abilities, disabilities, limitations, difficulties, and potentialities, as a basis for educational placement and adjustment, and for psychological, psychiatric, and social treatment. For a review of the extensive literature on the description and uses of these techniques the reader should consult the handbooks on tests, the texts on clinical psychology, and the extensive bibliographies now available.[3] A few brief comments must suffice here.

[3] The following references will supply leads to source materials:

Oscar Buros, *The Third Mental Measurements Yearbook,* New Brunswick, N.J., Rutgers University Press, 1949 (see earlier issues also).

Joy P. Guilford, *Psychometric Tests,* New York, McGraw-Hill Book Company, Inc., 1946.

Rudolf Lassner, "Annotated Bibliography on the Oseretsky Tests of Motor Proficiency," *Journal of Consulting Psychology,* 1948, January–February, 37–47.

Chauncey M. Louttit, *Clinical Psychology of Children's Behavior Problems,* rev. ed., New York, Harper & Brothers, 1947, 24–133.

James L. Munsell, *Psychological Testing,* New York, Longmans, Green & Co., Inc., 1947.

L. A. Pennington and Irwin A. Berg, *An Introduction to Clinical Psychology,* New York, The Ronald Press Company, 1948.

Stanley D. Porteus, *The Practice of Clinical Psychology,* New York, American Book Company, 1941, 154f., 200f.

"Psychological Tests and Their Uses," *Review of Educational Research,* Washington, D.C., American Educational Research Association, 1941.

David Rapaport, *Diagnostic Psychological Testing,* Chicago, Year Book Publishers, Inc., Vol. I, 1945; Vol. II, 1946.

Thomas W. Richardson, *Modern Clinical Psychology,* New York, McGraw-Hill Book Company, Inc., 1946.

Saul Rosenzweig and Kate L. Kogan, *Tests in Psychodiagnosis,* New York, Grune & Stratton, Inc., 1948.

Helen Sargent, "Projective Methods," *Psychological Bulletin,* 1945, 257–293 (references).

Miriam G. Siegel, "The Diagnostic and Prognostic Validity of the Rorschach Test in a

Some tests are designed for clinical (individual) use, others for group use. Many group tests, however, are also applied clinically, although the norms are derived from group administration. Some tests require oral responses to oral queries or test situations; others require motor reactions to verbal instructions or to written or pictorial materials. Some require written responses (words or checks) on paper-and-pencil blanks, while others require the manipulation of concrete materials, such as form boards or mechanical puzzles or contrivances. Some of these tests are based on self-estimates regarding the presence or absence of certain characteristics or on those regarding the amount of a trait possessed, while other tests require estimates or ratings by other persons. Some are based on objective observation by the clinician of the client's responses. Some measure the presence and amount of single or comparatively simple traits (one-dimensional tests); others are combined into batteries (multidimensional tests), supplying a more detailed clinical picture (a psychological profile). Some require responses to definitely controlled and standardized stimuli or test situations; others encourage the subject to respond ad libitum to the test situations that are not rigidly controlled and that may be either very simple or highly complex. Some are designed to explore the individual's deeper tendencies or the total structure or organization of the personality. Some explore the dynamic make-up or trends; others, the static structure.

Among the better known tests for clinical use are different versions of the Binet-Simon Scale of general intelligence, which is arranged in age steps from early infancy to adulthood (largely verbal); the Wechsler-Bellevue Performance Scale (partly verbal and partly nonverbal), for adolescents and adults; and the new Army Individual Tests. The individual scales or batteries of performance tests include the Stenquist Mechanical Aptitude Tests, the Arthur Point Scale Performance Tests, the Cornell-Coxe Performance Ability Scale, the Pintner-Paterson Scale of Performance Tests, the Porteus Maze Tests, the Leiter Performance Scale, the Oseretsky Tests of Motor Pro-

---

Child Guidance Clinic," *American Journal of Orthopsychiatry*, January, 1948, 119–133 (references).

Percival M. Symonds, "New Trends in Clinical Psychology," *American Journal of Orthopsychiatry*, January, 1948, 153–161 (references).

Theodore L. Torgerson, *Studying Children: Diagnostic and Remedial Procedures in Teaching*, New York, The Dryden Press, Inc., 1947.

Frederick L. Wells and Jurgen Ruesch, *Mental Examiners' Handbook*, 2d printing, New York, The Psychological Corporation, 1945.

See also "Roundtable on Diagnostic Psychological Testing," *Journal of Consulting Psychology*, January–February, 1948, 1–57; C. H. Patterson, "Is Psychotherapy Dependent upon Diagnosis?" *The American Psychologist*, May, 1948, 155–159; "The Psychologist's Contribution to the Study of the Mental Patient: A Symposium," *Journal of Personality*, December, 1946, 93–143.

ficiency. For infants there are the Merrill-Palmer Scale of Mental Tests, by Rachel Stutsman; the Minnesota Preschool Scale, by Florence Goodenough, Josephine Foster, and Marvin J. Wagenen; the Gesell Schedules for infants; and the Psyche Cattell Scale for infants.

The composite individual educational or achievement scales include the Wallin-Gilbert (now Cutsforth) Brief Educational Attainment Scale for Clinical Use, the Porteus Educational Attainment Scale, and the Jastak Wide-range Achievement Test.

A profusion of aptitude tests now exists for determining whether the individual possesses the traits, talents, or capacities needed for success in different occupations, or whether he possesses in latent form the potentials that will make it possible to train him for a specific job. As illustrations of existing tests may be mentioned those for clerical workers, stenographers, typists, riveters, sheet-metal workers, machine power press operators, sewing machine operators, precision lens grinders, pipe fitters, electricians, aircraft detail drafters, radio and telegraph operators, navigators, and bombardiers. . . . Some of the tests are designed to test general mechanical ability, usually through a battery of sub-tests. One of the best known of such group paper and pencil tests is the MacQuarrie Test of Mechanical Ability, given in its original form to over 5,000,000 persons up to 1943. Seven sub-tests measure accuracy of tracing, speed of tapping dots, speed and accuracy of dotting, the perception of space relations, and the accuracy of eye movements. Among other tests of this character mention may be made of the Detroit General Aptitude Examination (Baker, Voelker, and Crockett) and the Detroit Mechanical Aptitudes Examination (by the same authors). Other tests are highly specific, such as tests of finger dexterity, of precision of movement or fineness of motor co-ordination, and speed of muscular reaction. One of the best known speed of reaction tests is the Minnesota Rate of Manipulation Test, in which the subject (a) replaces 60 round blocks in round recesses as fast as possible and then (b) turns each block over and replaces it as rapidly as possible. This test is stripped of unnecessary complications to reduce the test to one of speed. Nearly all the well-known form boards are tests, in part, of the perception of spatial relations. The paper equivalent of such tests is the Minnesota Paper Form Board Test (revised by R. Likert and W. H. Quasha).

One of the significant developments has been the construction of batteries of aptitude tests to afford more comprehensive and accurate measurements of the traits needed for success in many occupations. The greatest spurt in the development of such aptitude test batteries has come since Pearl Harbor through the work of the war department and the war industries. Hundreds of jobs and vocations have been analyzed to determine the abilities and personality qualifications essential for success in different jobs. Few of the latest tests have thus far been released by the army or by industry. Aptitude batteries now exist for about 170 occupations. Moreover, many jobs and occupations have been broken down into job families. Breakdowns into about 85 families of related jobs and occupations are now available in employment offices for use in connection with transferring and upgrading workers (D. G. Marquis). These occupational breakdowns are based on job analyses and workers' traits—*e.g.*, dexterity, muscular strength, fineness of motor coordination, memory, and other needed traits. Some experimenters entertain the hope that it may be possible to subdivide all occupations into ten or fifteen basic families based on the presence of the same primary traits as shown by factor analysis. Should such reductions or combinations prove feasible, the problem of occupational testing would be greatly simplified. This job has not yet been accomplished.[4]

Personality tests and inventories are available in even greater profusion for determining interests, introversion, extraversion, ascendance, submission, dominance, aggressiveness, fears, worries, self-reliance, emotional instability, emotional maturity or immaturity, mood, neurotic make-up, submerged complexes, racial prejudices, social skills, and many other traits. A few of the best known of such devices (nearly all paper-and-pencil tests) are E. K. Strong's Vocational Interest Blank; Robert S. Woodworth's Personal Data Sheet (one of the earliest personality inventories, with many derivatives); Louis L. and Thelma Thurstone's Personality Schedules; Robert G. Bernreuter's Personality Inventory; Carl R. Rogers' Adjustment Inventory; H. M. Bell's Adjustment Inventory; Fred Brown's Personality Inventory of Children; Louis P. Thorpe, Willis W. Clark, and Ernest W. Tiegs' California Test of Personality; Starke R. Hathaway and J. Charnley McKinley's Minnesota Multiphasic Personality Schedule; the Haggerty-Olson-Wickman Behavior Rating Schedules; the Humm-Wadsworth Temperament Scale; and Edgar A. Doll's Vineland Social Maturity Scale. The latter consists of socially significant behavior competencies arranged in ascending age steps from the first year to the age of 25.

The expressive or projective techniques (the latter term suggested by Lawrence K. Frank), fundamentally based on the method of free association, have attained widespread vogue since the second decade of this century, both for the diagnosis of the total personality and for therapeutic purposes. In the projective-test situation the subject is allowed to give free expression to his thoughts or feelings and to project them into the experimental situation. The clinician interferes as little as possible with the client's responses, although he may seek interpretation through follow-up questions. The test situations are designed to stimulate the uninhibited, free play of the imagination and phantasy and the betrayal of the inner dynamic drives, needs, and motivations, and of the concealed anxieties, conflicts, and repressions. The varied methods employed include casual conversation; observation of behavior responses; free storytelling; free word-association tests (certain responses are leads to complexes) and psychoanalytic interviews (both are the forerunners of the

[4] J. E. Wallace Wallin, "The Psychological Aspects of the Problem of Vocational Preparation and Rehabilitation of Mentally and Physically Handicapped Civilians," *American Journal of Mental Deficiency*, January, 1945, 297*f*.

projective methods); manipulation of unstructured materials (such as clay or finger paints); play techniques with toys (especially dolls, used particularly to reveal family relationships and to release hostility feelings, the child projecting his feelings into the doll, which may play the role of a parent or of a sibling). Use is also made of the drama, in the form of puppet shows (which may be constructed by the children and in which the child can project his problem into the puppet characters) or in the form of Jacob L. Moreno's psychodrama (in which the child acts out problem situations in the therapeutic theater, and thus obtains catharsis), and in the form of pictures, especially as in Henry A. Murray's Thematic Apperception Test (in which the subject reveals his personality in writing dramatic fiction, explaining what the scenes are about in a set of photographs exposed serially, what the causes of the situations are, and what will be the probable outcome). More technical devices include the electrical recording of brain waves (which differ according to the condition of the brain), the use of ambiguous auditory stimuli or vowel patterns repeated by a phonograph (tautophone), and the Rorschach ink-blot test. Some of these techniques will be discussed in Chap. VI. A brief reference to the Rorschach must suffice at this point.

The examinee is asked to tell what he sees in the 10 intrinsically meaningless ink blots printed on cards (devised by Herman Rorschach, Swiss psychiatrist), shown one at a time. Five are in black, two in black and red, and three in various colors. The spontaneous responses and answers to questions are recorded verbatim by the examiner. The responses are carefully analyzed and classified according to certain categories, such as responses to the whole blot or to parts of it; to the shape, unusual details, shading, colors, positions, sensations of movements, or combinations of these elements. Note is also made of the contents of the responses—animals, human beings, or objects. Varying systems of scoring have been devised to determine the peculiarity of the individual's response pattern. The response pattern differs with individuals and with various types of individuals. The test has been used to determine the intellectual status of the client, his peculiar intellectual make-up and talents, the pattern into which his personality is organized, and his dynamic trends. It has been used to explore the richness or poverty of his psychic experiences and to reveal the presence of all kinds of maladjustments, fears, anxieties, worries, emotional instability, neurotic trends, compulsive neuroses, and different kinds of psychotic disorders. The test has been applied to all kinds of persons—to normal, abnormal, and supernormal children and adults; to mental defectives, neurotics, psychotics, psychoneurotics, epileptics, behavior cases, and others.

The value of many personality tests still remains to be determined. Most of them explore only a limited segment of the personality under artificial conditions and are subject to ambiguity of interpretation. The Rorschach, which still occupies the center of the spotlight among projective techniques, is concededly of little value in the hands of novices. Results of the studies of its reliability and validity are somewhat discrepant. The more conservative clinicians feel that the test is made to carry an excessive diagnostic load, as was the Binet-Simon test in the second decade. Most personality tests (and other tests also) while they are an aid to diagnosis, are in need of refinement.

4. To resume the discussion of the mental-hygiene elements of the school program, the next consideration is that the organization of adequate programs of social and recreational activities will tend to promote the pupils' and the teachers' mental health. Such programs should include cooperative school projects carried on by the students: dramatics, athletics, assemblies, entertainments, group discussions, literary societies, club and guild activities, student councils, and student self-government activities. Participation in such diverse school activities should further socialization, aid the student in becoming adjusted to the social order, and develop a sense of social responsibility and solidarity. Emphasis upon activities like these, which make for social adjustment and integration, is in harmony with the view that teaching children to live is of more practical significance for society than is teaching subject matter.

5. The pupil's mental welfare will be furthered by the elimination or the reduction of those physical and mental factors in the school that produce nervous strains, mental disturbances, or shocks. The constant aim should be to search for the causes in the school situations and procedures that may be responsible for difficulties and maladjustments in individual cases. Among the numerous factors to be considered are defective illumination, heating, or ventilation of the classrooms; defective seating arrangements with respect to size of desks, glare, and direction of light; defective construction of textbooks, especially with reference to size of type, length of lines, and finish of paper; improper length of class periods; unhygienic arrangement of study, rest, lunch, extracurricular, and recreation periods; constant interferences with undivided concentration of attention occasioned by street noises or commotions within the building; excessive teacher or pupil load; excessive competition or rivalry; or the use of improper incentives or methods of stimulation.

Different individuals react differently to different kinds of noises, according to differences in nervous constitution, attitude, and mind-set. But sharp, startling, and irregular noises are particularly irritating and injurious to sensitive, nervous systems. Such noises may tend to produce nervous shocks, fears, excessive muscular tension, and energy expenditure; even, sometimes, spasms, inhibition of the flow of saliva, increased blood pressure and respiration, trembling, paleness, partial deafness, and reduced work output. One experiment showed that typists used 19 per cent more energy and lost more than 4 per cent in speed while working under noisy conditions. One department store reduced errors in the bookkeeping department about 24 per cent by the use of sound-deadening devices. In an "experimental factory" in which measured noises of various kinds and degrees of loudness were produced, Donald A. Laird found that group conversation reduced the production in certain routine operations about 3 per cent. Complaints of muscular stiffness followed periods of loud clatter. The greater the noise, the greater the recourse to time-wasting rest periods. Buzzing noises continued in the workers' ears as much as 3 hours after work stoppage.[5] Working efficiency, comfort, and mental health can often be increased by the location of buildings away from noisy surroundings; by the establishment of quiet zones near hospitals and schools; by the adoption of earplugs, heavy panes of glass, or double windows; or by the use of absorbent materials, such as soft, porous tile, perforated metals, and felt. The campaigns against needless noise have led to the invention of noise gages and the organization of antinoise societies.

Many educators, especially of the progressive wing, object to the use of all extrinsic rewards, such as prizes, honors, scholarships, or marks, partly on mental-hygiene grounds. The competitive and prize systems are unwholesome, they say. They foster undesirable attitudes, arouse jealousy, produce undue emotional strain, and create improper motives for study. These educators would replace the extrinsic motives with intrinsic ones, namely, interest in the activity itself derived from the satisfaction that springs from the power acquired in the attempt to master the assigned tasks. Many educationists object to the use of tests and examination for the same reasons. They are merely artificial schemes for inciting effort by conferring artificial rewards, namely, recitation grades or examination marks. They engender a spirit of rivalry and often result in severe emotional upsets. They should be used only as a means to help the teacher and the pupil to check progress, to determine the direction of aptitudes, to discover weaknesses, to diagnose difficulties, and to discover cues for remedial and corrective work. They should be used as a natural means of guidance, not as artificial incentives. There can be no question that the use of the competitive and the prize systems is accompanied by many evils from the mental-hygiene point of view. But it would be rash to predict at this time what the schools of the future will do with the prize and examination systems. Perhaps they are a necessary evil that cannot be wholly eliminated, at least with regard to those who cannot be reached by intrinsic incentives. Moreover, measures of progress of some kind obviously cannot be dispensed with.[6]

6. The prevention of injury to the teacher's mental and bodily health and the crippling of her personality characteristics are of paramount importance for the successful prosecution of the human-engineering activities of the class-

[5] Donald A. Laird, "Noise Does Cut Production," *Forbes*, Aug. 15, 1932.
[6] For a further discussion of the system of examinations and marks, see the writer's "Scholastic Pottage," *Progressive Education*, 1936, 179–187.

room and the school. Restated in positive terms, the preservation of the teacher's mental and physical efficiency and the improvement of her personality make-up are prime essentials for the successful conduct of any public-education enterprise. If the sanity, wholesomeness, and efficiency of the individual teacher is the most important factor in the school education of children, what should be done to maintain the teacher at top efficiency? From the mental-hygiene viewpoint, teacher efficiency, adjustment, and happiness should be improved notably by the cumulative effect of the following suggestions:

(1) The properly qualified teacher is entitled to economic security or stability through a saving wage commensurate with her training, experience, efficiency, and the social prestige that she should enjoy in the community as a professional worker and an enlightened and patriotic citizen. It is notoriously true that many of the nerve-racking worries of teachers in the past (teachers are often described as chronic worriers) have been caused by the meager salary scales in effect from time immemorial in many sections of the country. The annual wages of many teachers have been less than those paid to unskilled laborers. Only a few years ago, the average annual salary of teachers of all ranks, including administrators, in the United States, was $1,260, or $500 less than the average salary paid U.S. civil service employees at that time. Although teachers' salaries have risen substantially since the Second World War, the disparity of the average wage for teachers was $238 as compared with industrial workers in 1946 ($2,000 as compared with $2,238). In 1947 the disparity amounted to $230 ($2,250 versus $2,480). Although the annual wage for the teaching staff had reached $2,550 in 1947–1948, industrial workers and civilian Federal employees are still greatly overpaid in comparison with the teaching profession.[7]

Low pecuniary rewards have kept many excellent prospects from entering the profession, have caused many of the most enterprising and progressive teachers to seek more lucrative occupations, and have made teaching a "procession rather than a profession."

In spite of the upward salary trends of recent decades, lack of adequate financial reward is still cited as the major handicap of the teaching profession. It is not necessary to present a brief here for more pay for teachers. But teaching efficiency cannot be envisioned merely in terms of dollars and cents, and there is a danger of placing undue emphasis on the monetary return of the teacher's vocation, the one issue with which some teachers' associations seem to be concerned. Education is, always has been, and always should remain, an idealistic and altruistic enterprise—one that always has attracted,

[7] *Leaders' Letter,* National Educational Association, October 10, 1945.

The Teacher's Economic Position, November, 1947, National Education Association, Washington, D.C., 1947.

and possibly always will attract (although perhaps in diminishing degree), some of the best brains and noblest humanists of the generations, because of its opportunities for exalted, unselfish service in the interest of human kind, irrespective of the recompense. It is unfortunately true that too many contemporaries are inclined to measure the value of educational service in terms of the pay check, which is the sole standard for appraising the value of services by many whose consuming goal in life seems to be the selfish one of "getting more and more money for less and less work." The educator is "worthy of his hire" in accordance with his efficiency and the value of his contributions to the public weal; but excessive compensation—if that is possible in education—is not an unmixed good. Necessity has always been the mother, not only of invention, but of application, growth, and progress in general. Affluence not infrequently has produced a letdown of personal effort, stagnation, the disposition to allow George to do the hard work, and resignation to the ease and comfort of the carefree life of the playboy. The easy accumulation of a competency in education might well tend to stifle the incentive toward growth and improvement and to attract to the profession the complacent and indolent drones whose primary interest is to find a comfortable way of life, at a comfortable wage, in a job that has short hours and long vacations and is free from the keen competition of private enterprise. "Job holders" looking for well-paid sinecures education has had its share of them—tend to gravitate into loosely supervised public organizations, where the possibility exists to "get by" with a minimum of work without much danger of detection.

(2) Teachers are entitled to occupational security, or job tenure, after a preliminary period of probation. They should be protected by properly drawn tenure laws that forbid dismissals or contract cancellations except after a fair, impartial hearing of charges, preferred in advance in writing. Most teachers now are rehired every year and can be fired or dropped without the formality of formal charges, for reasons that may have nothing to do with their teaching efficiency, on the demand of the superintendent, the principal, the Board of Education, or a coterie of taxpayers or politicians. Teaching is about the only profession in which a person can be found incompetent after many years of experience, often on the flimsiest pretexts. Job security will bolster the teacher's morale even more than a liberal stipend, and thus it will add to her competency, contentment, and serenity.

(3) Similarly important is the establishment of adequate retirement systems for teachers and systems of disability allowance, as well. Many states have been very slow in adopting such systems. In consequence, many teachers in both public and private schools have not enjoyed the security afforded ordinary laborers through the National Security Act, although they must contribute

their share toward the support of the Federal Retirement Systems. Efforts to include teachers in the Federal system have been defeated, partly because of the overt opposition of the teachers in the states that grant superior retirement allowances. Fortunately all states except one (Idaho) now provide more or less adequate retirement allowances, at least 10 states having adopted retirement plans in 1945. When adequate retirement and disability allowances have been provided, many teachers will continue in the profession who now leave for more lucrative work that will provide for the needs of old age.

(4) The administrative control of the schools should be thoroughly democratized on a cooperative basis. Teachers should not only be permitted but should be encouraged to offer suggestions and advice regarding the conduct of the school, to share in policy making, and to cooperate in planning the details of the program. They should be allowed reasonable freedom in planning the details of their own work and in exercising initiative, and should be granted authority commensurate with their responsibilities.

It is a curious paradox that the publicly supported schools established by our Democracy to proclaim, disseminate, and exemplify the principles of individual rights and freedom basic to the concept of that form of sovereignty should themselves become autocratic, authoritarian, and dictatorial. To quote William H. Kilpatrick,

> The school system is in its management too often autocratic. My large class this summer, which is a fair cross-section of the nation, estimated that 75 per cent of school superintendents run their school systems autocratically. Even where there are exceptions, it is too generally a benevolent despotism that grants it. . . . We cannot run schools on a factory basis or treat teachers as factory hands.[8]

Fear of incurring the disfavor of superior officers and the adoption of the defense mechanism of bootlicking have destroyed the initiative and independence of many resourceful teachers, reduced their work to mediocrity, and soured their lives. As the teacher must recognize the sacredness of each child's personality, so should the administrative officers recognize the inviolability of the teacher's personality and individuality. The techniques of mass production do not belong in the school. Teachers must not be treated as machines in a human factory, conducted on impersonal principles of factory efficiency. But the solution is not via the practice of the principle of *laissez faire*. The school system will not run itself. There can be no organized, unified system of schools if every teacher is a law unto herself. The solution lies in finding the golden mean between autocratic regimentation on the one hand and unbridled liberty on the other hand, by means of sensible, reasonable, cooperative adjustments.

[8] W. H. Kilpatrick, "The Future of Education," *Journal of the National Education Association,* 1937, 255.

(5) Among other essentials tending to further the teacher's happiness and healthy mental adjustment that the school authorities should provide are

a. A well-illuminated, well-ventilated, properly heated, relatively noise-free, and cheerful room for the class activities

b. Helpful, sympathetic supervision that will enable the teacher to achieve adequate intellectual independence and emotional maturity

c. Freedom from overdirection and unnecessary interference with classroom details

d. Relief from excessive or unnecessary clerical work

e. Advancement in salary and professional status at proper intervals, according to merit

f. Tactful and considerate criticisms only when necessary, by superior officers, free from sarcasm, arrogance, unreasonable faultfinding, or personal bias; and the prohibition of snubbing or censuring before pupils, parents, or other teachers

g. Reciprocal relations between administrators and teachers, on a plane of cordiality, tolerance, frankness, and sincerity—free from bickering and vengefulness; with scrupulous avoidance of trickery, hypocrisy, deception, duplicity, and dodging; and with faithful fulfillment of promises and agreements

h. Periodic health examinations as a means of furthering teacher efficiency (at public expense or as a requirement of certification renewal)

(6) The teacher should make every effort to lessen the numerous occupational hazards that beset her job, in order that she may keep maximally fit and healthy, mentally and physically, although teaching as such does not appear to be an unhealthy occupation, as judged by longevity statistics. Nevertheless, the teacher should do everything to ensure maximal mental health, for vigorous mental health tends to bring forth happiness, enthusiasm, and efficiency; while ill health is likely to produce discontent, irritability, and misery.

Reference has already been made to the importance of periodic health examinations. Among the most obvious desiderata are the prevention or avoidance of excessive fatigue and the recovery from unavoidable fatigue. Excessive fatigue, the bane of many teachers, tends to lessen capacity for work, it decreases the amount of effort one will expend in the preparation of the day's work and in its delivery; it produces lapses of memory, slips of attention, and motor clumsiness; it lessens interest, makes for impatience and irritability, incites outbursts of anger, and makes for dispirited, routine teaching. When tired out, the teacher becomes more impatient with the pupils' shortcomings and, at the same time, becomes more perfectionistic in her demands. Teachers, in general, tend to be very idealistic and perfectionistic—but they often demand perfection in the pupils rather than in themselves. Under conditions of excessive fatigue (there is, of course, a healthy, nonpathological fatigue) and ill-health they may become more exacting and subject the pupils to unjust disciplinary measures. Unfortunately, the pupil's resentment over the injustice may assume the form of hostility toward all persons in authority.

What are the causes of the teacher's exhaustion that should be minimized or removed? Her fatigue is due in part to the excessive amount of homework or of extracurricular assignments; or the pursuit of in-service courses in compliance with administrative suggestions, which often have the force of directives; or the mechanical strain of teaching; or the stress of maintaining order; or worries about her financial or social status. These factors admit of considerable control in the interest of teacher health. Often the teacher's fatigue is due to lack of emotional satisfaction in the work, because of improper placement (unsuitability of the job), lack of interest in the work, failure to receive recognition for her efforts, or failure to achieve the high goals that have been projected. The futile effort to attain high standards of workmanship in the pupils or in herself may produce feelings of frustration and fatigue. Failure to obtain joy and satisfaction from job performance will engender feelings of discontent, boredom, and tiredness. This is one of the primal sources of teacher dissatisfaction and inferior performance. If the teacher regards teaching merely as routine taskwork, she will probably become a victim of chronic ennui and fatigue, for teaching as hack work is one of the dreariest of occupations. On the other hand, as a skilled art it is stimulating, pioneering, adventuring, and one of the most inspiring of the professions. There is challenge, inspiration, and satisfaction in teaching as a creative profession, but not as a humdrum job. The teacher who gets joy and satisfaction from her teaching does not become a victim of frayed nerves, even though the teaching load may be heavy and exacting. Satisfactory emotional adjustment to one's job will serve as a powerful bulwark or buffer against the stresses and annoyances of life. The joy and inspiration that spring from satisfying accomplishments will serve as a perennial tonic and restorative. Job satisfaction is health preservative. Without it any job becomes distasteful and tends to degenerate into irksome, monotonous routine.

To keep mentally healthy, resilient, and vibrant, the teacher must find satisfying emotional outlets. One of the most important methods of finding re-creative emotional release is through satisfying task performance, or job satisfaction. The conviction on the part of the teacher as to the vital importance of her work to the growth and development of the nation's most precious asset, the leaders of the oncoming generation, will add greatly to her joy of achievement and her peace of mind.

Much of the teacher's weariness doubtless comes from the grind of the monotonous routine that is supposed to be a necessary evil of classroom learning activities. But the ingenious teacher will find little difficulty in circumventing this annoyance by varying the procedures, contents, and materials of her learning units and by other modifications. The teacher who adapts her work to the interests and capacities of her pupils, who discovers and removes the causes of their maladjustments and dissatisfactions, and who keeps them profitably occupied with challenging activity or experience units, will not be harassed by assumed insurmountable problems of discipline.

One important source of the teacher's discontent and fatigue is inadequate physical, mental, and social recreation. The penalty in many cases for adherence to the ideal of "all work and no play" has been the production of insipid, colorless, uninteresting, ineffectual, unwholesome, or neurotic personalities. The teacher should find emotional release from her tensions and disappointments in diversions, pastimes, recreations, and hobbies. Her recreational needs can be supplied by one or more of the following activities, indulgences, or avocations: muscular relaxation (see page 236), brief rest periods and "cat naps" during the day (let rest periods displace clerical routine after the noon lunch), walking, hiking, dancing, golfing, bowling, motoring; hobbies, gardening, housework; indoor and outdoor sports, games, club activities, parties, amusements, and pastimes; movies, theatrical productions, operas, musicales, and athletic contests; and aesthetic experience with the fine and plastic arts. Unfortunately the teacher is sometimes hampered in her search for diversional outlets by the community's proscriptions and taboos. She may not participate in some activities that other normal people indulge in just because she is a teacher and must occupy a segregated pedestal as an example to the pupils and the parents. There may still be places in the United States where the teacher must not dance or use rouge or play cards or express her own opinions on questions of social reform, politics, or religion.

Finding needed emotional outlets and intellectual diversion, stimulation, and enrichment through satisfying human contacts that will strengthen the feeling of emotional security, especially with adults in other walks of life, should be on the teacher's "must" list. One of the important reasons for this imperative is explained in the following paragraph.

(7) An important part of the teacher's "way of life" is to achieve emotional maturity, so that she can divest herself of childish survivals, and so that she will avoid, in the attempt to solve her own adjustment problems in the schoolroom, resorting to the immature reaction patterns that brought success in her childhood and that may be used by some of her pupils to solve their schoolroom problems. Such immature response patterns often constitute a bar to normal maturation including for example attitudes of dogmatism, cocksureness, intolerance, prejudice, oversensitiveness, irritability, peevishness, irrational jealousy or hostility, and impulsiveness. Regression to these and other kinds of infantile reaction patterns are often of the nature of defenses against one's inner conflicts and frustrations or the projection of one's difficulties upon

someone else. In the schoolroom, the blame projection often involves some pupil who resorts to irritating defense mechanisms for overcoming his unsolved problems or some pupil with whom the teacher has not established sympathetic rapport. The teacher, of course, is not the only one who has to wrestle with the problems of emotional immaturity, but the teacher is confronted with a special hazard in the achievement of mature emotional and intellectual patterns, because she must constantly deal with immature personalities. Because her life is spent in the world of childhood, she may fail to grow up emotionally and may adopt attitudes of complacency or condescension, on the one hand, or superciliousness or arrogance, on the other hand, toward the foibles and frailties of her young charges. The teacher must, of course, strive to keep young and plastic, so that she can get down to the level of her pupils in order to maintain effective rapport with them, but not at the cost of emotional fixation and stratification on the childhood level, or of an objective approach toward her problems and those of her pupils. She must strive to maintain a detached, objective, but, withal, sympathetic attitude toward her pupils, so that she can accept the child as he is and enter into an understanding relationship with his limitations without emotional prepossessions or involvements.

The teacher should balance her association with children by association with adults. To maintain mental equilibrium, we often have to balance one factor against another when we cannot avoid certain deleterious influences in the environment. We can often minimize or counteract inimical influences by balancing factors. We can balance factors that are a hindrance or a liability with factors that make for effective living. One of the important readily available balancing factors for teachers is fraternization with adults, especially with those engaged in other vocations. Contacts with adults from different walks of life develop maturity, adjustability, flexibility, catholicity, and poise.

(8) Faulty sex adjustment hampers the teaching efficiency of some teachers —both the married and the celibate—and produces health and personality problems that are in need of skilled treatment. For some the solution is normal sex life in marriage (which, however, must not be conceived as a cure-all for all sex or personality maladjustments), although this is still taboo for women teachers in many schools. Many will find satisfactory resolution of the sex drive in various kinds of social, cultural, and physical sublimations. A modicum require psychotherapeutic treatment by qualified therapists.

(9) As has already been emphasized (page 98), the vital first step in the improvement of teacher personnel should start in the process of selective admission to teachers' colleges of students who are normally endowed from the standpoint of personality make-up, who are emotionally mature and well balanced, as well as scholastically proficient and intellectually capable.

(10) It goes almost without saying that a search should always be made for any adverse situational factors in the school environment that may contribute toward the production of personality distortions in individual cases, and that may render the best psychological treatment futile; and every effort should be made to minimize or remove the inimical influences, whether they be scholastic, psychological, social, or physical. Some difficulties disappear completely as soon as the unfavorable factors in the school milieu are removed. Moreover, without the needed environmental underpinning, relapses sometimes occur in the improvements or cures that have been wrought.

Numerous educational applications are made in the following chapter, which deals with different kinds of handicapped children, as well as in later chapters, especially in connection with the discussion of treatment techniques.

Division of Functions and Cooperation Needed in the Work of Diagnosing, Preventing, and Correcting Personality Blemishes. The successful prosecution of an efficient program of mental hygiene is a cooperative enterprise between specialists and lay workers. On the one hand, many mental snarls, handicaps, and difficulties can be successfully handled only by persons who are highly skilled in psychological or psychiatric diagnosis and therapy. Some of the cases require the services primarily of a neurologist, some of a psychiatrist, some of a psychoanalyst, some of a specialist in clinical psychology or in clinical education. Many require the skilled follow-up ministration of competent special-class teachers of different kinds. Others require tactful and understanding investigation and follow-up work by competent social case workers, specially trained psychiatric social workers, visiting teachers, and guidance counselors. While the three outstanding kinds of specialists in this domain are recruited from the ranks of psychologists, physicians, and educators, it cannot be stressed too definitely that psychologists qua psychologists, physicians qua physicians, and educationists qua educationists cannot lay claim to being technically qualified to render reliable, expert services in the fields of mental hygiene, special education, or remedial and diagnostic teaching. Expertness in these fields requires much more highly specialized preparation than can be secured in the general courses in medicine, psychology, or education. Good judgment, academic erudition, acumen, and sagacity are indispensable assets in mental-hygiene work, but they are not substitutes for technical skill.

So varied and multitudinous are the mental, social, and educational handicaps and maladjustments to which children are subject, that any specialist who pretends to be fully competent to handle all types of cases can be safely classified as a pretender, although not necessarily a deliberate mountebank. No specialist, be he psychiatrist, psychologist, educationist, or sociologist, has any monopoly in the field. There are, indeed, vociferous specialists who are not backward about implying that certain self-styled "adepts" can handle all phases of examination and therapy work with equal expertness, that they themselves possess the right of "eminent domain" to this new "gold field," that the whole field belongs to one profession by a species of "divine right," and that all others are bungling interlopers. But no one profession ever has preempted, or ever can preempt, the whole field of mental hygiene for its own exploitation. In this multilateral domain there is room for many kinds of specialists of sound scientific training and adequate experience in their particular fields of specialization. To assume that one specialist is superior to another specialist of equal ability and training merely because the one possesses one degree and the other another degree is simon-pure psychological ballyhoo.

While there is room in this province of research and service for many kinds of specialists, there is little room for amateurs and mountebanks, at least so far as the more technical aspects are concerned. Incalculable injury has doubtless been inflicted on countless defenseless children by dilettantes and bunglers. There is, however, an abundance of work for both the trained specialist and the enlightened layman.

The chief work of the specialists is to analyze and describe the mental problem or difficulty, locate its primary and secondary causes, interpret to the client and to others the meaning of his defenses and symptoms, review all the findings, outline the required treatment, provide the expert therapy needed, or make the necessary recommendations and suggestions to the cooperating individuals and agencies. For understanding difficulties on the psychological, social, and educational level, training is required in mental hygiene; psychiatry; clinical, abnormal, and child psychology; the various disciplines dealing with mental and physical handicaps; neurology; diagnostic, remedial, and corrective education; sociology; psychological and social case work; counseling; therapeutic interviewing; and educational and vocational guidance. The personnel requirement for this phase of the work includes properly trained psychologists,[9] psychiatrists, physicians, educationists, psychometrists, psycho-

[9] For a discussion of the nature of the training required by the clinical psychologist, see J. E. Wallace Wallin, *Clinical and Abnormal Psychology*, 1927, 127–130, 172*f*.

For later discussions of this problem, consult the following authorities in the *Journal of Consulting Psychology:* A. T. Poffenberger, January–February, 1938, 1–6; David Shakow, May–June, 1938, 73–76; Simon H. Tulchin, July–August, 1939, 105–112; Edgar A. Doll, Carl R. Rogers, Metta M. Rust, and Rose G. Anderson, September–October, 1939, 137–152; Warren W. Coxe, May–June, 1940, 96–103; Symposium on Certification, March–April, 1941, 49–77; Symposium on the School Psychologist, July–August, 1942, 173–228; David Shakow, November–December, 1942, 277–288; and Committee report, January–February, 1943, 23–26. See also *Journal of General Psychology,* July, 1947, 87–92, Committee report in *The American Psychologist,* December, 1947, 539–558; Lawrence S. Kubie and Mary R. Harrower, Conference report, The Josiah Macy Foundation, 1947.

educational examiners, social workers, visiting teachers, counselors, therapeutic interviewers, and guidance workers. The director in charge of a mental-hygiene clinic, be he psychologist or psychiatrist, should possess a certain amount of training in all of the above disciplines, in addition to thorough mastery of his particular field.

While the services of the specialist are indispensable in this, as in any other complicated field of human adjustment, the work of prevention will make little headway without the intelligent cooperation of parents, teachers, general medical practitioners, nurses, social workers, clergymen, and, in truth, all who have anything to do with the rearing, care, or education of children. In fact, it is becoming increasingly obvious that substantial progress in any and all phases of mental-hygiene work, the preventive, the remedial, and the positive, cannot be brought about by a small corps of specialists who can see only a tithe of the individuals in need of advice and adjustment and who will be able to treat only a small number of these. Progress on a large scale cannot be achieved without the active cooperation of all these groups of lay workers.

The fact that lay workers have not been functioning very efficiently in mental-hygiene and mental-health conservation work in the past is not due to the fact that the principles of positive, preventive, and remedial mental hygiene cannot be formulated in simple, comprehensive terms. The primary reason is that these workers have received little scientific information or training in mental-hygiene problems, principles, and techniques. It has been frequently demonstrated that adjustment difficulties can often be successfully handled by tactful, sympathetic, understanding teachers and parents who possess a good fund of common sense and some understanding of human nature and mental hygiene. (For illustrations of tactful handling of child problems, see the case histories on pages 132*f.* and 145*f.* and also some reports in Chap. XVII.)

So far as the social and educational programs are concerned, the primary obligation for the execution of all three phases of the mental-hygiene program will devolve upon parents and teachers. The adequately trained teacher of the future will be not only a subject-matter specialist but an adroit practitioner of good mental hygiene and a wise guidance counselor. Trained in some of the essential disciplines listed on pages 256*f.*, the classroom teacher will become the mainstay of the experts in mental hygiene and counseling on the one hand, and of the parents or guardians on the other. She is the essential functionary who must establish primary contacts with the child, day in and day out, and who must serve as the coordinator between the experts on the one hand and the parents, social workers, or visiting teachers on the other hand.

CHAPTER V

TYPES OF CHILDREN WITH WHOM MENTAL HYGIENE IS CONCERNED

The Problem of Mental Hygiene in Relation to Handicapped and Normal Children. As has already been intimated, mental hygiene is concerned with the personal adjustment problems of all kinds of children (as well as adults), the normal as well as the abnormal, the dull as well as the bright, and those with disabilities as well as those free from disabilities. All children are or may become subject to personality deviations or adjustment difficulties on the psychosocial and educational levels. So far as the normal are concerned, mental hygiene is interested in the preservation of their normality and in the prevention of the growth of abnormalities in them. In the case of handicapped or deviating juveniles, the interest of mental hygiene is in remedial or curative treatment and in preventing the development of further abnormalities or undesirable behavior patterns. This chapter will be devoted to a consideration of some of the important mental-hygiene problems of some of the more obviously handicapped kinds of children, as well as of normal children who are subject to personality maladjustments or specific disabilities.

Great Variety of Types and Grades of Handicapped Children. It is pertinent to emphasize at the outset that the group of handicapped children who have mental-hygiene problems is a very heterogeneous one. It contains a great variety of types and degrees of deviation from the hypothetical normal. Nor does any one of the major types of handicapped children, such as the visually defective or the mentally subaverage, constitute a highly homogeneous group. Each group consists of many subvarieties and many grades of divergence from the normal standard. However, for our immediate purpose we can conveniently subdivide the entire group of the handicapped into four main subgroups: the physically handicapped, the intellectually handicapped, the intellectually normal who are subject to personality twists or disturbances or emotional conflicts, and the socially maladjusted and behavioristically unadjusted.

THE PHYSICALLY HANDICAPPED

This discussion will be confined to a brief statement of the main mental-hygiene problems affecting seven types of physically handicapped children that are of considerable concern to the schools.

172

1. **The Visually Handicapped.**   This includes children who are totally or partially blind.   The first interest of mental hygiene in the visually handicapped is in securing the organization of nationwide programs for the prevention of eye defects.   Most cases of blindness and of seriously impaired vision could perhaps have been prevented by proper eye hygiene at birth (*e.g.*, the application of silver nitrate to the eyes of the newborn) and by the application of proper health measures, accident-prevention measures, and visual-hygiene measures throughout life.   The present nationwide antisyphilitic campaign with Federal aid should make its contribution toward the prevention of visual handicaps.

All children with pronounced visual defects, however, become special education problems, either in residential schools or classes for the blind (Braille classes, for those whose vision is less than 20/200) or in sight-conservation classes (for those with uncorrectable, static acuity between 20/70 and 20/200 and certain other defects).   It is not the function of this book to discuss the standards for the admission of children to various types of special classes or the needed equipment, the program of remediation, or the qualification of the teachers for each kind of class.   References are supplied in this chapter to publications dealing with the problems of these and other types of handicapped children.[1]

2. **The Auditorially Handicapped.**   Most cases of impaired hearing originate in childhood from nose and throat infections and from certain specific infectious diseases of childhood (*e.g.*, scarlet fever).   Some otologists estimate that 75 per cent of impaired hearing is wholly unnecessary and could

[1] For comprehensive works on the psychology and education of different kinds of handicapped children, consult

Special Education, The Handicapped and the Gifted, White House Conference on Child Health and Protection, New York, Appleton-Century-Crofts, Inc., 1931.

Harry J. Baker, *Introduction to Exceptional Children,* New York, The Macmillan Company, 1944.

John E. Bentley, *Problem Children,* New York, W. W. Norton & Company, Inc., 1936.

Merle E. Frampton and Hugh G. Rowell, *Education of the Handicapped,* Yonkers, New York, World Book Company, Vol. I, 1932; Vol. II, 1940.

Karl C. Garrison, *The Psychology of Exceptional Children,* New York, The Ronald Press Company, 1940.

Arch O. Heck, *The Education of Exceptional Children,* New York, McGraw-Hill Book Company, Inc., 1940.

Norma V. Scheidemann, *The Psychology of Exceptional Children,* Boston, Houghton Mifflin Company, Vol. I, 1931; Vol. II, 1937.

Teacher's Guide to Special Education for Exceptional Children, State Department of Education, Austin, Tex. (undated).

J. E. Wallace Wallin, *Children with Mental and Physical Handicaps,* New York, Prentice-Hall, Inc., 1949; *Educational Psychology,* 2d ed., New York, Prentice-Hall, Inc., 1945, 533–554; *The Education of Handicapped Children,* Boston, Houghton Mifflin Company, 1924.

have been avoided by the prevention of colds and infections and by proper nose, throat, and ear hygiene before and after infection. The educationists and mental-hygiene workers are vitally interested in the institution of effective programs for the prevention of auditory defects.

All children subject to seriously defective hearing become special education problems. Those who are deaf and those who do not possess a usable degree of hearing should be grouped in special classes or should be sent to residential institutions for the deaf for the development, in the first instance, of speech and lip reading. Those who have a less pronounced degree of hearing impairment, but who are seriously handicapped in hearing spoken language (who have a minimum shortage of 20 decibels in the better ear as determined by the pure-tone audiometer), should be given the advantage of remedial instruction in hearing-conversation classes for the development of residual hearing (in which sound magnification apparatus is used); or in speech-reading or lip-reading groups, two or three times a week, provided that the hearing is not restorable by proper otological treatment (including the use of radium or the fenestration operation, in selected cases) or by means of properly fitted hearing aids. The mental-hygiene implications of visual and auditory defects are discussed on later pages.[2]

3. Orthopedic Children Who Are Subject to Various Kinds and Degrees of Muscular Weakness or Paralysis and Deformities of the Limbs. Most of the members of this extremely heterogeneous group can be subsumed under three major groupings, according to the causation: (*a*) prenatal or natal defects, including cerebral palsy (about 10 per cent of the entire group of the crippled), the group of nationwide interest at the present time, hip dislocations, clubfoot, and cleft of the vertebral column (*spina bifida*); (*b*) defects produced by bacterial or virus infections, including polio-

---

[2] References on the visually and auditorially handicapped:

Harry Best, *Deafness and the Deaf in the United States,* New York, The Macmillan Company, 1943.

Hallowell Davis, ed., *Hearing and Deafness: A Guide for Laymen,* New York, Murray Hill Books, Inc., 1947.

Merle E. Frampton, *Education of the Blind,* Yonkers, New York, World Book Company, 1946.

Winifred Hathaway, *Education and Health of the Partially Seeing Child,* New York, Columbia University Press, 1947.

Helga Lende, *Books about the Blind,* New York, American Foundation for the Blind, 1940 (annotated bibliography); *What of the Blind?* New York, American Foundation for the Blind, 1938, 1941 (2 vols.).

A. F. Niemoeller, *Complete Guide for the Deafened,* New York, Harvest House, 1940.

Rudolf Pintner, Jon Eisenson, and Mildred B. Stanton, *The Psychology of the Physically Handicapped,* New York, Appleton-Century-Crofts, Inc., 1941 (deals with all kinds of physically handicapped persons).

Mary W. Whitehurst, *Training Your Hearing,* Washington, D.C., Volta Bureau, 1947.

myelitis, or infantile paralysis (about 18 per cent), the most numerous group—which has been in the forefront of public interest for years—bone and joint tuberculosis, spinal meningitis, osteomyelitis, arthritis, and rheumatic fever cases (some of bacterial origin); and (c) defects caused by accidents or mechanical injuries after birth.

Here, again, the first interest of the mental hygienist is the prevention of orthopedic disabilities. Millions of dollars gathered from the Franklin Delano Roosevelt birthday balls and the "March-of-Dimes" campaigns, and from other sources, have been spent in the effort to devise effective vaccines or immunization agents to prevent poliomyelitis and also serums to prevent the crippling effects from infections. Scores of prophylactics and cures have been announced from time to time, but very few have fulfilled early expectations. Deformities caused by rickets are largely preventable by means of sunlight (or ultraviolet light), vitamin D, and an adequate diet. Some progress has been made in the prevention of birth injuries due to oxygen deprivation (anoxemia). Much progress has been made in the use of new chemicals for ameliorative, remedial, or curative purposes in the case of victims of infections: *e.g.*, sulfamerazine, sulfadiazine, penicillin, and Flexner's serum, in the case of cerebromeningitis; streptomycin in the case of tuberculosis of the bones; the sulfa drugs for osteomyelitis; prostigmine for birth palsy and infantile paralysis; and curare for birth palsy. The Kenney hot-pack treatment is particularly valuable for polio. The accident prevention campaigns waged by the schools have reduced traffic accidents among children; but much remains to be accomplished on the streets, in playgrounds, and in homes. Most accidents occur in the home. Of 100,000 children and adults killed in accidents in 1947, 33,500 deaths occurred in the homes and 32,000 from motor vehicles. A large proportion of crippled children require special educational treatment, including muscle training, massage, physiotherapy, occupational therapy, ultraviolet radiation, health improvement, adjusted literary instruction, occupational training, speech therapy, and morale building. Some can do satisfactory work in the regular grades. Others require the special facilities afforded in special orthopedic schools or classes. The subnormals require a differentiated program of instruction. Judicious psychological treatment is needed to prevent or overcome the emotional problems created by long periods of hospitalization or immobilization, the possible feeling of lack of affection because of removal from home and friends, anxieties regarding growing deformities, and the like (see also pages 185*f*.).[3]

[3] *A Selective Bibliography on Cerebral Palsy,* Chicago, National Society for Crippled Children and Adults, 1947.

Edgar A. Doll, Winthrop M. Phelps, and Ruth T. Melcher, *Mental Deficiency Due to Birth Injuries,* New York, The Macmillan Company, 1932.

(*Footnote continued on p.* 176)

4. Poorly Nourished, Pretuberculous and Tuberculous Children, and Delicate Convalescents. All these cases of so-called lowered vitality may conveniently be grouped together. They constitute special education problems in open-window classes, open-air schools, nutrition classes, preventoriums, sanatoria, hospitals, or camps. The favorable results of the nutrition, rest, and fresh-air treatment afforded in such classes and institutions demonstrate that these conditions are largely preventable and often curable.

5. Cardiopathic Children.[4] Many children subject to various kinds of organic heart disorders require a special educational regimen, including feeding, rest periods, and the avoidance of too-vigorous muscular exertion. Some of these children would profit greatly from the special regimen afforded in the so-called cardiac class. Heart disease, responsible for one of the most tragically neglected groups of physically handicapped children, ranks among the leading causes of child mortality. The mortality could be significantly reduced by effective programs of early discovery, care, and treatment.

Equipment for Cerebral Palsied Children, Chicago, National Society for Crippled Children and Adults, 1947.

Ernst Herz and Tracy J. Putnam, *Motor Disorders in Nervous Diseases,* New York, Columbia University Press, 1946.

Elizabeth E. Lord, *Children Handicapped by Cerebral Palsy,* 2d printing, New York, Commonwealth Fund, Division of Publication, 1945.

Morris Fishbein, ed., *A Bibliography of Infantile Paralysis, 1789–1944,* Philadelphia, J. B. Lippincott Company, 1946.

Romaine P. Mackie, *Crippled Children in American Education, 1939–1942,* New York, Columbia University Press (references).

Winthrop M. Phelps, *Cerebral Palsy and Poliomyelitis,* Springfield, Ill., Charles C. Thomas, Publisher, 1940.

Rehabilitation Facilities for the Severely Handicapped, Chicago, National Society for Crippled Children and Adults, 1947.

Bernice Rutherford, *Give Them a Chance to Talk: Handbook on Speech Correction for Cerebral Palsy,* Milwaukee, The Bruce Publishing Company, 1948.

Alfred Strauss and Laura E. Lehtinen, *Psychopathology and Education of the Brain-injured Child,* New York, Grune & Stratton, Inc., 1947. (This deals with the non-paralytic forms of brain injuries characterized by disturbance of perception, attention, thinking, learning, personality, and behavior.)

T. Arthur Turner, *Organizing to Help the Handicapped,* Chicago, National Society for Crippled Children and Adults, 1944.

J. E. Wallace Wallin, *Children with Mental and Physical Handicaps,* New York, Prentice-Hall, Inc., 1949 (references).

E. Louise Ware, *Mental Hygiene of the Orthopedically Handicapped Child,* New York, Association for the Aid of Crippled Children, 1947.

Norman Westlund and Adelaide Z. Palumbo, "Parental Rejection of Crippled Children," *American Journal of Orthopsychiatry,* April, 1946, 271–281.

[4] On the psychological implications of heart disorders, see John M. Johnston, "Psychosomatic Implications in Cardiovascular Disease," *Mental Hygiene,* April, 1948, 235–245.

6. Children Subject to Epileptic Seizures. Great differences exist in this group of afflicted children also in the matter of the character, severity, and frequency of the attacks, as well as in the causation and treatment. Fortunately, great progress has been achieved in the determination of the brain condition in epileptics by means of the electroencephalograph (an instrument that records brain waves magnified about a million times), which shows the nature of the electrical, cortical waves associated with different kinds of seizures (such as grand mal and petit mal, Jacksonian, or focal, and psychomotor attacks) and by means of the pneumoencephalograph (an instrument that gives an X-ray picture of air injected into brain cavities), which reveals cavities or areas of destruction that may be present in the brain. Great progress has also been made in the perfection of synthetic drugs for the control of the attacks. On the basis of the studies of the brain-wave disturbances (dysrhythmia) in epileptics and in their relatives, it has been concluded that from 500,000 to 700,000 epileptics are found throughout the country, and that 10,000,000 persons in the general population show the same brain-wave disturbances that are found in epileptics. However, only 5 per cent of those predisposed actually develop epilepsy.

The anticonvulsants found effective in the control of seizures include luminol (gardenal or phenobarbital) for grand mal, dilantin (phenytoin sodium) for grand mal and psychosomatic seizures, and tridione for pure petit mal. These and a few other chemicals must be given regularly and unceasingly under medical supervision, to prevent side effects.

Under effective medical treatment, from two-thirds to three-fourths of epileptics continue intellectually normal and are capable of pursuing the regular courses in the public schools. Many can do successful work on the college and university level.

Many epileptics are subject to a great variety of personality problems and maladjustments, produced either by the disrupting effects of the malady, especially the episodic convulsions—anxieties, fears, distrust, hopelessness, depression, inferiority feelings, feelings of disgrace or shame, attempts at concealment, emotional conflicts, and instability—or by the social treatment received from parents, siblings, or playmates, either in the direction of pampering, oversolicitude, overprotection, or indulgence, or in the direction of avoidance, shunning, ostracism, criticism, or snubbing. The psychological problems often require patient and expert handling.[5]

[5] References on children with seizures:
Paul H. Hoch and Robert P. Knight, eds., *Epilepsy: Psychiatric Aspects of Convulsive Disorders,* New York, Grune & Stratton, Inc., 1947 (references).
William G. Lennox, *Science and Seizures,* 2d ed., New York, Harper & Brothers, 1946.
(*Footnote continued on p.* 178)

7. Children with Speech Impediments and Handicaps. From 3 to 10 per cent of pupils in the elementary schools (depending upon the rigor of the criterion) are subject to a large variety of speech disorders, defects, and imperfections, which may conveniently be considered here, although only a small proportion are structural in nature, that is, due to physical causes. This group of child handicaps, largely neglected in years past as inconsequential, includes stuttering, stammering, defects of articulation and pronunciation, lisping, lalling, baby talk, sound substitution, cluttering, nasality, huskiness, tongue-tiedness, motor aphasia, and psychic mutism. Many speech handicaps (especially stuttering or inarticulate speech) may interfere seriously with the child's progress in school and may produce a great variety of personality disturbances, such as excessive self-consciousness, timidity, shyness, inhibitions, stubbornness, refusal to speak, withdrawal from social contacts, or aggressiveness (see page 183).

Children with speech disorders and defects should be given speech therapy two or three times a week by itinerant speech-correction and -improvement teachers. Many school systems now supply such services. All kindergarten and primary teachers should be required to pursue courses in speech correction and improvement, in order that they may supply treatment to uncomplicated speech cases, at the outset of their school careers, and thus leave the more difficult cases (such as stutterers and stammerers) to the speech therapists.[6]

Wilder Penfield and Theodore C. Erickson, *Epilepsy and Cerebral Localization,* Springfield, Ill., Charles C. Thomas, Publisher, 1941.

Tracy J. Putnam, *Convulsive Seizures, How to Deal with Them,* Philadelphia, J. B. Lippincott Company, 1943.

R. Rossen, "A Critical Analysis Obtained from 873 Electroencephalographic Examinations," *Medical Bulletin,* Washington, D.C., November, 1947, 494–503.

Oslwei Timkin, *The Falling Sickness: A History of Epilepsy from the Greeks to the Beginnings of Modern Neurology,* Baltimore, Johns Hopkins Press, 1945.

J. E. Wallace Wallin, *Children with Mental and Physical Handicaps,* New York, Prentice-Hall, Inc., 1949.

[6] References on children with speech defects:

Ollie L. Backus, *Speech in Education,* New York, Longmans, Green & Co., Inc., 1943.

Mildred F. Berry and Jon Eisenson, *The Defective in Speech,* New York, Appleton-Century-Crofts, Inc., 1947.

Mabel F. Gifford, *Correcting Nervous Speech Disorders,* Prentice-Hall, Inc., 1940.

Harry J. Heltman, *First Aid for Stutterers,* Boston, Expression Company, 1943.

Wendell Johnson, *The Influence of Stuttering on the Personality,* University of Iowa Studies in Child Welfare, Iowa City, University of Iowa Press, 1932.

Carney Landis and M. Marjorie Bolles, *Textbook of Abnormal Psychology,* New York, The Macmillan Company, 1946 (Chap. IX, Epilepsy; and Chap. XXII, Disorders of Speech).

(Footnote continued on p. 179)

The Mental-hygiene Problems Presented by the Physically Handicapped. The interest of mental hygiene in physically handicapped children is twofold.

1. Physical defects sometimes directly produce special educational, psychological, or social problems. Physically handicapped children are influenced by the same factors that affect the lives of normal children and also by specific factors connected with their peculiar types of physical defect. The problem of therapy involves needed adjustment for the defect itself, as well as for the emotional, social, intellectual, and personality reaction characteristics that may be associated with it. In general, no definite personality pattern is invariably associated with a particular bodily defect, although certain tendencies toward particular behavior patterns may attach to certain primary defects, such as blindness or deafness. The problem is to study clinically the reaction responses of each child in relation to his particular defect.

For example, total blindness and total deafness directly produce educational and psychological problems because of the complete lack of visual perceptions, in the one case, and of auditory perceptions, in the other case. In the case of the congenitally deaf and blind, whole areas of sensations and perceptions remain completely undeveloped, and compensatory or substitute modalities (separate sense departments) of perception must be developed and organized. The sensory black-out may also result in emotional vacuity. Blindness necessarily interferes with the arousal of the emotions that go with the perception of the beauty of color and form, and deafness with the emotional stimulation from melody, harmony, rhythm, beautiful tones, and voices. The deprivation of such aesthetic experiences may lead to dissatisfaction, emotional maldevelopment, and emotional immaturity or stagnation. Muscular disabilities may directly produce a sense of weakness, impotency, insecurity, emotional thwarting, and dissatisfaction. Similarly, specific brain

Mardel Ogilvie, *Terminology and Definitions of Speech Defects,* New York, Columbia University Press, 1942.

"Psychosomatic Study of Fifty Stuttering Children," *American Journal of Orthopsychiatry,* July, 1946, 100–133. (A roundtable by four speakers.)

Sara M. Stinchfield and Edna H. Young, *Children with Delayed or Defective Speech,* Stanford University, Calif., Stanford University Press, 1940.

Florence M. Teagarden, *Child Psychology for Professional Workers,* rev. ed., New York, Prentice-Hall, Inc., 1946.

Charles Van Riper, *Speech Correction: Principles and Method,* New York, Prentice-Hall, Inc., 1947.

J. E. Wallace Wallin, *Clinical and Abnormal Psychology,* 3d printing, Boston, Houghton Mifflin Company, 1928, 464ff.

Robert West, Lou Kennedy, and Anna Carr, rev. ed., *The Rehabilitation of Speech,* New York, Harper & Brothers, 1947.

lesions or structural cortical defects may be a direct cause of a profusion of sensory, intellectual, emotional, and motor disturbances.

2. Physical defects sometimes indirectly give rise to problems of personality maladjustment and mental hygiene. These problems arise from the subject's attitude toward his defects. He may have grown excessively sensitive about his deficiency. This morbid consciousness can often be traced to the attitude that parents, playmates, or teachers have shown toward the defect, such as attitudes of coddling, criticism, ridicule, or the application of derisive names. The subject's abnormal sensitivity regarding his defects may produce all sorts of unhealthy reactions, such as fears, timidities, secretiveness, shamming, seclusiveness, withdrawal, emotional outbursts and conflicts, repressions, hypersensitiveness, introversion, fear of inadequacy, fear of being different, feelings of disgrace, despondency, malingering, sullenness, behavior disorders, self-pity, brooding, fear of early decrepitude, efforts at compensation or over-compensation, daydreaming, suspicion of dullness, and sometimes tendencies to flaunt the defect as a bid for sympathy. These mental sequelae of the victim's attitude toward his handicap often constitute a far more serious obstacle to the child's ability to adjust himself satisfactorily to the social and vocational demands of society than does the physical defect itself.

Illustrations of Personality Maladjustments Traceable to the Morbid Consciousness of Physical Blemishes or to the Attitudes Shown toward Them. Our records are replete with instances showing concretely how personality defects and distortions similar to those referred to above developed from the consciousness of a physical blemish.

Eye Defects. Defective vision may be interpreted by others as dullness and thus evoke sarcastic remarks that may lead the victim to feel he is different from others. This may call forth compensatory reactions. In the following case, the vexation produced led to the happy resolution never to treat children sarcastically and to a determination to be content to make the best of an irremediable defect.

SEVERE CONGENITAL MYOPIA, INTERPRETED AS DULLNESS AND PRO-
DUCING SARCASTIC CRITICISMS OF RESPONDENT, WHO WAS LED TO
FEEL SHE WAS DIFFERENT FROM OTHERS; SHE EVENTUALLY COMPEN-
SATED BY RESOLVING SHE WOULD NEVER BE SARCASTIC TO PUPILS

I have a case of severe congenital myopia which is relieved very little by glasses.
When I was old enough to tell time and had to approach as nearly as possible to the clock in order to see, my people concluded that I was dull.
This handicap became more apparent when I entered school. I would wait for the teacher to put the work on the board when it was already there. My failure to

distinguish things that others talked about caused me to think I must be different from others.

When I was in the fifth grade I was fitted with glasses for the first time. Now occurred an experience that I have never forgotten and which led me to make a resolution that when I was old enough to teach, I would never be sarcastic to a pupil. When I was unable to read from the blackboard across the room even with my glasses, my principal shouted at me, "Why do you wear those glasses?"

The only way in which this handicap is noticeable now is the difficulty I have of recognizing other people beyond a certain range. This is a serious obstacle to a person in public life, but, as it is unsurmountable, I make the best of it. I resolutely exclude from my consciousness the things that I cannot possibly do. I realize I have my life to live, and that I must not bow down to difficulties, but must work determinedly and must maintain confidence in my ability to accomplish something worth while.   (M.H.; F.; E.S.P.; Age 49)

That derisive epithets and the taunts of playmates inspired by a blind eye may lead to a train of serious consequences is illustrated by the following case.

SULLEN, ANTAGONISTIC ATTITUDE, REFUSAL TO ATTEND SCHOOL, AND HOPELESSNESS PRODUCED BY PLAYMATES' TAUNTS AND NICKNAMES BECAUSE OF A BLIND EYE; BECAME WILLING VICTIM OF OLDER MAN WHO FLATTERED HER BY ATTENTIONS; ATTEMPTED SUICIDE BECAUSE OF FEAR OF CONSEQUENCES

A. was brought to the bureau to find out whether she had a psychosis, as she had set fire to herself. As soon as I entered the room I noticed that A. had a rather sullen, antagonistic air, which I ascribed to the fact that one of her eyes dropped. I conjectured at once that this blind eye had a good deal to do with A.'s troubles; and so it proved. When she reached adolescence, the other children's taunts and nicknames, including "wop" and "one-eye," became unbearable, and she refused to go to school any longer. On questioning her, I found that she had set fire to herself because, as she expressed it, "What is there for a girl like me?" I found that she felt that no man would ever notice a girl like her. One man, an old man, had noticed her, and, flattered by his attention, she had given him his way with her; and it was because she was afraid of the consequences that she had attempted suicide. A.'s I.Q. was not very high; but from the intelligent way in which she seemed to grasp the situation and the amount of insight she had, I concluded that she was more intelligent than the test showed and that she was not psychotic.   (From M.N.; F.; C.T. of Psy. and Ed.; M.A.)

Whether nearsighted and farsighted children develop abnormal personality characteristics cannot be definitely answered without further investigation. A. P. Wilkinson has concluded that nearsighted children tend to become lazy, mischievous, motor-minded, inattentive, and dissatisfied with school.

The nearsighted boy cannot play baseball; he cannot see the ball soon enough and so is unable to compete with his playmates. Therefore, he tends to become a bookworm, to acquire sedentary habits, and to become the teacher's pet. On the other hand, the farsighted boy can play baseball, is a good shot, and can hunt. Therefore he wants to leave school.

Deafness. Deafness or seriously impaired hearing is a prolific source of personality deviations, often producing suspicious and paranoid trends, aloofness, introversion, morbid sensitiveness, timidity, and attempts at concealment. Frequently the subject's morbid symptoms merely express his attitude toward the way people react, or the way he believes they react, to his deafness. The following case shows the state of mind of a very hard-of-hearing teacher and how she overcame her idiosyncrasies to a considerable extent by associating with others who, although similarly handicapped, had become emancipated and also by her determination to face the facts.

PERSONALITY DEVIATIONS PRODUCED BY IMPAIRED HEARING, LARGELY
OVERCOME BY DETERMINATION TO FACE THE FACTS

My deafness began about the age of sixteen or just before I finished high school. According to recent information from my mother, my grandmother thought that I did not answer because I was stubborn or just because I did not want to hear.

During my last year in college I became aware of head noises. But for some time I thought the noise was outside rather than inside my head.

I did not become especially conscious of hearing loss until after I had been teaching several years. When I did realize that I was becoming hard of hearing, I became sensitive and self-conscious. I would have spells of morbidness and crying. I was afraid to meet strangers and always wished to avoid a crowd. I could not muster up courage to tell people I was hard of hearing. Just why, I do not know, but there seemed such a stigma attached to it. I was misunderstood many times because I would not respond when people would speak to me. It was difficult for me to keep up with conversation in a crowd and consequently I had very little to say. I lived under a very great nervous strain, trying to hear and trying to keep people from knowing that I was hard of hearing.

Then I went away to study speech reading and was thrown with teachers and students who were laboring under the same handicap. All of my teachers were hard of hearing. They were not morbid or sorry for themselves: they had mastered the problems created by their deafness.

After studying and associating with these people, my attitude was changed. I realized it was no disgrace to be hard of hearing, and by facing the situation I found that most hearing people were willing to be patient and helpful.

I can't say all of my fear is gone and I still live under a great nervous strain, due, I believe, to head noises as much as to anything else. But I can say that I have learned how to fight fear and I have also learned that one must master deafness or be mastered by it.   (P.E.M.; F.; S.C.T.)

Speech Impediments.[7]   Speech defects constitute an equally prolific source of mental conflicts and behavior disturbances, often because of the ridicule the sufferer must endure at the hands of playmates and others.   The following are cases in point.

TIMIDITY, WITHDRAWAL, AND INTROVERSION FROM A SPEECH IMPEDIMENT

When I was young I had a slight speech impediment, a sort of stammer.   But it did not become a menace until I was about fourteen.

Neither of my parents stammered or stuttered although I was told my mother's uncle did all of his life.   A cousin, the son of my mother's brother, stammers now.

My difficulty lasted from about fourteen to eighteen.   During this time I could not even tell anyone the time of the day although I had a watch before me.   I could not even say "present" without much trouble when my name was called in school.   Sometimes I could not make a single sound.   Once I had uttered the first word I could usually go through with the sentence.   Although it was impossible for me to read in public, I could speak very well from the platform.   In fact, during this four-year period I won a gold medal in one oratorical contest and came out second in a second contest.   But shortly after these contests I was not only unable to speak, but I was afraid to speak before an audience.

Because of the embarrassment caused me, I had a great desire to get away from all those I knew, even those who had attempted to help me.   Such attempts had only made me worse by making me conscious of my defect and calling the attention of others to it.   I left my small town and went to Philadelphia, where I knew no one and where I felt I could carry out my plan for breaking the habit.   I was determined to break it.

In less than two months I returned home able to talk without any difficulty. To this day I am able to speak without any impediment unless I get unusually excited, angry, or run down physically, and then it is only when speaking with those who have authority over me.   I now have no fear of going into the office of any man, no matter how important he is, and carrying on a conversation with him, especially if I am not under his direct authority.   Outside of my own family, I have always done much better with strangers than with those I associate with regularly.   If I am in good physical condition, I will not stammer or stutter, whether or not the person has authority over me.

This is about the only fear I have had worth mentioning.

(B.D.A.; M.; U.S.)

FEAR OF APPEARING BEFORE AUDIENCES BECAUSE OF UNCORRECTED BABY TALK WHICH WAS MADE FUN OF; SUGGESTIONS FOR PREVENTION

Until I was a grown man I was always "stage struck" whenever I went before audiences to speak or to do my part in school exercises.

[7] See Joseph P. Blank, "My Adventures in Free Speech," *The Reader's Digest*, May, 1948, 7–9.

During my first three years in school I was called "Dutch" by my playmates because I could not pronounce certain words very plainly. The children made more or less fun of me because I often twisted the words. I pronounced "three" and "free" alike. A "th" was pronounced like an "f." I usually omitted the "r" sound in words. No physical defects caused me to mispronounce words. My parents and older brothers and sisters had talked "baby talk" to me at home. This may have accounted for my ailment.

I was very quiet in school and would not voluntarily recite. In my third year in school a sympathetic teacher assisted and encouraged me in correct pronunciation which resulted in a great improvement in my speech. I finally overcame the defect. However, I still did not like to appear before audiences or do anything which would make me conspicuous.

When about eight years of age I began to take lessons on the violin. Soon I was able to play in an orchestra which was composed of six brothers and sisters. I was not uneasy when playing upon the platform at church or in lodge halls. Finally, I was able to play violin solos in our concerts and was never nervous when the time came for me to do my part. I was not platform conscious in music but I certainly was in anything which had to do with a verbal presentation. Since it was necessary for me to appear before audiences in school programs, I attempted always to perform my part of the program by violin playing.

In high school I was influenced very much by a principal who was very adept in speaking before assemblies. He was very much admired by his students and when I grew up I wanted to be just like him. He encouraged me to welcome opportunities to recite and to take part in school exercises. During classroom exercises and discussion I would volunteer speaking after having rehearsed in my mind the exact words I was going to say. I volunteered and was given a minor part in a high-school play.

After one year of training in a normal school I became a teacher of vocational agriculture in a rural section. This afforded me many occasions to talk before audiences of farmers. By making a careful preparation of my subject matter, in order to give myself confidence in my message, and by speaking whenever an opportunity presented itself, I finally overcame my fear of audiences. At the present time I have no such fear, other than that of a speaker who is anxious to do his best and who desires to give a presentable talk.

Recommendations

1. Parents should talk to young children in the same kind of language that they use in talking to adults. While there is need to use simple words when talking to young children, these words can be pronounced correctly, for children are great imitators and the effects of baby talk will carry over.

2. Had my first-grade teacher possessed the proper kind of knowledge regarding speech defects and had she been trained to assist pupils to overcome impediments in speech, my ailment could have been corrected while I was still in the first grade.

3. In the latter part of the grades and especially in the first year of high school, courses in public speaking should be offered that will acquaint pupils with the

rudimentary knowledge about speaking before audiences. I believe that most of our fears of audiences are due to the fact that we do not know how to appear before them and how to deliver our message in such a way as to command their attention. This type of training would have been very beneficial in my case.[8]

(P.L.W.; M.; Jr. C.T.; M.A.; Age 35)

Orthopedic Conditions. The crippled child often becomes a victim of self-pity and self-glorification, frequently because of the pampering and spoiling processes to which he has been subjected at home and in school. He may become a victim of fears and inhibitions because of his unsteady gait or falls. His mother may contribute to his apprehensions by her own apprehensive behavior or by her expressed fear that he may hurt himself, by gloomy forebodings regarding his difficulties, and by doing everything for him. The inability to compete on equal terms with other children in their physical plays and social activities may develop feelings of incompetency, seclusiveness, or dissatisfaction, or the determination to overcome the handicap and to excel in other directions. Secondary traits often develop on the basis of this determination. These may include stubbornness, contrariness, or vanity.

Unless wisely guided, the crippled child may become a shirker or a tyrant and insist that the world owes him a living and that his every whim must be humored. One of the basic objectives of the educational program for the crippled child (as well as for any other type of handicapped child) is the development of the spirit of self-help and the willingness and resolution to face handicaps honestly and courageously, and to recognize that a physical handicap is not an insurmountable barrier to success but merely an impediment to overcome or compensate for by learning to do so well in something else in which the defect is not a handicap that he can compete successfully in the labor market with the average worker. To train the handicapped child to live contentedly and cheerfully with his defect is one of the first steps in making him a successful and satisfied citizen.[9]

That ideas concerning lameness are frequently more handicapping than the lameness itself may be seen from the following two cases. The first person largely overcame the mental effects of her disability by developing socially desirable qualities and other excellent traits.

[8] For suggestions regarding the psychological treatment of stage fright and other forms of fear, see Chap. XII.

[9] For a good illustration of the wise handling of a crippled child by an intelligent mother, see "My Child Was a Cripple," *The Reader's Digest,* July, 1937, 52–54; and the book by Earl R. Carlson (a spastic who became a medical specialist on spastics), *Born That Way,* New York, The John Day Company, 1941.

DEVELOPMENT OF CERTAIN SOCIALLY APPROVED TRAITS; STUBBORN-
NESS, INTROVERSION, SECLUSIVENESS, AND INTELLECTUAL APPLICA-
TION, DUE TO CRIPPLED CONDITION

I received an injury at the age of eighteen months which necessitated my staying
in bed for six months and afterward left me with a slightly shortened leg. This
did not worry me to any great extent in early childhood. I could do practically
everything my sister and the other children could do. At about the age of ten
I got the idea that being lame caused people to like me less and that seemed to
oppress me although the lameness itself did not, because it was not of a handicapping nature. The desire for social approval and the hope of compensating
for the disagreeable effect of the lameness on people caused me to try to develop
kindness and helpfulness and other socially approved traits. It was an attempt to
compensate for a felt inferiority. In later school life I could not compete with my
classmates in athletics, dancing, hiking, etc., and so concentrated upon mental
activities or physical skills in which I could hope to excel. Whatever success I
may have had in these lines I attribute to concentration on them rather than unusual innate ability. The fact that I have been fighting to overcome certain
obstacles has tended to develop a stubborn tendency which sometimes brings me
into conflict with other people.

I tend to be seclusive and introverted to a certain extent. I am often alone in
my thinking even in a crowd. I like people but am not dependent on them for
happiness. This feeling may have developed from the idea that I could not do
what they could and was not just like them and therefore must go my own way.
I have succeeded in overcoming this feeling to a certain extent. I can lose myself
in the lives of the pupils I teach, and in this way seem to have achieved a socialized
condition.   (W.E.; F.; S.C.T.)

MORBID CONSCIOUSNESS OF A PHYSICAL DEFECT AND FEELINGS OF
UNHAPPINESS, INFERIORITY, AND WORTHLESSNESS IN A HUNCHBACK,
ENGENDERED BY EPITHETS AND NEGLECT; DEFENSIVE SATISFACTION
IN A COMPENSATORY DAYDREAM

Until I was nine years of age my life was no different from that of the average
poor boy. I enjoyed the few privileges that were afforded me, such as the theater,
playground, school, and settlement house. I participated in school and church
concerts as did the other children. Life was enjoyable because I had no cares
and did not know the meaning of the word, worry.

One day during my tenth year, my mother noticed that I was developing a
spinal curvature. This curvature had begun about four years earlier but remained unnoticed. She took me to the hospital, where I was thoroughly examined
and given a curative treatment.

At first I did not pay any attention to the defect. I just felt that I was ill,
like thousands of others, and would become better after a short period of time.
However, one day as I was running down the street, I heard a boy yell, "Hunchback, Hunchback." This name caused me to become depressed. I sensed the

fact that I was different from other people. When I got home I slipped into my bedroom and began to cry, wishing and praying that I might die.

From this time on my life was unhappy. Children and even grown-ups would stare at me on the street as if I were a "curio" from the circus. Many of them, would indulge in ridicule. Whenever I was asked by a neighbor to go on an errand, something of this nature would be said, "If it's heavy don't bring it as you are a cripple." It seemed as if this word always made me feel that I was a liability to myself.

School life was really boresome. I seemed to have no pupil friends. They spoke to me at times but they were not chummy. On the playground I seemed to be an outcast. I was never invited to participate in the games. I had an inner urge to be active in school affairs. I wanted a chance to debate, to orate, to take part in dramas. But no one ever asked me to participate in any extra-curricular activities. I was always overlooked when a program was prepared It was about this time that I decided that I was a worthless individual born with a curse.

I had heard something about sins being visited upon the children of the third and fourth generations. I was suffering for something someone else had done. How unjust this seemed to be!

At home we were very happy. My mother did her best to keep the house attractive and make it enjoyable. I liked to be home with my brothers and sisters. But mental depression assailed me when my brothers and sisters would go out with their friends. No one invited me to go walking with them. The boys and girls of my age paid no attention to me and my brothers' and sisters' friends were either too old or too young. As soon as they left the house I began to wonder why I hadn't been born strong and healthy like other people. Why should I live the life of a hermit?

When I became a junior in high school I was elected class treasurer. This made me happy and I felt that life had reached a turning point for me. I kept my records very accurately and the class seemed to delight in having me take charge of their money. The class was getting ready for the prom. The month of June came and we were asked by the class sponsor to give the names of our guests. Except for myself, every boy seemed to have a girl as his guest. The boys "kidded" me when I said I was going alone. We were told to wear white flannels and dark coats. I had no flannels nor money with which to buy them. I was singled out (for what reason I don't know) and told most emphatically by the president not to come unless I had flannels. This caused me to realize definitely that going to the prom was out of the question, although I had paid my dues and had worked like a Trojan to collect the money for the prom. No girl to take, no flannels, no ability to dance!

All of this I blamed on my physical defect. If I had been physically well I would have been more popular; I would have had a job that paid enough to enable me to buy flannels and would have known how to dance. The thought of this gave me great mental pain and it had a harrowing effect upon my nerves. I tried to find relief by sleeping but I couldn't sleep. It was then that I began to fly to the world of fantasy through a daydream.

I imagined myself at the prom: popular, anxiously sought by the girls, each dance taken. I glided most gracefully across the floor. I was dressed in new oxfords, the latest style of flannels, and a dark blue coat. When I left the prom I took a crowd to a tea room near-by and here I treated them to refreshments. I had plenty of money in my pockets.

When I came back to myself I was repossessed with the inferiority complex. This complex remained with me until after graduation from high school.

Upon enrolling at a higher institution I was with a new group. All of the students were strangers to me. Someone asked me my name and introduced me to the rest of the group. They were very friendly to me. I was assigned as chairman of a study group. I was kept so busy that I had no time to think about my inferiority complex. A few months later I had forgotten about the defect. Since then I have learned to realize that life is what one makes it.

(M.A.J.; M.; Col.; Secretarial Work; Age 24)

The following respondent was not conscious of any detrimental personality effect resulting from her limp, although she was cruelly teased by boys because of it. This was due largely, she thinks, to wise parental guidance and the skill she developed in various motor activities. Nevertheless, the consciousness of her physical deformity seems to play an important role in the fear of growing old which now obsesses her.

CONSCIOUSNESS OF A LIMP WITHOUT ANY DETRIMENTAL PERSONALITY
EFFECTS, POSSIBLY BECAUSE OF WISE PARENTAL HANDLING OR CAPA-
BILITY IN MOTOR ACTIVITIES

Of course, I have always been conscious of my limping. Yet I don't think it has influenced my life in a detrimental way. I have been cruelly teased by boys at school because of it, but my mother has always been so sane about everything relating to my lameness that I have not really developed much of an inferiority over it. As a child I played on the class scrub team in basketball. I played a fairly respectable game of tennis, and have kicked and done everything else but skate and dance. I tried to learn to dance but was such a failure at it that I gave it up. I simply couldn't do the tango and the other wild hop-skip-and-jump dances everyone was doing at the time I should have been going to dances.

But I have developed a fear of old age. I don't want to grow old. I loath being in my thirties now, and really am dreading the forties and on up. As one grows older, one's physical defects grow more pronounced. I fear that my slightly curved back and my limp are going to be worse. I am going to be a fearful old woman; and unless I have a husband I will be alone in the world after my parents leave. I have often thought that, when I get old and these awful things happen to me that come with old age, I'll simply commit suicide. Now, don't laugh and say I will not because suicides never do anything when they talk about it. I wonder if my ego will ever recognize myself as being really as terrible as my thoughts project myself in the future.

Old age and its horrible consequences to a partly deformed, limping person, certainly holds its horrors for me at the present. As far as I know, this is my only real phobia.   (C.M.I.; F.; S.C.T. and Mental Tester; B.S.)

Physical Unattractiveness as a Source of Mental Upsets. Perhaps no other physical condition or circumstance can produce greater emotional perturbation or a greater variety of mental reactions, especially during the sensitive adolescent period, than the realization that one is lacking in physical charm, is ugly of face, ungainly in manner, too large or too small, too fat or too lean, well dressed or poorly dressed. This situation may fittingly be considered in connection with the question of physical defects. The following cases illustrate the causes and consequences of this kind of sensitivity. As will be noted from the reports, some of the mental maladjustments and vagaries cannot be ascribed solely to the factor under consideration but rather to a combination of factors.

SENSITIVENESS ABOUT PERSONAL APPEARANCE AND IDEAS OF SELF-REFERENCE; GOING INTO STORES TO AVOID THE FANCIED REMARKS OF STREET LOAFERS; ATTEMPTS AT CURE

At one time I could hardly walk a block without wondering what people were saying about me. When passing groups of individuals on the street, I was certain that I was the object of their discussion. If a group laughed just before or just after I had passed it, I became frantic. Thoughts like these rushed into my mind: "Are they laughing at the way I walk?" "Is anything hanging on me?" "Does my dress look funny?" "Is my face dirty?" "Is my hat crooked?" "Wonder why they are laughing at me?" "Are they laughing at my size?" And many other equally foolish thoughts. Usually I would manufacture some errand which would take me into a store and off the streets until I could regain a certain amount of composure. I find myself prone to be sensitive at the present time but I usually manage to allay my sensitivity by saying to myself, "Come now, don't be foolish; you're not so important that every one must talk about you." However, this remedy sometimes fails and I find myself living through the experiences of previous years.   (A.H.T.; F.; Col.; Univ. Instr. of Psy.; M.S.; Age 26)

INFERIORITY FEELING AND SHYNESS FROM UNFAVORABLE COMPARISONS OF HER HOMELINESS WITH SISTER'S PHYSICAL ATTRACTIVENESS, LEADING TO SUSPICION OF BEING AN ADOPTED WAIF; COMPENSATION THROUGH EARNING HIGH MARKS; DESIRE FOR ANNIHILATION TO ESCAPE TORTURE OF FACING AN AUDIENCE; PARTIAL RELIEF THROUGH EMULATION OF ADMIRED TEACHER WHO WAS CHARMING ALTHOUGH UGLY

The chief early difficulty which M. experienced was decidedly an inferiority complex. This condition may have been brought about by the fact that she had two older sisters who were unusually attractive both in appearance and in manner. M. began to realize that she was homely to an unusual degree when strangers commented on her sister's beauty and sometimes added, "Who is this little girl, she isn't related to you, is she?" Finally the thought came to her that she was a waif whom her mother and father, in the kindness of their hearts, had adopted. But she expressed this to no one.

Later on entering school M. was shy and self-conscious. She sought to bolster up her self-esteem by bringing home excellent marks in her studies. Occasionally she partook in little plays. Physical pain could not have caused her more torture. She can remember crossing a railroad track one evening on her way to take part in a Christmas program and wishing that an engine would run over her and thus relieve her of the necessity of reciting.

As M. grew to womanhood she realized that she was missing much in life that was worth while on account of this obsession. Admiration for a teacher who was charming in spite of lacking beauty taught her that there were other qualities more important than physical appearance.

She began to cultivate people and make friends, and they are now a source of great pleasure. But never to this day has she been able to overcome a feeling of panic when forced to confront even a small audience.   (G.M.; F.; S.C.T.; B.A.)

SELF-CONSCIOUSNESS AND INFERIORITY FEELINGS PRODUCED BY LACK OF BEAUTY, A PUG NOSE, FRECKLES, AND PERSISTENT DYSMENORRHEA; EXTERNAL PHYSICAL DEFECTS RENDERED MORE ACUTE BY APPLICATION OF NICKNAMES

I can't remember when I began to have inferiority feelings. I do remember that I was very young when I realized I wasn't pretty, and that hurt my feelings greatly. My sister and I were playing with older girls, pretending to be their little girls. Two of the girls quarreled over having my sister for their little girl. One of them said, "Oh, I will take Edith, she isn't pretty, but she will be good." Another hurt I well remember was when a boy called me "Pug," because my nose was so flat. I went home with the determination to do all I could to modify the nose. Every day I would spend some time in hiding with a clothespin fastened to the end of my nose. I can't remember where I heard of the clothespin remedy. One day when my sister found me with the clothespin on my nose she told mother. Mother said she would spank me if I used it again, because it might ruin my nose. That night father told me I had a nice nose and I was pretty to him, but I felt he said this only because he loved me. The clothespin remedy could not be consistently applied as someone always found me and reported to mother. Finally, father talked earnestly with me about this, telling me it was wrong and that I was trying to harm myself. Father could always get me to do what he wanted, but this did not lessen my feeling of inferiority. Soon afterward, I became conscious of also having freckles. A child called me "turkey egg." I did not know what that meant but upon inquiring at home, I found that a turkey egg was covered with little brown spots. Mother said if I would wear a bonnet I would not have freckles. So I endured a bonnet for some time. Although I did not wear it all the time, as it interfered with my play, I stopped worrying about looking nice, until it was time to be "dressed up"; then I felt very self-conscious. Nevertheless, the first twelve years of my life were the happiest.

My feeling of inferiority has been intensified by my persistent dysmenorrhea, described elsewhere, which led me to reject a teaching principalship. I felt I could not do the work of this position as it should be done because of this physical defect.

Of all the difficulties I have had, the feeling of inferiority has been my greatest hindrance. It has caused me frequently to change my natural way of living. And I believe this inferiority feeling is caused by my physical blemishes, especially the dysmenorrhea.   (R.E.; F.; E.S.T.; Age 35)

SHYNESS, SECLUSIVENESS, AND SENSITIVENESS ENGENDERED BY JOKES AND CRITICISMS LEVELED AT IMPUTED LACK OF PHYSICAL ATTRACTIVENESS; APPLICATION TO INTELLECTUAL PURSUITS AS COMPENSATION FOR ASSUMED PHYSICAL UGLINESS AND DEFECT; NATURE OF ATTEMPTED CORRECTION OF MALADJUSTMENTS

I was always made to believe that I should be able to control my actions wisely at all times. Being trained very carefully and strictly in order that I should be independent, I find that this training perhaps gave me my greatest personality defect. The experiences I went through may be briefly stated as follows.

It seems that I had the misfortune to be the most unattractive of five grandchildren, two girls and three boys. One of my earliest childhood memories brings the picture of my mother hugging me and saying, "You're ugly but you're sweet." I imagine that this must have been true, after comparing such a little brown child with the other curly-haired, blue-eyed granddaughter next door. To my dismay at about the age of six, I became conscious of the fact that my pet name around the house was "nigger." And when my uncle said that he believed some one took my mother's baby and left me instead, since I looked like no one in the family, I was ready to believe him.

My daddy was taking me for a walk one windy autumn day, when the uncle next door appeared with a heavy rope, and very gravely requested that it be tied to my leg or else I'd be sure to blow away. I had been sick a great deal, and that evening the mirror revealed the fact that I was skinny!

Mother had quite a problem when it came to choosing correct clothes for me. I wanted frills and bows, but she exclaimed they were impossible. Since I was such a plain child she solved the problem by buying me a boy's coat and hat (sport clothes then were in dark) just at the time when I thought boys an abomination. Can you picture me walking beside the other grandchildren, who had lovely rose coats (I remember the color) and a soft white neckpiece and muff? I did not go out many times; I stayed at home!

As I grew older, I began to grow taller, until I was the tallest person in my mother's family. My father's family were tall, but at my father's death, I went to live with my mother's people. Here I acquired the feeling of being gawky and I thought that I would never finish growing up.

I think the final climax came at about the age of fourteen. I had taken an inventory of any possible good points in my appearance. Fingernails and teeth were the only ones I could find. As I was laughing with a crowd of boys and girls one summer evening, one of them while running hit his head against my teeth and broke a moon in front of them. After the tragedy was over, the family laughingly said that possibly it would never have happened had I kept my big mouth shut. My mother then found herself faced with the problem of raising this tall, snaggled-toothed girl, who was very shy.

Among the attempts made to overcome my personality difficulties were the following:

When I was entering high school mother realized that I had taken to heart the jokes people played on me. To rid me of my self-consciousness, and to get me to associate with people, she finally gave me the dancing lessons I had longed for all my life.

To adjust matters I decided that if I couldn't be the prettiest grandchild, I would be the smartest one. When I was skipped a grade in school, I was able to face my uncle with a much stronger will.

My mother let me choose my own clothes with the thought that, if I felt contented, that was all that mattered. She took an apartment, and let me furnish it so that I might find self-expression. By doing this I realized that my thoughts were worth carrying out.

In college I realized that my height would never make me conspicuous. I learned to meet people and not to avoid them, even though I forced myself to do so. I became a more sociable individual and to the observer outgrew perhaps the ways of that little skinny girl.

And yet, I believe the mental patterns and early responses are with me to stay. The uncle reminded me this fall, after I lost weight at Hopkins, that he still had that rope.

I don't think that this is an inferiority complex in the true sense, since it does not carry over into my work. There I am completely at ease and happy. Even though I am without vanity, I had rather have the feeling of self-confidence than the thoughts I have to push into the background when I am with people. I have reasoned it all out with myself, laughed at it, and yet I am sensitive. The psychologist who said that all of our responses are the same as those we made to like situations at the ages from two to four years must have been correct. There are times when I still want to run into that corner and hide. (L.M.; F.; S.C.T.)

Mrs. Franklin D. Roosevelt in her autobiography describes herself as a "shy, solemn child who never smiled" because she was ashamed of her failure to inherit the pulchritude bestowed upon other feminine members of her family. The personality distortions produced by sensitiveness about looks are not always so subtle. The hero of Rostand's drama, Cyrano de Bergerac, famed for his bravery in the field, fought many duels because of uncomplimentary references to his elephantine nose. A young St. Louis chemical engineer committed suicide (in 1932) "because people couldn't let him forget that he had an uncommonly big nose." He said that he "feared the world but not death." A 17-year-old boy in New York City with a revolver fatally shot his 12-year-old cousin in the head (in 1936) whom he had invited to his home, because the latter taunted him with being skinny: "Skinny, skinny, you're nothing but a skinny." Brooding over one's physical limitations may even lead to such homicidal attacks as that of a 17-year-old St. Louis boy with a paralyzed left leg who killed one police officer and wounded two others in Oklahoma (in 1937) because his infirmity prevented him from "being a policeman and having excitement." [10]

THE INTELLECTUALLY HANDICAPPED

The second major group of handicapped children, the intellectually handicapped, is more numerous than the group of the physically handicapped, unless all degrees and types of physical handicaps are included. This group includes a great variety of grades and types of children who are subject to intellectual limitations or defects. It includes all children whose abilities are limited in some way. The intellectually handicapped group can be divided into two main subdivisions: the generically deficient and backward and the specifically handicapped.

1. **The Generically Deficient and Backward.** This includes the group of children who fall at the lower end of the curve of distribution of general intelligence, the 1 per cent, more or less, who are the most deficient in general ability and intelligence. This constitutes the mentally deficient group. It also includes the next higher level of ability, the 2 or 3 per cent who constitute the group of so-called borderline and backward children. All of these children are lacking in all-round ability or general alertness, some because of native defect, and some because of acquired handicaps. Some of these, however, may be merely apparently deficient (pseudoatypical).

The most important single cause of the deficiency in the mentally deficient group is defective inheritance. A cacogenic heredity is likewise the cause of the intellectual limitations in many of the borderline and backward cases. Various environmental factors also play important roles in the causation of the different degrees of mental retardation. The proper application of existing knowledge would prevent many cases of mental defect.

All of these children constitute problems for mental hygiene because (a) they require special training to enable them to make the most of their possibilities, and (b) they are prone to develop many personality difficulties and

[10] References:
F. B. Riggs, *Tall Men Have Their Problems Too*, Cambridge, Mass. (privately published), 1943.
Mildred G. Ryan, *Your Clothes and Personality*, New York, Appleton-Century-Crofts, Inc., 1937.

idiosyncrasies, largely as a result of the difficulties they encounter in the attempts to adjust themselves to the home and school requirements and to the demands made by parents, teachers, siblings, and playmates.[11] Repeated failures in school and the sneers, jibes, and jeers from children and adults may have caused great emotional upsets in these children and rendered them sullen, resentful, and discouraged. The reception frequently accorded backward children calls to mind the reply of the office boy. The office boy, when asked by the visitor, "Who is the responsible man in this firm?" replied, "I don't know who the responsible party is but I am the one who always gets the blame."

The following case is illustrative of how some backward children react to repeated failure in school.

THREAT OF DESTROYING HIMSELF IN A FURNACE BECAUSE OF FAILURE
TO WIN PROMOTION; SENSITIVENESS BECAUSE OF ADVANCEMENT OF
YOUNGER FOSTER BROTHERS

Henry S., colored, born of illegitimate parents, placed in a home because the mother disappeared, was sent to our school as a backward child. He was sensitive

[11] For a discussion of the educational and other problems of the mentally deficient and retarded group, consult the following

Harry J. Baker, *Introduction to Exceptional Children*, New York, The Macmillan Company, 1944, 244–272, 425–451.

Cyril Burt, *The Subnormal Mind*, New York, Oxford University Press, 1935; *The Backward Child*, Bickley, Kent, England, University of London Press, Ltd., 1937.

Leonard Carmichael, ed., *Manual of Child Psychology*, John Wiley & Sons, Inc., 1946, 845–885 (by Edgar A. Doll).

Roy M. Dorcus and G. Wilson Shaffer, *Textbook of Abnormal Psychology*, Baltimore, The Williams & Wilkins Company, 1935, 293–310.

John Duncan, *The Education of the Ordinary Child, Lankhills Method*, New York, The Ronald Press Company, 1943.

William B. Featherstone, *Teaching the Slow Learner*, New York, Columbia University Press, 1941.

Karl C. Garrison, *The Psychology of Exceptional Children*, New York, The Ronald Press Company, 1940, 157–233.

Philip L. Harriman, ed., *Encyclopedia of Psychology*, New York, Philosophical Library, Inc., 1946, 184–198 (by Elaine E. Kinder).

Arch O. Heck, *The Education of Exceptional Children*, New York, McGraw-Hill Book Company, Inc., 1940, 341–388.

Mary E. Hill, *The Education of Backward Children*, London, George G. Harrap & Co., Ltd., 1939.

Christine P. Ingram, *Education of the Slow-learning Child*, Yonkers, New York, World Book Company, 1935.

Annie D. Inskeep, *Teaching Dull and Retarded Children*, New York, The Macmillan Company, 1930.

(*Footnote continued on p.* 195)

because he has foster brothers who are younger but more advanced than he is. At times he appears to be mentally deficient; when irritated he is stubborn; he is inclined to be dishonest. He is very talkative and fond of reading, but only comprehends at times. He can spell and write well, but is poor in arithmetic. He was promoted to the fifth grade on trial, but failed of promotion. When he found this out he became greatly depressed, and especially so when he went home and learned that his brothers had been promoted. He completely gave up, saying that he had tried all he could and that he was going to get into the furnace and burn himself up. It was such a pitiful case that he was allowed to go up on trial. When he grows weary of the effort he falls back on reading, which seems to have a soothing effect.   (From M.L.A.; F.; Col.; E.S.T.)

Failure in studies or failure of promotion and overstudy have devastating effects on some students who have not learned how to resolve their worries and to avoid despondency. Such is the case of a Villanova, Pa., schoolgirl of 15 (in 1933), who telephoned to her mother at a bridge party that she was about to commit suicide because of two failures in the same subject at a preparatory school. Before the mother could return, the girl was dead from a bullet wound in the head.

Carney Landis and Marjorie M. Bolles, *Textbook of Abnormal Psychology*, New York, The Macmillan Company, 1946, 130–148, 253f.

Robert M. Lindner and R. V. Sellger, *Handbook of Correctional Psychology*, New York, Philosophical Library, Inc., 1947, 174–193 (by Gale H. Walker), 194–207 (by Effie C. Ireland), 208–225 (by Theodora M. Abel).

Chauncey M. Louttit, *Clinical Psychology*, rev. ed., New York, Harper & Brothers, 1947, 175–302.

Elise H. Martens, *A Guide to Curriculum Adjustment for Mentally Retarded Children*, Washington, U.S. Office of Education, Bulletin 11, 1936.

James D. Page, *Abnormal Psychology*, New York, McGraw-Hill Book Company, Inc., 1947, Chap. XVII.

Stanley D. Porteus, *The Practice of Clinical Psychology*, New York, American Book Company, 1941, 228–255, 403–420.

Mandel Sherman, *Intelligence and Its Deviations*, New York, The Ronald Press Company, 1945, 126–137, 236–245.

Charles E. Skinner, ed., *Educational Psychology*, New York, Prentice-Hall, Inc., 1945, 533–554 (by J. E. W. Wallin).

Florence M. Teagarden, *Child Psychology for Professional Workers*, rev. ed., New York, Prentice-Hall, Inc., 1946, 404–409.

Alfred F. Tredgold, *A Textbook of Mental Deficiency*, 6th ed., Baltimore, William Wood & Company, 1937, 449–476.

J. E. Wallace Wallin, "Mental Defectives," in *Encyclopedia of Educational Research*, New York, The Macmillan Company, 1941, 81–88 (revision with Harold C. Reppert); also, *Children with Mental and Physical Handicaps*, New York, Prentice-Hall, Inc., 1949; and *The Education of Handicapped Children*, 5th printing, Boston, Houghton Mifflin Company, 1939.

Ralph Winterbourn, *Educating Backward Children in New Zealand*, New York, Oxford University Press, 1944.

The record for one year (1936) contains runaways, murders, and suicides:

A 10-year-old Philadelphia girl who had been playing the violin since she was 2 years old ran away twice within 2 weeks because she was "tired of practicing."

A 13-year-old Harrisburg, Pa., girl, daughter of a district attorney, hitchhiked with truck drivers to New York to "hide the shame" of a flunk in Latin. Her identity was revealed after 3 days on "toast and cocoa," when her money was gone. "I worried a couple of days after my teacher said I'd get a D on my report card."

A Lehigh University student, 23, committed suicide after shooting his English instructor twice with fatal results, because he was refused a reexamination in English, in which he "rated less than 1 per cent short of a passing mark." (Are examination marks sufficiently accurate to justify a flunk on a deficit of one point?) "He was a diligent student but often graded low, and was unnerved by hard pre-examination work and the failure to pass."

A 21-year-old medical student at the University of Chicago, with a prior brilliant scholastic record at Columbia, "stabbed himself fatally with a scalpel in a fit of despondency." According to his roommate, "all he would say was that he was tired of school and life and would have ended it all long ago if it were not that he hated to hurt his parents. . . . When I am dead there will be no standards by which I can be judged."

A Pleasantville, N.Y., botanist, 22, son of a former Columbia and University of Wisconsin professor, with a brilliant record in botany, committed suicide with poison while in Massachusetts, because he was "despondent and suffering from overstudy. He was tired of living."

A 46-year-old postgraduate student in a Fordham University night class was held under $2,000 bail for "threatening by mail to bomb the school and kill the two professors who refused him a chemistry degree."

The following year chronicles the finding of an 11-year-old Indianapolis girl in a vacant house "suffering from frostbite and hunger, lying on blankets . . . because she was 'afraid to go home and show her report card.'" Another girl, 11 years of age, in Caldwell, Tex., who "had learned she failed for the second time to win promotion from the sixth grade was found shot to death in her parents' bedroom, a pistol by her side."

In Nutley, N.J., a 12-year-old boy "shot himself in the abdomen with his father's pistol because he did not want to take a guitar lesson" when his mother reminded him that it was the day for it. His mother had not taken seriously his threat: "If I have to take my music lesson I'll shoot myself."

In Muskogee, Okla., a high-school girl of 16 told the court she was "not sorry" she shot at her English teacher, because "she gave me low grades."

2. The Specifically Handicapped. On a very conservative estimate, from 10 to 15 per cent of school children manifest specific intellectual disabilities or limitations. These limitations may affect any intellectual function, such as memory; visual, auditory, or motor imagery; attention; association of ideas; and abstract thinking. Not all the limitations or disabilities are inherent or constitutional or permanent. Some are merely apparent or spurious (pseudoatypical). Some are temporary, transient, or correctable by effective therapeutic procedures. Doubtless, many specific intellectual handicaps are associated with disabilities in the types of curricular subject matter that are functionally related to the mental functions that are impaired, *e.g.*, disabilities in reading, spelling, arithmetic, writing, drawing, or singing.

We should, of course, recognize that not all children who are scholastically handicapped or deficient are intellectually handicapped. Those who are intellectually handicapped will be educationally handicapped more or less, but those subject to specific or general educational difficulties may not be subject to intellectual limitations. There are intellectually normal children who encounter difficulties in various types of curricular subject matter. Educational incapacities may be due to many causes other than intellectual limitations, such as inappropriate methods of teaching, lack of application, specific scholastic weaknesses, lack of learning drive, and unfortunate emotional conditioning.

Illustrations of Specific Scholastic Disabilities Due to Unfortunate Emotional Conditioning. We are beginning to realize more and more that adverse emotional conditioning may produce definite scholastic difficulties, as is shown by the following illustrations.

HATRED FOR SPELLING AND THE PRODUCTION OF APPARENT DISABILITY
IN SPELLING BECAUSE OF EMOTIONAL REVULSION AGAINST A BRUTAL-
IZING TEACHER WHO PADDLED THE HAND FOR EVERY WORD MISSED

My record throughout school has been a very pronounced case of scattering. I cannot recall a single week, month, or year of public school life that I did not stand at the foot of the class in spelling and at the head of the class in mathematics. While in the fifth grade I was compelled to stay in for spelling every day but three during the year. This condition grew out of an experience that I had during my first year in school. The teacher who was teaching that grade was unquestionably the most brutal and cruel I have ever witnessed. After more than twenty-five years I approached a group of students who had gone to her and I asked them whom they considered to be the meanest teacher they had ever gone to and they all said, "Why, Miss H. of course." To give an illustration of her brutality: A boy came into the room on a very cold morning a few minutes late. For his excuse he gave the reason that he had stopped in a house to get his hands and feet warm. She became furious and forced him to put his overcoat on and then encased him between some metal screens and a red-hot stove that was used for heating the room. She was so cruel that she was finally forced to resign during the period when discipline was considered the first law of all school virtues. It was with this teacher that I soon acquired my aversion for spelling and it was not until I met a real, genuine teacher of English in high school that I overcame my aversion and started to rebuild my spelling habits. The situation in particular that produced the disastrous effects was this: The teacher had made it a rule that when a child missed a word in the spelling lesson she would paddle his hand for each word that was misspelled. Naturally the day arrived when I missed a word and became a subject for punishment. The emotional fear that crept over me when I saw her coming toward me has never lost its effect. I had been corrected for misdemeanors by my mother but it was always in a humane and rational way. I knew why I was being corrected. But now I could not see where I had violated any rules of the social order (and I don't yet) and her fierce approach completely upset me for the moment. I didn't cry or do anything except to turn pale with fright and an hour later was sent home by the teacher because I was sick. Since that time I have learned that the sickness was probably due to an upset autonomic nervous system. That ended it with me for spelling or anything akin to it. My interest in spelling was so effectively killed that I literally hated the very thought of spelling. This condition stayed with me until I reached the high school. Here there was an English teacher who became very much concerned over my abuse of all the rules of spelling, so she called me to her for an interview. In the interview she stated that my work in English was above the average of the class as far as the content matter was concerned but my spelling was "atrocious." Further, she said that she knew I could learn to spell if I went at it the right way and she proceeded to assist me. The first word that she approached was "receive" and I found for the first time that it is possible to keep "e" and "i" in their proper order in spelling. Since that time I have acquired a fair proficiency in spelling although I find tendencies to revert back to a lot of old habits that I formed before I made any attempt to correct the difficulty.

(M.E.M.; M.; Director Vocational Guidance in T.C.; M.A.; Age 33)

DISLIKE FOR SPELLING ENGENDERED BY FALSE ACCUSATION BY A TEACHER, RESULTING IN A SPELLING DISABILITY

I started to school at the age of six years and three months. I will always remember my first teacher and my happy experiences in her room. My second year also was a happy one and I made an excellent report.

The trouble started in the third grade when we had a spelling test and I was the only pupil that made a hundred on the test. The teacher, Miss P., said to me, "I believe you cheated as you are the only child who made a hundred." I was crushed and shall never forget the feeling I had of being accused of cheating.

Then she said, "Now tell me, didn't you copy these words from something?" I said, "No ma'm I did not," but she would not believe me and went to the principal, Miss T., and told her that I had cheated on the spelling test and would not confess it.

Miss T., an ideal in my young mind and later my seventh-grade teacher, called me to her office and talked to me. She saw that I was telling the truth and believed me. She saw also my sudden dislike, almost hatred, for Miss P.

I may say here, in all my school experiences I have never cheated and was never accused of this awful thing but this one time. Of all the teachers I have had, ninety-one in all, she is the only teacher I ever disliked.

But to my query, "Why I cannot spell?" From this experience I acquired a dislike for spelling, and to this day I am a poor speller. I don't have any confidence in myself when it comes to spelling. At the end of the third year when promotion time came, I failed in spelling but was promoted on condition owing to the principal's influence. Spelling continued to be my weakness through grammar school. Of course, when I went to high school and college, spelling was not taught as a separate subject but I found I was more deficient in this than in any other subject.   (P.A.; F.; S.C.T.)

LOSS OF ABILITY TO READ IN SCHOOL BECAUSE OF EMOTIONAL DISTURB-
ANCE, SENSITIVENESS, EMBARRASSMENT, AND RESENTMENT AT BEING
CALLED THE TEACHER'S PET OWING TO THE FACT THAT THE TEACHER
WAS ENGAGED TO THE RESPONDENT'S BROTHER

At the time that I transferred from a delightful private school to a formal third-grade class, as explained elsewhere, I read better than any of the other children in the class, and the children thought I was wonderful because I read so well. Instead of giving me pleasure, this caused me embarrassment, no doubt due to the fact that I was very timid, and I became resentful because I was called the teacher's pet, owing to the fact that the teacher was engaged to my brother. I soon got so I did not want to read, became very much disturbed when asked to read, and finally got so that I could scarcely read at all at school. The teacher told my brother and he asked me to bring my reader home. I was delighted to do anything for him, and read him story after story. He and my teacher decided that it was the school experience that had upset me, and the teacher tried to help me. She had to be very cautious as she could not give me much attention without causing unfavorable comment. I became more adjusted as the year went on but I was never happy in that grade and was so glad when school was out in the spring.
                                    (D.M.; F.; E.S. Supv.; B.S.; Age 41)

Specific scholastic difficulties, which are found not only in intellectually normal children, but also in bright or talented children, often yield to properly adjusted and motivated instructional procedures. The following is an illustration of a reading disability, one of Marion Monroe's cases.[12]

Betty, aged 7, in the second grade, had not learned to read after 2 years in school, although she had a Stanford-Binet I.Q. of 135. She had memorized the primer in the first grade, but could recognize only a few isolated words in unfamiliar material. In a number of standardized reading tests her outstanding errors included difficulty of forming visual and auditory associations, the omission of sounds, the tendency to read backward, difficulties with

[12] Marion Monroe, *Children Who Cannot Read*, Chicago, University of Chicago Press, 1932, 159f.

vowels, and the refusal to attempt to read. She rationalized her difficulty by stating, "I don't happen to care for reading about little pigs. I would not mind reading about astronomy, though." This case is of interest in showing what can be accomplished by remedial reading instruction. After 60 hours of such instruction in 30-minute periods several times a week, from May to September in the following year, she improved 3.4 years in reading ability (in 1.3 years) and later added 1.5 years more in reading accomplishments without special instruction. Her reading index rose from 0.41 to 1.06, *i.e.*, from the condition of a severe reading handicap to a high average. At the time of the first test, she was 1 year retarded in reading, but at the time of the last test she was advanced almost 2 years. Her average reading grade at the age of 9 years and 5 months was 6.3.

The generically deficient or backward may also be subject to specific disabilities in reading or arithmetic or other subject matter. Specific educational disabilities are usually more severe in the intellectually limited than in normal individuals, because they are in the first instance more frequently based on real, specific mental disabilities than is the case with normal children. This, however, is not always true.

Only the high lights of one case from our clinic files can be given, for illustrative purposes—that of an intellectually backward boy with a reading disability. His Stanford-Binet ratings were as follows: at the age of 9-2, a Binet age of 7-0, I.Q. 78; at 10-2, a Binet of 8-8, I.Q. 85; and at 12-3 a Terman-Merrill Binet age (Form L) of 10-0, I.Q. 82. In the Wallin-Gilbert-Cutsforth Individual Attainment Scale at 10-2, he could read only a few words; he could spell none of the words in the first-grade list; he rated grade I in written language achievement, and grade II in arithmetic achievement. In the Monroe Diagnostic Reading Test, his average reading grade at that time was 1.2, spelling grade 1.3, and arithmetic grade 2.8. He knew four letters of the alphabet; showed extreme confusion with the letters *b, d, p, q,* and *n;* he had vague ideas as to the proper orientation of letters and words; and was a mirror reader and writer. His most frequent errors were faulty vowels and consonants, reversals, addition of sounds, and repetitions. He showed no eye preference, but seemed to be right-handed. In the Betts telebinocular test he scored normal, except for sharpness of image for distance and for reading distance.

The recommendations made for overcoming these difficulties were based on Marion Monroe's procedures, together with finger tracing of letters and words while pronouncing the letters and the words. Two months later he was admitted to a remedial reading group and received from the psychoeducational examiner 12 hours of remedial reading instruction during the next 4 months, in weekly periods of from 35 to 45 minutes each. Two weeks after the termination of the special reading instruction, his average reading grade had advanced from grade 1.2 to grade 2.1. His oral reading grade was 1.9, silent reading grade 2.2, word recognition 2.3, word discrimination 2.3, and ability in sounding words 2.7. About a year and a half later (while in the fifth grade), he rated III plus in reading and language, II plus in spelling, and II in arithmetic, on the Wallin-Gilbert-Cutsforth scale.

What are the effects of specific disabilities on school progress? Sometimes a specific disability may prove very disastrous to the child's school progress and adjustment to the school requirements for at least four reasons:

1. It may cause discouragement, indifference, hostility, or rebellion against the school because of repeated failure to overcome the disability.

2. It may develop a morbid consciousness of the handicap, which in turn may produce a train of maladjustments, due either to discouragement from the unsuccessful attempt to overcome the disability, to unwise criticisms of the child, or to the attitude displayed toward the handicap by other children, by the parents, or by teachers who do not understand the nature of the child's difficulty.

3. It may cause the pupil to develop a violent antipathy toward a certain branch of study and toward the teacher of that subject. Therefore, the child fails to make progress in that branch because of unfortunate emotional conditioning.

4. The disability may affect a pivotal type of subject matter on which scholastic progress intimately depends. Thus the child is unable to progress satisfactorily in school. For example, a reading disability would handicap the child in practically every subject that is dependent on reading. In a school in which the major source of information is obtained from the printed page, a child with a decided reading disability would suffer a very serious handicap and might, because of this handicap, be transferred to a class for the mentally deficient unless he were carefully examined psychologically.

Treatment of Specific Scholastic Disabilities. What is involved in the treatment of these disabilities? Briefly, (1) the discovery of the nature of the defects and their causes by a thorough case study, and (2) the removal or mitigation of the defect, usually by processes of remedial and diagnostic instruction. One of the major objectives of the program of remedial instruction and special education is the correction of specific disabilities. In addition, the correction often involves mental-hygiene treatment. The mental-hygiene treatment will concern itself not only with finding the cause of the handicap but also with determining the pupil's attitude toward it, overcoming injurious attitudes, and correcting any personality maladjustments that may have originated from the defect. Frequently it also involves the adjustment of the teacher's and the parent's attitude, as well as the attitude of other children, toward the defect and toward the child.

Attitude for Teachers to Assume toward Specific Educational Disabilities. In general, it is well to assume the attitude that specific educational disabilities are correctable, so that a reasonable effort to remedy them will be made before all effort is abandoned. The child should always be given the benefit of the doubt. Fortunately many specific educational disabilities are not due to inherent mental or brain defects but to adventitious causes that can be corrected, such as sensorimotor defects, maladjusted methods of instruction, excessive stupefying drills, and dislike for the subject matter. Dislike of subject matter may be due to unfortunate emotional conditioning, which is often produced by ridicule, punishment, criticism, or harsh treatment at the hands of parents or teachers or others. The harsh treatment referred to in two of the above case histories can be classified only as educational malpractice. Such harshness is probably less prevalent now than formerly. Disabilities based on such factors as the above are apparent rather than constitutional, and often temporary rather than permanent. By the removal of hampering sensorimotor defects, by the application of remedial teaching techniques that meet the child's peculiar needs (as revealed by clinical study), and by appropriate emotional conditioning, such disabilities can often be corrected if treatment is afforded before the disability becomes fixed.

The literature is strewn with records of specific educational disabilities which were diagnosed as irremediable, but which were eventually overcome by proper orthogenic treatment and motivated learning. For example, during a 3-year period 3,000 children in the New York City schools who were failing in their classwork received special instruction from "W.P.A. remedial reading teachers." According to a press summary, "2,700 were found to respond to treatment and a majority of them were returned to the classroom within a year." Most of the 300 who made little progress "were found to be emotionally starved," and craved affection. Almost all of the "true non-readers" in remedial reading groups in the Los Angeles public schools made notable improvements from the instructional techniques employed, according to Grace M. Fernald, who also reports almost 100 per cent of corrections in her clinic groups, consisting of both extreme and partial reading-disability cases, by the application of her kinesthetic approach (finger tracing of whole words from visualization, accompanied by word pronunciation).[13] The large majority of these children were intellectually normal or supernormal.

[13] Grace M. Fernald, *Remedial Techniques in Basic School Subjects,* New York, McGraw-Hill Book Company, Inc., 1943.

The literature on reading is so extensive that it is possible to cite only a few of the more important books:

Emmett A. Betts, *The Prevention and Correction of Reading Difficulties,* Evanston, Ill., Row, Peterson & Company, 1936.

(*Footnote continued on p.* 203)

It is undoubtedly true that many specific scholastic disabilities that have in past years been considered to be irremediable can be overcome by improved developmental, corrective, or remedial teaching techniques.   The author's use of kinesthetic and tactual methods in highly simplified form (finger tracing of elevated and depressed letters and words and Montessori's sandpaper letters, besides letter and word tracing in large script with a pointer in the sandbox) began with mental defectives in Pittsburgh in 1912.   Extensive use of these simplified procedures, as well as of the more elaborate methods of Grace Fernald, Marion Monroe, and Donald Durrell, have brought excellent results in some cases, moderate results in some, and little improvement in others.   Unfortunately, because of other exacting duties, time has not availed for close follow-up for determining to what extent the recommendations have been carried out.   In spite of the great progress made in the field of remediation of specific scholastic disabilities, we still find in practice in the schools (perhaps because of the application of faulty teaching techniques and lack of learning motivation) many children whose disabilities have not been corrected, but only mitigated.   Inherent or constitutional disabilities on a background of mental subnormality and disabilities produced by brain injuries are the most resistant to the processes of instruction.   Such disabilities call to mind the answer of the retiring college president to the query of the visiting alumnus.   The alumnus was curious to know what had impressed the president most during his many years of teaching.   To this query the president replied, "The thing that has impressed me most profoundly is the infinite capacity of the human mind to resist the introduction of knowledge."   Many teachers who have labored for years with the techniques that the specialists have supplied to overcome children's educational handicaps will reecho that reply.

By persistent drill the child with innate specific disabilities, especially when these are accompanied by varying degrees of generic mental defect, can sometimes be brought up to passing standard; but he tends to retrogress eventually to his inherent level.   Sometimes, because of the discouraging toil and trouble that persistent drill has forced him to live through, he may have developed attitudes that constitute greater handicaps to life success than the educational

Edward W. Dolch, *A Manual for Remedial Reading,* 2d ed., Champaign, Ill., The Garrard Press, 1945.

Donald D. Durrell, *Improvement of Basic Reading Difficulties,* Yonkers, New York, World Book Company, 1937.

Arthur I. Gates, *The Improvement of Reading,* New York, The Macmillan Company, 1935.

Samuel A. Kirk, *Teaching Reading to Slow-Learning Children,* Boston, Houghton Mifflin Company, 1940.

David H. Russell, Etta E. Karp, and Edward I. Kelly, *Reading Aids through the Grades,* New York, Teachers College, Columbia University, 1938.

disability itself offers. The child may have become so disappointed and cynical from years of failure and from the repeated admonitions and criticisms to which he has been subjected that he may have developed undesirable compensations and character traits that will constitute a far greater handicap than that of his educational disability.

The Existence of Specific Disabilities Not Incompatible with Normal or Superior General Ability. One thought may be emphasized in this connection that should give comfort to anyone who may be apprehensive that he is not "all there."   It is that there are many persons who have specific "shorts" but who are otherwise normal or even above normal. They may have achieved success or even eminence in many walks of life because of the possession of other social, mental, or physical traits, although they failed in high school or college because of one or more specific scholastic incompetencies, for which they may not have been responsible. The schools may have tried in vain to correct these deficiencies, and, when they failed to do so (often, no doubt, because of the use of inappropriate teaching methods), the child was penalized. Many instances can be cited of children and youth who failed in school for some reason or other and who became famous in after life.

Linnaeus, the great Swedish botanist, did so poorly in college that his father (a vicar) wanted to apprentice him to a tradesman. His gymnasium director advised the father to make a cobbler of him because he was unfit for a learned profession. However, a physician who recognized Linnaeus's industry and ability brought him to his lifework, and he became the greatest naturalist of his generation. Charles Darwin has reported the observation that he was singularly incapable of mastering any language and that he was considered by his masters and by his father to be a very ordinary boy. In fact, his father declared that he would be a disgrace to himself and his family; yet he became one of the greatest scientists that England has produced. Napoleon Bonaparte, the greatest military genius of his day, ranked forty-second in his class in the final examination. Can anyone name a single one of the forty-one students who surpassed him? Napoleon failed to distinguish himself in the military school, except possibly in mathematics. He was unable to spell words in any language with any accuracy. Isaac Newton, the great physicist and discoverer of the law of gravity, declared that at twelve, "he was extremely inattentive to his studies and stood very low in school." He showed so little ability in his schoolwork that he was put to work on a farm at the age of fifteen. He failed in his Euclid in the university. (Was this due to his unwillingness to conform to "approved" procedures?) Jonathan Swift, great British satirist and novelist, the greatest prose writer of the eighteenth century, manifested no brilliance or promise in his college studies. He was refused his degree because of "dullness and insufficiency," although the degree was granted to him later as a special favor. He failed in two out of three subjects in his final examination.

Robert Fulton, the great American inventor—designer of the first successful steamboat, in 1807—was considered dull by his teachers, who applied the rod liberally as a stimulant. Perhaps he was considered dull because his mind was preoccupied with other interests or because he had been unfavorably conditioned emotionally. G. W. F. Hegel, one of the greatest philosophers produced by Germany, the founder of Absolute Idealism, was considered mediocre in the lower schools. The certificate presented him on leaving the university stated that he was of average industry and especially deficient in philosophy. George Byron, the great satirical poet, was at the foot of his class in Aberdeen Grammar School. At Trinity College, Cambridge, he was "never anything but a poor scholar bestowing little care on the studies of the place." M. Pierre Curie, codiscoverer of radium, was considered so stupid in school that his parents withdrew him and placed him under private tutors. Many other cases could be cited, including Lowell, Beecher, Goethe, Pasteur, Webster, George Eliot, and John Adams.

The Necessity of Adjusting Curriculums to the Biological and Psychological Facts of Individual Differences. Some day, when we have made our educational theories and practices conform more fully to the biological and psychological facts of individual differences, and when we have provided courses of study sufficiently flexible to meet the needs of all children, we shall no longer attempt to force all children to conform to a narrow and rigid curriculum. Nor shall we continue the process of ruthlessly "flunking" normal children who may be innocent and helpless victims of incurable specific handicaps. On the contrary, in both the higher and the lower schools, we shall follow the sensible practice in vogue in the special classes for the mentally deficient, in which we do not "fail" children. In these classes we allow each child to progress just as fast as he can in each branch of study. When we encounter irremediable deficiencies, as we frequently do, we attempt to develop desirable compensations. We allow each child to develop proficiencies in substitute activities along the line of his special interests and aptitudes. We attempt to discover what potentials each pupil may possess, to capitalize his assets, to stimulate his creativeness, and to develop a success morale.

Application of the Doctrine of Creative Education to the Handicapped. Let no one infer that the program of creative education pertains only to normal or talented children. The precepts of the theory of creative education are applicable also to children subject to specific or generic handicaps, although, obviously, the generically deficient will possess less creative ability than will normal or bright children. Nevertheless, many handicapped children possess talents or aptitudes along certain lines, and there is danger that these aptitudes may be snuffed out by efforts to suppress spontaneity, or by failure to provide the pupils with opportunities for creative constructiveness, or by too rigid insistence on compliance with routine and stereotyped procedures. In order that she may not run the risk of extinguishing the spark of genius, the discerning teacher will be very slow to suppress or interfere with the child's spontaneous interests or attempts at creative work merely because these do not conform to her pet theories or because he does not follow conventional patterns.

One is reminded of Hugo Mearn's story of calling upon a young woman in London, who had become renowned as a portrait painter, to offer his congratulations upon her merited success and also to express pride in the fact that the excellent art instruction she had received in an American public-school system, of which he was superintendent, had started her upon her brilliant career. Imagine his chagrin when she turned upon him with the blunt declaration that her artistic success had been achieved, not because of, but in spite of, the art instruction she had received in the public school. She then related how the art supervisor, in the course of her periodic rounds of inspection, had glanced at her sketches and had repeatedly manifested her disapproval of them because they did not harmonize with her own ideas. She had crumpled the papers and cast them into the wastebasket, thus doing everything she could to discourage the embryo artist and stifle her spontaneity and originality.

The safe rule for teachers to follow when dealing with dominant trends and interests in children, be they dull or brilliant, is to vouchsafe a maximum of encouragement with a minimum of interference or suppression. For all the teacher may know, the child's dominant trend may be the expression of a latent talent that may set a new vogue or standard of value. Sympathetic, appreciative guidance should replace overdirection and insistence upon rigid accordance with traditional procedures. Even when the child's penchants seem to be undesirable, destructive, or antisocial, the positive method of substitution or diversion is usually preferable to the negative method of suppression. Certainly so far as constructive application is concerned, the child must be allowed the liberty of doing some of his tasks in his own way without undue outside interference. Constantly to correct, criticize, dictate, dominate, and control the child's methods of solving his problems is tantamount to depriving him of his inalienable birthright—the exploratory pursuit of his own tasks in his own way. Self-determination and self-direction in the mastery of an absorbing task make for mental concentration, integration, virility, and health.

THE INTELLECTUALLY NORMAL WHO ARE SUBJECT TO PERSONALITY TWISTS OR DISTURBANCES OR EMOTIONAL CONFLICTS

This classification contains the largest group of children who are subject to some kind of adjustment difficulties, not only because the group of the intellectually normal children is far more numerous than the combined groups of the physically and intellectually handicapped, but probably also because the normal and the bright, especially those with highly sensitive nervous systems, develop a larger ratio and a greater variety of minor personality problems than do the duller witted defectives. As has already been emphasized, inventories of personality maladjustments have demonstrated that very few intellectually normal or superior individuals are entirely free from some kind or some degree of personality difficulty or peculiarity. Some of the specific mental maladjustments that the intellectually normal are prone to develop have already been referred to in the foregoing pages, particularly in Chaps. II, III, and V, and others will be described in greater detail in Part II. Here it is sufficient to emphasize two conclusions, the importance of which has been brought out again and again in our autobiographies of maladjustment.

Lack of Recognition and Neglect of the Minor or More Insidious Types of Personality Disturbances. Many of our respondents have pointed out that no one ever knew anything about the inner conflicts and struggles that they endured. Even some of the older adults have stated that the first revelation of the mental difficulties they had experienced since early life was made in the "inventory" submitted to the writer. One reason for the lack of recognition by parents, teachers, or others of children's adjustment difficulties and minor personality disturbances is that subjective difficulties are often very subtle and develop so slowly that they are not easily recognized. Frequently the victims themselves do not clearly recognize their difficulties and, when they do recognize them, they often conceal them because they are ashamed of them. Childish pride leads to concealment or suppression. Therefore, since the victim is not known to present any special problem, no attempt is made by the parent, the teacher, or the subject to overcome the trouble.

Again, when the difficulties have been recognized, they have often been misunderstood, misinterpreted, or minimized. In consequence, they have been improperly or inefficiently handled. The remedial measures invoked have often been confined to the treatment of the symptoms, *i.e.*, attempts to remove the symptoms (such as fears, timidities, obstinacy, deceitfulness, nail biting, and the like) by advice, suggestion, command, reproof, ridicule, or punishment, in order that the child's overt behavior will conform to conventional social or educational standards. The treatment has been analogous to that employed by the doctor who treats headaches by removing the symptom through the use of an anodyne instead of tracking down and removing the cause. Little or no attempt has been made by the average parent or teacher to comprehend the dynamics of mental maladjustments. Mental idiosyncrasies are first of all symptoms. The important thing about any symptom (be it a phobia, an obsession, an anxiety, a conflict, or compensation) is not the symptomatic act itself, but the underlying disturbance of which it is the symptom. Symptoms are warning signals that must be comprehended and correctly interpreted. They point to some kind of underlying maladjustment, just as a headache is a symptom of the presence of some disturbing causative factor that must be removed in order that the condition may be cured. One medical authority, after perusing textbooks, encyclopedias, and articles, as well as recalling his own experience, listed 120 causes of headaches. Among them are gas pressure from the stomach and intestines, eyestrain, brain tumors, hardening of the arteries, worry, and lack of sleep.[14] Just as a headache is not a disease in itself, but a symptom that may point to an unsuspected or obscure trouble spot in some other part of the organism, so mental abnormalities often point to concealed causes. Mental symptoms are the natural effects of multiple causes, and ordinarily cannot be effectively treated until the causes have been discovered and removed. Often the real causes of mental symptoms are very difficult to locate. The causes are sometimes more obscure than the symptoms. Many mental abnormalities develop so gradually and insidiously that they are not recognized until they have become thoroughly ingrained, long after the causes have been forgotten, even if they were recognized at all. Sometimes a symptom is merely one phase of a complex network of related maladjustments based on a nexus of causes, some of primary moment, some merely contributory. Both the causes and the symptoms may appear in sequences or in simultaneous patterns or constellations.

Here, then, is a large borderland of adjustment difficulties and personality distortions that have been largely ignored, neglected, or minimized. Frequently they have been mishandled or maltreated, not of course intentionally or deliberately or maliciously, but because they have been misunderstood or have been considered as of no consequence. In general, our attitude in the past toward these adjustment problems has been one of smug complacency and *laissez faire*. As parents and teachers, we have not frankly faced these difficulties in ourselves or in our children. When we have recognized idiosyncrasies and maladjustments, we have tended to ignore them as trivial incidents of the day's work, or we have jested unconcernedly about many of them, often in the child's presence, as something "cute" or smart which is innocuous and which does not require prophylaxis or treatment.

Unfortunate Results of Policy of Neglect. It is true that many behavior idiosyncrasies or anomalies do not constitute a serious bar to social

[14] For a comprehensive treatise on headaches, consult Harold G. Wolff, *Headache and Other Head Pains,* New York, Oxford University Press, 1948.

or vocational success or a serious threat to the preservation of mental health. But we are beginning to realize that many personality distempers and difficulties, even those that produce little outward expression or disturbance, can color the individual's whole psychic background for life, and may eventually produce profound character distortions that may permanently mar and disfigure the personality. Sometimes disagreeable, limping personalities are produced, and these are harder to adjust than are limping, disfigured bodies. Frequently the repressed feelings and subjective distortions that are not reflected in outward expression may be more detrimental to mental health than overt maladjustments. The quiet, timid, repressed, introverted child who conceals his feelings and indulges in secret ruminations often constitutes a more serious mental-hygiene problem than does the active, demonstrative, boisterous extrovert. The quiet, repressed child, however, often arouses little concern in the home or school, because he creates little outward disturbance. The shy child may receive little attention, because he is a quiet conformist who remains unnoticed in the background.

Our case histories have shown in profuse and convincing detail that many apparently minor personality disturbances cannot be dismissed as inconsequential trivialities. Because they have been untreated or mistreated, they have frequently become the cause of poignant mental anguish, often unsuspected by parents or teachers. They have sometimes become the source of faulty adjustments of various kinds, bad habits of emotional and motor response, emotional upsets, detrimental attitudes toward the problems of life, feelings of dissatisfaction and discontent, and sometimes of mental disintegration or disorder. Not infrequently, the psychic disfigurements produced have undermined the individual's morale and have created handicaps that have continued throughout life to hamper his adjustment to the practical issues of life. Therefore, we cannot emphasize too frequently that no phase of modern education and mental hygiene is more fundamental than the prevention and cure of the minor mental maladjustments to which normal people (as well as those who are supernormal, subnormal, and abnormal) become victims.

The cataclysmic effects of emotional shocks, thwartings, conflicts, or frights on some persons are difficult to envisage fully without concrete examples. A few pertinent cases from the record will illustrate the point.

A woman in Kansas City, Mo. (in 1934), screaming a warning to a youngster who darted from his mother into the path of an oncoming truck, saved his life. "I called to him to stop," she started to tell the mother, and then she "became speechless from terror. Her lips moved but no sounds came from them." She remained speechless for 5 years. Her voice was finally regained with the use of sodium amytal, a sedative that dulls consciousness, and by suggestive treatment.   This was probably a case of fear-produced hysterical aphonia.

Gabriel Bernard, French writer of mystery books and plays, "acclaimed as an expert in the art of imparting vicarious horrors to audiences," is reported to have "died from fright" (in 1934), produced by the seemingly trivial prank of a youngster who suddenly shoved a paintbrush soaked in iodine under his nose.   M. Bernard apparently mistook it for a revolver.   He fainted, collapsing on the sidewalk, and died in the evening in the hospital, apparently from a heart attack.

In Omaha, Neb. (in 1937), a woman in an action in court for a divorce from her husband, testified that "they had lived together for a year without speaking to each other.   They ate their meals in silence, sat and read, evenings, in the same room without a word being said, and listened to the radio without comment."   These are probably cases of emotionally produced speech inhibitions or blockages.

For 45 years a woman in College Springs, Ia., had lived with her father, 81 years of age (in 1936), without ever having spoken a word to him.   "She talks with her brother, 43 years old, she chats with the neighbors, and bargains with the butcher and grocer," but she "always just sort of chokes up when she tries to talk to her father."   "Once the father and his wife were going away on the train before the girl was born.   The mother did not want to go.   When they got about a block from the depot she choked up and couldn't talk to him for some time.   That's the only way anyone ever has been able to explain her [the daughter's] trouble.   She was probably birthmarked."   This curious case of speech inhibition was, in all probability, caused by early emotional conditioning after the child's birth, probably a specific fright produced accidentally by the father.

For 50 years, bachelor "Silent Bill" of Audubon, Ia., who died in 1939 at 86, had remained completely speechless.   "He vowed after his fiancée left him at the altar that he would never speak another word," and he never could or would overcome the emotional blockage.

At West Milton, N.H., a man stayed in bed a half century because of a thwarted love affair.   "On one of his several trips from home [he was an authority on cattle] he met a farm girl.   He visited her often and fell in love. One evening at the glowing fireside, at the age of 22, he told his father of his love.   The father, showing evident displeasure at his son's new-found affection, ordered him to stop talking and to go to bed.   The son went to his room.   The next morning he refused to get up.   And every day for the rest of his life [he died when 72, in 1912] he remained steadfast in his resolve to stay in bed.   His beard grew to his waist and his fingernails were exceedingly long."   His mother died in 1873 and the father in 1881, after he had been in bed 19 years; but he remained in bed.   His two brothers never married.

Alfred Dreyfus at the age of 75 (in 1934) was still "haunted by nightmares of his imprisonment which often woke him from his sleep, although it has been 35 years since he was pardoned from an unjust sentence for treason."

THE SOCIALLY MALADJUSTED AND BEHAVIORISTICALLY UNADJUSTED

Reasons for the Interest of the Mental Hygienists in Children Subject to Conduct Difficulties. For obvious reasons, few groups of deviates exist in which the mental hygienist is more profoundly interested than in the group of children who are maladjusted or abnormal in social behavior. In the first place, children who are socially maladjusted and criminally inclined constitute a grave potential menace to the happiness and security of society. Genetic studies show that the swarm of delinquents and criminals that preys upon society is to a large extent recruited from the army of behavioristically abnormal children and juvenile social nonconformists. George Kirchwey's investigation in 1934 showed that 92 per cent of 3,000 first offenders hailed into the New York Court of General Sessions on felony charges had previously been in the children's court.

The modal age for male criminals under 25 in 1944 and the first half of 1945 was 17, followed by 18 and 19. The corresponding figures for females are 19, 18, and 21 in 1944, and 22, 21, and 19 in 1945.[15] Apparently unguided, misguided, discontented, and maladjusted children and youth furnish the taproot of our crime problem. In the second place, the understanding and treatment of behavior abnormalities and conduct disorders are primarily problems of psychology, mental hygiene, and education. For these and other reasons many so-called psychological, psychiatric, and mental-hygiene clinics devote a significant portion, if not the major portion, of their time and energy to the study of juvenile offenders or delinquents.

The Terms Applied to Offenders and Types of Offenses. The group of socially deviating children is referred to by a variety of names. In school they are perhaps most frequently referred to as problem children. This designation is not very apposite, because it is too generic; the mentally and physically handicapped also constitute distinct educational and vocational problems, and often social problems, as well. The schools are also prone to refer to these children as disorderly, mischievous, vicious, wayward, unruly, rebellious, unmanageable, ungovernable, disciplinary, or refractory; as behavior cases; as incorrigibles; as truants, when they "play hooky"; and, less frequently now than formerly, as moral perverts, degenerates, or imbeciles. The legal terms usually applied to those who have gone afoul of the law and who have been brought into the juvenile court are "juvenile delinquents" or

---

[15] *Uniform Crime Reports for the United States and Its Possessions,* Federal Bureau of Investigation, U.S. Department of Justice, Washington, D.C., 1945, Vol. XVI, No. 1, and 1944, Vol. XV, No. 2.

"juvenile offenders." Minors who have been convicted of misdemeanors or felonies by a judge or a jury are often referred to as juvenile lawbreakers or criminals.

In the concept of behavior or conduct disorders is included a great variety of forms of social nonconformity or of behavior patterns that are usually disapproved of or regarded as undesirable. These include (1) overt breaches of state and Federal laws, city ordinances, school regulations, business codes, neighborhood or home customs, and the like. Such violations may assume the form of thieving, stealing, trespassing, acts of vandalism, destruction of property, and physical or mental injury to persons. (2) The manifestation of behavior characteristics that are undesirable from the standpoint of potential or actual inconvenience or injury inflicted upon others and also because of the undermining or disintegrating influences exerted upon the offender himself. Among such behavior traits may be mentioned disobedience, rebellion, and defiance of authority; untruthfulness, deceitfulness, trickiness, prevarication, and cheating; irresponsibility or undependableness; indifference, indolence, sluggishness, inattentiveness, carelessness, and failure to study; excessive selfishness, egotism, conceit, and disregard of the rights of others; stubbornness, obstinacy concerning one's opinion, and the determination to have one's own way; lack of self-control, temperamental and emotional instability, and temper outbursts; jealousy, suspiciousness, and hatred of others; sullenness and sulkiness; unhappiness, depression, and moroseness; shyness, timidity, fearfulness, cowardice, tendency to withdrawal, shut-in-ness, introversion, introspective rumination, oversensitiveness, and daydreaming proclivities; cruelty, bullying, teasing, boisterousness, domineering attitude, quarrelsomeness, and destructiveness; whispering, disorderliness in class, meddlesomeness, and tattling; tardiness or truancy; bad sex habits, indecency, vulgarity, and profanity; smoking, drinking, and carousing. This list of character traits suggests the prolific crop of behavior anomalies that constitute problems of study by the mental hygienist.

Nature of the Interest of Mental Hygiene in the Forms of Misbehavior. To be sure, mental hygiene is interested in the forms in which social maladjustments appear; but its major concern is in the discovery of the causes and motives of social nonconformity as the necessary first step in any effective program for the prevention or correction of antisocial tendencies. Success in the prevention of delinquency is scarcely to be expected without the discovery and removal of the causative factors and the follow-up adjustment of the individual to the social requirements or the adjustment of the social and physical environment to the child's needs. Behavior disorders to the mental hygienist are problems to be understood, and not merely tendencies to be suppressed. Treatment that is concerned only with the form of misconduct is equivalent to treating symptoms and does not reach the root of the trouble.[16] The wise disciplinarian always tries, as a matter of primary concern, to understand the mental life of the child, and especially the causes, the motives, or the dynamics of his malbehavior.

What is involved in the study of the causes of behavior abnormalities? Fundamentally, it involves a thorough investigation of the physical, mental, and social characteristics of the child and all the influences that have affected his growth and development and his attitude toward social and moral questions. The factors that conduce to misconduct may reside in the child himself (the so-called internal or endogenous causes), or they may reside in his environment, in unfortunate home or neighborhood conditions (the so-called external, or exogenous, or situational causes). In the study of the child himself we should try to discover any physical handicaps that may bear on the situation; we should determine his general ability level, his special abilities or disabilities, his special interests or lack of interests, his frustrations or dissatisfaction, and especially the motives for his behavior eccentricities or conduct disorders. Why does the child behave as he does? What does he hope to gain by his conduct? Or avoid? Or evade? What is he trying to accomplish? What is the motivation for his cheating, defiance of authority, prevarication, or whispering? Many possibilities must be considered. For example: Is his conduct due to some fear, hidden or expressed? Does some concealed fear drive him to desperation or to some form of defense reaction? Is he trying to gratify some secret longing, say, an urge for power or recognition? Is his behavior in the nature of a compensation or an escape from some repressed impulse or handicap? Or is it a means of satisfying desires that cannot be realized normally because of poverty or denial of privileges or opportunities? Is the act a smoke screen, a disguise for a worse offense? Or is it a means of taking revenge upon someone for some fancied or real slight or grievance? A 16-year-old boy in Lemoyne, Pa. (in 1938), confessed setting at "least six fires to get revenge" on several persons for "making fun of me because I was in jail once." Is it a means of attracting attention, getting into the limelight, or achieving a feeling of security or superiority? Is that the motive of the boy's boisterousness? Is his mischievousness the breaking out of undesirable attitudes or habit patterns acquired in the home or in the school because of excessive disciplinary severity or repression, excessive laxity, false social standards, or feelings of dissatisfaction? Or is the misconduct the expression of some mental, emotional, or sex conflict, or some uncontrollable impulse? Or was the child led to commit an unlawful or a disapproved act by the suggestion, example, or command of his pals? Was he trying to help or shield one of his

---

[16] In this connection reference may be made to H. W. James's inflexible catalogue of punishments for various school offenses: "Punishments Recommended for School Offenses," *Elementary School Journal*, 1928, 129–131.

cronies?   These questions are merely illustrative of the great variety of motivations that influence child behavior.

It should be obvious that, if we desire to exercise rational and effective control over problems of social noncomformity or delinquency, the first step to take is to strive to understand the multitudinous motivating forces that precipitate antisocial behavior.   Even if the root cause is discovered, corrective measures will not succeed in 100 per cent of the cases; but much greater success will be achieved from treating causes than from treating symptoms.   Different forms of misconduct basically are symptoms—symptoms of some maladjustment or lack of adjustment.   We cannot hope to understand or control the child's conduct merely by studying or treating symptoms as symptoms.   It is much more important to obtain insight into the whys and wherefores of the child's behavior—an understanding of the nature of his acts —than merely to obtain a knowledge of what he did.   The child might have committed a dozen kinds of misdeeds on the basis of exactly the same motive. The form of his misdeeds may have been determined purely by the accidents or circumstances of the situation, although the motivating drive may have been the same.   Once the motives and causes have been discovered, we are in a position to map out a more effective preventive and correctional program.   We can develop intelligent plans for removing the causes, whether they are in the social or physical environment of the home, school, or neighborhood, or in the child's physical condition, mental attitudes, mental conflicts, dissatisfactions, or what not.

In cases in which behavior disorders or maladjustments have already been acquired, prolonged efforts are sometimes required to modify the viewpoints, attitudes, habits, and reaction patterns of the offender.   A patient process of socialization and personality reconstruction, based on a deep understanding of the individual and his surroundings, is often essential.   Without efficient cooperation from the home, school, institution, and other social agencies, uncertain success awaits our best efforts in many cases.   Family customs and patterns are often the important factor in need of reconstruction.   Sometimes the strategic line of attack is the modification of the school procedures to meet the child's needs, such as the individualization of the instruction, the introduction of multilateral courses, or the establishment of special classes.   Sometimes the needed personality reconstruction requires the effective application of one or more of the analytic, interpretative, client-centered, expressive, or release therapies discussed in Chap. VI.

To be genuinely preventive, the treatment of behavior disorders must begin in the incipient stages.   Much more can be accomplished in the early stages than after the tendencies have become confirmed.   Thus the places to begin are in the home and in the school.   Parents and teachers should form the habit of watching for early signs of social maladjustments and conduct disorders and should take immediate steps to prevent their development. One aid for the achievement of this objective in the elementary schools is the continuous individualized "behavior-record cards," prepared through the co-operation of the subcommittee of the Committee on Commerce, under the chairmanship of R. S. Copeland, dealing with rackets, kidnaping, and other forms of crime. On these cards, the antisocial tendencies, character anoma-lies, and behavior characteristics of the pupils are periodically recorded. Some of the tests of personality traits and maladjustments already discussed should be of value as screening devices for spotting various forms of incipient or advanced malbehavior.

The success thus far achieved by child-guidance, mental-hygiene, and psychiatric clinics in the prevention and correction of child delinquency leaves much room for improvement. The thorough investigation by Sheldon and Eleanor Glueck of 1,000 male juvenile delinquents handled by a good juvenile court, an outstanding child-guidance clinic, and trained probation officers—involving in some instances discriminating placement, when neces-sary, in foster homes or in industrial or reform schools—revealed that during 5 years after release from supervision, 88.2 per cent of the 923 who could be located had continued in their careers of delinquency. Those actually appre-hended (84 per cent of the 923 boys) had been arrested on an average of 3.6 times during the 5-year period. Two-thirds of the entire group committed serious offenses, mostly felonies.[17]

The record 10 years later was considerably better. "By the time our juvenile delinquents had reached an average age of twenty-nine, almost 40 per cent [of 938 offenders] had ceased to be criminals. Furthermore, even among those who continued to commit crimes, significant improvement oc-curred. The proportion of serious offenders dropped from 75.6 per cent in the period prior to the original contact of the group with the Boston Juvenile Court to 47.8 per cent at the end of the fifteen-year follow-up span." In the prevention and correction of antisocial or criminal tendencies the authors stress the importance not only of the child's home background and early emotional conditioning, but also of his congenital equipment and particularly of his capacity for normal, balanced "physical, mental, and emotional maturation" and personality integration. Conduct disorders may be linked not only with delayed maturity, but with the processes of deterioration incident to aging. "Misbehavior due to *un*integration gives way to misbehavior due to *dis*integra-tion, until the organism slows down and finally stops." A "sizable proportion of offenders" are so defective as to require permanent segregation from

[17] Sheldon Glueck and Eleanor Glueck, *One Thousand Juvenile Delinquents,* Cambridge, Mass., Harvard University Press, 1934. See also *500 Criminal Careers,* New York, Alfred A. Knopf, Inc., 1930; and *Later Criminal Careers,* New York, Commonwealth Fund, Division of Publication, 1937.

society. [18]   The Gluecks supply certain criteria for forecasting the outcome for any given case.

The greatest hope in the battle against antisocial conduct and crime apparently lies in the program of positive and preventive work, in the home and in the school, before the age when most children appear in the juvenile courts or in the psychiatric clinics. The latter agencies often get the child too late to do genuinely preventive work. Although they have been set up as preventive agencies, their mode of attack must, perforce, often resemble correctional and reformatory work.

[18] Sheldon Glueck and Eleanor Glueck, *Juvenile Delinquents Grown Up,* New York, Commonwealth Fund, Division of Publication, 1940, 264, 271; see also *Criminal Careers in Retrospect,* Commonwealth Fund, Division of Publication, 1943.

Consult also

Augusta F. Bronner, "Treatment and What Happened Afterward" (a second report), *American Journal of Orthopsychiatry,* 1944, 14, 28–36.

William Healy and Augusta F. Bronner, *New Light on Delinquency and Its Treatment,* New Haven, Yale University Press, 1936; also, *Treatment and What Happened Afterward,* Boston, The Judge Baker Guidance Center, 1939.

CHAPTER VI

PSYCHOTHERAPEUTIC METHODS

Scope of the Discussion. While detailed suggestions are offered in various parts of the book for the prevention or correction of specific personality maladjustments and shortcomings, a book in mental hygiene would be incomplete without at least a brief overview of various psychotherapeutic treatment techniques. The exposition that follows must, because of space limitations, be restricted to a very general discussion of the basic kinds of psychotherapeutic procedures in general use and a brief discussion of a few of the simpler and a few of the more specialized and technical psychotherapeutic techniques. The important questions concerning the precautions to observe in the administration of various kinds of therapy (treatment), the conditions necessary for successful results, the types of adjustment difficulties and types of maladjusted individuals to which the different techniques apply, and many related questions, cannot receive detailed consideration in this abridgment. The reader who wants these details should consult the footnote references or the references in the bibliography at the end of the book.

Meaning of Psychotherapy. Any psychological methods employed for overcoming or meliorating mental maladjustments, disorders, or difficulties, or for favorably modifying the individual's attitudes and reaction tendencies may be referred to broadly as psychotherapeutic methods or as psychotherapy. A considerable variety of psychological forms of treatment are in vogue, some very simple and easily understood and administered, others very complicated and difficult to apply successfully. Some, even among the simplest ones, prove very effective with certain cases under optimal environmental conditions, while some are highly efficacious both for preventive and for remedial purposes with certain individuals. Some possess temporary curative virtues but do not prove to be permanently effective. Some may remove the external symptoms —at least, the more annoying ones—but do not reach the underlying conflicts or motivations. Some may prove effective in removing the primary symptoms but not in preventing the emergence of secondary symptoms, which often serve the purpose of defense or escape mechanisms. Some prove to be potent only to the extent that the needed environmental readjustments are instituted and maintained. Exactly which particular treatment technique is applicable to a given child in a given situation will, in many cases, have to be determined by the competent clinical psychologist, psychiatrist, or mental

217

hygienist after due consideration of all the relevant factors.   Often trial-and-error experimentation is required to determine the most effective procedures. In many cases (in general, the less serious cases), the treatment will begin with some of the simpler or more superficial techniques, such as could be applied by the intelligent educator, parent, or social worker, and be followed, when these prove negative, by the more technical and penetrating procedures at the hands of the specialists in psychic therapy.

Types of Therapy.   Treatment techniques may be classified as superficial or symptomatic—those which are concerned with the removal of undesirable symptoms and the establishment of wholesome reaction patterns through the use of the simpler procedures—and the more basic causal kinds of therapy. Causal therapy, employed by the so-called "depth" psychology (psycho-analysis, analytic psychology, child analysis, individual psychology, thera-peutic interviewing, projective techniques, etc.), is concerned with the dis-covery and removal of the underlying causative factors of the mental diffi-culty and providing tension-releasing outlets (release therapy) through ade-quate insight and correlated emotional discharge (catharsis, abreaction).

Psychotherapeutic methods may also be classified as direct and indirect, or environmental.   In the environment approach, the attempt is made to bring about desirable adjustments in the child through the modification of the fac-tors in the environment that appear to be related to the child's particular mal-adjustment.   This mode of treatment is referred to by some writers as situa-tional therapy.   The factors in need of modification are almost limitless. Sometimes a better grade classification in school, a modification of the curricu-lum, placement in a suitable special class or in a residential institution (for defectives), remedial reading instruction, or exposure to new contents or a different teacher may solve the scholastic problems that appear to be at the root of personal difficulties.   Occasionally transfers can be made to special schools where there are psychiatric or psychological services.   Sometimes the primary problem may be solved by providing tension-relieving outlets through satisfying social activities.   Satisfaction-yielding participation in the activities of other persons constitutes a prime method of alleviating or removing fears, timidities, anxieties, feelings of inferiority, tendencies toward introvert rumi-nations, frustrations, hostilities, or aggressiveness.   Possible forms of social intercourse include school, church, or other club activities, camp activities,[1] scout trooping; programs of sports and recreations; craft, shop, and hobby work in curative work shops or in club centers; band, orchestra, and group singing; and the like.   Successful accomplishments in almost any kind of social activity will win social approval and social status or prestige, and will enable the child to evaluate his assets more realistically.   Opportunities for

---

[1] "Psychopathology and Psychotherapy of Camping," *The Nervous Child,* April, 1947, 127–231.

the assumption of responsibilities in the home, club, and elsewhere will make for the development of initiative, resourcefulness, and independence of judgment and action.

When intolerable conditions exist in the child's home, or when the home is inadequate, the best solution in many cases is to place the child in a properly supervised foster home suitable for his particular needs. The problem here is one of reeducation, retraining, reconditioning, the breaking up of undesirable habits, and the development of new attitudes and responsible reaction patterns by more competent parent surrogates. Treatment by a person who assumes the parental role has been called "supportive therapy" by Jeannette Axelrode.[2] The most important environmental factors of child maladjustments often inhere in the husband-wife, parent-child, and child-sibling relationships.

The recognition of the fact that the problem of childhood maladjustments is often primarily a problem of maladjusted parents has led to the attempt to correct injurious parental behavior patterns, attitudes, and methods of rearing the child, by helping the parents to understand how their own emotional needs and dissatisfactions, frustrations, ambitions, and motivations may be reflected in faulty methods of handling the child, such as overprotection, overdomination, excessive repression, rejection, overindulgence, excessive laxity, or ambivalent methods of discipline.

In the direct types of therapy, verbal stimuli or other influences are brought directly to bear upon the child to supply insight and understanding regarding the causes, motivations, and nature of his behavior reactions, to reorient him with respect to his personal problems, to relieve him of tensions, conflicts, and maladjustments, and to supply new motivations for the redirection of his energies and the modification of his attitudes and behavior patterns. The simplest procedures involve the offering of explanations, interpretations, enlightenment, suggestions, and advice; the use of persuasion or even commands; the giving of encouragement; provision for rest and relaxation (the rest cure); the use of music (music therapy); reeducation; art-craft activities and creative and art projects (occupational therapy); and religious enlightenment or consolation (religious therapy).[3] The more involved procedures include hypnotic and closely related forms of suggestion, psychoanalysis, psychobiology (as formulated by Adolf Meyer), expressive and interview therapies,

---

[2] Jeannette Axelrode, "Some Implications for Supportive Therapy," *American Journal of Orthopsychiatry,* 1940, 244–271.

[3] The following are among religious or semireligious forms of treatment: Christian Science (Mary Baker Eddy, 1866), the sect called the Peculiar People (John Banyard, 1838), the Emmanuel Movement (Elwood Worcester), New Thought, Spiritualism (1848), Dowieism, the system of "powwow," and the cults of the savage witch doctor and the Indian medicine man. Mention may also be made of the systems of Theosophy, Roscicrucianism (1610), and Psychiana.

and other variants of the so-called "depth" psychology. It should not be concluded that the direct and the indirect forms of treatment are necessarily antithetical or exclusive (some are), and that they are separately administered. Both forms of treatment often go hand in hand, although the emphasis may be placed on the one phase rather than on the other. Sometimes both approaches receive equal attention; sometimes the one plays a merely adjuvant role to the other. Sometimes the environmental treatment is primary while the direct therapy plays the adjuvant role; sometimes the reverse situation obtains, depending upon the complications presented by each child. The following paragraphs supply merely a brief outline of some of the more important systems of therapy in current use, without any attempt to outline detailed treatment techniques.

Suggestive Therapeutics. One of the most frequently employed methods of treatment is called "suggestive" therapeutics. It consists, in general, in arousing by appropriate suggestions firm convictions in the subject that he is all right, that he is well or will get well, and that his difficulties will disappear if he follows certain suggestions. The attempt is made to imbue the subject with desirable positive beliefs and attitudes.

The factor of suggestion accounts for the efficacy of many allegedly magical forms of cure, such as the laying on of hands; the application of health charms or talismans; the curative effects of health shrines and, frequently, of health springs; and ordinary or supposedly miraculous drugs that prove, on analysis, to be nothing but "bread pills."

In the system of powwow—a species of suggestive or faith healing which invokes the "good spirit"—currently in use by the Amish, a religious sect located in the Dutch section, near Lancaster, Pa. (they have spread to other states), supposedly potent words, usually drawn from the Bible, are muttered over the patient's head. The Amish also use the old family stand-by of sulphur and molasses and the onion poultice. The method of hexing involves the use of an "evil spirit."

Hypnosis and Hypnotherapy. In large measure, suggestion also explains the effectiveness of hypnotherapy—at least, in its simple form based on direct or indirect suggestion—for removing nervous symptoms or overcoming undesirable habits or attitudes. The efficacy of hypnotherapy is based on various factors. (*a*) In the hypnotic state, especially in deep hypnosis, the subject becomes so highly suggestible that he accepts uncritically almost anything that he is told and does almost everything that he is requested or commanded to do by the operator with whom he is "en rapport" or has established a condition of "transference" (to be explained on a later page). (*b*) Because of the extreme suggestibility (hypersuggestibility) and responsiveness to the hypnotist, resistances, inhibitions, and amnesias (memory gaps) can often be readily removed and early memories revived. (*c*) The revival of long-forgotten memories frequently enables the operator to reconstruct the client's early experiences, to discover the psychic causes of his idiosyncrasies or difficulties, and, on the basis of such insight, to remove the causes by means of appropriate suggestions or to reeducate the personality. (*d*) Through the revival of the traumatic emotional episodes and the free, uninhibited re-living of the original affect (which may manifest itself in such expressions as shouting, sobbing, shaking, trembling, cowering, raving, perspiring), the client is enabled to release, discharge, or "work off" his pent-up emotional tensions and conflicts. This process of cure is technically known as the method of catharsis or abreaction, which will be referred to again. The following citation from William Brown, psychologist at Oxford University, shows the use made of hypnotization for recovering buried memories.

Another one of my patients went to sleep in a barber's chair. He went out of the hospital one day to get his hair cut and didn't come back for three days. Then he came back with loss of memory and I had to hypnotize him to see what had happened. I found that with the barber "messing about with my hair" he went to sleep and his idea in the sleep was that he must go back to Suffolk to see if a friend had returned. When he got back to his ordinary surroundings he could not remember anything about it, but under hypnosis he could.

The detailed techniques employed to induce hypnosis can only be mentioned here: verbal suggestions or commands, concentration of attention, steady maintenance of ocular convergence, fixation of the eyes on a bright object, listening to monotonous sounds, monotonously stroking the forehead, and the use of various drugs (*e.g.*, sodium pentothal or one of the barbiturates) for inducing rapid narcosis (a state of deep unconsciousness produced by a drug) and for removing the resistances to hypnosis. The last-named method, known as "narcoanalysis" or "narcosynthesis," was extensively used with psychoneurotic combat casualties in the Second World War.

The process of direct verbal suggestion employed in the simple kind of hypnotherapy is designed not only to infuse positive attitudes of confidence and determination and to induce states of relaxation and ease in the agent, but, more importantly, to suppress or remove the obnoxious symptoms. By appropriate procedures the suggestions made during the state of hypnosis are extended into the posthypnotic period, thereby influencing the subject during his normal waking state, although he may not clearly apprehend the forces at work.

Many hypnotherapists do not limit their efforts to bringing about "symptom disappearance"—to removing the symptoms by subtly conveyed suggestions, entreaties, or commands—but try to give the client an understanding of his underlying difficulties and an insight into the causation and significance of his symptoms. They try to uncover the underlying emotional factors, to treat the basic difficulty, and to reeducate or recondition the total personality. They attempt to integrate, through adequate insight, the abreacted experiences into the subject's total personality pattern. This is accomplished through the supplementation of hypnotherapy by hypnoanalysis, a modified form of psychoanalysis.

Some hypnotherapists believe that the subject's "subconscious mind" can be reached by the process of hypnotization to release dynamic, subconscious healing forces. The subconscious mind is contracted with the conscious mind. The latter mind, which is connected with the cerebrospinal nervous system, controls the voluntary muscles and thought. It is connected with intellectual, rational, and memory operations; and it functions through the cortex of the brain and the sense organs. On the other hand, the subconscious, or unconscious, mind—so they allege—is connected with the autonomic nervous system and exercises control over the involuntary muscles and the internal organs, the normal functioning of which is essential for mental and physical health. The subconscious mind unconsciously records and indelibly retains the impressions and experiences that the conscious mind receives through the senses. Such unconscious impressions are the basis of "unconscious autosuggestion." By coming in contact with ideas of ill-health, the subconscious mind, unknown to the conscious mind, may thus through unconscious autosuggestion become the cause of mental and nervous maladies. The cure for disorders thus caused is by autosuggestion, through the subconscious mind.

It was the contention of Emile Coué that hypnosis is nothing but suggestion from the conscious mind of the hypnotized subject. Heterosuggestion thus reduces to autosuggestion. Therefore there is no need of a second person. The conscious mind of the patient can convey suggestions to its subconscious mind more effectively by "conscious autosuggestion." The patient needs only to expel extraneous thoughts from his conscious mind and repeat health-producing phrases (see page 3) which will exert an unconscious influence upon the unconscious mind. The most propitious time for this type of suggestive therapeutics is just before going to sleep, while the conscious mind is fatigued, or just before complete awakening. Coué maintained that minor ailments will readily yield to this treatment, that more serious ones can be conquered after several months of application, and that the method can also be used to overcome bad habits or moods.

Hypnotherapy in the form of hypnotic suggestion and hypnoanalysis and hypnosynthesis has been employed in the treatment of many forms of mental and nervous disorders—such as hysteria, hysterical somnambulism, neurotic depressions, obsessions, compulsions, kleptomania, homosexuality, alcoholism, speech disturbances—and many kinds of objectionable habits, such as excessive smoking and bad sex practices. It has been used to dispel fears and anxieties; to lessen or obliterate pain; to produce anesthesia in connection with surgical and dental operations; to remove amnesias; to resynthesize dissociated systems of ideas; to engender hopeful, restful states of mind; and to accomplish other ends.

Hypnotism has been referred to as the sovereign remedy for bad habits and morbid tendencies (August Forel). However, its effectiveness both in the simpler form (suggestive therapeutics) and in combination with psychoanalytic techniques varies greatly with cases. Even the shallower treatment, based merely on hypnotic suggestion, sometimes proves permanently successful in overcoming even stubborn habits and serious nervous maladies and in completely abolishing obnoxious symptoms. Sometimes the relief obtained, however, is merely temporary, even in the case of minor disorders and even when deeper techniques are employed (hypnoanalysis). In general, the combined technique (hypnotherapy and hypnoanalysis), now largely employed, produces more lasting improvement than hypnosuggestion alone. The method of hypnotherapy, which was largely superseded in the early part of the century by psychoanalysis, has staged a comeback since the Second World War, especially in the combined form, and is deserving of a wider utilization with selected cases than is now practiced.[4]

[4] On hypnosis consult

Colin Bennett, *Hypnotic Power: Its Cultivation and Application to Psychotherapy*, New York, E. P. Dutton & Co., Inc., 1937.

Margaret Brenman and Merton M. Gill, *Hypnotherapy*, New York, International Universities Press, 1948.

George H. Easterbrook, *Hypnotism*, New York, E. P. Dutton & Co., Inc., 1943.

Roy R. Grinker and John P. Spiegel, *Men under Stress; and War Neuroses*, Philadelphia, The Blakiston Company, 1945.

John S. Horsley, *Narco-Analysis*, New York, Oxford University Press, 1946.

Clark L. Hull, *Hypnosis and Suggestibility*, New York, Appleton-Century-Crofts, Inc., 1933.

Samuel Kahn, *Suggestion and Hypnosis Made Practical*, Boston, Meador Publishing Company, 1945.

Lesley Kuhn and Salvatorg Russo, eds., *Modern Hypnosis*, New York, Garrett Foundation for Psychological Research, 1947.

Leslie M. Le Cron and Jean Bordeaux, *Hypnotism Today*, New York, Grune & Stratton, Inc., 1947.

Robert M. Lindner, *Rebel without a Cause: The Hypnoanalysis of a Criminal Psychopath*, New York, Grune & Stratton, Inc., 1944.

Andrew Salter, *What Is Hypnosis? Studies in Conditioning*, New York, Richard R. Smith, 1944.

Silvan S. Tompkins, *Contemporary Psychopathology*, Cambridge, Mass., Harvard University Press, 1944, 479–516 (three reprinted articles).

Lewis R. Wolberg, *Hypnoanalysis*, New York, Grune & Stratton, Inc., 1945.

Lewis R. Wolberg, *Medical Hypnosis*, New York, Grune & Stratton, Inc., 1948.

Bernard Wolfe and Raymond Rosenthal, *Hypnotism Comes of Age: Its Progress from Mesmer to Psychoanalysis*, Indianapolis, Bobbs-Merrill Company, 1948.

Brief reference should also be made to the method of hypnoidization of Boris Sidis. Through proper processes of suggestion by the operator, the subject is induced to relax into a dreamy state, referred to as the hypnoidal state. In some subjects only a few seconds to a few minutes will be required to induce this state, which resembles the hypnagogic state just preceding or following sleep, in which the subject is half asleep and half awake. In the hypnoidal condition the subject is able to retain vague perceptual relations with his surroundings while his partially dissociated mind experiences vivid dream imagery as it is proceeding along the dream route toward sleep. In this vague state of consciousness, during which memory is diffuse, the emotions undisturbed, and the body and the mind at ease, fragments of forgotten reminiscences may come to the surface. Moreover, the subject's restful, relaxed, and nonresistant state is also highly favorable for therapeutic suggestions. Accordingly, because of the conditions of nonresistance, favorable recall, and high suggestibility, the operator may be able to unravel the causal nexus of the subject's troubles and suggest remedies for their removal or mitigation. If the subject has been able to free himself from his inhibitions, he may be able to reveal his suppressed memories and emotions, possibly at first in detached words and later in complete sentences, especially if given the necessary aid by the operator, who may suggestively guide the revelations from clues supplied by the subject's responses. Therein lies a possible danger. The operator may unintentionally suggest fictitious situations by his questions, leads, or attitudes, and thereby reach unwarranted conclusions. Much training is sometimes required before the subject can overcome his inhibitions and talk without restraint or conscious deliberation.

The hypnoidal state supplies an excellent starting point for reinforcing desirable impulses and for removing minor obsessions and fears (Hugo Münsterberg). It is an aid for tapping and liberating dominant or reserve energies, for breaking down inhibitions, for disintegrating painful systems of ideas, and for reintegrating them into wholesome thoughts and feelings (Sidis).

Lillian J. Martin has used a simplified form of the hypnoidal state for inducing relaxation, following a threefold method of suggestion. Thus the operator conveys a positive suggestion to the subject, such as "let your right leg relax." The subject responds with the autosuggestion, "my right leg is relaxed." The operator then offers the suggestion that the goal has been accomplished, such as, "your right leg has relaxed," or "your heart does not ache any more," or "your heart has stopped aching." Both hypnosis and hypnoidization require the services of the trained hypnotist.

The effectiveness of the ordinary, nonhypnotic form of suggestion, such as is usually employed by teachers, parents, and medical or psychological interviewers, varies greatly with the prestige of the adviser, the degree of responsiveness and suggestibility of the child, and the character of the transference established between the counselor and the counselee. In some cases rational persuasion and subtly presented suggestions may completely and permanently overcome a child's timidities, conflicts, or inhibitions; in other cases temporary relief may be afforded, but the original difficulties may tend to return. Removing difficulties by rational suggestion does not always prove to be permanently beneficial, because the individual is in need of emotional reconstruction rather than intellectual indoctrination or assurance. Filling the individual's mind by cues, hints, or attitudes with desirable points of view, motivations, and outcomes may not help him to gain insight into the nature of his difficulties and may leave the fundamental problem of adjustment unsolved. In fact, he may not even realize that he has an underlying problem that has not been touched. To instill assurance in order to develop the subject's confidence in himself is a valuable objective, unless it leads him to assume an attitude of smug complacency—"All's right with the world," so why bother?—and to make no effort to provide therapeutic outlets for his pent-up emotional tension. Suggestion, advice, exhortation, command, interpretation, and explanation (the line between them is ill defined; suggestion is one method of transmitting advice) are of value only to the extent that they are assimilated and emotionally accepted. Without adequate insight, explanations and interpretations may be intellectually apprehended without being accepted emotionally. The subject might not be able to act on the suggestions because of the emotional satisfaction, real or illusory, that he gets from his defensive maladjustments, or because he has not had the emotional release or experience needed to free himself from his conflicts and to help him get the insight needed to understand his deeper motivations and to make independent decisions. If he finds a frank intellectual probing and evaluation of his conflicts distasteful, as is often the case, the virtues of wholesome positive suggestions may be rendered nugatory by contrary autosuggestion. In general, the more suggestible the child is, the more readily will he respond to therapeutic suggestions. But ready suggestibility may also be a handicap, because it renders the subject amenable to later conflicting suggestions, which may undo the good effects of earlier beneficial ones. Simple suggestion is a readily administered and valuable form of psychotherapy when it works. But it does not always work.

When the simpler forms of treatment (interpretation, explanation, suggestion, advice, encouragement) prove fruitless, recourse may be had to some form of "depth" therapy. The basic objectives of all of these forms of treatment are to provide means for the free expression of the child's emotional tensions and conflicts and to provide the experiences that will enable him to gain adequate insight into his behavior mechanisms and to achieve a higher psychic integration in the light of the reorientation gained from his growing assimilated experiences.

Systems of Expressive and Release Therapies. The following groups of treatment techniques (largely the product of the years since the first edition of this book was composed), will be considered in this section because, although differing in various details, they are alike in the basic objective of providing release from emotional or psychosomatic tensions through some form of free or undirected expression by means of words or action; individual therapeutic interviewing or counseling, group discussions or activities (group therapy); play therapy; psychodramatics.

Therapeutic Interviewing or Counseling. This is a form of "relationship" therapy for the adjustment of personality or emotional problems. In its narrow, technical connotation, it provides a "permissive" relationship, in which the child is permitted and encouraged to give full expression through verbalization of his problem—his feelings, emotional conflicts, fears, worries, hostilities, resentments, guilt feelings, sex difficulties, aggressive trends—without any interference, criticism, or chastisement on the part of the interviewer.

The purpose of the free, uncensored recital is to permit the child to relieve himself (release therapy, catharsis) of any tensions, inhibitions, emotional conflicts, fears, guilt complexes, or resentments, as a condition for gaining the orientation needed for adequate insight, understanding, and objective acceptance of himself and his problems; and as an essential precondition for achieving growth toward self-mastery and the independent solution of his problems. The client is given every opportunity to talk out his problem, to get it off his chest, and to unburden himself of forbidden thoughts or desires and tabooed fancies. The primary purpose is to free the client from the obstacles, particularly emotional blockages, that interfere with his normal growth, and to assist him to attain the insight and integration needed to solve his own problems without dependence upon the therapist or the parent.

The successful therapeutic interview is conceived in terms of a growth experience in which the removal of the negative feelings should be followed by the emergence of positive impulses that make for the attainment of emotional maturity and the unfettered development of self-understanding and insight. Motivations that are based on deep insight become dynamic forces for personality reconstruction. With the gain in insight come genuine assimilation and increased self-confidence; and with increased self-confidence come more insight, capacity for self-direction, and improved personality integration.

While it is essential in this free, unregimented relationship for the interviewer to take deep personal interest in the child and win his confidence through the establishment of proper rapport, he must play a perfectly objective, detached, and passive role, as far as offering advice and suggestions is concerned. In this so-called "nondirective," client-centered form of therapy, the methods of suggestion, advice, evaluation, censure, prescription, command, and the issuing of directives that characterize the "directive" approach are taboo. When this technique is followed, the interviewer's or clinician's function is limited to assisting the subject to gain the insight needed for a correct evaluation of himself and his problem, and the independent solution of his difficulties. His function is objectively to accept the client (be he child or adult) as he is, without prejudice, criticism, moralizing, or undue sympathy, and help him to clarify his problem. His purpose is so to guide the interview situation that the child will be led to explore, recognize, and understand his real feelings and the nature of his maladjustments and their genetic background, instead of hiding them behind some form of face-saving defense, or projecting them onto other persons. The interviewee must be led to see himself as he really is, without his tricky defenses, and objectively to accept his spontaneous self with all his childish behavior patterns. When he has obtained the needed insight through his own evaluation of his problem and acceptance of himself, with his good and bad traits, he will be able to reorganize his "perceptual field," as well as his viewpoints and feelings regarding himself. The automatic results of the successful process of self-understanding and reorganization of his motivations, are, according to the theory, a unification or integration of the self or ego, changes in reaction patterns, release from tension and anxiety, and the emergence of a sense of freedom, repose, and power. Intellectual insight, however, is not sufficient. It must be accompanied by reduction of emotional tension and by emotional reintegration.

Phonographic records of actual interviews are now utilized for the purpose of training client-centered therapeutic counselors, particularly by Carl R. Rogers, who has made the greatest contribution toward the development of the system of nondirective therapy. Rogers's system is based on the assumption that the client possesses the capacity to explore his own feelings and attitudes better than the therapist and to gain insight into his own problems when the therapist provides the needed psychological atmosphere, a noncritical atmosphere of warmth, understanding, permissiveness, and acceptance of the good and the bad alike. The client, it is emphasized, possesses the spontaneity, the creative and integrative insight, and the desire and drive to grow and develop, to become emotionally mature, socially adjusted, and self-reliant; to choose new, health-preservative goals; to redirect motivations; and to reorganize attitudes, viewpoints, and behavior patterns without any "diagnostic shrewdness" on the part of the therapist. "Diagnostic knowledge and skill is not necessary for good therapy." [5] Good therapy, in such a system of self-discovery and evaluation, is not dependent upon diagnostic testing or case-history procedures.[6] Certain "basic attitudes and skills" can of themselves "create a psychological atmosphere which releases, frees, and utilizes deep

[5] Carl R. Rogers, "Significant Aspects of Client-centered Therapy," *The American Psychologist,* October, 1946, 421.

[6] Cecil H. Patterson, "Is Psychotherapy Dependent upon Diagnosis?" *The American Psychologist,* May, 1948, 155*f*.

strengths in the client." [7]   The outcome of effective client-centered therapeutic procedures can be predicted with a high degree of accuracy.   The process of therapy is essentially an educational one, as was emphasized with respect to all psychotherapeutic procedures in Chap. IV.

Controversy exists regarding the relative merits of the so-called "directive" method of treatment, a term suggested by Frederick C. Thorne, for the method of discovering causes by the diagnostician and overcoming them by interpretation, suggestion, reeducation, guidance, and other techniques, and the nondirective or passive approach.[8]   This controversy cannot be resolved until more satisfactory evidence is at hand than is now available.   The need doubtless exists for both types of treatment and for the avoidance of the extremes of each type.   Self-direction and rational control constitute the ideal in personality adjustment, and overregulation should be avoided.   But many persons with serious personality maladjustments are doubtless incapable of discovering the sources of their difficulties and of resolving them satisfactorily. They require the guidance of the skilled diagnostician and therapist.   The skilled therapist should be able to bring about readjustment and reeducation more expeditiously and more effectively than can be done by the trial-and-error explorations of the client.

Therapeutic interviewing in general may not be applicable to all who labor under emotional distress; it is not a panacea for all psychic disorders. The most acceptable cases are considered to be children of 10 and above who suffer from severe emotional conflicts engendered by incompatible strivings or by cultural demands, who are of approximately normal intelligence (above the dull normal level); who are not subject to extensive instabilities, particularly instabilities that rest on an organic or hereditary basis; who are not emotionally dependent upon the parents; and who are able to express their emotions through verbalization or action.   A feeling of dissatisfaction with present adjustments and the desire to be helped and to attain emotional maturity should be present, and cooperation from understanding parents and guardians is important.   Therapeutic interviewing is used chiefly in mental-hygiene clinics.[9]

[7] Rogers, *op. cit.*, 422.

[8] For a defense of the directive method, see Frederick C. Thorne, "Directive Psychotherapy," *Journal of Clinical Psychology*, I, 1945, 155–162, 228–240, 318–330; II, 68–79, 176–190, 261–266, 371–383; also, "Principles of Directive Counseling and Psychotherapy," *The American Psychologist*, May, 1948, 160*f*.

Certain phases of the controversy are aired in the symposium on "Research in Psychotherapy, Round Table, 1947," *American Journal of Orthopsychiatry*, January, 1948, 92–118.

[9] On nondirective therapy, see

Hadassah Peres, "An Investigation of Nondirective Group Therapy," *Journal of Consulting Psychology*, July–August, 1947, 159–172.

(*Footnote continued on p.* 229)

Group Therapy. The child is fundamentally a social creature and craves social contacts. Mere participation in social activities offers therapeutic possibilities. The winning of social acceptance and recognition makes for mental soundness and social efficiency. Almost any kind of group activity is replete with mental-health potentials (as well as possibilities of personality distortions): games, sports, play activities, puppet shows, dramatizations (psychodrama), social diversions, music, moving pictures, expression, art and craft activities, club activities, school exercises, church services, discussion conferences, courses of instruction (*e.g.*, on mental hygiene) [10] conducted in harmony with mental-hygiene principles, and the like.

Certain group-discussion procedures are specifically designed to mold and modify attitudes and behavior responses, to prevent or correct personality maladjustments, to provide emotional outlets, and to supply a "permissive environment" for optimal normal growth. Attempts have been made in public school "classes in human relations" by means of discussion techniques, to teach mental-health principles and concepts, to improve emotional adjustments, and to develop wholesome personalities. On the basis of interest-provoking stories from original sources, or from magazines or newspapers, dealing with problems of interpersonal relations, the leader (teacher) and the pupils join in a free, informal discussion of all sorts of sociopersonal problems, such as tolerance, teamwork, cooperation, getting along with people, unselfishness, fear, meeting difficulties, family relationships, inner dreads, emotional conflicts, and the like.[11]

Because of the shortage of psychiatrists and clinical psychologists in the U.S. Department of War, large use has been made, with gratifying results, of group-discussion therapy techniques and of specially devised psychothera-

---

Carl R. Rogers, *Counseling and Psychotherapy*, Boston, Houghton Mifflin Company, 1942 (references); "Electrically Recorded Interviews in Improving Psychotherapeutic Techniques," *American Journal of Orthopsychiatry*, 1942, 429–435; and "Therapy in Guidance Clinics," *Journal of Abnormal and Social Psychology*, 1943, 284–289.

Carl R. Rogers and John L. Wallen, *Counseling with Returned Servicemen*, New York, McGraw-Hill Book Company, Inc., 1946.

William U. Snyder, *et al.*, *Casebook on Non-Directive Counseling*, Boston, Houghton Mifflin Company, 1947; and "The Present Status of Psychotherapeutic Counseling," *Psychological Bulletin*, July, 1947, 338–340, 381–384 (references).

Articles by Carl R. Rogers, Arthur W. Combs, Harold H. Anderson, and Lawson G. Lowrey in the *American Journal of Orthopsychiatry*, October, 1946, 581–622.

On directive methods, see Thorne, *op. cit.*

[10] On the mental-health value of courses in mental hygiene, *cf.* Percival M. Symonds, "The Value of Courses in Mental Hygiene for the Personality Adjustment of Prospective Teachers," *Mental Hygiene*, 1941, 568–575; and "The Therapeutic Value for Teachers of the Course in Mental Hygiene," *Journal of Educational Psychology*, 1942, 561–583.

[11] H. Edmund Bullis and Emily O'Malley, *Human Relations in the Classroom*, Wilmington, The Delaware State Society for Mental Hygiene, Inc., 1948.

peutic cinema films among victims of war neuroses and psychoneuroses.[12] Paster's procedure in an army general hospital is, briefly, as follows: The patients who have been previously interviewed and their histories recorded are

assembled in a comfortably arranged living room.   The atmosphere is congenial, informal, and conducive to relaxation.   In a brief introductory talk the patients are reassured. . . . They are told that the primary purpose of our sessions is to afford them an opportunity to discuss their problems, air their grievances, and to help them get well.   They are urged to express themselves freely, and are told that the road to well-being and mental health lies not in forgetting or turning away from one's past, but in learning how to face one's terrifying memories calmly and courageously. . . . The number of sessions varies from 12 to 18.   During the first two or three sessions, each patient is called upon to relate the experiences which have led to the development of his nervous state.   The more extraverted patients are called upon first.   With some exceptions the more inhibited and withdrawn, encouraged by the examples of others, follow with comparative ease. Their stories, charged with emotion, are always dramatic and frequently interspersed with tragic incidents. . . . Encouraged by the presence of others who manifest symptoms similar to their own, most of the patients lose their defensive attitudes.   They talk much more freely about their painful experiences and reveal the inner turmoil they previously tried to repress. . . . The attitudes of the patients are not always the same during the group session as they are during individual interviews.   They are more outspoken during the group session. . . . The effect of the group sessions on most of the patients has been most favorable. Their attitudes of distrust and hostility disappeared.   Their tension and irritability diminished, and they have become more cheerful and friendly. . . . The psychoneurotic reactions precipitated in combat are in most instances not deeply rooted. . . . If these patients were treated promptly and placed on limited duty immediately following the onset of the symptoms, most of them would be salvaged and would continue to perform a useful function in the army.[13]

Paster's technique involved a combination of suggestion, indoctrination, and catharsis (release).

One other variant of group-discussion-therapy procedures deserves special consideration, namely, the "activity-therapy" method described most fully by Slavson.[14]   It is used with suitably selected children in small groups of from

[12] Howard P. Rome, "Motion Pictures as a Medium of Education," *Mental Hygiene,* 1946, 9–20.

[13] Samuel Paster, "Group Psychotherapy for Combat Neuroses," *American Journal of Orthopsychiatry,* 1945, 472–482 (references).

[14] S. R. Slavson, *An Introduction to Group Therapy,* New York, Commonwealth Fund, Division of Publication, 1943, 352 pp.

On various forms of group therapy, consult also

American Journal of Orthopsychiatry, April, 1947, 254–325 (a symposium).

Bruno Bettelheim and Emmy Sylvester, "Therapeutic Influence of the Group on the Individual," *American Journal of Orthopsychiatry,* October, 1947, 684–692.

(*Footnote continued on p* 231)

about 9 to 18 years of age. The treatment is intended for children who cannot get along with others; who are egocentric, seclusive (autistic), insecure, unassertive, or socially maladjusted; who are hostile, aggressive, or destructive; who have been rejected by the family, the school, or the street gang; and who tend to spend their idle time in the world of phantasy. The method is not

---

Ernest Fantel, *Psychodrama in an Evacuation Hospital,* New York, Beacon House, Inc., 1946.

Jacob H. Friedman and Lewis W. Gerhart, "The 'Question-Box' Method of Group Psychotherapy," *Mental Hygiene,* April, 1947, 246–256.

S. Gifford and J. Mackenzie, "A Review of Literature on Group Treatment of Psychoses," *Diseases of the Nervous System,* January, 1948, 19–24.

Margaret C.–L. Gildea, "The Social Function and Group Therapy," *Mental Hygiene,* April, 1948, 203–216.

Henriette T. Glatzer, "Selection of Mothers for Group Therapy," *American Journal of Orthopsychiatry,* July, 1947, 477–483.

"Group Therapy for the Young Child," *The Nervous Child,* July, 1945, Vol. 4 (a symposium by 12 writers).

Jose Gurri and Mignon Chasen, "Preliminary Survey of the Group Treatment of Psychoses," *Diseases of the Nervous System,* February, 1948, 52–54.

Jacob W. Klapman, *Group Psychotherapy, Theory and Practice,* New York, Grune and Stratton, Inc., 1946.

Gisela Konopka, "Group Therapy in Overcoming Racial and Cultural Tensions," *American Journal of Orthopsychiatry,* October, 1947, 693–699.

Abraham B. Luchins, "Methods of Studying the Progress and Outcomes of a Group Psychotherapy Program," *Journal of Consulting Psychology,* July–August, 1947, 173–183.

James Mann and Harold Mann, "The Organization and Technique of Group Treatment of Psychoses," *Diseases of the Nervous System,* February, 1948, 46–51.

Joseph I. Meiers, *Origins and Development of Group Psychotherapy,* New York, Beacon House, Inc., 1946.

Jacob L. Moreno, ed., *Group Psychotherapy,* New York, Beacon House, Inc., 1946.

Jacob L. Moreno, *Mental Catharsis and the Psychodrama,* New York, Beacon House, Inc., 1944.

Jacob L. Moreno, *Psychodrama and Therapeutic Motion Pictures,* New York, Beacon House, Inc., 1945.

Joseph H. Pratt, *The Group Method in the Treatment of Psychosomatic Disorders,* New York, Beacon House, Inc., 1946.

Nahum E. Shoobs, *Psychodrama in the Schools,* New York, Beacon House, Inc., 1944.

Samuel R. Slavson, *The Practice of Group Therapy,* New York, International Universities Press, 1945.

William U. Snyder, "The Present Status of Psychotherapeutic Counseling," *Psychological Bulletin,* July, 1947, 297–386 (a review of the recent literature on group therapy, traditional counseling, hypnosis, psychoanalysis, psychodrama, and relationship and nondirective therapy).

Edith M. Stern, "Ganging Up on Personal Problems," *Reader's Digest,* May, 1948, 93–96.

George W. Thomas, "Group Psychotherapy; A Review of Recent Literature," *Psychosomatic Medicine,* 1943, 166–180.

Lewis B. Wolberg, "The Hospital Treatment of Emotionally Disturbed Children," *Mental Hygiene,* 1945, 394–404 (references).

applicable to children who show serious behavior disorders or intense sibling rivalry, or to psychotics or frank psychopaths. These children need a haven of refuge from inner and outer pressures and restraints—a friendly, informal, "permissive" group environment in which they will be accepted with all their hostilities and faults without censure, threats, or punishment, and in which they will find opportunities for the unrestrained expression of their feelings and urges. Dynamic face-to-face relations with other children and with the therapist in a permissive social setting are conducive to emotional reorientation; to dissipation of fears, conflicts, and anxieties; and to normal personality integration.

In the therapy room the children are on their own. Freed from their inhibitions and guilt feelings, they are allowed to do what they like and comport themselves to one another much as they desire without suggestions or interference from the therapist. They can withdraw from activities, mingle with one another, quarrel, fight, construct things, or break things. External controls must be relaxed if the environment is to be therapeutic. The control is exerted by the group rather than by the leader. The children must learn to fashion their own controls. If adjustment is impossible, they need institutionalization. The program of activities—this is activity therapy—includes arts, crafts, cooking, sweeping, eating together, picnics, and excursions. These activities are intended to provide opportunities for successful achievement, for creative self-expression, and for acquiring feelings of confidence and security. The concrete work links them to reality and serves as a corrective of excessive phantasy indulgence. This form of treatment is often used as a supplementary kind of treatment rather than as an exclusive approach. Individual treatment might be carried on concurrently for selected cases.

Play Therapy. Extensive use is now made by psychologists and psychiatrists of play activities for diagnosing and treating certain kinds of maladjusted children. Play is the universal language of childhood. Children (and adults too) are most truly themselves when they indulge in spontaneous play. Psychologists for long have emphasized that we often get our most genuine glimpses of child nature by observing the spontaneous play activities of children—how they adjust themselves to other children; how they cooperate with one another; how they plan, imitate, follow, and lead; how they manipulate toys; what kind of play they are interested in; in what way they express their phantasies in imaginative plays and dramatizations; what is the nature of their play motivations; how they reveal their personal problems, frustrations and anxieties, and the home and school conditions through their spontaneous behavior, as well as the nature of their personal and social characteristics. The child's imaginative plays often symbolize his inner struggles. He is usually the suffering or the conquering hero in such play activities, which afford unconscious outlets for his inner tensions. His hostility toward his mother or his teacher shows itself in the spanking that he administers to the doll.

The use of the more refined play techniques for child diagnosis and therapy is of comparatively recent origin. Two types of therapy procedures are in vogue: free, or spontaneous, and controlled, or standardized. When the free-play method is pursued, the child, alone in the playroom with the therapist, is shown a variety of simple toys and is told that he may play with them as he likes. He may say what he wants and comport himself as he likes except that he must not break windows or lights or attack the therapist. Assured of the therapist's interest, he is encouraged to choose any toys and engage in any form of play that he chooses, without any interference on the part of the therapist. He is encouraged to give verbal expression in the form of a story to what he is thinking about and doing. He is permitted or encouraged to repeat a behavior pattern until he and the therapist acquire insight into its deeper meaning.

The purpose of the free play, of course, is to afford the child abundant opportunities to give unrestrained expression to his phantasies, fears, hostilities, sex conflicts, death wishes, and the like, in the expectation that the free expression will exert a desensitizing effect, offer release from emotional tensions (abreaction, catharsis), besides affording insight into the nature and meaning of his behavior mechanisms and the causes of his difficulties.

Because of its naturalness, the spontaneous-play method makes it easier for the child to enter into rapport with the therapist and to express his resistances. However, the development of rapport may be slow because of resistance to the therapist that is difficult to overcome. Suitable cases are inhibited children, children whose difficulties arise from disturbed family relationships, children with hostilities, excessively clean or neat children, and neurotics.

In the controlled, or standardized, procedure, the therapist chooses and arranges the play materials and describes to the child a particular play situation, which is designed for dramatizing or reenacting the episode that prior investigation has shown to be responsible for his particular problem. The child is encouraged to react to the problem situation after it has been explained to him. The following are illustrative planned play situations: A boy who had developed car sickness was shown a boy doll in a play car, which was pushed back and forth. He was told that the boy was riding in a streetcar and was asked to tell how the boy felt. A girl, subject to night terror, was asked what a doll in a toy bed was thinking about. A victim of a mouth tic, a sudden opening and closing of the mouth, acted out his compulsion in biting the play doll in the anal region. The child is encouraged to verbalize and dramatize his feelings without restraint. He assumes the role of the doll and answers for the doll in the period of questioning that may follow. Dolls constitute the usual play materials and may represent one of the parents, a sibling, the teacher, the therapist, or anyone else. This method (which may be combined with the spontaneous-play method for further exploration) is used to provide rapid clues to unconscious conflicts and wishes, a short cut to insight without much dependence on rapport with the therapist, and a prompt desensitization or a release outlet for the child's specific emotional disturbance. The method is particularly designed for children of 10 or less having normal family relationships, whose symptoms are traceable to some specific emotionally disturbing episode in the past. It is less applicable to family-produced disturbances (through rejection or severe discipline) or to neuroses of some standing. Little interpretation is supplied by the therapist. Insight and release are obtained from the experience involved in the free expression of the pent-up emotions—*e.g.*, the expression of obsessions about dirt (misophobia) or orderliness (overscrupulousness) in messy plays; the expression of aggressiveness in destructive activities, such as hitting or destruction of property; or the obtaining of infantile pleasure by sucking water from a nursery bottle.[15]

Psychoanalysis. Psychoanalysis is a highly refined (not to say esoteric) psychological method for discovering and removing the causes of mental or nervous difficulties, which, according to the psychoanalysts, are often hidden in the individual's past. Sigmund Freud, a Viennese psychiatrist, the dis-

---

[15] The literature on play diagnosis and therapy has become voluminous. Only a few references, which present disparate points of view, can be given here. Some of these contain additional references. Consult the symposium on play in *Understanding the Child*, June, 1938, 3–23; and *American Journal of Orthopsychiatry*, July, 1938, 466–524.

Virginia M. Axline, *Play Therapy: The Inner Dynamics of Childhood*, Boston, Houghton Mifflin Company, 1947.

Charlotte B. Buhler, "IV Play Therapy," in *Encyclopedia of Child Guidance*, New York, 1943, 308–312. (This brief statement contains an excellent bibliography.)

John E. Davis, *Play and Mental Health*, New York, A. S. Barnes and Company, 1938.

John E. Davis and William R. Dunton, *Principles and Practice of Recreational Therapy for the Mentally Ill*, New York, A. S. Barnes and Company, 1936.

Lydia Jackson and Kathleen M. Todd, *Child Treatment and the Therapy of Play*, London, Methuen & Co., Ltd., 1946.

Alfred Kamm, "Therapeutic Value of Recreation," *Occupational Therapy and Rehabilitation*, 1940, 237–245.

David M. Levy, "Trends in Therapy: III. Release Therapy," *American Journal of Orthopsychiatry*, 1939, 713–719.

H. W. Newell, "Play Therapy in Child Psychiatry," *American Journal of Orthopsychiatry*, 1941, 245–249.

Cuthbert H. Rogerson, *Play Therapy in Childhood*, New York, Oxford University Press, 1939.

Anna M. Smith, *Play for Convalescent Children in Hospitals and at Home*, New York, A. S. Barnes and Company, 1941.

tinguished originator of psychoanalysis, died in London in 1939. The year before, through the intervention of W. C. Bullitt and Franklin D. Roosevelt, he had been transported to London as a refugee, his fortune having been confiscated by the Nazis. References will here be made to only three psychoanalytic concepts or treatment techniques, as the theory of psychoanalysis will be discussed in Chaps. XIII to XVII.

Mental Catharsis. This refers to the dissipation of mental conflicts through the removal of disturbing attitudes or complexes by a sort of emotional purgation or purification. One of the processes for accomplishing this relief is abreaction.

Abreaction. Abreaction is a process of releasing dammed-up emotional energy by discharging it into some channel other than that employed in the formation of the symptoms. The subject is led back to the mental state or emotion in which the symptoms first appeared. He must recall the original experience, so as to identify the source of his trouble. Having made this discovery, he must communicate the recollection to the analyst under intense emotional expression.

Sublimation. This is regarded by some as the third stage of catharsis. It consists in the diversion of undesirable or inexpedient impulses or desires into socially approved forms of activity (see Chap. XVI).

Psychoanalysis in the hands of the skilled analyst doubtless has been a godsend to certain types of mental and nervous sufferers, although the value of the method is still in dispute.

The term "child analysis" is applied to a modified psychoanalytic technique employed with children, involving the use of free play and casual conversation with the examiner. Little or no use is made of the method of free association with dream or phantasy material, or of the method of abstraction in the recumbent position (see Chap. XV). The psychoanalytic goal of this kind of analysis remains the same, the discovery of the deeper, underlying, unconscious causes of the maladjustment.

Among the simpler forms of mental treatment mention may be made of the rest cure, occupational therapy, social diversion, and music.

The Rest Cure. This method was popularized years ago by S. Weir Mitchell for the treatment of nervous exhaustion and mental and nervous troubles. Prolonged rest in quiet surroundings is no doubt valuable in cases of genuine fatigue or exhaustion, in certain types of organic heart disease, in recovery from a severe cold, and during the period of convalescence from many illnesses, such as influenza, pneumonia, or chorea. Charles W. Manzer has recently inferred from experiments in lifting 10-pound weights that rests should be taken before, not after, fatigue. He found that, at the worst, the lifters accomplished four times as much when they took rests before rather than after the muscles had been fatigued. When they worked without rests, they suffered a reduction of 80 per cent in efficiency.

One of the outstanding exponents of the gospel of relaxation, Edmund Jacobson,[16] has outlined specific exercises of alternately tensing and relaxing almost all the skeleton muscles in succession, in order to establish the habit of relaxation. Fried [17] has employed with gratifying results a method of "purposeful relaxation as a first step in self-mastery" for unruly, overactive children in a private school for subnormals. The children, who were constantly running, jumping, scribbling, or breaking something, were required to relax half a minute every hour. In a game of "shut-eyes" they closed their eyes for 30 seconds, gradually relaxing the arms, legs, and feet. Through such practice, they gradually form the habit of complete relaxation. The relaxation was found to soothe the nerves, rest the body, and refresh the brain. To be able to teach the children to relax, the adults must first learn to relax themselves. Fried has the teachers sit on a comfortable chair or couch, with hands folded in the lap or resting on the sides and the body completely limp. The eyes are closed, the lips parted, the head allowed to fall to one side on the shoulder, the feet are crossed at the ankles, soles outward, and all muscles are relaxed.

Relaxation is the restorative needed by the overtense, the restless, and the high-strung. It is not a panacea even for all neurotics, as was once thought to be the case. In fact, the value of rest as a general treatment in nervous and mental difficulties is not held in such high repute today as formerly. Nervous patients are usually all too prone to adopt this form of treatment as a smoke screen for evading disagreeable situations in life. With nothing to do, they become more and more introverted and spend their time in unhealthy ruminations, constantly brooding over their unhappy fate. The rest treatment may thus aggravate the malady, instead of curing it. Nowadays, the substitutes for the rest treatment are occupational and recreational therapy and the work cure.

Occupational and Recreational Therapy and the Work Cure. To aid them to forget themselves and to become objective, mental and nervous

16 Edmund Jacobson, *You Must Relax: A Practical Method of Reducing the Strains of Modern Living,* New York, McGraw-Hill Book Company, Inc., 1942; also, *You Can Sleep Well,* McGraw-Hill Book Company, Inc., 1938.

For a recent evaluation of Jacobson's method of conditioning, see Dorothy H. Yates, "Relaxation in Psychotherapy," *The Journal of General Psychology,* 1946, 213–238.

17 Rudolph S. Fried, "Ten Years of Relaxation and Self-direction at Baily Hall and a Description of New Methods in Training of Children," *American Journal of Mental Deficiency,* 1941, 459–463.

See also Josephine L. Rathbone, *Relaxation,* New York, Teachers College, Columbia University, 1943; and Gerald R. Pascal, "The Use of Relaxation in Short-term Psychotherapy," *The Journal of Abnormal and Social Psychology,* April, 1947, 226–242.

patients (especially in institutions) are now provided with suitable forms of occupational training, such as knitting, rug weaving, basketry, brush and broom making, woodworking, leathercraft, modeling, sketching, painting, beauty-parlor work, gardening, farming, or housework. They are also encouraged to take part in suitable forms of social diversions, such as games, sports, movies, dances, dramatics, religious exercises, assemblies, entertainments, and house parties. Many institutions for the mentally disordered have introduced creative art expression (painting) as a means not only of discovering and developing talent, but of discovering and interpreting the mental conflicts and complexes of the patients and as a form of release therapy. During the depression, art classes were sponsored by the government in many institutions as Federal Art Projects. Many institutions now employ teachers of fine and industrial arts and of recreational therapy.[18]

That engrossment in satisfying, productive work possesses definite mental-health value is so well recognized that the term "work cure" has been

[18] References on creative art expression, occupational therapy, and physiotherapy:

Rose H. Alschuler and Le Berta W. Hattwick, *Painting and Personality: A Study of Young Children*, Chicago, University of Chicago Press, 1947 (2 vols.).

Jacob A. Arlow and Asja Kadis, "Finger Painting in the Psychotherapy of Children," *American Journal of Orthopsychiatry*, January, 1946, 134–146.

John E. Davis, *Rehabilitation—Its Principles and Practice*, rev. ed., New York, A. S. Barnes and Company, 1946.

William R. Dunton, *Prescribing Occupational Therapy*, 2d ed., Springfield, Ill., Charles C Thomas, Publisher, 1945.

Robert E. Johnson, "Fine Arts as a Means of Personality Integration," *The School Review*, April, 1948, 223–228.

Louis J. Haas, *Practical Occupational Therapy for the Mentally and Nervously Ill*, Milwaukee, The Bruce Publishing Company, 1944.

Nora Hayworth and E. M. MacDonald, *Theory of Occupational Therapy*, Baltimore, The Williams & Wilkins Company, 1941.

Richard Kovac, *Physical Therapy for Nurses*, Philadelphia, Lea & Febiger, 1940.

Edward Liss, "Pattern for Rehabilitation: The Role of the Educator," *Mental Hygiene*, 1947, 257–265.

Viktor Lowenfeld, *Creative and Mental Growth*, New York, The Macmillan Company, 1948.

Peter J. Napoli and Beatrice E. Gold, "Finger Painting in an Occupational Therapy Program," *American Journal of Occupational Therapy*, December, 1947, 358–361.

A. K. Rigast, "Inherent Therapeutic Values in Industrial Arts," *Industrial Arts and Vocational Education*, May, June, September, 1947, 198–201; 237–238; 282–285.

John I. Russell, *The Occupational Treatment of Mental Illness*, Baltimore, William Wood & Company, 1938.

Thelma E. Weisleder, "Establishing Rapport through Finger Painting," *The Elementary School Journal*, October, 1947, 82–87.

Helen S. Willard, *Principles of Occupational Therapy*, Philadelphia, J. B. Lippincott Company, 1947.

applied to this form of treatment.[19] As has already been intimated, many mental patients require the work cure rather than the rest cure. A definitely scheduled program of work, through the diversion and objectification of attention, arousal of new interests, and wholesome mental and physical activity, is of undoubted value in the treatment of both structural and functional illnesses, as well as imaginary troubles. The following case history supplies an excellent illustration of the value of the work cure used with proper insight in the case of a 20-year obsessional, imaginary, secret fear of having contracted tuberculosis. It also shows how such ills may arise from early processes of conditioning and how emotional hang-overs may continue for years to affect the individual's attitudes and behavior.

A DREADFUL OBSESSIONAL, IMAGINARY FEAR OF HAVING CONTRACTED TUBERCULOSIS, LASTING TWENTY YEARS, ASCRIBED TO CAUTION INSTILLED BY MOTHER WHEN TUBERCULOUS AUNT BECAME A GUEST IN THE HOME, KEPT SECRET UNTIL SHE MARRIED; EVERY COUGH AROUSED FEAR SHE HAD THE DISEASE; WHEN NEAR AN ILL PERSON, WAS AFRAID TO BREATHE THE AIR AND WASHED HANDS AND GARGLED THE THROAT AFTER LEAVING THE ROOM; REEXPERIENCING NAUSEA EVEN NOW WHILE RECALLING THE FACES MADE BY HER AUNT WHEN TAKING COD LIVER OIL; FASCINATED BY THE DISEASE ALTHOUGH IT WAS FEARED, READING EVERYTHING AT HAND ABOUT IT; SENT TO A SANITARIUM BECAUSE OF PERSUADING THE FAMILY DOCTOR AND THE CLINIC THAT SHE HAD THE DISEASE, IN SPITE OF THE NEGATIVE CHARACTER OF THE LABORATORY TESTS; CURED OF FEAR BY INTERESTING WORK AND PROPER ENLIGHTENMENT

From the age of four to twenty-four I was dreadfully afraid of tuberculosis. When I was about four, my aunt, who lived in a large city, contracted tuberculosis. As she was unable financially to go to a sanitarium, she came to our farm for a rest. My mother, fearing the result of our contact with her, admonished my sister and me before she arrived in no uncertain terms to play outdoors and to stay away from aunty. She succeeded in instilling in me such a fear of my aunt that during her entire stay, I am sure I never came into close contact with her or anything that she used. However, I saw her swallowing great heaped-up tablespoonfuls of thick, greenish cod liver oil. The faces she made and the odor of the foul stuff created such a nausea within me that I experience slightly the same sensations now again even as I write about it.

[19] For a summary of the investigations on work and behavior, see
David H. Fink, *Release from Nervous Tension,* New York, Simon and Schuster, Inc., 1946.
Henry Hart, "Work as Integration," *Medical Record,* December, 1947, 735–739.
Richard L. Solomon, "The Influence of Work on Behavior," *Psychological Bulletin,* January, 1948, 1–40 (little, however, on the mental-hygiene aspects).

From that time all through my childhood, adolescence, and young womanhood, I was dreadfully afraid of contracting tuberculosis. I was afraid of anyone who coughed. If I had to be near any ill person, I immediately suspected the person of having the dreaded disease. I was afraid to breathe while in the room with him and after I left I gargled my throat with any antiseptic at hand and washed my hands, but I still felt afraid.

Even though I feared the disease it fascinated me. I read everything I could find, mostly family health books and advertisements of cures, until I became fairly well acquainted with its symptoms. Then every time that I felt tired or had a little cough I immediately thought that I was headed straight for the graveyard, my aunt having died.

No one ever discovered my fear, I'm quite sure, until after I married and my first baby was a few months old. I did not regain my strength from the birth ordeal and with the care of a bouncing baby and my house I gradually grew thinner and weaker. Living in a large city without friends, I had plenty of time to think about myself. I persuaded myself, my doctor, and even the clinic at the hospital that I had tuberculosis even though none could find any signs of it from X-ray or sputum tests. I'm sure that my accounts of the symptoms were greatly exaggerated. I told of my aunt's visit but omitted telling them of the constant care exercised by my mother and myself. Finally they sent me to a sanitarium. Aside from the need of rest the specialist there could find very little wrong with me. As I did not begin to recover after a few weeks' rest treatment and as I remained very despondent, my doctor evidently began to scrutinize my mental health. After several long talks with me he advised me to take up typing, which I did. A little later he made it possible for me to become an associate editor of a monthly magazine published by the institution. Then he sent a priest to ask me to become organist of the institution's little church. In addition to this he gave me unlimited privileges to go to the rectory to study church history under the same old priest. Thus, outside of two hours' rest in the afternoon and one in the morning, my time was gradually filled with interesting things to do. This wise old doctor also gave lectures every week or so on tuberculosis, its causes, treatment, and cure. He constantly stressed the curability of the disease.

After living in this busy, enlightening atmosphere for eight months, I was sent home, now almost eleven years ago, cured of the disease (if I ever had it) and of all fear of the disease. Knowing more about the disease I lost all fear of it.

(M.J.L.; F.; E.S.T.; Age 35)

There is, however, another phase of the mental hygiene of relaxation that should not be lost sight of. One of the chief social characteristics of the present century is our high-gear living. Life's tempo has been enormously stepped up by Gatling-gun machinery, breakneck types of transportation, instantaneous methods of world communication, rapid multiplication of inventions, constant stimulation and excitement, especially in the large urban centers, keen business rivalry, the vast accumulation of knowledge to be mastered, and the heightened demands for efficiency and skill that must be satisfied during the formative period of life. What injury this high-pressure living may be inflicting upon the nervous and endocrine systems can only be surmised at present. According to G. W. Crile,

. . . the high activity of the brain, the thyroid, and the adrenal-sympathetic system (the kinetic system) of civilized man gives him not only his unique power and distinction, but also his unique diseases. . . . The human being is experiencing hyperkineticism, due to an excessive evolution of the energy-transforming system. . . . By the excessive action of the brain-thyroid-adrenal-sympathetic system . . . there are produced certain diseases which . . . may be considered as diseases peculiar to civilized man—neurocirculatory asthenia, hyperthyroidism, peptic ulcer, and probably diabetes. . . . These diseases trail man's ascent and the more highly civilized man becomes the more prevalent do these diseases become. [They are connected with] his incessant activity, especially mental and emotional [and not with his physical work, diet, climate, or infections. These diseases] occur most commonly among the most active, most striving, most worrying men and women. . . . Civilized man works all day and worries all night. . . . In both civilization and hyperthyroidism there is . . . greatly increased physical and nervous activity . . . increased emotional activity . . . high speeds and marked inhibitions . . . an increased incidence of peptic ulcer . . . of mental and psychic disturbances, of emotionalism, of intellectual acuteness. . . . Hyperthyroidism is a pathologic physiology of the mechanism of civilization. . . . African natives do not have peptic ulcers, nor do morons. Both are sheltered from the worries of civilized man. The highest incidence of diabetes in man is in the more highly civilized races. Diabetes has been made possible by the keen energy system of the civilization of which the diabetic is a member. [All these diseases, then,] are due to an overdevelopment of the energy or kinetic system [which may become] hyperactive, establishing a state of such excessive activity as to be termed hyperkineticism.

Organisms are either evolving or stationary or they advance according to the law of orthogenesis. [When a species begins to vary definitely in any direction, it cannot reverse itself, and the species continues to vary in that direction even if it is tending toward destruction.] In the case of man, the law of orthogenesis is applied to the controllers of the energy-transforming system, namely, the brain, the thyroid, and the adrenal-sympathetic system. The application of the law of orthogenesis would progressively involve especially the brain and the thyroid gland, which inevitably would reach a height of activity and speed that might destroy the individual. Thus man conceivably might be destroyed by the same tools that enabled him to reach the greatest height of his civilization.[20]

This is indeed a gloomy picture of the ruinous effects upon the nervous and endocrine systems of civilized man produced by the excessive emotional and intellectual activity incident to the high pressures of the forces of civili-

[20] Quoted, with the author's permission, from *Diseases Peculiar to Civilized Man,* New York, The Macmillan Company, 1934, 4–6, 10, 12, 92, 97, 104*f.*, and 395*f.*

zation. While we do not possess enough scientific knowledge to pronounce a final verdict on this question, it is doubtless true that the speed and pressure of modern occupational and social life are damaging to wholesome personality development and to the preservation of sound mental and physical health. Of course, this staccato-speed living does not affect all layers of the population or all individuals. Many groups of people and many persons who inhabit the United States still lead an easygoing, carefree existence, as did the imperturbable old Negro who, at the height of the depression, in response to the query how he was getting along, cheerfully replied: "Well, boss, I didn't have nothing when the depression started and I still have it." Perhaps these groups may in the end subserve vital eugenic ends. High-pressure living affects more particularly the workers in the more competitive pursuits, the overcrowded occupations, and the technical and intellectual classes—the more aggressive and progressive elements of the population.

The Atomic Age. Since the above picture of high-tempo living was drawn, civilization has been precipitated into the atomic age (dating from Dec. 2, 1942, according to a recent ruling of the U.S. War Department) by the cataclysmic technological advances produced by the Second World War. It would be idle at this time to speculate regarding all the implications for mental health, serenity, gene mutations, and survival, and for national and international peace of the sudden release of intra-atomic, or nuclear, energy—immeasurably the most powerful force ever unlocked by man's advancing technological skill.[21] Man apparently stands on the brink of a new age, but what that age will mean in terms of human adjustment or survival no one can now predict with certainty. We do know that every major technological advance has brought about an industrial revolution, with concomitant social dislocations. Witness the age of steam, electricity, the combustion engine, electronics, and radioactivity. The invention of new tools, self-directing, robot machines, and the introduction of mass production have meant greater productivity and more freedom and leisure, but

[21] For a discussion of the atomic age concept and the social pathologies of the present era, see

Franz Alexander, "Mental Hygiene in the Atomic Age," *Mental Hygiene,* 1946, 529–544.

Francis J. Braceland, "Psychiatry and Atoms," *Mental Hygiene,* January, 1947, 29–37.

Harrison S. Brown, *Must Destruction Be Our Destiny?* New York, Simon and Schuster, Inc., 1946.

G. Brock Chisholm, "Can Man Survive?" *The Nation,* July 20, 1946, 63–65, and July 27, 1946, 93–96.

Kenneth B. Clark, "Social Science and Social Tension," *Mental Hygiene,* January, 1948, 15–26.

Julia E. Johnson, *The Atomic Bomb,* New York, The H. W. Wilson Company, 1946 (references).

Public Reaction to the Atomic Bomb, Social Science Research Council, Ithaca, N.Y., Cornell University, 1947.

also more mechanization and technological unemployment. Man's adjustment in the past to the constantly shifting industrial scene has often proceeded at a much slower and more uncertain pace in terms of needed modification of habits of living, working, thinking, and feeling, and in educational and social adjustment than has the rate of progress achieved in the physical sciences. In the course of the Industrial Revolution of the last century man has remained fundamentally the same in his social and psychological behavior mechanisms. Will he be able to adjust to what may prove to be the most stupendous technological advance of all time? The atomic age may mean, on the one hand, a reign of illogical, irrational, emotionalized behavior—fear, distrust, suspicion, duplicity, hostility, envy, lust for power and revenge, and global internecine strife generated by the possession of the most devastating instrument of destruction ever conceived. How much peace and security can there be in a world in which atom bombs can now be delivered noiselessly, without warning, at a speed greater than the velocity of sound (V-2 bombs) without present possibility of interception? The bomb dropped on Hiroshima killed 78,150 persons and injured 305,000, while 13,000 were missing; and it leveled all the buildings within a radius of a mile and a half. Now far more powerful bombs than that can be manufactured.

On the other hand, if man succeeds in outlawing the atomic bomb and subsequent even more powerful derivatives for use as instruments of mass ruin, in order that he may survive at all, the harnessing of atomic energy for peaceful uses might create terrors of peace as bad as the terrors of war through mass unemployment in a scale hitherto unknown, and through the attendant loss of income and the inability to adjust to a life of leisure or idleness. If atomic energy is limited to industrial uses by international agreement, in accordance with the universal demand of the masses of mankind, if this produces industrial overproduction on a scale hitherto unsuspected, and if adequate subsistence can be obtained on a much foreshortened work day, the problem of health-preserving leisure-time occupation may become one of paramount importance in the decades just ahead. The evils of unemployment are not only economic, but also, as has already been pointed out, psychological, social, and moral. Inactivity spells physical deterioration, psychic stagnation, and possible moral degeneration.

What, then, shall be done with the energies freed by industrial technology? The challenge to the social engineers and the religious and educational leaders is to provide constructive cultural outlets in all kinds of socially useful pursuits that will contribute to mental soundness and the art of effective living on the psychological and social planes. This job will involve the development of the desire and the ability in the youths of the oncoming generations to apply the energies released from the production of food, clothing, houses, and all other kinds of material possessions to higher social and cultural aims in the fields of aesthetics, the creative arts (music, painting, dramatics, litera-ture, etc.); mental, social, and physical health; and ethics. It will also be necessary to foster in the body politic a deeper appreciation of the value of cultural contributions, as compared with material productions, and a willing-ness to make greater financial sacrifices for their support.

High-pressure Mass Education. Many neurologists and psychiatrists have for years condemned the schools for laying the groundwork for the development of nervous and mental disorders in the later lives of children because of overpressure in school. There is doubtless some basis of fact for the assertion that the schools have done irreparable injury to the mental and nervous health of countless children and youth, although overpressure is not the outstanding evil of the schools. Nevertheless, some teachers create undue nervous strain through overlong assignments—assignments that exceed the generally accepted standards of what an instructor has a right to demand per unit of credit. The overpressure is probably greater in the high school than in the elementary school and greater on the college than on the high-school level, partly because less inspectional supervision exists in the college than in the high school. In fact, the college is notorious for its lack of regi-mentation and control. If a speed enthusiast in college makes inordinate demands upon the student, he is usually left to his devices without inter-ference.

Whatever the truth of this indictment, it is indubitably true that over-emphasis in the schools and colleges upon the mere mastery of subject matter has wrought serious damage to wholesome personality development in many individuals. This condition will be remedied only when we learn to put first things first. In the words of the distinguished biologist E. G. Conklin, the aim of education is the development of "good habits of body and mind, not storing the mind with facts. If the acquisition of infor-mation is the chief aim of education it must be confessed that it is a dismal failure as measured by lasting results." After all, information and knowledge getting, however important ends they may be (if indeed they are ends in themselves), are of secondary importance in comparison with the develop-ment of mental, social, and physical health and efficient personality adjust-ment, and the acquisition of the mastery of the technique of unprejudiced, objective, factual thinking and the art of emotional control. The accumu-lation of vast stores of knowledge or even the acquisition of superskill is not worth the price of loss of mental balance. We may well ask, Of what good are knowledge and skill if the price is mental maladjustment, discord, and derailment? The student will have no use for the subject-matter contents if he "goes to pot" in cramming to obtain them and has to spend most of his subsequent days in battling his internal conflicts or trying to overcome his maladjustments. The highest function of public education is to conserve the nation's greatest assets, the brain power, intellectual and moral stamina, and desirable personality attributes of its citizens.

A Contrasting Phenomenon in the Recent Economic Depression. Reference may not be amiss at this point, by way of contrast, to the general economic depression in which we were engulfed during the third decade of the century. From early reports, it seemed that this wide-scale economic debacle would prove more destructive than any other occurrence in modern times to mental balance and health and would produce a larger harvest of despondency, neuropsychiatric abnormalities, ruined morale, and blasted careers. Roscoe Hall believes he found evidence that the depression developed a new ailment, comparable to the shell shock of the First World War, which he denominates "depression shock." In this disease the victim unconsciously magnifies some minor ailment because of the fears produced by his battles against economic odds and develops a disabling illness as a means of escape from disappointing and humiliating experiences. To be unable to earn his subsistence and to be forced to depend on charity is as disgraceful and cowardly to a formerly self-supporting, self-respecting person as was running away from the battle to the gallant soldier. But it will not seem to be a disgrace to avoid a futile combat with the depression if you are too sick to fight.

More recent reports seem to show that the severe economic dislocation of the thirties did not produce such great havoc to mental health and morale as had been anticipated. Many believe that this is due primarily to the fact that the government spent many billions of dollars to provide "made work" for anybody in need of financial assistance. In fact, the allowance was so liberal for a short work week that many did not want to get off the "dole." They preferred a snap, short-week, public job at good pay to a more difficult long-week job in private industry at no better pay or even at less pay. It did not seem to them disgraceful to continue on the dole, in view of the fact that they were rendering some service, even though the work was pure "boondoggling." They became reconciled to a comfortable, noncompetitive berth as a merited government "handout." Because of the complication of government relief, which changed the whole problem almost overnight, it is very difficult to assess the mental-health effects of the depression. It is equally difficult to determine the effects of the governmental coddling and overprotection that went on for several years. According to Edward A. Strecker and Kenneth E. Appel (quoted from press reports),

"Undue dependence on the government for support produced in individuals numerous unhealthy characteristics, such as loss of initiative, carelessness, boredom, restlessness, discontent, irritability, and an unwholesome need for help and support. . . . Continued dependency on the State by large masses of the population might create general irresponsibility and ineffectiveness among the dependent classes, just as governmental overindulgence of the entrepreneurs in the past bred frightful irresponsibility in that class.

What the ultimate effects on the morale of millions of our workers of our system of generous handouts would have been in the years to come is also difficult to determine, because of the sudden eruption of the Second World War. The new war developments provided abundant jobs for anybody who wanted to work, often at grossly inflated wages.

We have just emerged from an unparalleled period of long-hour, high-speed industrial production, the mental-health effects of which cannot as yet be correctly assessed. Vigorous demands have been made for a reduction in the hours of labor, for increased wages, and for provisions for social and economic security; but a drastic reduction in the work load might create more mental-health problems than it would solve. Long hours of idleness, instead of conducing to mental health, might actually create serious hazards to its attainment and preservation. Boredom and idleness might indeed become a greater menace to the nation's mental and social health than is poverty. A new problem in mental hygiene might have to be faced—that of providing wholesome interests and pursuits and healthy emotional outlets and intellectual interests to occupy the individual during his leisure time: hobbies, joyous creative activities, artistic constructiveness and appreciation, music, and the like.

Music Therapy. Music, through its rhythm, tempo, melody, and harmony, is one of the most powerful mediums for influencing man's feelings, attitudes, disposition, and morale; for creating unity of feeling in crowds or in whole nations; for socializing individuals; for energizing and harmonizing their muscular movements; and for arousing people to action. Nothing is superior to powerful martial airs for stimulating soldiers to vigorous attack on the battlefield or for arousing the populace in the home centers. Work songs and instrumental music (usually phonograph recordings) have been used to synchronize the movements of work cooperatives; to accelerate the work tempo in factories (the increase in output in one cracker-packing plant amounted to 11 per cent); to afford relief from fatigue or boredom in repetitive operations or relaxation during the noon or other intermissions; or to produce feelings of buoyancy, contentment, and cheer. Music can now easily be made available in industrial plants and in institutions of all kinds by means of radios, phonographs, bands, and orchestras, visiting performers, and talented institution inmates.

Music therapy has been used to some extent in general hospitals, in hospitals for the mentally disordered, and in institutions for social and mental defectives for a variety of therapeutic purposes.[22] It has been used in the

[22] Egyptian medical papyri discovered in 1889 seem to show that the therapeutic use of music was recognized at least as early as 2500 B.C.

treatment of almost all kinds of physical and mental maladies, even as a form of support therapy in operations. The most frequent employment of it has been in connection with the treatment of certain types of psychotics (mentally disordered or "insane" patients), neurotics, and emotionally and nervously unstable children and adults. For these cases music usually has been adopted as a sedative to quiet and soothe frayed and unsettled nerves, to relieve emotional and nervous tension, and to afford relaxation and rest. For this purpose, the music selected must, of course, be such as will have a quieting, sedative effect—Beethoven's *Kreutzer Sonata,* the Bach-Gounod *Ave Maria,* and Brahms's *Lullaby,* for example. While the mental effects of certain tempos are fairly general and constant (measurements show that the brisk, stimulating *Rhapsody in Blue* by Gershwin almost invariably accelerates the pulse rate), the exact effect of a given melody, air, or tempo upon a given person must be determined by clinical observation and study. The virtues of music are, of course, not limited to the melioration or cure of mental ailments. Its preventive value may be even greater.

L. C. Marsh, in an experiment in "group social psychiatry" at the Worcester State Hospital, which included occupational therapy, social diversion, daily morning assemblies with music and talks, dancing, and other activities accompanied by music, found that talks accompanied by soft music and tender love songs held the patient's attention. Music had a noteworthy quieting effect on the disturbed patients. Though none was cured by it, music supplied a form of emotional release that perceptibly improved the emotional tone of the patients. It proved an excellent device for treating disturbances that Marsh regards as basically emotional in nature. Since social-emotional experiences are the cause of mental disorder,[23] the treatment must be some form of social therapy. "The dance is one way of helping people to recover their sense of social security, which to my mind is the rationale of recovery." Tap dancing proved the best form of the dance, followed by social dancing, provided that the partners (volunteer high-school girls) were gay and conversationally inclined.[24]

According to A. F. Fultz (as reported in a magazine write-up) children with colic stopped crying when they heard the Brahms *Lullaby;* an anemic girl who had not been sufficiently interested in life to finish a meal manifested a new attitude after listening to a Judy Canova record of hill-billy ballads; a man suffering from a severe attack of shingles, a skin rash, recovered after listening to Rimsky-Korsakoff's *Scheherazade.*

[23]   "By the crowd have they been broken,
                        By the crowd shall they be healed."

[24] L. Cody Marsh, "An Experiment in the Group Treatment of Patients at the Worcester State Hospital," *Mental Hygiene,* 1933, 396–416.

Two of Laura S. Bender's cases may be briefly cited as illustrations of the effect of music on young malbehavior cases.

A violent ten-year-old mentally deteriorating "bull in a china closet" had been a menace to the other children until he was entered in the music class. There he got enjoyment from the music, was able to sing with his fellows, and even came to express concern as to whether the other fellows were having a good time.

An eight-year-old boy who had driven his parents frantic—they had been forced to lock doors and windows and to disconnect the gas when he was home—became the music teacher's darling for his exemplary behavior.

Music has, in fact, been hailed as the universal cure for crime and delinquency. Edwin F. Goldman has said, "I guarantee you that if our children were given a chance to play some musical instrument, within a few years we could drop the bars from our jails. Have you ever heard of a gangster who played an instrument or a musician who was in jail?" Exceptions to this extravagant statement readily come to mind. There was, for example, Snodgrass, the "king of the ivories," whose piano recitals were broadcast from the Missouri penitentiary, years ago. Another is Thomas Meryle Wofford, "song composing desperado," with a flair for cowboy songs, thrice-convicted and twice-escaped convict, whose sentences include 28 years for robbery and 15 years for kidnaping. Among North Carolina's 9,000 convicts in 1937, 11 were musicians, as against 2 dentists, 2 ministers, 3 artists, 4 teachers, 5 physicians, 5 newspapermen, 6 attorneys, and 13 engineers. Among these professional groups, the musicians rank next to worst. Music, with all its charms, is not a panacea for all the unruly passions and distempers of the mind. Nevertheless, it is more than a mere luxury to the mental hygienist. It is a vital necessity to many discordant natures. Music is the universal language of the emotions—a language that all can understand.[25] One of its great virtues is the keen pleasure and enjoyment derived from listening to it or from participating in it. Music induces a joyous, contented, wholesome emotional tone, which makes for mental and physical harmony. It provides one of the most satisfying outlets for the emotional life.

The strategic role that music can play in the dissemination of propaganda on a national scale in the interest of a political system was well understood by the Nazis. They did not hesitate to prostitute the use of music to bolster their doctrine of German supremacy. They accomplished their vile objectives, not only through the exclusion of worth-while music from other lands,

[25] Thomas A. Edison, Inc., has issued a pamphlet (*Mood Music*, 1921), which lists 112 graphophone records according to "what they will do for you." Included in the effects produced by the different selections are stimulation and enrichment of the imagination; excitation of energy; and the stimulation of moods of joyousness, wistfulness, good fellowship, love, tenderness, dignity, and devotion.

but by distorting the mythological characters in German operas to symbolize Nazi supermen. To overcome this perversion of a fine art, to rescue the great musical heritage of the Germans, and to use music as a means of reeducating the German nation, Fabien Sevitzky, conductor of the Indianapolis Symphony Orchestra, has proposed the appointment of an international board of psychologists, psychiatrists, and musicians who would apply "music therapy" in the program of directing Germany toward national sanity. This board, during a 20-year period, would reintroduce throughout Germany the great music of all races and nationalities, and would educate the Germans to "sing for construction, not destruction," and to "listen to opera as entertainment, not national politics."

The Music Research Foundation has recently been founded for the purpose of investigating the kinds of music that possess therapeutic value and the types of mental patients that are most responsive to music.[26]

[26] Those interested in the musical aspects of the mental-health problem will find material of value in the following references:

I. M. Altshuler, "Music in the Treatment of Neurosis," *Proceedings of the Music Teachers' National Association,* 1944, 154–163; and "Past, Present, and Future of Musical Therapy," *Educational Music Magazine,* 1945, 16–17.

D. K. Antrim, "Healing Children with Music; Occupational Therapy with Music Instruments," *Etude,* 1943, 651*f.*

R. Bradley, "Music in Hospitals," *Proceedings of the Music Teachers' National Association,* 1944, 453–455.

G. H. Cartwright, "Healing Art of Music," *Etude,* 1945, 81*f.*; and "More Musical Therapeutics," *Etude,* 1945, 136.

E. G. Gilliland, "Healing Power of Music," *Music Educators Journal,* 1944, 18–20; "Music for the War Wounded," *Music Educators Journal,* 24–25; "Music in the Treatment of the Sick," *Hygeia,* 1944, 896–897; "Let Music Pave the Way to Health," *The Crippled Child,* June, 1947, 12–13; "Today's Hospital Needs Music," *Hospital Management,* 1947, 116, 118–119.

Arthur H. Harrington, "Music as a Therapeutic Aid in a Hospital for Mental Diseases," *Mental Hygiene,* 1938, 601–607.

John W. Hausserman, "Music for Relaxation," *Spastic Review,* 1943, 8–10.

O. Irving Jacobson, "The Use of Music in an Educational Program of Mental Hygiene," *Journal of Experimental Education,* 1940, 399–402.

Willard A. Kerr, *Experiments on the Effects of Music on Factory Production,* Stanford University, Calif., Stanford University Press, 1945, 44 pp.

Sidney Licht, *Music in Medicine,* Boston, New England Conservatory of Music, 1946. "Music for What Ails You," *Rotarian,* 1937, 39*f.*

Edward Podolsky, *The Doctor Prescribes Music,* Philadelphia, J. B. Lippincott Company, 1939.

Frances Raperte, "Music in Military Medicine," *Mental Hygiene,* 1946, 56–64.

Robert Haven Schauffler, *Junior Poetry Cure* and *Magic of Music,* New York, Dodd, Mead & Company, Inc., 1931; 1935.

Willem Van de Wall and Clara M. Liepmann, *Music in Institutions,* New York, Russell Sage Foundation, 1936.

(*Footnote continued on p. 249*)

Range of Application of Psychotherapeutic Methods. Psychological methods of treatment have often proved helpful in the handling of both real and imaginary troubles and of both bodily and mental illnesses. Numerous cures have been wrought by psychotherapeutic methods, even when they have been based on fallacious assumptions. Many techniques lay claim to miraculous elements, but the miraculous tends to disappear as procedures are better comprehended. Many forms of treatment are merely different kinds of "suggestive therapeutics." Of course, psychological methods prove more successful with the lesser forms of functional difficulties than with organic diseases or with the major forms of mental disease (technically called psychoses) and defects. And yet, perhaps Bernard C. Ewer did not go far astray in his assertion that by far the larger part of human suffering can be reached more effectively by psychotherapeutic methods than by any other methods; or Abraham Myerson in his contention that drugs and physiological therapeutics are just as much psychic agents as are good advice and analysis. John M. T. Finney, distinguished Johns Hopkins surgeon, in an address delivered after years of practice, stated that he had reached the conviction that operations should not normally be performed unless the patients have the will to live and the desire to cooperate. "Hopeless cases," according to Finney, "have been made successful sometimes solely by the will of the patient to live . . . but minor or routine operations may result fatally if a patient is convinced he has no chance to survive. Success demands faith in the doctor, regardless of the surgeon's skill or experience." It is no exaggeration to say that the physician who desires to achieve maximum success in the treatment of bodily diseases will never allow himself to forget that he must treat the whole personality, the composite whole, rather than merely the liver or the kidneys or the wound. Certainly, the emotional shock resulting from an operation is often more difficult to treat than the wound itself, and the psychological skill and tact required are of a higher order than is the corresponding manual dexterity requisite for the operation.

Effectiveness of the Treatment of the Maladjusted. Although some types of mental and nervous disorders doubtless rest upon a hereditary basis and represent the belated expression of hereditary influences, nevertheless,

---

Willem Van de Wall, "Functional Use of Music in Industry and Therapy," *Proceedings of the Music Teachers' National Association,* 1944, 147–153; and *Music in Hospitals,* New York, Russell Sage Foundation, 1946.

M. Wayne, "Instrumental Music for the Maladjusted Child," *Music Educators Journal,* 1944, 33*f.*

R. Williams, "Music for What Ails You: Six Prescriptions for Emotional Moods," *House Beautiful,* 1943, 37*f.*

For four additional references, consult: *Bulletin on Current Literature,* The National Society for Crippled Children and Adults, January, 1947, 4.

the facts seem to show that only about one child in 100,000 under the age of 15 suffers from mental disease so serious as to require hospitalization. But one out of every 22 born in New York State eventually becomes a patient in a hospital for the mentally disordered in the lifetime of a generation (H. M. Pollock and B. Malzberg). In Massachusetts, one in ten has at one time been an inmate in an institution for the mentally defective or the mentally diseased, while one in every five or six in civilized society will become a victim of nervousness (Stewart Paton). The astonishing prevalence of mental disorders in our adult population is further shown by the fact that there are now as many patients in hospitals for the mentally afflicted as there are in all other hospitals combined. According to information received from the Veterans Administration, 61 per cent of the 72,729 veterans of all wars in the veterans hospitals on Oct. 1, 1945, were classed as neuropsychiatric cases. Of these veterans, 43,979 were from the First World War and 22,986 from the Second World War. The number of first admissions a year to all hospitals for mental disease has risen from 50,000 in 1920 to 92,157 in 1946.

Of 68,893 first admissions to hospitals for mental cases in the various states of the union, 47.7 per cent were classified as functional cases associated with faulty mental adjustments (W. L. Treadway). On the basis of this fact, one might be led to conclude that about one-half of all psychoses are preventable. However, the problem is not quite so simple, because some of the functional cases doubtless rest upon a hereditary predisposition, while some of the organic cases (such as those produced by syphilis, alcohol, and possibly arteriosclerosis) may be due purely to the stresses, strains, and dissipations of life.

It is practically impossible to hazard trustworthy answers to the questions in which the mental hygienist is chiefly interested, namely, what proportion of mental disorders can be prevented and what proportion can be cured by proper prophylactic and curative measures. It would be bootless, even if space permitted, to attempt to reconcile the contradictory views of the psychiatrists on these questions. In general, the rate of recovery will vary with the age at onset, and with the duration, severity, and nature of the malady. Functional, or acquired, mental disorders are, in general, more remediable than are the organic. According to the report of the Bureau of the Census for the year 1942, 30.3 per cent of the 52,677 patients discharged from state hospitals were recovered, 58.5 per cent were improved, and 9.2 per cent were unimproved. The condition of the much larger number who were retained is not revealed.

Doubtless more cases of mental disorder are curable today than was the case two or three decades ago. Under the newer medical treatment procedures, some of the types formerly regarded as hopeless are yielding more encouraging results. For example, the fever treatment (thermotherapy) has proved successful with a certain proportion of patients having the psychosis known as general paresis (or paralytic dementia), which is caused by brain syphilis. This brain disease used to affect from 10 to 15 per cent of first admissions to public and private hospitals for the mentally diseased. By 1938 the number had been reduced to 7.1 per cent; by 1945, to 5.7 per cent, possibly as a result of the government-sponsored campaign for the prevention and cure of venereal diseases. When the brain has been invaded, the disease ordinarily follows a rapidly progressive course of cerebral degeneration and mental deterioration (with serious disturbances of memory, judgment, disposition, character, orientation, speech, writing, motor coordination and reflexes, and delusions of grandeur) to a fatal ending within a few years unless the disease responds to the fever treatment. The elevation of the patient's temperature to from 103 to 105 degrees for several hours destroys the syphilitic germs (*Spirochaeta pallida*). This can be done by inoculation with malaria germs (the form of treatment originated in 1917 by Julius Wagner-Jauregg of Vienna), by vaccination with proteins, by the use of electrical cabinets or blankets or of instruments that shoot high-frequency wave lengths through the body, or by the use of prolonged hot baths. The fever treatment may be supplemented by the use of drugs (arsphenamines and bismuth). The percentages of reported cures and improvements from this fever treatment differ considerably.

In the case of dementia praecox (technically called "schizophrenia") [27]— one of the earliest forms of mental disease and one that includes about a quarter of new admissions to the hospitals for psychotics and that is often regarded as a hopeless constitutional mental disorder—a new form of treatment, the "sugar shock" treatment, was inaugurated by Manfred Sakel, Viennese physician, in 1928. The treatment consists in giving daily injections of insulin in progressive doses until the sugar in the blood is very low (the condition called "hypoglycemia"). Then a massive dose is administered and this, after a few hours, throws the patient into a deep coma. The return of consciousness is brought about by feeding the patient sugar (glucose). Upon the return of consciousness, the mental condition often clears up and mental reintegration is established.

[27] The victims of this disorder tend to become shut-in, seclusive, apathetic, introvertive; to lose contact with their surroundings and take recourse to the world of fancy or day-dreaming; and to manifest incongruity between their feelings and their thoughts.

For references on dementia praecox, see the books on psychiatry and the special monographs in the Bibliography at the end of the book. See also the following:

Leopold Bellak, *Dementia Praecox,* Grune & Stratton, Inc., 1948. (A review of the past 10 years' work.)

Roy G. Hoskins, *The Biology of Schizophrenia,* New York, W. W. Norton & Company, Inc., 1946.

David Shakow, *The Nature of Deterioration in Schizophrenic Conditions,* Nervous and Mental Disease Monograph 70, 1946.

Many other methods for shocking the patient into unconsciousness have been employed, such as the use of camphor, the inhalation of nitrogen, and particularly the injection of metrazol (a treatment devised by Ladislaus von Meduna of Budapest in 1934) and the shooting of an electric current (electro-shock therapy) of less than 100 volts through the head. A sufficient amount of metrazol is injected to produce epileptiform convulsions and unconsciousness. The injections are usually repeated 10 to 15 times. The treatment is rather drastic and is often preceded by the use of curare to lessen the violence of the spasms. Certain types of schizophrenics (the catatonic and paranoid forms) are said to respond better to the insulin than to the metrazol. The electric-shock treatment, introduced in its modern form by U. Carlotti and L. Bini in Rome in 1938, has superseded the chemical methods in many places because it is milder, more easily controllable, largely harmless, and apparently equally potent; but it causes more memory loss after treatment than does metrazol. Usually from ten to twenty treatments are administered two or three times a week. This treatment is being applied to other forms of mental disease, especially those characterized by depressions, such as manic-depressive psychosis and the psychoses incident to old age and the menopause. According to Kolb and Vogel, 94 per cent of 305 state mental hospitals have used some form of shock therapy.[28] The reports vary from glowing accounts of spectacular cures to records of moderate improvement or even failure.

The following reports on the use of insulin were issued in May, 1944. Of 316 patients treated since 1939 in the Trenton, N.J., state hospital, 60 per cent "had shown definite improvement." The results obtained during a 7-year period with 700 patients in the Central Islip, N.Y., state hospital were "not as effective as reports have indicated." Nevertheless, worth-while results were obtained with cases up to 2 years' standing. It is usually conceded that the shorter the duration of the malady the more effective is the treatment. The various forms of shock therapy seem to be ineffective with children. The patients must be in good physical condition to withstand the shock ordeal.[29]

[28] Lawrence Kolb and Victor H. Vogel, "Use of Shock Therapy in 305 Mental Hospitals," *American Journal of Psychiatry*, July, 1942, 90–100.

Edward N. Hinko and L. S. Lipschutz, "Five Years After Shock Therapy: A Preliminary Report," *American Journal of Psychiatry*, December, 1947, 387–390.

[29] The Committee on Therapy of the Group for the Advancement of Psychiatry has recently warned against the indiscriminate use of electroshock treatment.

On the shock treatment, consult the following:

Alexander Grulnick, "A Three-year Survey of Electroshock Therapy," *The American Journal of Psychiatry*, March, 1946, 583–593.

(Footnote continued on p. 253)

"Psychosurgery" is the term ordinarily applied to the form of prefrontal lobotomy (cutting into the lobe) introduced by Egas Moniz in Portugal in 1936. The operation consists in severing bilaterally the subcortical fibers (white) that connect the frontal lobes and the thalamus, a mass of gray matter at the base of the brain, which is supposed to be functionally connected with the emotions, a sort of physiological battery for "charging" ideas with emotional contents. No part of the brain is removed and the cortical areas are left intact. The implication is that the break in the neural connection between the intellectual and the emotional life reduces the emotivity or excitability of the subject and so renders him less apprehensive, fearsome, and impulsive.

Psychosurgery has been applied to intellectually normal persons who are subject to worries, depressions, fears, phobias, doubts, and delusions, and to different kinds of psychotics, with varying immediate sequelae, often unfavorable. The unfavorable results include confusion, restlessness, forgetfulness, loss of initiative and of planning capacities, and psychomotor retardation. The long-range favorable results include relief from anxieties, fears, inhibitions, and excessive impulsiveness. The method has also been used among psychotics, with varying results. One report issued in May, 1944, states that the operation enabled 50 per cent of schizophrenics to "lead normal lives." This rather drastic procedure invites analytical statistical validation on a large scale over a period of years.[30]

Edward J. Humphreys, Etem Vassof, and Suzanne A. L. Howe, "Ambulatory Insulin and Adjunctive Institutional Treatment of Mental Defectives with Psychiatric Disorders," *American Journal of Mental Deficiency*, April, 1943, 450–455.

Lothar B. Kalinowsky and Paul H. Hoch, *Shock Treatment and Other Somatic Procedures in Psychiatry*, New York, Grune & Stratton, Inc., 1946.

D. C. Lewis Nolan, "What's What about Shock Therapy," *Mental Hygiene*, 1946, 177–185.

V. Gerard Ryan and Lucie Jessner, *Shock Treatment in Psychiatry*, New York, Grune & Stratton, Inc., 1941.

Manfred Sakel, *The Pharmacological Shock Treatment of Schizophrenia*, New York, Nervous and Mental Disease Publishing Company, 1938.

Edward Stainbrook, "Shock Therapy: Psychologic Theory and Research," *Psychological Bulletin*, 1946, 21–60.

Gladys C. Terry, *Fever and Psychosis*, New York, Harper & Brothers, 1939.

[30] For references on psychosurgery, consult the following:

Harriet Babcock, "A Case of Anxiety Neurosis before and after Lobotomy," *Journal of Abnormal and Social Psychology*, October, 1947, 466–472.

H. M. Birch, "Prefrontal Leucotomy," *Medical Journal of Australia*, Oct. 25, 1947, 508–509.

Walter Freeman and James W. Watts, *Psychosurgery: Intelligence, Emotion and Social Behavior Following Prefrontal Lobotomy for Mental Disorders*, Springfield, Ill., Charles

Nevertheless, it is obvious from the statistics of discharges that the percentage of cures is relatively small, for institutional cases at least. Our main hope, therefore, lies in the preventive approach. It is obvious, of course, that practically all the cases caused by such factors as inebriation and syphilis are preventable by refraining from indulgence in alcohol and profligacy. It is the belief of many psychiatrists that a large number of the functional mental disorders can be prevented also by proper prophylaxis, even where a constitutional predisposition exists. Although it is impossible to venture anything like an accurate estimate, perhaps we shall not err greatly if we assume that about 50 per cent of mental disease can be prevented by the application of existing knowledge. If 50 per cent of major mental disorders can be prevented, is it not safe to assume that a larger proportion of minor mental maladjustments can also be prevented (and also corrected) by appropriate mental- and educational-hygiene procedures?

The favorable results of special classwork in the public schools for mentally handicapped children may be indicated very briefly by the following reports: "Out of more than 800 pupils who have gone through the atypical classes of San Francisco's school department, only four have appeared in the Juvenile Court." "Of 1,969 pupils enrolled in the St. Louis special schools during twelve years, only 3.3 per cent had been committed to a correctional institution because of conduct disorders. Of 787 pupils enrolled during a three-year period, only 4.5 per cent had been truant, many of these for only a half day or a day." [31] In Wilmington, Del., during the school year 1935–1936 only 3.7 per cent of the 242 children enrolled in the special and opportunity classes truanted one half day or more. Two boys (colored) were responsible for 86 per cent of all the days of truancy. There was only one girl (colored, Binet I.Q. 68) who was absent 8 out of 92 days. She had attended very irregularly in the regular grade, and finally refused to go to school at all. When she was returned to the regular grade (during the following school

C Thomas, Publisher, 1942; and "Psychosurgery during 1936–1946," *Archives of Neurology and Psychiatry*, October, 1947, 417–425.

Kurt Goldstein, "The Mental Changes Due to Frontal Lobe Damage," *The Journal of Psychology*, 1944, 187–208.

Milton Greenblatt, *et al.*, "Report on Lobotomy Studies at the Boston Psychopathic Hospital," *American Journal of Psychiatry*, December, 1947, 361–368.

George W. Kisher, "The Behavioral Sequelae of Neurosurgical Therapy (Bilateral Prefrontal Lobotomy)," *The Journal of General Psychology*, 1945, 171–192 (references).

Stanley D. Porteus and Richard DeM. Kepner, *Mental Changes after Bilateral Prefrontal Lobotomy*, Provincetown, Mass., Genetic Psychology Monographs, 1944, No. 29.

Stanley D. Porteus and Henry N. Peters, *Maze Test Validation and Psychosurgery*, Genetic Psychology Monographs, August, 1947, No. 36.

[31] J. E. Wallace Wallin, State Provisions for Mentally Handicapped School Children in the United States, *The Training School Bulletin*, 1934, 21–29, 51–57, 69–76.

year) by the principal, without the knowledge or approval of the director of the special-education department, she at once became a chronic truant again, being absent 22 out of 27 days. She soon got into conflict with the law and was sentenced to the girls' industrial school as a juvenile delinquent.

The importance of combating truancy by adjusted instruction is obvious. Truancy is both a result and a cause of maladjustments. It is frequently a mechanism of escape from a situation that the child regards as intolerable, a means of escape from a sense of boredom or a feeling of futility caused by the impending failure to master incomprehensible subject matter. Unlike the sit-down strikes of the last decade, in which the strikers substituted immobility for activity, the juvenile runaway strike represents a protest against the sit-down inactivity of the schoolroom. It is an attempt on the part of the child to satisfy his urge for activity, power, and prestige by indulging in forbidden out-of-school activities in which he can win recognition by assuming the role of the conquering hero, or by identifying himself with the leader and thereby sharing in his glory.

On the other hand, truancy leads to maladjustments of various kinds. It spells lack of opportunity for cultural improvement and often results in the formation of the habit of drifting, loitering, and shirking responsibilities. Sometimes it leads to indulgence, with others, in various kinds of antisocial conduct. Truancy is the gateway to juvenile delinquency and later criminality. The solution for this form of juvenile maladjustment is more special classes planned to meet the needs of retarded and motor-minded youth rather than more juvenile courts.[32]

The experience of the Los Angeles Institute of Family Relations is suggestive. About 70 per cent of divorces have been prevented among the 10,000 cases of domestic difficulties handled by the institute in less than 5 years. Ninety per cent of marital difficulties based on sex problems have been adjusted. The primary cause of the discord was "ignorance of marriage and its problems, most of which are based on complaints of sex maladjustments." Premarital instruction on the different problems connected with marriage had been given in less than 15 per cent of the cases (D. P. Wilson, according to a press report).

If we make our estimate conservative by assuming that only one-quarter of all child and adult mental and social disabilities and maladjustments can be

[32] For a further discussion of truancy from the mental-hygiene point of view, see:

J. E. Wallace Wallin, *The Nature and Implications of Truancy from the Standpoint of the Schools,* Proceedings of the Fourth Conference on Education and the Exceptional Child of the Child Research Clinic of the Woods Schools (Langhorne, Pa.), 1938, 19–30.

E. Y. Williams, "Truancy in Children Referred to a Clinic," *Mental Hygiene,* July, 1947, 464–469.

See also references under XIII in the Bibliography at the end of the book.

prevented or corrected by comprehensive programs of mental and educational hygiene and remedial and differential instruction, the savings in dollars and cents would still be stupendous—it would pay the expense of the required technical service many times over—while the increase in human well-being and happiness would be incalculable, for the human brain power of the nation is its most valuable asset.   Yet, so little money is spent by the schools and other social agencies for this essential type of human salvage as to constitute a crying national disgrace.   It has been estimated that the value of the population of the United States is five times greater than the nation's entire capital (L. I. Dublin).   Nevertheless, we are spending only 5 per cent of our national income on social health and educational service, as compared with 15 per cent in Germany and 11 per cent in England (René Sand), and this includes the paltry sum expended for mental-hygiene and special-education work.

Favorable Results to Be Expected with Normal Children When Parents and Teachers Have Been Adequately Trained in Mental-hygiene Principles.   Certainly no phase of the mental-hygiene program will yield richer returns than the prevention and correction of minor personality and adjustment difficulties in normal children.   But progress in this field will be halting until efficient, well-coordinated programs of training, differential education, and mental hygiene have been made available to children early in their careers before maladjustments have been formed.   The primary essential for the execution of such programs is adequately trained prospective and actual parents and teachers.   At the present time, the large majority of parents have received practically no systematic training in any phase of scientific child study.   Apparently we have acted on the assumption that mothers know by instinct how to rear and train their offspring.   As for the teachers, the vast majority of them have pursued only a brief one-semester course in educational psychology, possibly supplemented by a brief one-semester course in child study or general psychology.   So little time has been given to the psychology work they have pursued and so much has been crammed into the brief courses, that the modicum they have acquired has been of little practical value to them.   They have not been required to pursue any courses in mental hygiene; dynamic, abnormal, and clinical psychology; differential, remedial, and diagnostic teaching; on counseling; or on mentally deficient and retarded children, or children subject to specific mental, educational, social, or physical disabilities.   In fact, rather few institutions have included any of these courses in their offerings, and then merely as electives.   These optional courses, fundamentally important for the "child-centered school," have been forced to compete with the required courses, often with the ill-concealed opposition of conservatives.

The smattering of scientific information that teachers have obtained from the vast field of applied mental science constitutes a wholly inadequate foundation to prepare them for the difficult work of analyzing, understanding, and interpreting the behavior patterns and personality make-up of their pupils; of understanding their dominant trends, talents, defects, or subtle personality difficulties; of interpreting the deeper motivating forces that govern them in their acquisition of knowledge or in their adjustment to the personalities of the schoolroom; or of understanding their methods of forming healthy or unhealthy reaction patterns and attitudes or abnormal, hampering character traits.

With such superficial preparation, it is not to be expected that the average teacher will be able to handle skillfully the elusive problems of personality growth and integration or that she will be able so to guide and direct personality development that the child's personality will reach its maximum of efficient, symmetrical growth without suffering irreparable damage from the innumerable perils that beset the path of personal progress on every hand. Neither will she be able to individualize skillfully the processes of instruction to meet the needs of her varying pupil material, or to apply sound principles of mental hygiene in her management of all the classroom activities, or to perform skillfully the functions of a guidance counselor. Nor do we have a right to demand that the teacher shall be able satisfactorily to render this expert service, in view of the fact that the needed training has not been provided except on a small scale.

If it is true that the skillful teaching of the content subjects of the curriculum requires specific training—and on this point no dispute seems to exist between the subject matter and the "professional" educators—must we not concede that the art of personality development requires a vastly higher order of trained skill and proficiency? The task of developing a fine, socialized, and unified personality represents a far loftier type of teaching artistry than merely teaching children to read, write, or cipher. It requires a much deeper understanding of human nature and the mastery of a much higher technique of molding character. Moreover, the development of a well-rounded, efficient, contented personality, which is free from internal conflicts, emotional maladjustments, and intellectual schisms, and which is able to realize its highest potentials, is far more important for the welfare of both the individual and the state than is the teaching of cube root or quadratics. Teaching children the three R's or any other academic accomplishments is an excellent service to the child and to society. But, after all, such acquisitions are merely tools furthering the efficient development of the personality of the child to meet the conditions of modern life. In the hands of a warped personality, these tools may constitute a social menace rather than a social asset. Moreover, if the content subjects are not taught in accordance with the requirements of the mental hygiene of learning, they may be acquired at the expense of proper character and personality development.

Nowadays the child-centered school is extolled on every hand. But can there be genuine child-centered schools unless the schools are manned by teachers possessed of deep, sympathetic insight into the problems of childhood, especially with respect to the dynamics of trait formation and the sources, "latent" as well as "manifest," of childhood motivations? There will be no possibility of staffing the schools with such child-centered teachers unless we break away from the narrow, hidebound subject-content-centered training curriculum that has dominated the teacher-training schools in the past. We must devote more time to the fundamental study of the processes of normal and abnormal growth and development of the living organism around which the whole curriculum revolves. Teachers and parents cannot prevent the formation of intellectual, social, and emotional maladjustments in children unless they possess profound understanding of the subtle ways in which such maladjustments are often acquired. They will not be able to direct and safeguard the development of integrated personalities, possessed of the flexible power of adaptation and coordinated action required by a progressively changing social and physical environment, unless they possess a deep comprehension of personality and the dynamics of character formation.

Fortunately for the childhood of the emerging generation, society is gradually coming to realize that it is as much the legitimate and essential function of the school to teach and exemplify sound principles of mental health and wholesome personality development as it is to teach geography or literature. It is beginning to dawn upon at least some of the leaders in the teaching profession that the supreme function of the school, particularly so far as the lower levels are concerned, is to develop healthy, efficient personalities, rather than to teach subject matter, and that personalities can be developed just as are informations, understandings, appreciations, and instrumental skills. With this vital point of view, the traditional schools of the past, at least beyond the primary levels, have been only secondarily, if at all, concerned.

That mental hygiene is destined to acquire the importance implied in this discussion is indicated by the fact that the committee on teacher training [33] of Section III, Education and Training, of the Hoover White House Conference on Child Health and Protection, recommended that courses in mental hygiene, clinical and abnormal psychology, remedial and diagnostic instruction, and certain other subjects [34] be required of all elementary-school teachers, principals, and supervisors. (The committee did not deal with secondary-

---

[33] The teacher-training recommendations, drawn up by the author as a member of the committee, were unanimously endorsed by the committee.

[34] See Special Education, *The Handicapped and the Gifted*, 1931, 551–580. Also, J. E. Wallace Wallin, "The Baltimore Plan of Training Special-class Teachers and Other Workers in the Field of Special Education," *The Elementary School Journal*, 1931, 607–618.

school problems.) When this recommendation has been translated into practice, and when elementary courses in mental hygiene have been made available to high-school students and also to parents, we shall be better prepared to develop a generation of children and adults who will be relatively free from crippling personality handicaps that may hamper their adjustments throughout life. The essential prerequisites for the conservation of the nation's normal mental life are properly trained parents and teachers.

In spite of this pregnant recommendation of the White House Conference, and in spite of the high value that teachers place on mental-hygiene courses, teachers colleges and state education departments continue to accept these courses, if they accept them at all, merely as electives. The rating that teachers accord mental-hygiene courses is shown by the following inquiry. Four classes of students (mostly teachers in service in the elementary schools) who pursued a lecture course on personality maladjustments and mental hygiene were requested to list anonymously in writing the six courses on the college level which they considered had proved most beneficial to them (1) personally, *i.e.*, in understanding their own behavior and the behavior of others, (2) professionally, *i.e.*, in their work as teachers, supervisors, or administrators. The following tabulation shows the distribution of the rankings accorded work in mental hygiene. The figures indicate the number of votes cast for mental hygiene for each rank in comparison with the six most valuable college courses.

Rank position	1	2	3	4	5	6	Below sixth place
Personal value	54	10	9	3	2	0	2
Professional value	35	16	11	7	2	2	7

Mental hygiene is given the first two highest ranks by 80 per cent of the students from the standpoint of personal value and by 63.7 per cent from the professional point of view. "It was given the highest three rankings by 91.2 per cent of the respondents so far as concerns its personal value and by 77.5 per cent so far as concerns its professional value. . . . Based on the total figures for the six rankings, mental hygiene alone received almost one-fourth as many votes in both groupings as the combined figures for all the other subjects."

In a follow-up inquiry 2 years later, all the students who had pursued a course in mental hygiene

ranked it among their first five choices. . . . If only those students who have had a particular course are taken into consideration, mental hygiene is ranked higher than any other course offered in the curriculum [for elementary school teachers]. . . . This raises the pertinent question: Should not mental hygiene be included as a required course in teacher-training curricula, especially for elementary school teachers? If teachers' judgments are to be considered as a criterion the answer is in the affirmative.

The mental health needs of pupils and teachers cannot be adequately presented or championed by those who possess merely superficial knowledge of the field of mental hygiene. Nor can the problem be solved merely by offering to teachers courses of instruction in mental hygiene by persons who possess inadequate knowledge of the intricate problems of personality development and the complicated problems of mental health. If any discipline in the curriculum requires profound insight and sound erudition, it is the field of personality unfoldment and integration and mental health development and conservation.[35]

This chapter may fittingly be closed with a quotation from W. H. Kilpatrick: [36]

Mental hygiene—under that name or a better—is here to stay and on far stronger terms than we have yet known.

Also the education of the future will still more consistently respect child purposing as the strategic manifestation of child personality . . . and still further, the education of the future will put first before learning the improving of life qualitatively conceived. This shift will be as from Ptolemy to Copernicus. The central aim will be to make life good for all. . . . This must be the school's inclusive aim.

Particularly in the secondary school must the pursuit of the good life come first, and specialization no more than second.

[35] For further details regarding this investigation, see J. E. Wallace Wallin, *What Teachers Think about the Value of Mental Hygiene Courses*, Educational Administration and Supervision, 1938, 675–686; and J. E. Wallace Wallin and K. Brantley Watson, "An Appeal for a Thorough Investigation of the Relative Value of Teacher-training Courses Suggested by a Limited Study of the Evaluation of College Courses by In-service Teachers," *The Training School Bulletin*, 1944, 49–59.

[36] William H. Kilpatrick, "The Future of Education," *Journal of the National Education Association*, 1937, 254–256.

PART II

SYMPTOMS OF PERSONALITY MALADJUSTMENT AS
EVIDENCED BY INADEQUATE OR UNWHOLESOME
MODES OF RESPONSE TO DIFFICULTIES. SPECIFIC
TYPES OF FAULTY METHODS OF SOLVING LIFE'S
PROBLEMS, WITH PREVENTIVE AND REMEDIAL
SUGGESTIONS

CHAPTER VII

INTRODUCTORY DISCUSSION OF METHODS OF SOLVING PERSONAL DIFFICULTIES; NATURE OF INFERIORITY FEELINGS AND DEFENSE MECHANISMS

Modes of Responding to Problems as Criteria for Gaging Mental Adequacy. As was emphasized in the first chapter, one of the best tests of sanity is the ability of the person to adjust himself satisfactorily to baffling situations. If this is correct, it follows that one of the best ways by which the student can become familiar with the symptoms of abnormal or unwholesome behavior patterns is to study the various inadequate methods that people employ to solve their problems. How, then, do the methods used for solving problems differ among well-adjusted and poorly adjusted individuals?

Nature of the Solution of Difficulties in the Adjusted and Unadjusted. In general, the well-balanced, efficient person attempts to solve his problems in a frank, straightforward manner. He first tries to understand the facts of life and then faces them squarely as they are, no matter how disagreeable or forbidding they may be. He meets his obstacles openly, candidly, and unemotionally, or under conditions of emotional control. He attempts to make a direct frontal attack on the problem itself, instead of trying to sidestep or evade it or run away from it. Before reaching a decision or making a response, he tries to size up the whole situation and to evaluate its components, relations, and interrelations, so that he will be able to react to the situation in its entirety after due consideration of all the important relevant facts and circumstances. Another way of emphasizing these traits is to say that the well-adjusted person, in the handling of his problems of adjustment to his inner or outer world, tries to maintain a thoroughly objective or scientific attitude, the scientific attitude being merely the perfection of the objective method of approach in the solution of problems. He is objective-minded. He keeps his attention focused on the objective aspects of his problems—the objective adjustments that he must make, the tasks he must perform—instead of becoming preoccupied with his subjective states—his feelings, timidities, diffidences, prejudices, caprices, egocentric trends, and imagination. If he becomes subjective-minded, he focuses attention on himself merely in order to arrive at an accurate appraisal of his assets and deficits or to obtain self-understanding. In addition to all this, the well-adjusted person tries to respond in a manner reasonably consistent with the social goals and standards

263

of the community and not too inconsistent with his own convictions and personal integrity.

The outcome in the case of most normal persons who thus attack the vicissitudes and exigencies of life and who have reached the age of discretion and are fairly well adjusted is a reasonably satisfactory or victorious solution of life's ordinary problems and often of the more baffling ones also.

But the unadjusted or maladjusted or inefficient individual, instead of attacking his problems in a forthright, objective manner, resorts to a great variety of subterfuges, tricks, and blinds for concealing his failures, shortcomings, or dissatisfactions or for dodging reality and retreating from the ugly facts of life into an illusory, subjective nirvana of security. The numerous response mechanisms that unadjusted persons adopt for solving their problems (to be considered in detail in the subsequent chapters) are probably only variant behavior patterns for cloaking their inadequacies, for disguising their feelings, for evading their responsibilities, and for finding security and satisfaction in deceptive compromises. All of them can be classed as defense mechanisms which the individual consciously or unconsciously adopts to hide, avoid, or overcome his real or imagined deficiencies.

From the mental-health point of view, response mechanisms such as these, when frequently used as a means of escape from difficulties or as a means of solving shortcomings, are inimical to the preservation of mental efficiency and often are disruptive of mental integrity. To be sure, they often appear outwardly successful, for they enable the individual to "get by" temporarily. They may enable him to attain his immediate goals, however inferior or unworthy they may be, or however undesirable the means used to attain them, although frequently the immediate outcomes spell disappointment and frank failure. Even where some form of compromise solution yields temporary satisfaction, the ultimate effect is frequently ruinous to the individual's wellbeing. Transient victories are often obliterated by the ultimate boomerang of defeat. In the end these deceptive mechanisms may generate a host of mental conflicts and difficulties, which may lead to further dissatisfactions, other unhealthy or inadequate modes of response, mental distortions, and sometimes, eventually, nervous or mental derailments, such as frank neuroses or psychoses.

Nature of the Causes of the Individual's Difficulties. Although the number and variety of the specific causes of personal difficulties are legion, as already shown, all have their source either (1) in obstacles in the physical or social environment (exogenous factors), or (2) in personal defects or limitations based on real or imaginary physical or mental inadequacies, in antagonistic impulses and drives that produce thwarting of inner urges and ambitions, in conflicts between feelings, ideas, ideals, and attitudes, or in emotional repressions (endogenous factors). While most mental difficulties probably have their roots in both the external and the internal factors, the external factors serve merely as stimuli, or excitations. The essential or basic point is the way the individual reacts to the stimuli of his environment—how he is affected by his surroundings; how he responds emotionally to the situations of life.

Among the more pervasive and fundamental internal factors that are responsible for many difficulties of adjustment and personality distortions are feelings of inadequacy or inferiority.

These feelings constitute one of the most prevalent forms of personality disturbance among the intelligent as well as among the dull, among the young as well as among the old. Because they are a prolific source of personal difficulties and because they constitute the hidden core out of which various seemingly unrelated maladjustments may later develop, it seems fitting to introduce the discussion of specific types of unhealthy and inadequate behavior by a consideration of the so-called inferiority complex, together with a description of the general nature of the mechanisms that individuals use to defend themselves against their shortcomings, whether these are real or assumed.

Nature of the Inferiority Complex. In its most general sense, stripped of abstruse technicalities, the so-called inferiority complex [1] refers merely to a state of mind that is characterized by lack of self-confidence and by feelings of inadequacy, diffidence, and timidity resulting from exaggerated feelings of incompetency or unworthiness. The victim of inferiority feelings is afraid of failure, especially in competitive situations, because he is abnormally distrustful of his ability to succeed. He feels he is not equal to the demands that will be made upon him and, therefore, tends to develop feelings of insecurity and uncertainty regarding his future. He tends to become increasingly self-conscious, worrisome, and "touchy." Of course, the intensity of the feeling of inadequacy varies greatly among individuals and in the same person from time to time, from a vague feeling of discontented self-derogation to intense feelings of insecurity, fearsomeness, and self-despair. The inferiority complex is not a simple, or "pure," state, but a complex of many overlapping feeling patterns. Basically, it is an emotional reaction, the core element of which is the primitive emotion of fear [2]—a threat to one's social security; or a conviction that one lacks the social, mental, or physical characteristics without which one cannot win social approval or achieve a coveted goal. It is not based on mere intellectual apprehension of one's shortcomings. The clear intellectual recognition of the lack of a talent which has no connection or only a remote connection with one's ambitions or which is not regarded by society as important for winning social acceptance does not produce the inferiority pattern.

---

[1] The word "complex" is not used here in the technical Freudian sense (see Chap. XV).
[2] The distinction between feelings of fear and of inferiority cannot be sharply drawn.

Causes of Inferiority Feelings. The specific causes of the feelings of inferiority are multitudinous, but they may all be subsumed under two headings:

1. *Physical Causes.* According to Alfred Adler, who coined the term "inferiority complex," the basic cause of feelings of inferiority is organic inferiority, *i.e.,* a defective, arrested, or immature condition of some bodily organ. The results of organic inferiorities may be various, such as increased susceptibility to disease, increased mortality or morbidity, or feelings of inferiority or insecurity. Such feelings of inadequacy often engender attempts to overcome the felt deficiencies by some form of adaptation, such as evasions, compensations, or overcompensations. Occasionally the eventual outcome is the development of nervous or mental disorders, which frequently represent a form of attempted solution for the victim's sense of incompleteness and dissatisfaction.

Obersteiner believes he has found evidence for the existence of organic inferiorities in various forms of mental and nervous disorders, such as epilepsy, dementia praecox, or schizophrenia, juvenile general paralysis or paresis (these two prevalent forms of mental disorder were given brief consideration in Chap. VI), amaurotic idiocy (an infrequent type of mental defectiveness), and hereditary ataxia.

Doubtless some kinds of physical inferiority are more important than others in the production of inferiority feelings. Reference may be made by way of illustration to the condition known as gastroptosis (or enteroptosis), popularly called dropped stomach. A downward displacement of the abdominal organs, due to the lack of tone in the muscles and tendons, tends to pull the individual down mentally, so that he literally sags mentally as well as physically. He tends to feel unfit, lacking in pep, diffident, insecure, and craven. This condition affects lean people rather than stout ones and people who must stand a great part of the time. It can sometimes be overcome by appropriate exercises. A properly fitted bandage with the pressure above the pubic bone, while it will not cure the condition, will relieve the sufferer of the dragging-down sensations and will enhance physical and mental efficiency. Stunted development of the generative organs and inferior, abnormal, disordered, or thwarted functioning of the sex mechanism, real or imagined, also constitute a Pandora's box of feelings of inadequacy and insecurity.

Is organic inferiority an important cause of inferiority feelings? Adler, who originally seems to have held that organic inferiority is always at the root of these feelings, that the cause is always biological or anatomical, concedes in one of his later writings [3] that "psychological inferiority . . . may also be brought about by entirely different circumstances that have nothing to do with organic inferiority." Many authorities, however, are inclined to

---

[3] Alfred Adler, *Education of Children,* New York, Greenberg: Publisher, Inc., 1930, 92.

pooh-pooh the organic-inferiority explanation. In an investigation of inferiority feelings among a group of college students, 48 per cent of whom reported such feelings, 32 per cent attributed the feelings to social factors, 6 per cent to intellectual failures, 4 per cent to financial difficulties, and only 3 per cent to physical defects.[4] The author's observations have led him to the conclusion that organic inferiority may sometimes produce deep-seated feelings of personal inadequacy or unfitness, either directly because of subpar functioning on the part of the inferior organ and of other organs dependent upon its normal functioning, or indirectly because of the individual's attitude toward his physical handicaps, be they real or imaginary. The indirect effects of physical inferiorities or blemishes are more important in the production of feelings of mental inferiority than are the direct bodily effects. The important factor in most cases is the mental state or the emotional reaction that the consciousness of the physical defect produces. The physical factors most stimulative of feelings of inferiority and insecurity are external flaws which can be easily seen by acquaintances and which may tend to arouse ridicule or slighting remarks or to impair (so the victim imagines) one's social status, such as surface or orthopedic blemishes, homeliness or ugliness of countenance, and unbecoming clothes. That acute or morbid consciousness of a defect often serves as the starting point of feelings of personal inadequacy has already been shown (see pages 104*f.*, 137*f.*, and 180–193).

One case history may be introduced at this point as an illustration of emotional conditioning resulting from the consciousness of physical blemishes or unattractiveness.

MORBID SELF-CONSCIOUSNESS AND FEAR OF MEETING PEOPLE DUE TO FEELING OF BEING PHYSICALLY UNATTRACTIVE AND MENTALLY DULL AND INFERIOR; DOUBTS REGARDING OWN AND OTHERS' SINCERITY; AMBIVALENT, CYNICAL, AND CHARITABLE ATTITUDES; SELF-DEPRECIATION

As I think back over my childhood, the thing that stands out most prominently—not only then, but still—is that I have always had a very complicated inferiority complex which has colored my whole life and is still a very great handicap. I think that any other peculiarity that I have can be traced back to this dominant thing in my life—fear of people. For instance, I dread to have to meet people even on the streets; for I am thinking constantly of my appearance—I consider myself awkward and unattractive, not only in appearance, but in conversation, and that fact makes me so self-conscious that I am very rarely free from thoughts of self and what kind of impression I am making on other people. It is a curse, and I often think when I am alone how different my life would have been if I had not

---

[4] G. E. Gardner and H. D. Pierce, "The Inferiority Feelings of College Students," *Journal of Abnormal and Social Psychology*, 1929, 8–13.

had my thoughts so constantly preempted by this feeling of sensitiveness and inferiority. My very expression would have been different; for I do not dare to let myself go except in the presence of people who know me and like me because, I feel, they know me as I really am. Only under such circumstances, or when I am carried away by the enthusiasm of teaching or speaking of something in which I am deeply interested, do I ever forget myself and the impression—usually unfavorable—which I either imagine I am making on other people, or which, because of the peculiarities of my conduct and expression, I really do make. Because of this fear, I have grown very intuitive—have my tentacles out, so to speak, feeling the least change in the atmosphere against me, and I close up or blossom out—to mix metaphors—according to which way the wind blows, toward me or against me.

Another thing that increases my feeling that I am dull or unenthusiastic and a woman without a charm is that I have a dread of being thought to be insincere. If I should forget and let myself go enough to be cordial, I begin right away to question my own motives in doing so, to wonder whether I really feel cordially toward the person, or whether I am acting that way for some ulterior motive; and so I relapse into my former dull, unenthusiastic way of talking. Correspondingly, I am always questioning other people's motives in being nice to me. I so seldom see anyone's face really light up with genuine gladness to see me that when anyone's does, I wonder why. They surely want something from me. Bad, isn't it? I suppose that makes a cynic of me regarding human nature. I was early taught by my mother to fear the consequences upon others of what I said, and not to introspect too much as to my motives. Psychology, what I know of it, has increased that cynicism. But, although it sounds contradictory, psychology has also had the opposite effect on me. It has made me more charitable toward people and their foibles. For, although I see the defects and foibles of human nature very plainly, and all its shams, hypocrisies, and selfishnesses, I do not blame anybody for anything he does! Unless his behavior affects my own selfish interests too deeply, I just put it down to human nature, shrug my shoulders and say, "Well, that's the way it is." I do not expect too much of anyone, especially since I know I am just as human myself. Then, I don't want to convey the idea that I do not believe that there are any good unselfish people in the world. I am an idealist, in spite of my disappointment with the majority of people and with friendship; for it has been my good fortune to have an unusual mother, who typifies all that is best in motherhood and in Christian character. I know that she is real and genuine and that there must be others like her. In fact, I have met such people occasionally and nobody worships genuine goodness more than I do.

(M.N.; F.; C.T. of Psy. and Ed.; A.M.)

2. *Psychological Causes.* The large preponderance of feelings of insufficiency are caused by mental and social factors, even when physical elements are involved. They are traceable to episodes in the individual's past experiences and the attitudes assumed toward them. A great variety of circumstances and occurrences may establish the groundwork for the inferiority

complex. So far as the very young child is concerned, the following factors are of significance: (*a*) The infant emerges into the world in a state of great inadequacy. He is practically impotent except that he is able to cry, kick, toss, roll, wave the hands, and perform certain physiological processes. He requires aid in almost every aspect of his psychobiological existence. (*b*) After he is able to leave the cradle and the high chair and to creep or toddle about, he constantly stumbles and falls, bumps his head, and squeezes his fingers. All these episodes tend to develop feelings of insecurity and dread. (*c*) Very early in his career the youngster experiences all sorts of repressive social encounters. He is constantly prohibited from doing what he wants to do by parents, siblings, and playmates; he is reproved for engaging in forbidden activities; and he is restrained by superior force and punished if he rebels. He is often frightened by parents, playmates, animals, and natural phenomena. The eventual outcome of this sort of conditioning is that at the very beginning of his existence he is made conscious of his limitations and handicaps and may become a victim of inhibitions and timidities of all sorts. All of this may tend to implant in the child very early in life a sense of insecurity and make him distrustful of his ability to cope with the problems that confront him. Alfred Adler even goes so far as to assert that "all children have an inherent feeling of inferiority."

In later childhood, the child's contacts with his parents, comrades, teachers, and caretakers often tend to deepen his conviction of incompetency. Almost innumerable occurrences in his workaday life may conduce to this result:

a. He may be constantly scolded and ridiculed for his shortcomings rather than commended for his accomplishments.

b. His efforts may be disparaged by snubs and frowns, by jeering remarks, or by evidences of impatience because of his clumsiness or slowness. The following is a case in point.

LACK OF BACKBONE ASCRIBED TO LACK OF SELF-CONFIDENCE OR FEELING OF INFERIORITY ENGENDERED BY MOTHER'S LACK OF APPRECIATION, CONSTANT CRITICISMS, AND UNFAVORABLE COMPARISONS

Another trait that I despise myself for is lack of backbone. I don't know what causes this. When I was a small boy I had plenty of nerve. I would always do anything that called for nerve. But now, it seems, I'm not facing life as it is: I am afraid of it. I can plan what to do, but when the time arrives I evade the responsibility if I can possibly get out of it. I feel within me that I know what to do and how to do it, but when the time for action comes I am doubtful of myself. This may be due to my sensitiveness or lack of confidence in myself, or to an inferiority complex, which seems to be mine, or to lack of encouragement. In our family little encouragement is given and few compliments are bestowed. From mother we always receive criticism. She always has compared us with other children so that we look small in our own eyes. She compares their good points with our weak points, which sort of makes me feel that I don't care. I know she means to stimulate us to work, so she can be proud of us, but it doesn't have that effect on me. I wish I could eliminate these undesirable traits for better ones. I realize I'll never get anywhere at the rate I'm going, but I don't know what to do about it. I'm conscious of my shortcomings but that doesn't seem to help at all. I try to change my behavior patterns, but my traits are so fixed that I keep right on and never think about my responses until after I have acted. In other words, I just seem to be minus something. There seems to be a break between my thoughts and the carrying out of my thoughts. If you think that I'm rather worthless, you hit it about right. If you could offer any advice that you think will help me, I'd appreciate it beyond words. I need something that I haven't got but don't know how to get it.   (A.J.R.; M.; U.S.; Age 21)

c. Severe punishment or carping criticism may magnify his faults, render him unduly conscious of them, and lay the basis for an exaggerated sense of guilt and unworthiness.

d. Sometimes he is humiliated and embittered by uncomplimentary epithets or opprobrious terms. Offensive nicknames may make him embarrassingly conscious of some physical or mental defect that the derisive or obnoxious sobriquet symbolizes. Instances have already been cited (see especially pages 181*f.* and 186*f.*).

Being jocularly or ironically dubbed "Fatty" is not an innocent joke to an introvert mind. Such appellations may drive some sensitive natures to the most extreme measures, even suicide, as in the case of Mary Dane, 17, who weighed 200 pounds and who, as reported in the press, committed suicide because other girls called her "Fatty."

It took her a week to reach the decision, a week in which she remained away from high school and away from gibes and taunts, her parents unknowing.

When a card came from her principal Saturday, asking why Mary Jane was absent, she pocketed it before her mother could see it. Then she engaged a room away from home and called herself Dian Whitman.

They found her body yesterday, a self-fired bullet through her head, and a note which told her mother that she was sorry.

From a study of the effects of nicknames on 235 boys and 75 girls in a child-caring institution, Samuel Z. Orgel and Jacob Tuckman [5] concluded that "the nicknames studied have no value from either the individual's or society's point of view. All they do is to produce resentment, ill feeling, disagreement, quarreling, and fighting." "With the exception of nicknames of the affectionate form, the nickname is the source of much unhappiness." In the case of the

[5] Samuel Z. Orgel and Jacob Tuckman, "Nicknames of Institutional Children," *The American Journal of Orthopsychiatry,* 1935, 276–285.

boys, 39.9 per cent of the nicknames were based on personality defects, and 32 per cent on physical defects—most of these terms were derogatory—while only 3.7 per cent were terms of endearment. The girls fared better: while 30.2 per cent of the terms were based on physical defects and 11.6 per cent on personality characteristics, 32 per cent of the cognomens represented forms of affection. The large preponderance of the nicknames were obnoxious and provocative. In Stephen Habbe's [6] later investigation, based on 95 city boys (half of whom were hard of hearing) in New York public schools, the liked and hated nicknames were about equally divided. Here too the names most frequently hated related to physical shortcomings (especially physiognomic blemishes) and personality peculiarities. The inimical influence of name calling was less marked in this group.

e. Derogatory comparisons with superior siblings or playmates will arouse in some children resentment, hate, jealousy, and a feeling of inferiority, because of their continued luckless ineptitude. Illustrations of the effects of unfavorable comparisons have already been given (see pages 136–139 and 189–190).

f. Enforced competition with stronger or more able contestants often intensifies the victim's self-consciousness and timidity. That the situation may sometimes be initiated by a mere chance remark is shown in the following report.

LIFELONG LACK OF SELF-CONFIDENCE AND INABILITY TO ENTER INTO COMPETITION ASCRIBED TO A CHANCE, AND APPARENTLY INNOCUOUS, UNFAVORABLE COMPARISON

I find myself afflicted—and afflicted is right—with an inability to enter into competition of any sort, whether in games, scholarship contests, or what not. The fact that I am aware of proficiency along the line of the contest has no bearing whatsoever on the matter of my inability. For example: I am a pretty fair bridge player, and know that I am. I thoroughly enjoy playing a "friendly game" with two or three boon companions, but let any one "throw a party" with prizes and I am completely lost. My hands tremble, my mind will not work, and I forget the simplest rules of the game.

I may know the subject matter on which a test is to be given ever so well, but the test becomes a "nightmare" of trembling hands, blank mind, and difficulty in seeing.

Doing a little psychoanalysis of my own, I believe I can trace this disconcerting and inconvenient trait to a certain day when I was about six years old.

My sister, two years younger, and I were deputized to "watch the baby" who was peacefully sleeping on the bed, while we played a game on the floor. My

[6] Stephen Habbe, "Nicknames of Adolescent Boys," *The American Journal of Orthopsychiatry*, 1937, 371–377.

sister, I know now, was a very different and much more appealing type than I was. I was very reserved and inclined to "size up" people and situations before "making up," while she was a spontaneously friendly little body. I never talked about what I was doing, while she talked considerably and took everybody into her confidence.

On this particular day, I recall being decidedly annoyed because she would continually interrupt our game to run and look at the baby, and then run to the door and call to mother, "Mother, I looked at baby and she is all right." I considered this wholly unnecessary, since the baby was sleeping and we could see her all the time from where we were sitting.

That evening we had a guest, and, during the conversation between her and mother, to which I was not listening, my attention was suddenly and sharply arrested by hearing mother say, "She is much more dependable than J." She then related the incident of the afternoon, citing the fact that I was indifferent and careless in contrast to my sister's conscientiousness.

I remember the peculiar, helpless, numb sort of feeling that came over me. I have experienced it many times since. I was gaining my first knowledge of "individual differences." From that time on, I was always on the alert for remarks comparing my sister's ability with mine, and I treasured all of these in my mind and experienced that numb feeling when I thought of them.

As we grew older, I avoided doing anything that brought me into competition with my sister in any way, even though I knew I could do the thing as well as she could. If she started something I always stopped. For that reason, I did not perfect myself in many things although I enjoyed doing such things as tennis and dancing, and learned to drive a car at a time when not many girls were driving. The latter gave me a great deal of pleasure and a great impetus toward acquiring self-confidence. Gradually I found this feeling of inferiority extending to my relations with other people. I have never been able wholly to eradicate it, try as I may. In any unusual situation that involves competition it crops out, sometimes most unexpectedly. I had a very trying experience last summer with a rather different kind of course which I took at the university, and which included many time or speed elements.

If, according to psychoanalysis, the cure consists in getting things "out of your system," perhaps this unburdening may rid me of my trying handicap and permit me to go happily on my way, like Christian. Wouldn't that be nice? I really never have spoken of it before, although it has been in my mind for a long time. But speaking of it seems like treason toward a very dear and kind mother, who was not trained in the modern methods of motherhood.   (S.M.J.; F.; S.C.T.)

It would be difficult to exaggerate the effects of competitive situations upon sensitive natures with their ever-present opportunities for invidious comparisons. If the child has not been confronted with such situations during his preschool stage, it is likely that he will become aware of the meaning of competition the very first day he enters school, and that he will have to participate in competitive situations as long as he remains in school. The systems of grades, marks, medals, prizes, honors, rewards, promotions, demotions, demerits, failures, contests, recognition by commendation, and reproofs, which are almost universally employed in the schools and which are based upon comparisons and competition, stimulate rivalry and comparison and often induce keen frustrations and inferiority complexes. The observation of Bernard Clausen, as reported in the daily press, may be quoted in this connection: "The drive of twelve years spent in bitter competition for recognition at school, with success defined in terms of beating somebody else, on playing fields, in classrooms, and in examination halls, all result in producing such mean little individuals as curse the world today." But this competitive situation is even worse in the colleges than in the secondary or elementary schools.

g. The assignment of tasks in the home and in the school beyond the child's level of ability tends to deepen his sense of futility and inadequacy. One of the principal sources of discouragement, lack of confidence, timidity, and inferiority feelings is failure resulting from the inability to meet the personal and social demands of the home, the social expectations of the community, and the social and scholastic requirements of the school. Any failure that is acutely felt may produce a festering psychic trauma, the eradication of which may require prolonged expert treatment. Repeated scholastic failures often exert a devastating influence upon the child's morale. The basic importance of failure and success in the program of mental hygiene justifies the attention devoted to these factors in various parts of the book.

h. The child may have been pampered or oversheltered by too indulgent parents, grandparents, or caretakers, and may never have been allowed to make independent decisions or to shoulder his own responsibilities, as is shown in earlier autobiographies (see pages 139*f.*) and also in the following case.

PERSISTENT FEELING OF INFERIORITY AND INADEQUACY IN AN ONLY
GIRL, TRACEABLE TO OVERPROTECTION BY THE MOTHER

As I was the only girl and the youngest in a family of five, my mother was very careful of me and shielded me from all the hard things of life. I was not allowed to do many things that other girls of my age could do. My mother thought I must not go anywhere alone for fear something would happen to me. I was told I must not talk to strange men on the street. I suppose my mother was afraid I would be kidnaped. I was held in this dreadful fear. Because she made me think I could not do anything alone, and that she must always help me, I developed an inferiority complex. Everything I wore was determined by her, in fact, all of my affairs were decided by her even after I had grown up. My father often remarked that I would never have any confidence or know anything because I was always held back. I was never allowed to go ahead on my own initiative. This inferiority complex has followed me all my life. Since I have grown older I have overcome it to a certain degree but it still troubles me. Even now I do not feel capable of doing things so well as other people, although I may be able to do them better.

All of my timidity, fears, nervousness, and inferiority feelings I attribute to my early training. If I had been encouraged to go out into the world and meet people and had been allowed to fight my own battles I would have had more self-confidence and lived a happier life.   (T.E.C.; F.; S.C.T.)

i. Racial and sex discrimination often becomes a source not only of lasting animosities and antagonisms but also of rankling inferiority complexes. Sex discrimination constitutes the basis of Alfred Adler's "masculine protest" on the part of the female. Perhaps in the not distant future, as the female continues on her march, not only toward sex equality but dominance, we shall have a new complex to deal with, namely, the "feminine protest" on the part of the subjugated male. The following is a vivid picture of resentment engendered by reputed racial inferiority.

FURIOUS RESENTMENT AGAINST ASSUMPTIONS OF RACIAL INFERIORITY

Regardless of what may be said, the racial factor influences one's entire life. It seems to be taken for granted that one must not express one's views upon this situation, but must pretend that all is well. Since this is confidential, it is a pleasure to analyze truthfully the factors that make up one's individuality.

The deeper one feels family pride, the keener is the chafe produced by racial discrimination. This has been the superirritant in my life, which I learned from my ancestors. I am only two generations removed from slavery.

My maternal ancestors are traced to Africa, to a woman who was supposedly an African princess of the Nubian tribe. When they were brought to this country, they were sold to slave owners who lived in the county of Cometa, Georgia. My great-grandmother was a child of her master who treated her with the kindness of a real father. At his death he made a request of his dearest friend to take his daughter and got from him a solemn promise that she would never be treated as a slave nor sold to any other slave owner. This friend lived true to his promise, but his wife hated my great-grandmother and made life for her as miserable as possible. My great-grandmother, who was considered a beautiful woman, was quite indignant because of her birth, and could not become reconciled to the insults and humiliations she had to suffer. Owing to the mental conflict, she and her mistress clashed constantly. Finally, the mistress demanded that her husband whip my great-grandmother, in order to show her that she was a slave. Repeatedly he refused, but finally, realizing that she was his wife, he attempted to comply with her wishes. My great-grandmother became so enraged that she became "temporarily mad" and fought her master until she fainted from exhaustion. She fought and clawed and bit, but in spite of his bruises her master was kind and did not carry the process farther. Though she was of Negro blood, true to the promise given his friend, never again was she treated as a slave by any member of the household.

My great-grandmother married a "free man." In those days a "free man" was looked upon by Negroes as something almost marvelous. He was given the privilege of buying my great-grandmother's freedom at the time the Civil War broke out.

One of his children was my mother's mother, a tall woman, of a color slightly red, which turned into a very deep red whenever she became angry, which was quite often, although she quickly recovered. Grandmother wore her hair in two very long black braids. After I became older I asked her to tell me of her Indian blood. I took it for granted from her looks she must have had Indian blood. Very vividly do I remember her whispering as she feared she would be overheard, "I am so ashamed of my Indian blood that I never, never mention it. You must never admit that such exists in your mother's family, because Indians steal." I tried to explain to my grandmother in my childish way that I thought Indians were as good as any one else and that it was just as unfair for her to say that as it is for white people to say all Negroes steal. She was subject to deep racial prejudice.

The very first thing which my grandmother did after emancipation was to enter school in order to get an education. At that time Atlanta University was a grade school, starting in a car barn in Atlanta. My grandmother moved to Atlanta and entered the school, which was then known as Storr School. She felt that education would eradicate her feeling of inferiority, against which she fought so hard.

This problem attained triple intensity in my mother, who was not a slave. Her teachings were to rise in spite of racial handicap. Unlike my mother's people, all of whom became well educated, some receiving higher degrees, my father's people did not have the benefit of education. They attempted to make up for it by accumulating money. They bought every book they could afford and built up valuable libraries. Through sheer determination and self-education they became financially superior to many of their associates.

The determined fight against racial unfairness, which savored of a certain inferiority, had a definite effect upon my childhood life. Today any racial discrimination makes my blood actually boil and I experience the desire to tear to pieces any person who attempts to make me feel it. Education alone is all that saves me, for I am beside myself at the time.

(P.K.B.; F.; Col.; Vocational Counselor; A.B.)

j. The feeling of being unwanted (parental rejection), the bitter wrangling of mismated parents, separation, and especially divorce may undermine a child's basic moorings of security and engulf him in feelings of dejection, anxiety, and diffidence, leaving him in a state of bewildered quandary.

k. The lack of economic security and the low cultural level of the home might convince the child that he is of inferior stock, that he is worthless, or that he occupies an inferior social status. This might tend to impair or destroy his confidence in himself and in his ability to rise above the family level.

l. The riot of conflicting cultural ideologies and practices in the world of ambivalent, discordant adults into which he is plunged as he is approaching the stage of independent decisions and as he is getting ready to leave the shelter of the parental roof often creates numerous acute perplexities that tend to render him uncertain, cynical, and insecure. Such are the conflicts between the traditions and beliefs of the home and modern science and industry; the conflicts between profession and practice, in religion, morals, politics, and statecraft; the democratic proclamations of the schools and their occasional autocratic administration; the violation of political platform pledges; permitted law evasion by political henchmen or privileged chiselers; false advertising for the sake of profits; misleading propaganda for personal advantage; the widespread use of cover-ups, subterfuges, and "white lies" in social relations; pragmatism, materialism, hedonism, religious pietism, fundamentalism, or modernism; educational progressivism or essentialism; political liberalism or reactionarism; free enterprise or planned economy; isolationism or internationalism; atheism, agnosticism, free love, trial marriage, multiple marriage, monogamy, polygamy, birth control, nudism; bureaucracy, lockouts, strikes, labor dictatorships, rampantly unchecked racketeering, the control of legislation by arrogant, antagonistic minority blocs; and other cultural schisms ad infinitum. Is it surprising that youth experiences increasing difficulty in finding emotional and intellectual anchorage for a positive, secure, confident outlook in so chaotic a welter of ideas?

m. The feeling of inferiority itself may engender further convictions of inadequacy and doubt and may intensify the individual's feelings of distrust and insecurity. He may become more discouraged and fail to exert himself to overcome his shortcomings. The conviction of futility may keep him from making any constructive effort or may divert his energies into some other form of activity, beneficial or injurious, as the case may be, in an attempt to compensate for his feelings of dissatisfaction. Thus feelings of inferiority, once acquired, may become the nucleus of numerous other crippling feelings and convictions, in consequence of which the individual will suffer from cumulative injurious effects, unless he is able to resolve his difficulties.

3. *Unknown Causes.* Finally it should be emphasized that the causes may never have been correctly recognized or they may have been forgotten, possibly buried in the individual's forgotten past. According to some psychoanalysts, the causes of genuine mental or emotional complexes have always been submerged from the individual's conscious life. They have been repressed from the realm of conscious experience, but they have not thereby become exterminated. Since the conflicts and inhibitions that are at the basis of the real inferiority complexes always operate unconsciously, they can be removed or remedied, we are assured, only by being brought to the surface. If a cure

is to be effected, the circumstances that produced the complex must be made clear to the individual and this can be accomplished, so say the psychoanalysts, only by the methods of psychoanalysis. (Submerged complexes and psychoanalysis receive separate consideration in Chaps. XIII to XVII.)

Nature of the Reaction Patterns to Inferiority Feelings; Three Basic Types. How do people respond to their inferiority feelings? What sort of behavior do such feelings arouse? In attempting to answer this question it is, first of all, necessary to recognize the importance of the factor of individual differences. The responses will vary greatly in different individuals according to a number of factors:

1. Individual idiosyncrasy.

2. Constitutional make-up. The neurotic, introverted, and hypersensitive types of individuals more readily become victims of the inferiority complex than the nonchalant, extroverted, and nervously stable types.

3. Some persons experience transitory effects of inadequacy feelings and readily recover; some experience periodically recurrent attacks, while others remain in a more or less permanent slump. They tend to remain "down in the dumps."

4. The intensity of the reactions will vary, in general, with the severity of the affective disturbance and the social setting.

Recognizing the importance of all these modifying circumstances, the victim of the inferiority complex will, in general, however, set about to free himself from his mental shackles by some sort of protective or escape device. In the opinion of Alfred Adler, feelings of uncertainty, self-depreciation, and inferiority always arouse a desire for reaching a higher level of completeness and a status of equality; in fact, they engender an urge for superiority. Adler, in truth, goes so far as to maintain that the sense of inferiority and the striving for superiority are two phases of the same psychological mechanism. Possibly all manifestations of the inferiority feelings constitute efforts to achieve superiority. Be that as it may, we can distinguish three main response patterns to the inferiority complex. However, these basic types of adjustive response do not, as has been suggested, constitute watertight compartments. They are not mutually exclusive, but rather are reciprocally interactive. Some may function coincidentally, to reinforce or to weaken one another. Typical responses to given situations may, no doubt, exist; but a child who shows an avoidance reaction under one set of circumstances might show aggression or delinquent behavior under other external or internal conditions.

1. *The Flight Reaction.* The affected individual may become timid, fearful, and anxious, and in consequence may become suspicious, indecisive, submissive, and unduly sensitive to criticism. He loses confidence in himself, begins to worry about his reputed deficiencies, and may begin to indulge in atti-

tudes of self-depreciation, to "pick on himself," and to blame himself for his real or imaginary inferiorities. Thus he may become hyperconscientious; he may develop an exaggerated consciousness of guilt and blameworthiness; and he may begin to attach moral values to mere trifles. As a result of his preoccupation with his shortcomings or inferiorities, whether real or assumed, the victim eventually sets about to fortify himself by the development of some sort of defense mechanism. If his hypercritical attitude toward himself or his lack of confidence in himself has made a moral coward of him, he is liable to have recourse to some sort of flight reaction. This represents the first type of defense mechanism. In the flight type of solution, he tries to avoid the issues of life. Exactly what type of flight mechanism the victim will select cannot be readily predicted. Brief mention will be made of eight overlapping avoidance mechanisms.

a. The victim tends to become introverted [7] and withdrawn. He dreads social contacts and will shun them whenever possible. His tendency is to become seclusive and retiring.

b. Because of the fear of failure, he tries to avoid contests or any competitive situations in which comparisons will be made between the merits of the contestants.

c. Because of distrust in his competency and doubt regarding the outcome of his efforts, he tends to avoid making decisions. He postpones them as long as possible and thereby may eventually become a victim of chronic indecision and procrastination. He acquires the reputation of being a chronic shirker who has no taste for the fray. The following cases will prove instructive (see also pages 140–142 and Chap. VIII).

[7] A former student at Johns Hopkins University handed me this little attempt at versification with the query as to whether or not it was a correct characterization.

THE INTROVERT

Why must I be
Forever probing at my heart,
Investigating this and that,
Tearing it apart?

I want to know,
And yet what pain
Such seeking after knowledge brings,
And what is it I gain?

A little more bewilderment
To add to life's forbearing,
Less peace of mind and joy of heart,
And more despairing.

A CASE OF PROCRASTINATION, PARTICULARLY INVOLVING WRITING, TRACED TO EARLY SPOILING, CRITICISM, AND PUNISHMENT

I have suffered under the handicap of procrastination almost as long as I can remember. But I just considered it one of the human ills that flesh is heir to, hence did nothing about it, and continued to suffer.

I have lost money, time, friends, credit for work done, and precious opportunities because of my seeming indifference. At the same time, I have suffered untold remorse because of it.

I have had people owe me money but have put off the collection so long that I have been ashamed to ask for it.

I have failed to write friends or relatives even the one letter courtesy required after a visit at their homes, and I have been ashamed to face them when we would meet the next time.

I have bought things at stores and kept them for a month at a time before making an exchange, and then, to cover up my embarrassment, have deliberately lied by saying I had been out of town or had been ill.

Almost every month I have failed to pay my gas and electric bills until past the time limit, although I have known that every time I do this I will suffer a 3 per cent penalty.

I could go on and on and name many other facts illustrative of how I just put off doing things with no reason for doing so.

While taking this course I have read article after article and cut clipping after clipping that had a direct bearing on the lesson, but invariably put off making any mention of it.

Often I resolve to correct the error of my ways. I make a good beginning and then lapse back into the old ways.

I have tried to discover the cause for my abhorrence of writing, since much of my procrastination is directed along that line. I just hate to write.

I then dug these facts from some of my early training.

There were ten children in my family and I was considered about the worst penman of them all. Several of them were extra fine writers. They always made fun of my writing, made unfavorable comparisons, and criticized and ridiculed me. My stepmother even punished me often because I did not seem to improve in my penmanship.

As a teacher I never put work on the blackboard. I always have it done by someone else. I always have someone fill in the names on my report card and in my register.

My mother died when I was two years old. My dad was a Methodist minister and we lived next door to the church. I was spoken of as the "poor little motherless baby" and was consistently spoiled by everybody as a child.

When I married, my husband was much older than I was and had been one of my college professors. I was humored, indulged, and spoiled by him. I was treated as a child or a toy. He took all the responsibility and helped around the house with the cooking and cleaning.

We were married five years and during the whole time there was never a cross word in the family. When I began to "grow up" and wanted to outgrow some of my handicaps there was trouble.

Later when I was divorced and went back home to live with my family, out of sympathy and pity they resumed the old job of coddling as they had done before.

It is only about six or seven years ago that I succeeded in weaning myself away from the family crutch.

For the past few weeks I have been taking myself in hand and hope to stick this out until I overcome this one maladjustment.

This month I made out my own reports. I made out my checks and mailed my bills the same day they came in.

I have written sixteen letters within the past month and have renewed some friendships of long standing. I am corresponding with one friend I haven't heard from directly for nearly five years and another one I haven't heard from for seven years.

I have adopted the "Do It Now" slogan, as suggested in the course.

(P.B.E.; F.; Col.; H.S.T.; B.S.; Age 32)

d. In extreme cases the despondent victim may even elect to pass out of existence by his own hand. He prefers to "shuffle off" or have recourse to the supreme, unalterable flight rather than face his problem of defeatism. Instances are constantly chronicled of timorous souls who have attempted to find permanent deliverance from onerous or feared obligations through the irrevocable escape route of self-destruction. The following seems to be a case in point.

A would-be bridegroom of 26, "a man of nervous temperament, but a fine gentleman of good reputation" in the community, was seen to leave Shippensburg, Pa., one day in March, 1939, traveling fast in his car, toward Chambersburg near by, where he was scheduled to marry his fiancée. He told his father he intended to stop at a florist's shop for a bouquet for his bride-to-be. But he never showed up at the wedding ceremony, although he had leased and furnished a house for his future home, nor did he visit the flower shop. The wedding ring was found later in his desk. An extensive search was made in several states for a suspected victim of amnesia or foul play. Three weeks later the body was discovered in an automobile in the desert near Elko, Nev., 2,500 miles away. "A tube connected with the exhaust pipe was found in the car. Windows were closed and doors locked from the inside." "He undoubtedly committed suicide through the inhalation of carbon monoxide," was the verdict of the coroner. Apparently he could not go through with the wedding ceremony or face the duties of marriage.

e. Another mechanism of escape from the dreaded world of difficulties, a very popular one, is to resort to the world of phantasy, and let daydreams of power and success compensate for the bitter disappointments of the workaday world. In the world of imagination, the greatest weakling and the most abject coward can achieve success without effort or fear of failure. The daydream is a readily available, albeit illusory, means of satisfying the craving for prestige and superiority. To picture oneself as a remarkable fellow, as a conquering hero among one's associates, requires little real effort or prowess. Alfred Adler has not hesitated to affirm that "megalomania in daydreams is always a sign of a strong feeling of inferiority." In addition to illustrations of the daydream techniques already given (see pages 186*f.*) and those that will appear in Chap. X and elsewhere, the following autobiography may be introduced as a typical illustration of compensation in the world of make-believe for a humdrum existence.

COMPENSATION IN DAYDREAMING FOR A HUMDRUM, BARREN LIFE ON A FARM; DREAMS OF FORTUNE, COSTLY LACES, AND GRAND PARTIES; AVERSION TO MARRIAGE; AN EARLY REDUCING DEVOTEE

Building castles in the air started in early adolescence and continued for many years. I am not entirely cured yet of this habit. Living on a farm in the backwoods, doing the housework, weeding the garden, canning fruit, cooking for the hired help, and doing the many chores left little or no time for daydreams in the busy growing season, but the long winter months were very tedious to an adolescent girl. My sisters had made unfortunate marriages, so my father did not approve of my meeting any young men, and parties were simply out of the question. I grew up feeling that one thing that I must particularly avoid was marriage. Always a willing worker, I found plenty to do during the day, sewing, mending, doing fancywork, cooking, washing dishes, and endless cleaning. My father generally read aloud to us in the evening. This was a great treat. He was a fine reader, and this is one of the dearest memories of my girlhood days. There were very few visitors, seldom any of my own age. We all went to church on Sunday; we saw the circus parade every summer and attended the annual Sunday School picnic on the Fourth of July; that was about the extent of the time spent away from the farm. The first theatrical performance that I ever attended was *Uncle Tom's Cabin* when I was fifteen. I read again and again an old English edition of *The Children of the Abbey*. The principal love scenes were almost worn out by frequent reading. I had a cousin who furnished me with plenty of trashy novels which I read and reread many times, living through each as I read it. I felt the adolescent's urge to get out into the world and do great and noble deeds. But not for the world would I have breathed my yearnings to a soul. I had no pals in those days. I was a gentle, timid girl who craved affection, and was simply starving for praise and the outward expression of love. I longed to look pale and weak and therefore drank vinegar, and tried to adopt a woebegone, wan expression. I walked with a stoop so that I would not look so tall. I longed to be beautiful and have people admire me. Praise and appreciation was what my heart was yearning for. There is not much time for affection in a large family of limited means.

My parents were busy making a living for us. It never occurred to me to rebel or to run away.

But gradually I learned to compensate in daydreams. I longed to be a book-keeper in a small town where I could earn money to buy nice clothes and all the things needed in our humble home. My sex dreams at this time I have included in my description of sex adjustments. Later when I asked for new clothes and could not have them, I dreamed of rich materials and costly laces and also of accidental fortunes which would make their purchase possible. Instead of the party that I had set my heart upon, I learned after a few years to dream of a party far grander than the one that I had wanted so much to attend. I learned to compensate for many of life's hardships in this way.

My father died when I was nineteen and from that time I had to face reality. I would analyze the causes of my daydreaming as follows:

1. The humdrum, lonely existence on the farm.
2. Trashy novels, which filled my mind with sex longings.
3. Lack of companionship of boys and girls of my own age.
4. Naturally imaginative tendency.
5. Early formation of habit of suppression of feelings.

(S.B.R.; F.; H.S.T.; B.S.; Age 58)

f. Another kind of flight is to infantile forms of behavior. Thus the older child, the adolescent, or the adult may resort to childish deeds as a means of escaping responsibilities or realizing their ambitions. They adopt the type of behavior that brought them success during the helpless or dependent stage of life when every wish was satisfied by the oversolicitous parent. This so-called "regression" type of defense is discussed in Chap. IX.

g. Many seek safety in neurotic symptoms (to be discussed in later sections), many of which are merely regressions to infantile or childish forms of behavior. These are adopted as means for arousing commiseration, as bids for sympathy, or as defenses against the necessity of facing the stern realities of existence.

h. Predisposed persons may eventually develop very serious nervous or mental disorders, such as a neurosis or dementia praecox.

2. The Fight Reaction. The second type of reaction pattern against the inferiority bugbear is almost the exact opposite of the first. Instead of resorting to a flight escape, the victim may take recourse in some form of fight reaction. As an antidote or protection against his feelings of inadequacy or dissatisfaction, he may become assertive, aggressive, determined, or venturesome. Aggression is a natural result of frustration. The fighting spirit assumes two main forms.

a. The individual may resolve to try to overcome his defects or limitations. In a do-or-die spirit he may determine to wage relentless battle against his demons until he has subjugated them and become master of himself. This attitude of dogged determination has its values. It often proves successful provided that it is accompanied by action and persistent practice and does not end in mere resolutions or good intentions, or wishful thinking. A determined fighting spirit supported by actual performance may sweep away the intellectual restraints and emotional fetters and free the subject from his inferiority complexes.

Who is not familiar with the thrilling saga of the transformation of the youthful physical weakling, Theodore Roosevelt, into the aggressive, militant statesman and robust Rough Rider, as a result of a season of heroic "roughing it" in the "wild and woolly" mountains and plains of the West. The iron will to overcome the severe orthopedic disabilities resulting from an attack of poliomyelitis at the age of 39 may have transformed the rather easy-going and complacent, but physically robust, young Franklin D. Roosevelt into the dynamic, fighting Governor and President of later years. He met his "affliction with astonishing courage. I have seen him," said his secretary, Louis McHenry Howe, "lying in bed, concentrating his will to such an extent that perspiration literally rolled down his face in an effort to move a single little toe." "Tremendous will-power evoked slow recovery. Convalescent, he exercised tirelessly, hobbling to his desk on crutches."

When informed that he would lose his voice from the removal of a cancerous larynx, John Davis, New York attorney, determined to overcome his defect and began "to practice deep breathing and tamed his breath," with the result that "he could speak huskily from his diaphragm. He has organized the Lost Chord League for helping others similarly afflicted."

In January, 1942, two hemiplegic victims of poliomyelitis, both with right-leg paralysis, were given a testimonial dinner by the National Foundation for Infantile Paralysis and were also honored with an appearance on the Hobby Lobby radio program, in recognition of their outstanding achievements in overcoming the crippling effect of the disease through unflagging application. Jean White, 19, afflicted at 10, stimulated to put forth her best efforts by gifts of candy bars from her mother on attaining designated goals, was high "on the road to being New York State's roller skating champion. . . . She can jump, spin, and dance on skates better than any other girl in New York, where most of the skating championships are held." Nancy Merki (of Portland, Ore.), 15, stricken at $7\frac{1}{2}$, induced to "dog paddle across the pool" to get an ice-cream cone tantalizingly displayed by her mother, won her first swimming race at 9, and a 3-miler at 10. At 15 she held 28 titles. "She has broken one world record and four American records. The Amateur Athletic Association classified her as No. 1 girl swimming champion." Verily, physical defects do not constitute bars to the attainment of championship status in the keenest competitive contests, even in feats of agility dependent upon the use of a crippled organ! Annette Kellerman, the Australian "diving and swimming Venus," although handicapped by a crippling condition from childhood, through determination and practice developed a physique described as perfect.

The excessively vain, clubfooted Lord Byron was exceedingly sensitive about his lameness, possibly because his ill-disciplined, temperamental mother twitted him about it. "He would have moved the universe to suppress all evidence of his deformity." Nevertheless, his club foot drove him into such desperation that he became a crack swimmer, who was able to negotiate the Hellespont. He joined in all sports in which he was not hopelessly incapacitated, "made" the cricket team, and became an excellent horseman. He demonstrated the truth of his slogan, "ugliness is courageous," by achieving success in athletic competitions.

Immanuel Kant's gout and sunken chest, and perhaps his diminutive size, may have driven him into a life of isolation and contemplation, which bore fruit in the development of one of the world's greatest metaphysicians. Ludwig Beethoven's dissatisfaction with his pockmarked face, his snub nose, and his asthma, may have inspired him to win recognition for his wonderful musical compositions, in which, later, he doubtless found compensatory relief for his deafness. One of England's greatest philosophers and essayists, Francis Bacon, whose physical suffering may have channelized his energies into intellectual pursuits so that he eventually became one of England's outstanding intellectual luminaries, had an appreciation of the principle of overaction involved in the strenuous effort to overcome the feeling of humiliation or frustration from a defect. He expressed it in this way: "Whoever hath anything fixed in his person that doth induce contempt hath also a perpetual spur in himself to rescue and deliver himself from scorn."

Persistent practice freed the lisping, short-winded, and weak-voiced Demosthenes from his speech impediment and transformed him into one of the great orators of ancient Greece. He practiced with pebbles in his mouth; he learned to deliver many lines in one breath while running up hill; he acquired volume by trying to outshout the breakers at the beach. He practiced in a subterranean chamber sometimes 2 or 3 months at a time, shaving his head on one side to resist the temptation to go into the streets.

Many of our case records introduced elsewhere illustrate this method of frontal attack upon the difficulty itself (see pages 137*f.*, 145, and 182). One additional illustration will suffice at this point.

FEELING OF INADEQUACY AND UNCERTAINTY OVERCOME BY THE CHALLENGING COMMENTS OF A CLASSROOM TEACHER

In my thirteenth year, I always had a feeling that I could not depend upon myself. I always thought that everyone else was better than I was. At the crucial moment, a certain fear or feeling of undependableness seemed to creep over me and cause me to fail in any important thing I had to do. This fear held sway for many years until my high-school senior year. At that time I had a teacher who seemed to be much interested in me. One day in class she called on me to recite my Latin. But the fear crept over me and I told her that I wasn't prepared although I was. This led her to give me a lecture in which she said that I had a terrible case of inferiority complex. This little lecture hurt me quite a little because I was the only boy in a class of seventeen. As she talked on, I grew more ashamed of myself. She said many things about me which I had never heard before. As time went on, the thought of overcoming my complex was continually on my mind. I have overcome this great fault not merely by thinking about it; every time I found myself under the grip of this fear I would immediately force myself from it and complete the thing I was trying to do. Thus I have freed myself from this demon and now enjoy full control of myself at all times. I owe all to this teacher. In due time, I hope I shall see her so that I can show her my appreciation for what she did for me. Although I hated her at the time, what she did for me is probably the greatest thing that has ever happened to me, because overcoming my inferiority feeling has enabled me to reach greater goals than I ever thought possible.   (E.W.C.; M.; U.S.)

This type of adjustment will prove all the more valuable if the subject will attempt to discover and remove the causes of his inadequacies, whether they are physical, psychical, educational, or social.

b. A second type of fight solution is to develop some other qualities or traits that will more easily enable the individual to achieve success or satisfaction. He tries to develop talents in some other line of endeavor that will counterbalance or compensate for his weakness. This type of adjustment, technically referred to as compensation, often proves successful. It often enables the individual to obtain compensatory satisfaction in some other worth-while field of effort. Illustrations of the compensatory type of response have already been given (see pages 124*f.*, 180*f.*, 186*f.*, 189–190, and 191), and others will be introduced in Chap. XI, in which the compensatory mechanism is given detailed consideration. At this point, three striking cases of successful compensation will clarify the nature of the mechanism. One is achievement in physical skill by a college undergraduate; the second, compensation in an adjusted form of writing by a victim of psychoneurosis; and the third, compensation in intellectual achievement by a hyperkinetic college instructor.

"My father played baseball at Penn. He hoped I, too, would be an athlete. Do I have a chance to make the gym team?" This was the query Tom Glucker, victim of infantile paralysis at 5, posed to the Princeton gym director as he limped into his office as a freshman, with his will to conquer undimmed by his physical handicap. He never became a baseball player, but ceaseless, indefatigable effort and zeal won him the title of the world's "climb king" in his senior year.   In the

dual meet with the Navy he tied Jimmy Cruse, Annapolis ace, in rope climbing at 4.2 seconds.   No Princeton man had ever before climbed the 20-foot rope under 4.5!   Two weeks later, in a dual meet at Temple, Glucker did 3.9, a new world's record.   The previous record was 4.1.   In the Eastern Intercollegiate championships he scaled the hemp strand in the unheard-of time of 3.8 seconds. In competition against college stars from all over the country he also won the individual side-horse championship, a sort of anticlimax to his more sensational feat.

One illustration from contemporary life with a different background will be cited.   Oscar Odd McIntyre,[8] author of "New York, Day by Day," a syndicated hodgepodge column of chatter and reminiscences, received an income of $150,000 a year from 508 newspapers in all the states of the union and in Canada and Mexico, with a total circulation of 15,000,000.   He was, nevertheless, apparently a victim of a deep-seated inferiority complex.   The complex showed itself in his "odd" behavior (he lived up to his name), in his indecision (he would "rather face a tiger than a decision"), shyness, aversion for crowds (ochlophobia), avoidance of people, fear of open spaces (agoraphobia), dislike of daylight (photophobia), fear of poisoning (toxophobia), dislike of bankers (he lost a large part of his savings in 1929), fear of blackmail (one of his friends was blackmailed into suicide), and "terror of telephones."   His flair for bright red and for flamboyant haberdashery (loud "awning-striped shirts"), his extravagant wardrobe, and his penchant for curious, obscure, and foreign words probably were cover-ups of his phobic insecurity and were also means of attracting attention, enhancing the ego, and gaining prestige.   His dandyism was, accordingly, a smoke screen for his underlying defeatist timidity.   His wardrobe contained 200 neckties, 200 canes, 200 bathrobes, 100 shirts, 100 pairs of socks, 60 pajamas, 50 suits of Japanese silk underwear, 60 suits, 50 pairs of shoes, and three dozen hats.

Starting as a cub reporter on the Gallipolis, Ohio, *Journal* in 1902 at $5 a week, he became managing editor of the Dayton, Ohio, *Herald* at $12 a week in 1906.   In this early position, his feeling of insecurity was already evident in his "terror" of the editor.   Whenever he saw the latter coming toward him in the corridor, he "would break in a panicky gallop and rush past" him.   His employment record for years was one of constant turnovers.   Fired from the New York *Mail,* as dramatic editor, he had a "nervous breakdown" that prevented him from holding a regular job, as he would not leave his room. "Brinkerhoff and Weber would spend hours inducing him to come for a short

    [8] J. Bryan, III, "Gallipolis Boy Makes Good," *The Saturday Evening Post,* Nov. 20, 1937, 10, 11, 79, 82–88.

walk. Two blocks from the hotel he would break away from them and sprint home, arriving breathless and shattered." Thus the "column a day was his only resort," apparently a substitute, or compensatory, activity that he adopted as an escape from the necessity of going out and meeting people and encountering open spaces—although he was driven about in his car about 3 hours at night, "utterly aimlessly," on his news-scouting tours. His "compensatory drive"—he never missed a day or took a vacation—produced a column that brought him international renown, in spite of its occasional loose grammar, misspellings, and triviality of content, and in spite of his psychological inadequacies.

EARLY SENSITIVENESS AND FEELINGS OF INFERIORITY BASED UPON LACK OF PHYSICAL CHARM, LEADING TO LIFELONG DISTRESS AND COMPENSATION IN INTELLECTUAL PURSUITS

As a child, ever since I can remember, I must have been sensitive to the opinions of others; for I remember my acute embarrassment when I was about four at being called down in church by an old lady for swaying back and forth looking at my new white beaver hat, instead of sitting up decorously and listening to the preacher. My mother ruled me by simply withholding her approval. I was always ready to grovel at her feet and to admit I was wrong, whether I was or not, just to get her to smile at me again.

When I was about to begin school, unfortunately, I had a long spell of what used to be known as "slow fever," which resulted in my head's being shaved. My hair grew back in uneven stubby lengths all over my head—and it was not curly, but straight as a stick. Also I had such a ravenous appetite that I ate myself into becoming a fat child, just as I was about to enter school. I was also losing some of my temporary teeth at the time; and I can see myself now as I appear in a class picture—fat, shock-headed, snaggled-toothed, and dressed in the most unbecoming red and blue percales that my mother bought because of their durability, not because of their becomingness. Not long after I entered school, my father suffered reverses in business, and my mother felt it necessary to "take boarders," much against my father's protests, for he felt as if it were a reflection on him and his ability to take care of his family. My father's humiliation impressed itself upon us children, especially upon me; we lived in a fashionable neighborhood, and the children with whom I should have associated at school snubbed me—or so it seemed to me—on account of my mother's having to support the family and on account of my being different from them in appearance. They called me "Fatty," and, while I would smile and never let them know it hurt, I did not try to join them in their games, but either stayed off in a corner to myself or played with some child whom my mother considered my inferior; and when I went home, I cried myself to sleep. My mother was too busy to notice me much, and I went around half the time with my stockings down and my hair in my eyes and did not care whether I made good grades at school or not, just so I got by. I had started out making what were known as "star hundreds" in the second grade, to which I was promoted after one day in the first grade, because I already knew what the first-grade children were being taught. (I had been taught a little at home by my old black mammy's daughter who was unusually bright.) I remember having it brought home to me even that early that I was not so attractive nor so much sought after as other children, for whenever the teacher—whom I adored—sent someone across the street for her milk at recess, she always sent Annie or Odille, instead of me!

My teachers in the other grades took no notice of me. I never misbehaved, but just sat back in my corner, with my thoughts usually elsewhere—until I got to the seventh grade. The teacher of this grade—bless her heart—was a human being as well as a teacher, with a mother's heart, and she took notice of me enough to tell me that I was not doing so well in school as I could. Upon that, I began to pick up in my work. Then when I got to the first year in high school at the age of twelve, one of the teachers there—they had departmental work of course—who knew my family and knew that I had had a brother who had been given "first honor" seemed to expect a similar standing from me. I began to try, and ended up by getting first honor myself! I have an old diary kept at about this time, in which I very naively express my desire to compensate by my scholarship for other things I felt I lacked. Among other things I lacked, besides slimness and pulchritude, was, first of all, popularity with boys—which was a natural result with me of considering myself huge and ugly. I was so filled with the idea that I was unattractive that I was. About that time, one of the neighborhood ladies, who had a daughter about my age, took pity on my awkwardness and timidity and invited me to join the neighborhood boys and girls when they met at her house every Friday night for a dance. This was the first chance I had to mingle with my own kind; and it was a very thrilling experience to me, although I usually spent most of my time upstairs to keep it from becoming noticed that I was not being asked to dance. At other times, I would fill in by playing for the others to dance. Occasionally, a kind-hearted boy, who had nothing against me, would drag me around the floor—oh, I suppose I exaggerate my awkwardness, for I really learned to get around rather lightly on my feet. But I had no conversation —or chatter, for that is what it was, not conversation. I have since learned how to talk "small talk," and am not afraid to talk even to a man; but there are some kinds of people who simply paralyze me even yet—the kind who are not especially interesting themselves, for instance, but who let it be known shortly by their restlessness that you are boring them. If I know anybody expects me to be clever, I couldn't think of anything clever to say to save my life; but if I am with my friends who encourage and seem to appreciate what I say, I sometimes surprise myself at my easy and even wit. I almost get on a "high horse." I think perhaps this may account for many a person's "manic" phase after depression, the natural reaction to having been alone so long and having had nobody congenial to talk to, in whose presence one can "turn loose" and even be silly, without being criticized for it, but applauded.

Well, my getting first honor at high school helped my self-respect a good deal; and then when I got to college, where my reputation for scholarship had preceded me, and was "bid" to one of the sororities, that helped. I eventually became not only president of the local chapter, but Grand President, as it was called, of the National Sorority; and had more than one nice trip to conventions or to found chapters, where I was lionized and wined and dined, given corsage bouquets of Parma violets, and written up in papers—in fact was the center of attention. This might have swelled some girls' heads—for I was only nineteen when I graduated from college and became Grand President; but mine had such a long way to go to get swelled! I was just a little bewildered, and very grateful and happy. I had some wonderful opportunities about this time, but my mother would not let me take advantage of them—a chance to go on the yacht of a millionaire to Cuba, for instance. But I was still in school—normal school by this time—and my mother always taught me to put school first. At any rate, this little brief authority and honor did not do me any harm, I believe. It simply gave me the self-respect I had had too little of before. I found that I was competent and had executive ability, as well as sufficient intelligence to get along and make a success in life. So I turned my attention in the direction—as so many women who have not been successful in attracting men have done—of a career.

For a while, I was satisfied with pursuing my ambitions. I was going to summer school at the University of Chicago, and here I had two serious love affairs, the first of which ended by my own volition because I could not return the affection of the man, and the second for the opposite reason. About the time that this second love affair ended—disastrously for me—the war broke out. At the same time I was having family troubles, and my religious views were upset. Altogether, it was too much for me; and I developed an abnormal attitude toward life and love and marriage. I really did not want to marry, because I thought it was all futile. Why bring children into the world, just to become cannon fodder? I used to look at babies and think "Poor little things—they don't know what is coming to them" and I looked at people who married as fools. Like Adam and Eve in *Paradise Lost,* I questioned very seriously the wisdom of bringing children into a world like this. I have since regained a more normal way of looking at marriage, have regained my religious foundations (through my mother's life), and have been helped to understand myself by psychology; but there are still times when I am overwhelmed by a sense of the futility of it all, and even terrified by an indescribable nightmare of horror at the thought of annihilation, the unexplained mystery of life, and the seeming injustice of the scheme of things. Why evil is allowed in the world and why the good suffer with the rest and because of the rest still worries me.   (M.N.; F.; C.T. of Psy. and Ed.; A.M.)

3. The third basic type of response to inferiority feelings is the *development of undesirable personality or character traits*. This is merely another phase of the fighting attitude. The effort to overcome or counterbalance shortcomings often produces unfortunate character distortions. This is perhaps due to the fact that the effort put forth to overcome felt limitations is generally the product of an unhealthy mental attitude and thus results in excessive effort. The victim is frequently laboring under an intense emotional strain, owing to the keen dissatisfaction produced by his feelings of insecurity, doubt, or help-

lessness, and possibly influenced by the hatred and jealousy that he may have developed toward others more fortunately circumstanced. Because of the emotionalized drive under which he is laboring, he may become excessively aggressive and his actions may become more or less blind and impulsive. His inferiority feelings may operate like a constant irritant; thus he tends to become nervous, restless, irritable, and supersensitive. His excessive militancy may reveal itself in flashing eyes, a bellicose or intolerable attitude, boastfulness, dictatorialness, and immoderate ambition. He may resort to some form of excessive exhibition to bolster up his courage, to hide his inferiority feelings, to evade the necessity of facing the pesky humdrum issues of the day, or to attract attention to himself so that his comrades can discern that he is a very important or superior being. So we find that our weakling has developed a sort of superiority complex, a hypertrophied ego, as a masquerade for his inferiority complex. Having become imbued with exaggerated ideas of his power, he may have become inordinately ambitious to shine or to dominate others. The iron will, the keen intellect, the exaggerated ego, and the ambition to dominate the world manifested by William II, of Hohenzollern, late emperor of Germany, were, in the opinion of his biographer, Emil Ludwig, forms of overcompensation for feelings of inferiority produced by his withered left arm. He grew up "into the conceited prince who, in his early days, used his own bust for birthday gifts, and one can appreciate how, while the old, old emperor was still alive and the crown prince losing his battle with death, this heir presumptive could send his photograph to England, writing beneath it the words, 'I bide my time.' " [9]

The ambitions of persons who are driven to compensate frequently outstrip their talents or level of ability, as is illustrated by the following simple story of a crippled boy who apparently was stimulated by inciting comparisons to show his classmates that he was the "cock of the walk."

A SUPERIORITY COMPLEX DEVELOPED BY INCITING COMPARISONS AS A COMPENSATORY REACTION TO MUSCULAR PARALYSIS

Jack, a paraplegic of six years and four months mental age and ten years and six months chronological age, I.Q. 60, came into my special class. At first the class's attitude was one of great sympathy. Later the children became rather intolerant. This change was due, in great part, to the decided superiority complex developed by Jack.

He was determined to show the class and me that he could do just what the others did despite the fact that he'd often hurt himself and run rather dangerous risks. The following are some examples.

[9] Emil Ludwig, *Wilhelm Hohenzollern; The Last of the Kaisers* (translated by Ethel Colburn Mayne), New York, G. P. Putnam's Sons, 1927, 3.

Although Jack was excused from the formal setting up exercises, he'd throw himself into certain positions, raise his arms, try to keep with the counts, and call loudly for the class to watch him.

He had asked for the job of caring for the manual-training tools—putting hammers, saws, etc., back into their respective places. I suggested that some tools were hard to manage and thereupon substituted another duty for him. One day soon after this, the tools were not properly returned because the class had to leave the room hurriedly. Jack was left alone in the room until after recess. When I returned, I found him struggling to put up all the tools. He had fallen two or three times, but was most determined to show me he could do it. Although his face was bruised from his fall, he turned to me and said, "See, I told you I could. I'm just as smart as the others."

Upon interviewing his mother I came to the conclusion that the family, because of a desire to make him as useful and happy as possible, had overdone it. "Jack, you can beat that. Go ahead, try it, show them how." Such remarks were made to him in reference to the deeds of the other older normal children. He was beginning to feel that Jack was indeed the "cock of the walk."

(From W.W.V.; F.; S.C.T.)

If this aspiration or drive for superiority merely expressed itself in heightened aggressiveness—overaction or overcompensation—the situation might not be so bad. But these individuals frequently are concerned only with the end results, the winning of recognition for themselves and acclaim from others, and have little concern about the means they employ. Inclined not to be socially minded, they are not given to praising or appreciating others. In fact, they are made jealous and envious by the praise others receive; they are annoyed by their successes; they often wish them evil, and sometimes will do them harm when the opportunity presents itself. As youngsters they do not get along well with other children, as they want to dictate and lead. As a disguise for their weaknesses they often affect an arrogant, haughty, boastful, pompous manner. Not infrequently the tendency toward overcompensation for their lacks results in the excessive development of the opposite character traits. Thus we find that they often become vindictive, malevolent, cruel, and tyrannical, as measures of compensation for their own inferiorities. The henpecked or browbeaten husband sometimes finds relief or compensation for his belittlement in the home by becoming domineering, vindictive, or tyrannical in the factory or the office.

Careers of Adolf Hitler and Benito Mussolini as Phenomena of Overcompensation and Overreaction.[10] The consuming urge behind the savage vindictiveness and pitiless cruelty of the two European dictators who plunged the world into its most sanguinary and irrational war sprang, at least

[10] For a psychiatric study of the dictators, see David Abrahamsen, *Men, Mind, and Power*, New York, Columbia University Press, 1945; also, Gustave Gilbert, *Nuremberg Diary*, New York, Farrar, Straus & Co., Inc., 1947.

in part, from their dissatisfied, embittered childhoods. Both Adolf Hitler and Benito Mussolini had humble and unsatisfactory origins and harbored deepseated grudges against the social order. Both were victims of emotional immaturity and fixation, as was shown in their childish vanity, arrogance, boastfulness, intolerance, cocksureness, impetuousness, fanaticism, and lack of mature judgment. Diabolically clever in capitalizing on their exhibitionist and histrionic assets, and on the ready susceptibility of the discontented, starving masses; unscrupulous in the dissemination of their false propaganda and in the use of the techniques of intrigue, espionage, and sabotage, and in the "purging" or assassination of dissenters, they rapidly succeeded in securing, with no organized opposition, the power of absolute, irresponsible dictators.

The early Life of Hitler,[11] one of the most amazing and enigmatical human phenomena of the centuries, was a record of frustrations, tragedies, and failures. He was in constant conflict with his father, who was the illegitimate son of a lowly peasant. The elder Hitler, a shoemaker by trade, had risen to the rank of a custom's official. Adolf, who had a horror of regular work, rebelled against his father's insistence that he prepare to become a civil servant of higher grade. He was determined to become an artist, an ambition that was vehemently opposed by his father. Being forced by his father to attend school, where he found little to interest him, he was determined, so he says, to make unsatisfactory progress. He says he learned well what he enjoyed (*e.g.*, history and geography) but sabotaged what he despised. Some of his studies were "neglected, out of defiance." His school record, with grades varying from excellent to not satisfactory, grew steadily worse and his conflicts with his father, increasingly bitter. He wanted to quit school at 12, when his father died, but his mother induced him to continue. After he failed to pass his final examination, he remained at home for 5 years as a "mother's pet" (his stepmother is reported to have spoiled him), spending his time "idly and aimlessly," dreaming about his thwarted ambitions, and indulging his penchant for drawing. At 18 he went to Vienna to enter the Academy School of Art. "Crushed and disappointed" when he was denied admission on the ground that his "drawings proved unmistakably that he was not suited to be an artist," he spent several months of irresolution with his stepmother (whom he adored). She died in December, 1908 (his own mother had died when he was 5), leaving a "spoiled boy" who "had learned nothing and who had nothing."

For 3 years he lived in Vienna in destitution in a men's hostel among riffraff, down-and-outers, and political radicals of all kinds, eking out a miserable existence as a casual menial laborer. He made water-color pictures and drawings and read the writings of Marx and other radicals, and was "always

[11] Konrad Heider, *Hitler, A Biography*, Alfred A. Knopf, Inc., New York, 1936.

at loggerheads with his fellow-workers." The spring of 1912 found him, "aloof and furtive," in a furnished room in Munich, which was a center of German art and music, plying the trade of a house painter and continuing to turn out water-color picture post cards of mediocre quality, until the outbreak of the war, in 1914. This threw him into a "transport of enthusiasm. I sank down on my knees and thanked heaven from an overflowing heart." Apparently the outbreak of the war was the climactic event for which he had pined. It became "der Tag" for him. Enlisting as a volunteer in the infantry, he became an orderly to the regimental staff, was never in the trenches, and attained merely the rank of a corporal.

The collapse of the German empire found him back in Munich as a German civilian, communing with the radical forces and "railing against the republic and its Marxist founders." Here, after 3 years as a beer-hall soapbox agitator, he had (in 1921) to his credit six followers who swore fealty to him as their elected Führer (leader). His temporary incarceration in the fortress at Landsberg, Bavaria, for his seizure of the government at Munich in a conspiracy with General Von Ludendorff, brought him into the limelight and added to his political prestige as the leader of the Nazi party. The compensatory relief from his accumulated frustrations afforded by his army experience as a corporal, his status as a German patriot, and his Munich exploits (which at least got him into the spotlight) probably supplied the impetus needed to touch off Hitler's subsequent furious drives: his fanatical attacks on the social order and the capitalistic system; his harangues on racial prejudice, the master race, Nazi superiority, and other vagaries of the Nazi ideology. He found his early converts among the malcontents who were looking for a deliverer from their woes and who would help them realize their age-long dream of *Deutschland über Alles*.

It may be no exaggeration to say that Hitler spent most of his adult life trying to make up for the disappointments and failures in his early life. Be that as it may, his career as the Nazi Führer was that of a blustery braggart and egomaniac, an inveterate pledge violator and lawbreaker, a genius of duplicity and intrigue, a barbarian iconoclast, an irresponsible madman, and a sadistic criminal and terrorist, who apparently received compensatory satisfaction from his ruthless policy of universal "rule or ruin." His pathological behavior is explicable in part on the principle of reaction formation and in part on the assumption that his acts were those of a psychopath, an hysteric, a maniac, or a paranoiac, as he has been variously diagnosed.

Reaction Formation. What is involved in the concept of reaction formation? This term has been used by the psychoanalysts to denote the development or overdevelopment of a character trait that is the exact opposite of the undesirable infantile impulse that it holds in check in order to prevent its recognition by the individual. Thus kindliness may be a reaction formation against sadistic trends, sympathy against cruelty, and generosity against greediness. Of course, not even the extreme Freudians would explain all sympathy or kindliness by the mechanism of reaction formation. When the repressed urge is very intense, the reaction formation may become excessive and lead to overreaction or overcompensation. Kindliness may thus become overkindliness, generosity may show itself as lavishness, and cleanliness may become manifest as exasperating finicality. Illustration of the development of the latter type of exaggerated reaction formation may be seen in the young infant who has been unduly pressured to develop clean habits. Feelings of revulsion and shame may have been instilled in him by repeated severe reproofs for his dirty habits. As a result of excessive discipline, he may eventually become overfastidious, and his exaggerated nicety may extend to many things. It may show itself, for example, in excessively precise speech or in absurd fussiness about trivial matters, such as a speck on the garment or on the skin (misophobia). Later in life, his reaction formation might extend to disgusting sights and show itself in tendencies to vomit or in feelings of nausea. Such reactions would be construed as defenses against the feelings of shame produced in childhood when he was made to feel disgust toward his own early habits. Similarly, the child may have become unduly conscientious or painfully honest, or he may have developed exaggerated scrupulosity in trivial matters in the field of etiquette as a reaction formation against severe punishment because of lying or some other moral breach.

The dynamic force involved in the mechanism of reaction formation doubtless explains some of the most vicious and brutal behavior manifestations with which the psychologist has to deal, especially in the sense of the exaggerated, compensatory expression of the traits that are the opposite of underlying feelings of frustration and inadequacy. Other classes of delinquent and criminal behavior can be more simply explained as attempts to achieve superiority in some disapproved form of activity as a compensation for failure in some legitimate type of endeavor or for some felt deficiency. The motivating force in many cases is the desire to attract attention and win recognition. The following appears to be a case of compensatory misbehavior provoked by a hideous facial blemish.

AN UNRESPONSIVE PSYCHOPATHIC CASE WHOSE BEHAVIOR DISORDER MAY HAVE BEEN A COMPENSATORY REACTION TO A HIDEOUS PHYSICAL BLEMISH PRODUCED BY A BURN AND ALSO TO SPOILING AS A RESULT OF THE SYMPATHY EVOKED BY THE ACCIDENT; ANOTHER OBSTREPEROUS CASE THAT RESPONDED

There was an unusually intriguing problem case in a class I taught three years ago, age about fifteen, and mentally about ten. An Italian boy, Michael, was seriously burned by falling into a bonfire while quite a small boy. His face was so terribly scarred that he looked hideous. I pitied him and wished to be friendly with him, but he had developed a disposition to correspond with his face. He was unmanageable and had been so with several teachers. He would jump up at any time in the lesson, talk, throw down his pencil or book, say he didn't want to stay in school, or say anything that came suddenly into his head. He was loquacious and wanted to "hold the center of the stage" at all times. He was probably compensating for his physical defect. I called upon his mother who explained that the family had petted him so much on account of his suffering that he had become spoiled and unmanageable at home also. I could easily understand how the shock to his nerves might have made him erratic and emotionally unstable. I became hopelessly discouraged with that case. He was impudent, actually insulting me with profanity when I tried to reason with him. The principal of that school had a reputation for winning the confidence of the boys (the reputation having been established by himself) and I knew he would take sides with the boy, even though Mike had been openly scornful when I told him I'd inform the principal. It was the first time I really failed absolutely to control a pupil. He was a genuine example of the psychopathic type. When he obtained his working papers I told him I wished him luck but feared he would not learn to control his temper. I genuinely pitied him. I was glad to be relieved of the strain but regretted that I had been unable to exercise more influence for good in his case.

I had a similar type many years ago, Stanley, son of a white woman and a Negro. He had been the terror of five teachers, but eventually became devoted to me. Nearly ten years after he left school, he returned, a member of the navy department, a fine-looking pleasant young man. He told me he had never forgotten some of the things I taught him about making a gentleman and a useful citizen of himself. Just why I succeeded in one case and failed in another, I cannot fathom, though I have given the matter serious consideration.

(From V.E.; F.; S.C.T.)

For suggestions for preventing or overcoming hampering inferiority feelings, see Chap. XII.

Purpose Subserved by the Individual's Adopted Response Reactions; Defense Mechanisms Defined. Why does the individual adopt the above modes of response or other types of reaction to his difficulties or feelings of frustration? How shall we interpret his behavior patterns? Essentially they are defense mechanisms. What, then, is a defense mechanism?

As the word is ordinarily employed, a defense mechanism or defense dynamism is a mode of response adopted by the individual for the purpose of protecting himself from the knowledge or consequences of his own shortcomings. It is a method employed to circumvent or side-step the feelings of chagrin or disappointment that result from conflicts or feelings of inadequacy. Essentially it is a form of deception by means of which the individual hopes to conceal the real facts from others or to deceive himself into believing that he can find security, peace, and recognition by faking or bluffing his way through difficulties. The human mind has been extraordinarily ingenious in inventing a great variety of defense mechanisms, some transparently simple and clumsy, others exceedingly adroit and cunning. The following analysis and illustrations will show the great variety of defense mechanisms employed and will further elucidate the use of the concept. The introduction of concrete cases from normal individuals will be preceded by a brief description of some of the commoner types of defenses.

Illustrations and Concrete Instances of Different Kinds of Defense Mechanisms in Normal People. 1. *Lying.* The ordinary garden variety of prevarication is perhaps the most common defense pattern. Some persons try to escape the consequences of their weaknesses or responsibilities by deliberate deception. The motivation for this kind of untruthfulness is the desire to conceal the real facts, to cover up some shortcoming or dereliction, to shirk some onerous responsibility, to escape punishment or disfavor, to save one's face, or to win approval or favor by pretending that one has measured up to the requirements.

2. Excessive Display of Some Kind. Excessive indulgences or manifestations arouse the suspicion that the individual is defending himself against something. The man of weak intellect may try to conceal the fact or to defend himself against his feeling of mediocrity by bedecking himself with expensive or gaudy apparel, by becoming excessively scrupulous about his sartorial and tonsorial appearance, by attempting to look sage and solemn, by adopting certain speech affectations, such as a cockney dialect or Bostonian pronunciation, or by the use of high-sounding words that he has memorized or sesquipedalian compounds. Similarly the man with a physical deformity may affect superior erudition as a defense against his bodily blemish. In a similar fashion, the sinner who is conscious of his shortcomings and moral lapses may strive to convey the impression that he is a paragon of virtue by indulging liberally in public prayers and other religious observances. This species of defense is known as hypocrisy. Hypocrisy, undoubtedly, is often a defense against a prickly conscience.

The cynical attitude and irritability of the unromantic old bachelor of either sex may be only a defense against his or her repressed or unrequited affection. Morbid sensitivity about matters of sex is sometimes only a defense against the individual's own consuming sex interests and conflicts. Excessive talking may be motivated by the desire to keep out unpleasant thoughts— to defend oneself against one's own annoying ideas—or to divert attention away from something in himself that one wants to conceal.

3. Defenses against Being Ignored or Bids for Attention and for Adequate Recognition. Many behavior patterns are defenses against being disregarded or belittled; they represent attempts to get into the limelight. Thus the child who thinks he is not being adequately recognized may become incorrigible or may feign illness in order to become the center of attention. The neglected wife feigns sickness as a protection against her husband's coldness or as a means of arousing his affection. Similarly the young lassie who imagines she is inadequately appreciated may try to win attention or favor by throwing a hysterical fit or feigning a swoon. Many persons will endure incredible discomfort or distress to attract attention.

Petulance may not be what it seems to be—the expression of some physical disorder; often it is a device for protecting one's prestige or for augmenting one's domination over others. As will be shown later, the superiority complex is often merely a defense against the inferiority complex; it is a means of winning prestige.

4. *Mechanisms for Avoiding Irksome Tasks and for Securing Compliance with One's Desires.* The number of behavior patterns that are adopted to avoid the disagreeable and to secure the desired is legion. We have referred to the emotional defense mechanism against fear that many doughboys adopted to get out of the trenches, namely, shell shock. Industrial accidents are often merely a defense against the grinding drudgery of monotonous machine work. Alcoholic indulgence is a very popular form of defense against feelings of inadequacy, disappointment, anxiety, and frustration in love or business; it is a means of evading responsibility and escaping from irksome obligations. Amnesias also, no doubt, are often defense reactions against painful memories or they are methods that may be employed to save one's face because of negligence in discharging duties one desires to shirk. Some persons who forget their names or identities—amnesia victims, in the language of the newspapers—may be attempting, perhaps unconsciously, to protect themselves against disagreeable recollections or to shirk onerous duties. Often, no doubt, this attitude may be due to some kind of mental conflict. Accounts of amnesia cases occur constantly in the press.

In January, 1933, a woman in Tennessee "released her husband, an auto mechanic, who claims to be suffering from a twenty-two-year lapse of memory, to a wife and two grown sons in New Jersey, whom he mysteriously left years ago." He was identified by his brother whom he "immediately recognized, identified pictures of scenes and relatives at R., but only looked blank when his Tennessee wife and daughter hugged him and pleaded for recognition. . . . Numerous friends of the man called and addressed him as Mr. M. but he only muttered, 'I don't know you; I'm all mixed up.' . . . Mrs. M. said he was a devoted husband and father. . . . As the man left the building with his brother and son to return to New Jersey, his wife put her arms around him, looked into his eyes and begged, 'Don't you know me now, Ted?' 'Oh, you were here this morning,' he said blankly, pushed her aside, and walked away. The man told officers he was walking along the street here Thursday and suddenly remembered his name to be E. G. A.

He sent a message to his sister in New Jersey and the investigation followed." This prolonged "memory lapse" might have been a defense against some odious situation.

Later press reports from Tennessee (Oct. 9, 1933) relate that "E. G. A., fifty-seven, was divorced here Thursday from the New Jersey wife he married forty years ago and was rewed Friday to the Tennessee wife he married under the name of T. M. in 1912 while suffering from amnesia. They were reunited for the sake of their fourteen-year-old daughter. They left for their future home, M., New York, where A. met and married his first wife forty years ago."

In April, 1933, a one-time salesman for an Ohio bank-equipment company appeared at the police headquarters in Washington, D.C., a "confused and depressed derelict," with the query, "Who am I?" His memory was a complete blank for an 11-year period, from 1922 to 1933, although he was able to identify in 1936 the reporter whom he had seen only once, 3 years before. "He distinctly recalled Warren G. Harding's election as President, but not his death. The White House incumbencies of Calvin Coolidge and Herbert Hoover, Lindbergh's flight to Paris, the Wall Street crash, and other outstanding occurrences between 1922 and 1933 are entirely outside of his ken." A few months later, his identity was established when he was placed under hypnosis, was asked to write a letter to his wife, and was told to sign his full name when he had concluded the letter. He did this without hesitation but could not recall his name on returning to normal consciousness. A short time thereafter, he was identified by a Nashville, Tenn., woman from a photograph in a newspaper as the "brother of one of her neighbors." The identity was confirmed by a missing toe. Follow-up inquiry on December 7, 1945, at the District of Columbia Home for the Aged revealed that the victim had been retained in the Home until July, 1942, when, apparently, he had made a spontaneous recovery of his memory. Upon discharge he obtained a job as a night watchman in an apartment building. In December, 1944, when the last word was received from him, he held a district civil-service position as a guard in a Federal building.

"One of the most unusual cases on record" of a defense or escape phenomenon may be cited as an illustration of the great variety of ways in which the mechanism works. Mrs. H. W. L., 31, was convicted in Los Angeles, in 1937, of second-degree murder of her husband, a wealthy broker, because he refused to tell his mother of their secret marriage. The penalty would be from 7 years to life. She vowed, however, that she would never be sentenced, as she could will herself to die at any time. "I can sit in this chair or lie on this bed and kill myself by will power whenever I want to." A few hours after she was found guilty, just before she was brought into court for sentence, she lapsed into an "escape coma," in which she remained for 158 hours before she could be awakened. She was examined by many physicians during her coma. Her bodily functions, except those of breathing and circulation, remained paralyzed during the more than 6-day interval. Her arms, legs, bladder, stomach, and liver were inactive. She did not react to pinpricks or to ammonia fumes. She was forcibly fed milk and orange juice and was given intravenous injections of glucose and normal saline solution for a week, but lost 10 pounds, while her pulse grew constantly weaker. Her consciousness was finally restored after 5 days of suggestive treatment by a psychiatrist (Samuel Marcus), whose efforts were centered on "getting through to the deep recess of her subconscious mind" and on an effort to "reassociate her split consciousness." "He leaned over her as she lay on her jail cot. He stroked her cheek. He murmured into her ear: 'I'm coming in. Here I come. I'm knocking. Let me in.' He kept repeating it—then suddenly announced that within a minute she would be awake." "Her body quivered, grew rigid, her eyes opened with an expression of deep horror." Later she exclaimed, "I want to go back where I was, away from staring eyes, fingers that point at me, crying, 'You're guilty—you must pay.' "

The coma was variously diagnosed by the attending physicians as nervous exhaustion, catalepsy, suspended animation, hysterical coma, self-hypnosis, trance, partial suicide, mental dissociation, control by the subconscious mind, and malingering. Trances and comas, to which reference is made on a later page, represent one form of mental release and flight from reality. The trancelike states induced by the deep-breathing exercises of the Yoga, an East Indian cult, sometimes end fatally for neophytes. Instances have also been reported of superstitious Negroes who have been "voodooed, witched, or conjured and pined away" under the influence of the "voodoo curse."

A transient case of amnesia resulting from emotional conflict was cited on page 36 in connection with the inability to recall the name of chocolate drops. Other instances will occur on later pages.

Parenthetically, reference may be made here to the numerous defense mechanisms employed by some weak teachers to bolster up their prestige or to escape from the realities of the situation. Thus the teacher who is ignorant or lacking in the mastery of the subject may try to divert the pupils' attention from this fact by excessive talking about his personal exploits or things other than the perplexing lesson. The teacher who has not adequately prepared the day's lesson because she has been motoring, attending the movies, playing bridge, or what not, may try to kill time by introducing irrelevant and trivial topics until the bell rings. The teacher who is lacking in teaching skill may defend herself by becoming very rigorous, harsh, sarcastic, and domineering. The teacher who is conscious of feelings of inferiority or lack of disciplinary skill may try to build up prestige by "picking" on some younger children, by becoming overexacting, overcritical, or over-methodical. Or she may attempt to become popular with certain pupils, especially those from the better homes or the more attractive ones, by courting their attachment through the bestowal of special favors. The teacher who is not popular with other teachers sometimes resorts to this method of gaining prestige.

Instances of Various Kinds of Defense Reactions. The autobiographies here introduced illustrate the use of temper tantrums as a defense against cruelties and as a means of getting what is wanted; bluffing illness to escape work and the necessity of facing facts; throwing fits to escape whipping, disciplinary regulations, and work and to obtain special foods; and the cultivation of the conviction of worthlessness in a young girl by a jealous, timid mother as a protection against her own shortcomings. (For illustrations of similar and also different kinds of defense mechanisms, see the author's *Minor Mental Maladjustments in Normal People.*)

TEMPER TANTRUMS, STARTING AS A DEFENSE AGAINST BROTHER'S CRUELTIES AND DEVELOPING INTO A MECHANISM FOR GETTING WHAT WAS WANTED, THROUGH THE SYMPATHETIC ATTITUDE OF AN AUNT; OVERCOME WHEN AUNT LEFT AND THE TANTRUMS BROUGHT PHYSICAL PUNISHMENT

Up to the age of eight I was the oldest boy in the family, as my two older brothers attended school in a small town, while I remained on the farm. At that time a schoolhouse was built near our farm, and my two brothers returned home. I had been considered a good helper around the house and never had had any temper tantrums.

At the age of nine I went to school with one of my older brothers, who on the way used to thrash me a great deal. I could not defend myself and so came home crying several times. That year one of my aunts stayed with us on the farm. When my brother would hit me or thwart my acts or desires I would go into a temper tantrum and cry for a long time. My aunt sympathized with me a great deal and rebuked my brother for striking me. My aunt's sympathetic intercession increased my temper tantrums. Every time I wanted something I would go into tantrums, and generally received what I wanted, while my brother would sometimes be deprived of something or be punished to please me. I soon discovered that this was an effective method of getting what I wanted. Several times my tantrums assumed a vicious form, such as grabbing a knife and running after my brother and threatening to kill him. My aunt would then come to the rescue and sympathize with me. I remember very distinctly that I once approached my brother with a knife to kill him but he was not afraid, and my aunt was not present. I knew that I was only making vain threats and was afraid that my bluff would be called.

It is interesting to note that when my aunt left I continued my temper tantrums for only a short time. One day I had a tantrum and my mother became angry and told my father about it that evening. He punished me with a strap for acting as I did. The next time I was going into this tantrum my mother threatened to tell my father and I immediately changed my tactics. In a short while my temper tantrums disappeared and I have not had any since.

(K.A.S.; M.; T. Subn. Delinquents; Ph.B.; Age 26)

FEIGNING ILLNESS, INITIATED APPARENTLY TO ESCAPE WORK OR THE NECESSITY OF FACING REALITY; SUGGESTIVE OF HYSTERICAL MAKE-UP

Mildred, age nine, underweight, nervous, easily excited, agile, a leader in her school grade, from an impoverished family, attended a summer camp for girls. One morning during the second week, she and another girl were reported sick. I found them in adjoining cots, very solemn, glibly describing numerous symptoms. Their temperatures, taken very seriously, were found to be normal. I told them the doctor would come by in the afternoon, and they could just remain quiet on the sleeping porch. I had them wash their faces and clean their teeth; and had two older girls very solicitously bring in orange juice, soft eggs, toast, and milk on dainty trays, with sprays of flowers and napkins with bright-colored borders. The other children were out all morning, while my assistant stayed with the two little girls most of the time. She tiptoed around, wrote letters, and now and then rubbed their foreheads with camphor. About eleven (our dinner hour was twelve) I went in to inquire about them, and remarked casually that it was such a pity they had to be sick on Wednesday. Aunt Maria was giving us fried chicken and fresh peach ice cream for dinner. Of course, I'd be afraid to let them eat anything but soup and toast until the doctor came.

Not more than fifteen minutes later, I was not surprised to see two shining faces appear in the living room. They rushed toward me, giggling and jumping up and down and explaining that they were not sick at all; they just thought it would be fun to pretend. I explained that we had all been pretending that morning, but wouldn't we be distressed if Aunt Maria happened to be pretending about the chicken and ice cream! Then I told them the old story of the little boy who frequently cried, "Bears are coming!" Each time the neighbors ran and found there were no bears. Finally, they stopped coming when he called; and then, one day, a huge bear really did come.

It was during the early part of our last two weeks of camp that we found Mildred one afternoon seemingly unconscious on the porch floor. I could not rouse her. No one knew what had happened. I called our physician immediately. He examined her very carefully and beckoned to me to come to the living room. He said she wasn't sick, just bluffing, to leave her in my guest room, and when she decided to awaken to let her eat anything she wished. That night I put my cot near her door. She did not rouse during the night but once, only to collapse a few minutes later. This continued until the next afternoon when Mildred heard the children calling to each other, "Dr. B. is coming, I hear his car." Dr. B. was chairman of the camp committee, and adored by all the children, especially Mildred. She opened her eyes very languidly; wanted to know where she was; had she been very sick? She was feeling fine now. Could she get up? I had her stay in bed until the next morning, and allowed Dr. B. to come in for just five minutes after supper. He played with the children until nine-thirty, a half hour beyond their bedtime. Mildred never once gave me any more trouble.

I found later that at home she did the family washing alone nearly every Monday, and that she often had these "spells." The social worker learned that they generally occurred on Monday morning. (From M.C.L.; F.; P.; B.A.)

A BOY WHO HAD HIS WAY WITH A SCARED TEACHER AND LENIENT PARENTS BY THROWING FITS; PROMOTED TO "GET RID OF HIM," HE RESPONDED TO FIRM AND UNDERSTANDING TREATMENT

Melvin, age ten, 4A, during lessons would crawl all around the room on his hands and knees and make hideous faces and throw the class into disorder. The child's parents contended that he was subject to epileptic fits. The 4A teacher had fully made up her mind to promote this boy just to get rid of him. I realized that promotion would bring the child to me, so I decided to go to the 4A room at my free times to study and observe him during working hours. I also observed him closely at recess and I finally arrived at the conclusion that his trouble was three-fourths deviltry.

The morning Melvin landed in my room, I had an earnest talk with him and drew from him the admission that he threw his spells conveniently: at home, to avoid whippings, to receive special foods, etc.; and at school, to avoid work and disciplinary regulations. He realized, child that he was, that the 4A teacher feared him and that his parents were sympathetic toward him.

I laid out my plan of action to Melvin, with the result that he never threw one spell. He did his work well, although he often showed signs of temper. However, I realized something was wrong with him and had him examined at Hopkins, where he received weekly treatments. Because he did not respond satisfactorily, he was later committed to an institution, where he still remains. (From Col.T.)

THE CULTIVATION IN A YOUNG GIRL OF A CONVICTION OF WORTHLESS-NESS, INADEQUACY, DIFFIDENCE, AND SECLUSIVENESS BY A JEALOUS, TIMID, CRITICAL, DETERMINED MOTHER, AS A PROTECTIVE DEFENSE AGAINST, AND COMPENSATION FOR, HER OWN SHORTCOMINGS

From my earliest acquaintance with life's facts it was impressed upon me that as a person I was not a satisfactory investment. When I compare early pictures of myself with those of present-day children, I was not exactly one of God's projects.

My mother was a timid, determined, and jealous person. So far as I ever learned from her directly, she was not at all pleased with her daughter's appearance, facially or physically, disposition, temperament, or anything. In fact, all her criticisms were adverse, and all suggestions along developmental lines were negative. This triad of examples will illustrate: "Don't bite your lips. They are thick enough now." "Your hands are too big and awkward to fix that. You will spoil it." "If you looked like X—— (a delicate, frail daughter of a friend) it would be some pleasure to fix some things for you to wear."

The one thing that was satisfactory with me was the God-given gift of a retentive memory, which enabled me to retain the echoes of instruction and make good marks in school.

Now, growing up in this atmosphere of constant disapproval engendered in me the idea that, except for my brain, I was a dead loss to society. I dreaded meeting new people, and as far as possible avoided those whom I did know.

My first real success in the effort to overcome this deplorable personal condition (I mean this seriously) came to me in the early days of my teaching experience. I was the teacher in charge of a one-room school in a country community away from home (Baltimore). Suddenly it dawned upon me that the teacher belongs not to herself but to every one in her little part of the world. This is not the place or the time to recount the pains of re-creating myself. It may be of interest, however, to know that I am still a welcomed visitor in the homes of that section.

At times even now, I find myself a bit wobbly about advancing my ideas or methods of work. The only way I can strangle this feeling of diffidence is to give the very best that is in me and let people take it or leave it. Conquering a deeply rooted fear that perhaps one is inferior to his fellows is not an easy job. I know.

Analyzing my mother's influence upon her daughter I come to these conclusions:

1. Being a timid person she felt the need of having someone to lean upon, and prepared for this need by shutting outside interests from me.

2. Being determined to have her way in this matter, she saw to it that my reactions toward society kept me within her reach.

3. Being of a jealous disposition she may have thought that other people might see something to like in her child, and to circumvent this calamity she used as her weapon the poisoning of the mind of that child against society at large.

Many of my early ideas have been proved untrue, and I have worked on this condition until it is no longer a liability to me. But always, I suppose, the question will intrude itself: "Why did it have to be? Was it a necessary step in my development as a member of the human family?" (H.E.; F.; S.C.T.)

Mental and Nervous Symptoms as Forms of Defensive Malingering in the Functional Neuroses. It is when we study the manifestations of many nervous and mental disorders (the so-called neuroses, psychoneuroses, and psychoses) that we obtain the clearest pictures of the essentially defensive character of many behavior patterns. Mental and nervous disease symptoms are not always what they seem to be; often they are signs pointing to something quite different from what they are thought to be. Frequently they are merely a means by which the neurotic patient tries to defend himself against the imposition of some unpleasant duty or the necessity of facing some situation that he deems intolerable. Some nervous disorders are characterized by a great variety of defensive symptoms. Thus the defense mechanisms or disguises used by the victims of hysteria (a functional nervous disorder without organic basis) include temporary paralyses, muscular contractures, loss of sensibility, blindness, losses of memory, loss of will power, catalepsy, feelings of unreality, clowning, pantomimic dramatization, delirium, convulsions, swooning, emotional outbreaks, high suggestibility, and the like. Many neurotics develop a neurosis as an alibi for not doing what they do not want to do. The symptoms they have developed, consciously or unconsciously, enable them to make a plea for sympathy, to convince their friends and the doctor that they are unable to attend to their duties because of their nervousness, headaches, pains, aches, tiredness, feelings of numbness, or what not. The symptoms enable them to defend themselves against their self-criticism and to justify, so they think, their timidities, impotencies, withdrawal from social contacts, pusillanimity, or the herculean work they are accomplishing in spite of their infirmities. The symptoms enable them to blame their shattered nerves, backaches, or illnesses.

Neurotic symptoms are frequently highly symbolic in character and very difficult to unravel both by the sufferer and by the investigator. The paralysis that the soldiers in the trenches developed often proved to be merely a symbol of the fear of receiving injury in combat. Excessive scrupulousness regarding personal cleanliness and fussiness about dirt or offensive odors may be symbolic escape mechanisms for a sense of inferiority or moral blameworthiness. Blinking tics may represent an attempt to shut out painful memories. The functional inability of the child to swallow his food may often prove to be, as the psychoanalysts aver, a symbolic protest against the authority of the parent or parent surrogate. Many such symbolic sensory and motor phenomena occur, not only in the neurotic and psychotic, but also in normal individuals. In psychotics the defensive symbolism is frequently so grotesque as to defy analysis. Ordinarily the purpose subserved by symbolic symptoms is to supply a means of escape from mental conflicts or a plausible means of justification for one's beliefs, attitudes, or conduct.

It is apparent, therefore, that the real key to the understanding of many of the neuroses, and even some of the psychoses, is to regard them as attempts to evade the issues of life by taking refuge in symptoms, such as pains, paralyses, fears, anxieties, delusions, illusions, hallucinations, indecisions, doubts, obsessions, symbolic behavior, etc. These defenses are essentially flight reactions. The neurosis serves as a sort of shock absorber against life's real or imaginary hardships. It provides a means for self-deception and the deception of others. The motives that produce the neuroses, however, often act unconsciously, according to the psychoanalysts. The motive itself thus acts as a defense by shielding the patient from the painful knowledge of the real motive.

Accordingly, to understand a functional neurosis (or a psychosis) we must always try to penetrate the symptoms. What is behind the symptom?

What is the individual trying to defend himself against by developing various symptoms? What are the symptoms designed to hide? What is the individual trying to conceal? Again, in the course of the treatment the neurotic often develops new symptoms. These must also frequently be viewed as defenses. Paradoxical as it may seem, the new symptoms are in many cases essentially defenses against recovery. In plain words, the neurotic patient often does not want to get well. If recovery occurred, the patient would have to face life's difficulties and annoyances. Thus the neurosis becomes a defense against progress, just as, in the thirties, the dole proved to be a defense against progress in the case of those who wanted to continue on their easy jobs and made no effort to reestablish themselves. Progress means self-help, independence, self-sufficiency, and not self-pity and impatience. Frequently the neurotic is one who has failed to establish proper responses to difficult situations. He is afraid of life and does not want to grow up, so he takes refuge in his neurosis, which, as explained on page 353, is often a form of regression. Obviously, therefore, a childhood neurosis may constitute a real bar to intellectual and social progress and to emotional maturation.

"Chubby," a 23-year-old wife and mother (in 1918), supplies an extreme illustration of a person "who never grew up" (the Peter Pan motive). She left Lancashire, England, at 15, to act as nursemaid for two little girls in London, and grew so attached to them that "she never wanted to grow up" but "just remain a little tot that needs a lot of tenderness and care." She continued into adulthood to wear school-girl dresses, low-heeled shoes, ankle socks, to have her hair cut Buster Brown style, to play with children's toys, and to act like a child. Her emotional stratification did not prevent her from marrying at 21, "with only one adult habit, cigarette smoking." She received a doll as a wedding present from her husband. The arrival of her son had provided a "new outlet for her juvenile interest." When he died after a few months, she "longed to be a child again to escape from her sadness and from the care that accompanies adult responsibility." She began to play with the little children on the street and started going to school again as an 11-year-old, dressing and acting as a child. For 4 months she acted her part so well that her true age was not suspected either by the teacher or by her 11-year-old schoolmates. When she quit school upon being promoted to a higher grade and given homework that interfered with her housework, the threat of the truant officer to force her back led to the exposure of her "pretense of childhood." The attendant publicity soon brought her a contract from a London amusement company at $100 a week to toddle about or sit in a play pen in rompers, playing with toys and cuddling a teddy bear.

Detailed Consideration in Subsequent Chapters of Injurious or Inadequate Modes of Solving Problems. The chapters that follow give detailed consideration to the various types of faulty reaction patterns to which many people resort for solving their problems. These are to a large extent false remedies or deceptive defense mechanisms, which if persisted in tend to develop unwholesome social attitudes and unsuccessful methods of meeting the multitudinous issues of life, and which often lead to mental disintegration. A knowledge of the nature, causes, and remedies of these unhealthy reaction types should prove of practical value to the student, in enabling him to overcome handicaps or to avoid acquiring them in his social contacts with other human beings. This knowledge should help him to recognize and understand the symptoms as they occur in children, thus enabling him to take measures to correct unhealthy trends in their incipience, or, better still, to take the necessary steps to prevent them altogether.

The line of demarcation between many of these defense mechanisms, or behavior patterns, is not sharply drawn. Some of them are interrelated and overlapping. Some contain similar elements and may be evoked by the same or by similar excitations. A child may use one kind of mechanism at one time and another dynamism at another time, even when the environmental situation is the same. Moreover, a given response may contain elements common to two or more mechanisms and permit of multiple classification. The mechanisms can be more easily categorized in thought than in practice. These reservations should be kept in mind in studying the groupings and in reviewing the cases under each. These cautions will add weight to those given on pages 66–68, 109–112, and **277.**

CHAPTER VIII

(1) TRIAL-AND-ERROR ADJUSTMENTS; (2) DODGING RESPONSIBILITIES BY EVASION; (3) MINIMIZING DIFFICULTIES; (4) REFUSAL TO ACKNOWLEDGE DEFEAT OR FAILURE; (5) SELF-JUSTIFICATION THROUGH SHIFTING THE BLAME; (6) SELF-JUSTIFICATION THROUGH COMPARISON WITH INFERIORS; AND (7) PROCRASTINATION

1. TRIAL-AND-ERROR, OR HIT-AND-MISS, ADJUSTMENTS

Nature of Trial-and-error Adjustments. Hit-and-miss experimentation is a universal form of intentional (as well as unintentional) learning used both by the lower animals and by human beings when they are lacking the necessary insight, knowledge, or skill to solve their problems successfully. When confronted with novel or difficult situations, both the lower and the higher forms of animals resort to the method of random experimentation. They try one response after another until the right solution is hit upon more or less fortuitously. Through such experimentation, nonadjustive responses are weeded out and replaced by successful ones.

The classical laboratory illustration of this kind of learning is the experiment with a hungry cat confined in a strange cage or puzzle box with a dead fish outside as the bait to stimulate him to try to escape from the cage and satisfy his hunger. Careful observation has shown that in the effort to get out the cat tries all sorts of solutions. He jumps, throws himself against the sides of the box, tries every part of the cage, bites the slats, claws at everything, and finally, through the process of sheer experimentation, makes the right response by turning the knob and escapes. Although his series of movements appear blind and impulsive, they are directed more or less definitely by the controlling desire to escape from confinement and to appease his appetite. On again being replaced in the box in a similar state of hunger, the cat goes through the same process of trial-and-error experimentation. After 15 or 20 such trials, he is able to get out promptly and unerringly upon the first attempt, not, however, as a result of reasoning or learning by deliberate, systematic observation, but by indulging in a variety of chance activities, gradually eliminating the activities that do not give satisfaction or yield favorable results, and retaining those that prove satisfying and successful. The satisfactory responses become fixed because they are usually the last or more recent ones and thus they are more likely to recur on subsequent trials than are the early, unfavorable ones.

The human child has been observed to adopt the same method of attack in similar novel situations. He indulges in similar random, impulsive movements when confronted with puzzling, novel, or difficult situations. When he does not know how to solve his problem, he tends to experiment with one thing after another until success crowns his efforts, provided that the inner urge is sufficiently strong to induce the necessary effort. But he does better, in general, in the solution of his unmastered problems than does the animal, because he shows evidence of insight. After a certain amount of experimentation, the child often learns to see through the problem. After experimenting awhile, he may gain a more or less immediate apprehension of the general principle of the thing, and this insight will enable him to solve the problem thereafter very rapidly or at once. Such insight also frequently enables the child to solve similar problems without recourse to a period of slow hit-and-miss experimentation.

This hit-and-miss process of adjustment continues to be the mainstay of many mature humans with respect to their overt behavior, as well as their thought responses, when they lack the necessary knowledge, insight, or skill required for making rational adjustments to complex or difficult problems. Many persons all their lives rely entirely too much upon this primitive pattern of adjustment.

Evaluation of Trial-and-error Adjustments. Trial-and-error adjustments, while wasteful of time and energy, are not necessarily abnormal or inimical to mental health, unless the child persists in using them too long. If he prefers to continue to rely on hit-and-miss experimentation as an easy, indolent substitute for careful, planful, analytic procedures, he is acquiring attitudes and habits that will hamper his progress toward the rational control of his problems. Too many children after they have reached the junior- or senior-high-school stage prefer to solve their arithmetical problems by trying at random one solution after another until they accidentally hit upon the answer that corresponds to the correct solution supplied in the book. When older adolescents and adults make a practice of falling back on this primitive method of solving their problems at times when things go wrong or when difficulties arise, the method is readily transformed into a regression technique for dodging responsibilities. When things do not suit the child or the youth, he may revert to the early method of random discharge of energy over many motor pathways, resorting to beating, kicking, and crying as means of getting over his irritability or solving his difficulties, rather than to seek some sensible, rational form of adaptation. Such methods are essentially survivals of childish traits that were developed to dodge the necessity of solving difficulties. Similarly in moments of excitement, or when he is off guard, or when he is confronted with great difficulties, the adult of poor mental control or integration may resort to the primitive method of random, multiple responses and may indulge in unnecessary gestures or talking too loud or too much, or even moaning or crying. He believes he can solve his problems by the use of such primitive random hit-and-miss discharges, which, he hopes, will arouse sympathy or divert attention away from his perplexity.

In normal, well-adjusted persons, this method of excessive, non-adjustive discharge will be succeeded by the method of attentive, planful, objective study of all the details of the problem, in order that it may be clearly apprehended before any solution is attempted. This method of careful planning before acting, rather than acting before planning, is the method of critical analysis and rational control. One of the major obligations of all parents and teachers is so to train children that they will substitute rational forms of solution for mere trial-and-error experimentation. The planned, reasoned kind of solution proves in the end to be more satisfying and satisfactory. It yields more efficient and successful adjustments. In school we should lay the foundation for planned, analytic procedures by using problem-solving methods at the very beginning in the kindergarten and primary grades. The children should be given tasks to solve which come within their range of comprehension and which will require careful observation, analytic understanding of the different elements of the problem, and orderly, reasoned statements of observations and conclusions. The resourceful teacher can so arrange the settings in connection with any task that the child will form the habit of solving problems by thinking them through and by analyzing and comprehending them, instead of by following the line of least resistance and "toying" with them until some solution eventually emerges as the result of chance observation or experimentation.

2. Frank Dodging of Responsibility by Ignoring Issues, or Refusing to Face Them, or Childishly Denying Their Existence

Intelligent and Evasive Methods of Meeting Difficulties Contrasted. The contrast already drawn in Chap. VII between the responses of the well and the poorly adjusted obviates the need of any extended discussion of the differences between intelligent and evasive methods of solving problems.

The intelligent method of attacking difficulties is to recognize them and understand them. One must study the problem from every angle in order to recognize and appraise all the factors that have any bearing upon it. After the situation has been adequately sized up, one should then face the problem calmly, unemotionally, objectively, and understandingly. This sort of objective, intelligent attack of the problem usually leads to success and the development of a success morale; it develops a success psychology, instead of a despair psychology, and it engenders a positive attitude of confidence, determination, and effort, instead of a negative or paralyzing attitude of confusion, doubt, or surrender.

Some persons, however, think they can achieve success, or at least avoid open failure and "get by with it," by not meeting the issue at all. They believe that the best solution is to shirk the responsibility by some sort of flight reaction. Thus one person may refuse point blank to fulfill his agreements, either because he does not recognize the obligation as binding or merely because of the childish pretext that he "does not want to." He withdraws completely from the contest or the issue, no matter how incompatible or paradoxical the course of flat repudiation may be. Again, if the dodger does not want to commit himself, he evades the responsibility of answering your letter by conveniently forgetting all about it. Since he "completely forgot," it is perfectly all right to ignore the letter. No one, he argues, is justified in holding him accountable for a lapse of memory, although it was more imaginary than real.

Perhaps the best illustration of frank and shameless dodging of responsibilities by the refusal to acknowledge obligations is furnished by the international diplomacy of the past centuries. This record is strewn with notorious examples of the outright repudiation by many nations of the most sacred covenants. The present decade has witnessed a form of international outlawry without parallel in the annals of civilized life: the complete repudiation of international compacts and international law by certain nations, by the simple device of attacking without any scruples about declaring war on friendly nations whom they had beguiled into a false sense of security by deceptive propaganda; and by the repudiation of the articles of war in their wholesale extermination of innocent civilians and noncombatants. The strategy of German, Italian, and Japanese aggressors was to absolve themselves completely of any feeling of guilt by all sorts of rationalizations, trumped-up excuses, and bald lies, for violations of promises, agreements, laws, moral principles, or recognized modes of conduct.

One of the outstanding phenomena of the depression of the thirties was the jaunty—not to say, conscienceless—way in which many people repudiated their financial agreements and contracts. Thousands of people were willing to take advantage of lax bankruptcy laws—people whose word, a few years before, was as good as their bond and who formerly regarded such an act as dishonorable. The moral- and mental-health consequences of the recent gold decision of the Supreme Court will be tragic if people acquire the idea that it is perfectly honorable frankly to dodge their financial responsibilities. If it is legitimate to do that, it is just as legitimate to repudiate all social obligations. The populace is not slow to follow the example of its defaulting government; and promises to pay may be reduced to the proverbial "scraps of paper."

In extreme cases, this withdrawal mechanism may develop into an attitude of inaccessibility and detachment from reality. This is seen most clearly in victims of dementia praecox, who sometimes become totally inaccessible and unresponsive. In this negativistic attitude, the subject cannot be induced to say or do anything or to show the examiner the slightest sign of recognition. Sometimes such individuals become so resistant that they must be forcibly moved about, must be tube fed, and must be given the physical care required by infants. The complete refusal to face life's responsibilities by denying or ignoring the realities of existence represents an extreme regression phenomenon (see Chap. IX).

The unwholesome, disintegrating effect upon the personality that results from dodging obligations, flatly refusing to face issues, simply ignoring them, or glibly denying their existence is too patent to require comment. What is the motive behind this type of behavior mechanism? It is a form of defense, adopted often deliberately, sometimes more or less fortuitously, as a protection against feelings of cowardice, inadequacy, fear to face life, or self-distrust. It is a device by means of which the subject believes he can successfully circumvent the necessity of making the disagreeable efforts required for life adjustments, can completely avoid performing hated tasks, and can satisfy his cravings for comfort and ease.

This dodge, often adopted because of earlier failures or lack of success, practically always constitutes an illusory haven of security that should be avoided at all costs. The mental mariner who charts his life course into this treacherous harbor of imaginary mental safety faces the certain loss of the respect of his fellow men and the probable shipwreck of his mental composure.

3. MAKING LIGHT OF DIFFICULTIES

Nature of the Mechanism; Its Values and Evils. Many individuals are inclined to pass off their difficulties as jokes or trifles. They banter about them, try to laugh them off, and treat them as if they were bagatelles. They do this on the assumption that they will appear less menacing and do less damage if they minimize them. They assume that this laissez-faire attitude will enable them to save their faces and bolster up their morale.

The attitude of smugness may assume the form of the sour-grapes mechanism, so-called from the species of justification used by the frustrated fox. The fox, so goes the tale, saved his pride by asserting that the grapes he could not reach were sour and no good anyway, so why should he worry? Some people, similarly, belittle their failures by the rationalization that they are better off by not having achieved their goals. The position they failed to get was no good anyway. Thus the working girl who could not go to college consoles herself with the thought that college women are very impractical anyway. "Beautiful but dumb" and "bright but impractical" are familiar forms of this type of rationalization used by some as a defense against unattractiveness or dullness. In the converse type of justification, called the "sweet-lemon" defense mechanism by Arthur I. Gates, the sting of failure is met with the consoling rationalization that, no matter how humble or lowly one's position or success may have been, it is just what was wanted or what proved to be the best in the end; or, no matter how great the misfortune, it might have been worse. The disappointed husband may have "picked a lemon in the garden of love," but she possesses some good qualities and is quite "sweet," nevertheless. He could have picked a worse one.

The attitudes of nonchalance, minimization, levity, and jocularity may occasionally prove valuable, in that the individual may be heartened to continue his struggles against heavy odds until the battle has been won or lost. Such attitudes may serve as buffers against excessive anxiety and thus save the victim from consuming his energies in constant worry. By engendering a hopeful, optimistic, determined frame of mind, the victim may be able to overcome his defeatist attitude; this in itself will conduce to victory.

Value of Humor. In this connection a few comments on the mental-hygiene value of humor may be in place. Humor is one of the best forms of mental medicine. The ability to perceive the humorous or the seriocomic in the minor or major tragedies of life, as well as in its humdrum occurrences, is no mean mental-hygiene asset in this day of stern, not to say grim, realities. The ability to preserve one's sense of humor amid life's seething maelstroms of toil and trouble constitutes an invaluable form of mental-health insurance. Humor takes the sting out of defeat, disappointment, and criticism; it is a shock absorber against tension and irritability; it is an antidote for despondency and discouragement; it creates an atmosphere of buoyancy, serenity, and hopefulness; it is a magical touchstone against worry and frayed nerves. By providing emotional release and nervous and muscular relaxation, hearty laughter is a more potent sedative, tonic, or stomachic than many of the famed drugs of the pharmacopoeia. Humor helps us to see ourselves as others see us; it helps us to enter into the feelings and thoughts of others, and is an aid to objective self-study. The person with good humor is popular and admired, while the ill-humored person is disliked and shunned. The ability to see the comical side of life saves many of us from becoming too egocentric and from always taking ourselves too seriously. "Without vision the nations perish"; without humor life grows drab, stale, and boresome. Therefore, good humor and a taste for the humorous should be cultivated in the homes and the schools as prime characteristics of the healthy personality. Children's spontaneous love of the comical is shown by their insatiable cravings for the "funnies."

The following poem by Douglas Malloch[1] is not without mental-hygiene significance.

No Sense of Humor

The funniest thing, beyond all doubt,
Is someone with the fun left out,
A man without a sense of humor
Seems like a myth, at most a rumor.
I can't believe there can exist
A person like a pessimist,
Not here, not certainly hereafter,
A man without a soul for laughter.

There is more laughter on this earth
Than all things else of any worth.
The morning merrily uncloses,
And how God smiled when He made roses.
The laughing brook will presently
Be mingled with the smiling sea.
And even clouds are vagrant vapors
That cut the most amusing capers.

The kittens play before the fire,
The puppies romp until they tire.
I can't believe the bee's as busy
As he makes out he is—or is he?
The birds go singing through the skies,
And with a smile the daylight dies—
It must be wrong, a myth, a rumor,
This talk about no sense of humor.

Nevertheless, the attitude of undervaluation of one's difficulties is attended by possible evils. It is essentially a species of distortion of the facts, a species of bravado based on self-deception. Therefore, this attitude may invite eventual disappointment and failure because it does not lead to an adequate appraisal of all the elements of the problem; in fact, it leads to the belittlement of the entire problem, and so the individual may make little effort to overcome his limitations. He may try to go through life blissfully oblivious of his failures or blandly unconcerned about them. He consoles himself with the rationalization: "What's the difference anyway? My difficulties don't amount to much. I guess I can continue to stall along in the future as I have done in the past, laughing off my picayune troubles and worries." Thus he may become a chronic victim of the complaisant "I-should-worry" attitude, which has reduced many brilliant careers to mediocrity or failure.

[1] Copyright, 1934, by Douglas Malloch.

The best way to surmount difficulties is to recognize them and to prepare for them by a candid evaluation of all the factors involved. This makes for the development of a winning attitude. While some breaches or shortcomings may not be important, others are colossal, although the victim may use this dodge to persuade himself of their unimportance.

This excuse mechanism probably supplies the justification for many deliberate homicides. Many murderers, no doubt, minimize the gravity of their crimes. Murder to them is pretty much of a lark or a prank. The removal of an object, even a human being, in the path of one's progress is merely an "incident." "Life is cheap," why worry about one or more lives? That kind of sophomoric rationalizing motivates the conduct of some people. To illustrate: On Easter Sunday in 1937, in New York City, a self-styled sculptor nonchalantly murdered a woman, her daughter, Veronica, and a roomer. He announced very blandly upon his apprehension that these murders were merely an "accident." He intended to murder Ethel, Veronica's sister, but as she had not returned home at the time of his intrusion, those who were at home served his purpose just as well.

In the same city, a few years ago, a woman took her two children into a thicket near Brookhaven, L.I., and committed a most gruesome crime without compunction because, she alleged, she wanted to marry a restaurant worker who said her two children were in the way. She cut her 7-year-old daughter with a pair of scissors, hit her with a hatchet on the mouth, drenched her in gasoline, and set fire to her. She also tried to kill her 4-year-old son. She had a right, so she reasoned, to remove any obstacle to her remarriage, even if it involved the assassination of her own children.

The war lords and their cohorts of the aggressor nations, under a similar perverted ideology of utter belittlement and contempt for all human values, staged orgies of crimes on a wholesale scale, including mass murders, as mere unmoral incidents in their march toward the subjugation of all mankind. One medical perpetrator of fiendish atrocities expressed great surprise that he should be tried as a war criminal for his work in the furtherance of science! Human beings were nothing but guinea pigs in the eyes of prostituted science and the arrogant Nazi and Japanese sadists. Our generation affords a picture of self-styled "master races" for whom the most repugnant crimes against humanity had no more ethical significance than common horseplay or a disagreeable chore.

The widespread resort to the mechanism of minimizing the significance of faults and breaches and of compromising the established folkways of the nation may account, in part at least, for the extensive vogue of divorces in certain strata of society. Two or three decades ago, the obtaining of a divorce was a great scandal—something to be hushed up and handled in secret. Now multiple divorces are so frequently chronicled in the press as to arouse only passing comment. An Oregon woman recently won her fifteenth divorce and "still hopes to find the right man." She was married to and divorced from one husband three times. Going through divorce procedures has, in fact, become the grand sport or publicity stunt in certain circles, especially in the "gold-digger" class and among the denizens of filmdom, who know how to combine "chiseling" and the quest for thrills. Some feel so little concern about making and breaking marriage vows that they might as well not be married at all. Marriage to them means nothing but a legal form that can be used as a basis for legal claims for alimony and legacies. Otherwise, as a legal contract, it is regarded even more lightly than an ordinary business obligation that can be enforced at law. Marriage to some is essentially a species of tandem polygamy. A part of the psychology of today's "marriage racket" is the exaggerated "playboy" tendency that regards the issues of life, the major as well as the minor ones, as mere jokes and bubbles.

A closely related attitude is the following manifestation.

4. REFUSAL TO ACKNOWLEDGE DEFEAT OR FAILURE

Nature of the Mechanism; Its Advantages and Evils. Some people tend to become blind to the existence of their shortcomings, defeats, or dissatisfactions. They refuse to admit or acknowledge them. They, no doubt, adopt this attitude as a defense against disappointments and frustrations. They keep assuring themselves that there is nothing wrong with them. "They're all right. They're successful, they're going strong, they're delivering the goods," no matter how seriously they have blundered or failed.

Can there be any virtue in such protective bluffing? Yes, if the stubborn refusal to acknowledge failure incites the individual to redouble his determination and effort to succeed in spite of all his handicaps and discouragements, it may be a valuable attitude to assume. The attitude of unflinching determination in the face of bitter frustrations, no doubt, enables many persons to triumph over their failures and thereby become successfully adjusted. Instances of persons who achieved eminent success in spite of physical handicaps are given on pages 283*f*. and 400*f*.

But grave evils may attend the use of this mechanism of adjustment.

1. One of the dangers is that the child or the adult may be led doggedly to persist in spending his time in doing things that are beyond his powers and limitations, instead of applying himself to tasks that he can perform successfully. He may thus invite continuous disappointments and failures by this species of intriguing self-deception. It is better from the standpoint of mental health and practical life success that we should integrate our efforts about tasks that we can perform with distinction, no matter how lowly they may be, than that we should achieve mediocre success or suffer failure on a level of activity above our limitations. Continuous concentration upon the first

kind of pursuit serves as a corrective of unhealthy subjectivism; it makes for the salutary objectification of attention and for mental integration. Application to tasks impossible of fruitful mastery, on the other hand, tends to produce mental incoordination and disintegration.

2. Another possibility is that the subject may be led to ignore his present limitations and failures and to maintain a victorious attitude by mentally taking refuge in past successes. Instead of marshaling his resources for a valiant assault upon his present problems, in order to achieve an acceptable degree of mastery over them, he may spend his time in glorified rehearsals of his earlier conquests in dealing with relatively simple problems, such as confronted him when he was a child and when he enjoyed a protected existence. Moreover, "distance lends enchantment," especially when dealing with one's own hoary past; thus his reenvisagements of his earlier successes are often highly exaggerated. One tends to remember the pleasant experiences of childhood and to forget the unpleasant ones, the "Old Oaken Bucket" delusion. In all probability, he was not such a towering hero in "the good old days" as he imagines he was. After all, this type of adaptation is sometimes merely a species of deceptive rationalization or a cowardly device, by means of which the individual hopes to forget his present discouragements and failures or rid himself of the feeling of dissatisfaction they have engendered, by mentally substituting the real or imaginary successes of his earlier days. But satisfactions gained from the retreat or regression to an earlier stage crowned with victory usually prove deceptive. Thus when the boy who has been repulsed by the girl with whom he is infatuated returns to an earlier stage of mother fixation (the so-called Oedipus complex, discussed in Chap. XV), he may remain forever fettered in this infantile stage of mother adoration. Similarly, when the youth cannot have his own way with adolescent companions, he may select his playmates from younger children. But the satisfaction thus obtained often proves illusory. It may shackle him to a stage of immaturity, and prevent him from growing up intellectually and emotionally.

3. A third evil is the tendency of the individual to project responsibility for his failures away from himself to some external situation. Since he will not admit that he has failed, in spite of the evidence or the logic of the situation, he attempts to rationalize away responsibility for his failures by projecting the blame upon something or someone else. Even when he admits that he has not achieved distinctive success, he is not to blame. This method of excusing failures constitutes our fifth defense mechanism.

5. Self-justification through Blaming Other Persons or Untoward Circumstances for One's Blunders or Inefficiencies

Few protective or compensatory devices are more frequently used than this dodge. If anything goes wrong, why not absolve yourself of any responsibility by blaming the weather, some phase of the moon, the depression, bad luck, evil spirits, the "evil eye," the hoodoo, the banshee woman, the witch doctor, politics, the President, your parents, your teacher, your siblings, or playmates, God Almighty—anything or anyone except your impeccable self? If you fail to obtain a position or to retain your job, it is not your fault, but dirty politics, personal pull, favoritism, jealousy, or prejudice. The ball player was not responsible for his inaccurate batting, the trouble was with the ball or the bat. The pupil finds no difficulty in attributing his "flunk" to the "mean" teacher who "had it in for him" and who is "getting even" with him. The disappointed social climber feels no compunction about accusing her rival, whom she despises, of undermining her, although her lack of social success may be due purely to her own ineptitudes. Adam blamed Eve, and Eve blamed the serpent; and so it goes ad infinitum in this royal pastime of "passing the buck."

The human mind has an infinite propensity, doubtless acquired, to indulge in buck passing as a means of self-protection, as a means of defending itself against feelings of inferiority or guilt, as a means of asserting and defending its worthiness or vanity, or as a means of exalting the ego. One's own dear ego must be defended at all costs, irrespective of the injustice that may be done to others. This mechanism is constantly employed by many persons who have acquired a sort of superiority complex that makes it difficult for them to concede that they are ever in the wrong, and who always find someone else or something else in the wrong. They seem to have accepted for themselves the proverbial attribute of royalty, namely, "the king can do no wrong." This attitude of assumed superiority is often induced by their own sense of insecurity and fear, especially the fear of being blamed by others. The fear of being blamed is one of the most disturbing of the many fears that harass people. Our impulse to project blame on someone else often is nothing but a defense against being blamed ourselves. We attempt to divert suspicion from ourselves by blaming others, and we hasten to blame others before they have time to blame us. Fear of being blamed and resort to blaming often go together.

The blame mechanism is the stock in trade with children of all ages. The habitual excuses offered by children for their misdeeds, derelictions, and shortcomings run about as follows: "He did it" (when the fact is the accuser did it). "He did it first." "I did it because he did it." "Why do you pick on me when I only did what he did?" "He told me to do it." "I was afraid he would hit me if I had not taken it." "I couldn't help it." "Something made me do it." All kinds of extenuating circumstances are offered by children as excuses for acts of omission or commission.

Illustrations of the Blaming Impulse in Children. The following are typical illustrations of the naive way the blaming propensity manifests itself among children. In the cases cited, the process of blame rationalization amounts to downright fabrication, the form often adopted by children and by less clever adults.

FALLING INTO THE MUD FROM A GIANT STRIDE AND BLAMING HER COMPANION FOR THE ACCIDENT; RATIONALIZING AWAY RESPONSIBILITY FOR VIOLATING THE RULES

One day at recess as I came into my room I saw a little girl, age eight, in the third grade, near the radiator. As soon as she caught sight of me she exclaimed very indignantly, "Look what E. has done to me. Now my mother will whip me." I then saw that her clean dress, always spotless, was wet and splashed with mud. When I inquired how it had happened, she said E. had pushed her into the mud and she insisted she be allowed to go home at once to change her dress.

Upon further investigation I learned that she had been swinging on the giant stride. In trying to stop her chain, she had tripped and the little girl back of her naturally had bumped into her.

Her feeling of hurt pride at seeing her clean dress all mussed and the thought of what her mother would do or say led her to blame someone else for her mishap. She framed an excuse for her own wrongdoing in riding on the giant stride after a rain, to save herself from a scolding or whipping.

(From M.W.A.; F.; E.S.T.)

STUBBING AGAINST AN EASEL LEG, THEREBY SPLASHING PAINT ON HER DRESS, AND PROJECTING THE BLAME UPON A COMPANION TO RATIONALIZE AWAY FEELINGS OF GUILT

Four six-year-old children in the first grade were busy at easels with alabastine making the farmer, his wife, a pig, and an apple tree for our farm unit. Working rather close together and using the same jars of paint, each was absorbed in his own picture.

B., immaculate as usual in a beautiful yellow silk dress, stepped boldly out and dipped her brush in the green paint. As she turned around, her foot struck the leg of the easel, and a big spot of paint appeared on her dress. Quickly, with eyes flashing, she turned to M. and said, "See what you made me do." M., turning and looking at her in a wistful manner, said nothing, but went on with her picture.

I had witnessed the whole performance, but did not interfere. I occasionally glanced in their direction and could see that B. was very much disturbed. When the pictures were finished and the group had seen them and everything had been put away, B. came to me and said, "See what M. made me do." I said, "Did she? How?" She hesitated and then said, "Well, she got in my way." I replied, "Are you sure? I thought you walked into the easel. Didn't you?" Very sweetly she said, "Yes, I did, but mother won't like it." Then I said, "Mother will understand when you tell her how you got it on the dress. Besides, it will wash out." Thereupon she went quietly to her seat, still holding her dress. Later, at recess, she came running in, beaming as she exclaimed, "See, it is all gone. I washed it out." She was happy again. (From W.M.E.; F.; E.S.T.)

AN INVETERATE TENDENCY TO BLAME, POSSIBLY ACQUIRED FROM THE GRANDMOTHER; BLAMING AN INNOCENT BOY FOR A THEFT SHE HAD COMMITTED; PREVARICATION

My second-grade children had on their wraps waiting to be dismissed for lunch when I noticed one girl, M., age ten, quietly searching in her desk for something. Suddenly she told me that her lunch money, which she had left in her desk that morning, was gone. M. and I looked through her things again, but the money was not there. Then a boy, Bo., age seven who sat in front of M., said that during the recess period he had seen a girl, B., age seven, looking in M.'s desk. As soon as he said this B. looked at him and said, "You are telling a story. I didn't bother her things, but I saw you around her desk." Then she turned to me and said, "I haven't her money but he has."

I dismissed the class but asked M., B., and Bo. to remain for a few minutes. B. started out with the group. I called her and she pretended that she hadn't understood me. I thought she acted very strangely. Her face seemed almost colorless.

I asked B. to take everything out of her desk, which she did, but there was no sign of any money. Then I noticed that one of her coat pockets was buttoned, which was very unusual for B. I asked her what was in the pocket; she refused to answer. I do not know whether or not I did the right thing but I put my hand in her pocket and there I found the money. She had been blaming Bo. all the time.

The blaming attitude seems to be B.'s worse trait. She is always blaming someone else for everything, when most of the time she is the guilty one.

B.'s home life is not very happy. She lives with her grandmother, who blames B. for everything. I have been wondering if B. might not have acquired this blaming attitude from her grandmother.   (From S.S.N.; F.; E.S.T.)

A PENCHANT FOR EXCUSING TARDINESS BY PROCESSES OF RATIONALIZATION AND BLAME PROJECTION

About 9:15 A. came rushing into the classroom all out of breath. I questioned her in regard to her tardiness. In a lengthy explanation she told me how she had hurried to school, hoping all the while that she wouldn't be late. It was not her fault that she was late. Her mother was slow in getting up. She just wouldn't get up and prepare breakfast.

I accepted the child's excuse without further questioning, hoping that it would not happen again. The next morning A. came to school at 9:10. I waited for the explanation that I knew was ready for me. This time A. blamed her tardiness on her small brother, whom she brought to school with her each morning. She said that B. had been "poky" all the way to school. She just couldn't get him to hurry.

Several days after that I saw the child's mother and in our conversation mentioned the fact that A. had been tardy quite often lately. Then the mother explained that A. had just been contrary and wouldn't wear the dress to school that she wanted her to wear. A. had cried so hard that the mother had stopped her work and had ironed the dress which she wished to wear and therefore A. was late for school. Had I not immediately checked up on A.'s excuses, she probably would have developed a habit of tardiness as well as acquired the use of rationalization.   (From W.H.M.; F.; E.S.T.)

Many persons are perfectly willing to assume credit for meritorious performances. But when they fall short of their accepted ideals they are quite ready to blame others for their baser impulses. In consequence of this attitude they may refuse to heed the well-meant suggestions of others. They become negativistic and nonreceptive to advice.

Evils of This Kind of Justification of Personal Lacks. This kind of bluffing or deception is one of the most childish of childish survivals and it is one of the most pernicious, because it often works. Although the excuses may be nothing but more or less clever or stupid rationalizations, they are often believed by credulous people and accepted as genuine. As a result, the malingerer often becomes an object of misdirected pity and sympathy. Many parents, teachers, employers, and others do not realize that the explanations offered are mere inventions or subterfuges. Because the ruses succeed, the tendency is to make increasing use of this form of alibi, so that it often develops into a habitual mode of excusing personal lacks. Indeed, the tendency to rationalize one's failures and to project the blame upon something in the environment may become so fixed as to become almost an obsession, with the result that the individual will go through life always offering alibis and blaming others and his unlucky stars for his own shortcomings. If he grows satisfied with his deceptive stratagems, he becomes doubly handicapped, because he will not exert himself to overcome his defects. Why should he? He is not to blame. If he has been unable to free himself from the realization of his duplicity, he may still believe that he has been successful in "putting it over" on the rest of us. This belief frequently proves delusional. Eventually the camouflages fail, bringing censure, hatred, and scorn upon the dissembler, who develops heartaches, fears, and loss of self-respect. When the person who has become a slave of the impulse to blame others is found out, people will realize that he is merely satisfying the childish impulse to camouflage his own lacks, and he will incur their ill-concealed contempt.

How the blaming impulse may develop into a fixed and dangerous obsession is seen in the mental disorder called paranoia, which is characterized by systematized delusions of persecution and chronic suspiciousness of others, who are often blamed for the hapless condition of the victim. The paranoiac's belief that people are trying to persecute him is a species of rationalization. The delusions of persecution probably represent, in part, an effort to achieve superiority as a defense against the patient's feelings of fear, blame, insecurity, and inferiority. To counteract these feelings, he rationalizes that people are trying to persecute him. They would not persecute him unless they feared him, and they would not fear him unless he were a very important person; however, a very important person cannot fail. So the paranoiac blames his reputed enemies for his misfortunes and difficulties. Because of this conviction the paranoiac often attempts to annihilate persons against whom he nurses delusioned grudges. He does not realize that his superiority complex may be merely a compensation for his rankling sense of insecurity and inadequacy and a reaction against the fear of censure.

This blaming penchant in adults is essentially a reversion or regression phenomenon. It is the method employed by the child and by primitive man for escaping from the harsh demands of existence that they could not meet and for maintaining their self-respect by shifting the blame. Instead of assuming the blame themselves and trying to overcome their difficulties and shortcomings by personal effort, primitives found it more convenient to project the responsibility upon the environment and to resort to excuses, dodges, incantations, excoriations, exorcisms, and imprecations. They blamed the medicine man, the witch, the evil spirit, or his satanic majesty for their misfortunes, and so they indulged in elaborate rites of propitiation instead of bestirring themselves to develop the necessary skills to overcome their deficiencies. Evidence has already been presented (pages 127 to 135), in connection with the discussion of black magic, voodooism, and hexing, that many primitive minds still exist in the present-day culture of our own country who resort to the same kind of blame techniques employed by primitives. One more case that further illustrates the point was culled (during the year 1935) from the "Pennsylvania Dutch Country." A boy of 5 slashed his 8-month-old brother on the forehead because he had been "hissed to do things." Some of the neighbors blamed the hex, while the father is quoted as "blaming unfriendly neighbors for the spell, who had urged the youngster 'to be devilish.' The first attack upon the baby prompted the parents to call in a woman 'witch doctor' to break the spell of the hex. . . . The witch after mumbling her ritual ordered the boy left alone with his baby brother." The parents stole to a window and saw the boy slash his brother again, this time, however, with a butcher knife, even after he had, allegedly, been cured of the spell by the mumbled incantations of the witch doctor. "Belief in the magic of traditional phrases and symbols persists in many Pennsylvania rural districts. Signs of the 'hex' can be seen on many a barn and farm building."

Similarly, when the child carelessly stubs his toe against a stone, he does not blame himself but kicks the stone. He must protect his self-esteem at any cost, even when he deals with inanimate nature. By blaming the stone, he has freed himself of blameworthiness. The "mean door" squeezed his fingers, and so he vents his wrath upon the door by giving it a vicious slam or by punishing it with a hatchet. Many civilized adults still cling to this crude type of defense mechanism, although they may substitute a voluble flow of curses or expletives for the kick or the bang.

Preventive and Corrective Measures. The child, to become a self-reliant, responsible adult, must be led to discard this childish form of self-deception and projection as he grows up. He must be so guided and trained that he will assume responsibility for his own carelessness, shortcomings, failures, and acts of commission and omission. A few suggestions may be helpful in the attempt to realize this desirable goal.

1. The first step must be taken by the parents as a part of the important problem of emancipating the child from dependence upon them and upon external authority. The child must be so conditioned that he will gradually outgrow his dependence upon his caretakers. He must be led to realize that genuine success or failure in life depends largely upon his own efforts and accomplishments, and not upon his lucky tooth or lucky stone or lucky day or upon the prestige of his parents or the success of his siblings.

2. Parents and teachers must afford opportunities for training the child along the line of his capabilities and giving him the taste of success in things that he can do successfully. The successful child has no need or desire to project the blame for his triumphs upon someone else. He will be only too willing to assume credit for his successful accomplishments.

3. The child should be so instructed and conditioned that he will come to see that spurious arguments and excuses only lead to self-deception and eventual disillusionment, dissatisfaction, and failure in life, because they do not supply the essential groundwork for lasting success.

4. Do not reprove the child too severely, because this tends to develop an exaggerated consciousness of blameworthiness or a desire for revenge. The child who labors under an excessive feeling of guilt may seek compensation or relief from his prickly conscience by blaming others.

5. In harmony with the previous suggestion is the necessity of making a careful, critical investigation of the child's excuses, to determine whether they are genuine or manifestly false, or whether they are subtle rationalizations. Let no one imagine that this task is an easy one. The flimsiest excuses and explanations often possess every semblance of genuineness. Even when the child seems to be absolutely honest and sincere, he may be malingering shamelessly. We must be sure of our ground before making imputations of dishonesty or prevarication, in order that we may not be guilty of lodging false accusations against children. The consequences of these are often most tragic (see page 198). A false accusation may provoke an acute emotional upset, the effects of which may continue for many years. Not the least evil is the habit the child may form of making false accusations himself. "Why should not

I even the score by blaming others unjustly even as I was unjustly accused?" The invariable rule should be: Try to understand the child and learn the reasons for his tendencies to project blame before censuring or correcting him.

6. Closely related to the fifth suggestion, in fact a corollary of it, is the requirement that adults themselves cease practicing this dodge. The extensive use made by adults of all levels of competency of this defense mechanism, without regard to the facts, which is one of the most prevalent types of childish survivals found in adults, is little less than amazing. With some the blaming impulse has acquired the strength of an obsession. Children who acquire the blaming disposition early in life have, in all probability, almost always acquired it from their parents. Parents must, therefore, set the example and refrain from rationalizing their foibles and utilizing this shallow mechanism for protecting themselves against their own negligence or inefficiency. They should especially avoid blaming children, particularly unjustly. Some mental hygienists even go so far as to assert that elders should never blame children, because of the fear that the latter will acquire the same trait. They contend that punishment is preferable to blaming. Be this as it may, before any attempt is made to blame the child, one should first try to determine the cause of his faults. Often causes will be found for the child's misconduct or clumsiness that will absolve him of most of the blame. Moreover, it is often possible, without resort to blaming, to lead a child to understand that his undesirable acts do not conform with the standards of good usage observed in his home or in his school and that if he is to remain in good standing in the group he will have to modify his behavior patterns. The feeling of not belonging because of conduct that tends to ostracize often acts as a powerful brake upon tendencies toward nonconformity.

7. Try to condition and train the child so that he will acquire the right attitude toward blaming and being blamed. He should develop an objective attitude toward the whole problem of blaming and blameworthiness. This requires a careful, unemotional analysis of his own behavior patterns and motives, in order that he may understand himself, and an understanding of the blame motives of others, in order that he may realize why he is being censured. Through a proper understanding of the blaming impulse, he should be led to realize that one should not become too sensitive about being blamed.

The impulse to blame often springs from excessive sensitiveness about protecting one's own ego, reputation, or vanity. Therefore, when people blame others they may not intend to be so blunt or severe as may appear on the surface. Let the child realize that in the attempt to defend themselves some people seem to be more unsympathetic and critical than they actually are, their primary motive being to protect their own integrity or to safeguard themselves against being blamed. The knowledge that the impulse some people show to blame others is often a release from or a compensation for their own shortcomings and therefore is merely an effort to shift the blame should enable the child to grasp the humor of the situation. If he can laugh over the comical elements in the picture he will not be likely to take the criticism too seriously and to become abnormally sensitive. This suggestion should prove of particular value for spouses who often evince a special penchant for projecting the blame upon each other. When the child has been unjustly blamed, he will be less inclined to become unduly sensitive if he realizes that his critic may be trying to compensate for his own frustrations by making him the scapegoat. He should feel such a form of emotional release will not do any particular injury to himself, innocent victim that he may be. Understanding this, the child should not be likely to develop an unjustified sense of blameworthiness when he has done his best and is still subjected to blame.

Of course, many occasions will arise when the child is at fault and it is necessary that he mend his ways and improve his techniques. It is, therefore, equally important to develop in the child the right attitude toward merited criticisms. He should be led to look upon deserved criticisms unemotionally and objectively as well-meant aids for correcting his faults. When he finds his performance imperfect, just reproof should serve as a spur to improvement instead of making him excessively sensitive and resentful. If he assumes the right attitudes toward his failures, they will become opportunities for growth and stimuli to achievement on higher levels of integration.

Let children and adults learn to take blame with equanimity as it comes and not to become hypersensitive about it. Let them adjust themselves to the realities of the situation, correcting real faults and deficiencies when these are found, taking their just share of the blame, and looking for extenuating circumstances in the case of misguided critics. Let them marshal all the facts bearing on the situation and allow the logic of facts to convict or refute those who resort to the blaming technique on the basis of false premises. Inexorable facts are stubborn realities that cannot always be hoodwinked. They have a way of eventually "telling their story" and compelling recognition. This method of meeting blame situations is more valuable for the preservation of mental balance than finding outlets in emotional flare-ups. Whether they are justly or unjustly blamed, it is important that children and adults do not acquire an acute or morbid fear of being blamed, for people often compensate for fears by contracting the habit of blaming others.

If children and adults, as well as peoples and nations, would only stop blaming one another, what a forward stride would be taken toward the establishment of the millennium! A marked step toward the elimination of this vice would be registered if all accept as a part of their social philosophy the point of view that can be most fittingly expressed in the following paraphrase of a popular slogan: There is so much good in the worst of us and there are so many blemishes in the best of us that it behooves none of us to cast blame on the rest of us.

Nations are among the most vicious offenders in the practice of blame projection. Practically all the national propaganda organizations in the First World War blamed the opposing combatants for the perpetration of the most barbarous atrocities, but none ever acknowledged responsibility for any of them. As to the cause of the war itself, charges and countercharges were hurled back and forth for years by most of the belligerents, but none ever acknowledged any responsibility for precipitating what was at the time the world's greatest holocaust and crime against civilization. Germany, Serbia, Austria, Russia, France, and other countries vigorously proclaimed their own innocence and equally emphatically blamed one of the enemy countries.

In the Second World War, the dictator-controlled totalitarian powers had reduced their subtle, omnipresent "propaganda" (a euphemism for their highly perfected system of disseminating falsehoods through all conceivable mediums), which often assumed the form of blame projection, to an almost exact science. They were always in the right, while the enemy was always in the wrong and always to blame for instigating the war and for its continuance. Hitler repeatedly absolved himself from all blame for starting the war by accusing England, particularly, for its inception. He protested that he was only defending Germany against those who were plotting to destroy the fatherland. He attacked the Russians, with whom he had signed trade and non-aggression pacts, on August 19 and 21, 1939, because they were ready to attack Germany. He declared war on the United States, because it was responsible for the war with Germany's ally, Japan. Millions of credulous listeners "fell for" his buncombe that the warmongers among the capitalistic powers and the Jewish bankers were responsible for the war—not the innocent, persecuted Germans, who had to have "lebensraum." Fortunately, secret documents have completely refuted this blame projection on the part of a criminal who became the Chancellor of a great nation. These documents show that the world conflict was planned by Hitler and his conspirators as early as February 22, 1937, and that elaborate preparations for implementing the war started soon thereafter.

The detailed plans for the invasion of Czechoslovakia were made on April 21, 1938. On May 23, 1939, Hitler told his military commanders that blitz attacks would soon be made for the purpose of seizing Holland and Belgium as bases for smashing Britain and France, and that "declarations of neutrality will be ignored." On the following August 22, he ordered his generals to attack Poland and "to kill without mercy all the men, women, and children of the Polish race"; and he also told them that the pact with Russia was only a temporary device and that Russia would eventually get "just what I have predicted for Poland." The attacks on Czechoslovakia and Poland were justified by the most brazen pretexts: a border incident in the case of the former country adroitly instigated by the Nazis on Hitler's orders; and the ordered military attacks on a German radio station by Hitler's troops disguised in the uniform of Polish soldiers, to lend credence to the trumped-up charges. To induce Japan to make war on America, he promised the Japanese ambassador, on April 4, 1941, that Germany "would immediately take the consequences."

On January 21, 1948, the U.S. Department of State released for publication documents captured by the Nazis, which disclosed that Hitler and Stalin had, prior to Hitler's betrayal, agreed to divide Poland between themselves and also to keep the United States and Britain out of Europe, Asia, and Africa. Certainly, "there is no honor among thieves!" This amazing revelation immediately evoked the countercharge from the Soviet propagandists that the war was caused by the Anglo-French instigation of Hitler to attack Russia and by the "golden rain of American dollars" into Germany, which enabled Germany to rearm.

Since the close of the Second World War, the Russian totalitarians have persistently made use of blame-propaganda techniques, via the radio and the press, for the attainment of their supreme objective, the communization of the world and the destruction of all bona fide democracies. Many millions of people have been completely subjugated by the clever species of deceptive psychological warfare against the "capitalistic, imperialistic nations of the world," which are seeking to enslave the masses. These unscrupulous attacks have centered upon the United States, the stronghold of the democratic nations. It requires little intelligence for the unscrupulous mind to concoct specious accusations and tricky explanations (and that is the depth to which propaganda has fallen) to justify any course of action. The tragedy is that many persons cannot see through the ruses.

Blame projection is the grand strategy and defense mechanism used by the international brigands, as well as by the common garden variety of crooks and lawbreakers. The eradication of the blaming proclivity would represent a master step toward the attainment of more cooperative personal, national, and international relationships.

A somewhat similar type of rationalization by which persons seek to blind themselves to their present shortcomings is the following practice.

6. SELF-JUSTIFICATION THROUGH COMPARISON WITH CONSPICUOUSLY INFERIOR ACQUAINTANCES

Many persons are ever ready to console themselves with the thought that, no matter how inefficient or unworthy they may be, there are others who are even worse. This thought not only gives them comfort but it may be used as justification for their lack of ambition. Some persons derive a considerable amount of satisfaction and prestige from the knowledge or the assumption of superiority that this type of comparison gives, although they are gaging their attainments by very inferior standards. This form of justification is often used by children. John is eminently satisfied with himself because he can run faster than Jim, bat better than Tom, or read better than Charles, each one of whom may be several years younger than he is.

Examples of Justification by Comparison with Inferior Companions. The following actual cases will obviate the need of further elaboration.

A FAT, CLUMSY BOY WHO IS SATISFIED TO OUTRUN A LITTLE CRIPPLED GIRL

In playing an indoor game, B., a fat, clumsy, very slow boy of six in the first grade who is easily outrun by the other children, takes the nut and drops it on the desk of a little girl who is a cripple. He then runs as fast as he can and reaches his chair before she has hardly started the chase. B. says nothing, but his face plainly shows that he is satisfied with his success in outrunning one of his class-mates. The class, knowing that he has chosen to compete with one of inferior physical ability, does not applaud.   (From R.M.L.; F.; E.S.T.)

AN OVERGROWN, OLDER BOY WHO, SHUNNING COMPETITION WITH CHILDREN OF MORE NEARLY HIS AGE IN THE THIRD GRADE, GLORIES IN HIS SUPERIORITY IN PHYSICAL ACTIVITIES OVER YOUNGER FIRST-GRADE PUPILS

My first grade contains an eleven-year-old boy who seems to enjoy comparing himself with his inferiors, especially in physical feats. Because of his age and size he has the advantage over the little people of six in games and physical activities.

Noticing his unfair advantage when he came to me this year, I placed him in the third-grade group for games and activities, but he was not happy there and soon asked to go back to the first-grade group. Now that he is back with first-grade pupils he comments frequently on his ability to run faster, throw farther, drive nails better, etc., than the other children.   (From L.K.E.; F.; E.S.T.)

A HIGH-SCHOOL GIRL WHO MAKES LITTLE EFFORT BECAUSE SHE DOES AS WELL AS INFERIORS .

A high-school pupil, age fifteen, who is just barely passing her work, seems to be contented because she compares herself with those who are failing and those who are on her own level. Whenever she takes a test she says "Oh well, so and so got less than I did and practically the whole class failed." Her attitude really constitutes a handicap because she doesn't aim high and thus doesn't get high marks. She never worries about a poor grade, just taking for granted that she won't get above the passing mark. She is capable of doing better work, but doesn't make use of her abilities, as she is satisfied to compare herself with inferiors.

(From V.A.R.; F.; E.S.T.)

A BRIGHT BOY WHO WAS SATISFIED TO DRIFT BECAUSE HE WAS
SUPERIOR TO AN INFERIOR COMPANION AND WHO ADVANCED BY
LEAPS AND BOUNDS WHEN ENTRUSTED WITH THE LEADERSHIP OF
A GROUP OF DULL CHILDREN

Last year I had two or three fairly brilliant pupils in my room and I planned to have them do extra work since they were capable of doing much more than the average of the class.

Two of the three took to this work immediately and seemed to enjoy it but J., a boy of thirteen or fourteen, wanted only to do what the others were doing. He would do as little as he could to get by, just enough to try to show a little extra effort since he knew I expected it of him. At the close of the six weeks' marking period he had earned a low B whereas he was capable of getting A.

I called J. into my room one day and had a talk with him about his mark in mathematics. I told him he was capable of doing the same grade of work that the other two students were doing and asked him why he didn't try. He replied, "My mark isn't bad, why I have beaten H. who got C." I noticed that he seemed satisfied with the fact that he had beaten H. who was far inferior in ability to him. I spoke to his mother about the matter and she said the two boys had always been neighbors and that J. was always satisfied as long as he had beaten H. Whenever she questioned him about better grades he always remarked, "I think I'm doing very well, I always beat H."

It seemed from these facts that J. had chosen H. as a standard and had become smugly satisfied merely to keep ahead of him. Upon studying the situation, I found J., who was inclined to be lazy, had set H. as a standard because he realized that H. was inferior in ability and it would require little effort on his part to beat him and yet have a good alibi for his parents when questioned about marks.

Although this boy, who was not a discipline problem, had some qualities of leadership, he tried to do as little work as possible in the classroom. After trying vainly to stimulate him into more vigorous activity, I decided to make him a leader of a group of children who were very slow with their work. I told him I couldn't help all the students at once so I was going to divide the class into three groups and have three of the best students assist me. I talked the situation over particularly well with J., pointing out to him the necessity of his doing extra work so he would be able to answer their questions intelligently and help them solve their problems.

J. went at his work with much pep and became one of the best helpers I've ever had in that respect. Thereafter he progressed by leaps and bounds. His mother came to me one day to find out what I had done to him. She said they went away one evening and came home about nine o'clock and found J. at the desk working. She said, "What are you doing?" He replied, "I have some extra work here in mathematics which I must get finished before class tomorrow, so I'm going to do it now."   (From L.R.N.; F.; Jr. H.S.T.)

Values and Dangers of This Species of Justification. There is some virtue in this mechanism if it serves to fortify the individual against feelings of discouragement and despair, if it helps to maintain his morale, and if it spurs him to renewed effort to achieve and maintain a position of genuine superiority worthy of emulation. The danger is that the child continues to be satisfied with comparing himself with children very much younger or very much inferior in specific traits or in general ability, instead of comparing himself with normal children of his own age, group, or rank. In consequence of this he is likely to acquire an exaggerated sense of security and competency. Through such standards of measurement he may be led to forget about his limitations, and he may become convinced that he is a superior being; he may become smugly complacent with himself or extremely arrogant. Therefore, instead of trying to surmount his obstacles, he is satisfied with the laurels he has won on a low level, or with his pretended achievements, or with his real or fancied superiority over inferiors, or with dreaming about what he might have accomplished if he had been left to compete with his childhood comrades.

Corrective Measures. It is inevitable that child companions will make comparisons between themselves, irrespective of whether the home, school, or playground activities are conducted on a cooperative or competitive basis. Children cannot avoid noting resemblances and differences in their mental and physical characteristics. It is equally indisputable that such comparisons sometimes serve as powerful incentives for improvement (although they often arouse ugly jealousies and rivalries). But children should be taught that the proper measure of the standard of excellence they should strive to attain is emphatically not the standard set by younger children, or by children of inferior endowment, or even by children of normal or superior endowment. The true criterion of what any child should strive to attain is the realization of his own highest potentials or his own peculiar penchants or ambitions in the light of his own general ability, specific talents, and opportunities. The true measure of success in life is not the realization of the ambition to equal or surpass acquaintances of limited general endowment, or those who are handicapped in specific directions, or even those who are normal or superior, but the realization of one's own highest possibilities in worth-while forms of service. To rest content because one is not so poor as some acquaintances is merely one way of dodging the responsibility of giving a better account of oneself.

In general, the mechanism of comparison with inferiors is merely a defense against indifference and indolence, and its use tends toward stagnation instead of growth and progress.

Of course, a certain amount of comparison with others (which is unavoidable) should enable the child to arrive at a more accurate appraisal of his assets and deficits. Without such comparisons his own standard of perfection would be subjective and illusory—too vague and individualistic for one who must adjust himself to the demands of the society in which he dwells. A moderate amount of comparison is probably valuable, both in supplying standards and in furnishing incentives. But children should not be encouraged to compare themselves constantly with other children, especially inferior ones. Even too much comparison with superior children may create crippling feelings of jealousy, resentment, unworthiness, dissatisfaction, and discouragement. Let the child's major incentive be the attainment of his own maximum self-realization within the framework of activities that are compatible with the general social good.

7. PROCRASTINATION

Nature and Causes of Procrastination. One of the most prevalent symptoms of maladjustment is the tendency toward procrastination. What is the precept or rule of action followed by the inveterate procrastinator? It is, "never do today what you can postpone until tomorrow." "Do it not now, but later." "Wait until the last minute." "The accepted time is some other hour or day, never the present hour or day."

Douglas Malloch's poem entitled "In Just a Minute" [2] expresses the philosophy of action of the procrastinator very aptly:

IN JUST A MINUTE

She will—in just a minute.
　She'll be there—wait a bit;
She has a gown she can't lay down
　Until she's finished it.
A robin's in the plum-tree,
　A van before the flat,
She'll come to see—as soon as she
　Has finished what she's at.

There goes the hook and ladder,
　The beans are up today,
And she will come—but she has some
　Things first to put away.
The mailman brought a letter
　You need another nail,
She heard you trill, but wait until
　She reads about a sale.

It's just that way with women,
　In country or in town,
Whate'er you ask, she has some task
　She simply can't lay down.
When Gabriel blows his trumpet
　A man can safely bet
Some wife will state, "You'll have to wait—
　I'll come, but can't come yet."

[2] Copyright, 1932, by Douglas Malloch.

What are the causes or motives of the procrastinator's dilatoriness? Why is he so slow in reaching decisions or executing them, once they have been decided upon? Many explanations are needed to cover all types of cases. A few of the more important ones may be enumerated.

1. One of the most frequent causes is the example of other persons. It is comparatively easy to acquire the habit of drifting and postponing by following the dilatory practices of parents and associates and by justifying one's conduct by the behavior of others (see the examples on pages 140–142).

2. Another incentive to dilatoriness is the belief that by postponing action the necessity of performing the detested task can be entirely avoided, on the assumption that the other fellow may forget all about it or that somebody else will perform the duty. Thus pupils frequently allow their written work to slide unless they are constantly reminded of it. The explanation usually advanced —that they forgot about it—is often a subterfuge, the true explanation being the expectation or hope that the teacher will forget about the requirement and thus enable them to evade the responsibility. Some cases of bona fide forgetfulness are due to wishful thinking or active, purposive repression according to Freud.

3. Laziness, carelessness, and indifference are, perhaps, the explanations most frequently offered. But these traits of character are frequently merely symptoms of some underlying and often unrecognized difficulty. Slothfulness and indifference cannot always be taken at their face value.

4. A variety of other mental states often operate to produce doubt and delay. Among such states are lack of motivating impulse or drive, impairment of will, feelings of inadequacy, lack of self-confidence, fears, timidities, mental conflicts, inhibitions, and feelings of doubt and irresolution. The feelings of doubt and indecision produce a state of vacillation, excessive balancing of motives, and weighing of pros and cons. In states of indecision, or "blocking of the will," the victim may spend his time debating whether he should take this route or an alternate one, whether he should write the long overdue letter now or go to the tennis court instead, or whether he should prepare the algebra assignment or go joy riding. He cannot quite decide whether he should prepare his paper today or let it go until tomorrow. Or, if he has reached an affirmative decision, he just cannot get started, and so he keeps postponing the task until the very last moment. With many the chief difficulty is to overcome the initial inertia. Witness the great difficulty that many persons experience in starting the letter that they have decided to dispatch. If they could only overcome the initial torpor, many persons would be able to accomplish tasks fairly well.

In extreme or pathological cases the victim is unable to get over his state of irresolution, uncertainty, or impaired or blocked will (abulia), and so he spends all his time weighing the alternatives, mentally shifting between various courses of action, trying to decide what to do. When the decision has been reached, he changes his mind. Such states of vacillation are inimical to mental harmony and produce disintegration and discord.

Extreme degrees of impairment of the will, or abulia, are observed in some neurasthenics and in certain stages of some mental disorders, such as involutional melancholia (a psychosis of middle age), the depressive phase of manic-depressive psychosis (which is characterized by cycles of depression and excitement), and general paralysis or paresis. In these patients the springs of action sometimes seem to be completely paralyzed. The patient for hours or days may remain completely listless, inactive, and impotent, unable to form any decision to do anything, or unable or unwilling to execute any decisions that have been reached. Patients suffering from such "paralysis of the will" often attribute their impotence to some external influence (another instance of the blaming complex), such as a malevolent spirit; magnetism; an injurious ingredient in the air, food, or water which has rendered them powerless; some imaginary bodily disability; and the like.

The minor forms of this inhibitory complex are the bane of many persons, otherwise normal, who are habitually tardy in the performance of their duties, and who are a constant source of annoyance and irritation to their associates.

Illustrative Cases. Three typical cases of the procrastination complex occur on pages 140–142 and 279–280. In the following case, procrastination is merely one element in the picture of a self-satisfied, comfort-loving, regressive type of individual who has failed to outgrow her infantilism.

REGRESSIVE, INFANTILE TRAITS AND FAILURE TO GROW UP, POSSIBLY DUE TO EARLY SPOILING AND DESIRE FOR INFANTILE COMFORT; TOO INDOLENT TO OVERCOME REGRESSIVE TRAITS; RESORT TO RATIONALIZATIONS AND PROCRASTINATION; DIFFICULTY IN GETTING STARTED AND IN OUTGROWING CARELESS, SELF-SATISFIED, TOMBOY TYPE OF LIFE; VALUE OF THIS SELF-ANALYSIS TO RESPONDENT

Until B. (an only child) was fourteen she was always talked of as the baby of the family and was treated as such. An aunt spoiled her terribly, and her father made her feel she was perfect in all she did. Although at fourteen to sixteen she realized that she had not grown up, she seemed to make no effort to do so. Today many of her acts are infantile. In her, infantilism takes the form of following the line of least resistance, choosing the way which is likely to cause the least trouble to herself, and offering excuses. Another form of this is similar to that taken by older persons who become infantile, namely, that of always striving to be comfortable. Miss S., her former teacher, has told her that she "sags" all over, mentally as well as physically. Although much talking has been done about adjusting this, nothing but rationalization has been accomplished. She is too lazy to give up some of her pleasures, and much time is spent in dreaming and talking about what a great help she is going to be. But when the time comes she never quite measures up.

Procrastination has always been one of B.'s faults. As long as she can remember someone has always been saying "Hurry up" to her, which usually tended to produce a negative reaction when she was a child. She has been much overweight and is still 20 pounds over normal. It was always an ordeal to start to write the Christmas "thank-you" notes or to go to bed for there was usually something that would take just a minute longer to finish. In short, she really didn't like to start anything that entailed any work. This is another of her adjustment problems which is very evident at present. She really doesn't like to exert herself if there is any other way to get what she wants. For example, she will do anything rather than lean over to pick something off the floor. If she wants a thing badly enough she will do almost anything to attain it, no matter how much exertion is required, but when the end is attained she will settle back and rest on the glory of that accomplishment.

One of the first adjustments started by her intimate teacher nine years ago— which is still in progress because so many things seem to be snarled together with it and the correction of one thing leads on and on—was the change from a "slam-bang, tomboy" type of person to a more quiet, reserved, and inoffensive person. This required not only psychological but physical adjustment as well. When a person for the first sixteen to eighteen years of life has been permitted to wear overalls, flop into a chair, and sit with her feet either on some article of furniture or under her, there are bound to be drastic measures necessary when adjustment starts. B. found it quite a task to walk without striding, sit with her feet on the floor, talk in a modulated voice, and, above all, maintain a neat appearance at all times. She has always been one of those persons who could collect dirt without trying. All of these have been on the "correction list," but just as she thinks she has made some progress along one line or another, she discovers she has not. It has become apparent to Miss S., who is still trying to help, that B. doesn't really want the result badly enough to put in the extra effort necessary to maintain all these adjustments all the time.

Never in her life has B. wanted anything so badly as the position which she recently lost, and it would seem that this experience should have some effect upon her treatment of the entire problem, which shows: self-indulgence, self-satisfaction, incessant repetition of the same type of mistake, and careless inattention.

After writing this paper the facts of the case now seem very apparent to B., and she is going to start at the bottom of the ladder and first of all pay attention to details. With the habit of paying attention to details, both professional and personal, she will call to mind the habits of self-indulgence and self-satisfaction and adjust them as occasion arises. One wonders how the latter trait could continue at all after the affair of this past summer, when she learned very plainly that she had nothing to be satisfied about. The repetition of the same mistake occurs not only in professional tasks but in many, many things B. does.

(C.E.M.; F.; Grad. Reg. Nurse; Age 29)

Corrective Measures. Procrastination is not only an implacable, ruthless "thief of time," but it is often a sign that all is not well with the individual. It would be hard to exaggerate the difficulties that many people create for themselves and the financial and cultural losses they sustain because of their proclivity to put off and dillydally. As the writer entered the city of Boston the first time, he asked a fellow passenger how to get to Bunker Hill Monument. He learned to his amazement that his informer, a man in the thirties, although born in Boston, had never visited the monument and had seen it only from a distance. He explained that he had resolved again and again to make the visit but had invariably put it off. The writer knows a number of Washingtonians who have been repeatedly postponing for years their projected trips to the Library of Congress, one of the most magnificent libraries in the nation.

"I know of a young woman who wanted a scholarship in a summer colony very much. She inquired into it one year, realizing it was too late for that season, but in preparation for the next. She was found to be eligible and was advised to apply again in January. But the month slipped by and it was not until February that she awoke to the fact that she had not put in her application. She did it then with all speed, but her procrastination lost her the scholarship. She could not afford to enter, and so lost her chance through delay." In innumerable relations in life the adage applies, "a stitch in time saves nine." The housewife who delays about placing her winter apparel in moth preventives often pays for a new suit in the fall as the price for her dilatoriness.

Because procrastination is a hampering defect that seriously impairs the victim's practical efficiency, often causes him to lose the things he most craves, and robs him of many opportunities and pleasures in life, it should be permanently eradicated. The following suggestions should prove helpful in varying degree to different individuals.

1. A serious attempt should be made to ferret out and remove the underlying causes, whatever they may be, doubts, timidities, conflicts, inhibitions, overscrupulousness, lack of incentive, indolence, early habit formation, physical exhaustion, nervous disorder, etc.

2. On the positive side, the child should be trained to plunge vigorously into whatever he undertakes to do. He should begin by actively doing something, even if the activity merely assists him in preparing the way. He should attempt to shake off his lethargy or vacillation by becoming active, by doing something, no matter what—exercising, walking, talking, scribbling—anything to start the flow of activity in the cerebral mechanism. Nothing is more fatal to an attempt to overcome the handicaps of inactivity than the attitude of do-nothing-ism. The goal must be activity. Vigorous activity should enable the procrastinator to remove the stumbling block that constitutes the chief impediment with many people, namely, the initial inertia. So the first line of

assault in the attempt to vanquish this bugbear is to mobilize your energies and do something.

3. Adopt as your workaday motto the slogan "Do it now." The conscious envisagement of this work ideal will serve as a powerful spur to some through the power of conscious or subconscious autosuggestion. Let the procrastinator realize that the only opportunity for doing anything is the present moment. The past is irretrievably gone. Tomorrow is nonexistent. When tomorrow becomes existent it has become today. Today represents your only actual chance for accomplishment. "Now is the golden opportunity for work"; let that be your philosophy of action. The irredeemability of the forfeited past has been well expressed in verse:

> Lost, somewhere between sunrise and sunset,
> Two golden hours, each set with sixty diamond minutes,
> No reward is offered,
> For they are gone forever.

The same thought is enlarged upon in the following poem: [3]

THIS IS YOUR DAY

> This is your day. Not Yesterday —
> That day is done, your day no more—
> Nor yet tomorrow—though you lay
> Upon tomorrow's back a score
> Of burdens that today must bear.
> This is your day, and here, not there,
> And now, not then, things must be done—
> This is your day, the only one.
>
> This is your day—the past is through,
> The great unalterable past;
> And you have something more to do
> Than change a die already cast,
> Or cast a die before its time.
> There you may gaze, but here you climb.
> This is your day, the only hour
> Of earth within a mortal's power.
>
> This is your day—but not for long,
> This day yours now, or not at all.
> Today you cannot live it wrong
> And then tomorrow right recall,
> Whatever day this day shall be
> Tomorrow, till eternity,
> Depends forever on the way
> You live it now. This is your day.

[3] Copyright, 1932, by Douglas Malloch.

Until the bogy of procrastination has been fully overcome, adhere to the principle of never postponing anything until tomorrow that can be done just as well today. In fact, follow the practice of giving the right of way to the daily duties that must be performed. If these are given precedence and are attended to before the time arrives that has been set aside for diversion and relaxation, the unavoidable routine details of life will have been discharged ahead of time instead of behind time.

4. Establish a daily routine of work and play and adhere to it unflinchingly —at least until the habit of procrastination has been thoroughly uprooted. To follow this suggestion it is necessary to make out a time schedule for the various activities of work, recreation, eating, sleeping, exercise, etc., and to estimate as accurately as possible the amount of time required for each activity. Since the inauguration of "freshman week" by the colleges and universities of the country, the importance of budgeting one's time for the sake of mental and physical health and scholastic efficiency is receiving a modicum of the emphasis it has always deserved. To form the habit of doing things punctually, regularly, and invariably, it is necessary to plunge into the program vigorously and to admit no exceptions. One of the laws of habit formation, as formulated by William James, was never to allow an exception. The formation of a fixed habit of routine will solve the procrastination dilemma for many persons. But mere resolutions will not suffice for the establishment of a dependable routine. The indispensable prerequisite for converting an attitude of promptness and regularity into a fixed habit is practice, practice, and yet more practice. Safeguards must be taken, however, against a possible danger: the habit of promptness and regularity must not be allowed to develop into an obsession. It should be developed, not as an abstract end in itself, but as a means of combating a wasteful and injurious evil.

5. Develop in young children habits of prompt response in all routine matters. For example, with respect to answering the summons for meals, a warning signal might be used for getting ready, to be followed after an interval by a final signal for reporting at the table. If the child is dilatory and does not respond on time, apply some effective remedy in place of scolding or blaming. Thus, he might be required to occupy a chair away from the table for 10 or 15 minutes while the others are eating. The early routinization of habits of promptness in habitual matters should help to counteract the tendency to loiter.

Doubtless systems of rewards, both intrinsic and extrinsic, judiciously employed, can sometimes be effectively used in the development of promptness and dependability.

6. Introduce some rival stimulus that will provide a greater challenge and appeal than the tendency to follow the line of least resistance; this is in harmony with the principle that stronger stimuli tend to inhibit, overcome, or

remove weaker stimuli. This suggestion has wide applicability in mental hygiene and educational work. One way to overcome an undesirable trait, be it a feeling of timidity or indecision, an aversion, an inhibition, or an inclination to procrastinate, is by focusing attention upon a strong competing idea. The more vivid, desirable, or strongly alluring such an idea can be made to appear, the more effective will its influence be in the eradication of the contrary idea. Grant relates that his fear on the battlefield was overcome by the idea that the enemy was just as much afraid as he was. This competing thought served to instill a feeling of assurance. Many a youth has been heartened to undertake a difficult school task by the assurance that many of his classmates are just as much at sea as he is. The confidence that the child has that his mother will do him no harm will often overcome his fear of telling the truth. Thus a strongly implanted rival idea or a much-desired competing motive may become a new conditioning process that will exert a salutary effect upon the individual and put to rout opposing tendencies. This explains in large measure the effectiveness of the method of suggestive therapeutics. Strongly suggested or implanted rival ideas, especially if presented appealingly, often serve as powerful stimuli for the eradication of undesirable tendencies and the establishment of new processes of desirable conditioning. One way to remedy the child's disinclination to get up in the morning is to interest him in one of the morning radio programs and to turn on the radio as the "rising-bell" signal. The coveted experience of listening to the broadcast may be stronger than the inclination to stay in bed. The opportunity to participate in playground activities at 4 P.M. or to listen to Dick Tracy at 5 and to Terry and the Pirates at 5:15 may outrival the inclination to loiter until suppertime on the way from school.

There is, perhaps, no cure-all for the very disconcerting and baneful habit of procrastination which seriously handicaps many persons in the race of life. But the faithful application of the above suggestions will produce a marked improvement, even in stubborn cases, and may sometimes effect complete cures.

CHAPTER IX

(8) RATIONALIZATION AND (9) REGRESSION

8. RATIONALIZATION

Nature of the Mechanism and Types of Expedients Employed. Rationalization is a more or less clever species of prevarication or falsification, in which excuses, explanations, reasons, or motives other than the real ones are given to justify one's acts of commission or omission. It is a method of substituting explanations for one's conduct that are socially approved for the real, unacceptable reasons. It is a method of justifying our beliefs, sentiments, or conduct to ourselves and to others by offering excuses which seem plausible and convincing but which are not really the true ones. To escape the dilemma of injuring someone's feelings by telling the naked truth and of imperiling one's reputation for veracity by telling an outright falsehood, a plausible explanation is offered that does not seem like downright lying, since it possesses sufficient semblance of truth to be accepted as genuine.

Pertinent illustrations of everyday rationalizing spring readily to mind. The pupil, knowing full well that his low grades are due to his lack of application or to his inferior ability, may nevertheless offer the excuse that the teacher is inefficient, or that the teacher did not lend him sufficient assistance, or that the other pupils "cribbed" and thus were graded too high. The careless pupil may rationalize away responsibility for his failing by the explanation that his mother also is careless, that he "takes after" her and therefore cannot help being careless. The young swain justifies his evening promenades as a health measure, although the real reason for taking the walks is that he wants to meet a certain lassie. The jealous woman protests that she dislikes her rival because of her vulgarity instead of her dominating personality and magnetic leadership.

The screen star may constantly belittle the acting of the rising star, allegedly because of her lack of real artistry, although the hidden explanation is that she is envious of her meteoric progress. The exhausted businessman cannot attend church Sunday mornings because he needs to "rest up" in bed, although the real reason is that he is not interested in the services and wants to devour his Sunday paper undisturbed in bed. The victim of acrophobia excuses herself for not wanting to ascend Bunker Hill Monument because there are too many steps. The real reason is that she is subject to an irrational fear

338

of high places. Mamma's little darling boy ostensibly hates baby sister because of her squalling; but the real reason is that he has grown jealous because he has been dethroned by the new arrival. The pupil responds promptly to the teacher's question, as he has been urged to do, and then tries to rationalize his hasty answer.

A child is spiteful, not because he has been spoiled by unwise treatment but because he is nervous. The young man indulges his appetite for gin because he is feeling ill, and not because he relishes the taste of the liquor and the resultant mental exhilaration. The rolls turned out badly because the stove was not working right, and not because the cook mixed the ingredients carelessly or did the job poorly. The person who tends to indulge in self-depreciation and self-criticism is usually making a bid for praise, adroit or ill concealed as the case may be. He knows that common courtesy or practice requires his listeners to express their disagreement with him and thus he attains the prestige for which he yearns.

The young adolescent, torn by the emotional upheavals created by conflicts between his childhood views concerning questions of conduct, morals, religion, the teachings of science, and his growing experience, is confronted with the disconcerting dilemma of finding arguments by some crafty process of rationalization, either in support of his traditional, socially inherited creeds and prejudices to which he is emotionally attached and which he does not want to forsake, no matter how irrational or untenable they may be, or, having discarded his childhood emotional survivals, prejudices, and provincialisms, in support of his intelligent beliefs and a rational philosophy of life.

Illustrations of the more obvious use of this mechanism appear in a number of our case histories (*e.g.*, pages 140, 301–302, and 318–320). It is, doubtless, also present in many other reports, in which it does not appear to be a factor. The following is an interesting illustration of rationalizing a dislike for steam launches and gasoline engines.

RATIONALIZATION OF THE REFUSAL TO RIDE IN A STEAM LAUNCH AND A DISLIKE FOR GASOLINE ENGINES, THE ANTIPATHY IN BOTH CASES BEING REALLY DUE TO THE LOATHING OF LOUD NOISES

I do not remember any fears of high places, depths, or open areas. But a loud noise would quickly start me on a stampede. I loathed thunder, steam whistles, shooting, and hammering. When not over three years old, I refused a ride in a steam launch. My excuse was "it has hot water in it," but my reason was the fear of the whistle. Until I was nearly grown, I could not bring myself to admit the superiority of a gasoline engine over a steam installation. I argued that the gasoline engine ran irregularly since the exhaust was irregular. Secretly, I despised gasoline engines on account of their infernal noises.

(H.L.; M.; H.S.T.; B.S.; Age 38)

In the following case rationalized excuses were resorted to in order to defeat a candidate for a basketball captaincy.

ATTEMPT TO DEFEAT A CANDIDATE BY SPURIOUS ARGUMENTS—AN INSTANCE OF RATIONALIZATION

Last fall when the basketball season opened, everyone on the team started talking about whom they were going to elect as captain. Two candidates were nominated, M., a charming girl well liked by both students and instructors, and H., who had a very disagreeable disposition and was purely mercenary. H., however, was popular with some of the influential students in the school, largely because of the influential family from which she came. She always used this fact as a means of getting what she wanted.

During the few days before the election one could hear the students who patronized H. use various kinds of arguments as alibis for electing her. Some students would say, "M.'s mother is in the hospital and all of the household duties fall on her shoulders. She surely can't keep up with her schoolwork and come to practice as she should." Others would say that M. lived in the country while H. lived in town, hence it would be much easier for her to attend practice and go to the games. Still others would say that it was M.'s senior year and since she was already carrying a heavy program it would be an imposition to add to her many burdens.

These superficial arguments were merely due to jealousy on the part of H. and her adherents. Most of the girls saw through the flimsy excuses and on election day M. was elected by a large majority of the votes.

(From L.R.N.; F.; Tr. H.S.T.)

The process of rationalization may assume a variety of forms or utilize a variety of expedients. Among the numerous tricks employed, mention may be made of the following.

1. The rationalizer may resort to downright prevarication to win his point. Obvious unadulterated deception should, perhaps, not be listed as a species of rationalization but as plain, unvarnished lying.

2. Hypocrisy, a universally recognized form of inconsistency between one's profession and one's behavior, is frequently based on a series of cunning rationalizations. Through specious arguments or deceptive behavior, the hypocrite justifies to himself his hypocrisy as a legitimate means of obtaining cherished ends which he thinks he has a right to enjoy. There is, perhaps, more self-deception in the marginal field of consciousness in some cases of hypocritical behavior than conscious hypocrisy.

3. The telling of "white lies" is often rationalized on the hypothesis that one is not always required to tell the truth to any and everybody because the truth may be used for illegal or illegitimate purposes. Thus the murderer is not entitled to the information of where the man he wants to "put on the

spot" is concealed. I am not required, therefore, to reveal the information. Rather, perhaps, I am under moral obligation to deceive him and thus save a human life. Such rationalizations constitute fine casuistic questions in the domain of ethics. In this field it is not always easy to draw sharp distinctions or to determine the exact boundaries between truthtelling, prevarication, and rationalization. Primitive races usually justified deception as a legitimate means of self-preservation (sometimes referred to as "biological lying").

Occasionally the consequences of telling "white lies" are tragic. "A 'little white lie' from the lips of a pretty, dark-haired 15-year-old high-school girl was blamed today (in 1937) for the death of a 17-year-old military student" in a suburb of Chicago, who had driven during the night 300 miles from a military academy in Missouri to escape from a dreaded happening that proved to be illusory. The car, in an 80-mile-an-hour chase in Berwyn with the traffic cops in hot pursuit (the license number of the stolen car had been radioed), skidded on an icy pavement into a lamppost. When the police approached, they heard a shot, and found the youth's dead body with a bullet wound in his temple, a revolver clutched in one hand and a missive in his pocket addressed to the girl. He professed his deep love for her but said he was going to shoot himself because he had wronged her. The boy had apparently fled in consternation when informed by the girl that she was to become a mother, which she later told the police "wasn't true at all." She told him the fib "to make him feel happy." At the coroner's jury she testified, amid "avowals of undying love," that they had been secretly married some time before and were to keep the marriage secret until they had finished school.

4. Another device is to withhold some of the facts, perhaps minor ones, and to emphasize or exaggerate other facts, often irrelevant or unimportant ones. By such means desired attitudes or beliefs may be conveyed without resort to downright misrepresentation.

5. Facts may be distorted or embellished in a great variety of clever ways, so that they will not appear so forbidding, menacing, or important. Thus very significant issues may be facetiously glossed over as trifles or jokes, to the end that the subject will become reconciled to your point of view and do your bidding.

6. Many persons invent silly, ridiculous answers to conceal their underlying motives, to divert the inquirer's attention, or to fence for delay in the hope that the matter will be forgotten. An irrelevant remark sometimes saves the person from the necessity of making a direct reply.

7. One of the commonest forms of rationalization is to develop an illness or a neurosis as an alibi for shirking despised duties or as an excuse for blunders that have been committed or tasks left undone. The pupil who does not want to face unpleasant school situations finds it convenient to feign illness or to

develop a headache or a nervous convulsion. To the illustrations of the illness dodge on pages 103 and 301–302 may be added the following instance of a rationalized defense against attending church.

THE USE OF THE ILLNESS DODGE TO AVOID GOING TO CHURCH; SICKNESS PRODUCED BY THE EXCITEMENT OF THE SERVICES

Dodging my responsibilities never entered my childish mind. But now as I dig back into the past I realize how I did this on Sundays by feigning illness.

My mother was not by any means a religious fanatic but she believed in going to church on Sundays and being accompanied by the entire family. I never minded the beginning of the service. I always liked the deep tones of the organ, and enjoyed looking around at the faces "tuned" to a Sunday piety. In warm weather especially the swish of the gaily spangled fans on the deep purple dresses, silk, stiff and rustling, was music to my ears.

But near the end of the service when the minister, beginning to perspire, worked himself up to a noisy climax and stirred the sisters to follow a close second and when everybody was in a state of religious enthusiasm and fanaticism, I became actually physically sick.

Not letting my mother know my true condition, each Sunday morning I would feign illness. This illness continued systematically and regularly until suspicion was aroused. The ultimatum was "sick Sunday morning, sick Sunday afternoon also," and no pleasure.

I've forgotten how the real illness was cured or disappeared, but I do remember that my distaste for the services was as great as ever but the Sunday morning feigned illnesses completely disappeared.

(T.B.N.; F.; Col.; Asst. H.S.P.; M.A.; Age 45)

Motives for Rationalizing. Why do people try to rationalize away their difficulties? Why do they attempt to reconcile their conflicts or win their victories by processes of rationalization? Why do they invent spurious explanations or fallacious excuses for the true ones? Why do they resort to "fibbing"? Important among the motives are the following:

1. One purpose is to camouflage their real feelings, convictions, or purposes. They do not want others to know their true motives because they think that others have no right to know them or because they themselves may be ashamed to profess them.

2. They may want to avoid giving offense to others. They are afraid that if they disclose their real feelings or tell the bald truth they will cause embarrassment or arouse resentment. They argue that a tactfully presented trumped-up explanation is justified because it will arouse less ill feeling than the unvarnished truth. They act on the theory that the end justifies the means in social diplomacy.

3. They feel that the concealment of the real motive will cause the rationalizer less mental anguish than would the frank admission or pronouncement of the real facts. On both of these scores, therefore, they justify to themselves the use of white lies. International diplomacy in ages past has been notorious for its employment of clever rationalizations intended either to convey messages in such a manner as not to give offense, to conceal the deeper meanings of the message, or to deceive the other nation.

4. A very common motive is the desire to avoid performing irksome, distasteful tasks in all sorts of relations—business, religion, politics, school obligations, social affairs, etc. Some persons attempt by processes of subtle argumentation to rationalize away their feelings of duty so that they cannot be branded as deceitful and untruthful or as slackers, shirkers, and hypocrites.

5. Some want to enhance their egos, to seem more worthy than they are, and to appear in a more favorable light than the situation justifies. To induce themselves and others to esteem them highly, they rationalize their motives on a higher plane than is justified by their actions.

6. Doubtless the process of rationalizing sometimes springs from unconscious motives and may not be recognized as spurious by the rationalizer. The mechanism may have become so confirmed by frequent repetition that it operates almost unconsciously and automatically, like any fixed habit pattern. The practice of deception gradually becomes "the thing to do," and the habitual rationalizers become the "grand liars" of the community, so well known to many of us. Moreover, the emotional drives may have been so consuming as to obscure the perception of the nature of the act; or the process may have been repressed in the psychoanalytic sense.

7. The pragmatic justification supplies the conclusive motive with many. The deception works, they say. It brings success because people do not see through the camouflages, at least so they believe. Rationalization enables them to "get away with it."

Evils of Facing Situations by Rationalizing, with Corrective Suggestions. The evils of rationalization are due, in part, to the extensive use made of this method of adjustment. Few defense mechanisms are so persistently employed, from the cradle to the grave, as the process of rationalization for justifying one's emotional responses, prejudices, attitudes, and beliefs and for trying to bring one's ideals and acts into seeming harmony with one's profession and the requirements of the social code. In fact, nearly all the defense mechanisms might have been subsumed under the concept of rationalization. So inveterate is the urge to rely on this mechanism in all walks and stations of life—in the home, the school, the university, the business office or store, the legislative hall, and the international courts of diplomacy—that one is inclined to concede that the highest use some people make of their intelligence or reason is to find excuses by clever or clumsy processes of rationalization for their emotional attitudes, biases, practical decisions, or "sins of omission and commission." Having made unwise selections, inadequately considered decisions, or foolish, precipitate emotional responses, they refuse to admit the error of their ways or to make any effort to correct their mistakes, but proceed at once to find or fabricate excuses to justify their conduct by the easiest device available, namely, rationalization. The following represents some of the evils of this popular and illusory solvent of personal failings.

1. Rationalization at best is a species of attempted or actual self-deception and a tawdry effort to dupe, mislead, and impose upon others. It is a dishonest means of justifying what we want to believe or to do or to avoid doing, irrespective of the facts—a means of supporting our emotionally determined attitudes against our better judgments. It is a spurious method of finding reasons for our emotionally determined beliefs and cravings, a tricky device, impelled by motives that spring from our emotional fixations and traditional opinions and prejudices, for disposing of arguments that have won the approval of our enlightened understanding.

2. The rationalizing attitude is a great foe to genuine educational and intellectual growth and socialization. The habit of rationalizing one's prejudices and beliefs is a grievous admission of failure to grow up and to arrive at emotional and intellectual emancipation. It is a form of infantile fixation. A person who is fettered by emotionally predetermined preconceptions is unable to view his problems objectively and rationally. To him the adage is peculiarly applicable: "Convince a man against his will, and he'll be of the same opinion still." The practice of rationalization does not encourage the attitudes of frankness and sincerity, which are essential for a sound, wholesome personal or social life. Adjustments that do not result in intellectual honesty will not prove permanently satisfying. Insincerity means disintegration. An individual cannot permanently retain his self-respect and mental integrity upon the basis of deception; nor can society permanently endure upon the basis of universal deceitfulness.

The rationalizer eventually comes to grief. Clumsy rationalizations are easily detected, and the more clever ones are eventually found out if the rationalizer continues to fabricate. To this mechanism Abe Lincoln's aphorism, which has become familiar to the point of banality, applies: "You may fool all the people some of the time; you can even fool some of the people all of the time; but you can't fool all of the people all of the time." Outsiders have no difficulty, after they have learned to know the individual, in seeing through his shamming. The inevitable result of being found out is that the impostor's fellow men lose confidence in his intellectual and moral integrity.

The fabricator, himself, on discovering that his bluffs have been called and that his subterfuges have proved futile and delusive, becomes a victim of loss of self-respect, of self-condemnation for his shams and hypocrisies, and of growing mental conflicts. The habit of rationalization is one of the fruitful sources of mental conflicts and mental disintegration. Forming the habit of making hasty emotional responses and then searching for arguments in their support constitutes a grave hazard to the preservation of mental integrity.

The habit of rationalization, if unchecked, may become a serious bar to the development of sound culture and learning, which must be based upon the unprejudiced, objective study of the realities of life and the formation of policies, attitudes, and conclusions in harmony with the facts of existence.

The practice of rationalization makes it difficult to know oneself or to be oneself, because it is hard to tell whether one's traits are genuine or merely deceptive rationalizations; this, also, makes for the disintegration of the personality. Not only the outsider but the rationalizer himself may be unable to distinguish the real from the pretended (see page 118) or to recognize the true self, because the rationalizations may have been repeated so frequently that the deceit cannot be recognized. He may have become convinced of the correctness of his spurious arguments from the force of repetition. Having become thoroughly blind to his self-deception, he vehemently and perhaps innocently protests his sincerity. In many, perhaps most, cases the rationalizer started consciously to practice deception upon himself and others; the practice usually developed slowly and insidiously until it became a confirmed habit, and the victim eventually became a more or less unconscious dupe of his own machinations. Just as the individual may unwittingly acquire false beliefs, so may he also acquire a false personality. The problem of reconstructing a personality that has become distorted may be a far more difficult task than the correction of false opinions and bigotries, difficult as the latter task is.

In general, the cure for rationalization is so to condition children by instruction, precept, and example that they will reason instead of rationalize; that they will study all the facts of life, both personal and nonpersonal, objectively and dispassionately; that they will face facts and life situations as they are and not as their emotionally toned opinions would like them to be; that they will acquire the habit of impartial, analytical, factual thinking, in place of egocentric, wishful thinking; and that they will develop honest, forthright attitudes toward the problems of life, free from shamming and pretense.

The thorough acceptance of the objective attitude will in itself prove valuable for the prevention of the rationalization of emotional attitudes and for the control of emotional and instinctive impulses. The impulse to cover up or to atone for shortcomings or derelictions by offering trumped-up excuses or explanations will be weakened if the child has been reared to be himself, to be satisfied with himself, and to make the most of himself, free from jealousy of others or attempts to belittle them, in harmony with the philosophy that "every human being is intended to have a character of his own, to be what no other is, and to do what no other can do." The oft-quoted advice of Shakespeare is apropos:

> To thine own self be true,
> And it must follow, as the night the day,
> Thou canst not then be false to any man.
>
> (*Hamlet,* Act I)

9. REGRESSION

Nature of the Regressive Mechanism. Many defense mechanisms represent tendencies toward regression or retrogression, as it is sometimes called, that cling to many children and adults with lifelong pertinacity. What is the nature of the regression mechanism? In its widest connotation, regression represents a retreat by children, youths, or adults from baffling situations to childish behavior patterns or modes of behavior that brought satisfaction and success during the early years of life.[1] What are the detailed characteristics of the regression technique and the behavior responses in which it is exhibited? The following include the most important characteristics.

1. Regressions are reversions or recessions to more primitive or infantile forms of behavior. The regressionist returns to modes of feeling and thinking, attitudes, and action patterns which are characteristic of infants, of children, or of primitive people and which should have been outgrown and abandoned at the proper stage of maturity. Some of them may represent atavistic racial traits (phylogenesis), while others represent survivals of characteristics from the individual's early life (ontogenesis). The regressionist is a victim particularly of "emotional infantilism"; *i.e.,* the emotions more or less appropriate to infancy or childhood tend to become permanently stratified, while those appropriate to adulthood fail to develop or tend to become retarded or warped in their development. A person who remains infantile or immature tends to stick fast in the feeling, thinking, and behavior patterns that are characteristic of early life, such as those mentioned on pages 347*f.* and 353*f.* He is a child emotionally.

2. Regressive behavior patterns represent the substitution of lower levels of mental integration and primitive emotional modes of response for rational methods of solving problems. Instead of utilizing the method of careful, objective analysis and thoughtful, controlled reasoning, the individual falls back on behavior-pattern survivals from his earlier days. He recedes from the more delicate, discriminating, and complicated individual adjustments of

[1] In psychoanalytic literature, regression refers to the reversion of the libido (defined on a later page) to an infantile fixation or form of expression on the infantile level (a pregenital stage), because the individual cannot function at a higher level.

later life to the simpler, cruder, and more generic early-life modes of response based on native drives or emotional urges or on conventional or habitual behavior patterns.

3. Many regressions represent, basically, attitudes of surrender and retreat from difficulties or conflict situations. They are avoidance mechanisms, that is, attempts to evade the necessity of making needed adjustments. When some individuals are unable to adjust to the problems of life or are afraid to do so, they try, ostrichlike, to avoid facing them by taking refuge in the response mechanisms characteristic of their early emotional stage of infantile dependence upon the parents. They retreat to this early stage because they believe they will find greater comfort and security in some form of childish or dependent behavior, just as they did when they were young children. The retreat to the infantile stage of dependence represents the ultimate in the passive type of regression.

4. As a result of his regressive trends, the individual may resort to many childish ways of solving his problems, such as crying; weeping; pouting; sulking; swearing; lying; pretending illness; shrinking from obstacles; laughing; trying to tyrannize over his parents, siblings, or playmates; refusing to do things; coaxing or bribing others to do things for him; blaming others for his shortcomings; or displaying anger, jealousy, envy, sensitiveness, stubbornness, bad temper, excessive egotism, self-love, or self-adoration. Excessive self-adoration is technically known as narcissism, after Narcissus, the exceedingly handsome and conceited youth, who, according to Greek mythology, was caused by Nemesis to fall hopelessly in love with his own image, which he saw as a reflection in a spring. "Stuck on himself," he was doomed to pine away in adoration of his own image until he was changed into the flower, narcissus. The term "narcism," or "narcissism," is now applied to abnormal self-adoration, especially the deriving of sexual gratification from fixation upon one's own body. The narcissist is unable to love anyone who does not reflect his own adorable traits; and since it is difficult for him to find anyone who measures up to this requirement, he remains "wrapped up in himself."

Regression traits are not difficult to discern in the reaction tendencies of both children and adults. After the advent of a new baby, some 2- or 3-year-olds may suddenly become so helpless that they must be spoon-fed and given the same care as an infant. The adolescent who flings the geometry book into the wastebasket because he flunked in the test is guilty of an act of regression. The youth who, to punish the stone on which he stumbled, curses and hits it has reverted to the savage's primitive mode of response. Adults who indulge in emotional explosions or shouting or who give vent to exhibitions of sullenness or impatience when things go wrong, are, perhaps, merely regressing to their childhood patterns of behavior. The type of woman who meets life's trials and tribulations by orgies of weeping is well known. She is essentially reverting to baby acts as a method of attracting attention and securing compliance with her wishes. She employs the techniques of the little child as a means of avoiding the necessity of facing the unpleasant experiences of the home, or to regain her husband's affection. In order to shirk the responsibilities of married life and to revert to a more comfortable level of existence, some men regress to the stage of mother love and refuse to marry, while some who are married seek release from their marital obligations by the same regression technique. Some unmarried women, and some wives as well, revert to the stage of father love for the same reason. Of course, such male and female regressionists may not fully comprehend the nature of their difficulties, the mechanism they adopt in an attempt to solve them, or the underlying motivation. They may offer plausible explanations, but the explanations are often vaguely apprehended rationalizations. Such persons are striving more or less blindly to find the path of least resistance or the way that seems to lead them out of their perplexities in the easiest and most comfortable manner. This suggests an additional characteristic of some regressions.

5. According to some psychoanalysts, the motives for regression escapes are sometimes unconscious. They hold that the unconscious motive of the regression defends the reversionist against an intolerable situation by deluding him into believing that he is not really shirking or shamming. However that may be, it is doubtless true that many victims of regression do not clearly understand either the mechanism or the motivation of the regression dodge.

Genesis of Regressive Behavior. Resort to the use of regressive devices often begins very insidiously a long time before the beginning of adolescence and a long time before the child has any distinct comprehension of the significance of the response mechanisms that he is slowly developing. Two kinds of parental behavior patterns especially tend to foster the development of regressive tactics.

First, as the child grew up, he may have been permitted to continue those habits acquired as an infant that had led to conquests at that time. It did not take him a very long time as an infant to become aware that he could command, and tyrannize over, his mother by crying or shouting. He soon learned to grasp the idea that the way to become the cynosure of attention or solicitude was to pout, "act up," throw a temper tantrum, or play sick. Quite early in his career he became aware of the fact that he could secure the petting and pampering he craved by crying, moaning, and whining, and that if he became sick he would be amused, humored, idolized, and spoon-fed, and everything would be done for him. All this pampering may have so whetted his appetite and vanity that he eventually began to believe that he was the center of creation, that the world was made for him, and that his mother and others around him existed largely to cater to his every whim. By this type of strategy our little dear was able to get things done for himself without any effort on his part. As a result, he tended to grow increasingly egocentric and perhaps tyrannical. Having acquired a taste for his delightful, coddled existence, he may have come to prefer remaining a baby instead of growing up, in order to escape the irksome necessity of solving his own problems. Why should he elect to struggle with the many obstacles that thwart his will and defeat his clumsy efforts when he can more easily resort to some of the stratagems that worked so well in early childhood in inducing his mother. governess, or older sister to respond with alacrity to his every caprice?

The upshot of this whole process of conditioning is that, later on, when assailed by hardships and discouragements, our adolescent or adult may begin to dwell upon his golden period of early childhood, when he achieved success without effort by merely making his desires known through the clever use of some childish antic. Because of the satisfying recollection of those early successes, he may conclude that it will be easier to retreat from his present difficulties and fall back upon the same mechanisms that brought him satisfaction during his period of infantile dependence. Thus the adolescent and the adult may revert to childish reaction patterns to accomplish their desires. The yearning for the security and happiness of early childhood may have been in the mind of Elizabeth Aker Allen when she wrote:

> Backward, turn backward, O Time in your flight,
> Make me a child again just for tonight!
> Mother come back from the echoless shore,
> Take me again to your heart as of yore.

Second, infantile dependence and arrest of emotional development may also have been fostered by undue parental fixation. That is, the child may have become unduly attached to one or the other of the parents, often because of the attitude of the parent. Some parents cannot endure the thought that the child is becoming more and more interested in other persons and is gradually being weaned away from them. So they try to continue the child's dependence upon themselves by encouraging his infantile habits, by fixating his libido (attachment) upon themselves, or by exercising complete dominance over him, even in the period of adulthood, doing his thinking for him and solving his problems. Illustrations of such overprotection occur on pages 90–93, 134–135, and 140. When the object of such emotional fixation dies, the forlorn victim, whether child or adult, may fixate on some parent surrogate who, he hopes, will serve as a substitute for the mother or the father, so that he may continue through life in a state of smug infantile dependence, especially when things go wrong and life's fate becomes too cruel. If a girl thus fixated should marry, she is likely to continue to keep her love life rooted to the chosen parent, at least as long as the latter lives. It may be difficult, even after the parent's death, for her to transfer her affection to her husband.

Infantile fixations and regressions, therefore, are often the results of a species of spoiling, whether it be intentional or unintentional, by parents, relatives, siblings, and others, the effects of which have been to develop attitudes of continued dependence. Among the world's great, John Ruskin supplies one of the most tragic instances of parental overprotection, excessive repression, irrational and undeserved corporal punishment, and cruel, even if well-intentioned, deprivation of his inherent right to live his own life in his own way. Although he became a great art critic and a great prose writer of the nineteenth century, Ruskin—repressed, without the "joy of approved love," solitary, and unemancipated from parental dependence— 6 years after his marriage was divorced by his wife, whom his mother had chosen for him when he was 29; at 42 he complained of the "almost unendurable solitude of life." "The ceaseless authority exercised over my youth left me, when cast out at last into the world, unable for some time to do more than drift with its vortices." [2]

Illustrations of Early Fixations and Regressions. Instances of early spoiling have already been supplied (see pages 134f., 139–144, 273–274, 279f., and 332f.). The following illustrations of fixation and regression are appropriate.

FATHER FIXATION AND ADORATION; INABILITY TO FIND ANY MAN
EQUAL TO FATHER

From the cradle up, I was my daddy's joy and pride and he was my slave and lover.

When I was rather young (for my dad died when I was but eight) I was constantly aware of my love for him. If things went wrong at school, if I seemed to be left out of some game or ignored by my schoolmates, I clung to my daddy. His love made up for everything. His approval of what I did made me blissfully happy, his disapproval plunged me into despair and despondency. I doubt if he ever realized this.

No man I have ever met has measured up to my ideal of manhood as revealed or portrayed by my father, and I have never seemed quite satisfied with any other man I know. Although I have never been able to become reconciled to his untimely death, perhaps it was my salvation.

(F.E.D.; F.; Col.; E.S.T.; Ph.B.; Age 28)

[2] L. A. Nelson, "Why John Ruskin Never Learned How to Live," *Mental Hygiene,* 1928, 673–706.

A very rare case of progressive regression during a series of years to a state of fetalhood is described by Beverley R. Tucker.[3] At the time the woman entered his sanatorium, at 61, the medical findings were negative except for marked anemia, lack of hydrochloric acid, and inability or refusal to walk. She apparently was a woman of normal intellectual endowment who had a "fair noncollegiate education" and a "few cultural parlor accomplishments." She had grown up in a "protected environment of girls of the better class in Virginia" and had been waited upon and rather spoiled. When she married a corporation official, she was relieved of all responsibilities. He provided her with servants, managed her personal affairs, bought her railway tickets, escorted her on her trips, and helped to pick her hats and dresses. His death in life's prime left her completely unprepared to manage the estate or her three adolescent daughters. With the idea of becoming more like her children, she dressed and decorated herself as a young, unmarried woman. She entered into her daughters' lives, dressed like them, went out with them, and adopted their friends. Gradually she became more and more youthful, dressed more and more like a child, indulged in flippant speech, and required more and more care. When seen by Tucker, in April, 1932, she was a "nice little girl in short dresses rocking in her chair," with a mental level of 6 or 7 years. She read simple things poorly, craved attention, talked childishly, played with objects as if they were toys, and played jokes on the doctors and nurses. In a few months she had regressed to a level of 3 or 4 years, spilled her food, needed assistance with her feeding, soiled herself occasionally, spoke indistinctly, and had ceased to read. After a few more months, she was in bed, moving her limbs aimlessly, whining and crying like a youngster, hugging a rolled-up towel as if it were a rag doll, sucking the corners of her gown or sheet, soiling herself regularly, and frequently calling for "mama" (who had died 30 years earlier), the only word she could articulate distinctly. Unable to chew, she sucked liquids from a spoon, with which she was fed. She enjoyed fondling. Before she died (in another institution, to which she had been transferred), she had assumed the fetal posture, unable to make any movements except those involved in breathing.

The Virtues and Evils of Childish Emotional Fixations and Regressions. Not all reversions of adolescents or adults to habit patterns of primitive people are abnormal. Hunting and fishing, for example, are exceptions. Occasional returns to lower levels of integration or to normal, atavistic traits may serve useful purposes in affording diversion, recreation, relaxation, and relief from the monotonies, tensions, and harassments incident to the daily order of vocational and social cares.

[3] Beverley R. Tucker, "A Case of Progressive Regression," *Virginia Medical Monthly*, February, 1937.

Every one needs at times to drop back to a lower level of attention. . . . The confirmed conventionalist wearies of social custom and demands freedom. . . . The model teacher or judge for once would play the fool; and even the saint may feel the need of a holiday. . . . Leuba tells us that they (the priests, hundreds of years ago) protested against the abolition of All Fools' Day, maintaining that the abandon of the day and the relief from the strain of continued work enabled pious men to serve God the better by means of the relaxations.[4]

Although crying may be a regression, it sometimes constitutes a beneficial release. Wailing, weeping, and dashing about may constitute a valuable safety valve for a woman overcome by grief because of the death of her child. Expression, in general, is the safety valve of the emotions. Moreover, many of the traits of children are desirable and health preservative and should be continued into adulthood. Survivals in adults of such traits as enthusiasm, singleness of purpose, absorbed attention, interest in the realities of the present, naïveté, spontaneousness, straightforwardness, frankness, and absence of artifice, which are characteristic of child life, would conduce to mental efficiency and integration.

Nevertheless, many, if not most, of the regressions of adults or of adolescents to the behavior patterns of childhood are abnormal and injurious, especially if they have become habitual or persistent. The adult who is fixated in the childhood stage experiences the emotions that are more appropriate to children than to adults, and he is troubled by problems that he should have grappled with and learned to solve in childhood under the wise guidance of his parents and teachers. Persons emotionally undeveloped and fixated often retain survivals of childish characteristics as long as they live, although they may be intellectually normal. They tend to exhibit childish feelings and thoughts, such as impatience, jealousy, lack of emotional control, squeamishness, changeableness, selfishness, and vanity. They sometimes become petulantly domineering and exacting, or shirking and nonaggressive, because they are afraid to meet dangers squarely and thus avoid contests. Again, they sometimes tend to become socially indifferent, lethargic, unresponsive, irresponsible, or defiant. This defiance is regarded by some as the counterpart of the defiance the child assumed toward the father.

Regression should in large measure be regarded as a confession of failure; it shows that the person has not grown up mentally, especially emotionally, and that he cannot or will not lead an independent existence and solve his own problems but prefers to lean on others.

Regressionists tend to be exceedingly recalcitrant. Few persons are harder to arouse or reconstruct than those who are satisfied to remain children emotionally. Emotional regression must be rated as one of the most serious

[4] William H. Burnham, *The Wholesome Personality*, 1932, 279–281. Reprinted with the permission of Appleton-Century-Crofts, Inc.

barriers to attaining emotional poise and maturity and a healthy mind. This is especially true when the individual has regressed to the infantile level, which is characterized by complacency, autoeroticism, and self-adoration. It is almost impossible to arouse the infantile regressionists out of their state of inactivity and dependency.

Algernon Charles Swinburne, a victim of emotional immaturity and instability, was very conceited and intolerant.[5] He resented the slightest criticism. While spending the night with his former tutor, the Bishop of Oxford, the young man read aloud to his host the original draft of his play, *Rosamond*. The bishop, greatly impressed with its merits, nevertheless ventured some mild criticisms of certain amatory passages. These suggestions were met with a "long silent stare, followed by a scream that rent the vicarage." Then the poet bolted upstairs to his room, where he shut himself up for the night; but sounds emanated from the room throughout the night. When the bishop hastened to offer his apologies, the next morning, as Swinburne appeared very late and deathly pale, the latter said that he had burned every page of the manuscript in the grate, adding, however, that he had also rewritten the entire work.

Emotional infantilism is a striking characteristic of many nervous and mental disorders. Indeed, the regression mechanism helps to explain the cause of many of these disorders. Many neurotics or psychotics have stuck fast in, or reverted to, such infantile reaction patterns as pouting; whining; crying; shouting; complaining; laughing; exhibiting jealousy, anger, sulkiness, or fears; and indulging in temper tantrums. A hospital for the mentally ill is a kaleidoscope of exaggerated childish emotions. Many of the symptoms are patently designed to elicit the attention, coddling, or humoring that the patient craves. When the reversion proceeds to the infantile nursery stage, as sometimes happens, the individual becomes as helpless as an infant and requires the same physical care. This depth of regression is sometimes seen in hebephrenics, victims of a mental disorder belonging to the dementia praecox (or schizophrenic) group of mental diseases.

Many criminals also are victims of emotional infantilism, exhibiting traits of childish egotism, egocentricity, conceit, and utter indifference to the rights of others and the suffering they may cause them. Likewise many adult sexual abnormalities are due to failure of the normal development of the child's erotic tendencies, or to perverse sex practices in the child, or to adult regressions to infantile erotic traits. Homosexuality and masturbation in the adult represent regressions to early childhood forms of sex activity. Masturbatory excesses are frequently expressions of dissatisfaction and failure to adjust oneself, and represent attempts to find satisfaction in autoerotic forms

[5] Thomas V. Moore, *Personal Mental Hygiene,* New York, Grune and Stratton, Inc., 1944, 270.

of sex activity.   The following report (and the one in Chap. XI, pages 388*ff.*)
is a case of autoeroticism due, in part, to feelings of dissatisfaction and
discouragement.

LACK OF SEX DIFFICULTIES IN EARLY LIFE BECAUSE OF ENLIGHTEN-
MENT; MASTURBATION TRACED TO A LECTURE ON THE SUBJECT AND
TO THE LOSS OF SELF-ESTEEM AND SATISFACTION FROM CONFINEMENT
BECAUSE OF ILLNESS

With sex I have had few difficulties because of the fact, I think, that I was
very early in life informed about sexual matters.   I was seven years old when
my half-brother was born, and at that time I knew in an elementary way about
the creation and birth of children.   My mother always used the scientific names
for all such matters as ovary, embryo, etc.   To further my education along this
line a pair of rabbits was purchased for me.   I received no sex shock from observing the sexual acts of the rabbits nor upon viewing the birth of the baby
rabbits.   My attitude had been a very highly material one until I read several
books by Havelock Ellis and realized that there was great beauty attached to
the sex life.

I knew just what to expect at the onset of puberty and was most interested
in the changes in my body.   All of my associations had been 98 per cent with
boys, so that they have held no extraordinary virtues or attractions for me.   And
they have always accepted me on equal terms, apparently unconscious of the fact
that I am a girl, because of the rough-and-tumble life I have led.

The Catholic Church, of which I am a member, advocates complete continence
before marriage.   I am a devout Catholic and have observed that ordinance.
However, when I was in my last year at high school, I contracted scarlet fever
and had to remain in bed for some weeks.   Immediately before my illness, a local
physician gave a lecture on sex matters to the girls of our class.   The entire lecture
was concerned with masturbation.   He vividly described practices of masturbation among girls and predicted for all who indulged in the practice dreaded punishments.

I imagine the outcome of this lecture was the same with many other girls as
with me.   During my illness I began to masturbate.   The habit continued through
the summer when I was not very strong.   My illness had made me the laughing
stock of the town because I was exceedingly thin and my hair had been most
closely shaven.   My self-esteem was absolutely gone, and I persisted in masturbating in order to secure pleasure which I was not getting from other sources (having
no difficulty in experiencing the orgasm).   I am subject to a strong sex urge and
continued the practice for some time about once a month.

The dean of girls at our normal school gave a very different lecture on sex matters
upon our entrance to her school.   She said that there was little good to be derived
from masturbation, but also no harm.   If we had to eliminate our surplus energy
by masturbating, it was legitimate, but we should not permit ourselves to establish any habit of which we were afraid.   This put the practice in another light,

making it very ordinary to me. I soon overcame it with the total recovery from my illness, the regaining of my strength, and my program of athletic activities, and partly because of the sense of shame and weariness which it engendered.

Recently I have had no occasion for the recurrence of the habit owing to my strenuous activities in making a living. Besides, I am engaged to be married and see my fiancée very often. (T.A.M.; F.; E.S.T.; B.A.)

Prevention of the Acquisition of Regressive Trends. Few duties that parents and teachers owe young children are more onerous and important than freeing them from infantile fixations and behavior patterns, liberating them from dependence upon parents and others, and so training them that they will become normally self-reliant. Thus they will face the future resolutely and courageously, develop right attitudes toward the problems of life, and undergo normal emotional development. The following suggestions may prove helpful.

1. Map out programs of activity that will enable the child to live fully and satisfyingly the life of the present moment. Make the work of each day so interesting and appealing that the child will not spend his time living over in memory his past successes as a compensation for his present dissatisfactions or failures. To spend his time glorying over and magnifying his past exploits and conquests is detrimental to the child's normal development. It may lead to inaction, mere rumination, the killing of initiative and resourcefulness, or the use of childish methods of solving present problems. It is important to lead the child to understand that he may have developed an exaggerated impression of his early successes. Many of them were successes merely because his problems were very simple and they were often largely solved by his parents. He should be led to appreciate that to glory in past performances is often merely a form of deception caused by a distorted memory, that childish ways will not solve adolescent or adult problems, and that he should use past methods as a steppingstone for growth and improvement instead of as a childish refuge.

Perhaps it is equally bad for the child to spend his time projecting his infantile phantasies into the distant future, living in an imaginary future world where wishes come true without effort. The imaginary future is all too often a realm in which wishes are the proverbial horses, enabling all beggars to ride. To be sure, the child must have a forward look rather than a backward fixation, but the forward direction of his thoughts must be intent upon definite accomplishments in the world of reality. He must have a definite task to control and to direct his energies into fruitful channels, instead of being actuated by dreams and visions that serve merely as forms of escape from exertion and from realizing definite objectives.

Therefore, to counteract or nullify these two contrary tendencies, which will prove pernicious to wholesome personality development if indulged in overmuch or overlong, get the child thoroughly immersed in the life of the present through satisfying day-by-day accomplishments.

2. One expedient for accomplishing this objective is to make the work of each day an adventure in successful achievement. Assist the child in achieving success so that his efforts will be rewarded. Make each day more appealing than the day before by the satisfaction obtained from each day's victorious activities. Successful achievement will keep the child's attention on present joys and on real, immediate future programs of work and play, instead of on past triumphs or on imaginary, fictitious future conquests. A life spent in satisfying achievement should afford little occasion for reversion to infantile methods of achievement by tricking others into doing the work for you, as Tom Sawyer accomplished the whitewashing of his fence.

3. In line with the above suggestion, lead the child to see that in the long run no success is genuinely satisfying except that which is self-wrought. He should come to understand that success in life must be achieved by his own efforts and not by the efforts of his parents and teachers; that the tricks and stratagems of childhood will not win lasting victories in the real, workaday world; and that crying, pouting, whimpering, explosions of anger, and infantile excuses will not solve his boyhood and manhood problems as they did his babyhood problems.

4. Start gradually to accustom the child almost from cradle days to a realization that he is living in a real world in which the law of cause and effect determines the order of events, and in which results come as a consequence of effort and work, and that he is not living in a world of fancy where every whim can be satisfied merely by desiring and wishing. Parental treatment patterns are very important in the attempt to realize this objective. Parents should beware of spoiling the child by handling that will tend to foster in him the belief that the way to realize all his cravings is through ruses, such as whining, crying, pleading, or offering alibis. Parental treatment often encourages the child to believe that, if he persists long enough in whimpering, fretting, or supplication, the parent will eventually give in and he will be allowed to have his way. We should so condition the child by our manner of rearing that he will early realize that whining and offering trumped-up excuses will not bring victories in the workaday world and that only real merit and effort will bring true and enduring success.

Again, studied effort should be made not to pamper or protect the child too much. He should be trained to depend more and more on himself and to do things for himself. He should be given ample attention, recognition, and commendation when he attempts to "stand on his own feet." Parents should encourage him to try to solve his problems himself instead of insisting on doing everything for him. Overprotection tends to spoil the child and to bind him to the parent emotionally. This does not imply that one should not scrupulously protect the child from real menaces. One should, of course, take the necessary measures to remove the possibilities of serious injuries and dangers. Beyond this, however, one should allow the child to learn to extricate himself from the ordinary difficulties that beset his pathway. He will thus be induced to acquire the fighting, conquering spirit. It is easy to condition children so that they will become cowards and quitters. Overprotection and pampering educate them to use subtle devices to bribe others to fight their battles for them.

5. Do not force the child by neglect to become demonstrative or mischievous in order to receive attention. This may drive him to adopt exploits that will bring him into the limelight. Notice him and commend him when he is engaging in desirable activities.

CHAPTER X

(10) DAYDREAMING

10. Retreat to the World of Phantasy or Daydreaming (Reverie or Autistic Thinking)

Nature of Daydreaming. A daydream is a pleasure-yielding flow of ideas or images in which thoughts are combined into a story, or idle fancy. It consists of associations of ideas that are woven into a more or less coherent phantasy. In this form of mental activity the dreamer tends to enter into an imaginary or fictitious world. Through the daydream he has taken a flight from the world of reality into the world of make-believe, where he can linger unconcerned with the objective realities of life. This species of thinking is essentially autistic,[1] in the sense that it is sufficient unto itself. As mere self-contained reverie, it is immune to external tests. It can run on unhampered by any definite external goals or problems. Although the dreamer is not under the control of external goals or criteria, the daydream usually has some reference to the dreamer's future. The dream's hero or heroine is usually the dreamer himself or herself, although it might be anyone else, especially someone closely identified with the dreamer. Thus the fond mother may make her stunning daughter the heroine of her daydreams, to gratify her own pride in her offspring or in herself as the worthy parent.

The hero motive is perhaps the outstanding motive revealed in daydreams. On the basis of the hero motive, daydreams can be divided into two types.

1. *The Conquering-hero Type.* In this type of reverie the dreamer envisages himself as a conquering hero who has performed some outstanding act of daring, skill, or strength (the "display" motive); who has rescued someone from danger or oppression (the "saving" motive); who has rendered conspicuous services to someone whose patronage is desired (the "homage" motive); or who has become an imposing personage of great learning, wealth, or power (the "grandeur" motive). The conquering-hero dream is perhaps merely a mental mechanism for obtaining imaginary, vicarious compensatory satisfactions, and a sense of mastery, self-realization, or superiority, without the necessity of real exertion. This is the commoner and healthier type of phantasy.

---

[1] Autistic thinking refers to the imaginary gratification of desires that are not attained in the real world. Phantasy thinking, or daydreaming, contrasts with realistic thinking. Pathological forms occur in schizophrenia and in paranoid states.

2. *The Suffering-hero Type.* In this kind of dream the dreamer pictures himself as the hapless victim of discrimination, neglect, abuse, or mistreatment —the motive, perhaps, being to enhance his own importance by exaggerating his difficulties. In his imagination it is very easy to magnify any small slight that he may have suffered into a colossal insult.

The young adolescent, forced by the father to spend his late afternoons on his detested grammar, instead of roaming the streets with the gang, spends his time daydreaming about his unhappy lot instead of studying his assignment. The more he dwells in imagination on his plight, the deeper becomes his feeling of self-pity, the driving force behind the suffering-hero type of phantasy adjustment. In search for a form of release, he may begin to envisage himself as killed in an accident or as a runaway making his own way in the world under an assumed name, and to relish the great distress caused to his parents. He sees himself as a runaway scrawling a farewell note to his father, whom he pictures instituting a nationwide search for him, and he imagines the great joy experienced by the parents when he is eventually found; the generous acclaim by parents, neighbors, and teachers for his many fine qualities; the profuse expressions of remorse and regrets offered by the father for the wrongs inflicted upon him; and the promises that his liberties will be restored. Through the mechanism of the martyr reverie, our young, suffering hero may thus have obtained temporary relief from his frustrations and also compensating ego satisfaction from the sufferings endured by the parents.

The political reformer who has been assailed and who has suffered repeated failure will not find it difficult in his daydreams to convince himself that his wounded self-respect and pride prove that he has been outrageously abused and that, since he has been so grievously wronged, he must be a very superior person. In flights of fancy he can easily augment his importance or satisfy his craving for self-assertion by magnifying his injuries. Through some imaginary substitute for actual doing or fighting, he fancies that, as a preeminent suffering hero, he is achieving the outstanding recognition he deserves and the mastery that goes with it. His self-esteem is further exalted by the fact that he is inclined to picture himself as always being in the right and as being actuated by the highest motives. Since his motives are belittled or misunderstood by others, there can be little doubt that he is a real suffering hero, a real martyr of a just cause, who is deserving of pity and recognition instead of persecution. Thus by playing the role of a suffering martyr, the dreamer obtains satisfaction for his wounded pride and a feeling of superiority. Surely, he says, no one would bother about him unless he were a very important martyr.

Since the daydream is concerned about the dreamer himself, George H. Green has concluded that all phantasies are egocentric and relate only to the individual's selfish ends.

The Psychoanalytic View of the Daydream. According to many psychoanalysts, every daydream is essentially a wish fulfillment or an expression of a wish from the unconscious, just as is the sleep dream. It differs, however, from the nocturnal dream in that it is less absurd or grotesque and has a greater tendency to recur in stereotyped form. This is particularly true with respect to systematic daydreams. While these broad differences exist, the distinctions should not be drawn too sharply. Some daydreams may be just as absurd as night dreams, and some daydreams among normal persons just as bizarre as the reveries of psychotics. Moreover, some daydreams are purely casual, while others are highly systematized, as has been pointed out by Mandel Sherman.[2] The casual or nonrecurrent type of daydream, in which all people indulge more or less, varies from time to time, depending upon transient interests. The persistent, perseverative reveries, which often point to some deep-seated maladjustment, tend to recur in systematized form, such as dreams of wealth, power, or success in love or business. Many sleep dreams may also consist of recurrent phantasy. According to Sigmund Freud, many night dreams merely repeat the phantasies of waking consciousness.

Source of Fascination in the Daydream; the Mechanism of Identification. What is the source of the satisfaction and fascination derived from indulgence in daydreaming? It can be explained, at least in part, by the well-known and widely employed mechanism of identification, or the tendency to identify ourselves with the objects and persons of our interest and admiration —the motive, perhaps, being to gain protection, security, prestige, and power and to become like those whom we respect and admire. Thus the boy tends to identify himself with his paternal parent. Since the father often is a very wonderful person to his young son, the son aspires to be like the father. The tendency toward identification must be rated as one of the most important factors in the child's cultural development since it supplies a powerful drive toward emulation.

In his play the child similarly identifies himself with the role he enacts, be it that of parent, nurse, teacher, preacher, or racketeer. This is accomplished by what the German psychologists would call a process of empathy (feeling the part one is performing or "feeling oneself into" what one does, contemplates, or observes). Through this mechanism, at least in part, the college graduate identifies himself with his alma mater and exults in her traditions and ideals. The adolescent identifies himself with his club, fraternity, and teams, and takes pains to publicize the fact, thereby acquiring feelings of superiority as compensation for his shortcomings. The ordinary voter doubtless feels some of the prestige of his ward boss or his presidential candidate by identifying himself with his leader. Identification with his regiment enables the soldier to

[2] Mandel Sherman, *Basic Problems of Behavior*, New York, Longmans, Green & Co., Inc., 1941, 187.

bask in the reflected halo of the regimental commander. Symbolical means for enhancing the ego call to mind the practice of some people of attending only the best shows; the outstanding meetings, conventions, balls, or race meets; the most exclusive soirees; and the most select style displays. Patronage of the most expensive places and identification with big events are symbolical of greatness, so it is thought. Accordingly, one seeks to magnify the importance and the prestige of the ego by identifying oneself with the grand or the great. The identification mechanism plays an important role not only among normal people, but also among abnormals. It explains many hysterical phenomena. This type of reaction pattern is, no doubt, responsible for much of the pleasure derived from the reading of stories, novels, biography, and history; from viewing scenarios; and from play and work activities. How early this mechanism comes into play may be shown by the following interesting recitals.

PERSISTENT IDENTIFICATION WITH A PLAYMATE BY A YOUNG CHILD, ALARMING TO THE PARENTS, OVERCOME BY IGNORING THE MAKE-BELIEVE AND BY REDIRECTING ATTENTION

J., a normal child of two and a half years, has recently shown some symptoms of identification that seemed quite alarming at the time.

Her mother has made it a practice to recite all sorts of nursery rhymes and child stories to her. She liked the stories of Cinderella and Little Red Riding Hood best. Playfully her parents would occasionally call her Cinderella or Little Red Riding Hood. After she knew the stories well, she would dramatize them, taking the different characters in the stories and acting them out. Encouraged by her parents who thought her very clever, she would call herself Mother and call her Mother Daddy and her father J., and she would retain these mixed-up identities faultlessly for an entire morning or afternoon. No amount of argument could make her change these identities.

Very shortly after this period J. met G. She admired and liked this little girl so much that she began calling herself G., her belongings were G.'s belongings, her house was G.'s house, her mother and dad, G.'s mother and dad, and everything was G.'s.

At first her parents thought it was "cute." But the identification lasted through an entire day, and the following morning when she got up she still retained G.'s identity more tenaciously than ever. This caused the parents to become alarmed and they tried to talk it out of her. But this didn't work very well. She went to bed that second day still G. and got up the morning of the third day more G. than before.

The parents, thoroughly alarmed and fearful that their child would completely and permanently lose her identity, then chose a different method of attack, that of ignoring her references to G. entirely and changing the subject every time J. mentioned G. That night she still went to bed as G. but upon arising in the morning she was J. again and G. (and her three days' life as G.) was forgotten completely and has never been referred to again. In fact, that ended all her make-believe identities and she has never indulged in this particular peculiarity since.

(From B.N.; M.; Mn. Tr. T.; B.S.; Age 29)

IDENTIFICATION BY A FOUR-YEAR-OLD WITH AN IMAGINARY ADULT
AND ASSUMPTION OF ADULT INTERESTS AND BEHAVIOR PATTERNS

When Henry M. was about four years old, he told the family one morning that he was "Mr. Stickerson, of Gap." Occasionally for over a year he assumed the same role. Whenever he came to breakfast with the greeting to his mother, "Good morning, Mrs. M.," she knew that Mr. Stickerson was present. On these days Henry took his orange juice without having it strained and ate other food that he would not eat when he was Henry. As "Mr. Stickerson" he owned two cars, a Packard and a Chevrolet, and spent much time keeping them in order. He had a wife who couldn't drive the car but often told him how to do it (one of those back-seat drivers). He had four children, Nancy, Barbara, Bobby, and Jacky. These were always named in the same order. The youngest was just the age of Henry's baby sister. He also had a father-in-law and a mother-in-law, Mr. and Mrs. S. The whole family and the in-laws often came to visit Henry's family. During this interval when he was not "Mr. Stickerson, of Gap," he had several imagined playmates. One was "Bossa Tinn" and her brother was "Timmy Tinn." When he grew tired of playing with Bossa he would have her die, and when she was wanted again, he would resurrect her with the greatest of ease. But he finally allowed her to stay dead. One day Mr. Stickerson told Mrs. M. that he was going out to Gap and would leave one of his cars for her to use and drive out to see them. At the present time, at the age of seven and a half, when we ask about "Mr. Stickerson," Henry looks rather sheepish but says nothing.

(From Mrs. M.M., housewife.)

Since the daydreamer in similar fashion identifies himself with the hero of his imaginary world (see page 358), the conquering hero represents the successful envisagement or projection of his deepest longings. By identifying himself with the successful hero of his phantasy, he is able to enjoy a vicarious gratification of his craving for power, wealth, security, beauty, health, or recognition. The hero-identification mechanism thus, apparently, yields a satisfying expression of the mastery motive. The suffering-hero kind of identification doubtless also affords gratification for the dreamer's wounded pride and affords opportunities to display his importance, for reasons already suggested.[3]

---

[3] The word "introjection" also is used in the sense of identification with persons or objects, so that one obtains a sense of oneness with them and ascribes to oneself the virtues of others. The opposite term is "projection," imputing one's faults or motives to other persons or outside forces. These words also have other connotations.

Evaluation of Daydreaming. The daydreaming activity in itself is neither wholly good nor wholly bad. Indulgence in reverie is not wholly to be deplored, as it often is. Let us consider both the merits and the demerits of daydreaming.

The Daydream as an Intriguing Normal Activity. Some forms of daydreaming represent fascinating, intriguing, and normal mental activity which is innocuous, which may afford the individual harmless pleasure and satisfaction, and which may also serve useful purposes. In early childhood, the daydream apparently represents a normal, spontaneous form of mental exercise, similar to the child's play activities in its directness. It represents a direct wish fulfillment, without the disguised symbolism that often obscures the meanings of the reveries of older persons. A considerable part of the child's early life is lived in the world of phantasy, possibly because of the fairy tales and fables with which he is regaled; because of the stories, legends, and novels he reads; and because of the scenarios he beholds. The delights of fanciful reverie are reflected in such imaginary exploits as *Alice's Adventures in Wonderland, Through the Looking Glass, Andersen's Fairy Tales,* and *The Arabian Nights.* Myths and legends perhaps represent the phantasy material of the race—delightful exploits of whole nations or races in the world of the imagination. The young child takes delight in such phantasy material and draws upon it for answers to many of his queries, no matter how absurd the myths may be.

But why is daydreaming inherently pleasurable? Because it affords a release from the boredom and drudgery of life and from the restrictions of its stubborn realities, and also because it provides an outlet for free, spontaneous, creative activity, unfettered by the rules of logic or by obstinate facts. Moreover, in the world of make-believe the dreamer can realize his dearest wishes by a mere flight of fancy, a mere wish. Nothing is too difficult or too complicated to overcome in this delightful fairyland in which a magical watchword or a "magic carpet" or an Aladdin's lamp will bring all desires to immediate fruition without any effort or drudgery. In this magical, subjective realm the poor boy can obtain temporary surcease from the frustrations of his niggardly existence and can live the life of a Prince Charming or of a scion of wealth, as he may prefer, in harmony with his deepest aspirations. The homely maiden can experience the rapture of becoming the beautiful princess of the enchanted golden palace, adored by all the Prince Charmings and knights-errant from near and far. As a haven of escape from the hardships and disappointments of life, the world of autistic thinking may serve a useful purpose in easing the pain of unrequited love or of disappointed ambition. Many a daydream has served as a successful buffer against frustrations that the daydreamer would not have been able to cope with on the reality plane. The sense of satisfaction from the temporary solution of the problem in a new world, subject only to autistic control, may supply the necessary incentive and technique to surmount the difficulty in reality. Successful daydream solutions of conflicts may dissipate the individual's hypochondria, diffidence, and dissatisfaction and may thus serve to prevent the development of neurotic compensations. Examples that illustrate, at least in part, such use of the daydream occur on pages 281*f.*, and 368.

Another possible virtue of daydreaming is that success in the world of imagination may serve to incite effort to achieve success in the world of reality. The glow of success from imaginary conquests doubtless sometimes stimulates the ambition to make the dreams come true. Indeed, the successful ambitious man must be somewhat of a dreamer. Through an act of constructive imagination he must be able to envisage ideals, plans, and solutions and to project them into the future as accomplished results. His imagination must be sufficiently active and fertile to visualize something better than the status quo. Through the visualization of better possibilities he becomes dissatisfied with present conditions and thereby he may be induced to attempt improvements. The daydream doubtless has proved an inspiration to genius; it has stimulated imagination and creative phantasy in literature and art and has led to discovery and invention in many fields of science. Creative thinking is essentially an act of imagination; and the visionary daydreams of today often become the practical accomplishments of tomorrow. Phantasy is at the base, not only of literature (stories, legends, myths, scenarios, romances, the drama, poetry, etc.), but also of music, painting, and scientific hypothesizing.

Therefore, the indiscriminate attempt to suppress the phantasy life of the child would close an outlet that affords him tension-relieving recreation and some of his most delightful experiences; it would tend to stifle his spontaneity, imaginativeness, vivacity, creativeness, romantic insight, poetic fertility, and scientific inventiveness, and thereby would produce dissatisfaction, lack of interest, inattention, and dullness.

Example of Salutary Effects from Indulgence in Daydreaming Activities. Some of the beneficial or at least uninjurious results of gratifying the proclivity to indulge in reverie are shown in the following report.

ACHIEVING GREAT AMBITIONS IN THE WORLD OF FANCY; DAYDREAMING ABOUT HOW AS A TEACHER TO AVOID MISTAKES COMMITTED BY HER OWN TEACHERS; PLEASURE FROM BUILDING IMAGINARY HOMES; MORE PLEASURE FROM IMAGINARY THAN REAL ACTIVITIES

I do a great deal of daydreaming, planning for the future great things that I can never achieve. As a child, I would sit by the hour and plan what I would do when I taught school. Mistakes and poor teaching on the part of my own teachers rankled in my mind and I planned how to avoid them. As far back as I can remember I have always wanted to teach, and after ten years of experience the desire is just as strong. I still like to sit and dream about what I will do when the time comes. I dream about getting my degree in two more summers and then taking a trip to Europe, with enough money to buy this, that, and the other thing, to be followed by a trip to Alaska. Where the money for all this is coming from I do not know, but I love to dream about it. My family has always enjoyed my daydream homes. I build large beautiful homes in my mind, such as I some day hope to possess. The chances are ten to one that I never will build a house, but I love to plan them. The joy that I get out of the anticipation of a good time more or less comes from daydreaming, because I love to sit and figure out mentally everything that will take place when the time comes. Many times this daydreaming is far more enjoyable than the actual event.

(B.C.V.; F.; E.S.T.; Age 31)

Although daydream activities thus possess many virtues, they may constitute handicaps and often create serious adjustment problems.

The Evils of Daydreaming. Most of the detrimental effects of daydreaming are probably due to excessive indulgence and to the adoption of daydreaming as a method of defense, escape, or compensation or as a method of solving problems or difficulties. The tendency to conceal the practice, because it is often regarded as a childish activity or as an indulgence of weaklings, adds to the difficulty of coping with the problem. The reticent, inveterate daydreamer may not be discovered. The tendency to indulge excessively in reverie is due to the fact that the activity itself is inherently pleasurable, not to say intensely fascinating, and to the further fact that the activity affords not only an outlet for deep, underlying cravings but also a sense of achievement and superiority, however illusory the latter may be. Hence the individual may become so enamored with the life of fancy that he tends to spend his time in futile, introvert ruminations—in mere dreaming. The following are typical experiences.

DAYDREAMING OBSESSIONS UNCURED

My whole life has been filled with daydreaming. It started when I was playing with dolls, I think. I would sit for hours building air castles and playing with fancies. Even when I was doing my little duties around the home I always imagined I was someone else doing something else. Instead of dealing with realities as they actually were, I lived in a dream world; instead of living, I dreamed. Right now I am working hard to break myself of this. I wonder if it can be done? I didn't realize I was missing anything and thought I was having the best time possible. I have read that daydreams will eventually fail to satisfy and daydreamers are the most miserable people in the world when they get old. This caused me to resolve to break myself of the habit.

(N.M.; F.; H.S.T.; A.B.)

PAIN AND PLEASURE FROM DAYDREAMING PROCLIVITIES; HERO, CHIV-
ALRIC, SUCCESS, AND INVENTIVE DREAMS; SPENDING MORE TIME
DREAMING ABOUT SUCCESS THAN IN ACHIEVING IT

Daydreaming has caused the subject much pleasure and more pain. Even as
a child he seems to have indulged considerably in phantasies as all children do,
the nature of the phantasies changing with maturation. One that stands out in
memory is the dream of driving an automobile at an excessive rate of speed.
Travel to distant lands helped the subject as a young child through many otherwise boring days in school. As he grew older, came dreams of success in first one
field and then in another. Quite naturally, he was always the hero. He was
saving some helpless person from danger, whenever an account of a heroic deed
came to the attention of the general public. The boy's books that formed such
an important part of each Christmas supplied enough material for dreams through
the remainder of the winter. As adolescence was reached there came dreams of
saving some member of the other sex from some imaginary danger. With increasing age came dreams of success in various fields, a type of dream which has persisted so thoroughly as possibly to handicap the subject's chances for the very
successes he dreamed of. He has spent far more time in dreaming of success than
in activities actually making for success! Of late years will power has come to
his rescue to a certain degree, but it requires no effort at all for him to sit for
hours even now and dream. The dreams are of a varied nature. It cannot be
said that they have been totally without profit, for in these daydreams have come
stimuli for many subsequent activities. One of the chief characteristics of them
now is their inventive nature; however, upon investigation it has been found that
all of his ideas have been previously patented by someone more fortunate. These
ideas are generally of a mechanical nature. (B.O.I.; M.; C. Instr. of Psy.; M.A.)

As a result of excessive indulgence, the dreamer may become more or less
impractical and visionary. He may form the habit of substituting mere play
of imagery and mere wishing and hoping for actions, mere thinking for doing,
mere desires for facts, or mere fictions for realities. He may become satisfied
with imaginal achievements and with autistic, wishful dreaming, instead of
depending on straight, logical, realistic thinking and on objective accomplishments for the solution of his problems. This deceptive method of solving life's
problems becomes particularly dangerous when the recourse to it becomes so
frequent as to interfere with the individual's ability to adjust himself to his
personal, social, and vocational responsibilities. The practice may fasten upon
him attitudes and habit patterns that will tend toward the disorganization and
disintegration of his personality. He may become nonobservant, seclusive,
taciturn, and even shut-in to the point that he may become a victim of mental
abstraction and may lose contact with reality. He does not want to be
bothered by practical outside affairs that strike him as too common or base
for his exalted ego, but he prefers to spend his time "building castles in

Spain." Such a person may eventually become so detached from the workaday world that he fails to distinguish between fact and fancy and between fancied and real achievement.

Because it is so easy to solve difficulties in the realm of solitary dreaming, the daydreamer may adopt the daydream as the method of retirement from the sordid facts of life. Thus the dream technique becomes a cowardly method of retreat into a world of fiction, a method of avoiding the necessity of making disagreeable adjustments by replacing distasteful external situations with pleasurable but deceptive internal states. As a result of these practices, the dreamer will tend to form the habit of depending upon fictitious solutions of his practical problems, in consequence of which he may prefer to live in the land of make-believe so that he will not have to face the disagreeable task of transforming his reveries into realities. He may elect to become a solitary, visionary recluse and then will resort to all sorts of reality-dodging devices in order to withdraw into his own private world. But he cannot subsist as a self-contained, autistic recluse unless he can get others to make his external adjustments and provide for his physical needs. Necessarily, therefore, he will have to be disillusioned later, and this may prove to be a difficult task. He may not want to forsake his blissful subjective Elysium, in which the only alchemy needed to transform base metals into gold is a magical word or wish. It may prove no easy matter to abandon that paradise for the mean, troublesome realities of mundane existence. It should be apparent from this that the daydream may become an illusory method of surrender, a subjective method of escape from objective realities, or, as it has been defined, a "wish-fulfilling flight from reality." Myths and legends share this common characteristic with the daydream, according to Oskar Pfister; they are essentially "distorted wish-phantasies of whole nations."

Among the specific evils of excessive indulgence in daydreaming, mention may be made of the following:

1. Persistent daydreaming tends to confirm the individual in the use of artifices, subterfuges, and reality-dodging devices by which he hopes to evade his practical responsibilities. As a result of such an attitude, he may eventually become an expert victim of clever methods of distorting reality, of faking, or of practicing deception, thereby becoming essentially dishonest in his attitudes. All this will not tend to develop the ability to make sane, successful adjustments to the facts of life.

2. Persistent daydreaming tends to fix upon the victim the habit of taking refuge in illusory methods of compensating for his feelings of incompetency, lack of courage, or frustrations. Since daydreaming often has its roots in feelings of dissatisfaction and despair, as already has been emphasized, it is often employed as a defense against such feelings, as well as against unresolved

conflicts or the blocking of overpowering urges. Because the victim does not find permanent relief from his anxiety, he tends, however, to continue to use the device for such temporary tension release as it may yield, until it becomes a fixed habit. The following case histories illustrate this use of the daydream.

INCESSANT DAYDREAMING, BEGINNING IN CHILDHOOD AS A DEFENSE REACTION AGAINST FRUSTRATIONS, OR AS A MEANS OF ESCAPE FROM DIFFICULTIES; PRESENT GRATIFICATION FROM IMAGINARY PLANNING SOLUTION OF PROBLEMS AND FIXING THINGS AS RESPONDENT WOULD LIKE THEM TO BE

I am an habitual air-castle builder, planning modes of action for the distant future. I get an enormous amount of pleasure from just planning things and imagining certain happenings in my mind. When unoccupied, I often lapse into periods of daydreaming in which I fix things up as I would have them be. Scarcely a day passes in which I do not indulge in daydreaming. This habit began when I was very young. My associates were older than I and enjoyed much more freedom of action. When I was thwarted or restrained from participating in certain group activities I indulged in daydreaming. In my fancy I could be whatever age I desired. Consequently the daydream began to furnish for me a mode of escape from actual life situations. At the present time my daydreams are usually based on some objectives I wish to accomplish and I usually work toward their accomplishments in my daydreams.

(A.H.T.; F.; Col.; Univ. Instr. of Psy.; M.S.; Age 26)

DAYDREAMING AS A DEFENSE AGAINST UNHAPPINESS AT HOME OR AS A MEANS OF RELAXATION, PRODUCING THE CHARGE OF INDOLENCE, BUT APPARENTLY SAFEGUARDING THE SUBJECT FROM PESSIMISM ENGENDERED BY FRANK, UNROMANTIC FACING OF HARSH FACTS

Is it daydreaming to lie on the grass and watch the clouds, listen to the birds and drift away into a space of color and music? If so, I daydreamed through all my childhood. Except for the time in school, which was always full of joy for me, I daydreamed every moment I was alone. At home I was able to carry on an elaborate daydream while performing a required task. Naturally I was considered lazy and incompetent because my mind was far off. I only did this when an uninteresting situation had to be lived through. Later I would throw myself into a state of daydreaming as a means of relaxation. I seldom daydream now because my life is very full of interesting and happy experiences.

As a child I was constantly in an atmosphere of unhappiness and discontent. My parents despised each other and their many quarreling, crying children (I am the second of seven). When I think of my pessimistic, repressed older sister, who faced her childhood squarely and did not daydream, I am thankful for my daydreams.   (W.W.A.; F.; S.C.T.)

3. In adults, daydreaming represents a regression to a childish mechanism of adjustment, that of attempting to satisfy unmet needs by a dubious indulgence in pleasant reveries, by ignoring unpleasant realities, and by wishful thinking.

4. Certain rather definite evils are likely to accompany identification with the conquering- or suffering-hero roles. Assuming the part of the conqueror in the life of phantasy may lead to excessive arrogance and egotism in the social give-and-take of mundane affairs. He may become convinced that he is an extraordinary fellow because of his stunning make-believe accomplishments. In extreme cases—such cases are rare—the individual's judgment may become so impaired or confused that he fails to distinguish between his imaginary and his actual station in life and he may become subject to paranoid delusions of grandeur. He may become a conquering Don Quixote, fighting phantom armies. It is significant that the composition of this extravagant romance started while Cervantes was confined in prison, because of monetary deficiency in his accounts, and while his spirit wanted to take free wings. On the other hand, by realizing his craving for self-pity and self-assertion through identification with the suffering or abused type of hero, the daydreamer may become sullen, cynical, or faultfinding; in extreme cases he may develop delusions of persecution or may commit acts of martyrdom, in order to attract attention to himself and to demonstrate his greatness. Only a superior person, as has already been stated, is of sufficient importance to become an object of persecution or martyrdom. Martyrdom is prima-facie evidence of eminence.

D. B. Kline [4] has described a special kind of reverie, which may be productive of severe inner conflicts. He calls it the "debating-hero daydream." This type is provoked by the desire for revenge or retribution. The individual carries on an acrimonious dialogue or debate with the reprimanding parent, teacher, or employer. Freed from outer restrictions, he resorts to vituperative statements that he would not employ in reality. The more he indulges in his private feud, the angrier and the more upset emotionally he becomes. The mechanism may be employed in anticipation of real arguments that he expects to use in the future, or it may follow verbal clashes between siblings, spouses, employer and employee, and teacher and pupil. It is obvious that such heated inner controversies, because of the lack of release from emotional tension through motor expression, and because of the ease with which they can be indulged in at any time in the world of subjectivity, may exert a very pernicious influence upon health and efficiency.

5. Excessive indulgence in reverie may stimulate the development of tendencies toward certain mental and nervous disorders and abnormal mental

[4] D. B. Kline, *Mental Hygiene*, Henry Holt and Company, Inc., 1944, 342*f*.

states that essentially constitute flights from reality. Such tendencies naturally develop more frequently in predisposed individuals and in those who indulge excessively in dreams that serve as escapes from harsh experiences. Should mental abnormalities develop in such individuals, they may tend to assume flight characteristics. Included among such flight characteristics are the following phenomena.

Swooning. Some people avoid facing disagreeable situations by swooning. A temporary loss of consciousness provides an effective escape from painful feelings, although the relief may be quite short-lived. Swooning may be resorted to as a defense against great emotional and nervous upsets, but it may also result from such upsets, even when great happiness is experienced. According to the press reports of July 27, 1934, "Mrs. Connor cried out with happiness when Sergeant Hogan rushed in the house and gave her back her kidnaped Bobby. Her speech was incoherent in her happiness. Then, bursting into sobs and becoming slightly hysterical, she rolled Bobby on a divan, fondling him. Unable to stand the strain longer, she fainted." Even the shock of delirious joy may place too great a strain on overwrought nerves. A Missouri share cropper residing in a two-room log cabin, when informed by the doctor that his wife had given birth to quadruplets, one boy and three girls (in 1936), escaped from the emotional shock of the unexpected and perturbing news by fainting. Later, when asked if he had named the children, he gasped, "I'm hardly able to count them yet."

Normal Sleep. Of course, there are far more people who sleep off their troubles than there are of those who obtain oblivion or escape via the fainting route. The sleeping propensity of misdemeanants immediately after arrest and incarceration has been noted. The automobilist responsible for a fatal accident may awaken in his cell after a night of deep slumber without any recollection of the accident, an amnesia somewhat similar to the retroactive or retrograde form of forgetfulness which often follows a serious cerebral concussion and which is limited to the occurrrences immediately preceding the accident. The protective function of sleep in the case of the autoist responsible through carelessness for the fatal accident is obvious. The selective tendency to oversleep to escape from some irksome duty is illustrated in the reply, in the late war, of the private to the reprimand of the sergeant. The sergeant asked the private why he was late for guard duty. The private replied that he overslept. "You say you overslept in all that bombardment?" "Yes," replied the private, "I'd be sleeping yet if some guy hadn't been writing a letter with a scratchy pen." The tendency of the youngster to oversleep to escape from a boring chore is of like tenor.

Lapses of Attention or Periods of Absent-mindedness. Some persons become so preoccupied with their ideas, images, or feelings that they may become more or less oblivious of their surroundings. While they are listening to a lecture or conversation or indulging in some activity, their attention may be observed to wander. They evince periods of absent-mindedness in which they go off into trancelike states. In such states they appear blank, unobservant, or staring into space; they may have to be aroused by a sharp call, or they may spontaneously return to normalcy with a start. These states of absent-mindedness resemble the daydreaming flights that are characterized by detachment from reality. Of course, daydreaming may be due to excessive preoccupation with problems of consuming interest, as well as to efforts to avoid the disagreeable. In the following case, mind wandering seems to be due to pressure of ideas. Whether this pressure is the result of the boredom of the speaker, to the preoccupation of the listener with more interesting thoughts, or to something else, cannot be determined from the report. (Consult the discussion of absent-mindedness and fugues in Chap. XIV.)

HABIT OF MIND WANDERING OR INABILITY TO LISTEN ATTENTIVELY TO CONVERSATIONAL REMARKS, POSSIBLY DUE TO PRESSURE OF IDEAS

People accuse me of being indifferent. I have formed the habit of indulging in elaborate thoughts when talking to other people. I look intelligently into their faces and murmur, "Oh, yes," "I see," and such phrases but my thoughts are running riot while the conversation is in progress. After a time, I forget to make these murmurs and I am startled to hear the conversationalist say, "What do you think of that?" Then I am confused and must ask that the preceding remarks be repeated. Many times such a repetition is refused, for, they say, "Oh, you're not interested in what I was saying; you were not paying attention to me." What causes this I do not know, for I am sympathetic toward the difficulties of others, but this habit persists. (A.H.T.; F.; Col. Univ.; Instr. of Psy.; M.S.; Age 26)

Hallucinatory experiences (*i.e.,* perceptions that have no external reality; the projection of centrally aroused ideas into space without any relevant external stimulus). Excessive daydreaming might intensify the dreamer's mental imagery and cause it to be projected into space. His exaggerated emotions and the stimulation of his image-making phantasy might tend to distort his images and make them appear as lifelike and real as eidetic images (very clear images projected into space so that they assume a perceptual or objective character, usually limited to early childhood). He may thus hear nonexistent voices or see persons or things that exist only in his imagination. He may hear voices bidding him do certain things that he wants to do and thus he can justify his acts as commands of God, of the king, or of some other superior person; the threats or intimidations that he fancies he hears constitute justification for his fears. Many hallucinatory images are doubtless symbolical expressions of the victim's fears or wishes. They are projections of his emotional and moral struggles, and serve as defenses against them or as methods of escape.

Delusions. The transformation of reveries into delusions may not be so difficult as it appears on first thought. The repeated, persistent wishing for something in the land of dreams, where anything may be true just because it is desired or experienced, may eventually lead to the conviction that it is real and true or that the wisher, a powerful wizard or an affluent mogul, can make it come true by a mere wish or resolution. When the dreamer begins to place credence in his false beliefs, in spite of the external evidence as to their falsity, he has become a victim of delusions (false opinions that are impervious to logical arguments or to facts). To acquire delusional trends in harmony with one's desires is relatively easy, just as it is easier to believe that one was born great or had greatness thrust upon him than it is to achieve greatness by dint of laborious application. If the dreamer adopts a false belief of greatness as a defense against his failure to adjust himself satisfactorily to his task, he has become a victim of delusions, particularly if the delusion is not amenable to correction by objective facts. Should the daydreamer tend to become more or less mentally disordered, the delusional tendencies will be strengthened. Similarly, delusional daydreaming will provide a fertile soil for the development of tendencies toward mental alienation.

Romancing Confabulations of the Pathological Liar. The fictions in this kind of romancing, which is not instigated by any particular motive for gain, doubtless sometimes result from excessive indulgence in similar wish-fulfilling imaginal flights from reality.

Somnambulism and Double Personality. Possibly excessive indulgence in the daydreaming type of detachment from the workaday world may further the development of these dissociated secondary states of consciousness, which will be given further consideration in Chap. XIV.

Hysteria. According to Freud, hysterical symptoms are often traceable to phantasies that are unconscious distortions of memories.

Manic-depressive Flights. The "manic" flights in the manic-depressive type of mental disorder may be viewed as attempts to escape from the patient's limitations and inhibitions into a state of exhilaration and omnipotence. They represent a means of gratifying the patient's deeper cravings.

Dementia Praecox. This form of mental disease supplies one of the best illustrations of the flight technique. In this disorder the victim retires to an inner world of fancy, in which, apparently, his desires become subjectively satisfied. At times he gets so absorbed in his inner world that he becomes wholly inaccessible to outside influences. He becomes totally unconcerned with outside events and will not respond to external suggestions or commands.

He has become completely estranged from the world of objective facts, to which he has been unable to adjust himself. This condition of extreme unresponsiveness and introversion is technically called "inaccessibility."

Correctives for Excessive or Detrimental Indulgence in Reverie. What can be done to prevent or to overcome the injurious effects of daydreaming? A number of simple, homely suggestions are offered, such as fit the needs of simple, childish minds. They are proffered not as "universal solvents" but as more or less closely interrelated aids.

1. Make an effort to discover the cause of excessive daydreaming proclivities and of queer phantasies and abnormal behavior patterns suggestive of detrimental daydreaming tendencies. In the effort to accomplish this objective, the child should be encouraged to relate his dreams. Until his confidence has been won and until he has been led to realize that daydreaming is a very common thing, indulged in by most children, and that there is nothing disgraceful or reprehensible about the practice, he will probably continue to conceal his reveries. He should gradually be led to understand that he has had recourse to the phantasy world for the solution of personal difficulties that have annoyed him and caused disagreeable conflicts and that when his conflicts have been resolved the necessity for daydreaming escapes will disappear. Lead him to see that his difficulties are no different from those of many other children who master them by persistent effort instead of spending their time in idle musing.

The causes of some daydreams are readily indicated by the nature of the reveries. It is transparently patent that some phantasies are the expressions of the desire for power and prestige or for ease and contentment, while others are expressions of the desire to escape life's hardships. Such dreams often originate in the dissatisfactions, disappointments, and frustrations experienced in the everyday round of cares and tasks in the home and in the school. Sometimes, however, it will be necessary to unravel the meaning of the peculiar symbolism in which the dream occurs. Since the symbolism is often designed to conceal the emotional or mental disturbance that lies at the base of this kind of defense mechanism, the deciphering of the true meaning of the hidden symbolism may prove to be difficult. The dreamer himself may be of little assistance, as he may not grasp the meaning of the symbols that occur in his phantasies. A phantasy about crushing the head of a serpent may be a symbolic expression for the desire that a hated rival playmate may be crushed to death. Although daydream symbols may seem inscrutable and meaningless to the novice, they often possess deeper meanings than does the symbolism of most nocturnal dreams. However, when the cause of daydream indulgence is unearthed and the situation is treated understandingly, the daydream tendencies may abate and the bizarre daydreaming manifestations may disappear.

2. Make daydreams your servant and not your master. Dream in order to make your dreams come true. In the words of Rudyard Kipling's poem, "If,"

> "If you can dream—and not make dreams your master,
> If you can think—and not make thoughts your aim,"
>
> Then you can divert impending disaster
> Into channels that lead to ultimate gain.

Let your daydreams stimulate you to accomplish real results in your daily living, not merely imaginary ones. Let them fire you with the ambition to experience the glow of success in the world of reality that you experienced in the world of imagination. Daydreaming should prove a valuable device if it becomes a dynamic force for constructive achievement in literature, science, invention, commerce, industry, and art, instead of being a refuge for unsatisfied longings or blasted ambitions. It is of value when it aids us to become better adjusted to our social and vocational pursuits and when it ceases to be a form of imaginary compensation for limitations that ends in futile ruminations or in mental delirium.

Let us, therefore, strive to get children and youths to realize that the pleasures derived from excursions into fairyland will not prove permanently satisfying unless they incite the dreamer to make better adjustments to the practical demands of life and to achieve worth-while results in the objective world.

3. Strive to secure a proper balance between imaginal satisfaction and active adjustment, between the life of fancy and the life of reality. One expedient for doing this is to make reality not only tolerable but so attractive that the satisfactions derived from contact with people and things will yield deeper and more abiding contentment than the temporary thrills secured from building air castles can. Make the joys of living more attractive than the joys of dreaming and the joys of actual conquest greater than the delights of fancy. Let the child realize that real contests are more exhilarating and infinitely more worth while than are futile imaginings. The acquisition of this point of view should prove helpful in overcoming the contempt for practical affairs that some dreamers feel, in consequence of which they try to withdraw from the active world. Therefore, as a preventive measure, provide encouraging social contacts and satisfying objective tasks as balancing factors to beguile the child out of his dream world into the world of reality.

Another closely related expedient is to provide the child with abundant opportunities for experiencing satisfaction through successful achievement.[5]

[5] Certain remedial suggestions are reiterated in various parts of the book for the reasons stated on page 398, rather than for the purpose of reemphasis, although naturally

The bright pupil finds relief in revery from the boredom of the slow, monotonous grind that offers no challenge to his alert mind; the dullard obtains relaxation in his phantasies from his exasperating struggle with unintelligible abstractions and symbols. The successful, satisfied child does not spend his time daydreaming. Training children for success can be most successfully done by affording them every opportunity to develop along the lines of their greatest potentials and interests and by inspiring them with the ideal of service to society according to capacity as the surest road to lasting satisfaction.

4. Avoid inveterate indulgence in myth, story, and novel reading. Unless we subscribe to the doctrine of the realists, that the only things a child should be taught are real facts or truths, and not idle fancies or mythological falsehoods, there probably exists some place for the judicious employment of fairy tales, myths, and legends in early life. Observation shows that they not only afford the child keen satisfaction and enjoyment, but they also widen his horizon, stimulate his interest, develop his imagination, and possibly discipline his emotions. Some writers believe that myth and fairy-tale experiences may function beneficially as a means of emotional catharsis. By means of this kind of imaginal experience, the child is enabled to live through certain emotional experiences that it may be beneficial for him to experience vicariously. Such vicarious experiences may provide a way of sublimating in symbolical form his tabooed fancies and thoughts.

Be this as it may, it is equally important to emphasize the fact that the child's imagination is also in need of disciplining so that he may learn to distinguish between what is real and what is unreal, and so that his fancy will not run amuck but will show some conformance with the facts of life. It is altogether probable that excessive reading of fairy stories, folklore, and legends may develop an inordinate fondness for the unreal and may stimulate frequent resort to compensation in daydreams for shortcomings and to regressions to infantile and primitive modes of wish fulfillment that will not work with adolescents and adults.

Moreover, excessive infatuation with stories of the hero type should make us suspicious that all is not well with the child. A child who continues to be unduly preoccupied with such tales may finally become convinced that he is a very extraordinary person (the Jehovah complex) and thus he might eventu-

---

this function may also be coincidentally subserved by the repetitions. A poll of students using the book as a text revealed a decided consensus in favor of repeating the suggestions under the different related categories, rather than resorting to cross references. Without repetition, it would not be apparent to many that the same remedial or preventive treatment procedures would be applicable to different maladjustments that are closely related from the standpoint of causation or motivation.

ally become a victim of delusions of grandeur. The acquisition of such false beliefs should be prevented before they become a habit of thought.[6]

5. Imbue the child with the courage and willingness to face the struggles of life, to become reconciled to life's inevitable changes and vicissitudes—in fact, to be ready to start all over if need be. Lead him to appreciate that life is a continuous process of change and adjustment and that victory comes only to the brave, the quick, the strong, the adaptable, and the capable. Show him that disappointments and frustrations are a part of the normal ups and downs of life and may play an important role in the development of the mental virility, initiative, and resilience that are needed for satisfying success in the world of reality and active adjustment. Help him to realize that reality is an enormously complex and complicated thing, that our conception of truth must necessarily undergo marked transformation and expansion as life progresses, and that he must be ready and willing to readjust his philosophy of life and his behavior patterns in accordance with his expanding insight and acquaintance with the facts of existence, instead of clinging, through the mechanism of daydreaming fancies, to his childish survivals. Inspire the child to believe in his ability to achieve his visions on the reality plane. Show him that, properly used, the daydream is a dynamic mechanism for meeting the issues of life constructively and explain that it should not be used as a smoke screen to hide from those issues and thereby evade the necessity of meeting them at all. Lead the child to realize that when romancing is used as a dodge the daydreamer is headed for inevitable eventual disillusionment, disappointment, and defeat. Acquaint him with the fact that life's stern actualities usually do not measure up to childhood's and youth's romantic projections into the future, but that this is not a cause for alarm or discouragement, or for taking flights into fairyland, because genuine achievements are possible in all kinds of endeavor for people of all kinds of ability—achievements that yield lasting satisfaction and that meet with social approval.

6. Do not pamper or humor the child too much or deprive him of the opportunity to face obstacles and develop courage. Since the overprotected, pampered child tends to substitute daydreaming for aggressive combat, induce him to participate in the real battles of life, but under wise guidance, so that his combats will make for the development of resourcefulness, fortitude, and strength, instead of an attitude of introversion, defeatism, and surrender. This kind of tutelage should begin in the nursery; the reality-dodging ruses are among the earliest of the child's acquisitions.

7. Avoid unnecessary or harsh criticisms or invidious comparisons with more successful siblings or companions—treatment that tends to drive the sensitive,

[6] On the influence of fairy tales, myths, or legends, consult Sandor Lorand, "Fairy Tales, Lilliputian Dreams, and Neurosis," *American Journal of Orthopsychiatry*, 1937, 456–464 (references).

introverted type of child to take refuge in the illusory paradise of his phantasy, where he will be able to surpass his mates, no matter how brilliant they may be, without the necessity of making any struggle, and where he can obtain imaginary redress for his injured feelings. Effort should be made to become friends with the withdrawing dreamer and to lead his fancy into fruitful channels. He should be accorded appreciative recognition for every effort to translate his visions into fruitful actualities, without having to suffer the discouragement of listening to discriminatory comparisons with comrades who are more successful or who are free from adjustment difficulties.

8. Foster the development of sociability in the child. Begin early in his life to nurture an interest in people and social activities. Mingling among and fraternizing with other human beings will act as a safety valve, through the objectification of attention by diverting it away from self. Social participation will tend to develop healthy outside interests and prevent unhealthy preoccupation with oneself and the tendency to live in the world of subjective imagery; it will act as an emotional stabilizer.

9. Write down the details of the daydream while they are still fresh in mind. This will require effort. The effort required—perhaps an annoying chore— might serve as a counteracting irritant to the tendency to overindulgence in reverie. This practice will, moreover, induce a state of activity that may serve as a corrective for the daydream passivity. An objective, analytic study of each and all of the daydream records should possess further virtues. It should lead to a better understanding of the mechanism and the motivation of a given phantasy and of series of phantasies. Such analyses should reveal the chimerical and absurd character of many daydreams and the waste of time and futility of absorption in them. If such a study can be carried on objectively, it might prove of value as a form of release and insight therapy, and also as a fruitful form of intellectual activity that might lead to discovery of some nuggets of value in the mass of images and symbols that may be reflections of some of the deeper motivations and attributes of the personality.

CHAPTER XI

(11) COMPENSATION

11. Adjustments through Compensatory Reactions

Nature of Compensatory Drives. What is meant by a compensatory reaction? In mental hygiene the term "compensation" refers to the psychological mechanism by which undesirable traits are concealed or overcome by the development of some type of camouflage or of counterbalancing quality. Compensation represents an effort to cover up or to overcome some physical, social, psychic, or economic shortcomings, whether real or imaginary, with their attendant feelings of inadequacy, timidity, or frustration, fear of failure, and emotional conflicts, and to achieve feelings of security, superiority, and social status, either by a strenuous effort to overcome the defect or maladjustment itself (direct compensation) or by the development of some counteracting or compensatory trait (indirect compensation). Thus, in order to protect the ego (self) from the awareness of a fault or to conceal its presence from others, the individual may develop some desirable personality trait, often in exaggerated degree, as a protective screen against the underlying undesirable characteristic. Strictly interpreted, compensation should be limited to the latter phenomenon, but the term is usually given a wider connotation. The mechanism is extensively employed by both the young and the old of all levels of ability for achieving social status by superior performance in substitute activities.

When the difficulty is attacked with extreme vigor, an excessive development of the trait itself or of aggressiveness or assertiveness is likely to occur. This phenomenon is referred to as overcompensation or overaction.

The effort to compensate may be undertaken consciously and deliberately; it may develop from the gradual and insidious acquisition of attitudes and habit patterns of which the individual may be unconscious or only marginally conscious; or it may be due to conflicts that were once conscious but that have been forgotten.

Illustrative Situations Showing the Varied Use of Compensatory Devices. The great variety of uses made of the compensatory type of adjustment can be shown by reference to situations of almost daily occurrence. Who is not familiar with the undersized man who attempts to compensate for his stunted physical growth by the development of a domineering, stentorian voice and a wise- and impressive-looking demeanor, or who tries to magnify his importance by wearing a high hat, by sporting a walking stick, or by assuming a strutting air? Who does not recall the young civilian subalterns during the First World War who tried to make up for their lack of military training by the affectation of an erect posture, a sawed-off mustache, and military swagger? The resort to whistling by people who shrink from facing their problems, in order to bolster up their courage or, at least, to put on a bold front, is a trite device. Who is not familiar with the child who displays an exaggerated tendency to be naughty because of a fear of being called a goody-goody or a sissy? One reason why tale bearing or tattling is discouraged is the well-recognized tendency of many children to use this device to magnify their own goodness. The person who feels socially insecure or who cannot win social recognition because of lack of "oomph" may seek to attain status by becoming very proficient in rummy or bridge. Some parents who suffer from inferiority complexes or who entertain very poor opinions of themselves compensate by demanding brilliance or perfection in their offspring. The following report from a woman auditing one of the writer's courses of lectures before a popular audience is a striking case in point. She was severely beaten by her hyperexacting father because she did not bring home perfect grades; as a result of the brutal treatment she endured, she developed such rankling inhibitions and feelings of resentment and inferiority that she failed to receive the class appointments in her senior year for which her earlier scholarship had naturally predestined her.

A SENSE OF RANKLING INJUSTICE AND DETERIORATION IN SCHOLAR-SHIP IN A SUPERIOR STUDENT PRODUCED BY THE DEMANDS OF PER-FECTION BY A PARENTAL MARTINET, WHO MAY HAVE BEEN COMPEN-SATING FOR HIS OWN SHORTCOMINGS

As a child I thoroughly enjoyed being in school. In all subjects except drawing and sewing I maintained high grades. During my six years in grammar school I led my classes. I was spoken of at home as a bright and quiet child of whom much was expected. For fear of being made vain I was seldom praised. It was impressed upon me that I had never done anything extraordinary and that I could be perfect if I tried. In my thirteenth year in grade 8A I brought home a report card which I confidently thought would be well received. It was the best I had so far received, with 100 per cent in four subjects, 95 per cent in another, and 92 per cent in the sixth, giving me an average for the term of 97.8 per cent and putting me at the head of the class by a considerable margin. Because of the flattering remarks made in school I was in fine spirits as I went home. But my elation did not last long. When my father saw my report that evening, he flew into a rage because my report was not perfect, and I was whipped with a cat-o'-nine-tails until welts appeared on my body. My protestations that no one else ranked higher did not help any.

The whipping did more than raise welts; it gave me an attitude of "what's the use." Feeling deeply the injustice of the frequent whippings I had received, for the good of my soul, I decided that trying was not worth while. I told my father that no matter what I did it was wrong, that I didn't care any more, and that if I had to take whippings I would give him something real to whip me for. I think this sudden revulsion in a meek, quiet child frightened him. But my life had been damaged for quite a number of years. Instead of standing at the head of my class when I graduated I had dropped to a low-average pupil. Teachers and principals tried to find out what was wrong, what had caused this sudden indifference and listlessness in the previously eager pupil, but I was too proud to talk. Something was dead in me. I was helped by going to high school, but I was never again able to attain the standing I reached in the lower school, although I received A's through high school in some subjects. However, no matter what grades I brought home from high school, I was never again whipped even though praise was still withheld.   (M.A.; F.; Housewife)

Sufficient data are not available in this sketch to state positively that this particular parent who demanded perfection in his offspring was overcompensating for some frustration or handicap.

Some unfortunates who have spent their youth in riotous living attempt to overcome their feelings of condemnation by becoming crusaders against the forms of indulgence by which they were once enslaved. To try to reform others from your own weaknesses is a well-known form of compensation. Many child-loving women who have no children of their own compensate by dedicating their services to child-welfare work or teaching. Many of the unhappily married seek consolation and compensation in religion instead of escape via the divorce route. Many a wife, ungratified by her husband, obtains compensatory satisfaction through the bestowal of excessive affection upon her child and thereby, incidentally, runs the danger of arousing in him erotic feelings and laying the basis for a crippling emotional fixation upon herself. Some dull children try to mask their dullness, or compensate for it, by excessive cramming or indulgence in some other form of hyperactivity. The expectation doubtless is that this form of defense or compensation dodge will create the impression of successful industry.

Compensatory Tendencies among Dull and Bright Children. On the basis of observation during a period of 30 days of the behavior characteristics of 140 problem children (of whom 60.7 per cent were boys) in a child-guidance home, who had been tested by means of the Binet and the Vineland Social Maturity Scale, the conclusion was reached that "children with low intelligence quotients tend to compensate for their retardation by the development of a social maturity beyond the level of their intellectual status, while those with higher intelligence quotients tend to overemphasize their intellectual qualities at the expense of their social development." Thus "intelligence quotients and social quotients apparently compensated for each other." [1] This conclusion challenges verification from a study of a larger number of non-problem children.

The Virtues of the Compensatory Drive. Doubtless, when it is normally and reasonably applied, the method of compensation is a valuable technique for surmounting personal limitations, for "cushioning" personal dissatisfactions, for developing substitute competencies, or for meeting life's problems positively. At its best, it represents an active, aggressive, fighting attitude, instead of an attitude of surrender. It connotes effort and determination to overcome and conquer, instead of effortless abnegation or supine retreat, which usually leads to the adoption of regressive or other dodges.

Nature's method of adjustment has been said to be compensatory in character. Thus, we are told that the sensory defect of the blind man is compensated for by the superior sensitivity of the auditory or the tactile receptor; but this hypothesis is not literally correct. The alleged superiority of the tactual or the auditory senses in the blind is not due to any innate superiority or hypersensitivity of the nervous structures in these organs; it is due to training. The blind develop superior auditory or tactual receptivity or discrimination by the persistent use and training of the organs of hearing and touch. Thus the blind man's compensations are the result of persistent personal effort.

The numerous illustrations already presented [2] have demonstrated very clearly that the lack of physical charm or health or the possession of physical, social, or mental handicaps that engender feelings of dissatisfaction and insufficiency cannot always be regarded as unmixed evils, because they often incite the individual to put forth dogged efforts to overcome them or to become highly efficient in some other field of endeavor. The aggressive determination to succeed in the face of impediments may enable the victim to tap latent reservoirs of energy that may even carry him to higher levels of accomplishments than he would have reached without the handicap. It is fundamentally important, therefore, to lead the child to realize that successful, worth-while compensations may go a long way toward helping him to become

---

[1] Louis A. Lurie, Florence M. Rosenthal, and Louisa C. Outcalt, "Diagnostic and Prognostic Significance of the Differences between the Intelligence Quotient and the Social Quotient," *American Journal of Orthopsychiatry*, 1942, 104–114.

[2] Some of these instances are the development of interest in debating as a compensation for an emotionally conditioned aversion to singing (pages 124*f.*); dedication to the service of the living through the ministry, as a means of combating the wretchedness produced by the fatal burning of an adored sister (pages 145*f.*); intellectual application to compensate for the limitations produced by a crippled condition (page 186); application to intellectual or scholastic pursuits as a means of counterbalancing the effects of physical unattractiveness (pages 189*f.* and 191–192*f.*); and resort to hero daydreams as a compensation for the humdrum life on a lonely farm (pages 281*f.*). See, particularly, references to the persons who attained distinction on pages 283*f.* and 400*f.*

satisfactorily adjusted to his environment and to becoming hopeful, optimistic, contented and well-balanced emotionally.   Thus successful compensations should tend to bolster up his morale and exert a prophylactic influence.   They may prove of value in preventing the development of further dissatisfactions and unhealthy trends, which sometimes terminate in such pathological forms of compensation as appear in some of the neuroses and psychoses.

The Multifarious Evils of the Compensatory Type of Adaptation Explained and Illustrated.   While the compensatory method of overcoming difficulties and solving perplexities sometimes proves a health-preserving mechanism, it must frequently be regarded as an abnormal or vicious type of reaction from the points of view of its origin and of its outcome.   The compensatory urge usually springs from some mental maladjustment, such as lack of self-confidence, feelings of distrust, fear, impending failure, frustration, hatred, emotional conflicts, or inhibitions.   Since it emerges from an unhealthy mental soil, the subject's attitude toward his shortcomings or defects, whether physical or mental, real or imaginary, is usually highly emotionalized, owing mainly, perhaps, to the attitude manifested by parents, siblings, playmates, or teachers toward the hated blemish.   The child may have become unduly sensitive because he has been subjected to ridicule or criticism or unfavorable comparisons with other children because of his imputed deficiency.   In consequence of such treatment, he tends to react excessively, his intense, compelling emotions often driving him to overcompensate.   To overcome his emotionally toned inferiority complex he may develop an exaggerated superiority complex, some other type of aggressive behavior, or some type of self-deceptive masquerade or dodge by means of which he believes he can hide his inferiority or evade the necessity of facing the issues.

Of course, he may not be clearly aware of the fact that he is resorting to ruses and tricks to cover up or overcome his shortcomings, and he may not fully comprehend the real motives of his conduct.   In fact, the psychoanalysts hold that conflicts which are at the base of the compensatory urge frequently are unrecognized because they have been "repressed into the unconscious." Irrespective of the merits of the detailed assumptions of the doctrine of psychoanalysis, we can at least grant that the original conflicts, which may be at the base of the compensatory urge, have frequently been forgotten.   It is sometimes true, too, that the individual may not clearly apprehend just what the defects are that drive him to compensate.   He may merely be conscious of some vague, inexplicable feeling of dissatisfaction that leaves him no peace of mind until he has done something to get rid of it.   Therefore, the victim of the compensatory drive may not understand the motives back of his behavior or of his attitudes.   In consequence, he acts more or less blindly.   Beneath the surface he may be warring with desires that he considers irreconcilable with his social ideals or with the social ideals of the community. These must accordingly, he feels, be smothered. He may attribute his difficulties to some irrelevant or unimportant circumstance because he may not fully realize that it is his own inner conflict that supplies the motive for his attitudes and behavior tendencies. Thus, the grouchiness that the chronic grouch attributes to indigestion may be only a form of compensation for his deep-seated discontent over his failure to face frankly his own personal problems. If he does not realize this he will not understand the reason for his mean disposition. The lonely girl in a large family of boys may not understand that she is trying to compensate for the lack of a sibling of her own sex by the invention of a sister.

That compensations which are adopted more or less unconsciously to overcome some vague or misunderstood dissatisfaction will often fail to remove the dissatisfaction need occasion no surprise. The probability is that blind compensations usually fail, although outwardly they may appear to be successful. Such compensations usually prove to be merely illusory substitutes for what is wanted.

Extreme emotional reactions or exaggerated characteristics arouse the suspicion that the person is overcompensating because of some lack or defect or because of some trait that he deems unworthy or considers socially disapproved (see pages 289 to 294). Frequently the exaggerated reactions consist in the development of traits that are the exact opposite of those he wants to conceal (see pages 293f.). Sometimes the compensatory reaction manifests itself in a tendency to find fault with and to criticize others. The psychologist is well aware of the fact that it is difficult to tolerate in others characteristics persistently repressed in oneself. Violent condemnation of foibles and follies in others is often a tacit admission of the critic's own feelings of guilt, although he may be unaware of the deeper significance of his actions, and although he may vociferously protest his innocence.

Illustrative Situations Productive of Emotionalized Compensatory Drives The varied manifestations and evils of emotionalized compensations can be best shown by referring to certain typical situations fairly well recognized by the average reader.

Fanaticism on questions of morals and social customs is sometimes a refuge for or defense against the individual's own suppressed voluptuousness. The person who is horrified by nudity may be merely compensating for his own impure thoughts. "Unto the pure all things are pure," is a sagacious Biblical observation. Similarly, prudishness is doubtless sometimes a form of compensation for intense and prolonged suppression of the sex urge.

The satisfaction some reformers derive from making derogatory or condemnatory remarks about others may, unwittingly, compensate them for earlier, shame-producing experiences that they are striving to counterbalance or conceal.   In the zealous attempt to reform others, the reformer may really only be defending himself against his inner conflicts or his own guilty past, real or assumed.   The excoriating, relentless jeremiads against sinners by one of the greatest of latter-day evangelists, an admitted onetime victim of John Barleycorn, may occur to the reader.   Someone has said that the best reformers are those who have been "seared by sin" and that it takes a reformed toper to reform drunkards.   Be that as it may, many a perfervid reformer or religious fanatic may be merely unwittingly projecting his own problem into the person or group he has singled out for attack.   In a similar way, the piousness of some church deacons may be a cloak for their own hypocrisy.   That the cruel villain on the stage is sometimes presented in the role of a pious deacon is doubtless due to the frequent use of this particular type of defense mechanism.   The psychological effect of hypocritical conduct in some church elders is well illustrated in the following report.

AVERSION TO ATTENDING CHURCH, PARTLY DUE TO THE LOUD SHOUT-
ING AND GRIMACING OF THE PREACHERS, THE DRYNESS OF THE SER-
MONS, THE PIOUS ATTITUDE OF THE ELDERS, AND THE SUPERCRITICAL
ATTITUDE OF AND BETRAYAL OF CONFIDENCE BY THE PREACHER

I never liked to go to church.   The preachers did not say anything that interested me and many of them shouted so loud that my head ached.   But I liked one minister very much.   He and his wife were kind to me, and their daughter, a golden-haired cherub of six, was my most beloved classmate.   But I hated to hear the man preach.   He shouted and grimaced like a wild man.   Later, when I was about eleven, we had a minister who understood boys.   The elders said he wasn't very spiritual and had him moved on as soon as possible.   A large number of boys joined the church under his pastorate.   I was afraid I would be refused membership and humiliated.   In a way I felt unworthy to sit at the Lord's Table, but the real fear lay in the person of one of the trustees.   I once inadvertently asked him how he could blaspheme during the week and pray on Sunday.   He became very angry.   I received no satisfactory answer and a lack of adjustment ensued that required many years to resolve.

I was haunted by thoughts provoked by revival sermons dealing with how "the dear departed are looking down on the wayward loved ones" until I was convinced that going to heaven was not all that was claimed for it.   I was thoroughly glad that I was alive and on earth where I could throw snowballs, track rabbits, fight, and have a good time generally.

As I grew older, my dislike to go to church grew on me.   After I was received into membership, I took the attitude, "Well, I'm here, there is nothing to do but play the game." I endeavored to meet the formal requirements of the church, but all the while I felt a sense of unworthiness. I was not a bad boy in the generally accepted sense. I was not profane, nor did I have the sexual habits I knew other boys had. I respected my parents although I frequently disobeyed. Nevertheless I felt unworthy. The pious attitude of the elders, and the supercritical attitude of the minister made me feel that I was chief among sinners. I finally revolted, and the combined efforts of my mother and brother were necessary to get me to attend services.

Not infrequently, the constant bickering about attending church drove me into a rage. One pastor made a monkey of me by warming up under a mask of sympathetic friendship until he found out why I didn't like to attend services. Then he told "a few of the brethren." The next Sunday he preached a sermon on the stiff-necked sinner who is too proud to repent. I had already heard the sermon twice, so he may not have thought of me at all, but I thought he was preaching at me. I knew by that time he had betrayed my confidence.

After that, a pitched battle was necessary to get me to go to church. I was in a state of open rebellion. Frequently, after my Sunday-morning tantrum had been quelled by sheer force, I would walk submissively toward the church only to disappear at the door or in the vestibule.

Some of the older people whispered around that the devil had at last gained control of my body. I now marvel at the strength of the inferiority complex, and feel ashamed when I contemplate the rabid violence my tantrums assumed. Some years after my church-going difficulty, I came to know a country doctor of a remarkably loving disposition. He conducted a Sunday school, and ministered to the soul as well as to the body. Under his ministrations, I was able to work out a religious rationale that still strengthens me as I reach out to grapple with the Infinite. But the complex of unworthiness and the accompanying rebellion against tyranny left scars on my personality that time has hardly effaced.

(H.L.; M.; H.S.T.; B.S.; Age 38)

All zealots who are actuated by the compensatory drive (and reference is here made only to that type) are not confined to the field of morality or religion. Political bigotry or radicalism is frequently essentially an expression of excessive compensation inspired by deep-seated social or mental maladjustments. Doubtless some revolutionists are consciously or unconsciously projecting their venom upon society because of the repressed memories of their failure to adjust themselves to the social order or because of the bitter thwartings they experienced in childhood or adolescence. The fierce hatred of the anarchist for people of power or position or for the social order may be largely an expression of his own unrecognized self-hatred or of the unapprehended or misapprehended emotional turmoil that may be seething within him. This same psychological mechanism probably furnishes the key, in part at least, to an understanding of some of the modern dictators whose exhibitions of autocratic dictatorialness (let us call it the "dictatorialness complex") afford them an outlet for their consuming emotional fires kindled by bitter dissatisfactions, suppressions, and defeats in early life. Violent antagonism to authority as manifested in the uncompromising iconoclast, agitator, rebel, or anarchist is frequently a compensation for an early fixation or regression due, perhaps, to the early conflicts, jealousies, hatreds, and vindictiveness produced by brutal suppressions or cruelties inflicted by martinets in the home or elsewhere.

The victim of the compensatory drive often develops a nihilistic or anarchistic complex because he tends to blame the restraints and prohibitions of the social order for his troubles. He becomes very impatient with legal restraints and conformity to conventions and often revolts openly against the existing order when discipline is relaxed. This revolt may take the form of excessive belligerency or contentiousness or carping criticism. The victim is ever on the alert for opportunities to agitate, find fault, argue, criticize, make cutting or derogatory remarks, gossip, slander, muckrake, or show ill will or hatred toward people.

Harsh and despotic parents and teachers are, in turn, probably overcompensating more or less unwittingly for their own feelings of inadequacy or frustration. They may be merely reacting against their own internal conflicts and repressions produced by the repressive measures of their own parents or teachers. Such taskmasters may be wholly oblivious of the source of their rigorousness or of their "perfectionist complex" or "autocracy complex." The more unconscious the domination drive, the more insistent and uncompromising it tends to be. The "domineering complex" in the parent often has its roots in unconscious or vaguely conscious feelings of inferiority. Such feelings in the adult may express themselves in the desire to become the unquestioned, imperious master of the child. The same unconscious motivation sometimes explains the harshness of some teachers who do not understand their austerity or bitterness because they do not comprehend the nature of the underlying drives. They may not realize that their severity may be the expression of a compensatory strictness or autocracy complex, of which the pupils become the guiltless victims.

What are the effects upon the child of overdomineering, repressive parental behavior patterns? The victim of a repressive, domineering, autocratic parent of either sex may become either a timid, submissive, withdrawing, or sycophantic "yes man," or he may begin to hate his father or mother and all others who occupy any position of authority over him. The natural consequence of this kind of treatment is that both the submissive and the rebellious types of excessively repressed child may eventually become defiant of all authority, legal, moral, or personal. Thus the child who has been autocratically disciplined in the home or at school may compensate by developing traits that are antithetical to submissiveness, and he may become an adult tyrant like his father.

Among men of outstanding distinction whose personality traits were undoubtedly greatly warped by harsh parental treatment may be mentioned John Ruskin (see page 350), Lord Byron, and Arthur Schopenhauer. Byron began life by hating all women, ostensibly because of his hatred for his mother, who mocked him as a child and stoned him because of his club foot. Schopenhauer's entire philosophy of pessimism may have had its inception in hatred of his mother. Thrown downstairs by her because of his criticism of her manner of living, he left home, never to return, a woman hater and a world hater.

The rebellious complex may also furnish the drive for those peace-at-any-price pacifists who are trying to overcompensate for an inner raging rebellion against all authority—personal, governmental, or religious. In such cases excessive submissiveness or pacifism may represent the development of the trait that is the opposite of rebelliousness. Of course, this is only one source, a minor one, of pacifism. Another defense mechanism that may issue from a contrasting trait is excessive humility or contrition, which may be a disguise for excessive conceit—the conceit of power or of knowledge. Such hypocritical assumption of a self-depreciatory attitude is, after all, merely a clever means of feeding one's vanity. While superficially humble, many exemplars of humility, as is well known, are liable to be very presumptuous and arrogant about their opinions. They suffer excessively from the conceit of knowledge. Such persons are liable to exhibit unconcealed impatience and resentment should anyone presume to question their opinions. Often the appearance of excessive humility is affected to cloak the individual's depravity or rascality and avarice, as in the case of Uriah Heep in *David Copperfield*. In many cases, therefore, exhibitions of humility must be regarded as masks for concealing the opposite traits, for which the individual is trying to compensate. As is well known by every intelligent mother, the angelic behavior of the small boy is sometimes merely a mask for his mischievousness. These are instances of reaction formation.

Occasionally the victim of dissatisfactions and mental conflicts may seek compensation in some form of misconduct, such as stealing or various forms of sex indulgence. The following case and the one cited on pages 354*f*. are instances of autoerotic practices indulged in as a form of compensation for feelings of dissatisfaction.

AN EARLY ACQUIRED MASTURBATORY AND SEXUAL URGE AND INFERI-
ORITY COMPLEX; THEIR GENESIS AND ATTEMPTED RESOLUTION; MAS-
TURBATION BEGINNING BEFORE THE SIXTH YEAR AND CONTINUING AS
AN IRRESISTIBLE URGE FOR YEARS; LIBIDINOUS TENDENCY AROUSED
PARTICULARLY BY DIFFICULTY OF FALLING ASLEEP AND BY READING
UNPLEASANT STORIES, ESPECIALLY OF ATTACKS UPON WOMEN, OFTEN
ACCOMPANIED BY DISGUSTING HYPNAGOGIC IMAGES AND BY FEELINGS
OF DISAPPOINTMENT AND DEPRESSION; HABIT OF DECEPTION AND
FEELING OF SHAME AND SHYNESS FROM MASTURBATION; COMPLETE
DEVOTION TO AFFLICTED SISTER WHO BECAME THE CENTER OF INTER-
EST IN THE HOME AND LATER IN THE SCHOOL; SISTER'S OVERSHADOW-
ING POPULARITY RESULTING IN INCREASED SHYNESS, INFERIORITY
FEELING, WITHDRAWAL, CONCEALMENT, RETURN TO MASTURBATION,
APPARENT UNCONCERNEDNESS, APPLICATION TO STUDIES, AND DREAMS
ABOUT WONDERFUL MARRIAGES (AS DEFENSE MECHANISM AND WISH
FULFILLMENT); FEELING OF REPULSION TOWARD MEN BECAUSE OF
ENFORCED EMBRACE WHICH RESPONDENT HAS HITHERTO KEPT A
PROFOUND SECRET; EFFORTS AT RESTORING FAITH IN SELF AFTER
BEGINNING INDEPENDENT LIFE AS A TEACHER AND AFTER SISTER'S
DEATH; FIGHTING ATTACKS OF DEPRESSION

At 15 months I had an attack of spinal meningitis and had to learn to walk
and talk all over again.   At intervals for four years I had mild convulsions, which
were usually precipitated by emotional upsets or crying spells.   Hence I could not
be punished as were other children.   The convulsions were outgrown eventually,
and apparently my brain and intelligence were unimpaired; in fact, they were
considerably above normal.

My first punishment stands out with great distinctness in my mind.   I was
about six years old.   We were visiting and I had been put to bed in the afternoon
for my nap.   Because it was very warm, I was lying on the floor, but I could not
go to sleep.   Sometime before, how long I do not remember, I had discovered
that by rubbing myself I produced a queer pleasurable sensation.   As I experi-
mented that day, the door opened and my mother discovered me.   She took me
to the bathroom where she spanked my hands with a ruler.   But the punishment
did not break up the bad habit, for I practiced it in secret occasionally for many
years.   Mother explained to me that children who did "that naughty thing" lost
their minds, and she pointed out several horrible examples as proof.   Whether or
not there was a connection, I do not know, but even the fear of losing my mind
seemed not to deter me.

Sometimes when I was alone in the house or after I was in bed at night, if sleep
were slow in coming, this irresistible impulse would come over me.   I was ashamed
of yielding to it, and each time I would say to myself, "that is the last time it
shall happen."   But invariably I did it again.

As I grew older, reading an unpleasant story would suggest the habit to me. *Oliver Twist* is one book I recall as being particularly upsetting. I could read it for only a little while at a time. Newspapers, in particular, which for the most part I was forbidden to read, contained horrible tales which had this same strange effect. Curiously enough, though there was no connection in my mind, it was the stories of the attacks upon women or their disappearance which seemed to rouse me.

At the same time, especially at night, my practice was accompanied with the strangest thoughts. One might almost call them dreams, since they came just at the border of sleep. The people of my dreams were usually robbers and lived in the most degraded surroundings, preying on their neighbors. They ate the most disgusting things, even human excreta. As I look back now, those dreams did not continue nearly so long as did the habit.

I was not a particularly active child. I liked to stay in the house and read, rather than to play out of doors. Of course hearing my elders' comments upon my fondness for reading did not help the situation materially. I had to live up to my reputation.

This habit of mine was the basis of my deceptiveness. Shame at my inability to conquer myself was at the root of my deceit which was directed more at the concealment than with a positive intent to misrepresent facts. Moreover, I was shy and very sensitive.

There was another big reason for my ingrowing disposition. My sister, who had been born during my babyhood illness, at seven years developed a paralysis of the left side. As she walked along the street one day, her left hand suddenly slipped out of my mother's hand. When mother reached for it, she found that S. had no power to lift it. In addition to that, her left foot dragged. That was the beginning of a three-year siege. The thought, the entire life of the whole family, centered about the little sick sister. I can remember how I wheeled her in her chair; my mother tells me how I entertained her and read to her as she lay on the floor, how I shared my lessons with her. My memory of that time revolves about S. My thoughts, my feelings, anything that I did apart from S. does not enter into my mental picture of that period at all. S. was the center of all attention and my job was to make her happy, to wait on her, and to help her to get well. Such a situation could not help but leave an imprint on my sensitive mind.

She got well, and eventually passed through the grades and entered high school with her class. Happy-go-lucky, pretty, liked by everybody, her occasional temper tantrums forgiven because she had been so ill, S. was the center of my world.

I entered high school at twelve and acquired the reputation of being the smartest child who had gone through high school up to that time. But socially I was not so successful. For one thing the other girls were all older than I. Furthermore, though I was asked to a number of parties, I was not allowed to go unless S. was included in the invitation. I grew shyer. I much preferred being with older people than with those of my own age. One way in which my shyness manifested itself was an unwillingness to make an attempt to do something new for fear of failure and of being laughed at. I never have learned to play tennis for that very reason. Even today the fear of being the object of ridicule follows me. It seems to be much more apparent in connection with childhood out-of-door pursuits. During the past two years I have been president of a club of over 700 members, and have conducted the meetings and introduced speakers to the gatherings with apparently more than usual success. It was an ordeal, but I conquered.

When S. came to high school, she was an immediate social success. There was always an admiring boy to carry her books home from school. Wistfully I looked on, not knowing exactly what to do about the situation. I do not recall being exactly envious except on one or two occasions when S. went to parties without me, but I crept farther into my shell. I built up a defense of appearing not to care, though many times my heart ached with longing. I took refuge in my old habit of masturbation and in dreams of the wonderful man who would some day marry me and take me to live in the most beautiful house to be imagined. As I look back now, I realize that there were boys who tried to break down the barrier I had set up, but, so sure was I that I could not dance, that I was not pretty, that I could not entertain so well as S. could, that I took it for granted that they came to see S., and she proceeded to fill the breach while I looked on.

Because I had a scholarship I went to college, but did not have money enough to live in a dormitory or in a very good room. Here again to choke off my longings to do the same things that the other girls were doing, to wear the same kind of clothes and to have the same pleasures, I worked harder than ever. Strangely enough my mother never urged that I take part in other activities. My sister was the social butterfly of the family who were satisfied with my scholastic achievements and never tried to discover the undercurrents of my thoughts. I was too proud to show my heartache.

An incident which occurred during the summer after my first year in college did not help me materially. A former high-school teacher, of whom I had been very fond, had a garden, the produce of which he sold to the neighbors. When I went for our purchases one day, his family were all away. We went into the house where he washed the vegetables off before putting them into my basket. As we laughed and talked, he suddenly caught me to him and held me so tight I could hardly breathe, though I fought vigorously. It was the first time that I had ever felt a man's body so close to mine. I went home considerably shaken. The way was long enough for me to regain my composure. I tried to forget the incident of which I have never spoken to this day, but it was years before I could have a man near me without a feeling of repulsion.

My first teaching position, in a private school away from home, made a distinct change in my life. For the first time I was on my own. I was also accepted at my face value because no one knew what a charming sister I had at home, who had overshadowed me, or that I had not been a social success at college. I went tobogganing, against which I had no inhibitions, and enjoyed it to the fullest extent. One day the principal said to me, "Miss A., I like to meet you. You have such a sweet smile." That was the first time that I was made conscious that there was any attraction in me. It was not much of a beginning, but it was a beginning.

My sister married and I began to drive our car, which I had never done while she was at home. She had wanted to drive, and, as usual, I did not want to reveal my inexpertness. Now I found I was quite as capable a driver as she was. It helped me. One cannot be introspective while driving a car.

After fifteen months she died when her baby was born. My mother was ill for almost a year afterward, and I gave up my teaching to take care of her. During that period my feeling of inferiority increased as I thought over the wonderful things that S. could do. I never went anywhere without mother. Ever since that time she has been most dependent upon me. In spite of the advice of my friends that I be more independent, I cannot seem to break away. Both my father and mother have always seemed hurt when I have failed to spend as much time with them as they thought was due them.

Though I was very closely tied at home after my sister's death, quite by accident I got a teaching job in the next town. That was the turning point. Though I was still living at home and administering to my mother, self confidence began to grow. When an alumni association was formed and I was elected an officer, it suddenly occurred to me that I had ability.

I was invited to go on a canoe trip and I found I liked the out of doors, and out-of-door people liked me. That was the thing that thrilled me, the realization that people liked me, that boys liked me. The chief remnant of my former feeling of inferiority lay in the fact that I was older than some of the boys who liked me. I lied about my age and that lie was a canker sore in my efforts to have a good time. Its discovery almost broke up one of my most valued friendships. However, the disturbance was entirely due to my shame and embarrassment. My friends never referred to the situation in any way.

Though I must admit I still have attacks of terrible depression without apparent reason when the world looks very black, I can jerk myself out of them. I go out and call on a friend; I go downtown or do something else to take my mind away from myself. It is only at these times that my old desire to masturbate still recurs and cannot be resisted. It results in a sense of shame and exhaustion; I have experienced strong sexual urges from childhood, and still do occasionally. After the death of my fiancé just three weeks before the date set for our wedding, I had a very real battle with this depression, but I conquered. Now these attacks occur rather infrequently, not oftener than five or six times a year. And I think I am growing consistently in my efforts to overcome them.

(A.G.; F.; H.S.T.; B.S.; Age 33)

Of the two following cases, the first shows the attempt of a boy to become the "worst kid in school" as a compensation for being held in contempt because of scholastic excellence, while the second supplies an instance of leadership, acquired, perhaps, through overcompensation for an underlying timidity, which resulted in misbehavior when the leader was deprived of his leadership.

EARLY REALIZATION THAT THE SCHOLAR IS HELD IN CONTEMPT AND
THE LOUT LIONIZED, AND AN ATTEMPT TO COMPENSATE BY BEING
THE WORST KID IN SCHOOL, WHICH PROVED UNSUCCESSFUL BECAUSE
OF THE UNNATURALNESS OF THE ROLE ASSUMED

I was required to do my schoolwork at home.   Consequently, I had no trouble
in leading my class.   But it was not long before I learned that the scholar is
frequently held in contempt while the boor and lout are often lionized.   I wanted
to skip a grade, but that was unheard of.   I thought, if one were denied the
natural rewards for labor and penalized for being the best in his own set, I
would try being the worst for a while.   My attitude was unreal, so it led to disciplinary difficulties.   I realize that the school difficulties arose out of a desire on
the part of my classmates to embarrass me.   I easily led my class, and I wasn't
a tough like some of the boys who were allowed to run the streets all their lives.
The same attitude obtains in the adult world.   I cannot understand why the public
will go wild over a football player, a prize fighter, or hijacker, and assume a sour,
disparaging attitude toward a scholar, philanthropist, or genius.

(H.L.; M.; H.S.T.; B.S.; Age 38)

REACTIONS TO DISPARAGING COMPARISONS; ACQUISITION OF TEND-
ENCY TO BICKER FROM HOME ATMOSPHERE; LEADERSHIP AS A SYMP-
TOM OF OVERCOMPENSATION; MISCONDUCT MOTIVATED BY DESIRE FOR
THE LIMELIGHT AND AS A DEFENSE AGAINST BEING IGNORED; DISCI-
PLINED BY BEING IGNORED

L.K., I.Q. 68, was thirteen when he entered my group, the lowest of four groups
in the school, all Polish boys, with two exceptions.   L. came from what might
be termed a good Polish family.   His mother died when he was very young.   The
stepmother, an excellent housekeeper above the average in intelligence for that
group of people, could tell me little of her except that she was sick a great deal
and very "nervous."   She seemed distressed because of L.'s slow progress in
school.   She dilated on the success of the other children.   I fear this constant
disparagement had operated to give L. deep-seated complexes.   L. had been taught
at home to be careful of his personal appearance, and resented it very much when
his classmates came to school untidy and had to be sent to the washroom to wash
and comb their hair.   As cleanliness is one of the pet hobbies in special classes,
L. set a good example to the other boys.   L. was very much undersized but not
underweight for his height.   His greatest physical defect was his teeth.   He had a
few short teeth in his mouth that barely protruded out of the gums, but had never
had a full set of teeth.   On entrance L. scored zero in reading.   He sprinkled "yes"
and "no" on the pages and seemed to be well pleased with his effort, indicating that
he was determined to try to get something on his paper, a matter of self-preservation.   His effort at most times was above par.   In arithmetic his work was quite
accurate up to abstract subtraction in the test used.   Naturally he could not spell

but could write copy work very well, showing that his muscular control was good. His handwork and manual-training work were very good.

I had L. for almost four years and in that time he learned to read up to about the third grade fairly well and to spell about second-grade words. He also learned to write simple sentences, simple letters, telegrams, and checks.

In the elementary school, L. had been "sitting" in various grades up to the fifth, where he was merely an onlooker and not a participant. What saved him from utter annihilation was the fact that he was a splendid leader, and even the children in the normal group respected his ability to boss and lead. The boss appears to have his place in the scheme of things. Was this display of aggressiveness a compensation for an underlying timidity or self-consciousness? I think so. At least it was his road to self-expression.

As we wished to train others in the group to "lead" and not to "lean" we had to pass the honors of "captains," "monitors," etc., to others and not give L. a monopoly. This created our problem of discipline. L. became like a madman when deprived of any of his offices. He would swear, disobey, and sulk, not for a short time but for days. When given his pencil and paper and requested to do his lessons, he would throw his pencil on the floor and mutter in Polish. At first I sent him to the office, but I soon found out that he came back from his visit to the principal in a greater fury than before he was sent there. So I decided to try a plan of my own.

As each of these children has to be handled differently, it is often difficult to find a happy solution to the various problems that arise almost daily. When L. was in his tantrum, I utterly ignored him and asked all the children to do likewise. They were glad to do so as they feared him tremendously. The fist of this very small boy seemed to terrorize even the big boys in the class. Finally after some time of being left alone, L. would take paper and pencil and begin to do his work. We seldom took any notice of the renewed effort, but occasionally we would remark that the sun was shining once more. L. did not like being ignored; he enjoyed attention.

Other things would also precipitate tantrums. L. was very prompt and hated to be tardy. Once or twice he was late and his rage was directed against his stepmother who had forgotten to awaken him. L. was apparently responding to a situation in the only way he knew, namely, by means of tantrums. Because he was the best leader in the whole school, it was a temptation to allow him privileges. Except for his uncontrolled temper, L. was a good boy, honest, truthful, and very reliable. Self-control is a hard lesson for a Polish boy of low mentality to learn. Quarreling is a habit with them, and Polish families make no effort to stop bickering and quarreling. These traits seem to be embedded in the family drama of the Polish immigrant. The lack of control was probably learned at home. L. was probably just going his elders "one better." I believe that he did learn in school to some extent the utter futility of his tantrums. That was the lesson I was trying to put over.

Recently I learned that he had a position on the truck that brings the evening paper to the dealers. I am sure he is very faithful and efficient. His knowledge of all the principal streets of the city (from our geography projects), combined with his honesty and reliability, should make him very valuable in the distribution of the daily paper. L. was fond of earning money, and is very happy riding around in a big truck. It gives him a feeling of "bigness." L. no longer feels inferior, but rather very superior. Hence in his present work there is no occasion for a tantrum. The school did fit him for a job, and L. is now self-supporting and happy.

(From M.F.M.; F.; S.C.T.; B.A.)

That stealing and other forms of delinquency can sometimes be traced to sex difficulties, possibly as substitutions or compensations for the sex drive, has been convincingly shown by William Healy. To cite one of his cases:

Ada, age 9, had been addicted to petty stealing for two years, purloining money from her home and candy and fruit from the children in school. A year later she was referred to the clinic when brought to the court on the complaint of the school that she had pilfered pencils, handkerchiefs, and money, and also articles for which she had no use. The facts elicited in the examination showed that she was first told about stealing in school by an older boy, John, when she moved to town at about the age of six. Another classmate, Sam, who had a bad reputation with girls, informed her about sex matters and had attempted to enter into sex relations with her. Further inquiry revealed that she stole because she was afraid of John, who threatened to get Sam after her if she refused to steal for him. She found it difficult to sleep at night because of thinking about her stealing and about what Sam would do to her. She was troubled by the words they used which would come into her thought at night. Another boy, who had used even worse sex words, had offered her money if she would go with him. In addition, a delinquent brother had once come to her bed, but her screams brought her father. She gave a vivid description of her endeavors to repress her sex thoughts and efforts to master the impulse to steal. After analyzing all the circumstances in the case, Healy's conclusion was "sex affairs and stealing were most intimately mixed in this girl's experiences and in her mental contents." [3]

Apparently, these two offenses, intimately connected by processes of emotional conditioning, were at the basis of her mental and moral conflicts. The filching indulged in probably had continued because of the sex conflict. Suggestions given to the mother and the teacher were not carried out, as neither felt able to tackle the problem.

As we have already seen, the victim of the inferiority complex often attempts to root out his feelings of frustration by some compensatory device, such as an exaggerated "will to power," a violent "masculine protest," and an exaggerated assumption of superiority which is not only fictitious but which may lead to the development of antisocial characteristics and ugly character traits, such as arrogance, braggadocio, vaingloriousness, impudence, contumaciousness, contempt for the rights of others, obstinacy, and defiance

[3] Quoted from William Healy, *Mental Conflicts and Misconduct*, 1928, 174*ff*., with the permission of Little, Brown & Company, Boston.

(see pages 289–294). Feelings of inferiority constitute a prolific source of the reaction-formation type of maladjustment already discussed. One of the worst forms of conceit is sometimes exhibited by those who blindly and ruthlessly seek security and recognition through some form of compensation for their thwarted ambitions. Who is not familiar with the coward who flatters himself that he has concealed his poltroonery by loud boasting, but who fades away the moment his bluff is called? Bravado and bluster frequently cannot be properly appraised unless they are understood to be a protective armor against timidity and shyness, a mechanism for hiding a detested defect (often some fear) by pretended superiority in the trait which the bluffer regards as the opposite, namely, courage. Who is not familiar with the office boy who can outstrut the manager and surpass him in ostentatiousness? Through such vaingloriousness he is striving more or less consciously to attain feelings of importance to compensate him for his lowly position.

When the feeling of inadequacy is incited by invidious comparisons with siblings or playmates, the compensation is likely to assume the form of detesting, belittling, misrepresenting others, or feeling jealous of them. The child thus aggrieved fancies that he can exalt himself and satisfy his craving for power and recognition by debasing others. The natural fruits of the hatred and jealousy feelings have been well expressed by the popular writer, Edgar A. Guest, in his poem, "He Gave Himself to Hate": [4]

> He gave himself to bitterness and hate
> And found, too late,
> Good judgment fled
> And pity dead.
> Malice and cruel wrath
> Laid waste his path.
>
> It pleased him once to think revenge is sweet,
> But time is fleet
> And hatred lingers long.
> Soon choice of right and wrong
> With what is best at stake
> His temper could not make.
>
> Who gives himself to hate himself destroys!
> For lacking poise
> In moments of great stress
> And reason's helpfulness
> He wrecks his own renown
> By trampling others down.

[4] Copyright, 1935, by Edgar A. Guest. From the Wilmington, Del., *Journal-Every Evening*.

In extreme cases the compensatory drive against mounting feelings of inadequacy may develop a pathological "Jehovah complex." Through the development of delusions of grandeur the victim has become convinced that he is a very commanding person, a great captain of industry, a great inventor or scientist, a mighty ruler, or perhaps the savior of mankind (see pages 291*f.*, 320*f.*, 369, and 372). These delusional trends are, of course, most fully developed in some of the psychoses, such as paresis, alcoholic psychosis, senile deterioration, cerebral degeneration, and paranoia.

The motivation of the delusional urges in many cases is the effort to conceal, or the determination not to admit, inferiority. It is essentially a device for attaining security by self-deception and denial of the facts of existence. When the patient undertakes to blame his parents or defective inheritance for his misfortunes, he may attempt to overcome his limitations or to compensate for them by laying claim to divine parentage or noble lineage.

When the compensations assume the form of persecutory delusions (see pages 320*f.*), the patient wants the reputed plotters apprehended and punished, less perhaps for the purpose of punishment than for personal vindication and proof that they have been plotting against him, trying to undermine him because of the jealousy and fear they harbor toward a commanding person of unblemished reputation. In the paranoiac, the victim par excellence of persecutory delusions, the persecutory ideas are so thoroughly organized and systematized as to be immune to logic or fact.

A type of excessive overcompensation in which the individual enters into frequent litigation with his supposed persecutors is referred to as litigious paranoia. Compensatory delusions, whether of grandeur or of persecution, as found in various mental disorders, represent the deepest pathological form of compensation, namely, compensatory mental disintegration. It must be admitted that the tendency of many compensations is toward the disorganization or disruption of the personality, largely, perhaps, because they are specious, faulty, or only partial solutions of the individual's difficulties. Persons who have resorted to faulty compensatory methods of solving their problems will probably evince exaggerated and bizarre forms of the same mechanisms should they become mentally diseased. In general, it is perhaps no exaggeration to affirm that all forms of compensation that are insufficient or excessive or that are of the nature of rationalizations, evasions, or delusions may become inimical to the maintenance of sound mental integrity and health and may eventually lead to serious mental discord or personality disruption. Even successful compensations frequently fail in crises, with the result that the victim will tend to revert to fear reactions. It is obvious, therefore, that the use of the method of compensation as a means of overcoming personal limitations, or as a protection against weaknesses, or as an escape from difficult issues, is attended by grave dangers, however valuable the mechanism may sometimes prove to be. This being the case, what can the parent and teacher do to counteract the evil influences of injurious compensations? This question will be discussed in the next chapter, in connection with the consideration of the prophylaxis and cure of hampering inferiority feelings, since the treatment of pernicious inferiority feelings and compensations is closely related.

The use of the method of compensation for constructive purposes will receive further treatment and amplification in Chap. XVI, on substitution and sublimation. Although elements of compensation exist in both of these mechanisms, they can function in the absence of any strong or recognizable compensatory urge. Some substitutive and sublimative activities are intensely compensatory; others are not.

CHAPTER XII

SUGGESTIONS FOR PREVENTING OR OVERCOMING HAMPERING INFERIORITY FEELINGS, COMPENSATORY MALADJUSTMENTS, STAGE FRIGHT, AND FEARS [1]

OVERCOMING INFERIORITY FEELINGS AND COMPENSATORY MALADJUSTMENTS

Although 14 suggestions follow in seriatim order, there is nothing sacred about this particular number. The number could have been reduced by combining some of the suggestions, or it might have been increased by further division. This comment, it is almost needless to say, applies to the preventive and remedial suggestions offered in connection with the maladjustments considered in other sections of the book.

It will doubtless become more and more obvious to the reader that much overlapping exists, not only between different remedial procedures but also between different kinds of maladjustments. This is a fortunate circumstance, from the point of view of treatment, at least: the same remedial and preventive suggestions will often prove to be equally applicable to different kinds of difficulties. While we can draw sharp distinctions in thought between different handicaps and different treatment techniques—indeed, it is desirable to do so from the standpoint of clarity and completeness of systematic exposition—nevertheless, the differences that exist in nature are less sharply drawn. Mental traits, normal as well as abnormal, merge into a complex, indissoluble, unitary tangle or gestalt of traits that can be isolated conceptually only by processes of abstraction. Many treatment techniques, therefore, will prove of value for a number of mental conditions.

As has been emphasized on earlier pages, problems in mental hygiene cannot always be solved merely by proffering advice or by offering a series of "do's" and "don't's." Offering suggestions and advice as to what the child or the parent or the teacher should or should not do may prove to be barren of any good results. To suggest or to adjure is one thing; to put the sug-

---

[1] Although this chapter might logically more properly follow Chap. XVII, it does not seem advisable for practical reasons to shunt to the end of the book a chapter dealing with practical mental-hygiene suggestions. Moreover, brief courses in mental hygiene may not allow time for the consideration of the material in Chaps. XIII to XVII, largely psychoanalytic in nature, or the instructor in certain courses may prefer to omit this material.

gestion across effectively is quite another thing. Moreover, information, exhortation, and advice do not always reach the root complex; they do not provide the kind of enlightenment and penetration afforded by the different kinds of "depth psychology" that are needed for the treatment of many neuroses, psychoneuroses, and serious personality or behavior disorders. Nevertheless, suggestion and advice have a place in the treatment of many minor mental ills and, in the program of prophylaxis, the first step always in any program of improvement is to know what to do. When this has been learned, the skill and knack of doing the job most economically and effectively must be acquired. The practical art of putting mental-hygiene suggestions into effect is, perhaps, best acquired through actual experience in adjusting personality difficulties in oneself and in others. Many of the suggestions offered, singly or in combination, will prove effective in many cases for preventive and therapeutic purposes.

1. It is pertinent to reemphasize at the outset that it is just as important in the treatment of these maladjustments as of any others that each child be considered a unique, complex personality to be fully studied and understood (see pages 109–112 and 154). Children react quite differently to the run-of-the-mine experiences of daily life. One may be depressed, another elated, by the same outward occurrence. The same happening may produce an inferiority complex in one child and a superiority complex in another. Therefore, our first job as parents, teachers, and examiners is to determine how each child reacts to our differing types of treatment and to adjust our methods accordingly.

In connection with the inferiority complex, our purpose should be to discover the attitudes that the child entertains toward himself—whether he undervalues or overvalues himself; whether he is of a sensitive, introverted, and shrinking type or of a carefree, nonchalant, extroverted disposition. In such a study we must depend primarily on the method of careful, discriminating observation of his behavior patterns, rather than on the method of interrogation, the interview, or the use of the so-called standardized personality tests, however valuable the latter approaches may be in certain cases.

Because of childish pride or for other reasons, children will try to evade, conceal, or misrepresent. We should particularly observe how the child attacks his problems, whether in a positive, decided, confident manner or haltingly, falteringly, or confusedly. Perhaps he stops altogether and shirks his job. Look for evidences of shirking, timidity, withdrawal, anxiety, diffidence, or brooding. Is the voice firm or wavering? Is the glance direct or shifting? Is the carriage erect and self-reliant or is the child always leaning on or against something to overcome his trepidation or unsteadiness or to bolster up his courage? The suggestive leads offered above are merely symptom indicators. Any particular act must always be interpreted in the light of the entire unity of the child's personality, of the genetic background, and of the whole objective situation; not as an isolated symptom or event. The child must always be considered as an organismic whole in relation to the total physical and social environment.

We must also view the child's problems from the child's point of view if we want to appraise correctly his behavior patterns. Especially important is it in this observational study to remember that the traits that the child exhibits may be a masquerade to conceal his real feelings. He may be displaying compensatory courage, nonchalance, blusterousness, arrogance, or extroversion in order to cover up his real cowardice and timidity. The observer must, therefore, always strive to pierce through the superficial or manifest traits to the underlying reality if he would avoid incompetent or blundering handling of problems of maladjustment. What is of primal importance for the child's wholesome development is not so much the objective situations or even his ability, important as these factors may be, but the attitude he assumes toward his experiences or the interpretation he gives them. This kind of individual study, we may repeat, requires penetrating psychological insight on the part of the teacher, parent, or investigator.

2. Prevent or overcome, as far as possible, physical inferiority and defectiveness. This possible cause of maladjustment and compensation can frequently be removed, to some extent at least, by adequate health education and hygienic living and by appropriate remedial and corrective treatment. If physical handicaps can be removed, the need for compensating for them will disappear, unless the habit of compensation has become thoroughly ingrained, in which case a follow-up program of reeducation will be required.

3. When physical defects prove to be irremediable, lead the child to realize that his handicap does not constitute an insurmountable barrier to achieving commendable success through worthy compensatory development in other directions in which he has interest and ability. Impress upon the child the truth of the statement that he "who best can suffer, best can do"; that a fine personality is frequently the happy outcome of the struggle to overcome handicaps; and that a defect may be a "blessing in disguise" through the challenge it may offer to the mastery motive and the stimulation it may arouse to vanquish it, which may raise the individual to higher levels of achievement. Make your presentation dynamic by citing an abundance of bona fide cases from different walks of life. The roll of the physically handicapped who have achieved distinction is a notable one. A partial list would include, in addition to the names listed on pages 283f., the following—among poets and writers: Alexander Pope, a hunchback and dwarf, who may have been a victim of Pott's disease; Aesop, a hunchback; Victor Hugo, a "limping cripple during his later years"; and Robert Louis Stevenson, a victim of tuberculosis. John Milton, who was blind; Elizabeth Barrett Browning,

who was for years confined to bed with a spinal affliction; and Walter Scott, who was crippled from youth by infantile paralysis—these became three of the great figures in English literature.

Prior to wearing a brace, Scott was moody and melancholic and shunned public places. Because of the fact that his lameness prevented him from winning popularity on the playground, and because he had to spend a large amount of time in the house, he attempted to compensate for his limitations, according to his frank admission, by developing an "indefatigable appetite for books" and formed a great admiration for the wonderful deeds recorded in the tales of knight-errantry, in the reading of which he obtained a vicarious satisfaction for experiences denied him on the reality plane. He spent much of the "winter play hours" relating tales to an "admiring audience" and thus became an "inexhaustible narrator" and a "prince of story tellers." He acquired social status through compensation.

The great musicians include Charles Gounod, who was "lame," and Wolfgang Mozart and Edward Grieg, both deformed. Among noted religious leaders were the Apostle Paul, perhaps a hunchback; Pope John XXII, "a growth cripple"; and Blessed Bernadette, a "deformed cripple." Speech imperfections of one kind or another have been reported among such prominent persons as Virgil, Aristotle, Napoleon (an undersized military genius), Moses (who was "slow of speech and of slow tongue"), and King George VI of England.

When King George VI was still Duke of York his life was made "miserable because when he had to make a speech, no matter how short, he stammered and stuttered." For years he "dodged speech-making and avoided meeting people because of his stutter," to which one writer attributes the "subdued nature which was evident in his earlier years." Expert treatment has enabled him to overcome the handicap in large measure, but radio listeners have noticed that he "reads slowly and hesitatingly. . . . Frequent pauses, some of ten seconds' duration, break the sentences." "Through carefully selecting words containing letters easy for him to articulate," and "having near him an expert to check his speed if necessary," he is able to short-circuit his handicap to a considerable extent.

Some outstanding military figures are Alexander the Great, the greatest warrior of his day, who had a "distorted and deformed neck"; Julius Caesar, brilliant soldier and statesman, who is believed to have suffered from some kind of epilepsy; Frederick, Prince of Hamburg, who continued his career as a fighter even after he had lost a leg in battle; and Lord Nelson, who, called back into service after he had lost an eye and a leg, led the British Navy to victory. Inventors of prominence include Elias Howe, inventor of the sewing machine, who was crippled; Charles Steinmetz, the electrical wizard, who was a deformed hunchback; and Thomas A. Edison, an inventive genius of extraordinary productiveness, who had very imperfect hearing.

These illustrations [2] and many others that could be adduced lend much support for the apparently extravagant declaration of Lord Tweedsmuir (formerly Canadian Governor General) that "very few of the great figures of history were healthy and normal people . . . most of these famous figures did their work under grave physical handicaps for which there was no medical relief." Although it is not easy to determine how much a handicap had to do with their attaining eminence, to convince a child that physical defects are not a bar to the highest success by recitals of the accomplishments of handicapped persons who have won universal acclaim (because of the compensatory drive, in many cases) will often produce an almost complete transformation of his outlook on life. Four further suggestions may prove helpful in the attempt to realize this aim.

a. Teach the child to become reconciled to his handicap, to accept inevitable defeats, and to become a "good loser" in the field he enters with a handicap. Lead him to appreciate the fact that there may be many other fields in which he can win success, and that the success he can reach in such fields by dint of study and application may be just as great and worthy. The acceptance of this philosophy should serve to prevent the child from becoming mentally crippled by the feeling that he has been forced by ruthless circumstances to select an inferior outlet for his ambitions. The child should realize that the essential, creditable work of the world is so multitudinous and varied as to supply desirable outlets for people with all kinds of mental and physical abilities and disabilities.

b. Careful guidance must be provided so that the child does not select a substitute in which he lacks ability and thus becomes foredoomed to eventual failure. Such a form of compensation will deepen his sense of inadequacy and discontent, instead of reestablishing his self-confidence. We must keep constantly in mind the fact that the child's strivings must be suited to his type of defect. The organ that must bear the burden of compensation necessarily cannot be the same for the auditorially handicapped as for the visually or orthopedically handicapped. Visually handicapped children can render efficient service in certain vocations where auditorially handicapped individuals with the best training would be foreordained to failure. A blind boy would not make a satisfactory messenger or delivery boy; but a deaf boy would not be seriously handicapped in that type of work.

The reader may feel that danger exists in overstressing this point, for did not the deaf Ludwig van Beethoven compose music and lead orchestras, in

---

[2] For further data on some of these, see Bernard J. Ficarra, "Famous Cripples of the Past," *The Crippled Child,* 1943, 86–89.

spite of his deafness? True, but he manifested his love of music when he was a hearing child of only 4 years and he acquired his musical technique while he was able to hear. Had he become deaf before he received any musical training, the story might have been quite different. He did not grow deaf until he was about 44 and he doubtless retained full use of his accumulated auditory musical imagery. Without his storehouse of imagery he could not have continued to compose the symphonies, concertos, overtures, and sonatas that we cherish today.

c. The child must be wisely guided so that he does not become a victim of the evils of overcompensation or of misdirected, destructive, or deceptive compensations. It is important that he understand that compensatory devices should be a means for solving his problems in a frank, straightforward, effective manner, and should not be bluffs by means of which to fool people or deceive himself. He should not seek to evade his obligations and enjoy a satisfaction based upon futile, imaginary victories, which in the end will prove to be deceptive or fallacious.

d. These warnings apply equally to compensatory strivings against socially produced feelings of incompetency.

It is apparent that successful adjustment of the permanently physically handicapped requires skilled educational guidance and psychological insight. Outlets exist galore for these unfortunates, provided they have been efficiently educated or trained.

4. Correct undesirable compensations as early as possible before they have become fixed by repetition. That many compensations are undesirable has already been emphasized. The superiority strivings aroused by inferiority feelings only too readily become misdirected into injurious excesses, over-compensations, or behavior disorders. Sometimes the crippling mental disfigurements produced may get worse and worse with the passage of time.

The preventive implications of this recommendation should not be lost sight of. People who have remained free of injurious compensation complexes during their normal life do not ordinarily manifest delusional compensation as a prominent characteristic if they suffer the misfortune of developing a mental disorder. Manifestly, the ideal course is to remove by positive measures the necessity for developing any undesirable compensations. Many of the suggestions that follow possess prophylactic virtues.

5. Begin in early life to increase the diffident child's confidence in his ability and courage to meet the issues of life. Mental growth and development proceed normally when the child is able to look joyfully and hopefully upon the future. A confident, optimistic, positive attitude tends to remove self-imposed inhibitions and to free the springs of energy for constructive achievement. Therefore, lead children to believe that they can successfully achieve and become gradually more and more independent and self-reliant

by dint of application, perseverance, and courage. Even if the child should become overconfident by such conditioning, overconfidence is preferable to underconfidence. The following suggestion also possesses practical value for the realization of this objective.

6. Be generous in the bestowal of appreciation and encouragement for good efforts and intentions. Children thrive on appreciation and encouragement. If they are encouraged to have faith in themselves and to believe that they can do worth-while things, many will respond. As Emerson expressed it, "self-trust is the first secret of success." Offering appreciative encouragement is one of the sacred obligations of all teachers and parents. What children primarily need when their handicaps are merely apparent, as is frequently the case, is encouragement and the opportunity of regaining their shattered confidence.

Dale Carnegie's recital of straight-standing Lloyd C. Stark's method of overcoming round shoulders in his two daughters, aged 6½ and 5, furnishes an apt illustration. The former governor of Missouri, a graduate of Annapolis and an officer in the Navy and the Army for 10 years, could not tolerate round shoulders in his young daughters. Calling attention to their poor posture only once, "he made them want to stand straight . . . by giving them praise instead of criticism. When he saw them standing round shouldered, he would appear not to notice it. Looking in the other direction he would say, 'Come here, girls, and let me see how you are standing.' Naturally, by the time they got to his chair, they would be standing as straight as an Admiral; and he would praise them lavishly," instead of nagging and scolding them. He did this day after day until they had acquired an erect posture.

7. Provide children with abundant outlets for joyous, successful achievement in approved activities and pursuits. Compliance with this recommendation is one of the most important factors in the development of a healthy morale. Ordinarily a wholesome morale is the natural product of confidence born of success. Success inspires a tone of optimism and determination that constitutes the best guarantee of further success. Success makes for mental integration, while failure implants feelings of inferiority, dissatisfaction, and discontent that make for eventual disintegration. So it is appropriate to emphasize the success psychology, not only as a solvent of the inferiority complex, but as an educational principle of the broadest application. Although the attitude of confidence is an essential condition of success and although this attitude can be most quickly and firmly engendered by supplying opportunities for successful achievement, it is well to emphasize the reservation that success will not prove to be a valuable stimulus to mental growth and integration from the mental-hygiene point of view unless it is genuine, attainable success. If the tasks are pitched beyond the child's capacities and

require too much effort, the result may be a feeling of despair, inaction, and further self-depreciation, instead of a feeling of success. On the other hand, if the success comes too easily, it may lead to overappreciation, vanity, arrogance, and the conceit of knowledge. Therefore, our aim should be so to adjust the child's work that it will require him to work at a healthy tension but without undue strain, hustle, or worry, in order to avoid the growth of discouragement on the one hand and the development of conceit on the other hand. To steer a safe course between the Scylla of excessively difficult assignments and the Charybdis of excessively easy tasks represents the golden mean of the mental hygienist.

8. Direct the child's strivings into fruitful, worth-while, socially approved channels. Success in socially approved activities is an effective way of winning recognition. Social recognition, *i.e.*, recognition by others, is what the diffident child often needs to overcome his inferiority feelings. The removal of this source of undesirable compensations will conduce to mental contentment and health.

For evaluating the child's strivings, the following criterion may be suggested. Will they prove beneficial to society as well as to the child himself? Egoistic considerations cannot be accepted as the sole justification for the child's choices. The bearing of his activities upon communal life is another almost equally important consideration, in view of the fact that the child must live in society. The child should be so trained that he will become not only personally competent, but also socially minded, friendly, tolerant, cooperative, and free from envy or the urge to surpass others by degrading them or by dominating them. Successful socialization possesses distinct virtues from the mental-hygiene point of view. Social-mindedness, as emphasized in Chap. I, is a good barometer of mental normality. It is also a good antidote against inferiority feelings.

9. Encourage the child to tackle all his problems in a frank, unbiased, and courageous manner, and also to be fearless in criticism of himself. However, it is equally important to stress the point that his attitude toward himself must be fair and objective, so that he will not become hypercritical toward his shortcomings or demand a higher degree of perfection of himself than of anybody else. The cultivation of an attitude toward oneself that is excessively critical may stimulate the development of pathological compensatory self-accusation or self-condemnation, such as appears in certain forms of mental disorder (*e.g.*, melancholia). All of us need accurate insight into our own limitations, but we must avoid the dangerous pitfall of becoming overconscientious regarding trifles. It is important, therefore, that children be so guided in childhood that they will not get into the habit of "picking on themselves" and attaching moral culpability to innocent acts or feelings of incompetency. As W. S. Sadler has emphasized, conscience may well be left

to the domain of morals. The frank, straightforward child who is not bur-
dened by unjustified feelings of guilt concerning peccadilloes is not so likely
to become a victim of unhealthy compensations. (The guilt complex will
be referred to again on later pages.)

10. Do not let failure operate as a deterrent or an inhibitor of further
action, but use it rather as a stimulant to redoubled and renewed effort. Show
the child by examples and otherwise that mistakes need not become a barrier
to success but may be steppingstones to victory, and, that mistakes, in point
of fact, render education possible. If the child did not commit errors, there
would be nothing to improve. Growth and advancement presuppose limitations and shortcomings to be removed and to be replaced by more efficient
response patterns. If the child accepts this attitude, failure need not work
the devastating havoc that so frequently follows in its train. Instead, it
may become an incentive to mastery.

The illustrations of persons who have become outstanding in spite of serious
physical handicaps (pages *283f.* and *400f.*) and scholastic failures (pages
204–205) may be supplemented by the stirring examples of businessmen
whose early failures did not "get them down," but rather served as spurs
to renewed determination to succeed. David Margesson, whose mother is a
sister of the Earl of Buckinghamshire, once tramped the streets of Chicago
looking for work. "Sacked" in less than a month from his first job as a clerk
in a department store, he found another opening as stocking salesman in
Marshall Field's, a job usually handled by girls. He made good on other
jobs and in time rose to the position of head of the land force of the British
war effort in England in the late war.

Fred Harvey, another Englishman, was fired after a week from his first
job as a dishwasher in a Chicago restaurant because the manager did not
like the way he washed the dishes. He got another job and later went to
Topeka, Kan., where he launched his first restaurant in an upstairs room.
The Fred Harvey system now includes about 20 hotels and 66 restaurants.
Harvey relates that the loss of his first job aroused in him the ambition to
make good.

Milton Hershey, who gave the country its first chocolate bar, failed twice
before he "struck pay dirt." He was dismissed from his first job as a printer's
devil for incompetence, and his pushcart caramel business in Philadelphia
also came to an early end when a streetcar demolished his cart and stock.
In 1886 he "clicked" in Lancaster, Pa., in the manufacture of caramel.
After 15 years he disposed of his equity for a million dollars. Later, he
determined to give the world plenty of chocolate from his "factory in a
cornfield," "not for the money but for the satisfaction of doing something
interesting." Before he died, in October, 1945, he had created his "dream
town," Hershey, Pa., with its junior college, palatial hotel, luxurious theater,

museum, spacious parks, amusement center, model factory, and big-league hockey; besides a model town in Cuba—all at a cost of $60,000,000 or more.

Frank W. Woolworth, originator of the five-and-ten-cent stores, left his farm home for the first time in his life at 19 for Watertown, N.Y., looking for any kind of job in salesmanship. He canvassed every store, but no merchant would employ an inexperienced, gawky bumpkin. Determined to learn the business of selling, he persisted in his efforts until he learned of a freight agent who ran a grocery store on the side and closed whenever shipments required his attention at the station. The merchant said that he could not afford "one cent of pay," but that the youth might sleep in the rear of the store and help himself to cheese and crackers. So young Woolworth took the job without pay, for the privilege of learning the business in the school of hard knocks. After 4 years of experience and studying merchandising, he got the idea, at 23, of starting a "five-cent store." His first store was a miserable failure; the second one, launched with the aid of a backer, and the third and the fourth stores also failed. Undismayed by repeated failures, Woolworth was determined to put his big dream across and started a fifth store, which "struck fire." The subsequent record of his "five-and-ten" contributes one of the most dramatic chapters in the history of modern retail merchandising. When Woolworth died, in 1919, the corporation of which he was president controlled a chain of 1,000 five-and-ten-cent stores in Canada and the United States and 75 in Great Britain, besides the Woolworth Building in New York City, which, at the time of its erection, was the tallest building in the world (792 feet). The lesson of Woolworth to the easy quitter is the potency of a dynamic, irrepressible idea (motive) to overcome obstacles in the path of progress.

The tenth suggestion applies with peculiar pertinency to the timid child, who is all too prone to regard failure as a confirmation of his incapacity and as justification for his discouragement, instead of as something that should be hopefully attacked in the light of a new problem to be solved.

The attitude to be inculcated toward failure is well expressed in Edgar A. Guest's little poem of optimism entitled "If in the End." [3]

> If in the end all things prove well,
>   What matter failures here and there,
>   Or hours of anguish and despair,
> Or the rough ground on which we fell?
> If out of trial's darkening spell
>   We come at last to sunsets fair
>   And find the peace which follows care,
> We'll have adventurous tales to tell.

[3] Copyright, 1935, by Edgar A. Guest. From the Wilmington, Del., *Journal-Every Evening*.

'Tis this which adds to life its zest:
The future's an unwritten book,
And into it 'tis vain to look,
One never knows what's worst or best,
Upon our cares we'll proudly dwell,
If in the end all things prove well.

A few detailed suggestions may prove valuable to the teacher in her efforts to overcome the child's failures.

a. The first suggestion is to provide substitute activities in which the child can achieve success. The best way to reestablish the child's shattered morale from failure is to give him a taste of success in some activity in which he is interested and can achieve gratifying results without painful effort. The fruits of victory usually supply the best incentives to renewed effort. Essential for the carrying out of this suggestion in school is the establishment of multilateral courses to meet the needs of children with special physical or mental abilities or disabilities. While it is important to attempt to overcome scholastic deficiencies through remedial instruction, it is equally important to recognize that, if the child is required to spend most of his time trying to overcome ineradicable defects, he may fail to develop his special talents. The development of special talents usually gives the keenest sense of successful accomplishment. We must, therefore, not stake the child's future on the persistent attempt to develop superiority in his weakest traits, thereby neglecting the development of his special talents. Moreover, the persistent attempt to overcome an incurable handicap may intensify the child's consciousness of his disability and inferiority, and may result either in bitter disappointment and acute anxiety or in a degree of compensatory overconfidence in his capacities that is not justified by the facts. (For a further discussion of the values of the success incentive, see pages 322, 355*f.*, and 374*f.*)

b. Recognize and commend the child's success in other worth-while lines of endeavor. This may entice him to put forth effort to achieve success in activities in which he is more competent.

c. Do not predict failure for those who have blundered or lost their prestige or strayed from approved modes of conduct. Such treatment will merely tend to confirm their conviction of worthlessness and cowardice and cause them to become more apathetic, to withdraw further within themselves, and to develop ineffective compensations or behavior disorders. Therefore, inspire children with the hope of ultimate success, even though this might sometimes result in making them too self-confident and give them an exaggerated idea of their ability. We cannot be sure of children's real ability until we have built up their self-confidence, courage, and industry to a certain point. Frequently we cannot be sure that a given child is genuinely deficient, either specifically or generically, until he has made a genuine, resolute attempt to overcome his handicap.

11. As a corollary of the point just emphasized, encourage the child to make decisions, to assume responsibilities, and to obtain some experience of the meaning of authority. If the child is deprived of the opportunity to assume responsibility and to develop the feeling of authority that should go with it, his sense of weakness, indecision, and inadequacy will become further fixed and deepened. Perhaps the sovereign remedy for the state of indecision is to make decisions and then actually carry them into action. Therefore, provide challenging opportunities that will evoke thought, stimulate action, compel decision, and induce children to engage in activities that will make them plan, decide, and carry their share of responsibility. Interest them in participating in games, athletics, social and literary activities, class projects, socialized recitation programs—in fact, any kind of activity that demands decision and activity.

In this connection, it is important to determine whether the child's timidities, inferiority feelings, and compensations may have been produced by excessive overprotection or excessive sympathy in the home or in the school. Undue sympathy, like oversheltering, fosters the tendency to withdraw within oneself, to magnify one's misfortunes, and to let others solve one's problems. Sympathetic encouragement will prove more beneficial to the diffident child than voluble expressions of sympathy.

Important as it is to develop a sense of responsibility and authority, it is also important that the exercise of authority be regulated. We should recognize that, although deprivation of all opportunity to exercise authority leads to indecision, excessive submission, inaction, and resultant introversion, the excessive or unbridled exercise of authority is equally undesirable, in that it may tend to make the individual dictatorial, overbearing, and despotic. Having thus developed an overweening superiority complex, such persons soon become unpopular with everybody except fawning sycophants, the masochistically inclined, or weaklings who cannot stand on their own feet.

The state of indecision may, of course, be a case of chronic fatigue, brain fag, or ill-health, or a definite nervous or mental malady that requires expert physical or psychotherapeutic treatment. For example, the child's diffidence and indecision may be due to an anxiety neurosis, definite or vague as the case may be. This affliction is characterized by vague feelings of uneasiness and dread or morbid anxieties, particularly about the results of committing mistakes; feelings of indecision, sometimes amounting to a paralysis of doubt; feelings of impending doom; nervous strain and tension, shown in a drawn facial expression and muscular tenseness; nervous and emotional irritability; feelings of insecurity and inadequacy, with resultant attitudes of suspiciousness; inability to concentrate; withdrawal from social contacts; and lack of ambition.

There can be little question that the school situation is definitely responsible for the development of many cases of anxiety neurosis through overlong and overdifficult assignments; the competitive system; the systems of merits and demerits, failures, sharp rebuffs, and criticism; sarcasm of the instructors; and exaggerated emphasis upon mere scholastic excellence rather than upon the prevention of personality disorders and the development of balanced, harmonious personalities. With all the good that the schools have accomplished through their deification of scholastic perfection and insistence upon scholastic conformity, unfortunately many of them, particularly the high schools and colleges—especially the colleges—have also inflicted irreparable damage on the most priceless thing in human nature, the wholesome development of personality. Be that as it may, the mental conflicts at the basis of cases of morbid anxiety and anxiety neurosis require judicious investigation and treatment by experts in mental hygiene, clinical psychologists, and psychiatrists. Cases of this kind are more frequent among older adolescents and adults than among young children.

12. As an antidote for the inferiority feelings engendered by competitive situations, for individual rivalry substitute group competition on a cooperative basis. The zest of active cooperation with a hustling, determined group may, through the force of example or psychic contagion, serve to mitigate or cure the self-distrust, hesitancy, and fickleness engendered by individual contest.

13. So far as possible, remove the social causes of the feelings of frustration and inadequacy, which may lead to unwholesome compensations. It may be an exaggeration to affirm, as has been done, that every compensation spells faulty education and training, but there can be little doubt that many, if not most, minor mental maladjustments and feelings of inferiority and dissatisfaction are socially produced by unwise or severe social treatment of the kind to which reference has already been made: frequent, captious, or severe criticism; insulting rebukes; sarcastic snubbings; ridicule; depreciation; unjust punishment or repressive discipline; magnification of defects; arousal of fears of failure or other fears or anxieties; and implantation of an acute and unjustified consciousness of guilt or unworthiness. The obvious remedy, namely, to refrain from unnecessarily severe or frequent employment of any of these forms of correction or castigation, may be expressed in two important "don'ts":

a. Do not resort to excessive or stern measures as a means of frightening the child into conformity or into effort. Children who have been treated with undue harshness tend to develop antisocial compensations because of their resentment, and they may become hard, embittered, jealous, spiteful, and malevolent. Often unable to bear seeing other children happy, they may become envious of them, try to vent their hatred upon them, and, figuratively speaking, attempt to poison their lives. They thus seek to compensate for their own unhappiness or shortcomings by oppressing other children, usually weaker ones. Not infrequently child cruelty is merely an attempt to compensate for animosities and jealousies ultimately traceable to personal handicaps and frustrations unwisely treated by the caretaker. The insight of Pliny, of old, into the psychology of envy is in line with modern hygiene thought: "Envy always implies conscious inferiority wherever it resides."

To be sure, there may be occasional justification for expression of sharp reproof or for the application of stern measures, but the chief reliance always must be placed on the establishment of friendly, sympathetic, understanding relationships with the distrustful, misguided, or errant child.

b. Make little use of the processes of humiliation, ridicule, or sarcasm as incitements to effort. The shaming technique may perhaps spur a few to greater effort and achievement (see pages 284*f.*). But its common results are to quench good will, to deepen the feeling of worthlessness and cowardice, and to arouse resentment and hatred, in consequence of which the child may become suspicious, jealous toward those who are praised, combative, hostile, and ambitious to surpass others by degrading them. He will sometimes attempt to bolster up his prestige by resort to mischievous tricks. The most infamous form of brutalizing technique, perhaps, is sarcasm. Few attitudes are more effective in creating feelings of degradation and rankling hatred. The resort to sarcasm by teachers is peculiarly unsportsmanlike and reprehensive, because the child, being subordinate, is in no position to defend himself. Moreover, the sarcastic tongue is frequently merely a cover for the teacher's lack of knowledge or of understanding, or a compensatory defense against his own irritations and maladjustments, although he may be only vaguely conscious of this fact. Ernest H. Wilkins, in condemning the use of sarcasm, has fittingly referred to it as a species of "spiritual brutality," equivalent to adult hazing.

14. *Let adults set good examples to the childhood of the nation.* It is important to emphasize this suggestion because of the enormous vogue of the compensatory drive among modern adults, and because of the probability that the majority of children's compensatory reactions have been imitatively absorbed from the society of adults in which they live and move and have their beings. Manifestly, the child cannot be held personally accountable for all his faults and foibles, although he is, no doubt, responsible for some of them. Born into an enormously complicated social structure, which is highly maladjusted and from which he cannot extricate himself, the child must, inevitably, become to a large extent merely a reflection of the social customs

and habit patterns of his surroundings. He is usually more to be pitied than condemned. We may, therefore, conclude by emphasizing another precept:

Let adults deal with the problems of children candidly and undogmatically, and stop resorting to compensatory arrogance, defiance, sophistication, evasion, double-dealing, and excessive severity. In child rearing, the factor of chief importance from the mental-hygiene point of view is the way adults behave and the way they react emotionally to their own adjustment problems, rather than what they believe, think, or profess.

OVERCOMING STAGE FRIGHT AND OTHER FORMS OF FEAR

Stage fright and fears have been discussed in various parts of the book and much of the advice already proffered in connection with other problems possesses remedial and curative value for these annoyances.[4] It seems desirable, however, to bring together in one place sundry suggestions bearing directly on the overcoming of the fear of appearing before audiences. Much of the advice here given will apply in varying degree to other fears and timidities. There is, as will be apparent, considerable overlapping among the eight suggestions that follow:

1. Assume an attitude and demeanor of confidence. Walk to the rostrum in a self-possessed, self-controlled, confident, and buoyant manner. Stand erect and avoid a weak, cringing posture. The right kind of carriage will produce desirable action currents from the neuromuscular system and will supply the needed bodily reenforcement to bolster up the speaking morale. If the nerves are very frayed and shaky, the necessary somatic reenforcement may be secured by assuming an erect, energetic, well-poised carriage, by stiffening the muscles, and by getting the diaphragm and chest muscles under control. Energetic innervation of the musculature to counteract shaky knees, trembling hands, fluttering diaphragm, and heaving chest walls often yields the organic bracing required for voluntary control. However, when the muscles are too tense, better results sometimes accrue from efforts to relax the muscles or from actually assuming an appearance of ease and self-control free from any intimation of nervousness. Resort to gesturing and walking about may exert an adjuvant influence in a limited number of cases and may prove disturbing in other cases. To start speaking in a confident, self-possessed manner, or even merely vocalizing, will prove helpful in many cases. In the words of one of my students, "Just about the time I am to present my part of a program, I have a feeling of nausea and trembling of hands and knees. Though thoroughly prepared, I never know just what my opening sentence will be nor have I any idea of how my voice will sound. The sound of my voice, however, always reassures me and carries me through."

---

[4] The brief references made again to these problems in subsequent chapters are incidental to the discussion of psychoanalysis.

A high-school teacher of speech in commenting on this section in her term paper makes the following suggestion:

One of the best methods of overcoming stage fright is for the speaker or performer upon his entrance on the stage to stand for a moment before his audience and get his "bearings." Before saying a word, he should take a deep breath and "size up his audience." Amazingly enough, when he begins to speak his stage fright is gone. This method has proved effective in public speaking with me, with fellow students, and especially with my own pupils, and also in musical recitals. I know of a case in which a scared performer lost all stage fright and played with the utmost ease after that initial moment of halt or delay.

The embodiment of an assured, winning air and posture often aids in casting out fear, and stage fright is merely one form of fear. The appearance of success is one of the best antidotes for fear, which is largely an escape reaction. It is a mechanism by means of which we strive to avoid what we do not think we are able to cope with. It is a means of getting away from situations that appear dangerous because, owing to our feeling of insecurity, we do not think that we are prepared to handle them. Innumerable stimuli and situations may serve as exciting causes of fears, such as noises and lack of support, apparently the two inherited causes; violent changes; the sense of insecurity or anxiety; feared responsibilities, the necessity of doing things, threatened or actual loss of a job, or failure; oncoming tests and examinations; the awareness of physical defects or diseases; loss of articles; the realization of one's violation of the conventions or taboos of society; criticism or blame; natural phenomena; animals; parents, teachers, strangers, people in general under certain situations, such as the audience situation; the unknown; the giving up of cherished beliefs or traditions in spite of the fact that they may be based on fallacies, prejudices, or superstitions; and the like. The large preponderance of these fear-producing stimuli are subjective. In all such situations an attitude, demeanor, and carriage of confidence and success will often help to overcome the feelings of doubt, insecurity, timidity, and inadequacy for the task.

2. Since stage fright is a form of fear, as has already been emphasized, remedies should be tried that have proved useful in overcoming other forms of fear. One of the most generally applicable and useful suggestions is actually to face the fear-producing situation and do something in relation to the feared activity itself. A direct, drastic, frontal attack upon the fear-inspiring situation itself is apt to prove far more effective than a flank attack or an attack on the fear emotion. Thus, if the youthful tyro in roller skating has become timid and reluctant to continue his practice because of suffering a hurt in a spill, the best form of cure is to induce him to face at once the disagreeable situation itself by proceeding to practice guardedly, observing

how the more successful ones go about it, getting more and more interested in the objective situation itself, and thus forgetting all about the fall. Often when the child has acquired a fear of a dog because he has been bitten by it, the best method of cure is to get him to learn to know the dogs by direct contact, by doing something to them, such as feeding them, taking them out on walks and rabbit chases, and putting them in the kennel at night. Getting better acquainted with dogs and learning to know their habits and characteristics may cast out the fear of dogs. If the child has been thrown by a horse, instead of trying to force him to "down" his fear of horses, the better plan usually is to bring him into successful contact with horses. Let him lead them, water them, curry them, feed them, and ride them again under proper safeguards.

On the other hand, merely to resolve to be courageous often proves ineffective. Fighting the fear itself may not only prove futile, but it often invites failure. Fears often evaporate when the fear-producing situation is directly faced, fought outright, and subjugated. This is especially so if the problem is attacked before the fear is confirmed. The time for a successful forthright attack is in the incipient stages. According to current reports, when an army aviator suffers a forced landing because of some mishap, he is required to take off at once again, unless he has been injured.

Illustrations of the Vanquishing of Fear-producing Situations by Boldly Facing Them. Illustrations have already been given of the success that has crowned the practice of directly and courageously facing the disagreeable situations themselves, such as overcoming the fear of swimming (page 82), the fear of a dead father (page 129), the fear of ghosts (page 133), morbidity from deafness (page 182), and a horror of corpses (page 526). The following case report is apropos. It is a graphic portrayal of audience fear, which the victim has largely succeeded in overcoming by methods he fails to describe, but it can be inferred from other parts of his inventory that he repeatedly faced the disagreeable situation itself. He offers various suggestions of value for overcoming stage fright.

HOW STAGE FRIGHT AFFECTED ONE PERSON; METHODS OF CURE

For a long time I was afraid to speak in public, and that fear has not entirely disappeared. I am told that with our best platform speakers stage fright comes and goes. I felt my legs would not carry me to the platform. I imagined every eye was upon me, that everyone knew my subject matter better than I, and that, if I should forget something, my auditors would know it. I was tempted to repeat when I forgot portions of my talks, and this added to the fright. After I had received some instruction in gesturing, a new worry came into existence. I was always trying to give just the right gesture. The appearance of a former teacher or someone whom I deemed well informed in the audience was almost fatal to me. The appearance of my critic teacher was the greatest bugbear of all. The pronouncing of words disconcerted me. I would recall that a certain word pronounced one way was correct; and another way, incorrect. I would debate between the two ways and forget my lines. I would finally pronounce the word both ways to make myself sure. This illustrates the fallacy of teaching things by contrast— one way proper and another improper.

The position of my feet and hands gave me no little annoyance. Instead of moving about, I would stand riveted to one single spot. My circulation would fail me and my head would become dizzy. My hands gave me more worry than anything else. They appeared so large, and just how to place them was a problem. Should I put them in my pockets, fold them in front or back of my body, or let them hang, were the queries flitting through my mind. The perspiration on my brow bothered me. My major motive was not to get the thought over in a presentable manner, but to get through the ordeal and scamper back to my seat. In my first discussion talks I used no organized manner of presentation of the subject matter, and my discussions were very scattering. This was largely due to fright. From many of these stage inhibitions I have now fairly well extricated myself.

The cures for stage fright are, in general, confidence in oneself; much more talking in public, before less critical audiences at first, and then before more critical ones; and then grounding oneself well in the subject matter and organizing the same around large topics. Much of the lack of confidence in a speaker comes from overcriticism of parents, teachers, and classmates. Many a prospective speaker is ruined through the inhibitions resulting from criticism. The technique of criticism is begun before the novice has learned to express himself. Just how to give criticism that does not inhibit independent, free expression is the art in coaching public speaking. We should encourage pupils in all our schoolwork to do and say things, and not inhibit their expression with too much criticism. Suggestions like the following tend to develop confidence in young speakers:

"Do not be afraid."

"No one knows the subject matter save you."

"Do not repeat, the audience will not know you have forgotten."

"Take time and do not be in a hurry."

"Try to be just as natural as possible."

[The writer offers many other suggestions of value for young speakers which cannot be reproduced here.]   (M.M.L.; M.; S. Supt.; Ph.B.; Age 55)

One way, then, of overcoming stage fright is to speak or perform before audiences whenever it is possible to do so (see page 472). One must not rely merely on the resolution not to be embarrassed or afraid, but must actually "face the music." The virtues of this mode of attack are due partly to the success morale which it instills, which will prove directly curative, and partly to the effects of repeated experiences with the fear-producing situation. Since repetition of stimuli ordinarily exerts a dulling effect upon the emotions, repeated facing of the distasteful situation will produce rapid or eventual immunity to many fears.

3. As a corollary of the first suggestion, prepare your talk thoroughly before you appear before the audience. Nothing will so brace, steady, and fortify the performer as the assurance that comes from having mastered the task, whether it is a vocal solo, an instrumental rendition, a recitation, a speech, or participation in a debate. The assurance that you possess the necessary knowledge and skill or technique to "do your bit" will often dispel timidity and lack of self-confidence.

Therefore, to gain proficiency in one's task and the morale that this will engender, one should prepare well. If the speech is to be memorized, write it out in detail and recite it by the method of recall. Or prepare a good outline and get this outline thoroughly fixed in memory. It would frequently be found advantageous to practice aloud before an imaginary audience, vividly imagining the audience while rehearsing. Some will find it advantageous to practice before a mirror. Rehearsals before a small audience of sympathetic and appreciative friends will in some cases be found an excellent method of overcoming the initial shyness and reluctance and of bolstering up self-confidence. . This expedient is in harmony with the suggestion that fears can be overcome by gradually introducing the feared object in an agreeable situation. To illustrate, J. B. Watson, after having produced a conditioned fear of a rabbit in an infant by producing a sudden loud noise every time the child attempted to touch the animal, later overcame the fear by another process of conditioning. While the child partook of a tasty dessert, the rabbit was permitted to appear at a safe distance as a minor element in an agreeable situation. By thus repeatedly introducing the rabbit as a component of a relished situation, the animal situation acquired the same emotional tone, and the child overcame his fear of the pet.

4. Become thoroughly immersed in your task while you are delivering your message or rendering your selection. Become objective minded by keeping attention steadily riveted on what you are going to say or do. The performer will approach the ideal situation when he becomes oblivious of his body, when he is able to keep attention off the shaking knees, trembling hands, palpitating heart, heaving chest, unsteady nerves, or obtruding nose. If the performer can get thoroughly absorbed in the execution of his task, instead of keeping his attention on his body or on his fright or fears, he will be on the road to mastery. Some persons are definitely helped by holding some object, a book, a roll of paper, a pad of notes, or a pointer, as a means of objectifying attention. As one of my students remarked, "I have found that if I can have something in my hands with which to demonstrate my talk I do not have any difficulty."

It may prove to be of value to some persons to develop a vital curiosity about the fear-producing situation itself. It is, however, imperative for the success of such advice, as has already been emphasized, that the problem be studied objectively and that attention be kept away from the fear reaction itself.

It may prove helpful in the accomplishment of this objective to get absorbed in the audience and to stop thinking about oneself. There are many things in the audience situation to challenge one's interest, such as the panorama of intriguing faces, some attractive, others homely, some alert, some dull, some attentive, others inattentive; the apparel worn by the auditors; the furniture and decorations in the auditorium; and other details. At the zero hour, as the performer is about to appear before the audience, it is particularly important that he should keep engrossed with other things than with thoughts about himself.

5. The victim of stage fright should assume the right attitude from the start toward his assignment to appear before an audience. The task should be regarded not as a cruel misfortune, a hated commission, or a dire penalty, but as a privilege, a natural and wholesome means of self-expression and self-realization, an opportunity of giving something of himself to others, a prized means of rendering service to the social group. It should be looked upon, not only as a valuable means of mental growth for the performer, but also as a superior method of winning desired recognition or approbation.

The performer's morale will be greatly strengthened if he will assume the attitude that he is going to face a sympathetic, interested, and appreciative audience rather than an inattentive, critical, or cynical one. To make such a heartening assumption, even erroneously, will constitute a better preparation than to assume that one is going before a hostile, carping group. To establish rapport with the audience through preliminary fostering of the right attitude of mind is just as important for the speaker as it is for the psychological tester to get *en rapport* with the child to be tested. To establish rapport with the case is the first requisite for any psychological examiner. The reason for this suggestion is, in part, that the performer will not fear situations to which he is harmoniously adjusted. The right initial attitude or mind-set will tend to generate the self-assurance indispensable for success in the audience situation. The aphorism "well begun is half done" is equally applicable to the preliminary preparation of the skill required by the rendition, emphasized in the third suggestion, to the generation of the needed air of self-confidence, emphasized in the first suggestion, and to the development of the right attitude toward the task. This suggestion is perhaps merely another instance of the doctrine that "love casteth out fear." Love and fear are largely incompatible concepts.

6. The victim of stage fright, as well as his counselors, should try to discover the underlying cause of the affliction. In searching for the causative

factors, which may be legion, it is essential to keep in mind the fact that stage fright is occasionally merely a disguise for some other unsuspected fear or conflict. It may be only a mask for something else. To deal with such fears understandingly, it is necessary to get behind the mask. For example, to cite a case in point, a son's intense fear that his father was going to die proved to be merely a mask for his desire that his hated father would die. But the son did not dare openly to divulge or confess such an unworthy wish. Since he would not be able to reconcile such a shameful desire with his moral ideals, he disguised the wish under a fear which he could readily entertain without any compunction of conscience, just as Uriah Heep apparently found camouflage for his avarice and dishonesty in his pretended humility. The boy's fear was only a cloak for a tabooed desire that had produced a deep-seated inner conflict. When a stage fright is, in similar fashion, an irrational expression of a hidden fear (in some cases, perhaps, a hidden fear or hatred of people in general), an attempt must be made to discover the nature of the fear-producing situation and to remove or overcome it. The ordinary remedies for fears will generally prove ineffective with disguised fears. The more vague and shadowy the fears and forebodings, the more difficult it will be to find their causes and to understand them. Moreover, the more exaggerated, bizarre, and silly the fear is, the more likely is it to be a symbol of something else.

The general principle on which this suggestion is based is that adequate knowledge and understanding of the fear-producing situation will overcome many irrational fears. Correct scientific information has, in point of fact, destroyed a legion of fears based on imperfect knowledge, error, or superstition. Perfect knowledge, like perfect love, often proves to be an adequate remedy for many kinds of fears. Most civilized people no longer fear ghosts, goblins, mysterious "signs and wonders," or visitations of mystical diseases. Science or knowledge has to a large extent made our fears rational instead of irrational. Thunder is no longer Thor's hammer or the sound of the fighting of rival belligerent gods, but the operation of natural forces. Winds are no longer the fury of avenging spirits, but natural meteorological phenomena amenable to rational understanding even though they are beyond man's control. Civilized man has not yet completely freed himself from ignorance and superstitions and from the fear of knowledge or of persecution by the traditionally minded, who often do not hesitate to resist change with the most brutally oppressive measures. Galileo, it will be recalled, saved his life only by repudiating his theory that the earth moved around the sun. Hundreds of martyrs have paid the penalty on the pyre for their refusal to recant beliefs now a part of the common social heritage. Many educated moderns still do not possess the courage to profess their convictions because of the fear of the vengeance of the traditionalists. Nevertheless, man has gone a long way in vanquishing fears of natural phenomena by understanding the laws of nature. Our fears of such phenomena have to a large extent become rational. For example, our fear of exposing ourselves to the germs of influenza, tuberculosis, smallpox, or diphtheria or to cyclones or dust storms has become rational caution instead of irrational, emotionalized fear. While fear often is the product of ignorance, it is also true that "fear is the beginning of wisdom," provided it is reasonable fear based on genuine knowledge, which will incite to intelligent effort because it is founded on a correct understanding of the situation. However, man still has a long journey ahead, not only to obtain mastery of his fears of the natural and the supernatural, but, more particularly, before he will be able to conquer, by a proper understanding and control of human nature, the fears implicit in human relationships. These socially engendered timidities and fears may be more serious today than was the case centuries ago, because of the cumulative effects of the repressions and inhibitions fostered by the relentless demands of advancing culture and civilization.

To summarize: let us try always to discover the true basis of a case of stage fright. The mere insight into the cause will sometimes remedy the situation. If it does not do so, the victim is at least in a better position to make an intelligent effort to remove the cause of his handicap.

7. Precautions should be taken to eliminate the more obvious causes of stage fright, such as threatening children with placing them on programs as a form of punishment; programming them so frequently that the strain of preparation or the interference with their own legitimate interests and recreations will arouse bitter resentment and repugnance against public appearance; laughing, scoffing, or poking fun at them or subjecting them to ridicule while they are performing or because of their performance; destructive instead of constructive criticism; making them stage conscious, self-conscious, timid, diffident, or embarrassed by any other ill-advised form of treatment or attitude; etc.

8. Suggestive therapy will prove effective in some cases. The value of our first recommendation depends in part on the power of suggestion. To carry out this advice one should convey to the child in a confident, convincing, persuasive manner the suggestions that he is fully equal to the task, that he possesses the ability to master his part and to deliver it effectively, that he will be able to speak clearly and convincingly, that he will feel courageous and at ease, and many similar suggestions that will readily occur to the resourceful teacher and parent. Positive suggestions should be employed rather than negative ones. Hypnotic suggestion at the hands of specialists, which will doubtless prove of value with many older adolescents and adults, cannot be made available in many sections of the country, nor can it readily be used in connection with the public schools.

CHAPTER XIII

MENTAL CONFLICTS

Before attempting to treat the remaining adjustment mechanisms, it is advisable to discuss briefly the concepts of mental conflict and dissociation and to point out their bearings on the problem of mental health.

Nature of Mental Conflicts. A mental conflict is a rivalry or struggle between two or more opposing or incompatible psychophysical tendencies. Under modern conditions, the individual is constantly forced to adapt himself to the complex environmental situations with which he is confronted. He is frequently obliged to make a choice between a number of courses of action which may be quite incompatible. He is bombarded from morning to night by alternatives of action and by the necessity of making choices. In the morning the child is torn between the desire to remain unmolested in his drowsy slumbers in bed and the feeling that he must arise and face the toil of the day. During the day he is caught between the opposing struggle to prepare the assignment and the desire to go swimming. In the evening he must battle with the urge to remain up and listen to the radio and the peremptory injunction of the parent to retire. The toper halts at the street intersection in a state of indecision, trying to determine whether he should follow his cravings to enter the grogshop for a drink or whether he should heed the voice of duty and immediately repair to his home with his pay envelope intact. The student is torn between the evolutionary hypothesis of the origin of life and the theory of creationism.

Whenever the individual is confronted with two alternatives of action, two contradictory ideas or ideals, experiences mutually conflicting, or antagonistic impulses, a state of indecision or vacillation (a more complex state of indecision) inevitably arises, provided that the opposing urges or ideas are about equally strong. It is the experience of mutually antagonistic impulses, motivations, or ideas that supplies the groundwork for possible mental conflicts. If one motive to action is appreciably stronger than the opposing motive, little delay in reaching a decision will ordinarily be experienced; nevertheless, a mental conflict may eventually arise from the chosen course of action.

Causes and Results of Mental Conflicts. In general, mental conflicts or emotional disturbances are produced by the attempt to banish or suppress one of the conflicting cravings, motives, or ambitions. The ideas or desires that clash may or may not be clearly apprehended by the subject to be antagonistic, and the nervous strain produced by the conflict may be more or less unconscious. Nevertheless, the conflict may exert a very injurious effect upon the individual's mental and emotional stability. The ordinary individual doubtless experiences throughout life a multiplicity of conflicts of all kinds that do not produce any serious physical or mental consequences. Some conflicts are trivial and evanescent, can be readily resolved, and do not leave any permanent crippling. In fact, many conflicts doubtless exert a salubrious influence because they stimulate the individual to overcome them or to develop beneficial compensations. They may serve as a spur to achievement, excite curiosity, stimulate the imagination, develop initiative and resourcefulness, and make for personality growth and enrichment. Persons entirely free from mental conflicts probably develop drab, colorless, complacent, mediocre personalities that have no conception of what the mastery motive involves.

Although mental conflicts when properly utilized and resolved may thus become a valuable stimulus to forceful, dynamic personality development, it nevertheless remains true that mental conflicts constitute one of the primal sources of personality difficulties and distortions. Intense, deep-seated, and pervasive conflicts are frequently very difficult to dissipate and often occasion the most serious psychic disturbances. They play the central role in the causation of the neuroses, according to some authorities. The detailed causes of mental and emotional conflicts are multitudinous: business reverses, religious qualms, unfortunate love episodes, scholastic or occupational failures, frustrated desires, unrealized goals, personal failures felt to be disgraceful, and the like. Investigation seems to show that the most serious and disruptive conflicts arise from deep-seated antagonisms between the individual's psychobiological urges and his egoistic desires and ambitions, on the one hand, and, on the other hand, the social and moral inhibitions that spring from the conventions and laws of the social order. These socially engendered conflicts may produce in the individual a retinue of disturbances, such as fears, inhibitions, anxieties, introvert ruminations, shut-in proclivities, feelings of inferiority and failure, feelings of shame or guilt, or neurotic disorders. The feeling of guilt may sometimes produce in the victim paralyzing feelings of self-condemnation, which in turn may produce further conflicts.

According to the psychoanalysts, one of the chief preoccupations of the unconscious is to escape from this guilt feeling (Barbara Low). Be that as it may, it is probable that the severity of the mental conflict will vary directly with the severity of the feelings of inferiority and frustration and the guilt complex. The greater the feeling of frustration or shame or guilt, the greater will be the tendency to suppress or inhibit it. If the individual continually strives to inhibit the feelings of guilt, the results of the conflict will be aggravated. The more deep-seated and intricate conflicts, according to the psychoanalysts, are produced by warring clashes between conscious and unconscious forces, between the "Id" (the true unconscious stratum of primitive libidinal impulses, demanding immediate gratification) and the "Ego" (the rational, perceptual self in contact with the outer world, which seeks to control the primitive urges of the Id).[1] In fact, in the terminology of the psychoanalysts, a conflict is limited to a painful emotional state that is produced by the forcible prevention of an unconscious wish from entering consciousness.

The Freudian Conception of Mental Conflicts and the Stages (Autoerotic, Homosexual or Bisexual, and Heterosexual) of Sex Development. According to Freud, the chief causes of deep-seated and devastating mental conflicts are sexual inhibitions or shocks (traumas). The sexual traumas, however, are due less frequently to violent sexual aggressions or assaults than to overrepressions, sexual perversions, or abnormal fixations of the libido, especially in childhood. The libido (from the Sanskrit, *lubh,* desire) is variously interpreted by different writers. To Freud the libido represents the dynamic psychic force that springs from all forms of the sex urge, or all that is included in the word "love" in the broad sense.[2] The word, therefore, is not limited to sexuality in its narrow relation to genital activity, although this is the main component, but includes self-love (ego libido in early life); love for parents, children, and others (object libido); attachment to concrete objects and even to abstract ideas. Freud bases much of his system of normal and abnormal psychology on the development of the libido, although he also emphasizes the importance of the self-preservative instinct. Carl G. Jung, on the other hand, gives the term a wider connotation, apparently identifying the libido with the all-inclusive vital urge or the life and growth energy (asexual) and also with creative energy, or horme. The libido manifests itself both in progression, or a striving for differentiation, and in regression, or a retreat to the undifferentiated condition and irresponsibility of infancy. The libido, to William White and I. H. Coriat, is the energy used for both nutritive and sexual ends. H. L. Bergson's term, *élan vital,* has a somewhat similar connotation, designating the vital force, or impulse of life—the creative principle inherent in all organisms.

To understand Freud's theory of the sexual origin of mental conflicts, it is necessary to give at least the framework of his theory of the three genetic stages of sex development and to point out how interference with the normal evolution of these stages may create profound behavior disorders.

1. *Autoerotic or Infantile Stage of Sex.* In very early life, when the libido is undifferentiated, it is diffusely connected with all parts of the body—the

---

[1] For further explanation of these terms, see pp. 477*f*.

[2] For a recent interpretation and defense of Freudianism by his first American protagonist, see A. A. Brill, *Freud's Contribution to Psychiatry,* New York, W. W. Norton & Company, Inc., 1944.

skin, the muscles, and especially the orifices. In other words, in early life the child's own body is its sex object. Certain practices that do not seem to be specifically sexual are given a sexual or quasi-sexual significance by Freud; these include tickling, self-fondling, thumb sucking, sucking objects, and related mouth activities. Kissing is traced to these primitive lip movements. Included also are erotic anal and dermal practices and motor restlessness or muscle eroticism.[3] The infantile form of motor restlessness is regarded as a presexual stage of motor impulses. Stimulation of any of these not sharply differentiated zones has a quieting effect. Specifically included are certain definitely sensitive areas, called "infantile erogenous zones," the stimulation of which supposedly gives sexual gratification; such regions are the mouth, breasts, and especially the genital organs. Manipulation of the latter gives rise to the form of autoerotic practice known as masturbation, onanism, or self-abuse.

Many writers, including Jung, deny the existence of this infantile stage of sexuality.

Precocious abnormal sexual development. Perhaps the strongest evidence in favor of Freud's doctrine of infantile sexuality springs from the study of distinctly abnormal cases of sex development. Pathological cases of precocious sex development (pubertas praecox) have conclusively shown that it is possible for secondary sex characteristics to mature and for the gonads to begin to function during the first few years of life in either sex. These cases of sex precocity are caused by overfunctioning in early life of some of the endocrine glands, due to tumors (neoplasms) or hyperplasia (abnormal multiplication of normal elements in an organ), especially of the gonadal or puberty gland (hypertesticularism and hyperovarianism), the pineal gland, the adrenal cortex, and possibly the pituitary gland (excess secretion in early life of the master sex hormones) and the thymus. Some cases probably stem from pathological brain conditions, such as cysts in the ventricles, hydrocephaly, tuberous sclerosis,[4] and injury to the hypothalamus (an organ at the base of

---

[3] Other allegedly sex-satisfaction-yielding activities (neuroses or perversions in extreme form) include exhibitionism (the impulse to expose erogenous parts of the body, especially the genitalia), and inspectionism or voyeurism, or scopophilia, or the Peeping Tom complex (the impulse to look at the nude form, particularly the genitals, or at articles of apparel), and necrophilia (morbid sex attraction toward cadavers). Inspectionism and exhibitionism, and sadism and masochism (to be considered later), are illustrations of Freud's basic principle of dualism, or polarity, or contradictory trends (such as femininity and masculinity, the id and the ego, pleasure and pain).

[4] Jean P. Pratt and Robert L. Shaefer, "Sex Precocity, Virilism, Adrenal Cortical Tumor," *American Journal of Obstetrics and Gynecology,* Vol. 49, May, 1945, 623–633 (references; see remarks by J. G. Greenhill).

the brain), which may impair the inhibitory function of the pituitary gland.[5] Emil Novac, however, maintains that the most common form of sex precocity is the constitutional type, in which a healthy girl without evidence of endocrine or other defects may bear children when she is between 5 and 9 years of age, but who does not differ from other girls after the age of 10 or 11. Such allegedly normal cases of extreme sex precocity, perhaps more common than is usually assumed, are consistent with Freud's doctrine of infantile sexuality, which, apparently, has been confirmed by an extensive investigation along nonpsychoanalytic lines of the sex life of 12,000 American males in all walks of life.[6] This investigation has also confirmed many other facts of sexual behavior well known from earlier, less extensive researches.

By way of contrast, lack of secretion of the sex hormones, in early life, or of hormones that stimulate the development of the sex hormones, retards or prevents sex development and may produce hypogenitalism, hypogonadism, and pituitary eunuchism or eunuchoidism.

The picture presented by excessive early hyperovarianism includes (1) the beginning of menstruation during the first few weeks or months of life; (2) the development of the adult female secondary sex characteristics of face, form, and hair distribution; and (3) diminished stature. Signs of early hypertesticularism may include (1) precocious enlargement of the prostate gland and seminal vesicles and seminal discharges, (2) early male distribution of hair, (3) a deep voice, and (4) marked physical strength.

Hyperactivity of the adrenal cortex in females may give rise to a condition known as adrenogenitalism or adrenal virilism or masculinism, the development of well-defined masculine traits in women. Such activity in early life may result in the growth of a beard, masculine hair distribution, a deepening of the voice, marked muscular development and strength, a skeleton of adolescent proportions, overdevelopment of the clitoris, and sex precocity. Excessive cortical secretion after puberty may result in a deepening of the voice, failure of the development of the primary and secondary sex characteristics, dwarfing

[5] Bernard M. Scholder, "The Syndrome of Precocious Puberty, Fibrocystic Bone Disease and Pigmentation of the Skin: Eleven Years' Observation of a Case," *Annals of Internal Medicine,* January, 1945, 105–118 (references).

Albert E. Goldstein, Seymour W. Rubin, and John A. Askin, "Carcinoma of Adrenal Cortex with Adrenogenital Syndrome in Children: Complete Review of the Literature and Report of a Case with Recovery in a Child," *American Journal of Diseases of Children,* Vol. 72, November, 1946, 563–603.

Karl J. Karnaky, "Premature Sexual Precocity in Young Girls," *The Journal of Clinical Endocrinology,* April, 1945, 184–188.

Helmut P. O. Sekel, "Precocious Puberty in Children," *The Medical Clinics of North America,* January, 1946, 30, 183–209.

[6] Alfred C. Kinsey, Wardell B. Pomeroy, and Clyde E. Martin, *Sexual Behavior of the Human Male,* Philadelphia, W. B. Saunders Company, 1948.

of the uterus, enlargement of the clitoris, and regression toward the masculine type (male type of hair distribution, narrow hips, broad shoulders, and the appearance of a beard). The characteristics of adult (female) virilism include excessive hairiness, muscular hypertrophy, regression of the sex organs, loss of the feminine configuration, hypertrophied clitoris, amenorrhea, and eventual sterility. Virilism may also follow disorders of the pituitary and pineal glands and possibly of the thymus. Masculinism, or virilism, can be imposed on the feminine structure at any time. The antithesis of virilism, adrenal feminization, may occur in the male sex from excess of cortin. It is characterized by the development of the breasts, atrophy of the external genitals, loss of libido and potency, loss of hair, gain in weight, and the assumption of the feminine form.

A few illustrative cases of puberty praecox will lend needed concreteness. A 5-year-old boy with a tumor of the left testis had grown rapidly, possessed a deep bass voice, and had developed a beard and pubic hair. At the age of 9 he was 56 inches tall and weighed 97 pounds. Four months after the removal of the growth, his beard disappeared, the genitals diminished in size, his emissions ceased, and his voice and mental characteristics became child-like again (Joshua H. Leiner). A girl with an ovarian tumor began to menstruate, developed breasts, and grew pubic hair at 7. A boy with a pineal disorder was subject to emissions and was markedly precocious mentally at 17 months; at 44 months, he answered questions in a loud, bass voice; was independent and self-possessed with strangers; and spurned toys for small children (Leiner). Another boy of 8 with a pineal disorder possessed the sex development and functions of a boy of 15 or 16. An adrenal case from recent literature, a mentally retarded, bad-tempered boy, was normal at 6 months. At 12 months he had a deep voice, large hands, great muscular strength, a dental age of about 3 years, a bone age of 5 years, and a sex development of 8. His prostate was the size of a walnut and the penis was markedly enlarged. He practiced self-abuse frequently. He did not survive the removal of a tumor the size of a golf ball from the right kidney. (From Roy G. Hoskins' summary, p. 58). A girl of 4 to 6 with a cortico-adrenal disorder, had a markedly enlarged clitoris and required shaving because of the growth of a beard (William Bulloch and James H. Sequerira). Another girl of 7 looked like a young man with silky black beard (E. E. Glynn). The cortico-adrenal cases are five times as prevalent among females as among males (Norma V. Scheidemann), while the cases that originate in pineal or pituitary disorders are more common in the male (J. P. Greenhill). Overactivity of the adrenal cortex before birth may result in pseudohermaphrodism (*e.g.*, the possession of the external male genitalia and feminine ovaries and uterus).

Many observations and the few available examinations by means of objective psychoclinical tests seem to show that the precocious sexual development is not paralleled by a corresponding mental precocity. On the other hand, marked tendency toward mental retardation and immaturity (infantilism) characterizes the group as a whole. On the basis of the references (largely based on subjective impressions) to the mental status of 62 of 190 cases reviewed from the literature by Stone and Doe-Kuhlmann,[7] 21.3 per cent were classified as above average, 37.7 per cent as average, and 41 per cent as below average. Roger Williams, on the basis of the review of 104 cases, concluded that these children "have the childlike psychical qualities of their age, or they are usually dull, mentally defective, or even idiots" (Stone and Doe-Kuhlmann). A battery of psychological tests showed that all of the girls studied by Arnold Gesell were intellectually retarded, some being of imbecile grade; nor did he find "any radical increase of affectivity or sociability."[8]

This evidence on precocious sexuality may be supplemented by reference to authenticated medical records of pregnancy among young girls. According to Morris Fishbein, editor of the *Journal of the American Medical Association,* a precociously developed Ukrainian girl of 6, a Mohammedan girl of 7, a third girl of 8 years and 10 months, and many girls of 10, 11, and 12 have given birth to babies.

Regardless of the disagreement on the issue of infantile sexuality, let us follow Freud. At about the age of 4 occur the specialization and differentiation that establish the true primacy of the genital organs. While psychologists and physicians are in disagreement on this point also, autoerotic practices or the functional activity of the sex glands have been traced in several of the writer's case histories, from mentally normal people, to the age of 6 or 7 (see pages 328*f.* and 433*f.*).

The narcissistic stage (referred to as narcissistic libido) follows in the path from the autoerotic to the object libido. It is a condition of erotically tinged self-infatuation or sexual attraction toward oneself, and not mere selfishness or egocentricity. This narcissistically directed libido stage is, according to Freud, fairly normal for early childhood. According to the nonbiological (nonsexual) interpretation of Karen Horney, it is not a derivative of an instinctual drive, but is a "neurotic trend . . . to cope with the self and others by way of self-inflation."[9] Its cause lies in disturbed human relationships. The victim admires himself for nonexistent qualities, in order to magnify himself as a defense against alienation from others produced by fears and

[7] Calvin P. Stone and Lois Doe-Kuhlmann, "Notes on the Mental Development of Children Exhibiting the Somatic Signs of Puberty Praecox," *The Twenty-seventh Yearbook of the National Society for the Study of Education,* Nature and Nurture, Part I, Their Influence Upon Intelligence, 1928, 389–397 (see additional references).

[8] Arnold Gesell, "Precocious Puberty and Mental Maturation," *The Twenty-seventh Yearbook of the National Society for the Study of Education,* 399–409.

[9] Karen Horney, *New Ways in Psychoanalysis,* New York, W. W. Norton & Company, Inc., 1939, 88–100.

against felt inferiorities. He expects admiration from others for virtues he does not possess. To Freud, however, narcissism is a transitional stage that must be outgrown. If it is not outgrown during adolescence, sex practices assume the nature of a regression to autoeroticism. Such a regression is often referred to as "infantile fixation of the libido." That is to say, the libido is held fast in an early stage of sex activity, which may lead to the development of perversions, impotency, neuroses, sexual neurasthenia, and mental conflicts and difficulties. Some individuals may stick fast in this autoerotic stage and never reach sexual maturity. They remain, as it were, sexually infantile.

2. *Bisexual or Homosexual Stage.* This stage may be subdivided into two forms.

a. In the bisexual phase, the child is attracted indifferently by the members of either sex. It makes little difference whether the object of his attraction is of the same or the opposite sex. Bisexuality, according to Freud, accounts for the strong attachment of boys for boys and girls for girls, and for their homosexual perversions. Homosexual practices, of course, are not invariable concomitants of bisexual trends. Bisexuality is regarded as fairly normal during the early period following the autosexual stage, before the child reaches the heterosexual level. It is usually terminated spontaneously during the early stages of adolescence with the awakening of interest in the opposite sex, or because of aversion to homosexual inclinations due to social disapproval.

b. True homosexuality represents a form of neurosis in which the individual of either sex is sexually attracted only by members of the same sex. The homosexual syndrome may so affect the person's general demeanor that he will prefer the activities and dress of the other sex. Thus the male homosexual may paint his lips, rouge his cheeks, and add feminine touches to his clothes. The whole mental make-up may become that of the opposite sex, the male invert showing preference for feminine tasks, interests, and occupations, and displaying modesty toward men. Such tendencies tend to crop out at the puberal period. This is sometimes referred to as effemination in man and viraginity, or virilism, or masculinism in women. Some homosexuals even resemble the opposite sex in physical characteristics, such as body contours, shape of the shoulders and breasts, muscular development, distribution of the hair, and pitch of the voice. In men this condition is sometimes referred to as androgyny and in women as gynandry.[10]

Finally, homosexuality often manifests itself in homosexual perversions. Some believe that true homosexuality always leads to perverse erotic amours or sexual practices with members of the same sex. The male homosexuals make advances to men, especially adolescent boys, and the female inverts to

[10] These words are also used as synonyms for the condition of hermaphroditism, the presence in the same organism of the male and the female sex organs.

women. While the law classifies such practices as revolting crimes and inflicts stern penalties upon the offenders, whom it views as moral degenerates (in some states confinement in the penitentiary for a period of 10 years), many homosexuals are highly intellectual, idealistic, altruistic, and just as devoted in their attachments as heterosexuals are in theirs. Their conduct in other respects may be quite irreproachable. The fact that this form of sex inversion occurs among geniuses and men of refinement, especially those of sedentary habits, and is not confined to degenerates, psychopaths, paranoiacs, or neurotics seems to lend support to Freud's theory that we are all, in early stages of our development, "polymorphous perverse" [11]—that is, we can attach sexual interest to any object in the environment that gives sexual satisfaction. Whether or not this generalization is literally correct, true homosexuality should be regarded as a "fixation" or "regression" that will frequently lay the foundation for the development of a neurosis and the growth of abnormal attitudes and maladjustments. This, no doubt, is due in part to the severe condemnation by society of this form of sex perversion.

Homosexual males have at times been brought up as girls and married to men, and in some cases the fact has been discovered only from a postmortem examination. Instances of the marriage of two persons of the same sex are occasionally chronicled in the daily press. Thus the papers of July 7, 1934, record the marriage on June 2, in Portsmouth, Va., of "James" Erdman, 19, who proved to be Effie Erdman, female, masquerading in a man's attire, to Margaret Zerby, 19, both from Pennsylvania.

Effie met Margaret at a dance a short time after "he" began wearing masculine attire. The "bridegroom" was returned to the prison yesterday to await court action on the complaint that she posed as "James Erdman" when she married Margaret. When told by the warden that she must put on women's clothes, she snapped, "I will not," with a stamp of her foot that went well with her masculine garb.

Such marriages arouse the presumption that at least one of the contracting parties is a homosexual.

A few years ago it was discovered that a Fred Thompson under arrest in Chicago was a Mrs. C., who had been masquerading for 13 years as C.'s wife.

One of the strangest impostors was that of a "stalwart Amazon" in London who posed as a war hero and an officer who had suffered terrible wounds. She was first a captain and then promoted herself to major and colonel. She kept

---

[11] The term refers to the pregenital multiple sex manifestations of the child (anal, oral, sucking, touching, looking, etc.) from which normal sex behavior develops through the suppression of some of the impulses by the processes of education and socialization. If the tendencies continue into youth and adulthood, they become morbid or pathological phenomena (technically called "sex perversions").

a set of fine razors, with which she pretended to shave daily. She was known as a keen sportsman, cricketer, horseman, and boxer, and she moved in good society with a cool bravado. Apparently an unhappily married woman, she adopted male costume and induced a girl to elope with her. The outraged father pursued the pair and forced their marriage (in 1923). The true sex of the colonel was revealed when misfortune overtook her and she was forced into bankruptcy. Her "wife" testified that she had lived with her for 6 years without realizing that "her husband was not a man." This may be a case of sex inversion brought on by prior unsatisfactory marital relations.

A 10-year masquerade of a "slight" man who had posed as a woman was discovered (in 1937), when he was committed on some charge to the woman's house of detention in New York at the age of 26. For 4 years he had worked as a waitress, chambermaid, hospital attendant, and chorus girl, and had lived for 6 years as the wife of a steamfitter, who was "all broken up over the discovery." The " 'husband' never suspected the deception." This probably was a genuine sex invert.

A husky, 25-year-old, 6-foot grinder in a foundry in Seattle, Wash., was arrested on a tip (in 1945) from her "wife" of 5 months, who began to suspect that her husband was really a woman. The homosexual admitted that she had previously lived in Oregon for 3 years with another girl, whom she "married" in 1940. "She had worked alongside men for years, and fooled everybody, including herself." Her statement that she had been "raped at the age of fourteen and had had an aversion to men ever since" may supply the clue to her homosexual attachments. These may have been induced by a morbid repulsion for the normal sex relationship.

The sex of a 21-year-old Ottawa girl, who had successfully masqueraded for 2 years as a male worker in a munitions plant near Montreal, was revealed when she married a fellow girl employee, who later complained to the police (in 1942). Investigation showed that a curate had refused to marry the pair upon the statement of the alleged "husband" that he was "neither man nor woman." She probably was an hermaphrodite.

The sex of "Alfred," a model butler, chef, and major domo for 14 years in the home of an Oyster Bay, N.Y., millionaire, was not discovered until she died. She had never permitted a medical examination when sick, and she kept her 15 fellow servants at a distance by her air of austerity. With her abstemious habits and perfect record—she had never requested a day off in 13 years—she was regarded as the perfect servant. No clues are available for the interpretation of this case of inversion.

The reason for the masculinism, or virilism, in the following case is not difficult to discern. For 16 years Katherine had lived in Chicago as George, "because her mother wanted a son and not another daughter when she was born." So she proceeded to dress her as a boy and treat her as one. But when the "movie fever" struck her (in 1938) she resumed her natural status, because she thought a "pretty girl would have a better chance than an ordinary boy." While the quick-change beauticians brought a lightning transformation in her external appearance, "she still walks, talks, and acts like a boy." Boyish mannerisms acquired throughout years are not so easily discarded as boy attire.

3. *Heterosexual Stage.* Heterosexuals are sexually attracted only by members of the opposite sex. The manifestation of heterosexual trends and inclinations represents the normal condition from the time of puberty or early adolescence onward, although some adolescents give little evidence of the urge and although all retain to some extent, according to Freud, the earlier autoerotic and bisexual or homosexual tendencies. Most people reach this stage of sexual maturity normally and naturally; some reach it abnormally (via perverse or antisocial practices); others do not reach it at all, remaining fixated, perhaps, in an earlier stage and thereby becoming victims of regressions or infantile modes of behavior and frequently, in addition, of ensuing mental conflicts, maladjustments, neurotic maladies, and frank sex perversions.

Why Sex May Play a Central Role in the Production of Mental Conflicts. Freud, above all others, has emphasized that the sex life is the outstanding source of mental conflicts and neuroses, largely because of the way sex problems are handled by society. From time immemorial, sex has been vigorously and persistently suppressed by primitive taboo [12] and by the social mores and religious teachings of civilized man. Society has attempted to subordinate the sex activity of its members to the requirements of the social group and to shunt it into approved substitute activities, such as productive work, literary and artistic creativeness, athletics, and the like. It has inflicted severe penalties on the violators of its accepted social code in order to curb the illegitimate gratification of the sex impulse.[13]

Thus early in life the child has been made cognizant of the demands made upon him for social conformity, and he has frequently developed a morbid emotional attitude early in life toward the problems of sex because of the air of mystery, secrecy, uncleanness, and vulgarity with which sex activities have been enshrouded by parents, caretakers, and teachers. At the very onset of his sex interest he is made to feel that sex is filthy and obscene, a prohibited subject that must not be discussed, either openly or covertly. His earliest sex curiosity, his queries about the origin of life, are met by an attitude of

---

[12] A parallel fact should be borne in mind, namely, that the generative organs were regarded as objects of veneration and worship by primitive phallic religions.

[13] These statements should not render one oblivious of the converse fact: sex laxity and promiscuity enjoyed a holiday in this country and elsewhere during both of the world wars, and have been rampant for years in certain quarters where sex control seems to have been swept into the limbo of forgotten concepts.

emotionalized silence or by emotionalized reproaches or by false statements. Frequently the adult's response to his natural curiosity about sex has been an attempt to arouse a feeling of shame or disgust at the mere mention of the subject. The natural result of these attitudes of silence, mystification, or suppression has been to leave the child's imagination to feed upon ignorance, obscene pictures, or ribald songs; the smutty jokes, allusions, or misinformation of his playmates; or the vicious sex practices of his comrades, nursemaids, servants, or depraved adults. In consequence of this conditioning, the child has come to feel thoroughly ashamed of sex. Sex has become something nasty and degraded that must be concealed at all costs. So far as girls are concerned, they have in general been brought up as if they were sexless and as if they should not be consciously concerned with their most distinctive biological function. Nevertheless, like the boys they have also often secured their enlightenment surreptitiously, sometimes with disastrous results.

How children first obtain their sex knowledge is shown convincingly by the following investigations. Katherine B. Davis [14] in an investigation of the sex life of 2,200 women, found that only 13 per cent had as girls received complete information about reproduction from their parents. In 62 per cent of the cases in which the parents had imparted this knowledge, the information had already been anticipated by servants or other children. Sixty per cent found the information conveyed by the parents, such as it was, helpful; 37 per cent reported that it merely served as a stimulus to seek further information; only 3 per cent found it harmful. In their investigation of 200 male college graduates, Peck and Wells [15] found that 34 per cent obtained their first sex knowledge primarily from their companions.

Illustrations of How Sex Information Is Frequently Conveyed to the Young and the Effects of Unwholesome Enlightenment. The following case reports show the ways in which information may be acquired and the effects that such information may produce.

CHILDISH SEX ANXIETY DUE TO IGNORANCE

When I was six years old my oldest brother was about ten and my other brother about eight. The three of us played frequently in a cow pasture. Upon one occasion I remember my older brothers had taken off most of their clothing and played that they were male and female cows and were mating. This made a profound impression upon me. I was sorely afraid that the younger of the two brothers would give birth to an illegitimate baby (I didn't realize that only females

---

[14] Katherine B. Davis, *Factors in the Sex Life of Twenty-two Hundred Women*, 1929.

[15] M. W. Peck and F. L. Wells, "Further Studies in the Psychosexuality of College-graduate Men," *Mental Hygiene*, Vol. 9, 1925, 502–520.

See also M. F. Ashley-Montagu, "The Acquisition of Sexual Knowledge in Children," *American Journal of Orthopsychiatry*, 1935, 290–300.

bore babies) and thus bring everlasting disgrace upon himself and the rest of the family.

I did not mention my fear to any member of my family. Some months later, however, I was with a cousin several years older than I. I related the incident to him and asked him if he thought my brother would "have" a baby. He said that he would, perhaps, after he was married. I did not get the true meaning of this brief explanation at all, and lived in great fear that my brother's disgrace would be postponed merely until after the marriage ceremony was performed.

A year or so later this brother fell ill and died of blood poisoning. While I mourned with the rest of the family, there was a great relief in my young heart, for I felt that God had taken him in order to save him and us from an impending disaster.   (T.B.J.W.; M.; E.S.P.; M.A.)

SMUTTY SEX INFORMATION AND SCORN OF MEN

I received my knowledge about sex life from a cousin whom I visited every summer. She was two years my senior and acquired her information from the boys with whom she had always played. Perhaps it was the smuttiness of this and its concomitant associations that shamed me into my aloof scornfulness of men. It was a much discussed topic among my schoolmates, and "we wanted to know facts."   (W.H.; F.; S.C.T.; A.B.)

AUTOEROTIC, INFANTILE, AND HOMOSEXUAL PRACTICES, CULMINATING IN INTELLECTUAL HOMOSEXUALITY AND REPUGNANCE TO THE IDEA OF HETEROSEXUAL RELATIONS

Sexually, I would probably be diagnosed as "repressed" or "arrested." At an early age I practiced self-abuse, a habit taught me by playmates at the primary school. In the beginning, each of these acts was followed by a sense of fear of God and a promise to myself "never to commit it again." However, the acts were committed again and more or less regularly until I went to military school. Here, and later at home, I was introduced into the rites of homosexuality which had a strong appeal, possibly because they were initiated by one for whom I had an especial liking and admiration. This period was followed by one of "intellectual homosexuality" and later by complete indifference to all sex. (I have never had sexual relations with the opposite sex nor any desire for such a relationship.) On the contrary, although very fond of the company of girls and women, especially very elderly women, and completely at ease with them, the thought of sexual satisfaction is repugnant to me, as is the idea of "spooning" or "necking," its more recent term.   (H.H.W.; M.; U.S.; Age 22)

SEX DIFFICULTIES AND OVERDEVELOPMENT ASCRIBED TO THE PRE-COCIOUS TEACHING OF UNDESIRABLE SEX FACTS AND FALSEHOODS BY SERVANTS

In the matter of sex the subject has had his chief difficulties. As a young child he was cared for to a great extent by servants, both white and colored, who taught him many undesirable facts, as well as falsehoods regarding sex. His father having in his employ a considerable number of unscrupulous laborers, it is natural that they exercised an influence which was not wholesome. As he grew he made a friend of a child about the same age, or probably a little older, who had two sisters of rather uncertain morals. These girls taught the boy many undesirable things, which he in turn passed along to the subject, as well as to others of his acquaintance. Therefore this knowledge led him into difficulties at a very early age, for which he was thoroughly reprimanded. This one experience led to his only infantile fixation, which perhaps should not be called a fixation because it now exists in the form of a repulsion. But as he progressed through school he learned more and more from other children, resulting in curiosity which was bound to be satisfied. After puberty sex became the dominant factor in his life, with a consequent disastrous effect on his moral tone. This continued for years, yet, strangely enough in some ways, but not at all strange in view of his home teachings, he was quite averse to girls and women known to be of a low moral nature.   (B.O.I.; M.; C. Instr. of Psy.; M.A.)

VARIED SEX EXPERIENCES BEGINNING WITH AUTOMASTURBATION AT THE AGE OF SEVEN AND ATTEMPTED SEX RELATIONS WITH A GIRL AT THE AGE OF TEN, CONTINUING FOR YEARS WITH MUTUAL AND AUTOMASTURBATION AND SEDUCTIVE INDUCEMENTS TOWARD PER-VERSIONS, CULMINATING IN PERSISTENT STRUGGLES AGAINST HOMO-SEXUAL AND PERVERSE TRENDS, AND LEADING TO THE DEVELOPMENT OF INTROVERT TENDENCIES

In order to give the background for the fear or obsession which has more or less dominated my life, I will start with my first recollection of sex experiences, and try to trace them through a period of twenty years.

I can faintly remember experiencing sex sensations at about the age of six. Although my recollection is not perfect, I believe I began to practice masturbation at the age of seven. At this age, I was also afflicted with enuresis, which continued for about three years. I remember that I was terribly ashamed of this weakness and would cry for hours when this happened.

My only playmates at this time were the children of a very poor family. The father was a drunkard and the children were of low mentality. I believe that much of the blame for my abnormal sex consciousness was due to this association. The boy was older than I, while the two girls were of about my age. This boy led me to practice mutual masturbation with him. The excessive practice of masturbation seems to have dominated my sex life between the ages of seven and ten.

At the age of ten this boy and I took his two sisters to an out-of-the-way place and attempted sexual intercourse. The act was incomplete but the idea was there and the contact. Between the ages of ten and thirteen I was still a slave to the habit of onanism.

My next sex episode arose from meeting a young man who soon became my ideal. He was about twenty-one years old and I was thirteen. He was a leader in the scout movement with which I had just become affiliated. We became great friends. Now I realize that he lacked education and that he was not very intelligent, but at the time I did not know this. He was big and strong and seemed to me the perfection of manhood, while at that time I had a rather weak body and had been living entirely too much within myself. I associated with the gang of boys but I always kept my thoughts to myself. My parents were even strangers to me. As this man and I became better friends, we began to practice mutual masturbation. This was initiated entirely by him. I had begun to break myself of the habit because I had imagined that such a perfect man would not do such a thing. When I found that he also practiced this habit I was no longer ashamed of it. I reasoned that it must be the natural and right thing to do. I slept with this chap frequently for about three years. He was a real friend to me in many ways but I shall always feel that he did me more harm than good. Had there not been the difference in our ages, I could excuse him. He finally left town and I have seen him only occasionally since that time. Whenever I have seen him, I have experienced a feeling of disgust and pity for he has degenerated physically into a weak worn-out person.

I began again to live within myself. I had no very close friends, but many acquaintances. I felt much older than most of the fellows of my age. Girls did not bother me nor particularly interest me. I didn't go in for sentimentality or "necking" with girls. It just didn't seem to appeal to me, although I was far from being bashful or afraid of girls. I did go quite steadily with one girl simply because she suited my moods. She was quiet when I wanted to be quiet and talked when I wanted to talk. Any other girl would have suited me just as well. During this time, however, I began to worry about my sex life. I was ashamed of the habit of masturbation but I didn't seem to be able to stop it. I tried, but it seemed to have too strong a grip on me. I began to fear that I was developing into a pervert. I had a dreadful horror of this. I had never practiced any form of sexual abnormality other than masturbation, but I felt myself slipping into a perverted state of mind. Certain men attracted me. I fought the impulse by constantly reminding myself that I was subject to the weakness. I tried to force myself to stop thinking about it, but found that, instead of keeping it out of my mind, I was thinking about it more than ever. However, I kept striving to get rid of the impulse.

The knowledge of my susceptible nature helped me to keep my balance until I was old enough to overcome the tendency.

The idea of perversion was so disgusting, so obnoxious and repulsive to me that I could hardly live with myself. I grew moody. I was terribly afraid of myself. My body was not strong enough to allow me to go in for athletics, but I did much hiking. Usually I went alone. I was not unpopular in high school. I held several positions of prominence and went in for dramatic work. My grades were satisfactory. I associated with a group of fellows my own age and apparently seemed one of the gang. But all this time I kept my thoughts and fears to myself.

After graduating from high school, I became a day student at a college near home. I made up my mind to break myself of the masturbation habit which still bothered me, but did not succeed entirely until I went to a large city to work.

Here in the city I came in contact with perverts of various types. I worked in a large movie theatre and came in contact with them every day. Because of my susceptibility, my fear of perversion increased. I believe if I had ever succumbed to the practice I would have committed suicide. I cannot describe the feeling of horror that it arouses in me.

As I became accustomed to seeing both men and women of the sexually abnormal type, my attitude began to change. Gradually my feeling of hatred and disgust changed to pity. So many nice-looking strong young men who were apparently healthy and normal turned out to be perverts that I couldn't help but pity them and feel sorry for them.

My phobia of sex perversion has never left me. The thought of it in connection with myself nauseates me. Association with women and leaving the city have dulled my dread to some extent. I have tried to eradicate the thought from my mind altogether, and I believe I am succeeding slowly. I believe I am sexually normal, but this fear has made me abnormally sex conscious.

I trace my obsession to two causes: excessive association with men in early sex experiences and lack of a natural interest in girls during the high-school period. If my resolution had not been strong enough and if the fear had not been present, I am afraid that I might have become a pervert. In this case, fear may be said to have done good. (R.E.H.; M.; U.S.)

SEX CURIOSITIES SUPPRESSED AS VULGAR; SEX STIMULATION FROM GUSHING LOVE STORIES; FEELINGS OF GUILT

It is not easy for anyone to write about anything as personal as sex adjustments, although most normal people have had them to make.

By the time I was six years old I began to wonder about boys and girls. I asked my mother why one could see one's sister naked but not one's brother. She told me that I was naughty and not to ask such questions any more. The next remembrance I have was when I discovered that my little nephew was different from his little sister. Their father shamed me for my discovery and told me that a nice little girl never thought of those things. My sister told me about the birth of babies. This was no particular news to me as the animals on the farm often gave birth to their young in my presence. She neglected to tell me anything about conception. The big mystery to me was how the baby got where it was before it was born. I could get no more information from my sister and as this was too vulgar a question to ask my mother about, it was several years before I really understood the mysteries of the reproduction of the human race.

I began to menstruate when I was thirteen. My mother explained to me as well as she could the process of conception and birth. She also added a warning that boys must keep hands off; that it was a mortal sin to give in to a boy; that there was no disgrace greater than to have an illegitimate child; that I was too young to think about those things yet; that a girl must keep all these thoughts to herself. This satisfied me for the time being. As I grew older a Prince Charming entered my dreams.

During this time I read novels and really gratified my passion to some extent in reading gushing love scenes over and over. It produced feelings and longings that only real intercourse could satisfy. I learned to suppress these feelings by the greatest effort. I told no one about them. I felt wicked and degraded and was in mortal terror for fear I might in some way reveal my wicked thought to my father or my mother. I became very cautious in my conversation and withdrew to my room whenever possible. Tears relieved me somewhat but prayer helped me most. Gradually I learned to throw myself into the work at home and kept with my mother as much as I could because I had a horror of being alone. I do not deserve much credit for this control, because there was little or no opportunity for me to gratify my passion even had I been weak enough to yield to it.

This was a very bad way for any young girl to pass her time and God only knows what might have become of me if I had not at this time been thrown upon the world of reality.

My life as a teacher has thrown me more with women than with men. I think that my greatest protection was the feeling that everything connected with sex was vulgar, and my firm belief that God would always help you if you asked Him. Since my marriage I never think about this stuff. I am really, I think, sex adjusted.   (S.B.R.; F.; H.S.T.; B.S.; Age 58)

The results of the processes of early sex conditioning through lack of candor, evasion, taboo, misrepresentation, exaggeration, or excessive shaming and condemnation are most varied, depending on the intensity of the sex drive, the difficulty of sublimating it, or suppressing the feelings of shame or guilt that may have been aroused, the extent of autoerotic or perverse practices that may have been engendered, the kind of misinformation, and similar factors. In general, however, the result has been that sex matters have acquired abnormal emotional values. The eventual results have sometimes taken the form of morbid sex repulsion, sexual anesthesia or frigidity, sex repression, or perhaps morbid sex fascination. Sometimes compensation has been sought by means of indulgence in sex phantasies, erotic daydreams, or regressive, infantile sex practices. Or the morbid sex trends may have been transferred to other forms of activity, such as neurotic forms of indulgence, which also are to be regarded as morbid compensations or defense mechanisms. These neurotic outcroppings may sometimes take the form of vexatious obsessions or compulsions, such as the following case of obsessional washing.

OBSESSIONAL WASHING FROM FEELING OF GUILT

A young man of twenty came to the writer complaining of a number of symptoms. Among these was the impulse to wash his hands many times during the day. Associated with this impulse (or compulsion) was a feeling that his hands were unclean. The compulsive habit was easily traced to masturbation, which always gave him a feeling of uncleanliness and shame. He endeavored not to think of his masturbatory practices, to forget them, in fact to pretend that he was not guilty of them. After he had admitted the practice and clearly recognized its relation to his hand-washing compulsion, the latter disappeared.[16]

Sometimes the sex conflict may express itself in some type of antisocial behavior, such as stealing (see page 397), pathological lying, committing rape or murder, making sadistic attacks, or masochistic indulgence. Sadism (or active algolagnia) in its more developed form is a species of sex neurosis or perversion in which the individual obtains sexual satisfaction from inflicting beatings or pain on another person of the same or opposite sex. The abnormality is named after a French Count (de Sade), a writer of prurient romances who was condemned to death because of his vices. Loosely applied, the term refers to any abnormal tendency to maltreat or inflict extreme cruelty on others.

The press reports of October, 1933, recount the story of a terrific beating of a blond actress by a male actor. According to the news account, Miss W. testified that W. beat her so at her home after a party that her face was "frightfully disfigured," her eyes swollen until she could not see, and that she had to have a plastic surgeon work on her nose. She said W. struck her without warning, then threw her down in front of her house and sat on her. "He beat me up all over the street and grabbed me by my hair. I was ill in bed four days, and it's a wonder I didn't die." She testified that Mr. W. seems to like to hit women, having previously blacked both of Miss T.'s eyes.

The circumstances of the above case point to a sadistic attack. A prominent millionaire who frequently made the headlines years ago was the slayer of architect Stanford White. He was incarcerated for some time in a hospital for the mentally disordered and gave evidence of being a sadist. According to press reports, he inflicted merciless beatings on his protégé, a youth from Kansas City whom he had made his pal.

Freud offered various explanations of the sadistic complex: the impulse toward cruelty may have been stimulated (1) by the denial of gratification, aggression being the natural result of the blocking of the pleasure-seeking drive; (2) by the young child's witnessing of amatory advances on the part of adults that were misconstrued as attacks on the woman; (3) by skin contacts through fighting and wrestling with playmates; (4) and by the death instinct. According to Wilhelm Stekel, the sadist is driven to the "utter annihilation of the love object. Every sadist properly speaking is a murderer." Masochism (or passive algolagnia) is the opposite of sadism. The masochist obtains a sex experience by submitting to indignities at the hands of someone else, such as beatings, being cruelly treated, or being touched or daubed with the saliva of the consort. Flagellation over the genital region represents the

---

[16] V. E. Fisher, *An Introduction to Abnormal Psychology*, 1929, 188, with the permission of The Macmillan Company, New York.

preferred form of stimulation. Masochistically inclined children will commit repeated provocative acts for the sake of the pleasurable excitement aroused by the whippings. Jean Jacques Rousseau relates that as a boy of 11 or 12 he obtained keen satisfaction from the whippings received from his woman tutor and that he tried as an adult to provoke punishment from women whom he admired. The perversion may be a prelude to normal sex relations or—and this is more common—it may take the place of them. In a derived sense, the term "masochism" is applied to any form of behavior in which the individual seems to crave punishment and to enjoy suffering and helplessness. This type of punishment, devoid of sexual components, is referred to as social masochism. The word "masochism" is derived from Leopold von Sacher-Masoch, the Austrian novelist, who described the abnormality in some detail.

Algernon Swinburne, the childishly conceited devotee of the lure of pleasure, who drank himself to death and died in isolation, lived out on the reality plane the sadistic philosophy of death of Marquis de Sade, which he extolled in his poetical effusions.[17] His sadistic-masochistic cravings doubtless were the cause of the "incessant" punishments he received in school and the "frequent" punishments at Eton, which he relished. His masochistic trends are revealed in many phrases in his poetry, such as "the sharp and cruel enjoyment of pain," "sharp lips and fierce fingers," "fierce and bitter kisses," "our Lady of Pain," and "acrid relish of suffering." Swinburne was apparently also a necrophile (one subject to morbid, usually sexual, attraction toward dead bodies), at least in his phantasy life. One of his favorite themes was dead love:

> Yet am I glad to have her dead
> Here in this wretched wattled house
> Where I can kiss her eyes and head.

As is well known, some sadists will kiss and embrace the lifeless bodies of their love objects. Swinburne rationalized his abnormality thus: "I am cruel, but so is nature, and nature is God, and therefore I am like unto God. The more cruel and wicked I am, the closer do I come to nature." The bitter conflicts with his father may have been a factor in the development of Swinburne's abnormal sex life and his irreligion. As has been pointed out by Thomas V. Moore, "Those who later develop antireligious tendencies have [had] in childhood more or less bitter conflicts with parents and teachers." [18]

According to one hypothesis, the paradoxical masochistic, pain-pleasure complex is due to some peculiarity of the nervous system whereby a painful stimulation affords sensory pleasure through a process of emotional conditioning. Through conditioning, sex satisfaction becomes associated with some painful

---

[17] Thomas V. Moore, *Personal Mental Hygiene,* New York, Grune and Stratton, Inc., 1944, 267–285.

[18] *Ibid.,* 270.

experience. Freud propounded various theories: painful stimulation of an erogenous zone, particularly the buttocks; a transformation of sadism (which Theodore Reik revived after Freud abandoned it); and a fusion of the "death instinct" with sexual drives. To Karen Horney [19] masochism represents a tendency toward self-deflation, while narcissism is a tendency toward self-inflation. It is a "self-minimizing" tendency, a tendency to exaggerate "insufficiencies," a feeling of "being absolutely subjected to another's domination." Reik rejects these postulates. The essence of masochism is defiance. The masochist demonstrates the futility of punishment to control him by transforming the intended punishment into gratification. The punished child visualizes scenes of vengeance in which he plays the role of the torturer and the victim, playing at first the active role and then the passive role. The juvenile masochist obtains satisfaction from having witnesses observe the powerlessness of punishment over him. Revolutionaries and Christian martyrs have been social masochists, in part, who rejoiced in the multitudes of witnesses to the fact that they could not be deterred by suffering.[20] These varying explanations possess the value at most of plausible hypothetical constructs.[21]

[19] *Op. cit.*, 246*f*.

[20] Theodore Reik, *Masochism in Modern Man*, New York, Rinehart & Company, Inc., 1941.

[21] Another sex perversion should be mentioned, namely, fetishism, an erotic attachment to some object without intrinsic sex interest, such as an article of clothing worn by the adored person (a glove, a shoe, a handkerchief, etc.) or some part of the body other than sexual parts (the hair, a dimple, a mole on the face or neck, the eyes, teeth, or the nose). The contemplation or handling of the fetish tends to arouse erotic impulses. It is the result of emotional conditioning (*e.g.*, extreme fondness during childhood for some person with a dimple) or of the attempt through moral scruples to conceal or repress sexual attachment to some person. The sex attachment may thus unconsciously transfer to some article or feature associated with the person. In a broader sense, a fetish refers to any object of unreasoning devotion or of worship.

For treatises on some of the above sex aberrations consult

Henry Havelock Ellis, *Studies in the Psychology of Sex*, Philadelphia, F. A. Davis Company, 1897–1928 (Vols. 1–7).

Sigmund Freud, *Three Contributions to the Theory of Sex*, New York, Nervous and Mental Disease Monograph Series, No. 7, 1916, 2d ed. (translated by A. A. Brill).

George Godwin, *Peter Kürten: A Study in Sadism*, London, The Acorn Press, 1938.

George W. Henry, *et al.*, *Sex Variants, A Study of Homosexual Patterns*, New York, Harper & Brothers, 1941 (2 vols.).

Samuel Kahn, *Mentality and Homosexuality*, Boston, Meador Publishing Company, 1937.

Wilhelm Stekel, *Bi-sexual Love; the Homosexual Neurosis*, Boston, Richard G. Badger, 1922 (translated by J. S. van Teslaar).

Wilhelm Stekel, *Sadism and Masochism*, New York, Liveright Publishing Corp., 1929 (translated by Louise Brink).

Wilhelm Stekel, *Sexual Aberrations*, New York, Liveright Publishing Corp., 1930 (2 vols.) (translated by S. Parker).

Sometimes the outlet that the sex conflict may take is indulgence in slanderous gossip—an attempted defense, perhaps, against morbid preoccupation with the evils of sex—reading vicious meanings into innocent events or cantankerous condemnation of trivial infractions, due, doubtless, to the sour-grape attitude produced in the victim by unsuccessful sex repression or sublimation or by his desire to parade his own impeccability.

Freud, then, to summarize, finds the chief source of mental conflicts in the sex life. In the view of many psychoanalysts, the most important factors in producing morbid sex conditioning are the prejudices and morbid emotional attitudes of parents, teachers, and caretakers, superinduced by their own sexual infancy and unresolved sex conflicts.

Alfred Adler's Concept of Emotional Conflicts. Adler split with his mentor, Freud, and became the founder of a system of "individual psychology," which substituted inferior organs for Freud's libido as the source of character traits. In opposition to Freud, Adler finds the chief source of the more violent emotional conflicts in the thwarting of the "ego instincts," or the instinct for self-assertion, and in the urge for power, security, and dominance over one's fellows. The main drive in life is the striving for superiority. Sex conflicts play only a subordinate role in the manifestation of this drive or in its thwarting. On the other hand, the attempt of the individual to assert his own individuality and to dominate his associates often produces conflicts with authority. Innumerable occasions exist for deep-seated clashes between the individual's multitudinous egoistic cravings and the ruthless antagonistic demands of the social order, including hostile encounters with parents, teachers, playmates, and others.

It should be reemphasized that, according to the view of Adler, the "will to power" is often due to feelings of inferiority superimposed upon a background of physical inferiority and that it represents a fictitious goal, the pursuit of which may result in disagreeable character traits and social maladjustments.

Normal persons resolve their conflicts; they are oriented by reality. But neurotics set up goals (guiding fictions) that are impossible of attainment, and this tends to intensify the conflicts. The conflicts are not between the conscious and the unconscious, both of which are directed toward the same goal. For effecting a cure, the fictional egocentric goals must be replaced by attainable, approved social goals. Neurotic symptoms (all compensations) stem from present conflicts with the environment rather than from repressed infantile conflicts.

Conclusions Regarding the Nature of the Causative Factors of Mental Conflicts. The conclusion that the writer has reached regarding the causes of mental conflicts, stated very briefly and rather dogmatically, although based on the study of actual cases, is that the causative factors cannot be restricted to the sex and power urges. Occasions for mental conflicts may arise in any phase of the individual's social and psychobiological activities. Whenever there is lack of internal unity or integration or whenever lack of harmony exists between the individual's desires and the cultural demands of society as expressed in its social code, conventions, and laws, conflicts may arise between one urge and another urge, between one emotion and another emotion (as between the emotions of fear and anger, or between love, ambition, or the feeling of duty and timidity), between one attitude or ideal and another, between ideals, "instinctual" or organic cravings, habit patterns, conditioned responses, etc. But whatever the particular source of any conflict may be— and the particular sources may be legion—the root of the trouble in all probability usually can be traced to the individual's difficulty of reconciling his selfish personal desires with society's inexorable social taboos and demands. Just as the specific causes of mental conflicts may differ enormously, so the severity of the conflicts will vary tremendously. Some conflicts will produce trivial and negligible results, while others may precipitate acute mental distress and eventually lead to serious psychophysical disturbances.

Symptoms of Mental Conflicts and the Consequences of Serious Unresolved Conflicts. Sometimes mental conflicts are converted into, or expressed in, various overt bodily manifestations. The suspicious somatic signs that sometimes (although, of course, not always) serve as conflict indicators include restlessness, fidgeting with the fingers, moving the feet, scribbling quasi-automatically with a pencil, scratching the head, wringing the hands, picking the nose, nail biting, tics, or other automatisms and choreiform movements (see page 508 for an illustration of such choreiform movements). In more serious cases of unresolved conflicts one may at times observe dizziness, cardiac palpitation, frequent micturition or defecation, paralysis, and nervous maladies. As has already been noted, the physical symptoms in hysteria are explained as "conversion phenomena," that is, the conversion of psychological difficulties into bodily disorders, such as paralyses, anesthesias, coughing, or vomiting (see page 303). Some authorities regard the phenomena of conversion as the outstanding characteristic of hysteria. Some hold that neuroses are due solely to mental conflicts— they are acquired, not inherited— usually as the result of years of emotional repressions, although the exciting cause may have been some definite emotional crisis. In the view of some neuropsychiatrists, a neurosis is essentially a defense against an inner conflict, an attempt on the part of the victim to seek security in childish reactions (neurotic regressions), so that they may be treated like children (see pages 282*f.*). Of course, the physical manifestations of mental conflicts will vary enormously with the individual's constitutional make-up, as well as with his acquired disposition and attitudes. This observation applies also to the mental symptoms of mental conflicts. Neither the physical nor the mental symptoms listed here should be regarded as pathognomonic signs of mental conflicts.

Rather, they should be regarded merely as suspicious signs or indicators of conflicts.

The mental symptoms include anxieties, worries, phobias, and fears; apathy, idleness, and distaste for work; inability to respond freely and stuttering; sensitiveness; amnesias; disintegration; mental disabilities; inhibitions; irritability and hostility; tendencies toward secretiveness, concealment, withdrawal from social contacts, shut-in-ness, introversion, and infantile regressions; other mechanisms for escaping from the dreaded world of reality with which the individual may be in conflict, and overcompensation or exaggerated development of the opposite traits. In extreme cases, mental dissociation may ensue, followed, perhaps, by definite mental and nervous diseases.

CHAPTER XIV

MENTAL DISSOCIATIONS

Meaning of Mental Dissociation.[1] Negatively considered, mental dissociation is the opposite of mental integration, synthesis, or wholeness. Positively, dissociation refers to the detachment or disjunction of certain mental processes from the main mental current, so that the split-off ideas or processes appear to be more or less unrelated to the main stream of mental integration and also uninfluenced by the latter. When the disruption is serious, there appears to be no reciprocal influence between the two streams of mental activity. The dissociated processes may operate outside the subject's awareness, and so he is unconcerned about them and is unable to exercise conscious control over them. The dissociated elements lead a more or less independent, autonomous existence and function more or less automatically. It is obvious, therefore, that dissociations as thus defined represent very serious degrees of mental disintegration or cleavage, although there may, of course, be various degrees of dissociation. The word "disintegration" might be reserved for the slighter degrees of mental dissociation and disharmony in which contact is maintained between the disintegrated elements and no loss of personal identity is involved, but such a restriction of the term is not now generally observed.

Types of Dissociated Activities. The mechanism of dissociation has been invoked to explain a great variety of psychic phenomena, both normal and abnormal. Dissociation is thought to occur in varying degrees in all of the following split-off states. The so-called normal split-off states include sleep, dreams, fatigue, inability to concentrate, absent-mindedness, loss of memory, and extreme grief.

1. *Sleep.* Dissociation is a normally recurrent phenomenon in sleep. The brain activities that go on in sleep are detached from the conscious activities of the waking state. There is a complete cleft between the unconsciousness of the sleeper and the consciousness of the person who is awake. Fortunately the successive diurnal conscious states are reunited or reintegrated upon the awakening from sleep, so that the individual is enabled to maintain his personal identity, in spite of the profound mental schisms that occur daily or almost daily throughout his existence.

2. *Dreams.* Dream experiences are almost always dissociated from the waking experiences, although one can and does dream about one's waking

[1] From Pierre Janet.

experiences, and although the dream experiences can often be integrated with the waking experiences upon awakening, just as the sleeper's conscious, personal identity is reestablished when he reawakens.   Dissociations also occur in the dreams themselves, so that certain ideas or emotions become detached from the main dreams.   While dream states are, no doubt, connected with the same brain areas as waking thoughts, memories, and sensory perceptions, they lead an automatic, detached existence, completely or almost completely dissociated from the dreamer's primary consciousness.

3. *Fatigue*.   Temporary and mild degrees of dissociation may obtain in conditions of extreme fatigue.   The impulsive and inconsistent behavior sometimes observable in such states may be due to the process of dissociation that they produce.   States of excessive fatigue and loss of sleep, it may be added, tend to produce inattention, memory lapses, motor incoordination, and speech disturbances.   In persons of weak mental integration they may reduce mental efficiency as much as can be done by intoxication, and may even produce momentary states of mental aberration bordering on mental alienation, such as transitory hallucinations or delusions.

4. *Absent-mindedness, Loss of Memory, Distractibility, and Flights of Attention*.   The process of dissociation is doubtless present in and responsible for some cases of absent-mindedness, inability to concentrate, flights of attention, periods of abstraction, or lapses of memory.   Mild dissociations heighten distractibility of attention, while serious dissociations constitute serious obstacles to persistent concentration of attention.   The following case of temporary amnesia during periods of emotional excitement produced by excessive self-consciousness and embarrassment may be explicable, at least in part, on the dissociation hypothesis.

A ROYAL ENTERTAINER IN THE WORLD OF DREAMS WHO WAS UNABLE
TO TAKE A GIRL PLAYMATE TO THE TABLE WITHOUT EMBARRASSMENT
LEST HE COMMIT SOCIAL BLUNDERS, AND WHO WAS SO EMBARRASSED
IN THE PRESENCE OF THE BEAUTIFUL MOTHER OF ANOTHER PLAY-
MATE THAT HE HAD TO WRITE WHAT HE WANTED TO PURCHASE TO
AVOID FORGETTING HIS ERRAND AND ALSO HAD TO STOP PLAYING WITH
THE DAUGHTER

I was overfastidious in matters of social behavior.   I was afraid to take my classmate to supper at our home lest I make some social blunder.   I royally entertained my grand creatures of phantasy.   I conducted them through the maze of a court reception with far more grace than I could command when I took my golden-haired playmate to the table.   In my daydreams, I was like the centurion. I said "Come" and he came; I said "Go" and he went.   But in reality, I was a different creature.   I had to conform to custom, and I was not sure of my ground. The girl did not embarrass me.   She was the only little girl playmate I ever had.

She was not a sister to me, nor a "best girl"—she was my good fairy. I loved her cornflower eyes and her pretty hair. Her voice was rich and clear; and I had shyly quaffed the sweet nectar of the lips that praised me. But taking her to the table and serving her with mush and milk were feats outside the pale of my powers.

Some years after, I had another girl friend or playmate. But I was then at an age when caressing provoked other emotions. I felt at ease in the girl's company, but her mother, a very pretty woman, embarrassed me beyond words. She was cordial and kind, but her beauty caused me so much confusion that I stopped playing with the daughter. The lady conducted a small store, to which it seemed I had to go on innumerable errands. I finally reached the point where I would write a list of the things to be purchased to keep from talking. I couldn't trust myself to speak. I would forget what I was saying in the middle of a sentence.

One day I discovered that the daughter had become much prettier than her mother. The timidity left me, and I still felt at ease with the daughter. But alas! Both the daughter and I had grown older. For us, no more long tramps in the woods, no more rainy afternoons playing in the hay.

(H.L.; M.; H.S.T.; B.S.; Age 38)

5. *Extreme Grief.* Evidences of dissociation in extreme grief, even in assumedly normal persons, are occasionally seen in incoordinate and inconsistent movements, such as laughing, crying, and disheveling the hair.

More Extreme Conditions Giving Evidence of Dissociation. The following are some of the more distinctly abnormal or pathological conditions that show evidences of dissociation.

1. *States of Recovery from the Effects of Anesthetics.* As the patient emerges from the anesthetic he may enter a "no man's land" of clouded consciousness, unaware of who he is or where he is. But with the return of consciousness the sundered associations are reunited. The dissociation phenomena connected with recovery from nitrous oxide gas (laughing gas) are well known.

2. *Narcotic States.* States of mental and motor dissociation of varying degrees can be produced by alcohol and other narcotics and habit-forming drugs, such as cocaine, morphine, and heroine.

3. *Automatic Writing.* Buried or dissociated ideas may explain the spontaneous or automatic writing that some persons are able to do with the aid of the planchette or the Ouija board.

4. *Hypnosis.* No conscious connection exists between the hypnotic and waking states. The hypnotized person on awakening has lost all memory of what transpired during the hypnosis. When rehypnotized, he again loses contact with his real self but may establish contact with his prior hypnotic associations. The hypnotized and dehypnotized person is like a person with two separate and independent selves. The characteristics of the hypnotized personality may differ radically from those of the normal personality.

5. *Dual or Multiple or Alternating Personalities.* In these infrequent conditions, the personality dissociations or cleavages are so extreme that the victim may exist in two or more separate selves or mental integrations. He may have a main, or primary, state or integration corresponding to his real self, usually the more lasting one, and a secondary state, corresponding to his dissociated or detached personality, which usually is the less enduring. When he develops three or more personalities, he is referred to as a case of multiple personality. He may alternate more or less periodically between the two or more personalities or may remain a long time in each state. He may eventually return to the primary state and retain his real self permanently. His behavior characteristics may be markedly different in the different states. Each personality pattern constitutes a distinct personality integration. The two-in-one usually cannot recall in the primary personality what happened in the secondary state. In the secondary phase he may be able to recall what he did in the primary integration, but he may attribute the acts to someone else. Usually the memory images are vague and dubitable. Most of those subject to the malady betray a history of some psychoneurotic weakness, excessive fatigue, and emotional stress (the precipitating factor).

The limits of this volume do not permit a detailed discussion of multiple personality or of many other abnormal mental phenomena that properly receive extended consideration in works on abnormal psychology and psychiatry.[2]

Brief reference may, however, be made to an apparent case of split personality reported in the daily press in April, 1934, involving an express truck guard who was under arrest in Chicago for having absconded with

[2] For a more adequate discussion of multiple personality and other mental abnormalities, consult

Edmund S. Conklin, *Principles of Abnormal Psychology,* 2d ed., New York, Henry Holt and Company, Inc., 1935.

Roy M. Dorcus and G. Wilson Shaffer, *Textbook of Abnormal Psychology,* 3d ed., Baltimore, The Williams & Wilkins Company, 1945.

V. E. Fisher, *An Introduction to Abnormal Psychology,* New York, The Macmillan Company, 1937.

Shepherd I. Franz, *Persons One and Three, A Study of Multiple Personality,* New York, McGraw-Hill Book Company, Inc., 1933.

William McDougall, *Outline of Abnormal Psychology,* New York, Charles Scribner's Sons, 1926.

Morton Prince, *The Dissociation of a Personality,* New York, Longmans, Green & Co., Inc., 1930; and *The Unconscious,* New York, The Macmillan Company, 1921.

B. Sidis and S. P. Goodhart, *Multiple Personality,* New York, Appleton-Century-Crofts, Inc., 1905.

J. E. Wallace Wallin, *Clinical and Abnormal Psychology,* Boston, Houghton Mifflin Company, 1927.

$39,000 from an express company. This man was identified as three different persons. When confronted by his mother from Columbus, Ohio, who identified him as R. L. H., he bowed stiffly and said: "I'm sorry, madam, I never saw you before. I'm glad to have met you, however." " 'The only thing I can say is that he's my son and he doesn't know it.' The mother reached up, kissed him, and murmured, 'Good-by, son.' Led from the room, she said: 'It's a shame to send a sick mind to the penitentiary.' " When confronted by his Chicago wife, the mother of five of his children, who had married him as A. R. H., his reply was: "Lady, I never saw you before." He was also identified by a New York divorcée as B. A., and he himself insisted he was B. A., a New York real estate man. "The authorities brought Mrs. R. L. H. from Cincinnati last night. She talked with him for two hours about their two children. 'Lady, you're mistaken, I don't know you,' said the three-in-one." Investigation showed that R. L. H., "one-time 'Handsome Bob' of the Columbus force, was injured in a motorcycle accident before he disappeared in 1918, leaving his wife and two children. His brother in Columbus said that he suffered an amnesia spell after the accident, in which his motorcycle struck a parkway while he was chasing a speeder, and that during the months he was in the hospital he would forget the daily visits of his relatives from one day to the next."

This appears to be a bona fide case of triple personality primarily traceable to a brain injury, although elements of mental conflict may be involved.

Minor alteration and alternation of personalities within the framework of the same self in so-called normal persons, who retain their identity and maintain their continuity throughout all the fluctuations, are fairly common, as contrasted with the rather infrequent losses of complete identity, such as are involved in the complete dissociations in "dual" or "multiple" personalities. For example, the type of person who is exceedingly upright on Sundays but unscrupulous on weekdays, and yet retains his identity, is fairly well known. The type of person who is alternately in high spirits and then down in the dumps but remains Madam X throughout her emotional oscillations need not be sought in the pages of fiction. She (or he, as the case may be) is a familiar figure in the homes of almost every countryside. The disintegration evidenced by such mutations does not amount to dissociation in the technical connotation of the word.

6. *Severe Amnesias.* No sharp lines exist between changes of personality, severe amnesias, fugues, and somnambulism. These bizarre conditions shade into one another. Two instances of prolonged memory lapses involving loss of identity and some characteristics of dual personality occur on pages 297f. A few additional cases of apparent amnesia, some of which also involve the development of secondary personalities, may be quoted in abbreviated form from press accounts.

May 13, 1934: Army authorities returned Sergeant A. B., twenty-six, an apparent amnesia victim to Boston today to face a charge of being absent without leave. He will be placed under hospital observation.

B. told police when he appeared here last Sunday he was unable to remember his identity. He was identified several days ago by M. S., who said they were to have been married on the day he disappeared. The youth, however, is married and has two children. [From the facts related above, this case of amnesia seems clearly to have served as an escape mechanism.]

Apr. 26, 1934: A woman who recalled clearly the many lands in which she has traveled, but could not remember her own name and address, was under treatment today at Bellevue Hospital, where she was taken when she told a police officer that she felt ill. In her purse were a number of photographs taken in the Virgin Islands, from which she said she returned only three weeks ago; an envelope addressed to E. E. D. of Essex, Conn., and a bill for $50 marked paid, from Dr. J. L. R., of Port of Spain, Trinidad, but her name was written in such a scrawl that it could not be deciphered. The woman, well dressed and about thirty-eight years old, wore two wedding rings. A handkerchief in her pocket was initialed "R."

March 9, 1934: A well-dressed man appealed to the police in Baltimore to help identify himself. When his wife subsequently appeared to identify him, he looked at her blankly and replied: "I'm sorry, I haven't the pleasure of your acquaintance." He proved to be a 46-year-old superintendent of a large ink concern in Boston. No clue was revealed as to the cause of the loss of identity or as to his subsequent recovery.

Oct. 10, 1935: A 53-year-old man wandered into police headquarters in Cleveland unable to recall his name or address. The use of the word "Otto" by one of the policemen in addressing a co-worker reintegrated the split psyche. "Otto," said the amnesia victim, "Why, that's my name—Otto S. I'm from Baltimore."

Nov. 22, 1935: P. C. C., on visiting Kansas City, his boyhood home, suddenly recalled his identity. He had, as disclosed by army fingerprint records, lived in the army under two names, for sixteen years as F. A. Adams. Soon after his induction in 1917, possibly due to severe emotional conflict, he remembered nothing until he received his discharge as Adams. He was reunited with his mother in Luray, Kan., for the first time in 18 years, and disclosed that he had a wife and daughter in Baltimore.

Dec. 2, 1937: A man recovered from the oblivion of amnesia in a jail cell today and remembered for the first time in 30 months his name, his wife, and his home. He had been picked up by a policeman in Redwood City, Calif., at 1:30 A.M., wandering aimlessly around in the streets. After having a displaced neck vertebra adjusted by a chiropractor, he went to sleep and upon awakening exclaimed: "Where am I, and why am I in jail?" He was able to recall everything up to May 18, 1935, when he sold the restaurant he operated with his wife in Cincinnati and had left with two male friends, whose names he recalled, for Akron and Cleveland, looking for a job. He expressed a desire to return to his wife, a waitress in a Cincinnati restaurant, who had not given up hope that he would return. Another amnesia victim, a 20-year-old boy, regained his memory in the city prison hospital in Columbus, O., when his "neck was given a twist," by Dr.

D., whose hobby is criminology. There was a snap, "things began to clear up," and he remembered that he was J. M. of Chicago. Upon return to normalcy, he expressed his elation in terms of "earning a million dollars."

May 11, 1939: 56-year-old "Frank Miller" applied for relief at Santa Ana, Calif., and was recognized by the administrative clerk as F. C. McC., who had left his home at Lompac 19 years earlier on a business trip to Los Angeles, from which he never returned. Reunited with his wife the fog of amnesia was dissipated after a week of patient repetition of past experiences. Because he had been declared legally dead 12 years ago, he and Mrs. McC., parents of six children, "eloped" to Yuma, Ariz., and were remarried.

Among cases of amnesia, one that attracted national attention was the sudden disappearance of Raymond Robins, militant dry leader, social worker, and philanthropist, on September 3, 1932, in the heat of the presidential campaign in which he was an active campaigner. After starting to keep his appointment with Herbert Hoover at the White House, he completely vanished and was thought to have been kidnaped by bootleggers, in reprisal for his prohibition activities, or by Russian imperialists because he favored the recognition of Russia. After a ten weeks' nation-wide search he was identified as one Reynolds H. Rogers, a purported mining engineer from "out Kentucky way," wearing overalls and boots, his face covered with a long shaggy beard. He had been "prospecting" for gold in the mountains of Swain County, N.C., where he had built a lookout tower in a tree on the summit of a mountain back of his boarding house. He was found to be in "sound physical condition and perfect control of his ordinary mental faculties, except for his affliction with amnesia." When his nephew and wife reached the scene he denied his identity and failed to recognize either one of them. "When Mrs. Robins greeted him a few minutes after she arrived, he looked at her and said: 'I don't know you, lady.'" "Not a glimmer of recognition followed Mrs. Robins' second visit to a hospital where her distinguished husband, stricken with amnesia, is seeking to recover his memory under the care of specialists. 'We had a pleasant, friendly chat,' she said, 'but he did not recognize me. One could see that, aside from his inability to recall events beyond the time he reached Whittier, he is well and healthy in every way.'" The hospital psychiatrist found that "he recalls early features of his own personal history as Robins but is under the impression, nevertheless, that he is Rogers." His nephew reported that Robins "feels that we have made a tragic mistake in identification. However, he has resigned himself to the situation, believing, apparently, that he may soon convince his physicians and Mrs. Robins that he is not Colonel Robins and be free to again take the peaceful life at Whittier that he learned to love so well. He disliked to leave Whittier 'and have the best peace I have known in ten years torn up.'" After her third visit on the third day Robins "recognized his wife after an obvious effort and regained his memory. 'Do you say, this is my wife?' he was said to have asked the doctor. After a half minute's silence, during which the patient was reported to have shown evidences of great strain, Mrs. Robins approached him," and he recognized her and called her by name.

According to a press release under date of Dec. 11, Robins is quoted as saying:

I have come through a terrible experience. Here in my home, surrounded by my family and the friends and associations I have loved since I was a boy, I am being fully restored. Those who are wise in matters of this sort assure me that the darkness that overtook me in the midst of my day's work was a provision of nature to save me from a serious collapse. Those who meet me in the future therefore will be able to judge of my mental clarity. Those who have known my life in the past will not believe that I have been a quitter.

For the generous and tender helpfulness of many dear friends in these hours of suffering for my wife and family I am grateful beyond words. For the competent and kindly cooperation of the officers of government and the immense aid—and in the main truthful and fair treatment—accorded me by the public press, I cherish abiding gratitude.

In so far as there has been untrue and unfair comment I forgive its authors and accept it as the cost of a life spent in battle for causes I hold dear. All that I ask for the future is judgment upon the facts of my way and work from day to day.

One feature of unusual interest to the mental hygienist in amnesia cases, so well illustrated in this case, is the regression of the victim to an earlier period in his life in which he made his fortune. Robins participated very successfully in the Klondike gold rush of the nineties. It was to this period crowned with successful achievement that his secondary personality reverted. This afforded him an opportunity to experience again the joys of prospecting for gold, but this time in North Carolina. This vicarious experience gave him the "best peace he had known in ten years." The amnesias of dual personality often must be interpreted as flights away from one's own personality to a different personality in which one can achieve success in a field of endeavor unknown to the primary personality and thus freed from the conflicts, inhibitions, and dissatisfactions of the latter.

7. *Fugues.* A fugue is a sort of hysterical attack in which the individual forgets his identity and past life and flees (*fuga*, "flight") from his accustomed haunts to which he is unable to adjust. He is dominated by the impulse to run away from a menacing situation that he is unable to face. The fugue, in other words, is an escape dynamism that enables the individual to take flight from his distasteful physical surroundings and from his own consciousness. The mechanism represents the bursting forth, more or less automatically, of painful repressed elements. The amnesia protects him from self-condemnation for his cowardice. The episode may continue from

a few hours to several months, or even years. Usually it is of considerable duration. On superficial examination, the victim of this malady may not appear to be abnormal. He may travel about and keep fairly well in touch with his surroundings, although perhaps less successfully than does the victim of double or multiple personality. He may awaken some morning with his identity and his memory fully restored, but with no recollection of the intervening fugue experiences. There is none of the detachment from the surroundings in this condition that is characteristic of some of the psychoses (*e.g.*, dementia praecox). The condition has been referred to as an amnestic hysterical episode and also as an advanced sleepwalking episode. According to some authorities, there is only one step from the fugue and somnambulism to multiple personality. Obviously, the line of demarcation between these pathological conditions has not yet been clearly drawn. They may all be phases of a general hysterical diathesis. Those subject to the malady betray a history of nervous instability and excessive worry and fatigue. Victims sometimes snap out of fugues or out of amnesias, thus reintegrating the personality, when reference is made to their past lives or when they are called by their right names.

8. *Somnambulism.* This term is sometimes used in a more comprehensive sense than sleepwalking (noctambulation). In states of hysterical somnambulism (classified by some writers as fuguelike states that occur during sleep), the victim, as in the case of ordinary sleepwalking, walks around in a trancelike condition and executes various complicated movements while usually avoiding obstacles in his path. The actions relate to a single idea or closely related groups of ideas (monoideic) or to two or more ideas or groups of ideas (polyideic), all, however, expressions of a single dissociated system.[3] According to one theory, the somnambulist is controlled by a secondary, disintegrated system of ideas, which is detached from his waking consciousness. He is intent, so it is held, on attaining some goal. Oblivious of his surroundings, he is reliving or reenacting some actual prior emotional experience, without any recollection of his exploits upon reawakening. This is an instance of amnestic dissociation. According to our records, awareness of the objective to be realized, if it exists, is dissociated from the primary mental integration.

Somnambulism is distinguishable from the fugue in that it is a phenomenon of sleeping or of a trancelike or sleeplike state; it probably involves a smaller segment of the individual's psychic life, and it is perhaps largely restricted to the dramatic reenactment of some definite past experience.

Illustrations of Cases of Sleepwalking and Talking in Sleep. Instances of sleepwalking are not difficult to obtain. It will be noted that none of the

[3] From Pierre Janet.

following somnambulists, except one, were aware of the purpose of their sleepwalking, that none connect the activity with any prior emotional experience, and that the activities apparently were automatic and unconscious in practically all cases, being controlled by dissociated cerebral activities. The methods used to overcome the compulsion are not without interest.

A CASE OF UNEXPLAINED SLEEPWALKING; CURE OF A CASE OF NIGHTMARE BY REMOVAL OF ADENOIDS

Beginning at the age of five years I often walked in my sleep. My parents would often find that I was not in my accustomed place in bed. Sometimes I would walk through another room and climb into the bed of an older brother. Mother would often hear me walking in my sleep and would attempt to awaken me but I was very difficult to awaken. She soon learned that cold water placed upon my face would shock me and thus cause me to awaken. This sleepwalking was not in the nature of a nightmare because mother reported that I did no talking nor was I in any kind of a delirium. Upon one occasion I opened a screen door and was sitting down upon the porch steps when I was found. At another time, when we were visiting my grandparents, I was found walking in the yard in my sleep. This sleepwalking continued until I was twelve years of age.

I have not walked in my sleep since that time except once when I was a grown man. One night I walked into the room of a friend, who was rooming at the same Y.M.C.A. in which I roomed, and asked him to get a doctor "quick." The friend went for a doctor who found me in a delirious state and it was necessary to give me a hypodermic injection before I would quiet down. I awoke the next morning and remembered nothing of the occasion. However, about a week later I had a nervous breakdown and was confined to my bed for several weeks.

I have not been able to ascertain any causes for this ailment. It may have been caused by a general nervous condition since I was very nervous when I was a child. Neither have I been able to ascertain why I stopped sleepwalking at the age of twelve years.

Since I do not know the cause or remedy for my sleepwalking I will relate the case of my young son (seven years old) who seemingly has been cured of nightmares. He began having nightmares at the age of five and a half years. His case was somewhat different from my own for he would sit up in bed, wildly throw his arms and make such exclamations as "They're getting me," "Help me hold this down," "Isn't this a wonderful airplane ride," "Daddy, don't let me fall," "I am just as strong as you are," etc. At times I barely had enough strength to hold him in my arms, as he would fight wildly. Sometimes it would take as long as fifteen minutes to awaken him. If we could get him completely awakened, the occurrence would not repeat itself again during the same night.

About two months ago his adenoids and tonsils were removed and he has not had a nightmare since. I cannot state that the adenoids were the cause of the nightmares, but the physician said that the pressing of the adenoids upon the back of the nose produced a feeling of pressure which caused the boy to have very fantastic dreams.   (P.L.W.; M.; Instr. in Jr. C.; M.A.; Age 35)

SOMNAMBULISTIC ESCAPADES WITH TALKING IN SLEEP AND ABILITY TO ANSWER QUESTIONS MORE OR LESS RATIONALLY, INDICATIVE OF DISSOCIATION

According to reports from various members of my immediate family—parents, brother, and sisters—I was what one might call a sleepwalking artist. I would arise from my bedroom at almost any time in the night and find my way to almost any part of our place. After wandering around to my heart's content I would usually find my way back to my room and bed without ever waking or becoming aware that I had left the room. This happened particularly between the ages of five and seven and continued at less frequent intervals up to seventeen. In fact, even now I get up and walk around in the house about once in three months.

I awoke one morning to find that my right leg had a number of deep scratches upon it. Later in conversation with the family I learned that I had been running in the yard between one and two o'clock in the morning and had got into a rose bush where I remained crying until my mother came and took me out and put me back to bed. I knew nothing whatever of this occurrence.

Sometimes in the night I would awake in the yard or on the lawn or garden, never knowing how I got there. On these occasions I would make exceedingly quick work of getting back into the house for I was terribly afraid of the dark.

On one of my walking excursions I was suddenly awakened from a fall on a paling fence that surrounded our yard. In the daytime I had frequently walked on top of this fence. I suppose I had been trying it that night in my sleep, slipped, and fell on the sharp-pointed palings. This accident awakened me and I immediately scampered away to my bed without arousing any of the other members of the family.

Another thing that may be of interest in my sleepwalking exploits is the fact that members of the family often conversed with me on some of these occasions and I answered them with such sensible words that they never knew that I was asleep until several days afterwards. I think that generally they did know that I was asleep, but there were times reported when I seemed to be able to carry on a very sensible conversation with different members of the family. I understand that I almost invariably talked when I was walking around. By this I mean that I uttered many sentences, both rational and irrational.

(L.I.S.; M.; Instr. in T.C.; M.A.)

SLEEPWALKING, WRITING POEMS WHILE ASLEEP, AND PREDICTING THE END OF THE WORLD WAR IN A DREAM

I was a sleepwalker as a child. On one occasion I carried a lamp about the house. My mother, hearing the sound of walking, got up and took the lamp from my hand. She said my eyes were wide open and staring, but I gave no sign of recognition. On another occasion, I got up, took my books from the dining room table, and put them under the bed. Next morning, having no recollection of this, I searched for my books and was late for school as a result. Frequently, I have put things away during waking hours without being able to remember where I had put them. I finally discovered that I needed only to shut my eyes and sit calmly and then I would be able to go directly to the place where I had hidden or misplaced the article. This is commonly characterized as "absent-mindedness" but to me it seems like "sleepwalking" while awake. I do not know how somnambulism is usually cured, but my mother effected a cure in my case which lasted for many years. She placed chairs alongside my bed. Thereafter, when I climbed over them while sleepwalking, she heard the noise and got up and woke me. For many years there was no recurrence of my somnambulistic performances until the summer of 1914 [when she was in the late twenties]. I awakened everyone in the house by walking about and screaming "fire and blood!" When they all stood about me, my mother holding me to keep me from falling, I awoke and became very hysterical. In a couple of months, war broke out in Europe. In October of that year my sister was drowned.

In 1918, while war was in progress in Europe, I got up and wrote part of a poem while asleep. When I arose next morning, the sheets lay on the chair beside my bed with the following words faintly scrawled:

> When sleep had borne me out upon its stream,
> Swift flowing, as the fabled river Lethe,
> And cast me on the shore of Oblivion's realm,
> Like ship-wrecked sailor, cast upon a reef;
> Rising, I seemed to wander aimlessly
> As one in darkness, seeking some human haven;
> My spirit searched in vain for light to lead
> Or hand to touch and give me aid . . .

For several years I tried to complete this poem, but was unable to do so until after I had had some peculiar dream experiences. I dreamed that same summer that the war would end before Christmas. I related this dream at Cornell University to students and one of the professors. Subsequent events harmonized with the dream.   (V.E.; F.; S.C.T.)

[The ability of some minds to do constructive work in dream states or in the drowsy states just before going to sleep or just before awakening, such as solving puzzling problems, composing music, writing prose or poetry, or perfecting inventions, is well known. The *Devil's Sonata* was composed by Giuseppe Tartini in a dream. Many of Wolfgang Mozart's musical scores were dream creations, while his *Magic Flute* was a hypnagogic inspiration. Samuel Coleridge's *Kubla Khan* and *Rime of the Ancient Mariner* took form in dreams. Many of the stories of Robert Louis Stevenson, including his *Dr. Jekyll and Mr. Hyde,* were conceived in his dreams. Henri Poincaré in a dream solved the hypergeometry of the Fuchsian functions, while Kekule discovered the benzene ring of organic atoms while he fell asleep on a bus in London.]

Sleepwalkers sometimes perform amazing feats and allegedly exhibit un-canny aptitude for avoiding dangers, such as walking around the eaves of the house without falling, climbing over difficult obstructions, or avoiding hazards while crossing treacherous paths. Nevertheless, instances of fatal mishaps are frequently recorded, such as the following tragedy, reported in a dispatch from London in the papers of March 15, 1933:

Anny Ahlers, one of the outstanding actresses in Europe, although she was only twenty-six years old, who died last night, was understood to have come to her death as the result of a concussion suffered in a fall while sleepwalking.

The German actress, it was said, had long been a somnambulist. Recently her maid said she had saved her as she was about to climb through a bedroom window while asleep.

In the first act of "The DuBarry," in which she had been starring here, she climbed through a window onto a balcony.

Many other abnormal phenomena that occur in both normal and ab-normal mental conditions are explicable as dissociated elements over which the individual is able to exercise little control. These include irrational obsessions, compulsions, phobias, delusions, hallucinations, and hysteria. Brief consideration will be given to obsessions, compulsions, and hysteria.

9. *Obsessions and Compulsions.* Obsessions are persistent, coercive ideas or urges that keep obtruding themselves upon the subject, while compulsions are similarly recurrent compulsive acts or tendencies to repeat certain move-ments again and again. Compulsions are often complicated ceremonials. Both are automatisms or automatically active dissociated elements over which the victim has little control. He is aware of them, sometimes acutely so; he knows he is enslaved by them; he often regards them as preposterous and silly; nevertheless, he possesses little control over them. The experiences he must endure are uncomfortable and disagreeable and often are characterized by haunting fears, phobias, and lurking doubts. Giving way to the impulses usually affords the sufferer a measure of relief. Symbolical motor expression often proves temporarily tension-reducing; its suppression increases the dread and anxiety. The symbolical expression supplies an outlet in the form of an apparently indifferent diversionary substitute for a severe emotional con-flict that the victim has failed to resolve. The compulsive activity is less morally objectionable than is the frank indulgence of the incompatible urge.

An obsessional neurosis is interpreted by the Freudian psychoanalysts as an unconscious regression to disapproved infantile forms of sex indulgence.

The catalogue of obsessions and compulsions is a very long one, from the harmless vagaries to which normal children and adults are subject—such as yielding to the urge to count steps and posts, to start with one foot first in ascending staircases, to step over cracks in the walks, and to touch every lamppost, and the recurrent tendency of a certain tune to run through the head—to distinctly distressing, uncontrollable, irrational uncertainties, fears, ritualistic behavior symptoms, or imperative criminalistic impulses—such as stealing (kleptomania) or setting fire to things (pyromania). All the manias are compulsions.

Illustrations. The following illustrative cases will show the variety of obsessional and compulsive impulses that annoy and frequently dominate normal persons.

INSATIABLE COUNTING MANIA, LASTING FOR YEARS, POSSIBLY DUE TO BEING TAUGHT TO COUNT VERY EARLY IN LIFE, OR TO THE SATIS-FACTION DERIVED FROM THE PRAISE RECEIVED FOR PROFICIENCY IN COUNTING; LED TO ABILITY TO MAKE RAPID ESTIMATES OF NUMBER OF OBJECTS; TENDENCY OVERCOME FROM OVERHEARING AN EMBAR-RASSING REMARK

The principal in our town wanted to experiment with some small children and so I with three others of preschool age was put in a class and taught at different periods of the day. The rest of the time we were free to do what we pleased, just so we did not disturb the room. The other pupils were quite old and were preparing for college.

I learned to count to one hundred in this room. When sent to the board one day to write one hundred, I was the only one of the four to do this correctly and I received quite a bit of praise from the teachers and the grown-up pupils.

From then on I began to count everything I saw, stairs, fence posts, letters in advertisements, etc. Nothing escaped me. I could only count by ones until one day I heard my father say to my sister that it would be easy to count by threes. I asked my mother what he meant, and she told me. From then on I'd count by ones, by threes, and then by fives. It became an obsession to count. I'd count the people at church or at concerts, those who were baldheads and those who had gray hair, the tucks or plaits in the dresses of the persons in front of me, the windows, the flaws in the woodwork, in fact everything that was countable.

After I went to high school I continued to count much to the amusement and disgust of some of my friends. I had learned to look at a row of things and very quickly tell how many there were. This obsession did that much for me. I went through college still obsessed with the counting mania.

I did not, however, realize what effect this obsession had on other people until one day I heard someone say: "I would not sit in front of her for anything and have her count all the tucks in my dress and find fault with what I had on."

This was the first time it had ever dawned on me that I was making people uncomfortable, so I immediately set about overcoming this mania. In a short time the intense desire to count was gone, although I occasionally find myself still counting.   (C.L.E.; F.; E.S.T.; Ph.B.; Age 40)

OBSESSIONS ABOUT OBSERVING HOUSE NUMBERS, COUNTING TELE-
PHONE POSTS, RUBBING HEAD WHEN READING, AND MAKING OUT
MONTHLY BUDGETS WITH METICULOUS CARE MONTHS IN ADVANCE

Observing House Numbers

Watching numbers on houses as I ride past them is undoubtedly one of my obsessions. Especially do I do this when I'm on streetcars. If something obstructs my view I almost feel like getting off the car and going back to see what the number was.

Counting Posts

I also count the telephone posts as I ride past them on the train. I always wanted to see how many there were between small stations especially. I remember one time when I was about twelve years of age, I decided I'd count all the telephone posts between Baton Rouge, Louisiana, and Dallas, Texas. It worried me because I knew I couldn't see when night came on. Of course I didn't succeed in my attempt to count the posts, and the journey was miserable, but as soon as morning came I awoke very early and began counting. I tried to imagine how many posts I had passed during the night. When I was small, I'd almost cry if my mother called me for any purpose (including the eating of lunch) while I was busily engaged in counting posts. This obsession is not so great as it was when I was a child, but traces of it still remain.

Compulsion to Rub Head and Pull Hair When Reading

Rubbing one particular spot on my head and pulling my hair when I read seems to be an obsession or a habit I've developed within the past four or five years. I may have had it before but I have just noticed it since that time. I feel that I'm not getting the thought unless this act accompanies the reading process. I know it is foolish but I unconsciously do it all the time.

Exaggerated Punctiliousness in Making Out Budgets

Making budgets has really become an obsession. At this very moment, August, 1930, I can tell you how much I plan to spend for miscellaneous expense, clothing, amusements, or 'most any item, during June, 1931. I always carry a small note book in my purse and at the most unexpected times I'll open this book and jot down some item which I forgot to include in my budget for say, April, 1931. I may be in class, in church, or on the street. I usually revise my budget every month; in fact, hardly a day passes that I do not feel called upon to make some changes. Maybe I bought an extra item that day so I'll suddenly decide that I may want to buy that same item on Jan. 10, 1931, so I forthwith open my book and add this to my January, 1931, budget.

I suppose economic pressure would cause almost anyone with limited means to make budgets, but why be so extreme about it? In a measure I attribute that to a trait which I have of wanting to do whatever I do in extreme degree. I have a tendency toward a one-track mind. Sometimes I wonder if at some time I will not suffer from monomania in a very pronounced form. This trait no doubt also contributes to my absent-mindedness.

(D.C.N.; F.; Col.; E.S.T.; B.S.; Age 29)

COMPULSIVE RHYTHMICAL COUNTING AND MOVEMENTS OF THE TOES IN DEFINITE PATTERNS, OCCURRING DURING MOMENTS OF FATIGUE

This obsession is so very absurd I almost refrained from including it in this inventory. For a long time I have had the habit of counting from one to thirty-two in patterns of four. For instance; one—two—three—four, five—six—seven— eight, etc., until thirty-two is reached. In unison with the counting I work certain toes on my feet in a certain order. I begin with the left little toe, go to the right big toe, back to the left big toe, and thence to the right little toe. The counting is done silently, one toe movement accompanying one count. When I reach nine I begin with the right little toe and proceed in the reverse direction until twenty-five is reached; then the reverse order is reinstated. These rhythmic counting and toe movements usually are employed when I am fatigued, when I will go through the performance once or twice. This is utterly foolish but it happens even now and to stop it I must forcefully inhibit the tendency.

(A.H.T.; F.; Col.; C. Instr. of Psy.; M.S.; Age 26)

UNEXPLAINED FEAR OF LOSING TICKET AND COMPULSIVE TENDENCY CONSTANTLY TO LOOK IN POCKETBOOK FOR IT, ALTHOUGH KNOWING THAT THE TICKET IS IN THE PURSE; SATISFACTION WHEN AT LAST CONDUCTOR COLLECTS TICKET

Whenever I am riding on the train I am always afraid that I shall lose my ticket. I am never afraid of losing my money, but just my ticket. For that reason, from the time I board the train until the last conductor takes my ticket, I look into my pocketbook at least every thirty minutes, just to make sure that my ticket is there. I may know perfectly well that there is no reason for it not to be there. Still I must look for it repeatedly. When the last conductor has taken my ticket, I always breathe a sigh of great relief.

(J.W.A.; F.; Col.; E.S.T.; B.A.; Age 30)

COMPULSIVE TENDENCIES TO JUMP INTO WATER AND URGE TO JUMP FROM HIGH PLACES

Urge to Jump into Water

Whenever I am near bodies of water, whether large or small, I want to jump into the water. Often, if I stand on a bank more than a minute, I must definitely set myself to the task of not jumping in. Sometimes I do this by repeating over and over to myself these words, "I must not jump in."

Urge to Jump from Heights

The same kind of feeling overwhelms me when I am on a high place, or looking out of a window above the first story of a building. That is, the desire to jump grows more intense as the height increases. Often I wonder if this desire to jump is not the explanation of some of the suicides. These unfortunate people have killed themselves for no apparent reason. Was this desire to jump and their inability to withstand it the reason? (J.W.A.; F.; Col.; E.S.T.; B.A.; Age 30)

AN OBSESSIVE "GAME" OF STUDYING CLOUDS AND FINDING ANIMALS IN THEM AND NAMING THEM ALOUD, YIELDING EXTREME SATISFACTION; TRACEABLE TO A CHILDHOOD GAME

Whenever I look into the sky and see a cloud, there is a feeling that impels me to inspect the cloud in order to determine just what animal it resembles. If I am with someone, I seem to be compelled to interrupt the conversation, regardless of its importance, call that person's attention to the cloud and name the animal that it resembles. If I am alone I seem constrained to name the animal aloud. When I have named the animal, the cloud immediately disappears or takes on another form. With the naming of each form a feeling of extreme satisfaction comes over me and I am ready to attend to matters more earthly and tangible than clouds. I used to sit for long periods during my playtime and play this game with the clouds.

UNEXPLAINED COMPULSIVE TENDENCY TO GO THROUGH CERTAIN FINGER EXERCISES IN ROTATION, WITH AN URGE TO CONTINUE UNTIL THE LITTLE FINGER IS REACHED

Often when my hands are idle, I find myself indulging in the following exercise: First, I pass my thumb over the nails of my other fingers, then I pass each of my other fingers over the nail of my thumb. Sometimes this is a slow movement and sometimes a swift, gliding one. Again, sometimes, I pass my thumb over the finger and then immediately pass the finger over the thumb before passing on to the next finger. This forms a kind of rotary movement. If I have not reached my little finger when I discover that I am doing this finger exercise, I feel that I must continue until I have reached the little finger and so conclude the performance. I don't know how long I have had this habit, maybe three or four years, maybe longer; nor can I imagine how it originated.

UNEXPLAINED COMPULSIVE TENDENCY TO MOVE HANDS FROM HAIR-LINE OF FOREHEAD TO TIP OF CHIN OR NECK, EVEN IF IT IS KNOWN POSITIVELY THAT NOTHING IS ON THE FACE

Another act that seems to be as much a part of me as some part of my body is the act of passing my hands over my face, beginning at the hairline on my forehead and continuing to the end of my neck. Sometimes I will terminate the act at the end of my chin. I seem to prefer to engage both hands in this activity but I will use only one hand if necessary. I may know positively that nothing is on my face, still it seems that I must perform this act in order to brush something off that doesn't belong on there.

(Above three reports from J.W.A.; F.; Col.; E.S.T.; B.A.; Age 30)

A study of these compulsions and other symptoms and facts contained in the original report or revealed in personal conference led the writer to conclude that the client's antics were the conversion phenomena of a guilt complex produced by the dread that the clandestine relations with a dentist in a neighboring town, which had gone on for some time, would be discovered.

From the current scene the highlights from one compulsive attempt at self-destruction, one compulsive murder, and one phobic retreat into hermitage will show the extreme manifestations sometimes assumed by these morbid impulses.

In September, 1941, a 22-year-old state unemployment commission employee plunged from the Golden Gate Bridge in San Francisco into the swirling waters 265 feet below—the only one of 35 who have taken the "suicide leap" to survive at the time of rescue. The impact against the water broke her back and both arms, caused severe bruises, tore her silk stockings into fragments, tore off her shoes, and wrenched a ring from her finger. Her explanation to the physician at the hospital for her leap was: "It was just an irresistible impulse. I just had to jump. I didn't feel anything when I fell. I was just numb." This kind of monomania is referred to as hydromania, in contrast with the following homicidal mania.

At East Lansing, Mich., in December, 1936, a 25-year-old stenographer in the Michigan relief administration fired five shots into the body of her lifelong chum, high-school and college classmate, and sorority sister, the daughter of a dean in Michigan State College, as she was helping her address her wedding invitations. To the state policeman she explained: "I had to shoot her. I did it on an impulse and can't explain why, but I couldn't help myself. I had my father's gun with me . . . all of a sudden I felt I wanted to kill and I emptied the gun. Then everything went black. For about a year I've frequently had an impulse to kill." Located at the home of a friend, she stated to the police medical adviser: "I've had the lust to kill since October of last year. Suddenly I looked up and stared at Bessie. Then that feeling came over me." She said that "she would do the same thing again if she had a chance." One week later, while confined in the county jail, she hanged herself with a silken noose fashioned from her pajamas, leaving behind a number of barely legible notes scrawled with a burned match on the margins of magazine pages to the effect that she felt she would be "left out of the picture" after her friend's marriage (all the other girls of her social set had married), that she was torn by "jealousy and disappointment," and that she "couldn't stand being the only one left." According to the report of one of the commission psychiatrists, she "suffered from an anxiety neurosis based principally on feelings of inferiority and insecurity. When she was with her chum she was plagued with the terror of the social contacts awaiting her that evening when she was to have been a hostess at a bridal shower. . . . She watched the bride-to-be who was in a very happy state of mind and realized . . . that her closest friend was getting away from her. She felt numb with fright and because her chum looked at her and commented on her queer expression the only thought she had was to shoot."

Among well-recognized monomanias are dipsomania (an overwhelming, periodic craving for alcoholic drink), dromomania (an unreasonable urge to roam about), kleptomania (an irresistible impulse to steal articles without thought of profit), megalomania (excessive egotism), mythomania or pathomania (pathological lying or morbid tendency to exaggerate or to report imaginary adventures), and xenomania (irrational admiration of the foreign).

William E. Leonard, poet, writer, and professor in the University of Wisconsin, author of *The Locomotive God,* had been confined within six blocks of his home (which he describes as his "phobic prison") for 27 years (at the age of 61, in 1937), because he is seized "by a terror of being left alone" even though he walks only a few blocks from his home. He attributes his phobia to a serious emotional shock suffered in childhood when a train rushed past him while he stood on a railroad platform. The phobia seems to have remained dormant until he was about 35 years of age, appearing after the tragic suicide of his first wife.[4]

Morbid fears assume a great variety of forms, to which mystifying technical terms have been applied. But the particular name and expression of a phobia are of minor importance. The basic cause and motivation of the phobia are the significant considerations. These may be the same, irrespective of the particular form of the fear.

Among the well-known phobias may be mentioned the following:

Acrophobia, a fear of high places. This phobia, according to report, keeps Joan Crawford out of airplanes.

Ailurophobia, morbid fear of cats.

Anthropophobia, fear of people.

Bacteriophobia, a morbid fear of germs.

Claustrophobia (or clitrophobia), morbid fear of enclosed spaces. It is reported that this fear keeps Joseph Hergesheimer, the author, out of movies and subways. His fear is ascribed to a tunnel accident.

Mysophobia, fear of dirt.

Nyctophobia, a morbid fear of darkness. Joan Crawford burns a light all night, so it is reported, because of this fear.

Ochlophobia, fear of crowds. This fear may be the basis of Greta Garbo's comparative reclusiveness (she avoids large crowds), and of the stage fright which is reputed to have affected Ethel and John Barrymore.

[4] William E. Leonard, *The Locomotive God,* New York, Appleton-Century-Crofts, Inc., 1927.

Photophobia, a morbid fear of strong light.

Pyrophobia, fear of fire.

Thanatophobia, a morbid fear of death, to which Guy de Maupassant, Leo Tolstoy, and John Bunyan are reported to have been subject.

Henry VIII is said to have trembled when he saw a dead fish; Henry III of France became sick at the sight of eggs; and Arthur Schopenhauer, the German philosopher, singed his beard because of the fear of razors.

The distinction between a phobia, an obsession, and a compulsion is not always clear. All are characterized by elements of irrationality, coerciveness, uncontrollableness, inscrutability, and anxiety.

The phobic element is very prominent in some obsessional and compulsive states. Some phobias are characterized by a dominant compulsive action trend, while others tend to inhibit action. On the other hand, some compulsions do not manifest any concurrent phobic factor.

Causes of Obsessions and Compulsions. *a.* The cause of an obsession or a compulsion may be some specific process of emotional conditioning of which the subject is painfully aware. Having been emotionally upset by some experience—for example, a tragic event or accident—the subject may suffer from a continuance of the emotional disturbance because he dwells upon the incident, elaborates upon it, begins to blame himself or someone else, lets his imagination conceive what might have happened as a result of his negligence, becomes self-conscious or sensitive about it, begins to worry, becomes timid and inhibited, tries to suppress the recollection of the unpleasant episode, etc. So it comes to happen that a pertinaciously recurrent idea or impulse may have been set up on the basis of a persistent emotional undercurrent, perhaps a vague dominating dread. Instances of obsessions and compulsions produced by recognized causes appear on preceding pages.

b. The circumstances occasioning the emotional disturbance may be unknown. They may never have been recognized or they may have been forgotten. Possibly they were repressed because of their painful character. The attempt may have been made to solve the conflict between a strong tabooed desire and the fear of surrendering to it by indulging in meaningless symptomatic acts designed to divert attention away from the disapproved craving. Even if the recollections were successfully repressed, the suppressed emotions may continue to exert a subtle, dominating influence upon the victim; thus the repressed ideas may express themselves in apparently absurd, irrelevant, or bizarre obsessions or compulsions. While the subject recognizes the ridiculous and fantastic character of his impulses, he may not at all understand their meanings or dynamic character. He may not comprehend the fact that the odd idea or the curious, annoying movement is merely a distorted symbol for the original disconcerting experience. The forgotten or repressed experience may have had some unpleasant moral implication, being regarded by the subject as an act of folly or a moral breach. Thus the obsessive idea may become the voice of conscience, super-induced by a feeling of guilt, although the subject may be unaware, or may be only vaguely aware of the cause of the feeling. In the ordinary experiences of conscience, the subject is well aware of the circumstances that produced the feeling of guilt; but in obsessional experiences, the fear or the guilt feeling attaches to an apparently meaningless symbol. For an excellent illustration, turn to the case of obsessional washing on page 436. Repeated washing of the hands is frequently an expression of repressed anxiety or guilt feelings occasioned by autoerotic practices that produced a feeling of shame or guilt. Lady Macbeth indulged in hand washing as an atonement for her murders. In certain rituals, washing the hands is a purification rite. Neurotic hand washing may have the same significance.

c. Some obsessional tendencies may represent the by-product of frequent repetition or of habit formation. The habit may have developed into an automatism, easily released by the interplay of nervous currents, or into an irresistible urge that may make itself felt at any time. Irresistible urges are more likely to result when the habit yields deep satisfaction. Habit bonds are more firmly established when the outcomes are pleasurable or satisfying.

Treatment of Obsessions and Compulsions. Only three suggestions of general application can be offered here.

a. When the specific causative factor is known, let the victim study his problem unemotionally and objectively, not to say jocularly. In a spirit of banter and *sangfroid* frankly admit the facts in the situation and rationalize the situation to yourself in a soliloquy somewhat as follows: "My mind has played me a foolish trick. Because of being disappointed or frightened or shocked, I began to seek some kind of release through some form of expression, repeating certain things again and again, doing certain things over and over again, until the tendencies became so fixed that I began automatically to think certain things and to say or do certain things until I became an unwilling victim of certain obsessive or compulsive impulses. But I realize that these bizarre outlets I have chosen are silly. They really have nothing to do with the cause of the trouble and therefore they cannot afford any lasting cure for my difficulty. In addition, these ideas or actions often make me look peculiar, odd, or ridiculous to my friends, and this causes me to become self-conscious and embarrassed. Since they are so senseless and baseless, I'm going to quit clowning and banish these fantastic antics from my mind."

The above thoughts are merely illustrative suggestions of ways of employing the rational, understanding method in attacking difficulties of known causation; this method often proves successful when the causes have been correctly apprehended. The "rational" method of subjugating difficulties involves the direct facing of the problem by means of emotionless, objective study of all its elements, and sometimes by means of the shaming technique, which is designed to make the subject feel that he is setting himself apart from others by some unnecessary oddity or caper. The same sort of rational attack on obsessions and compulsions due to habit formation often proves successful. The expedient of persistently directing attention away from the peculiarity by becoming absorbed in something else may prove beneficial with both types of impulsions—namely, those due to a definitely known specific process of conditioning, as well as those due to habit formation. The best form of treatment for many minor conflicts and disturbing ideas or impulses is to ignore them. Time, rest, and preoccupation with matters of absorbing interest often exert a subtle healing influence.

b. When the causes are unknown, the suggestions offered for the treatment of dissociations and fears should prove valuable (see page 467 and Chap. XII).

c. Tackle the problem in its early genetic stages before the obsessive and compulsive trends have become deeply fixed by constant repetition. Apropos of this connection is the second suggestion proffered in Chap. XII for overcoming fears and stage fright by directly and immediately facing and attacking the fear-producing situation.

10. *Hysteria.* Space permits only a brief reference to this protean psychoneurosis—a psychically produced (psychogenic) nervous malady without obvious organic basis—to which reference has already been made in various places. It was with this psychosomatic disorder that Freud achieved his most brilliant successes with his psychoanalytic techniques, as far as concerns etiological (causal) diagnosis and therapy.[5] A brief description of the disorder is difficult, because of the multiplicity of symptoms; the variation of the symptoms in degree and complexity between individuals; and the lack of a definite, fixed syndrome. The symptoms vary more or less with the subjective and the objective circumstances surrounding the genesis of the malady. To constitute true hysteria, the hysterical symptoms must be differentiated from similar symptoms connected with organic defects or produced by deliberate shamming or malingering. While the cause of hysteria may begin with conscious malingering (feigning some illness or disability as a means of dodging responsibilities), eventually the symptoms become unconsciously and automatically operative and uncontrollable. The malady has nothing to do with the *hystera* (uterus); it affects both sexes, but it is more

[5] For a more complete treatment of the disorder, see the references to Conklin, Dorcus and Shaffer, Fisher, McDougall, Prince, and others on page 446, particularly, to Pierre Janet, *Major Symptoms of Hysteria,* 1913, and to Joseph Brewer and Sigmund Freud, *Studies in Hysteria,* New York, Nervous and Mental Disease Publishing Co., 1936 (translated by A. A. Brill).

common among females; and it occurs most frequently between the age of puberty and about 25.

Pierre Janet groups the symptoms into two categories: (1) Certain stigmata, which are more or less persistent, such as functional anesthetic (insensible) or hypersensitive (supersensitive or painful) areas, including hysterical blindness or deafness; paresthesias (morbid skin sensations, such as tingling, pricking, burning, and numbness); functional paralysis of certain muscle groups, with contractures, including astasia-abasia (inability to walk or stand); involuntary hyperkinetic muscle innervations, such as tremors, spasms, or tics (spasmodic intermittent jerks, affecting any muscle group in unbelievable varieties of forms, such as facial contortions, grunting, hiccoughing, squirming, jerking); hysterical aphonia; lack of ability to execute decisions (abulia); hypersuggestibility; amnesias; egocentricity, sometimes amounting to ethical callousness and indifference to the rights of others; anxiety ("anxiety hysteria"); emotional instability; and alternation of personality. (2) Certain accidental concomitants (hysterical attacks) which are transitory, such as attacks of emotional depression and elation; outbursts of laughing or crying, which are what the lay public thinks of in connection with hysteria; and certain dramatic episodic outbreaks—the "grand attacks" of Charcot, infrequent major attacks that resemble epileptic seizures (but differ in various respects); epileptiform attacks; and various more frequent minor abortive attacks. The latter include attacks of vertigo, nausea, loss of appetite (anorexia); cataleptic seizures (in which the muscles become semirigid and remain in any position where placed,[6] with suspension of voluntary movement and sensibility); pronounced absent-mindedness; trance or stuporous states, fugues, and somnambulisms. These symptoms are regarded as phenomena of dissociated ideas or affects produced by unsuccessful repressions.

The dissociations that produce the automatically active symptoms of the malady result, according to the psychoanalytic theory, from severe emotional conflicts between the individual's ethical ideals (imposed by society's imperious demands) and his incompatible, egoistic urges. The rejected affects, in the process of forcible repression from consciousness, become detached and freed from conscious control. But the repression is only partially successful. The distressed affects continue a dissociated, dynamic existence. Denied an outlet through the conscious life, they burst forth automatically in some unrecognized, disguised form that is symptomatic of some illness or defect that can serve as a protective device. When the symptom is physical—such as a tic, spasm or paralysis, a sensation of pain, or the loss of visual, auditory, or tactual sensibility—it is called a "conversion symptom." A conversion

---

[6] The automatic tendency for the limbs to remain in position is called *flexibilitas cerea* (waxy flexibility).

symptom thus becomes a dynamism, that is, a mechanism of adjustment, a means of escape from or protection against the effects of the emotional trauma. Thus a right-hand paralysis makes it impossible for the subject to sign a document that he does not want to endorse. Hysterical vomiting may become a symbolical expression of an effort to rid oneself of thoughts that are repugnant to one's feeling of self-respect. A hysterical throat affection may function as a face-saving device against the frustration of being rejected from the music course because of lack of singing ability. An attack of hysterical mutism relieves the subject from making the dreaded speech or from revealing her treasured secret. Although apparently meaningless, every symptom is an adjustment dynamism. It possesses a more or less definite meaning, although this meaning is unrecognized by the subject. It is a means of expressing some basic wish or affect in a symbolical form that has no moral implications or that is less objectionable than the direct gratification of the urge. The fact that the symptom represents the realization of a wish and may give some comfort may explain why the hysterical person is not perturbed by his symptoms.

Although Freud does not deny the influence of the individual's constitutional make-up (his chemical, physiological, and anatomical structure), the hysterical symptoms are "psychically determined" by motives that have become unconscious through processes of repression. Psychic processes are never fortuitous, according to Freud.[7] The most important cause of the repression is conflict produced by sexual trauma, real or fancied, in early childhood. This is doubtless one cause; but any other severe emotional conflict may produce the same results in persons whose mental integration is weak through inherited nervous weakness or instability, or through defective discipline or habit formation in early life, or through mental or nervous exhaustion.

According to Janet, the hysteric is a person who has failed to develop normal mental synthesis because of defective heredity (an innate weakness of mental synthesis), emotional stress, and exhaustion. Emotional shock and fatigue aggravate the preexistent weak integration. The malady is a form of mental depression that starts with exhaustion and is characterized by dissociation and the narrowing of the field of consciousness to the point where the subject cannot respond in a unified, integrated manner to a complex environment, but only to one part of it. A person with deficient mental synthesis might be able to adjust on a simple level of functioning but not on more complicated human levels. The retracted field of consciousness accounts for the hysteric's extreme suggestibility and absent-mindedness. The dissociations and amnesias account for the volitional paralysis (abulia) or the

---

[7] This is the doctrine of psychic determination, one of Freud's basic tenets.

inability to ideate the movement of the dissociated muscle groups. The hysterical disturbances are the resultants, then, of a hysterical diathesis, emotional stresses, and dissociation.

The Central Role of Dissociated Processes in the Explanation of All the Pathological Phenomena Discussed in This Section. All the abnormal symptoms considered in this section are explicable on the hypothesis that they represent dynamisms or mechanisms that have been rendered automatically active by conflict-produced repressions, which function as compromise solutions of the dilemmas in which the individual has been ensnared. They are designed to yield substitute satisfactions and to rid the distressed individual of painful elements in his experience by dissociating them from the rest of his consciousness, in order that he may forget them or lose sight of the source of his disturbing or compulsive ideas or affects. But the process of dissociation does not necessarily remedy the difficulty, for the dissociated elements may continue a more or less independent and uncontrollable existence and thus produce all sorts of difficulties. Some of these may continue to plague the victim for life as humiliating annoyances or obnoxious habits. Others may greatly impair the individual's efficiency or disrupt his mental soundness. Dissociation, therefore, is essentially a deceptive, illusory mechanism for evading the disagreeable or painful experiences of life. If uncorrected, it may lead to further mental disintegration or mental chaos. Manifestations of dissociative tendencies in children should be watched for and steps should be taken to check them in their incipiency.

Suggestions for the Treatment of Disintegrative Dissociations. The application of many of the remedial measures offered elsewhere in the book will conduce toward the development of the type of wholesome mental integration that will serve as the most potent buffer against the psychobiological ravages of emotional storms and dissipations. Among the more important of these positive and preventive suggestions mention may be made of the following: absorbed concentration of attention upon successful work and play; dynamic, purposeful, coordinated pursuit of tasks suited to the child's interest and capacities; freedom from unnecessary interference with children's plans, purposes, and projects; opportunities for the development of self-confidence, self-direction, security, and sufficiency; opportunities for the development of initiative and self-expressive activities; objective, orderly, unemotional thinking; normal growth, expression, and control of the emotions; freedom from wasteful expenditure of nervous and mental energy, fatigue, excessive haste, severe repressions and conflicts, fears of all kinds, superstitions, worries, jealousies, suspicions, and blameworthiness because of being blamed or because of wrongdoing; and freedom from reliance upon artificial defense mechanisms and habits of rationalization. Two additional suggestions of general applicability may be emphasized.

1. Try to discover the causes of the emotional disturbances and conflicts that are at the root of the symptoms. One must not rest content with the recognition of the symptoms, which often are nothing but disguises or misleading distortions, but should penetrate to the very roots of the disturbance. The sooner the causative factors are disclosed and the meaning of the symptoms is revealed, the more effective will the curative and preventive treatment prove to be.

2. After this has been accomplished, it is necessary to develop a new attitude toward the causative circumstances and the personal difficulty. They must not be regarded as issues to be circumvented or camouflaged but as issues calling for definite corrective adjustments by being squarely faced and by being subjected to a straightforward, frontal attack of the objective situation. When the bugaboo is faced confidently, boldly, and critically, it will frequently prove to be nothing but a mirage that will vanish like the mist before the rising sun. If emotional complexes are resolved in time, they will not continue for years to torment the victim in disguised form as split-off segments of the psyche.

CHAPTER XV

THE RESOLUTION OF MENTAL CONFLICTS BY THE METHODS OF (12) INHIBITION AND (13) REPRESSION INTO THE UNCONSCIOUS

12. Inhibitory (or Suppressive) Adjustments

Nature of Mental Inhibitions and the Reasons Therefor. What is meant by an inhibitory activity or urge in psychology? In general, it refers to the interference or the extinction of one activity or impulse by an opposing activity or impulse. When one idea or impulse serves to impede, completely or partially, the expression of another idea or impulse, it exercises a so-called suppressive or inhibiting influence.

The method of inhibition is one of the commonest devices used to dispel mental conflicts produced by antagonistic motives or impulses. Stronger urges, of course, tend to suppress or restrain weaker desires or intentions without any effort on the part of the subject. The motives or cravings that naturally tend to dominate or control the child's behavior are the egoistic ones, namely, those that express his primitive urges and his selfish demands. But the child's egocentric demands often run counter to the social demands of the family and the social codes and practices of society. As a consequence of this antagonism, the child is early trained to curb his egoistic impulses and to restrain his desires when they conflict with the wishes of other people, particularly adults. From early infancy the child has constantly been told what he may do and what he may not do. He has repeatedly been required to refrain from boisterousness or levity, to suppress his curiosity in many things, and to remain inconspicuous. He may have been ridiculed because of his naive remarks and snubbed because of his mistakes. His spontaneity may have been congealed by sarcastic cuts and his activities restricted by the demands for orderliness and uniformity. Other inhibitions may have been produced by fears of examinations, of low grades, and of failure to achieve promotion. As the result of years of these and similar processes of negation and suppression in the school, in the home, and elsewhere, he may have become a bundle of inhibitions and feelings of conflict and inadequacy. He may have acquired the fixed habit of inhibiting or suppressing feelings, thoughts, and attitudes not in harmony with the views of his elders or of accepted social usage. He has by multitudinous processes of conditioning learned the lesson that inclinations that are socially disapproved must be suppressed if he is to win approval.

It is apparent from this recital of typical situations that the child's inhibitions have been, in the main, socially produced. They constitute an important chapter in social psychology as well as in mental hygiene.

To illustrate: Why does the child gradually learn to inhibit frequent expressions of anger? Is it not mainly because of the lack of esteem shown by society for temperamental weaklings? Civilized man does not highly regard persons who cannot control the exhibition of their anger. For this reason civilized man, to a considerable extent at least, has learned to inhibit or suppress the expression of anger, although the feeling may still be felt most acutely. Similarly with respect to the sex drive, the tendency to gratify sex impulses is controlled or restrained in many, if not most, people by the fear of social condemnation. The instinctive sex promptings are held in check or suppressed by a stronger motive, namely, the fear of social taboo or of prosecution.

There doubtless exist some inhibitions or suppressions that are not socially produced. However, the most serious ones can, in all probability, be traced to deep-seated conflicts between the individual's emotionally determined, egoistic drives and the taboos and prohibitions of society.

The Virtues of Inhibitory Adjustments. The practice of subjugating socially disapproved tendencies by the method of suppression is not wholly to be condemned, Rousseau and certain psychoanalysts notwithstanding. Many egoistic and antisocial propensities must be eliminated for the good of society. Certainly, inhibition or suppression may be a lesser evil than unbridled license. Moreover, the method of suppression is often effective, especially so far as the weaker desires and less fundamental urges are concerned. Experience shows that some undesirable tendencies can be gradually weakened or eliminated by processes of repeated suppression or repeated resolution without serious harm to the individual, or with less harm to the nonconforming individual than would be inflicted upon innocent people by the uninhibited expression of the individual's antisocial proclivities. In other words, the mere casting off of inhibitions and taboos, the solution proposed by some writers, would not solve the dilemmas this expedient would create. The adoption of a policy of laissez-faire license as a substitute for restraint would, in the long run, prove disastrous both to the individual and to society. In the field of sex, it would lead to unbridled licentiousness, with its possible train of venereal disease, physical exhaustion, satiety, revulsion, illegitimacy, loss of the finer sensibilities, degradation, and moral collapse. It would produce conflicts with the laws and mores of society which would in the end accentuate the free lances' feelings of guilt and produce further emotional upsets and antagonisms. Perhaps the recent crusades on the part of the nudist cultists are essentially an attempt to cast off distressing or irksome taboos and restraints rather than a quest for fresh air and ultraviolet rays. The demand that they be permitted untrammeled freedom in stripping themselves of clothing may be merely a symbolic act, the underlying and perhaps unrecognized motive being the desire to strip themselves of conflict-breeding inhibitions and repressions. Whether or not liberation from the fetters of this type of conventional restraint would make for mental catharsis and serenity, it is doubtless true that unconfined emotions tend to run riot and lead to emotional and physical exhaustion and disintegration. So it is quite probable that mere freedom in all fields of social relationship will lead to eventual disappointment, disillusionment, and mental and social disaster.

For these and other reasons inhibition is probably a lesser evil than unbridled liberty. But whether it is or not, unrestrained freedom would not be tolerated by organized society for long. Society would eventually check the individual's asocial or antisocial activities by restraints of some kind in the interest of the orderly performance of its necessary collective functions. Whether it satisfies the individual or interferes with the free exercise of his ambitions or cravings, society will not for any length of time tolerate arson, theft, assault, rape, or murder. Witness how many states in rapid succession not long ago met a widespread social menace by "cracking down" on kidnapers by the enactment of the most drastic statutory prohibitions and penalties. The inexorable demand of the state is restraint of individual prerogatives for the good of the whole, irrespective of the inhibitions and suppressions that may be engendered in the individual.

But the negative virtues of restraint are not the only ones to be considered. Positive values also attach to inhibitory adjustments. Some positive virtues, no doubt, accrue from the discipline involved in fostering competing ideas or motives to the point where they become conditioning stimuli strong enough to overcome antagonistic urges or fears. Perhaps the effort to overcome undesirable traits by sheer determination—the determination to root them out, to replace them with desirable traits, and to attack doughtily the situations with which the hampering trait is associated—may constitute excellent character training. This kind of discipline should lead to the development of such qualities as resourcefulness, resoluteness, aggressiveness, and the determination to become master of oneself or of circumstances, instead of the inclination to succumb submissively to the attitude of defeatism. There is some justification for James Dixon Ryan Fox's castigation, "the greatest curse that has come upon us is a theory that we are all victims of something or other. . . . Anything that saps the sense of individual responsibility will rot the American character. With rare exceptions one's individual future is in his own hands. The person who tells a youth he is the creature of circumstances is doing him no favor." William Ernest Henley, after he had lost one leg, suffered serious infection in the other and was brought to the Old Infirmary in Edinburgh for an examination by the noted Joseph Lister, who asked him whether he had the courage to undergo another ordeal, which was likely to prove fatal. Henley told them to go ahead and, while awaiting treatment, he penned his challenging poem, "Invictus" (unconquered), which concludes with two lines that Frank Crane called the "greatest spiritual declaration in English":

> I am the master of my fate;
> I am the captain of my soul.

The spirit of Henley's "Invictus" has enabled many a mortal to survive the crisis of death and has carried human culture to higher levels of attainment.

A positive frontal attack is, of course, not an inhibition unless it is viewed as an inhibition of an inhibition; but it may be inhibition inspired (or "aim-inhibited," in Freudian parlance) and inhibition shattering.

Value of the Positive Attack in Sweeping Away Inhibitions Illustrated in the Case of Stage Fright. The value of the attitude of resolute determination in ridding oneself of hampering limitations and in achieving satisfactory practical adjustment was shown on pages 413*ff.* and may be illustrated with one additional case of stage fright. Many are able to vanquish this bugbear by facing the problem forthrightly and unflinchingly, by resolutely bucking up one's courage and downing one's timidity by stiffening the muscles, by aggressively launching upon the task, and by convincing oneself of the importance of one's message or of one's ability to present it.

INTENSE FEAR OF SPEAKING IN PUBLIC OVERCOME BY BEING FORCED TO APPEAR BEFORE AN AUDIENCE; STAGE FRIGHT NOW SUPERSEDED BY STAGE DELIGHT

I feared to speak before any assembled audience, especially until I reached the junior year of high school. During that year the high-school principal made it obligatory for every student to participate in the weekly literary programs. My turn came to participate in a debate. Rather than face the group, I broke the perfect attendance record by staying away from school entirely. The principal then told me that I would have to take part in the next program or I would be expelled. I finally made the attempt and when I went onto the platform my knees shook until I couldn't stand without support. Mentally and emotionally it was a torture. The group multiplied in front of my eyes until it seemed that half of the county was present. Thoughts went blank. I even forgot the subject of the debate and had to get it from the secretary. Finally, in desperation, I threw back my head and made two short disconnected statements and went to my seat. It was the best thing that could have happened for from that time on I overcame that type of stage fright. Since then I have indulged in lecturing to a considerable extent. I now literally enjoy speaking in public. The only time that I have experienced any return of the stage fright came during my sophomore year in college when the head of the public-speaking department selected me to represent the public-speaking department in a chapel assembly. Attendance at the chapel session was compulsory, so the larger part of the student body was present. To my complete surprise, I found that the same condition was present that I had experienced in my early conflict in the high school. My knees shook (I have heard of people who claimed that, but mine did). I finally braced myself against the speaker's stand and decided to see it through then and there. One difference existed between the two experiences. This time I was able to think as clearly as I ever had before, and I found no trouble in presenting the matter. In fact, I concealed the condition so effectively that the instructor questioned it when I told her what I had gone through. I have never experienced anything of the kind since and now I enjoy public speaking more than any other hobby that I have.

(M.E.M.; M.; Director Vocational Guidance in T.C.; M.A.; Age 33)

The case of Edward Sothern, the great Shakespearean actor, is also instructive. As a youth he was forced to appear in a New York theater.

The boy had only one line to speak, but when he faced his father on the stage his tongue clove to the roof of his mouth and he did not mumble a word. Instead, he fled from the stage, frightened and brokenhearted. His father, a trouper of the old school, determined that his son should be an actor and sent him to Boston to study. After a few months of practice, the father placed Edward with John McCullough, the tragedian, and the youth started working his way from minor parts to majors.

Evils of the Method of Inhibition. It must be admitted that the method of inhibition, whatever its virtues, also has its limitations. Excessively or unwisely employed, it tends to foster unwholesome attitudes and to arouse feelings of unworthiness and guilt, fears, and conflicts. It may weaken the child's aggressiveness, suppress initiative and the impulses to self-expression, block spontaneity, and produce paralyzing suppressions. Moreover, the method of inhibition often degenerates into arbitrary suppression and restraint by processes of punishment and by the arousal of fears and timidities. With what results? Frequently when emotions are arbitrarily suppressed by threats, fears, and external restraints they may burst forth later with volcanic explosiveness. It cannot be too emphatically emphasized that merely preventing the manifestation of a mental activity by sheer force does not guarantee the extinction of that activity, but it may cause the smoldering fires to burn all the more fiercely. Even when the suppression may result in an outward expression of calm and resignation, a marked inward tension or upheaval may continue to annoy the individual, as is shown in mild degree in the last paragraph of R.R.'s case history on page 89. The volcanic outbursts of the emotions that sometimes result from severe inhibitions or suppressions cannot be regarded as innocuous or trivial events from the standpoint of wholesome personality development. In point of fact, such outbursts often prove to be directly damaging, mentally, morally, and physically, to the individual concerned and indirectly to society.

Nor can the method of arbitrary inhibition be relied upon as a dependable stand-by in the management of the fundamental biological or biosocial urges, whose misdirection often creates the deepest feelings of unworthiness and self-accusation. The attempt to inhibit the deepest rooted impulses, cravings, or desires by sheer suppression may exacerbate the mental conflict, instead of removing or alleviating it. In consequence of this, the final result may assume the form of violent attempts at overcompensation, either in the direction of (*a*) explosive emotional outbursts, (*b*) antisocial conduct, or (*c*) the development of a special type of defense mechanism which the Freudians refer to as repression.

13. Repressive Adjustments (and Submerged Complexes and Psychoanalysis)

Importance of Acquaintance with Psychoanalytic Concepts in Spite of Their Controversial Character. That heated controversies continue to rage respecting the validity of psychoanalytic doctrines and concepts and the usefulness of psychoanalytic techniques for psychological diagnosis and treatment must be freely conceded. The controversies are no longer confined to the Freudians *vs.* the Anti-Freudians, or to the psychoanalysts *vs.* the antipsychoanalysts, but now involve the protagonists of different schools of "psychoanalysis," of different schools of "individual psychology," and of different schools of psychopathology and neuropsychiatry. It is obvious, therefore, that any highly condensed exposition of the psychoanalytic doctrine will not prove satisfactory to all schools or cults, or even to any one school of psychoanalysis. In spite of the enforced brevity of our discussion, no treatment of the mechanisms of adjustment to mental difficulties would be complete or satisfactory without at least a sketch of the main outline of the psychoanalytic doctrine of the repressive type of reaction. In spite of its enforced brevity,[1] the exposition afforded in this and the following chapter will, it is hoped, reflect the essential elements of the more orthodox (and perhaps traditional) writers of the Freudian persuasion, however inadequate it may prove to be to some of the warring elements of the left and right wings of "psychiatrists," "psychoanalysts," "individual psychologists," "clinic psychologists," and the ordinary garden variety of psychologist.

The Psychoanalytic Distinction between Suppression and Repression. Many psychoanalysts draw a sharp distinction between two methods of

---

[1] The student who desires to obtain a more adequate knowledge of psychoanalysis should familiarize himself with the earlier and more recent writings of Freud and other psychoanalysts. The references supplied in the bibliography contain more extensive reference lists.

attempting to banish inner conflicts, namely, the method of suppression and the method of repression. They arbitrarily limit the use of the word "suppression" to the conscious exclusion of a painful idea from consciousness, while the word "repression" is applied to a similar unconscious process. In the deliberate suppression of a desire, in order that it may not control action, we are conscious of the process of suppression. Nor does the suppression necessarily render us oblivious of, or insensible to, the desire or yearning. Although we may be able to suppress or control the desire voluntarily, we are quite cognizant of its imperious sway. We are keenly aware that it is at the basis of our struggle for mastery. We know perfectly well that we are waging an open battle against some inner urges that must be subjugated.

But repression is, by definition, a different kind of process. To be sure, at the beginning, the individual's effort to rid himself of painful memories or intolerable feelings may be deliberate and conscious—he knows what the nature of the mental conflict or shame-producing idea is that is upsetting him — but eventually he represses the painful affects into the "unconscious," in the language of the psychoanalysts, so that he finally becomes completely oblivious of the source of his struggles. Through the process of repeated repression into the unconscious, the source of the mental conflicts becomes obliterated. Ostensibly, therefore, the process of repression serves as a defense mechanism against an intense wish (which in psychoanalysis means any urge, yearning, desire, or ambition) which the individual regards as incompatible with his moral standards and with the mores and sanctions of society. Because they are too distressing or unethical to remain in consciousness, they are banished from the "conscious to the unconscious mind," in the expectation that such banishment will afford the individual relief from the feelings of shame, anguish, guilt, or anxiety which are at the root of his conflicts.

But, although repression into the unconscious may cause the ideas and cravings to lose contact with the conscious mind and thereby prevent the individual from being conscious of their demands, nevertheless the desires or painful affects continue to lead an active existence in the "unconscious mind." All that repression has accomplished is to render it impossible for these ideas to reach consciousness except in some form of disguised symbolism that the individual cannot understand. In other words, the painful contents that have been completely repressed cannot get by the so-called censor in their original, unmasked form. The censor (perhaps equivalent in general connotation to the "voice of conscience") is the defensive, repressive force that prevents the emergence of the distressing, unsublimated wishes or ideas except in some distorted, esoteric masquerade that is meaningless to the victim. It is obvious, therefore, that one must not consider that the repressions have been rendered inert and sterile when they have been expunged from consciousness, for they may continue to rankle in the unconscious, and may thus become a veritable dynamic source of continued irritations, conflicts, and tensions that make themselves manifest in misleading symptoms. The submerged emotional conflicts do manage to elude the censor and reach consciousness, but they do so surreptitiously by becoming attached to some other activity that is seemingly wholly irrelevant, as well as innocuous. This displacement of affect from one idea to another or from one person to another is referred to as "transfer of affect" or "transference."

In the view of Freud, then, repressive adjustments are motivated by intensely disturbing affects, the sources of which have been concealed by a process of "dissociation" from the conscious mind. Only unconscious materials, in the opinion of some psychoanalysts, can operate pathologically.

The Freudian Conception of the Unconscious. The "unconscious" is something different from, apart from, and independent of the conscious mind. It is a sort of dormant storehouse in which our historic past is preserved. In this reservoir of memories are preserved the individual's past experiences that have been banished from consciousness because of their antagonism to the individual's ethical conceptions. The unconscious is, they say, the ultimate repository of human experiences, the realm of the individual's accumulated repressed desires and cravings, which frequently date from early childhood, the abode of repressed infantile wishes that should have been outgrown in early life. These interred infantile wishes constitute a serious bar to the individual's intellectual and emotional progress. In this unconscious museum of feelings and cravings—the sole function of the unconscious is wishing and wanting, they say—most psychic life exists in latent form.

This secondary mind, be it noted, is not like a dead, inactive volcano. It is not a split-off element that repression has rendered as dead as the proverbial dodo. On the contrary, it is vibrant with life. It is, in fact, an active, dynamic, "molding, creative force," which is the primal source of wit, humor, myths, folklore, and dreams. Restless with tabooed desires and wishes, the unconscious is the mischief-maker in the realm of mind. It is the wellspring of anxieties, fears, mental conflicts and disturbances, neuroses, and the primitive and antisocial desires that demand immediate gratification.

This submerged region, finally, constitutes the individual's real self, because the unconscious is the domain of the fundamental appetites and primal emotions from which spring the overwhelming unconscious motives of conduct. In this domain is to be found the fountainhead of our character traits and of our deepest interests, likes, and dislikes. That the ideas and desires that germinate from this region should possess a strong obsessive, compulsive character is due to the fact that they are unconsciously and emotionally determined and that their true nature is not recognized. It is for this reason, it is explained, that these underlying unconscious trends can dominate the individual's life. Moreover, they are not directly accessible to consciousness.

They cannot be brought into awareness by an act of memory or of volition. It is obvious from this brief characterization that Freud attaches basic importance to his doctrine of the unconscious.

The complexity of the psychoanalytic mental mechanisms may be illustrated, in a measure, at this point by reference to the concepts of the Id, the Ego, the Superego, and the Preconscious; and to their interrelationships. The Id is the deepest unconscious stratum of the psyche discussed above, which is dominated by the pleasure-pain principle. It is the primal source of the libido. It is a dynamic turmoil of unmoral, blind, impulsive wishing that demands immediate gratification. It is ruled by primitive impulses, based on the needs of the organism to live, to procreate, to be happy, and to dominate. The strivings of the Id, although unconscious, are reflected in consciousness as desires, cravings, or wishes. A blind striving goes on to remove the tension created when these impulses are thwarted. It is the task of every child to bring the selfish Id impulses into harmony with the cultural demands of the environment. It is the thwarting of strong desires from the instinctive unconscious by the Ego and Superego that creates mental conflicts and subterfuges by which the urges seek satisfaction. What, then, are the Ego and the Superego?

The Ego develops out of the Id. It is the superficial part of the Id, which has been directly modified through perceptual experiences with the external environment and which has become imbued with consciousness. Its function is the testing of reality—it is governed by the reality principle—it mediates between the demands of the Id and the requirements of reality. It represses some urges and grants outlets to those that prove acceptable to the Superego.

The Superego, which develops out of the Ego, and operates largely unconsciously, is a sort of overego, whose function is to criticize the Ego and to cause distress and anxiety whenever the Ego accepts impulses from the Id. It causes the Ego to curb the Id. The Superego represents society's cultural demands for the curbing of primitive urges. It represents the moral notions that the child has acquired from the parents or from early guardians. It is "a precipitate of all the prohibitions and inhibitions that were originally inculcated into us by our parents, especially the father." [2] The child, through identification, adopts the parents' ethical and cultural standards and thus learns to censor his conduct. He acquires self-criticism of his behavior, an inner monitor, or a censor, or, as it is usually designated, conscience. The child's problem is to establish a satisfactory compromise between the Id (primitive) impulses and the requirements of the surrounding culture.

If the primitive cravings are held in leash too firmly by the Superego (conscience), the child may become too hard-boiled or relieve his tension in emo-

---

[2] A. A. Brill, *Freud's Contribution to Psychiatry*, New York, W. W. Norton & Company, Inc., 1944, 153.

tional explosions. On the other hand, if the Ego follows the primitive impulses without restraint, a state of anguish and condemnation may ensue.

The Preconscious, or Foreconscious, which consists of latent mental processes of which the individual is unaware at the time, but which can be recalled more or less easily when wanted, is contrasted with the "Unconscious." The Unconscious, as has already been explained, consists of certain dynamic processes which do not reach consciousness, in spite of their dynamic character, and which cannot be recalled by voluntary effort.

The main "censorship," which prevents the emergence of distressing memories or impulses into consciousness from the Unconscious, is imposed between the Unconscious and the Preconscious, while the weaker censorship exists between the Preconscious and the Conscious.

Personality development, then, in terms of psychoanalytic theory, represents the growing control of the Id impulses by the Ego and Superego.

The nuggets of truth embodied in these dynamic agencies are, of course, explicable on other hypotheses. The reader will realize that the explanations offered above are hypothetical constructs.

The Language of the Unconscious. How does the unconscious life express itself? In general, it betrays itself by the acts, signs, or symptoms that will be discussed briefly in connection with the consideration of the suspicious modes of expression of submerged complexes.

The Submerged or Repressed Complex. It would be difficult to comprehend Freud's dynamic psychology without some understanding of his theory of the submerged complex. (The term "complex" was suggested by Jung.)

When strongly emotionally toned ideas or memories have been repressed into the unconscious, whether partly or completely, they become a center for a group, or constellation, of ideas or feelings. Such a pattern, or system, of repressed emotionally toned ideas is called a "submerged or repressed complex." In repressions, the feelings that are attached to ungratified wishes sink to the unconscious and form a complex. The ideas that cluster about the complex are bound together by some process of strong emotional conditioning, rather than by mere repetition. All the associated ideas acquire the emotional tone of the complex, so that when they are consciously revived they produce the affective reaction of the buried complex. The complex may thus be "touched off" by the arousal of any of the associated ideas through the recollection of past experiences or through fresh experiences. According to some psychoanalysts (e.g., E. Hitschmann), a complex is always at the basis of a neurosis, using the latter term in its technical psychoanalytic connotation. From what has already been said, it can be readily understood that it is the unconscious wish of the complex that is at the basis, not only of neurotic symptoms, but also of dreams, mental conflicts, slips of the pen or tongue, obsessions, phobias, myths, and the like.

The Oedipus and Electra Complexes. Worthy of special mention are two parental complexes that play very important roles in psychoanalytic lore. They are due to strongly emotionally toned groups of ideas and feelings that the child has formed more or less unconsciously [3] toward the one or the other of the parents.

The Oedipus Complex. The Oedipus complex refers to a son's overattachment to his maternal parent—his falling in love with, or fixing his libido upon, his own mother. It refers to a boy's sensuous affection for his mother and antipathy and jealousy toward his father. The allusion of the term is to the Greek legend concerning Oedipus, the son of Laius, king of Thebes, and his wife Jocasta. Because the king had learned from an oracle that he was doomed to perish by the hand of his son, he had the child exposed after birth on a mountain with his feet pierced through. Here the child was discovered by a herdsman of the king of Corinth who was childless, and who brought him up as his own son. The boy was given the name Oedipus, from his swollen feet. Being told as a young man by the oracle of Delphi that he was doomed to slay his father and commit incest with his mother, he fled in horror to Thebes, to escape this dire fate, in the belief that he had been living with his parents. On the way he met Laius (his real father) and his servants, who tried to force him off the highway. A fight ensued, in which Oedipus unwittingly slew his father and also all the servants. In Thebes he solved the riddle of the Sphinx, who devoured every passer-by who failed to solve it. He slew the Sphinx, and in gratitude received the hand of Jocasta (his real mother), which had been offered to anyone who would solve the riddle. After some years of prosperity, a pestilence came to Thebes, which the oracle attributed to the murderer of Laius, who, accordingly, had to be expelled from the country. Oedipus, upon learning from the seer Tiresias that he had murdered his father and married his mother, put out his own eyes and wandered toward Athens, where he was charitably removed from earth, while his mother and wife hanged herself. This particular myth, according to the psychoanalysts, represents the realized incestuous cravings of early childhood.

This complex is biologically determined, universal, and normal in childhood, according to Freud. While it is a disappearing phenomenon, it may continue unconsciously to influence vitally the lives of both normal and neurotic individuals, but especially the neurotics. Instead of regarding the attachment as biologically determined, many would ascribe it to unwise parental treatment, such as sexual stimulation by sexually tinged caresses, or more frequently the development of dependence upon the parent or parent attachment as a means

[3] The word "complex" in this connection (as in many other connections) is, perhaps, often used rather loosely to include both conscious and unconscious elements.

of allaying the anxiety that may have been produced by parental domination, criticism, prohibitions, or punishment. Most boys have been able to free themselves from undue attachment to the mother and jealousy of the father. In fact, it is probably safe to say that the vast majority of boys have never become serious victims of any Oedipus complex in the Freudian sense. Nevertheless, it may be conceded that, if the mother has been too caressing and indulgent, excessive emotional fixation upon her may have been fostered and the boy may begin to imagine that some day he might become his mother's paramour or husband. In consequence of such libidinous phantasies, he might grow jealous of his father and the antagonism thus engendered might persist more or less unconsciously into adulthood. To a boy thus fettered by excessive maternal fixation, his mother might become the ideal by which he would judge other women, upon growing up. In consequence of this abnormal attachment, he may never marry unless he finds a duplicate of his parental model. This type of fixation often eventually develops feelings of shame and repressions, and may incite abnormal sex practices and sexual inversions. It is the basis of many neuroses, according to Freud. Undue fondness of the boy for his mother or of the daughter for her father, to which reference will now be made, probably will not prove very injurious, provided it is later replaced or supplemented by other attachments.

The Electra Complex. The Electra complex,[4] the complement of the Oedipus complex, refers to overfondness of a daughter for her father and antagonism to the mother, in consequence of which the father may become the daughter's beau ideal, the object of sexual fixation. The attachment may result in such an excessive father fixation that the victim will refuse to cultivate love for any other man or for anyone not closely resembling her father, and thus may refrain from marriage. The continued father fixation may operate more or less unconsciously, as is the case with the correlative mother complex. Secondary sequelae may include the development of repressions, infantile sex indulgences, and nervous maladies.

The sexual fixation in the Electra complex may be due to the same factors as in the Oedipus complex, namely, excessive demonstration of paternal affection and caressing, and the arousal of the need for affection through the excitation of anxiety feelings.

The process of spoiling involved in undue parental fixation may also lead to excessive compensatory self-love (narcissism; see page 347), in consequence of which the child may become vain, egocentric, wrapped up in himself and so "stuck on himself" as to be unable to fall in love with anyone else. He may thus more readily become a victim of infantile forms of sexuality, homo-

---

[4] From the classical Grecian myth concerning Electra, the daughter of Agamemnon, who induced her brother, Orestes, to avenge the murder of their father, to whom she was greatly devoted.

sexuality, childhood sex phantasies, or nervous disorders during the period of pubescence, adolescence, or adulthood.

Suspicious Signs of Submerged Complexes. Among the alleged symptoms indicative of the presence of submerged complexes may be mentioned emotionalized actions; emotional outbursts without any external cause (an infallible indication, according to O. Pfister); overcompensation, due to the readiness of the neurograms to discharge; touchiness, particularly concerning the topic connected with the complex, in consequence of which weak stimuli may produce great effects; discontent and cantankerousness; and many of the symptomatic acts and complex indicators mentioned in the following section (see also page 441).

Modes of Expression and Results of Repression of Submerged Complexes. The submerged complex, so the theory maintains, exerts a profound influence upon consciousness without its action's being known to the subject. Since the direct outlet for the expression of the subject's submerged (and thus unconscious) thoughts and impulses is barred by the censor, they must appear in unrecognized substitute formations. While the energy is diverted into channels other than the natural ones, the same emotions may attach to the substitute or distorted expression as would attach to the natural or undisguised outlet. The great variety of alleged symbols or distortions in which the repressed thoughts and desires may appear includes the following: jokes, puns, and attempts at humor; amnesias, the psychic forces producing the repression being resistant to memory recall, thus producing forgetfulness through active, purposive repression and not through memory weakness; absent-mindedness and inattention; slips of the pen, mispronunciations and speech mistakes; inability to think well, clearly, or forcibly; blocking of the creative impulses; motor incoordination, paralyses, nervous tension, restlessness, and uncontrollable muscular automatisms; anxieties (every anxiety corresponding to a repressed wish, according to O. Pfister); consciousness of guilt, often traceable to masturbation; incomprehensible, peculiar aversions; political, social, and moral prejudices, often based on unrecognized complexes; character distortions, such as feelings of hostility, hate, and revenge; reality-dodging escapades; sensations of pain, tingling, headaches, poor appetite, insomnia, somnambulism, multiple-personality, delusions, hallucinations, obsessions, and other neurotic manifestations; regression to infantile forms of activity, due to the blocking of the libido; "incapacity for sexual love," especially sexual frigidity in women, the affections being held fast in the unconscious because of painful childhood incidents, dependent "without exception on repressed processes" and fixations, in the opinion of Pfister, who declares this to be one of the most frequent results of such fixations; indulgence in trains of imagery, sometimes resulting in sexual ruminations, or in literary or artistic productions, or in the phantasy formations of daydreams and nocturnal dreams. In daydreaming, the form frequently taken when the expression of the complexes causes much pain, the wish-fulfilling fictitious creations in harmony with the individual's cravings are designed to replace painful external situations, as has already been pointed out (Chap. X).[5]

Nocturnal Dreams. Sleep dreams, says Freud, are the most common symbolic representation in images of repressed desires. They are fulfillments in symbolical form of unconscious wishes. The following is an excellent illustration of such a dream, for which I am indebted to Frink,[6] who has also supplied the interpretation.

An acquaintance of mine once dreamed that he was kicking a skunk and that that animal, instead of emitting its usual odor, gave a strong smell of Palmer's perfume.

In discussing this dream with me the dreamer, whom we may call Taylor, was reminded by the idea of Palmer's perfume that he had been employed as a clerk in a drugstore at the time the dream occurred. This brought to mind the following episode which, as will readily be seen, was what gave rise to the dream. There had come to the drugstore one day a man who demanded ten cents' worth of oil of wormseed, and, as this drug is not classed as poison, Taylor sold it to him without asking him any questions. The man went home and administered a teaspoonful of the oil to his six months' baby. The child vomited the first dose; a second was given, and thereupon the child died. Then, instead of taking the responsibility upon his own shoulders, the father sought to blame Taylor for the child's death. The town in which the occurrence took place was a small one and in a day or so most of the inhabitants had heard this very untrue account of the affair. Then Taylor, who was naturally very unwilling to be thus exposed to public censure, sought to defend himself by setting forth his version of the matter to every customer that entered the drugstore. In a few days the proprietor, annoyed by this constant reiteration, said to him: "Look here, Taylor, I want you to stop talking about this affair. It does no good. The more you kick a skunk the worse it stinks."

That night Taylor had the dream I have related. . . . By the proprietor's command Taylor had been robbed of the only means at his disposal for squaring himself with the public, and in consequence he went to bed that night very much worried and disturbed. Though he dropped off to sleep, these tensions persisted

---

[5] The reader need scarcely be warned against the uncritical application of these criteria or symptom indicators by amateurs and laymen. Because some child or adult manifests some of the above traits, one must not immediately jump to the conclusion that he is the victim of submerged complexes of a sexual or other character. "Symptom indicators" are at best suspicious signs, which it is well for all teachers to note in the observational study of children, but the interpretation of such signs should be essayed only after a comprehensive study of all the factors in each case. In all complicated or involved cases, psychological diagnosis should be left to the experts.

[6] H. W. Frink, *Morbid Fears and Compulsions,* 1921, 99, with the permission of the publishers, Dodd, Mead & Company, Inc., New York.

sufficiently to disturb his rest. He therefore dreams that he is still kicking the skunk but without any unpleasant results, for it has a sweet smell instead of an evil one. In other words, the meaning of the dream is that he continued to defend himself and that good rather than ill came of it.

Through the mechanism of a wish-fulfilling dream, Taylor apparently was realizing his desire for vindication and exoneration.

Freud's doctrine is that all dreams are wish fulfillments. The wishes from the unconscious supply the motive for the dream. Such motives come to expression in the dream. One of the dream motives may belong to the dreamer's immediate past experiences; in fact, the "stimulus always lies in the experience of the preceding day." Not only that, recent experiences also supply the materials of the dream. In spite of all this, the true basis of the dream lies in childhood wishes stored in the unconscious, often dating back to the first 3 years of life. In fact, the symbolism of the dream may antedate the child's life, for we are told that the symbolism of the dream is identical with that of the myth and the legend (and the daydream); they are all wish-fulfilling phantasies that spring from the remote past, and thus they are fragments of the life of prehistoric ancestors.

The symbolism of the dream, since it springs from the unconscious, is often incomprehensible to the dreamer, as may be seen by the dream of Taylor. The symbols are absurd, fantastic, grotesque, or meaningless because they have been distorted, highly condensed, regrouped, or greatly elaborated in cryptic form, so as to conceal the real meaning of the dream and enable it to get by the censor. However, a distinction must be drawn between latent and manifest wish contents. When the wish that causes the dream appears in disguised form or content, the wish element is referred to as a latent wish content. The true meaning of the wish in such dreams is missing and must be supplied by the analyst. The manifest wish content, on the other hand, represents the wish as it appears to the dreamer in his recall. It is the remembered dream. In children the ungratified wish often appears in manifest form as fulfilled, because they are relatively free from repressions or disguises. The girl's dream about a doll expresses her undisguised craving for a doll. The child's dream about a resplendent party at which he received all the angel-food cake and ice cream that he could eat ostensibly is the "manifest" expression of his appetency for those goodies. Many dreams are of this kind; the nature of the wishes they express is perfectly apparent or manifest. They have not been concealed in fantastic, distorted symbols. In children there is little attempt at repression or disguise, hence the ungratified cravings are ordinarily represented as fulfilled.

Why do dreams appear in mysterious, disguised symbols? Because of the fact that the dreamer wants to dismiss from consciousness by the mechanism of repression into the unconscious forbidden desires which have produced feelings of shame or which have become very painful to him.

The dreams of adults abound in profuse sex symbolism because most adult dreams express erotic wishes, according to Freud. This is due in part to the great suppression of sex imposed by the forces of civilization. One of the results of the painful repression is forgetfulness of the shame-producing elements (the most significant part of the dream) and the elaboration of the dream in disguised form. In spite of disfigurement, however, the emotions experienced in the dream are genuine. It is the affects of the dream that constitute its unyielding component, no matter how much the symbolism may be altered from time to time.

The symbolic disguises serve a valuable purpose, say the analysts, in protecting the sleeper from the consequences of his baser self, except in the case of nightmares or anxiety dreams. (Nightmares are regarded by some as anxiety dreams.) In anxiety dreams, the distortion of the repressed erotic wish has failed in the dream, allowing the sexual element to break through in the dream, thus awakening the dreamer. Whenever the tabooed dream is correctly apprehended, the dreamer is awakened by feelings of disgust or shame. Ostensibly, therefore, the distorted symbol serves the purpose of a defense mechanism.

Every dream is egoistic, being concerned with the dreamer himself, particularly his repressed desires. Persons who appear in the dreams represent aspects of the dreamer's character. The dream may be either a statement in symbolical form of the dreamer's problem, or a criticism of it, or a form of compensation.

Many psychoanalysts frankly admit that many dreams are peripherally aroused, such as dreaming about being impaled through the foot and finding a straw between the toes on awakening. The peripheral stimulation would explain the genesis of the dream, but not the particular configuration of the dream story. This would depend, in the more conservative view, on the varying degrees of kinetic readiness of various neurograms to become activated by differing cortical tensions, or on the responsiveness of the association mechanism to varying degrees of stimulation from different cortical areas and the reciprocal influences of association processes upon one another; and, in the view of the psychoanalysts, on the influence of repressed wish-fulfilling motivations in the unconscious.

With such significance ascribed to the dream, it is readily comprehended why the Freudians attach basic importance to dream analysis in the attempt to discover the causes of nervous maladies. The unconscious motives at the bottom of the neuroses and of some other maladjustments betray themselves in dreams. The fundamental task of psychoanalysis, therefore, is to penetrate the subject's unconscious life in order to discover the unconscious springs of his conduct, normal as well as abnormal. Dream analysis furnishes one means, if not the chief means, of achieving this objective. In fact, some psychoanalysts hold that dream analysis is absolutely essential in psychoanalysis, on the premise that the unconscious can be penetrated and the latent content unearthed only through dreams. To effect a cure, the unconscious motive at the root of the neurosis must be discovered and revealed to the subject.

Nervous Symptoms and Neuroses. It is the effort to find an outlet for the unsublimated, repressed cravings, according to orthodox Freudian principles, that produces the neuroses. At the root of the neuroses is the overmoral repression of the libido.

Incestuous desires, says Freud, are at the basis of every neurosis. As we have already seen, both the Oedipus and the Electra complexes represent such desires. Freud's sweeping conclusion is reechoed by many Freudians, although perhaps in slightly different form. Thus, to quote one of his American admirers, I. H. Coriat: the "primal instincts," hunger and sex, constitute the "root complex of every neurosis," "the sexual components of the child's instincts produce all the neurotic symptoms in later life," and the real secret of the neuroses is "childhood phantasies," ordinarily attaching to the father or the mother. According to this doctrine, therefore, there can be no neurosis when the sex life is normal. These sweeping Freudian generalizations are challenged even by many psychoanalysts.

However, since the patient has forgotten the source or cause of his repressions, Freud is led to remark that amnesias also are always at the bottom of the formation of neurotic symptoms. The repressed wish impulses at the base of the neurosis become active, as we have already seen, in a host of masked substitute formations, such as infantile fixations, anxieties, phobias, erotic phantasy formations, compensations, obsessions, hysterias, etc. The obsessions and compulsions (in the so-called compulsion neuroses, which are characterized by doubts, compulsive thinking, and obsessions, and which were formerly called "psychasthenia") [7] are interpretable as a transferred self-reproach for something repressed into the unconscious (see pages 462*f*.). It is the repressed ideas (erotic in character, according to some psychoanalysts), or more properly, perhaps, the failure of the repressions, that are responsible for the dissociations, amnesias, and physical symptoms of hysteria (see pages 303*f*., 420*f*., 441*f*., and 464*f*.). Some psychoanalysts find a repressed erotic complex even at the base of a mental disorder like dementia praecox.

The attempt by many analysts to trace all of the so-called neuroses and psychoneuroses, not to say all of the major functional mental or nervous disorders, to repressed unconscious elements, particularly those of a sexual nature, is regarded by most psychologists and psychiatrists as one of the most vulnerable elements of the Freudian system.

---

[7] They often show themselves in calamity dreams, in which harm happens to others.

How the Psychoanalyst Tries to Discover the Unconscious Causes of Mental and Nervous Difficulties. Three methods of causal diagnosis employed by psychoanalytic workers will be briefly outlined.

1. One of the techniques most frequently employed, perhaps the fundamental one, dream analysis, has already been referred to in this chapter. Child analysis as known today began with Freud's system of dream interpretation. Since dreams and the neuroses allegedly originate in the same unconscious source, dreams afford the most direct entrance to the unconscious springs of neurotic and mental disorders. Some do not hesitate to proclaim that the unconscious can be known only through the dream. The interpretation of dream symbolism, therefore, becomes the most important aid to psychoanalysis. But the correct interpretation of the dream symbol is no "playboy" undertaking. The interpretation must be based on all the circumstances revealed by the analysis of many dreams, as well as on all the facts discovered in the study of the case, although it is true that some examiners depend more or less on standardized symbols for the explanation of dreams. The following will serve as illustrations of such standard key words. Small animals and insects in dream imagery represent brothers and sisters; dream images of God, kings, or superior persons refer to a parent; dreams of the death of someone probably implicate the dreamer's father, toward whom the dreamer entertained animosity or jealousy as a child. A house represents a man or a woman; the sun is the dreamer's father; dreams about women refer to the dreamer's mother or wife. Innumerable symbolic representations are provided for the generative organs. The same symbols appear in myths, sagas, maxims, and wit as in dreams, according to Hitschmann, such as kings, queens, bulls, and serpents. Typical dreams exist, we are informed, which spring from emotions that are common to all and thus possess the same significance. These include dreams of flying, of being insufficiently clothed, and of the death of parents and near relatives. It must be admitted that the psychoanalysts' interpretation of dream symbolism has met with widespread condemnation because of its subjective and fantastic character. The extreme critics dismiss the method of dream interpretation as so much rubbish. One of Freud's severest recent critics, Karen Horney, nevertheless, considers "the working hypothesis that dreams are the expression of wish-fulfilling tendencies" Freud's "most important contribution on this score" (his theory of dreams).[8]

2. The second method consists of the use of free association tests in two variations, namely, the free-running association in the form of a spontaneous narrative or reverie, and the association-reaction test.

In the running-association test the subject is asked to sit quietly or, more frequently, to lie down on a couch in a quiet room free from any interruptions

[8] Karen Horney, *New Ways in Psychoanalysis*, New York, W. W. Norton & Company, Inc., 1939, 31.

or disturbances. In a condition of perfect relaxation, free from worry or inner conflict, he is asked to close his eyes (preferably) and get into a state of reverie, allowing his thoughts to run on more or less automatically, without any control, compulsion, or inhibition. In such a condition of relaxed and unin-hibited abstraction or reverie, he is encouraged to communicate any thoughts or images that may flit through his mind, talking out his thoughts in a running narrative. The analyst (who usually is stationed behind the subject) mean-time records whatever is spoken—single words, phrases, sentences, exclama-tions—and also observes the subject's behavior responses. The analyst may occasionally offer certain cues and ask questions regarding certain images or episodes during or after the narration. It is not sufficient that he should make an accurate record of the reports; he must also make a searching analysis of the contents of the running associations, comparing the materials gathered in the different "sittings" or "readings" and also comparing the association-test materials with dream materials.

The hidden meaning may be revealed by comparing the free associations that the subject makes with the dream material. Frequently many narrations and dreams must be analyzed before facts of any diagnostic significance can be gleaned. Before the causative factors can be excavated, the subject's resistance must be overcome and proper rapport or transference must be established, often a very difficult and wearisome undertaking. Suspicious items must often be subjected to prolonged investigation, including the use of the association-reaction test.

The assumption on which this technique is based is that the deeper, for-gotten, or repressed mental contents can be dug up by the process of free association. In the free recital, involuntary processes are given a chance, so it is said, to press to the surface and betray the complex. The materials revealed in spontaneous associations are largely phantasies of early childhood, sometimes going back as far as the second year of life (Stewart Paton). While the associations are referred to as "free," they are not causeless or fortuitous. On the contrary, they are strictly determined, according to Freud's theory of pandeterminism of psychic processes, by the subject's unconscious motivations.

Should the reader want to try a little self-analysis on himself by the method of continuous free association or spontaneous reverie, he should get into a rested, relaxed frame of mind while occupying, preferably, a recumbent posi-tion in a room free from interruptions, and he should record all the ideas, images, words, dislikes, timidities, fears, obsessions, or symptoms that well up spontaneously. After the experiment, he should analyze and classify the different items. On subsequent experiments he should record additional ideas, images, or recollections that may bob up, comparing the different items in his lists which have recurred and which may be factors in some complex or in some maladjustment. Many of the items should be subjected to further critical analysis by the association method. From daily attempts of this nature for an hour each during 2 or 3 weeks, the subject can often recall an amazing amount of detail and thus unfold a panorama of the unconscious, or at least the forgotten, components of his past experiences.

The value of self-analysis for diagnosis and therapy, questioned by many psychoanalysts, is stoutly defended by E. Pickworth Farrow. Farrow achieved far greater success from autoanalysis than from the analysis by two psycho-analysts, being able to reenvisage clearly incidents that occurred at the age of 6 months, 11 to 14 months, and 6 to 7 years of age, which proved to be at the basis of his psychic disturbances. The mental revival enabled him to "work off" or dissipate his mental difficulties. The self-analysis does not turn the patient into a neurotic (as introspection may), but tends to overcome neuroticism. His method consists in the uncritical writing down on paper (and later talking out quietly to himself) everything that flashes into consciousness at any moment during the analysis, no matter how apparently irrelevant, absurd, painful, or humiliating, and especially the most insistently recurring conscious thoughts (completely unhindered conscious associations).[9] Successful autoanalysis may require as great skill as heteropsychoanalysis. The knack of analyzing oneself psychoanalytically, while it differs greatly with individuals (as is also the case with heteroanalysis), can doubtless be improved by training and experience.

In the second form of association test, the free-association-reaction test (Carl G. Jung) or discrete-association test, the subject is presented with a series of stimuli words, one at a time, and he is told to respond to each word with the first word that comes to mind. Thus the experimenter may pronounce the word "red," while the subject responds with the first thought that enters his consciousness, for example, the word "blue." He is advised to respond with single words rather than phrases or sentences. The stimuli words are usually presented auditorially rather than visually. For the purpose of an analysis, lists of words are drawn up in advance containing assumedly neutral or nonsignificant words and certain key words that are regarded as suspicious or pathognomonic signs, based on the results of the dream analysis, the analysis of the waking reveries, or other investigations. As the words are presented, the experimenter records the reaction words to each stimulus word and the time required to respond; he also observes the reaction characteristics of the subject. Later the responses are subjected to detailed analysis. Items regarded as significant in the association responses are blockages, delays, accelerations, perseverations, and commonplace, favorite, egocentric, and irrelevant responses.

[9] See E. Pickworth Farrow, *Psychoanalyze Yourself,* 2d ed., New York, International University Press, 1945. See also John Dollard, *Victory over Fear,* New York, Reynal & Hitchcock, Inc., 1942.

3. The third method consists of the observation of such symptomatic acts or aimless automatisms as were referred to on page 481. These are regarded as indicators of unconscious impulses and buried complexes.

Before any psychoanalysis is possible, the subject's resistance must be overcome. This is a requirement of pivotal importance for successful analysis. One of the basic sources of the resistance inheres in the phenomenon of transference, or the emotional attitude of the patient toward the analyst. This may express itself in the form of affection or admiration for the analyst (positive transference) or antipathy toward him (negative transference). This ambivalent attitude represents a reactivation of similar buried infantile feelings toward one parent or both parents, or toward siblings. Others ascribe it to the analytic situation that may create feelings of anxiety or hostility. In any case, the transfer must be dissolved before successful analysis is possible. According to Freud's procedure, this is achieved chiefly by an adequate explanation of the situation to the patient. The transfer ends when the patient understands that his attachment to the analyst is impersonal, that the analyst plays the role to him of a surrogate or substitute for an infantile parental fixation, and when he has been freed from slavish dependence upon the analyst. As long as excessive attachment to the analyst continues, the neurotic (neurotics crave sympathy) cannot emancipate himself from his complexes. After rapport has been established and resistances have been removed, the analyst must free the client from emotional dependence upon him. When the transfer has been completed, the patient is able to recreate his earlier infantile experiences and thus free himself from his fixations. The achievement of proper rapport will enable the patient to study his own mental life with the aid of one who understands him.

The establishment of satisfactory rapport is frequently very difficult, because the analyst, not having resolved his own conflicts, arouses opposition. The analyst can lead the patient only so far as he has gone himself. Before he can analyze others successfully, he must free himself from his own conflicts, fixations, and complexes; he must adopt a sympathetic, impersonal, noncritical attitude; he must also refrain from showing vexation and impatience, although some subjects are very trying to the analyst. Criticism tends to aggravate the neurosis and renders the efforts at analysis nugatory. Another factor that may block transference is the subject's opposition to getting well. Recovery would force him to face the vexations of life from which he has escaped by the development of the neurosis. Resistance is always present in the analysis, although it may operate in disguised form. The unwillingness to recover may be an unconscious resistance. Such resistance may betray itself by exhibitions of boredom, depression, anxiety, selective amnesia, exaggerated criticism, and irritability, while proper transference is shown by the rapidity with which these and other symptoms subside. One of the first jobs of the analyst, therefore, is to discover and overcome the subject's resistances, not only because they block analysis, but also because they distort the associations obtained during the analysis. The greater the resistance, the greater is the distortion.

Psychoanalytic Treatment Techniques. In psychoanalysis the methods of diagnosis and treatment are largely the same. The primary purpose of the analysis is to unearth the forgotten or hidden causes of the individual's conflicts and repressions. To do this the analyst must not only penetrate into the subject's unconscious life or forgotten past, but he must also make the subject aware of his concealed motives; he must get him to relive the episode at the root of his difficulty. The subject must be led to project himself back to the mental state in which the symptom first appeared, and he must be able to communicate his recollections to the analyst under intense emotional expression. In the presence of the analyst he must again live through the disagreeable experience in feeling, action, or speech. He must reestablish the connection between the emotion and the object that originally caused the conflict. This produces a discharge of the dammed-up energy (already referred to as abreaction, page 235), so that it may be released through other channels than those employed in the formation of the abnormal symptoms. Through this mechanism the repressed emotions are liberated and the energy attached to the repressed ideas is made available for useful pursuits. Every psychoanalysis, says Freud, is an attempt to free repressed love that has found inadequate compromise outlets in distorted symptoms. This liberation can be effected only by making the subject fully aware of the causative factors of his complexes, by making the unconscious sources of the difficulty conscious, and by abolishing the amnesias. Unless all the memory gaps are obliterated, there may be a recurrence of the symptoms. A partial analysis may remove some symptoms, but it will not effect a complete or lasting cure.

Psychoanalysis, then, according to the psychoanalysts, is the only method that effects a permanent cure of the neuroses or mental disorders arising from submerged complexes, because it is the only method that discovers and removes the basic causes. It is, so to speak, a radical form of mental surgery that cuts out the roots of the noxious psychic growths. Other methods concentrate on the removal of the symptoms and are largely confined to treating symptoms. The cure is due solely to the psychoanalysis and not to suggestion, advice, or encouragement, which only change the patient's attitude toward the symptoms without abolishing them. The method of psychoanalysis is most successful, so its votaries assert, in cases of hysteria, morbid fears, compulsions, obsessions, neuroses, sexual neurasthenia, homosexuality, sadism, masochism, and impotency. It may also effect improvement in the early or mild stages of schizophrenia (dementia praecox) and paranoia. The unprejudiced reader will, of course, balance these claims against the claims of the newer kinds of psychotherapy discussed in Chap. VI.

While the discovery of the hidden causes of mental or nervous maladies is the basic component of the psychoanalytic method of diagnosis and treatment, psychoanalysis also employs other treatment techniques, especially the methods of sublimation, which will be discussed in the next chapter.

CHAPTER XVI

SOLUTION OF DIFFICULTIES BY THE METHODS OF (14) SUBSTITUTION AND (15) SUBLIMATION [1]

Cursory references have already been made in preceding chapters to the resolution of mental conflicts and the solution of problems by the methods of substitution and sublimation. These methods deserve more detailed consideration, although the discussion must, perforce, be brief.

14. THE METHOD OF SUBSTITUTION

The Nature and Virtues of the Method. The substitution of new outlets or the sidetracking of the individual's energies into more acceptable forms of activity is one of the most commonly employed forms of adjustment to personal difficulties and frustrated ambitions. The expectation is that the new activity will enable the individual to achieve success in a substitute line of endeavor in which he possesses more interest and ability, or that the substitute task will provide a more wholesome or desirable outlet than the displaced activity. Sometimes the substitution consists essentially of the replacement of one set of motives or attitudes by other motives that will sweep away obstacles and enable the child to become victorious. To be sure, substitution may be regarded as a negative process, because it implies the restraint or inhibition of the contrasting ideals or tendencies. Nevertheless, instead of attempting to deny a forbidden tendency any outlet whatever by forced suppression or extinction, as is done by the method of inhibition or repression, the attempt is made to supplant the undesirable activity by a more desirable one. The method of substitution, when thus employed, is superior to the methods of sheer inhibition and suppression, of obstinate determination to engage in forms of activity in which the subject lacks interest or ability, or of the development of overcompensations—all of which frequently prove either futile or injurious directly to the subject or indirectly to society or both.

Illustrations of Successful Use of Substitutional Activities. The virtues of the method of substitution may be shown by the following illustra-

---

[1] These mechanisms here numbered separately could be subsumed under the eleventh adjustment dynamism, compensation, under its more inclusive connotation. It has seemed wise to accord them additional, separate treatment for the reason given on page 397.

tions of the successful use of substitute activities for overcoming a dislike for school and a querulous, bolshevistic attitude in school.

DISLIKE FOR SCHOOL ON ENTRANCE BY A SPOILED, ONLY CHILD, LEADING TO CONSTANT CRYING SPELLS BECAUSE MOTHER WOULD NOT REMAIN; READILY OVERCOME BY BEING GIVEN PLACE OF LEADERSHIP

It was very hard for me to become accustomed to school life when I first started. Being the only child and very spoiled I would cry every day on entering the schoolroom. The only reason I can recall was that my mother could not stay with me in school. I was told interesting stories by the teacher and everything was done to make me happy, but yet I would continue to cry. One day on entering the schoolroom crying as usual, the teacher called me and said, "You sit here at my desk, and be the teacher of the class." Immediately I stopped crying, as this just suited me, and from that day I began to like school. When a child I always desired to lead everything. I was very quick and if I could not be the leader when playing I would not play at all. I also loved to sing and was always singing and trying to play the piano. (B.E.I.; F.; Col.; E.S.T.)

IDEAS OF PERSONAL REFERENCE OR PERSECUTION; QUERULOUSNESS; OVERCOME BY APPEAL TO INTEREST IN ATHLETICS AND HOBBIES

G. entered high school at the age of fifteen and was considered to be slightly above normal in intelligence. He was a perfect specimen of boyhood in physical development, good looking, and very likable once you had established a point of contact with him.

The father and son were devoted pals, but the father was continually in a quarrel or brawl with his fellow workers in the railway service.

When G. entered high school, he was bolshevistic in his every tendency. He felt that every regulation was designed to entangle him, that every teacher was "picking" on him, and that every boy of every team or club was doing his best to see that he was not of their group. Every speech or program at assembly, given for the purpose of developing school morale and student acceptance of necessary regulations, was for his benefit and humiliation. With it all he had a heart of gold and qualities that would arouse the sympathies of any school principal.

During his first year, he was continually in trouble. He was punished in every way conceivable, including corporal punishment. There was no improvement and he was suspended toward the close of the first year because of his habitual grouch.

His second year started off as was to be expected. By Christmas his principal had concluded that his main objective would have to be to try to develop in him qualities of good school citizenship. This he attempted to do by catering to his interests in athletics and practical sciences. The principal gave him every article he could find stressing the qualities of the good sportsman, the value of teamwork, subordination of self for the good of the group, etc. He read them with zest, and began to try to exemplify many of the suggestions on the field. His temper at times would often cause him to revert to earlier attitudes, but he gradually developed a feeling of disgust with himself. Eventually the suggestion was accepted by the boys of the team that he be elected captain for the following year.

Another line of appeal was through his hobbies. He was used as an electrician and a repair carpenter for odd jobs, and he was given opportunities to tinker in the laboratory on the excuse that he was getting ready apparatus for coming class exercises. A fondness for schoolwork gradually developed, and by the end of the year he was doing work only somewhat below the level of the normal boy.

In his third year, as a result of his own inborn tendencies, he was involved in a town affair in which his father was killed. About a week later he confided to the principal that he was probably to blame, and expressed his resolution to make good. He did good schoolwork, was accepted by the students in all their functions, and was an influence for good student morale throughout the entire school.

Last fall, his fourth year in high school, he was forced to go to work in December to support the family. He now has a worthy job as an electrician's helper and is putting his sister through high school. The boy is on the road to becoming a good citizen. He feels that the principal has rendered him a great service. The principal feels that the good work accomplished is due, in major part, to utilizing his love for athletics and certain hobbies.   (From W.E.I.; M.; H.S.T.; B.A.)

The positive method of substitution can often be successfully employed, in place of the negative method of denial or suppression, in various fields of endeavor as a means of diverting impulses or ambitions away from destructive or useless channels into wholesome and fruitful ones. This may be shown by a number of banal illustrations. Thus, instead of chastising a boy who has a tendency to whittle school furniture and denying him any outlet for his energy, it is wiser to provide opportunities for the expression of his energies in some constructive form of industrial arts work. As is well known, the mere impulse to activity and self-expression impels some children to become mischievous and antisocial, although they have no desire to become nonconformists. The cure is to supply approved substitute outlets. Similarly, to cite another commonplace example: the child who has no ability to think in abstract terms or to live a life of intellectual contemplation can achieve a more satisfactory adjustment by devoting his preparation to more objective pursuits, such as those of a craftsman or a tradesman.

To cite an illustration from a wholly different field: the social climber, whose ambition to cut a conspicuous social figure has been frustrated because of lack of the necessary money or the requisite social graces, will achieve greater mental security and recompense by finding another outlet for her desire to bask in the limelight. She may take up some kind of social service, rather than spend her time trying to crush her impulses or consume her emotional energies in suppressed jealous feelings or in spiteful fulminations against her more successful rival. Again, the mother's poignant grief over the loss of her child can sometimes be more easily assuaged by the adoption of another child as a surrogate than by the attempt to follow the advice to stop grieving. Similarly, fears, anxieties, and apprehensions can be more readily and effectively eradicated or controlled if the child is led to engage in some activity designed to cast out these emotions and to assume the attitude, demeanor, and stance that will inspire confidence and courage, than if he is simply enjoined to forget the object of his fear (as was pointed out in Chap. XII).

Many inhibitions can be overcome by the simple expedient of implanting more potent ideas or motives, which will serve as rival stimuli. The desire for recognition and applause sometimes serves to displace stage fright. The passion for truth and right doing often sweeps away embarrassment and timidities. This method of adjustment may be referred to as the "expulsive power of a new affection." Instead of adjuring the neurotic to stop worrying and to forget or fight his neurosis, or to spend his time in travel—these usually prove to be futile as methods of cure—it is better to effect a spontaneous recovery (to follow the psychoanalytic theory) by means of proper analysis, emotional catharsis, and abreaction. The child's fear of or disgust for animals can often be overcome by leading him to see their harmlessness or beauty. To expel the aversion, however, such substitute or rival ideas must be made potent by a clever process of emotional conditioning (see pages 415*f.*).

The method of suppression should be supplanted by the method of substitution whenever it is practical or feasible to employ the latter. In general, a positive method is to be preferred to a negative method. Doubtless situations arise which render it desirable to obtain immediate results by the method of suppression or inhibition. For example, the imminent peril of a physical assault must be immediately checked by vigorous repressive measures. The automobile thief must be restrained instantly when "caught in the act," or the unfortunate owner may have to walk to his office. The child rushing headlong toward the abyss or reaching for the hot poker must be immediately forcibly restrained to avoid physical disaster. Imminent social or moral calamity often calls for immediate restriction rather than slow diversion. "Time and tide" cannot always wait for the well-considered application of the slower method of substitution. Physical perils or moral dangers must often be met by methods of certainty and celerity, however drastically inhibitory the latter may be. Moreover, the method of suppression is often effective without proving to be seriously subversive to personality integration, as has already been pointed out (see pages 470*f.*).

Nevertheless, the method of substitution should, in general, be preferred to the method of suppression or restraint. Controlling impulses by providing desirable, or at least not injurious, positive outlets is, in the long run, healthier and preferable to denying them any outlet whatever, by the method of suppression. The method of substitution (or sublimation) should, therefore, replace the method of suppression whenever possible. That the method of substitution, however, is subject to certain limitations is apparent.

Limitations of the Method of Substitution. 1. The method of substitution may be adopted precipitately or without adequate experimentation as the line of least resistance for meeting problems or as the easiest means of escaping difficulties. As a consequence, the child may never put forth enough effort to realize his highest potentialities. He may be satisfied to continue throughout life to substitute the easier for the better way of solving his perplexities. Precautions must, therefore, be taken lest the child quit trying to overcome his shortcomings because a more convenient outlet has been discovered. Many of his difficulties may not be due to inherent incapacities at all, but merely to adventitious or fancied causes that can be surmounted by determination and effort. It has doubtless often happened that a golden talent has been concealed in a temporary difficulty. The child must not be permitted to abandon the difficult path too hastily.

Again, the parent or the teacher might not be able properly to fathom the deeper values inherent in the spontaneous expression of the child's interest. This constitutes another reason why they should not be too hasty in sidetracking the child's energies into other channels. This may prove to be a means of robbing him of one of his most sacred rights, namely, the right to pursue his own spontaneously imposed task. To divert a child rashly, ignorantly, and forcibly from the pursuit of his deeper inner goals, which may lead him to higher levels of accomplishment, constitutes not only an act of disservice in general, but a specific infringement of a child's inherent rights which may play havoc with wholesome, efficient personality growth. Substitution has an important place as a method of child rearing, but it may prove pernicious if blindly adopted.

2. The second warning follows as a corollary of the first. The mere substitution of one activity for another may prove to be a futile gesture so far as accomplishing any useful end is concerned. Mere substitution may not lead to any better adjustments than the original activity. The substituted activity may be just as difficult, undesirable, or pernicious as the replaced one. Stealing, which is sometimes a substitute for sex activity, certainly is not a desirable activity, although it may not be so reprehensible as a sex offense. Many symptomatic acts which, according to the Freudians, are disguised outlets for painful affects, do not remove the conflict or increase the individual's ability to adjust himself. On the contrary, mischievous compulsive acts often seriously interfere with successful adjustment. It is apparent, therefore, that one cannot stress too strongly the careful discrimination that must be exercised in the choice of substitutions, so that the new outlets afforded the child will yield desirable satisfactions and make for effective integrations.

3. The substitutions adopted may prove only partially successful. That is, they may merely serve the purpose of a stopgap or temporary solution of certain incidental problems or difficulties that develop along the rough road of progress toward mastery. Some substitute tasks may be like some drugs that prove beneficial for a limited time only and then lose their potency or become positively injurious because of oversaturation or habit-forming characteristics. However, this weakness of the method of substitution is not very serious if parents and teachers will exercise the necessary surveillance and introduce from time to time new substitutions for those that have become outworn or injurious.

To recapitulate: we may conclude that, all in all, good substitutions often provide the child with beneficial outlets for his ambitions and urges, while inappropriate or ineffective substitutions will not only not solve the old difficulties, but may create new ones.

15. THE METHOD OF SUBLIMATION

Nature of the Process. What is meant by the word "sublimation"? Etymologically (from *sublimare,* to elevate, or *sublimis,* high, as in sublime) the word refers to any process of elevation, exaltation, or refinement. In the fields of education, mental hygiene, and psychiatry the word is technically employed in two related senses.

1. In the more general sense, sublimation is merely a specific form of substitution. It signifies the substitution of higher, socially approved forms of activity for disapproved, baser, or selfish desires. To state the matter somewhat differently, sublimation in its general connotation refers to the redirection of primitive urges into ethically and socially acceptable and useful behavior patterns. The attempt is made to replace the original egoistic aims with ethically approved vocational or social aims, such as approved commercial, industrial, humanitarian, artistic, literary, or religious activities. On a still higher plane, altruistic devotion to one's friends is sublimated into service to the race. Therefore, the method of sublimation may be described as a form of glorified transformation and resolution whereby the individual is liberated from the tyranny of antisocial impulses and ambitions and is thereby enabled to reach higher levels of mental integration and social effectiveness than would otherwise have been possible.

2. In the narrow Freudian sense, sublimation refers to a process of deflecting or sidetracking the libido from its original gross form of expression to higher nonsexual, socially approved goals. It is a process of refinement or purification of the repressed libido, or, stated more broadly, a process of socialization of the sex urge (which, in our opinion, may justifiably be classified as an instinct). The new interests are described as "aim-inhibited," because they have become desexualized or because their object is no longer

sexual in nature. Sublimation is the preferred method, in fact the only method, it is alleged, of conquering or subjugating the instincts and the neuroses. The process of sublimation should replace the process of repression or that of directly fighting the neuroses, which aggravates the difficulty.

Sublimation in terms of psychoanalysis is an unconscious emotional process, rather than a conscious intellectual process. In fact, for it to be successful, the libido must be dissociated from the person's intellectual processes. It is the end result of the process of psychoanalysis. The end result itself is an unconscious transformation of the repressed affects into more useful goals. Sublimation is difficult to effect when the patient fights the neurosis. Therefore, the assumption of a passive, noncombative attitude toward the neurosis is important for success. If successfully achieved, sublimation, then, will make for the reintegration of the personality and ultimately will lead to mental integration and health on a higher level of mental synthesis. In the final sublimation (which, as stated, is an emotional rather than an intellectual process) the unconscious, the real self, will be unfettered and freed for higher accomplishments.

Practical Implication for Child Counselors of the Psychoanalytic Doctrine of Sublimation. The psychoanalyst emphasizes as a matter of primal importance that parents and teachers must learn how to sublimate their own fundamental drives and conflicts before they can competently guide and direct the child's development. Unless they have sublimated their own impulses and desires, they may become a positive hindrance to the child's development, because their attitudes toward children will inevitably be colored unconsciously by their own unresolved complexes. The smoldering irritation caused by the tension of their own unrelieved conflicts will be reflected in grouchiness, listlessness, impatience, and intolerance; in childish prejudices; and in tendencies to criticize. As in the case of the analyst, therefore (see page 489), the teacher or the parent can lead the child in wholesome personality development only so far as he himself has gone.

Merits of Solving Problems by Sublimation. The general usefulness of this type of adjustment technique is attested by its wide-range application for the solution of personal difficulties and for the achievement of cultural ends. The diversion of intense ambitions and desires into higher forms of service, when it can be successfully accomplished, will vitalize and ennoble the performance of duty. Sublimation may prove to be an invaluable means of tapping the individual's hidden reservoirs of physical, mental, and moral energy and of converting it into higher forms of service and culture than could ever have been achieved without utilizing in sublimated form the irresistible, inveterate drives that emanate from basic life forces. The surge of emotional energy from deep-rooted drives, when harnessed to sublimated goals, may carry the individual to new heights of conquest. The Freudian thesis, that all culture is due to sublimation of the libido, may be an exaggeration, but it doubtless contains a germ of truth.

Illustrations of the Multifarious Uses of the Mechanism of Sublimation. The varied uses of sublimation for the control or refinement of antisocial impulses or egoistic desires can be readily shown by examples, banal and otherwise. The gross physical manifestations of the pugnacious disposition can sometimes be successfully sublimated into approved warfare against social and moral evils. A brutal, surly disposition can sometimes be diverted to harmless banter. A better outlet for the energy of the school bully who has a passion to dominate is to make him a leader in useful activities. Desirable leadership activities provide opportunities for the acquisition of feelings of importance and superiority, for the exercise of the authority urge, and for the desire to bask in the limelight; they may frequently prove to be a successful form of sublimation, as is shown in the following illustration.

THE EXERCISE OF AUTHORITY IN THE FORM OF BRUTALITY AND MIS-
BEHAVIOR AS A COMPENSATION AGAINST HOME DOMINATION AND SUP-
PRESSION, OVERCOME BY SUBLIMATING THE AUTHORITY DRIVE INTO
LEADERSHIP AND CONSTRUCTIVE WORK THAT TAXED HIS STRENGTH

The very first day that I entered the teaching profession I was warned that a problem child was being sent to me because I was to teach the dull group of the fifth grade. His former teachers confessed that it was impossible to handle him or to get any work done by him. This fact did not help my frame of mind any, and it was with some fear that I began my teaching.

The first week of school I kept a watchful eye on N., but I could not find anything particularly wrong with his behavior. He was over-age, fourteen at the time, with an I.Q. of 68, a healthy child, tall and muscular, with a clear complexion, an attractive smile, and good general appearance. I began to believe that I had been "kidded," and that he was no problem child after all. But I soon learned differently.

He probably had maintained his reserved attitude during the first week because I was a new teacher and he had been engaged in watching me as closely as I had been observing him. One day two of my smaller pupils came in crying with bloody noses. Upon inquiring I discovered that N. had taken the two and batted their heads together for his own pleasure. I sent for him and had a long talk with him. He was overbearing and sulky and tried to frame an excuse for his conduct.

From that time on I found that N. was at the bottom of all the troubles in my room. I had had enough psychology in normal school to know that there was some basis for his domineering attitude that should be disclosed. My inquiry showed that N. had an older brother who was humored at home. His father was a large domineering person who enjoyed bullying N. and who forced him to do all the farm work. Under unpleasant home conditions N. had been made the "goat" of all rebukes and abuses.

After discovering these facts I began to understand N. He was larger than anyone else in the class, and since he could not boss at home he was determined to have some authority at school. Through chance remarks I let N. understand that I knew him to be bigger and stronger than the rest of the boys, but that he should put his strength to good use. I made him group overseer in manual training, not to satisfy his whims but because he really was good in this work. When he fell down in his work, I would put someone else at the head. This never failed to make him work harder. I began giving him duties that required strength, and I found that if he was given work that kept him busy he forgot about his overbearing and domineering traits.

N. stopped school last year, because his father could see no reason for his continuing. During the three years that he was my pupil I found him very agreeable to work with and very original in his ideas, in spite of his low I.Q.

(From E.E.P.; F.; S.C.T.; Age 22)

Vigorous, stimulating participation in playground and recreational activities often supplies an effective antidote for tendencies to steal and commit depredations. Angered by intense dislike for some person because of a fancied or real slight, the wounded ego may sublimate its aroused energy by the determination to achieve superiority over the despised rival. The fury aroused by unjust or repressive social conditions may stimulate the ambition to develop a higher order of democracy or social organization. The ardor of the reformer indubitably represents in many cases a refinement of the anger aroused by the evils of society. Doubtless much of the finest creative productivity in the field of letters, art, and science represents sublimations of hatreds and wounded pride. Likewise the emotions aroused by deep disappointments sometimes find positive outlets in forms of service that ennoble the performance of duty.

The application of the principle of sublimation in the field of sex adjustment is proverbial. According to the Freudian psychology, this is par excellence the field for the application of sublimatory treatment techniques. In fact, Freud largely limits the concept to the redirection of the pregenital, libidual drives into aim-inhibited, nonsexual aims, a limitation that we regard as arbitrarily and unnecessarily restrictive. Nevertheless, practically all instinctive sex tendencies toward the other sex must be sublimated, since the frank, promiscuous expression of the sex urge is repugnant to many individuals and is not tolerated by society. Accordingly, the energy of these biological forces must be turned aside from the sexual goal to more approved objectives.

Illustrations of the more commonly employed methods of sex sublimation spring readily to mind. The physical directors of the high schools and colleges of the country encourage their adolescents to sublimate their sex drives by means of vigorous physical exercise of all kinds. With some individuals this expedient proves valuable. Equally common is the advice given young people to sublimate their sex life in wholesome fads, hobbies, avocations, music, and other interests, and in active participation in desirable social activities organized for youths of both sexes. Some oversexed persons succeed in adjusting themselves reasonably satisfactorily by plunging into literary, scientific, artistic, religious, or commercial activities, thus utilizing the enormous reservoir of energy from the sex drive for constructive purposes. This may be referred to as the sedentary type of work cure, as contrasted with physical work. Scientific curiosity is, indeed, regarded by some authorities as a sublimated form of sex curiosity. Be that as it may, the value of concentration upon a stimulating, worth-while task as a means of dissipating conflicts, controlling impulsive promptings, sweeping away impediments, and effecting inner reconciliation and integration can scarcely be questioned. For many people, physical labor is far more successful than intellectual labor in draining off the sex energy. Many spinsters, no doubt, sublimate their maternal instincts by playground or nursery activities, while the ungratified mating urge of the bachelor of either sex sometimes finds compensation in teaching. They may adopt teaching, perhaps more or less unconsciously, as a glorified substitute for parenthood. The conclusion that the new interest always must be a "special primary component of the sexual interest," as taught by some psychoanalysts (*e.g.*, Barbara Low) will scarcely prove acceptable to many psychologists. There are doubtless many forms of curiosity and interest that do not spring from the libido but are the result of the individual's prior experiences and processes of conditioning.

Limitations of the Sublimation Type of Adjustment. As compared with the method of forced negation or suppression, sublimation doubtless is a more effective technique for controlling deep, tabooed urges, but its limitations should be clearly recognized. Attention will here be directed to two of the most serious ones.

1. In some cases the process of sublimation is only partially or temporarily successful, while in other cases it fails entirely. Although some persons can sublimate only to a certain extent or for a limited period of time, that may, indeed, prove to be a gain, provided the impulses do not return in intensified form or provided the individual has been lifted to a point where he can tap new reserves of energy and utilize new approaches for the solution of his problems. Unfortunately, some individuals cannot sublimate at all, particularly those who are defective or those who are subject to consuming impulses.[2]

2. The sublimation may assume exaggerated, vicious, or pathological forms. Excessive sublimations often develop disagreeable attitudes and lead to

---

[2] The difficulty of sublimating the sex urge among males is shown in the following investigation: William S. Taylor, *A Critique of Sublimation in Males,* Genetic Psychology Monographs, 1933, 1–115.

undesirable forms of compensation. The results of such exaggerations sometimes appear in excessive programs of social uplift, excessive prudery, malicious gossiping, or extravagant condemnation of evil (sometimes traceable to an intense sex craving). Religious, moral, or political fanaticism, bigotry, and narrow-mindedness may be the fruits of excessive attempts at atonement or purification. A pathological fear of death may be transformed into morbid attachment to fantastic healing cults. The individual who attempts to sublimate his anger in daydreams may become an inveterate daydreamer and may spend his time in futile introvert ruminations and in devising means for the humiliation of his adversary. Many other evils of sublimation could be mentioned; but the above will suffice as typical illustrative situations.

Nevertheless, broadly conceived and at its best, sublimation often constitutes a valuable and efficient technique for adjusting the individual's inner drives to the demands of his environment. It is positive and constructive, while repression is negative and often paralyzing. Certainly one of the important obligations of every parent and teacher is to provide outlets in wholesome and socially approved forms of cultural activity for the child's impulsive and emotional drives and intellectual interests. The problem is one of so guiding and conditioning children that they will attach their interests to the less selfish and the more altruistic aims of their emotional, social, and intellectual cravings. Indirect means must be found for gratifying native drives through socially acceptable and worth-while outlets for the child's emotional, intellectual, and social interests and energies. Socialization of the original urges must be effected in new, satisfaction-yielding patterns and combinations. In general, the child must learn to substitute more remote for immediate satisfactions. He must sublimate his interests and wants with reference to more ultimate goals. As has been intimated, this is not purely or primarily an intellectual process; it is also, to a considerable extent, a process of emotional reconditioning, which may proceed more or less unconsciously.

CHAPTER XVII

SUGGESTIONS FROM PSYCHOANALYSIS OF VALUE IN CHILD GUIDANCE AND TRAINING

General Evaluation of Psychoanalysis. The most discordant views still exist regarding the value of psychoanalysis. On the one side, in this pitched battle of experts, are the psychoanalysts of various persuasions who unhesitatingly proclaim psychoanalysis to be the greatest contribution that medicine and psychology have bequeathed during the last half century for the correct understanding of mental mechanisms and for the diagnosis, prevention, and cure of mental and nervous disorders. In the opposed camp is found a motley array of physicians, psychologists, philosophers, ethicists, literary critics, and men of the street who are equally emphatic in proclaiming that psychoanalysis is little better than a system of fantastic, mystical dreaming or visionary philosophizing. Some of the criticism directed against psychoanalysis is transparently flippant, ignorant, biased, jejune, or insincere; but some of it is well grounded, searching, and trenchant and cannot be dismissed in a spirit of supercilious disdain.

A large wing of the opposition emphatically objects to Freud's doctrine of pansexuality from the infantile period onward, to his emphasis upon sex as the primal source of serious mental conflicts and of neuroses, and to his concept of the unconscious mind. Objection is also lodged against his theory of the instincts as out of harmony with the devaluation of the role of inherited adjustment patterns by modern psychology; to his one-sided emphasis upon the infantile genesis of the neurosis (out of instinctual-drive-generated conflicts and repressions); to his lack of sociological orientation; and to his lack of recognition of the importance of actual extant conflict situations (disturbances in human relations) and of the individual's character structure.

The writer is in agreement with the criticism that many causes of mental conflicts and maladies exist and that sex is only one source, although an important one; that recent conflict situations cannot be slighted in the attempt to diagnose or treat mental maladjustments, even when the primal source may lead to early-life experiences; and that the concept of an unconscious mind as a distinct entity, separate and apart from the conscious mind, is a convenient fiction. The latter admission, however, is not tantamount to the denial of the existence of unconscious or subconscious processes that can profoundly influence one's attitudes, disposition, and beliefs. Doubtless sub-

503

marginal or subliminal cortical processes or traces exist that can produce mental states which are not clearly conscious but which influence the individual's psychic life. Such processes have been variously referred to as the "penumbral region of consciousness," "fringe of consciousness," "subattentive states," or "unconscious cerebration." There are

neural processes which are too weak to reach the higher brain levels, but which prepare or "set" the nervous systems so that other nervous processes may reach the cortex, or which affect the "background" or "fringe" of consciousness. [These processes correspond, however,] not only to weak, nervous impulses (derived from subliminal stimuli), but to inherited and acquired neural dispositions or "patterns" and connections between neuron tracts. . . . Memories are the retention of vestiges or dispositions in, and of connections between, the neurons, and not deposits in a hypothetical subconscious [or unconscious] mind. Both the recording of the impressions and their retention are a matter wholly of unconscious cerebration.

The sudden revival of dormant memories which could not be recalled consciously is not due to the obliging activity of a secondary mind, the museum of innumerable memories, but to the activation of certain neuron tracts, changing adjustments between "neurograms," changes in resistance between certain neural synapses, the removal of neural interferences, and the facilitation of the passage of the nervous impulses over certain pathways. . . . There are many secondary automatic processes which were once conscious but which, through frequent repetition, can at length be carried on with very little or no consciousnessness. While attention is directed to the total activity, the part activities function almost automatically. . . . It is also recognized that there are many subattentive, marginal states near the "fringe or background" of consciousness far removed from its clear focus of which the individual may be barely conscious, but which may give color, continuity and meaning to the conscious processes. . . . The deeper tendencies of our thoughts and the tone of our feelings may be dependent, to no slight degree, on the many incipient impulses and wishes, and inchoate, unorganized attitudes and tendencies which well up from this penumbral region of consciousness.[1]

After all is said and done, it would be rash and premature to attempt at this stage of conflicting theories to offer a final and complete evaluation of psychoanalysis. The evidence is not all in as yet, and it is the best part of wisdom to reserve judgment on many moot issues in psychoanalytic lore. Doubtless the sources of mental disturbances have been discovered and removed and cures effected in many nervous and mental cases by psychoanalytic practitioners. But this does not prove incontestably that current psychoanalytic explanations and interpretations are adequate or correct. The process of cure might, after all, be reducible to terms of suggestion, in spite of the repudiation of this explanation by psychoanalysts, or to some other form of

[1] J. E. Wallace Wallin, *Clinical and Abnormal Psychology*, Boston, Houghton Mifflin Company, 1927, 439–441.

therapy involved in a complex treatment procedure, such as interpretative insight, expressive or release therapy, or therapeutic interviewing. Doubtless many modifications and simplifications of the doctrine or system will be effected with the progress of psychological research, which will result in a diminution of the tendency to hypostatize abstractions and a vigorous debunking of the present pedantic jargon of its devotees (of which only meager evidence has been given in our abbreviated and simplified treatment of the topic). Nevertheless, in spite of the theoretical or practical objections, the psychoanalytic movement is deserving of much credit for the aid it has rendered in making psychology dynamic and an instrument of service in the adjustment and harmonization of the mental life of man.

However, at its best, psychoanalysis represents a therapeutic luxury in the major surgery of psychotherapy which is available only to the favored few who can afford the costly expense of a protracted course of treatment from a psychotherapist thoroughly versed in psychoanalytic technique. Whether, in the hands of a competent analyst, it can be employed as successfully with children as with adults is problematic. Certainly it cannot be employed en masse with children in the homes or in the schools as an individual investigative technique; nor would it be expedient to use this means with school children without parental consent. In many cases the parental consent would be withheld, and vigorous protests would probably be lodged against the attempt to probe into the inmost recesses of the child's life. Nor could the method be employed by amateurs, as were the individual intelligence tests during the first decade of their use in the schools. Blunderingly employed with children (and with adults as well), psychoanalysis would doubtless do more harm than good. In fact, even its expert employment might entail injurious consequences through unfortunate conditioning. Through forced interpretations it may implant alien ideas from which the child might find it difficult to extricate himself, and in this way it might arouse needless fears and anxieties. Moreover, most nervous and mental difficulties in children can be helped by simpler methods, such as proper enlightenment, interpretation for the child of his problem, tactful suggestion, persuasion, healthy emotional conditioning, right-habit formation, employment of various forms of expressive and release therapy (play in a "permissive" environment, spontaneous sketching and craft activities, dramatization, puppet shows), relationship therapy (therapeutic interviewing), group therapy, and modification or removal of environmental handicaps (see Chap. VI). In many cases, perhaps in most cases, the causative factors at the root of the difficulty can be revealed without resort to difficult psychoanalytic procedures.[2]

[2] It should be stated, however, that Anna Freud, a daughter of Sigmund Freud, maintains that lay analyses of children can be successfully practiced by teachers who have been trained in psychology and in psychoanalytic procedures, and that medical training

Nevertheless, whatever the ultimate verdict of science will be regarding psychoanalysis, we are indebted to it for many suggestions of peculiar value for child study, development, and guidance. While psychoanalysis cannot arrogate to itself sole credit for all the values that are set forth in the following pages, it has rendered significant service in respect to the following points, which should not be underestimated. There is some overlapping in the items enumerated, but it is believed that the overlapping is justified.

Brief Summary of Valuable Facts and Suggestions Contributed by Psychoanalysis to Child Guidance. 1. Many, perhaps most, nervous and mental maladies have a long incubation period. The psychoanalytic investigators have shown that a recent episode allegedly at the basis of many mental difficulties may merely play the role of an immediate excitant; the basic cause may be some remote occurrence, often entirely forgotten. The demonstration that the dynamic motives which control conduct, both normal and abnormal, may be long-forgotten experiences, redounds to the credit of psychoanalysis, although this had previously been indicated by hypnosis. In attempting to unearth the taproots that may lie buried in the individual's early experiences, one must never, however, blind oneself to the importance of tracking down and evaluating all the internal and external factors of the client's present adjustment situation.

2. Many, perhaps the large majority, of mental and nervous difficulties are environmentally produced, the most important environmental focus being the home, followed by the school, the street, and the playground of the child's immediate community. In other words, they are of psychogenic origin, being produced by the individual's own earlier experiences and reactions to the forces in his environment and to his organic needs.

3. Many minor mental maladjustments and many major nervous difficulties are due to "psychic trauma" in childhood. These traumata, produced by intense emotional or nervous upsets or by insidious or subtle conflicts in the fields of the emotions, appetites, acquired habits, attitudes, beliefs, and ideals, have laid the basis for the development of anxieties, feelings of guilt, inhibitions, attempts at concealment, repression, perversions, early fixations, regressions, inability to grow up and adjust oneself to the social order, and nervous and mental maladies. Psychoanalysis has emphasized the relation to health

---

does not constitute an indispensable prerequisite for this type of service for children. Possibly analysis can be applied if caution, tact, and discreetness are exercised, and if the child is safeguarded against the dangers that lurk in the radical application of the method. *Psychoanalysis for Teachers and Parents,* New York, Emerson Books, Inc., 1935 (translated by Barbara Low). See the symposium on "Psychoanalysis with Children," in *The Nervous Child,* Vol. II, 1946.

and disease of the fundamental emotional urges and early habit patterns and has shown the necessity of obtaining complete insight into the child's early psychological history if symptoms are to be understood and cures effected. This is all to the good, provided that no relevant phase of the *status praesens* is neglected. The processes of trait formation, whether normal or abnormal, are, in the judgment of the author, essentially processes of conditioning.

4. Chief reliance for achieving successful results in the field of mental health and mental hygiene must be placed on the application of positive and preventive mental-hygiene measures in early childhood in the home and in the school. This will be achieved through a proper understanding of child development, of the mechanisms of character formation, and of the methods of furthering wholesome development and preventing abnormal deflections.

5. The most effective and expeditious way of resolving many mental difficulties and maladjustments that have already been formed is to understand them and help the child to understand them—how and when they originated, how they grew and developed, what forms of expression they have assumed, what recognized or unrecognized purposes they have subserved, and how they are operating at the time. Without this mutual understanding and insight, the child's counselors cannot minister effectively to his needs and the child cannot solve his own problems. Psychoanalysis has especially emphasized the necessity of acquiring an understanding of the remote dynamic causal mechanisms responsible for abnormal behavior patterns and the significance of disguised symptomatic acts.

That many aversions, dislikes, fears, eccentricities, and conflicts will, in point of fact, disappear when the subject finds out what is back of his difficulty—when it is properly explained to him, when he realizes on the basis of this understanding that the trouble is a slight one, as is often the case, and when he is given sympathetic guidance—is shown by many of our case reports. They have at least demonstrated conclusively that many personality difficulties of obscure origin can be cleared up without resort to complicated, esoteric, or mystical procedures. A few illustrative cases may prove illuminating.

Illustrations of How Difficulties Can Be Resolved by Simple Explanations and by Enlightened, Sympathetic Understanding. The following maladjustments (the nature of the origin of which, however, was known in most cases) include a fear of beholding lids placed on boxes, a state of terror induced by the horror of a burning death, a state of apprehension aroused by a sermon on the judgment day, bashfulness, excessive timidity, stage fright, and terrifying dreams about death.

CRYING TANTRUMS PRECIPITATED BY SIGHT OF LIDS BEING PLACED ON BOXES, DUE TO OBSERVATION OF MOTHER'S HYSTERIA WHEN LID WAS LOWERED ON FATHER'S CASKET; DESTRUCTIVE OUTBREAKS WHEN WHIPPED IN PUNISHMENT; FACIAL GRIMACES AND TICS AS SUBSTITUTES FOR CRYING; EMOTIONAL CONDITIONING LASTING FOR YEARS, BUT OVERCOME BY DISCOVERY OF CAUSE AND RATIONAL EXPLANATION

No personal difficulties of adjustment dawned upon my horizon until I was four years old, when my father, after a week's suffering from blood poisoning, died. From this event evolved two marked fears of my childhood.

My mother told me quite simply that my father was going to have a very long sleep and that I would not see him for a great length of time. I remember none of my feelings at that time, owing to my lack of understanding and not to lack of fondness for my father. My mother's sorrow was full of anguish and almost hysterical when the top of the casket was lowered after the services at our house. In my mind were associated the two, my mother's hysteria and the lowering of the top.

Much trouble resulted until my tenth year. During the intervening years, I was unable to adjust myself to the situation of seeing anything closed which was rectangular in shape. I would cry frightfully whenever I saw a top put on any article. My mother could not even do the very simple thing of taking a hairpin from a cardboard box and replacing the top, without my going into one of my crying "spells."

My crying apparently at nothing soon aroused the anger of the family, and the result was that, every time my crying was provoked by the shutting of a box, chest, or trunk, I was spanked. The spanking cure brought absolutely no results other than bad ones. I developed hatred for the entire family, would pull down curtains, push over chairs, break the china, and knock my head against the wall whenever I was spanked. I was then deprived of privileges instead of being spanked, but this had no effect. To stop from crying I would go through a series of choreic movements of the facial muscles, such as twitchings of the mouth, biting of the lips, and peculiar grimaces of the entire face. Never was I able to say what caused the crying even when I was carefully questioned.

I was ten years old before my mother made any effort to discover the cause. We were selecting a pair of shoes, and I, anticipating that the clerk was going to cover the shoe box after our rejection of the shoes, hid my face in my hands so as not to see the action. He laughingly inquired why I was afraid. It was then that I told my mother that I would scream if I saw him cover the box. My mother continued the questioning. She wanted to know if that was what made me cry so frequently, and why I hadn't said before what was the cause. "When did I first cry when a box was closed?" This last question it took some time for me to answer. My mother had to go back in my earlier life and question me about every incident of any importance. Finally, she got to the event of my father's death. We talked about it for some time before I could really remember, but I at last recalled the scene and described it to my mother.

The foolishness of the whole idea was shown to me, and most explicitly developed was the fact that my mother's hysteria and the closing of my father's casket should not be at all related because my mother just could not restrain her sorrow any longer and its outburst might have occurred anywhere and at any time.

After this, I did not have serious trouble when I saw a box closed, but I was unable to close one myself. This action was taken for obstinacy and stubbornness. Although at first timid about performing this dreaded deed, I did eventually react normally to the closing of a box and was able to close one without any emotional outbreak.   (T.A.M.; F.; E.S.T.; A.B.)

A STATE OF TERROR AND INSOMNIA INDUCED BY THE HORROR OF A
BURNING DEATH FOR HAVING COMMITTED THE UNPARDONABLE SIN;
DUE TO "HELL-FIRE-AND-DAMNATION" SERMONS

During my early childhood days and until well into the adolescent age I believed that I had committed "the unpardonable sin."

My father and mother were very religious people and as a result the children were brought up in a church atmosphere. During my early childhood days we had regular family worship, at which time my father would read the Bible and then the children would kneel and each would say his prayers. We lived in a small rural town. We were very faithful in our attendance at church meetings, especially on Sundays when the entire family would go to Sunday School in the morning, and remain during the morning worship. We would return again for the Epworth League meeting and for the regular Sunday evening church meeting.

It was the custom of the church to have a revival of a "Billy Sunday" type once each year. Our family attended regularly. Our minister during the year was also a revivalist who preached the "hell-fire-and-damnation" type of sermons. To this we children necessarily had to listen. Thus early in life we had a horror of death and of the events that might take place in the event of our death unless we were "saved souls." This formed an excellent background for the event which was later to happen.

It was during one of the revival meetings that I received an impression that I had committed "the unpardonable sin." Emblazoned on a large billboard in front of the church appeared each day of the revival the topic for the sermon. For this particular night the billboard read: "Have You Committed the Unpardonable Sin: Come Tonight and See." During the day the matter was discussed between playmates and myself as to the nature of this great sin for which there was no pardon. We could not arrive at any conclusion but each said he would certainly be present in order to be enlightened upon the subject. Our minister had preached so much about hell fire that we wanted to be certain we had not committed the sin.

Upon arrival at the church that night I eagerly awaited the minister's solution to the problem. The evangelist preached on and on, begging people to join the church and be saved; but to my immature mind there came no answer from the sermon as to the real significance or meaning of the unpardonable sin. I began to worry, even before leaving the church, and went home that night fully convinced that I had committed this great sin, even though I did not know what the sin was. Naturally, I said nothing about my feelings to my parents or brothers and sisters for I was ashamed. I was the "black sheep" in the family. They all had an opportunity to go to heaven when they died but I was doomed throughout all eternity. I was ashamed to go to them for I thought this would be the same as an admission of my guilt and I did not wish to confess to those whom I loved.

Each night thereafter, to the best of my knowledge, as I said my prayers to my parents I would add silently "Oh God, please forgive me for committing the unpardonable sin." But I knew it was of no use to pray for forgiveness because unpardonable meant that the sin could not be forgiven even though God wanted to forgive me. So no matter what I did I was a doomed boy. As a result I began to lie awake at nights. I have often heard my mother say that I was a very nervous boy at nights but I seemed to be a normal, healthy boy during the daytime. Mother would sit by the side of the bed each night and hold my hand until sheer fatigue caused me to fall asleep. Since I was so nervous, she would also leave the light in my room burning.

And what were my thoughts during those sleepless hours? I felt I was disgraced and had brought disgrace upon my family. But I would not tell anyone. I would carry my secret to my grave. Well, since I was going to hell I wondered what kind of a place hell was. It was terrible. The minute you arrived there Satan threw you in a raging furnace and your body burned on and on forever. I could picture myself being tossed into this terrible furnace and burning but never dying for my punishment was to be forever. But why all this injustice to me when I didn't know the time I committed the sin? What kind of a God was this who would allow a boy to commit a sin that would send him to eternal damnation? Our minister had told us that God was "just" but that we must not arouse his "wrath."

I went to church Sunday after Sunday in a state of terror. The minister continued his "hell-fire" sermons and my belief was confirmed that I was lost. I looked through the Bible many times in the hope of finding a solution to my problem. I looked through many different Bibles, consulting the index in an attempt to find the words "unpardonable sin." Then I would look for the words "hell," "fire," etc., in the dictionary.

During my hours of play when I was happy because I had temporarily forgotten about my predicament, suddenly I would remember that I was not like the other boys for I was doomed and they were not. However, I grew somewhat bolder for nothing so far had happened to me that was in any way different from the experiences of my playmates. If I lived as long as my father had lived it would be many years before I had to answer for my sin.

But I was still nervous at nights and as a result was now sleeping with an older brother in a room adjoining that of my parents. I was very much afraid of the dark and would not venture out after nightfall. I began to be very careful in all that I did. When I went swimming I would not go in deep water for fear of being drowned. The only way I could "beat the game" temporarily was to be extremely careful in all that I did.

The year arrived when Halley's comet came so close to the earth that it could be seen.[3] The St. Louis papers, in large headlines, commented upon the fact that the comet would not directly strike the earth, but that its tail composed of poisonous gases would envelop the earth. There were Sunday supplementary features about the coming of the end of the world. I was desperate, for soon I would have to face the penalty of burning because I had committed the "unpardonable sin." In my desperation I went to a young minister, who had recently been transferred to our church, and told him my story. He informed me that so far as he knew the only kind of a sin that could be unpardonable was not to believe in Jesus Christ, for if I did not believe in him I would have no opportunity of living the right kind of a life. I left that conference a happy boy (for I had joined the church and I did believe in Jesus Christ). I had not committed the unpardonable sin after all.

Recommendations

My suggestions for preventing similar occurrences in the lives of other boys are as follows:

1. Until approximately the age of ten years, children should have a church service of their own which is conducted in a language that their immature minds can interpret. Further, instead of being taught to fear God they should be taught to obey God through the virtues of love, kindness, etc.

2. A minister for young children and for those of intermediate grade should be kind and sympathetic. He should be one in whom children can confide. Had this been true in my case, I would have confided in him at the very beginning and my problem would have been solved at an early date in my life.

3. It is very doubtful whether the immature minds of young children should be exposed to the vicious journalism that is often found in the biweekly and weekly supplements of many of our large city newspapers. Suggestion is a powerful force. While the literature for children should no doubt be partly fanciful, in order to draw out their imaginations, it should not be of such a nature as to cause great fear, especially in such matters as religion.

4. Parents should teach children that their confidences are sacred and that anything told the parents would not be scoffed at or repeated. A spirit of mutual helpfulness in my case would have assisted me in overcoming my great fear.

(P.L.W.; M.; Jr. C.T.; M.A.; Age 35)

[3] This comet, which swings into view once in nearly 76 years, appeared on May 18, 1910. This recital reminds one of the sixteenth century stanza:

> Eight things a comet always brings:
> Wind, famine, plague, and death to kings,
> War, earthquakes, floods, and dire things.

UNSUSPECTED YOUTHFUL TERRORS AND APPREHENSIONS PRODUCED
BY THE SERMON OF AN EMOTIONAL PREACHER REGARDING THE JUDG-
MENT DAY; FEAR OF LOOKING UP INTO THE SKY AFTER SUNSET BE-
CAUSE OF DREAD OF BEHOLDING SIGNS AND WONDERS; PARALYSIS OF
FEAR FROM BEHOLDING A RED MOON AND OTHER UNUSUAL CELESTIAL
PHENOMENA; OVERCOME BY A DIFFERENT TYPE OF SERMON AT THE
BEGINNING OF THE HIGH-SCHOOL PERIOD

Mine was a home of strong Christian influence and we were required to attend
Sunday school and church regularly. I never thought of questioning the requirement or the teachings of the Bible.

When very young I listened to a very emotional minister who portrayed the
horrors of judgment day, and who gave a detailed description of the moon turning
to blood and of other signs and wonders in the sky which would foretell the advent
of that dreadful day.

My childish heart almost ceased to beat for I was simply terrified. I did not
know that I would live to see another day. The sun shone the next day and my
fears were somewhat allayed. I did not dread the day for the signs were to be
seen at night, or at least that was what I had learned. After the sun had set I did
not dare to look into the sky.

In the autumn or spring when smoke or haze caused the moon to have a deep
red color, I was paralyzed with fear for I was sure that it was blood. The only
time I ever saw the Aurora Borealis I almost went into convulsions for I thought
the heavens were in flames. My mother told me what it was but did not explain
it. I was glad to know that the last day had not arrived, and was told not to
bother about the phenomenon.

I remember waking in the night and seeing that the moon was not all there.
What had become of the rest I had no idea; I only thought it was one of the
"signs and wonders." The next day I asked my mother about it. She tried to
explain it, but she had no conception of the depths of my fears. I suffered, I am
sure, as no one ever dreamed.

One evening just at dusk a meteor crossed the sky and, while the other members
of the family watched, I burst into tears and ran to my mother. My father scolded
me, but he didn't understand. I was nearly ready for high school before I thought
of the heavens except as something in which I should see some awful sign of an
awful doom.

Strange to say the release from my fears also came through the same channel
as the cause. A minister, a man of superior qualities, spoke of the beauties of the
sky. From him I learned that there was nothing to fear but much to enjoy in
the heavens. He read the nineteenth Psalm which begins:

> The heavens declare the glory of God,
> And the firmament showeth his handiwork.

Considering how close my mother was to me I have never understood why she
did not know how great my fear was. Perhaps it was due to the fact that, like
most children, I tried to hide it.   (C.L.E.; F.; E.S.T.; Ph.B.; Age 40)

HOW BASHFULNESS IN A BOY WAS OVERCOME BY AN UNDERSTANDING
TEACHER

As a beginning teacher, I had an average boy in the fifth grade who was too
painfully bashful to participate in the Friday-afternoon rhetoricals. Since this
work was required of each child, it was my business to see that he took part. After
thinking about this problem, I decided to find a selection that would make a special
appeal to him. My efforts in that direction were successful. On Friday afternoon
he took the customary position, facing the room. He spoke so low that only those
in the front seat heard him. About this, I said nothing, for I felt that he had
accomplished much in taking his position and going through without forgetting it.
The next week, he did better and gradually improved until he was quite satisfactory.
I instinctively felt that compulsion would not solve this difficulty and that I must
stimulate his interest. (From M.H.; F.; E.S.P.; Age 49)

A CASE OF TIMIDITY AND STAGE FRIGHT OVERCOME

Catherine, age thirteen, was a member of the second-year high-school English
class. She sat in class with eyes alive to all that went on, she smiled at the funny
things, she was neither daydreaming nor listless. But she either could not or
would not talk in class, either in reply to a direct question or to present topics
that she had chosen, prepared in outline, and written out in full. In conference she
insisted that she never had been able to speak in any of her classes, although she
knew the material well and could write anything required. This last statement
was true.

The teacher decided to develop the ability to speak in this class, thinking she
could in some way appeal to Catherine. There were jokes, humorous experiences,
Negro readings, etc., given besides the discussions of the lessons. The teacher
joined in this work by frequently giving short readings. Comments were made
as to the work of each student. Soon Catherine was drawn into the spirit of this
work and before the first month was over she was giving some of the best talks.
She soon learned that she was gifted in expression and now her greatest pride is
to entertain her friends by some dramatic presentation.

(From M.R.; F.; H.S. Supv.; B.A.)

TERRIFYING IMAGES AND DREAMS ABOUT DEATH ATTRIBUTED TO A
CHANCE REMARK ABOUT DEATH; OVERCOME BY IDEALISTIC VISIONS
OF HEAVEN

One unavoidable circumstance of my childhood has left impressions that will
probably never be entirely erased. From the time I was five until I was eight,
much of our family life centered about our plans and activities for the physical
comfort of my father, who was smitten with an incurable disease. I suffered much
mental anxiety and depression because of my lively imagination and the fact that
I constantly overheard remarks from grown-ups which were not meant for my
ears. One was a chance remark about death, and, never having seen death in any

form, I built up for myself and for my brother some very terrifying pictures. I had some horrible dreams about it too, none of which I can recall now, and I used to wake up, screaming "Where is my father?" Everyone was so busy at our house then that I was allowed to suffer some time before I was helped out of my difficulties. Then it was in the good old-fashioned way with a beautifully idealistic picture of heaven.

My father was a patient sufferer and very much devoted to his children. I was warmly attached to him and used to slip in by his bedside to tender childish bits of service and to repeat poetry or scripture with him—his favorite method of diversion from his pain. I am sure that those sad and little understood experiences and the overbalanced spiritual or religious awakenings which accompanied them have had much to do with the shaping of my life. Some of it I do not regret— some of it, I know, might have been more wisely handled. When I had to pass through much the same experience with my mother a few years ago, I was glad for the vivid recollections of childhood faith to nerve me then. However, what I needed was more experience of a practical and realistic nature in the days between these two great episodes of my life to offset the idealistic turn which my imaginative thoughts took.   (W.C.H.; F.; Nursery Kg. Supv.; Ph.B.; Age 37)

6. Psychoanalysis has shown the value of treating the child's mental perplexities openly and honestly, training the child to face his problems frankly without evasion and compromise. The most difficult field in which to apply the doctrine of sincerity and frankness is that of sex education. A brief excursus on this point may therefore be in order.

Application of the Doctrine of Frankness to Sex Instruction. The difficulty of dealing with the great primal instinct of sex effectively is due partly to the fact that it is a very hard impulse to sublimate, and partly to the fact that the taboos and inhibitions thrown about it have led the child to feel that it is something coarse, unclean, and shameful—something that should not be discussed, but should be indulged in secret and suffered in silence when it has been misdirected and abused. It is also due to faulty sex instruction, beginning with injudicious handling in the nursery (such as repression of toilet habits), resort to snubbing when the child shows sex curiosity, and responding to his queries with lies or transparent evasions. But it is far easier to point out defects in our present methods of sexual enlightenment than to introduce satisfactory substitutes. This the Freudians believe results far less from lack of knowledge regarding the mental and physical hygiene of sex than from the fact that many parents and adults have not solved their own sex conflicts, in consequence of which they are not able to handle the topic sanely, coolly, judiciously, and without embarrassment. Sexually unadjusted or with their own sex drive unsublimated, they are unable to conceal from the child their own abnormal emotional attitudes toward the problem, and thereby they may aggravate the difficulties they are attempting to overcome.

Approved programs of sexual enlightenment have been frequently outlined. To epitomize some of the more important elements in such programs is not a difficult task. For example:

a. Handle the facts of sex, from the beginning, like any other matter, objectively, understandingly, and unemotionally.

b. When the interest first appears teach the child the facts regarding birth truthfully but in a way that he can understand. Teach the facts of animal procreation in the upper elementary and high-school years, in connection with the courses in botany and biology.

c. Safeguard the child in early life from precocious sexual stimulation by protecting him from inflammatory situations; by avoiding the excessive fondling often indulged in by ungratified parents; by having him sleep alone in a separate bedroom after the first year, instead of in the parents' room; by abstention on the part of the parents from caressing before the children, which may cause precocious sexual awakening; and by safeguarding the child from contact with contaminating playmates and lascivious nursemaids, who often inflict untold injury on children (the vast majority of young children feel little sexual urge without stimulation); and by preventing the influences of suggestive pictures, sex movies, sex novels, obscene markings and verses in toilets, salacious conversation or literature, and sex dances. Undue propinquity with members of the opposite sex should be avoided: the impulse toward sex attraction with most people is predominantly physical and is stimulated by physical contact. Any part of the body may become a sexual fetish or an object of unreasoning devotion (see page 439). Especially stimulating are spooning, petting, or necking, which are regarded as preparatory sex acts. Unsupervised dances easily degenerate into sexual debauches.

d. In this connection, let parents, teachers, and child workers realize that sex is sometimes an important factor in social and life adjustment long before the period of adolescence or the onset of puberty ordinarily starts. Even if the Freudian concept of infantile sexuality is repudiated, well-authenticated cases show that definite erotic or sex activities in some children antedate the average period of pubescence by several years. It is important to keep in mind, therefore, that sex guidance may be needed during the preadolescent period and that children need to be safeguarded from contamination and injurious habits before the usually recognized pubescent period.

e. Inculcate in children the attitude that sex activity is normal and not pathological but that it must be properly regimented and sublimated in the interest of mental and physical health and social morality. Foster ideals of wholesome restraint, proper habits and ideals of sexual morality, and higher ideals regarding the relations of the sexes. Certainly mere teaching of the facts of reproduction is not enough. Knowledge itself may serve as a definite inducement to immorality. The higher aesthetic and moral values of the sex life must be inculcated. Without these higher psychic components, sex becomes coarse and vulgar, a mere exercise of animal passion or a mere barter transaction. In sex the physical should be subordinated to the psychosocial give and take. Few things are finer than clean, pure sex life; and nothing is baser than the grosser forms of sexuality.

f. Provide wholesome mental and physical activity as forms of sublimation —an abundance of physical exercise, mental and physical games, interest-provoking work, and social diversion. Constant companionship with clean, high-minded persons of the opposite sex of suitable age will keep the child's mind wholesomely occupied and free from the unhealthy ruminations that flourish in conditions of unoccupied isolation.

g. Direct the child's thoughts and imagination into healthy channels. Keep his mind busily occupied with interesting, worth-while, satisfying personal pursuits, directed by some lofty life purpose. It is the empty mind that becomes the "devil's workshop" in the field of sex adjustment. Many sex difficulties originate in the field of the imagination. Salaciousness is the fruit of salacious imagery.

h. Give due attention to the hygiene of food and bathing, taking care to withhold sexually stimulating foods, drinks, and narcotics (such as alcohol, wine, condiments, and eggs); remove genital irritants, such as a constricted prepuce in either sex; and supply necessary treatment for hyperirritation of the verumontanum. Needless to say, cases of nymphomania, satyriasis and other pathological sex difficulties must be referred to the experts.

i. Supply correct information regarding the dangers of venereal infection and the evils of excessive masturbation or excessive indulgence. Implant in the child a proper realization of the sacred duty he owes to himself and to posterity to keep his body healthy, clean, and free from the type of pollution that will produce corruption, not only in his own organism but possibly also in his offspring. The child should get a vision of his supreme duty to the race, namely, to pass on the sacred stream of heredity free from any degenerating contamination. Wise, discriminating sex education is one of the most important phases of the education of youth. Children need to be protected from the evils of ignorance, misinformation, baffled or unrequited sex curiosity, undue stimulation, bad sex practices, sex inversions, and sexual aggressions. It is far better that the child should be forewarned and protected by wholesome and reliable enlightenment than that he should be deceived by concealment, misled by ignorance, and debauched as the result of the studied observance of a policy of *laissez faire* in matters of sex. According to M. J.

Exner,[4] 91.5 per cent of college men received their first permanent impression about sex from unwholesome sources at the average age of 9.6 years. Seventy-nine per cent reported that the effects of this information or misinformation were bad. Only at the average age of 15.6 years, or six years later, was instruction received from proper sources. Attention has already been called to the faulty sources from which sex information is usually received and the effects of such information (see pages 431ff.).

While the cogency of the facts and arguments adduced above may be freely admitted, the important problem in the field of sex education still remains unsolved, namely, how to do the job efficiently, with the least amount of harm and the greatest amount of good for each individual concerned. It must be conceded that the amount of reliable knowledge available in well-documented publications for putting across the program of sex education is far in advance of the skill, tact, and understanding possessed by parents, teachers, physicians, social workers, and others for imparting the information effectively and for wisely guiding and directing the child's sex strivings. In response to the query put to a class of 31 students (nine of whom were men), pursuing a graduate course offered by the author in the University of Chicago, as to whether or not they were ready (and prepared and willing) to offer sex instruction to children in the schools, nine responded in the affirmative, five stated they would be willing to do so if and when they possessed the necessary training, and one was willing to undertake the task if the instruction could be given in a biology course. Thirteen answered in the negative; one was noncommittal, stating that the problem should be handled in the home, while two failed to register their reactions.

In other words, 44.8 per cent of these men and women, nearly all of whom were mature graduate students, did not feel ready to assume this function. The percentage would be increased to 58 if we include those who were not willing to undertake the task before they had secured special preparation. All the answers were submitted in anonymous notes. The same inquiry, directed in a similar manner to 68 students (of whom 11 were men), all teachers in service, eight with degrees, pursuing an extension course offered under the auspices of the University of Delaware, yielded the following results: 40 students, or 62.5 per cent of the 64 who answered the query, stated that they were not ready to offer sex instruction to school children. This includes two who stated they might be willing to do so after having obtained the necessary training. The ratio of negative answers is smaller for the group of academically more mature students, although many of the extension students were chronologically as old as the students in the graduate course.

[4] M. J. Exner, *The Problem of Sex Education in Schools,* Washington, D.C., U.S. Public Health Service, 1919.

The attempt was not made to determine the reasons for the respondent's reluctance to supply hygienic sex advice, but many volunteered the opinion that they were not adequately prepared for the work. A considerable number of those who gave negative replies, however, expressed the view that sex instruction is very important and necessary. What proportion of those who professed readiness to give sex instruction are competent to supply guidance that will prove genuinely helpful and not injurious is problematic. Without the necessary emotional poise and freedom from emotionalized sex consciousness, childish affective survivals, and evidences of embarrassment, the attempt to proffer personal advice, however sound, in the field of sex hygiene may prove worse than useless. Teachers, parents, psychologists, nurses, and doctors who cannot handle sex matters without obvious emotional excitement or without betraying a flippant attitude cannot render acceptable service in this field. Personal probity, proper temperamental disposition, and freedom from unresolved sex conflicts are as essential in the mentor as scientific knowledge.

7. Do not develop an exaggerated feeling of guilt in children by harsh or repeated criticisms of their faults, by violent emotionalized condemnation of their foibles and follies, by nagging or even flippant or heedless remarks, by excessive prohibitions, by unwise or superstitious indoctrination designed to foster the idea that mishaps are penalties imposed by natural phenomena, or by any form of behavior that will develop an abnormal guilt complex. It may be conceded that children should acquire justifiable ideas of what is right and proper. But clinical investigations have shown that it is very easy by unwise management or suggestions to make mountains out of molehills and to make minor indiscretions and slips appear like unpardonable sins to sensitive natures. Through careless or thoughtless conditioning the child may acquire a deep-seated sense of guilt which is not justified by the facts and which may develop into a more or less permanent habit pattern of fears, mental conflicts, inhibitions, overscrupulousness, overfastidiousness, and nervous or mental disturbances.

Illustrations of the Exaggerated Guilt Complex. The following reports will illustrate the varied ways in which an exaggerated guilt consciousness may develop (see also pages 384*f.*, 388*f.*, 433*f.*, 436*f.*, 462*f.*, and 475*f.*).

AN EARLY REPROACH FOR "MURDERING A CAT," RESURRECTED THREE
YEARS LATER AS A DREADFUL FEELING OF GUILT

When visiting relatives in the country at the age of five, I dropped a cat down a well. I did not intend to hurt the cat. I only wanted to hear it splash. When my father remarked, "Now, Miss, you have murdered a poor pussy cat," I was sorry, but did not worry over the matter until I was eight. We had a lesson in Sunday school on the commandments, with a talk on "Murder" and on how a murderer would feel. This recalled the cat and my father's words. For days I suffered from a dreadful burden of guilt. One night when my parents had gone to the theater, it got beyond endurance. I could not sleep, but lay awake utterly miserable. When my parents returned, my mother came to look at us before going to bed. When she came to my room I sat up and exclaimed, "Mother, did I murder that cat?" She thought I had been dreaming, but when I explained the situation she sat near me and set my mind at rest, and I went to sleep, a happy sinner! (B.L.A.; F.; S.C.T.)

INTENSE SECRET WORRY FROM FEAR OF THE FLOOD BECAUSE OF WRONGDOING AND OF GABRIEL'S TRUMPET HERALDING THE DAY OF JUDGMENT, DUE TO EARLY RELIGIOUS TEACHINGS AND READINGS; OVERSCRUPULOUSNESS ABOUT PUNCTILIOUS TRUTHFULNESS ENGENDERED BY EXAGGERATED GUILT FEELINGS

Other fears from which I suffered were more or less a result of religious teaching and from reading Bible stories, which had a great fascination. I was afraid the Lord would send another flood upon the earth if I did not do what was right. The story of the rainbow had no significance. This fear existed from a very early age, perhaps five or six. Later, fear of the judgment day obsessed me. I really expected it at any moment. Any strange horn or whistle filled me with terror lest it be Gabriel's trumpet. It troubled me a great deal when I was away from home and it really caused me intense mental suffering, but I never mentioned my fear to anyone and I continued to read my favorite book in the Bible, *Revelation,* with the same torturous pleasure that most children get from tales of horror. The awful book of God in which all our misdeeds were recorded was another cause of endless worry. It made me overly conscientious and fearful of doing any wrong thing. Among the chief sins, a lie was uppermost. To avoid telling an untruth when asked a question about which I was uncertain, I most cautiously added "I believe so" or "I think so" to my statement. This fear gradually disappeared about the age of twelve or thirteen. (S.R.S.; F.; U.S.)

FIRST CONTACT WITH DEATH BY A SENSITIVE, INTROVERT BOY OF SEVEN IN THE ACCIDENTAL DROWNING OF A CHERISHED PLAYMATE, ENGENDERING FEELINGS OF GUILT AND SHAME BECAUSE THE RESPONDENT HAD DISOBEYED HIS PARENTS IN GOING TO THE HARBOR, AND RESULTING IN CONSTANT RUMINATIONS, DREAMS ABOUT THE VICTIM, NIGHTMARES OF THE SEA, TENDENCIES TOWARD SILENCE, REPRESSION, AND SLEEPLESSNESS

[The writer after having described his sensitive, introvert, poetical nature, refers to the following as one of the early life tragedies responsible for his emotional trends.]

I was seven years old and lived in what was known as the East Side in B. Within three or four squares of my home was the harbor where fleets of vessels came in periodically. The boys in my neighborhood were for the most part Italians, the sons of working men. In some cases both parents were compelled to work, so that these boys grew up with very little parental guidance and largely had to train themselves. Many of the boys went to the harbor almost daily in the summer to swim and in the winter to watch the few ships come in and go out. I went with them and participated in their games, although I did not know how to swim. When my parents discovered where I was making my playground, they strictly forbade me to go near the harbor again. My mother was quite emotional about the whole situation, and I clearly remember the expression of fear that was on her face when she spoke to me graphically of the horror of drowning. For a while I discontinued going near the water, but I finally succumbed to the taunts of my friends and furtively slipped out with them from time to time.

And then came a gruesome episode which terribly upset me. My next door playmate, who was considered a good swimmer, was drowned. I had never come in contact with death before. The little that I knew about it was so emotionally toned with terror that I had thrust the thought of it completely out of my life. And here it stalked before my very eyes in all its hideousness. Remembering the admonitions of my parents, I said nothing to them about what I had seen. I repressed the whole matter, ignorant at that time that repression merely submerges the fear episode into the unconscious mind and may lay the foundation for future mental and emotional conflicts which torture one's personality for years to come. The accident was soon known throughout the neighborhood, but I said very little. Somehow, a feeling of guilt and of shame possessed me. I began to think of myself in terms of a disobedient son who might have saved this boy's life if I had listened to my parents. For this boy was very much attached to me, and I led myself to believe that if I had stayed away from the harbor he might have done likewise. In the weeks and months that followed, I could not dismiss the picture of my chum from my mind. I would think of him by day; I would dream of him by night. I would awaken in my sleep, troubled by nightmares in which the sea played an important role.

Although I finally managed to dismiss the feeling of culpability, two definite reactions remained. The first was a tendency toward silence. The second was the habit of sleeplessness and of much dreaming. Both of these reactions have remained throughout life.   (S.A.A.; M.; Clergyman; M.A.; Age 37)

As a result of even slight or merely implied criticisms, the sensitive or conscientious child may become a victim of overconscientiousness, overpreciseness, or overscrupulousness in any field of activity. According to Freud, adult victims of the guilt complex represent a form of narcissism. That is to say, they have become victims of a species of glorified self-pity. One of the most important and delicate problems of parents and teachers is to liberate the child from the burden of supersensitive guilt or unjustified self-condemnation, which in some cases requires the discovery of the unconscious sources of the guilt feelings. However, this must be brought about in such a way as to conserve the interests of society. This can scarcely be done if the child's feelings of responsibility and accountability for his acts are destroyed and his sense of social values is impaired.

8. The control and socialization of the child's urges are essential for the harmonious, integrated functioning of his psychosomatic organism and for contented and successful social participation. In the effort to direct deep-lying biological urges, two extremes must be avoided: first, the negative method of blocking impulses and urges by harsh rebuffs and thwartings or violent repressions, which tends to produce emotional disturbances, mental conflicts, fixations, regressions, and maladjustments; and second, freedom from all restraint, or the unbridled license to do as one pleases, which would result in the disruption of society and produce inner discord. The method of finding outlets for the child's drives in desirable positive, constructive activities should replace the method of inhibition and repression whenever possible. Genuine mental development comes from releasing the child's spontaneous creative forces in constructive accomplishments and not from extinguishing them. This point of view of psychoanalysis is, in the main, in harmony with the tenets of progressive education. A minor reservation may be registered, however, to the effect that some inhibitions or suppressions may be quite neutral in their effects, or compatible with the demands of mental health, or at least not significantly deleterious. There may be healthy repressions as well as injurious ones.

9. Most of the child's fears, conflicts, and inhibitions are due to artificial conditioning, often purely accidental. A neutral stimulus through a process of conditioning thus may acquire the qualities attaching to an adequate stimulus. If an adequate stimulus is connected with intense affective reactions, the conditioned response will be similarly affected. Since the neutral stimulus may acquire the attributes of the adequate stimulus, originally neutral stimuli may become the source of intense emotional upsets. This conclusion is in harmony with psychoanalytic principles, although reached independently of psychoanalysis.

A number of the illustrations already presented have shown that perfectly neutral stimuli may become emotionally toned through artificial conditioning and thereby become the source of mental conflicts and maladjustments. Two additional illustrations may be introduced to corroborate this conclusion.

Illustrations of How Emotional Values May Become Attached to Neutral Stimuli through Artificial Conditioning. The first report seems to show that the fear of the croaking of frogs was induced by the emotional setting produced by a vivid chance encounter with snakes. The terror of the innocent feather in the second case was due to its association with a feather duster, which had become an object of fear from early emotional conditioning.

REVULSION AGAINST SNAKES DUE TO EARLY VIVID CHANCE EXPERI-
ENCE, AND AGAINST FROGS DUE TO EMOTIONAL SET; DREAMS INDUCED
BY THIS EMOTIONAL UPSET

When I was about six years old I went to the country for a visit. It was the
first time I had ever stayed overnight without my mother.

On the afternoon of my arrival my two cousins and I wandered down to the
water mill where we spent the time playing. While near the paddle wheel we
saw eight big water snakes. To me they were the most horrible, repulsive things
I had ever seen. After dinner and on through the quiet of the summer evening,
which remained quiet except for the croaking of the frogs, I grew more and more
homesick. The sound of the frogs only seemed to accentuate my loneliness and
I grew more miserable.

That night I cried myself to sleep and then dreamed of frogs and snakes all
night. I stayed in the country for several days and the dislike grew stronger
every day. To this very day the thought of a snake or the sound of a frog makes
me depressed. (S.E.; F.; S.C.T.)

AN OBSESSIONAL FEAR OF FEATHERS; FALLING OVER IN A FAINT UPON
BEHOLDING A WIND-BLOWN FEATHER; AN EXAMPLE OF A NEUTRAL
STIMULUS THAT HAD BECOME INTENSELY EMOTIONALLY TONED
THROUGH EARLY CONDITIONING

During a class period in one of the Philadelphia schools a feather blew through
the window and passed directly in front of the face of one of the pupils, a boy
about seven years of age. The child fell over in a dead faint. After being revived,
he was taken home, and subsequent investigation supplied the following explanation. When the child was quite young the family lived in a second-floor apartment. The mother was extremely afraid that he would creep to the top of the
stairway and tumble down the long flight of stairs. In order to prevent this
calamity, the mother placed her feather duster at the top of the stairs and at the
same time described vividly to the child what terrible things the duster would do
to him if he approached it.

As a result of this the boy developed an intense fear of feathers, causing him
to become extremely nervous at the mere sight of one.

(From S.M.E.; M.; T. in Trade School)

**The Mental-hygiene Implications of the Conditioned Reflex Theory
of the Acquisition of Affective Maladjustments.** Various implications of
the conditioned-response theory of the origin of mental traits and maladjustments have been stressed in earlier pages. Four practical considerations may
be briefly mentioned for the sake of emphasis at this point. First, on the
positive side, the aim of the program of mental hygiene may be stated as that
of forming beneficial associations by desirable processes of conditioning.

Second, on the preventive side, the aim of mental hygiene is the safeguarding of the child from the formation of harmful associations of stimuli or from injurious processes of conditioning. Third, on the remedial side, the aim of mental hygiene is overcoming by the process of reconditioning deleterious associations already formed. The process employed must frequently be one of emotional catharsis or reconditioning rather than one of rational or intellectual adjustment. The associative bond between conditioned stimuli that produce maladjustments is emotional in nature, rather than intellectual. Emotional bonds frequently cannot be dissolved by mere argument, intellectual analysis, or sheer determination. Such bonds must be loosened or dissipated by substituting other emotional bonds that are more potent by a process of emotional reconditioning. An excellent illustration of the effectiveness of the process of conditioning for the elimination of anesthesias, paralyses, and hampering habits is supplied by V. M. Bekhterev.[5] Bekhterev's method in the case of refractory kleptomaniacs was to associate a disagreeable, defensive reflex produced by an electric current with the words "do not take." By means of such a process of artificial conditioning, it was possible to eradicate the fault after several treatments at weekly intervals, apparently because of the inhibitory effects exerted by the affective tone superinduced by the painful electrical stimulation and the adjuration "do not take."

Two other pertinent illustrations of the use of the conditioned-response technique for overcoming undesirable habits may be cited. The first relates to the cure of enuresis by the establishment of a conditioned response to an artificial stimulus, the ringing of a bell. A dry pad consisting of two layers of goods (muslin, Indian head, or soft cotton) interlaced with copper wire and separated by a plain layer of cloth was securely fastened to the child. Whenever the inner layer became moistened from "bed wetting" the electrically connected bell would ring as a signal for the child to go to the bathroom. It was explained to the child that when he started to urinate the bell would ring and he must go at once to the bathroom, empty the bladder as much as possible, remove the wet pad and replace it with a dry one. In the case of very young children, similar instructions were given to the caretaker. Three chronic enuretics responded favorably to from four to six applications of this process of conditioning, and one child after 14 trials. The method was ineffectual with only one child, who had bladder trouble. The cured enuretics improved in personality characteristics and behavior.[6] The child could be conditioned, similarly, to a postural signal (being placed in a certain position before the

[5] Vladimir M. Bekhterev, *Emotions as Somatomimetic Reflexes,* The Wittenberg Symposium on Feelings and Emotions, 1928, 270–283.

[6] John J. B. Morgan and Francis J. Witmer, "Treatment of Enuresis by the Conditioned Reaction Technique," *Pedagogical Seminary,* 1939, 55, 59–65.

cycle of reflex discharge) associated with a verbal stimulus when the process of micturition begins.

The second illustration relates to the treatment of alcoholic addiction by the conditioned association of alcoholic beverages with a drug producing vomiting and nausea. The alcoholic beverage and the drug were first administered together until the conditioned reflex had been established. Thereupon, the perception of the alcohol alone through sight, taste, and smell produced nausea and vomiting and a dislike for the drink. According to Joseph Thimann, nine addicts treated in 1942, 25 of 47 treated in 1943, and 24 of 37 treated in 1944 still abstained from the use of liquor in 1945. Neurotics failed to respond to this process of conditioning,[7] although the treatment proved an aid to psychiatric treatment of the neuroses.

Fourth, the view that efficient emotional education and reconditioning of children is as much a part of the functions of parents, teachers, and all who are responsible for the care of children as are intellectual enlightenment and motor training is reenforced by the data presented in this volume bearing on the genesis of character traits. Normal emotional growth is to a large extent dependent upon the development of proper affective attitudes by wholesome emotional conditioning. Similarly, the remediation of many mental difficulties must be based primarily on emotional reconditioning rather than on intellectual enlightenment. In many cases, the intellectual, or rational, treatment occupies merely a secondary, or supplementary, role.

Illustrations of Difficulties That Apparently Required Emotional Reconditioning Rather Than Rational Treatment. Illustrations of various annoyances, such as fears, worries, anxieties, and hampering habits, which could not be conquered by mere determination, effort of will, or reasoning, or which responded only in part to such treatment, may prove illuminating. These difficulties would probably have yielded more successfully to processes of emotional reconditioning coupled with the discovery of the causative factors. Indications exist in a few of the cases that the difficulties were eventually overcome by emotional reconditioning.

FUTILITY OF TRYING TO OVERCOME PRACTICE OF BITING FINGERNAILS BY PUNISHMENT; LAPSES AFTER CURE

While I was punished constantly for nail biting I did not really try to overcome this habit until I was about thirteen and it had become a source of great embarrassment to me [thus producing emotional reconditioning]. After I had overcome the practice it would crop up in times of great mental exertion or physical pain, even after I had reached adulthood.   (W.W.A.; F.; S.C.T.)

[7] *Science News Letter,* 1945, 277.

STOPPING THUMB SUCKING BECAUSE OF BEING TEASED

I was a bottle baby almost from the onset. I developed the thumb-sucking habit very early, too, and was seven years old before I finally gave it up, though much remonstrated with. I remember very well that I did it then of my own free will, because I did not like to be teased in school [emotional reconditioning through ridicule]. (W.C.H.; F.; Nursery Kg. Supv.; Ph.B.; Age 37)

ATTEMPTING TO OVERCOME A HORROR AT BEING HEMMED IN BY FIGHT-ING THE IDEA; CLAUSTROPHOBIA

Miriam was a brilliant and highly sensitive little girl of six or seven. She had from infancy been afflicted with claustrophobia. When six years old, she was placed in a private academy. It soon became known to her friends there that she had a horror of being hemmed in or locked up by anyone in any sort of room or closet.

Miriam grew to adolescence. Her friends teased her about her fear, but not so seriously until one day a number of boys and girls locked her up in a closet. Notwithstanding the fact that the closet was large, well ventilated, and partially lighted by daylight, Miriam fainted. When the closet was opened Miriam was wholly unconscious. She was soon revived, but after that there was no more serious teasing along this line.

From this time forward she began to make a conscious effort to overcome this fear. She "fought the idea" and reasoned to herself that there was no danger. Yet, when a young lady, she fainted again when she became tightly jammed in a crowd at a ship launching, even with nothing but the blue sky overhead. She again took in hand the matter of overcoming this fear and says she has succeeded. She says she succeeded by fighting the idea and making herself realize that there was no danger [emotional reconditioning probably involved].

(From T.B.J.W.; M.; E.S.P.; M.A.)

VICTIM OF UNCONTROLLED WORRY; INEFFECTIVENESS OF EFFORTS AT RATIONAL SOLUTION

My inclination is to worry about almost every conceivable thing. I frequently stay awake until late in the night worrying about some school problem or something which is purely imaginary. While I realize that this is a very foolish thing to do, it seems to be beyond my control. (DeH.S.A.; M.; H.S.P.; B.S.)

Reconditioning through Emotional Shock. Overcoming or removing difficulties by the production of nervous or emotional shocks is merely one form of emotional reconditioning. Sometimes this is the most effective method of reconditioning the individual and removing inhibitions and dissipating conflicts; it is a kind of emotional allopathy. Sometimes this type of treatment merely consists in fearlessly forcing oneself to tackle the difficult situation and live through the emotional turmoil thus produced until the bogy is vanquished. While the drastic shock type of technique often succeeds in removing the major difficulty, injurious by-products doubtless occasionally supervene from such emotional treatment. The expulsive power or remedial efficacy of this kind of conditioning is shown in varying degrees in the following case reports.

HORROR OF THE DEAD, LEADING TO REFUSAL TO PLAY THE ORGAN AT FUNERALS; OVERCOME BY BEING FORCED TO FACE THE DISAGREEABLE

Margaret was a precocious and highly capable child, but also very sensitive. She had always been very much afraid of the dead. At eleven she became the church organist but would never play for a funeral because of her horror of the dead.

At the age of seventeen, the sweetheart of a girl friend was killed. A week later she went to spend the night with the girl friend to comfort and console her. About eleven o'clock that night a very old lady, living in the home of the nearest neighbor, died. Margaret's hostesses, both mother and daughter, were asked to come and enshroud the body. It was impossible for Margaret's girl friend, in her bereavement, to go and help in such a task. It fell to Margaret and her girl friend's mother to go. While the mother was detained, talking to some members of the bereaved family, Margaret went alone into the room of the corpse. She suffered untold agony in the presence of the body. But, with the other lady, she went ahead with the task and, from that day to this, has never again feared the presence of a corpse.   (From T.B.J.W.; M.; E.S.P.; M.A.)

VIOLENT PHYSICAL COMMOTION PRODUCED BY THUNDER AND WIND, OVERCOME BY FORCING HERSELF TO STAY ON DECK DURING A VIOLENT STORM

As a child I suffered miserably during thunderstorms and high winter night winds. I experienced miserable sensations of trembling, chattering of teeth, nausea, and sometimes vomiting. This gradually subsided, and four years ago, when crossing the Atlantic, I forced myself to sit out on deck during a violent storm. I then knew I had conquered that fear forever. I have never been troubled or annoyed since.   (R.S.; F.; Home T.)

FEAR OF FATHER BECAUSE OF GROWTH OF BEARD DURING SICKNESS ISOLATION; DREAD OF CORPSES CAUSED BY SEEING THE DISTORTED, DISCOLORED FACE OF A DEAD MAN, PARTLY CURED BY SLEEPING IN A HAMMOCK NEAR A CASKET

When I was about five years old my father contracted typhoid fever. I was not allowed to see him until he was pronounced out of danger. When I saw him he had a heavy beard. Mother reports that I screamed and ran out of the room refusing to have anything to do with him. I remember the strange feeling I had even after he was up.

Another fright I had in early life was caused by seeing a dead man. Even now I can still recall the distorted features and discoloration of his face. Memory of him was with me constantly in my dreams and in my play. Soon I began to think of my father in connection with him, and this, augmented by the fact that my father lost a leg in a railroad accident, caused me to dread seeing him go to work. He was a district agent for the railroad. When I was twelve years of age an aunt, who lived with us, died. I could not look at the corpse without shuddering. The body was prepared for burial and placed in the parlor, and, in order to try to rid myself of the feeling a dead body caused within me, I asked permission to sleep in the hammock on the porch just outside the parlor window. I could see the casket from the hammock. For some time I could not sleep, but finally rid my mind of all thoughts of the corpse and slept soundly until morning. I have never had the same feelings toward death or a corpse since, but I do not like to look at one now, preferring to remember the departed as they appeared to me in life.   (G.D.Q.; M.; H.S.P.; B.S.)

TERROR OF STORMS DUE TO SECRET FEAR THAT A MEMBER OF THE FAMILY WOULD BE STRETCHED OUT IN RIGID DEATH IN A STORM; FINALLY OVERCOME WHEN FORCED TO SLEEP ON A PORCH WHILE CAMPING DURING FREQUENT THUNDERSTORMS

The notion that some member of the family would some day be killed in a storm, added to the fear of the thunder and lightning, made a storm really terrifying to me. If any member of the family were out in the storm, I pictured them as struck by lightning. I would sit and suffer for hours, seeing in my imagination all the horrors of the death agony of my father, brother, or sister as they finally stretched themselves in cold rigid death. This was another fear that I kept to myself. On one occasion I slipped out of the house unnoticed after the storm and went to the spot in the woods where I was sure that I would find my sister dead. Needless to say, she was not there but peacefully sleeping at a neighbor's house, where she had arrived before the storm. I crawled home wet to the waist and almost exhausted. This is a sample of my fear of storms. I assure you that it is not exaggerated.

During my first term in a rural school I began in earnest to overcome the storm dread. I was forced to keep calm in order to quiet the children. Over and over I would repeat to myself, "Isn't God the same upon the water as on the land." At first I learned to show no outward sign although I felt badly frightened. As time went on I became more calm, but it was some years later before the real cure was accomplished. I slept on an open porch while camping on an island in the Mississippi River. There was an unusually large number of storms that summer and as I was forced to lie there with the lightning flashing in my face and the thunder roaring in my ears I finally bid good-by to the storm terror.

I believe that the causes of most of my storm fears were the following:

1. The effect on a nervous, timid, imaginative child.

2. I did not understand the phenomena of storms.

3. Those around me were usually afraid of storms.

4. Stories were vividly related of dire disasters that had occurred in previous storms.   (S.B.R.; F.; H.S.T.; B.A.; Age 58)

CONFLICTING DESIRES AND FEARS OF HIGH PLACES, CROSSING BRIDGES
AND RIDING IN AMUSEMENT CONTRIVANCES, POSSIBLY TRACEABLE
TO AN EARLY EXPERIENCE DURING THE SECOND YEAR; RIDICULED
BY RELATIVES UNTIL THE VICTIM FAINTED IN A SOMERSAULTING CAR;
ATTEMPTS TO OVERCOME PHOBIA AFTER MARRIAGE TO PREVENT POSSI-
BILITY OF PRENATAL INFLUENCES; CURE THROUGH EMOTIONAL
SHOCK; DREAMS OF FALLING; ACROPHOBIA

Since early childhood, I have had a fear of high places, particularly bridges. I experienced a sensation of dizziness and of being about to fall. When my mother took my sisters and me on a trip to Niagara, we were going to walk across the suspension bridge. I was the oldest but I became almost hysterical with fear. Mother afterward declared that it reminded her of the time she visited Niagara when I was a little over two years of age. She said I pulled away from her hand and tried to climb through the side braces. She quickly grabbed me by the dress or I would have fallen off the bridge. Possibly my fear is a result of this early experience, although a psychologist once told me it was doubtful if it could be traced to such an early experience.

The peculiar thing connected with my fear is that it has always been associated with a conflicting desire to climb and cross bridges. At the age of ten when I visited my aunt in New York, I asked her to take me across Brooklyn Bridge, but when we arrived there I was afraid. She was greatly amused and told my uncle and father that evening that I was afraid but that my little sister and cousin were not. I was so ashamed I cried myself to sleep. Later on while visiting relatives in Pennsylvania, I wanted to climb the mountains. When some of their neighbors' children took me, however, I soon wanted to return. When the Pan-American Exposition was held in Buffalo, I watched the Ferris wheel, fascinated, but I was afraid to ride in it, although I saw many people ride on it and knew it was comparatively safe. My brother laughed at me. Later I beheld a roller coaster whose cars, filled with people barred into the seats, turned a complete somersault. I wanted to "show" my brothers, who dared me to go up in it, that I was "game." I sat beside a stranger. The "Flip Flop" turned us all upside down. When the coaster arrived at the starting point, I was held unconscious in the arms of the man who sat next to me. He had the presence of mind to grasp me as I fell forward in the first fainting spell of my life. After this incident, none of my family teased me any more about the matter which they had formerly characterized as silly, cowardly, "just imagination," etc. Later, I went on a number of roller coaster rides at the beach, but trembled with terror although I tried to laugh it off.

After my marriage, I decided to remove any possibility of prenatal influence as I did not want a child with such cowardly emotions. So I went many times to the bridge spanning Passaic Falls and gazed down at the water and rocks below.

I visited Buffalo and took a trip to Niagara. I forced myself to stand there in spite of the old recurring dread. I am glad to say that my son has not "inherited" my fear (to use a popular expression, although I know it is a misnomer). He learned to walk and climb the stairs on his hands and knees before he was one year old. One day at the age of eighteen months, while I was talking to a friend, he was playing contentedly in the yard. The painter had left a ladder standing at the side of the house. Suddenly my friend cried, "Oh, look! Don't scream, you'll frighten M." He was nearly at the top of the ladder. As quietly as I could I crept up the ladder and got him in my arms. He was so intent on going up he had not noticed my approach. When I reached the ground and the reaction came, I cried. My friend said, "I don't blame you for being excited. That was a narrow escape for him." She didn't know that under ordinary circumstances it would have been impossible for me to climb that ladder, but the urge to "save my child" had completely dispelled my fear of height. This may sound melodramatic, but it is not half so much so as was the occurrence. The so-called "maternal instinct" to protect its offspring (which modern psychology discounts) must have conquered the fear.

Many times in dreams I have had this fear of falling. A friend once asked me if I ever seemed to strike bottom. I said, "No." She said, "If you did the shock might kill you." This fear is expressed in the following poem which I wrote:

> With eyes that seemed to draw within my head
> And heavy limbs, my erstwhile lightness fled,
> As once, in illness, under ether I had lain
> And heard a Voice which said "Emal" (away from pain; fainting sensation),
> So now, I seemed a weighty, congealed mass;
> Falling! Falling, through endless space, to pass
> At length into a different atmosphere.

(V.E.; F.; S.C.T.)

OVERCOMING RESISTANCE TO GOING TO BED BY THE METHOD OF PHYSICAL SHOCK, INVOLVING CORRELATIVE EMOTIONAL RECONDITIONING

At the age of five, my son, now seven, exhibited a tendency to go into an hysterical tantrum whenever his mother would try to get him to do something he did not want to do, particularly when she tried to get him to go to bed at seven o'clock in the evening.

Since we both felt that he should go to bed at this hour, I determined to do something to break up this nonsense. On the next evening the usual performance took place, kicking, dancing up and down, and refusing to get undressed. I waited until the exhibition got well under way, and then went upstairs and took hold of the young man by the back of the neck and the seat of his pants, and marched him into the bathroom where I put him under the cold shower, clothes and all. Following this I undressed him and dried him, and then in order to warm him up and prevent him from catching cold I applied the palm of my hand vigorously to the place intended by nature for that purpose. I do not know whether this proves that shock as a treatment is effective, or whether it bears out the old proverb that more knowledge goes in through the tail end than through the ear; but at any rate the young man now marches off to bed at seven every evening without comment or discussion.   (From S.M.E.; M.; T. in Trade School)

10. Even if the Freudian concept of the unconscious be completely repudiated, the conclusion of psychoanalysis that the child's conduct is sometimes dominated by hidden, suppressed, forgotten, subconscious, or unrecognized motives, and that the ostensible motives are not the real ones, has been abundantly substantiated by the original investigations supplied in this book. Child counselors should always try to determine whether any hidden or suppressed motives or complexes may be responsible for the child's behavior. This ordinarily involves the search for affective rather than intellectual factors. If it is true that such hidden factors usually cannot be reasoned away by appeal to rational or logical considerations, but must be overcome by a process of emotional reconditioning, it is important to reemphasize that the emotional reconditioning cannot become maximally effective until the hidden sources of the difficulty have been unveiled.

11. The work of the psychoanalyst has demonstrated the fundamental importance of giving prime consideration to the "individual equation" in all mental-hygiene work. This valuable contribution psychoanalysis shares in common with clinical medicine, clinical psychology, and psychiatry. The original data presented in this volume have demonstrated conclusively and brilliantly the enormous differences produced in the mental reactions of different individuals by the same stimuli, settings, or treatment. Maximum results in mental-hygiene work cannot be secured by the wholesale application of stereotyped formulas or procedures, however valuable such methods may be in the positive and preventive programs of mental hygiene. In addition to the teaching of mental hygiene to all parents, teachers, child counselors, and pupils (which must come in time) and the general lay application of mental-hygiene precepts and principles to the management of individual and social life, a need will always exist for the services of the skilled specialist who not only possesses deep insight and knowledge concerning the nature and causes of mental difficulties, which rank among the most complex and difficult adjustment problems with which man has to deal, but who also possesses the diplomacy and tact to apply his skill effectively to individual cases.

BIBLIOGRAPHY

Because of the prolific literary productivity during the last decade in the numerous areas covered by this book, many of the references in the first edition have, through sheer necessity, been deleted in order to provide space for the newer publications. Concededly many of the earlier publications thus eliminated still possess great value. The eliminations include nearly all of the shorter contributions (journal articles) and books and monographs not intimately related to the problems of mental health and mental hygiene. A few works have been retained because of the paucity of later materials in the particular area concerned or because of the vital role they have played in the literature.

Essentially, the bibliography is limited to textbooks and major treatises and monographs. The limited number of articles included have, perforce, been restricted largely to problems of educational and social relationships and to areas not adequately covered by recent books.

There is, of course, no sharp line between some of the groupings of the references. Some of the listings would fit equally well in other classifications. With few exceptions, references cited in the text are not repeated in the bibliography. So vast has the output of literature in mental hygiene grown that there is need for a major volume of carefully annotated references in all its major fields. The few books of readings in mental hygiene now available are highly selective and do not include all the important references. In fact, these books are just as conspicuous for their omissions as for their inclusions.

I. MENTAL-HYGIENE TEXTS AND TREATISES

(See Also Psychotherapy and Psychiatry)

ANDERSON, CAMILLA M.: *Emotional Hygiene,* Philadelphia, J. B. Lippincott Company, 1937.

BAKER, HARRY J.: *The Art of Understanding,* Boston, Christopher Publishing House, 1940.

BURNHAM, WILLIAM H.: *The Wholesome Personality,* New York, Appleton-Century-Crofts, Inc., 1932. (Bibliography.)

CARROLL, HERBERT A.: *Mental Hygiene,* New York, Prentice-Hall, Inc., 1947.

CLARKE, ERIC K.: *Mental Hygiene for Community Nursing,* Minneapolis, University of Minnesota Press, 1942.

CROTHERS, BRONSON: *A Pediatrician in Search of Mental Hygiene,* New York, Commonwealth Fund, Division of Publication, 1937.

CROW, LESTER D., and ALICE CROW: *Mental Hygiene in School and Home Life,* New York, McGraw-Hill Book Company, Inc., 1942.

———, and ———: *Our Teen-age Boys and Girls,* New York, McGraw-Hill Book Company, Inc., 1945.

CUTTS, NORMA E., and NICHOLAS MOSELEY: *Practical School Discipline and Mental Hygiene,* Boston, Houghton Mifflin Company, 1941.

DUNLAP, KNIGHT: *Personal Adjustment,* New York, McGraw-Hill Book Company, Inc., 1946.

EWER, J. H.: *Mental Health: A Practical Guide to Disorders of the Mind,* Baltimore, The Williams & Wilkins Company, 1947.

FENTON, NORMAN: *Mental Hygiene in School Practice,* Stanford University, Stanford University Press, 1943.

GRIFFIN, JOHN D. M., SAMUEL R. LAYCOCK, and WILLIAM LINE: *Mental Hygiene,* New York, American Book Company, 1940.

GROVES, ERNEST R.: *Understanding Yourself, The Mental Hygiene of Personality,* New York, Greenberg: Publisher, Inc., 1935.

HARRINGTON, MILTON: *The Management of the Mind,* New York, Philosophical Library, Inc., 1945.

HARTWELL, SAMUEL: *Practical Psychiatry and Mental Hygiene,* New York, McGraw-Hill Book Company, Inc., 1947.

HOHMAN, LESLIE: *As The Twig Is Bent,* New York, The Macmillan Company, 1940.

HOWARD, FRANK E., and FREDERICK L. PATRY: *Mental Health: Its Principles and Practice,* New York, Harper & Brothers, 1935.

JASTROW, JOSEPH: *Getting More Out of Life,* New York, Emerson Books, Inc., 1940.

JOHNSON, WENDELL: *People in Quandaries: The Semantics of Personality Adjustment,* New York, Harper & Brothers, 1946.

KLEIN, DAVID B.: *Mental Hygiene, The Psychology of Personal Adjustment,* New York, Henry Holt and Company, Inc., 1944.

LAIRD, DONALD A.: *The Technique of Personal Analysis,* New York, McGraw-Hill Book Company, Inc., 1945.

LINDEL, A. ADOLPHE: *A Study in Reconstructive Mental Hygiene,* Boston, Meador Publishing Company, 1946.

MCKINNEY, FRED: *Psychology of Personal Adjustment,* 2d ed., New York, John Wiley & Sons, Inc., 1949.

MCLEAN, DONALD: *Knowing Yourself and Others,* New York, Henry Holt and Company, Inc., 1938.

MENNINGER, KARL A.: *The Human Mind,* New York, Alfred A. Knopf, Inc., 1937.

Mental Hygiene in the Classroom, Report of Joint Committee on Health Problems in Education of the National Education Association and the American Medical Association, 1939.

Mental Hygiene in Old Age, Family Welfare Association of America, New York, 1937.

MIKESELL, WILLIAM H.: *Mental Hygiene,* New York, Prentice-Hall, Inc., 1939.

MOORE, THOMAS V.: *Personal Mental Hygiene,* New York, Grune & Stratton, Inc., 1944.

MORGAN, JOHN J. B.: *How to Keep a Sound Mind,* New York, The Macmillan Company, 1946.

MYERS, C. ROGER: *Toward Mental Health in School,* Toronto, Canada, The University of Toronto Press, 1939.

PRESTON, GEORGE H.: *The Substance of Mental Health,* New York, Rinehart & Company, Inc., 1943.

RENNIE, THOMAS A. C., and LUTHER E. WOODWARD: *Mental Health in Modern Society,* New York, Commonwealth Fund, Division of Publication, 1948.

RICHMOND, WINIFRED V.: *Personality, Its Development and Hygiene,* New York, Rinehart & Company, Inc., 1937.

RIVLIN, HARRY H.: *Education for Adjustment,* New York, Appleton-Century-Crofts, Inc., 1936.

RYAN, W. CARSON: *Mental Health through Education,* New York, Commonwealth Fund, Division of Publication, 1938.

SCHACHTER, HELEN: *Understanding Ourselves,* Bloomington, Ill., McKnight & McKnight, 1945.

SHAFFER, LAURANCE F.: *The Psychology of Adjustment,* Boston, Houghton Mifflin Company, 1936.

SHERMAN, MANDEL: *Mental Hygiene and Education,* New York, Longmans, Green & Co., Inc., 1934.

SHOOBS, NAHUM E., and GEORGE GOLDBERG: *Corrective Treatment for Unadjusted Children,* New York, Harper & Brothers, 1942.

SYMONDS, PERCIVAL M.: *Mental Hygiene of the School Child,* New York, The Macmillan Company, 1934.

THOMPSON, LORIN A.: *Mental Hygiene, Brief Guide to Self-understanding,* Columbus, Ohio, School & College Service, 1934.

THORPE, LOUIS P., assisted by JAY N. HOLLIDAY: *Personality and Life: A Practical Guide to Personality Improvement,* New York, Longmans, Green & Co., Inc., 1941.

TIEGS, ERNEST W., and BARNEY KATZ: *Mental Hygiene in Education,* New York, The Ronald Press Company, 1941.

TRAVIS, LEE E., and DOROTHY W. BARUCH: *Personal Problems of Everyday Life,* New York, Appleton Century-Crofts, Inc., 1941.

WALLIN, J. E. WALLACE: *Minor Mental Maladjustments in Normal People,* 3d printing, Durham, N.C., Duke University Press, 1946.

WHITE, WILLIAM A.: *The Mental Hygiene of Childhood,* Boston, Little, Brown & Company, 1919.

WITTENBERG, RUDOLPH: *So You Want to Help People,* New York, Association Press, 1947.

WITTY, PAUL A., and CHARLES E. SKINNER: *Mental Hygiene in Modern Education,* New York, Rinehart & Company, Inc., 1939.

WOOD, THOMAS D., and MARION O. LERRIGO: *The Healthy Personality,* Bloomington, Ill., Public School Publishing Company, 1935.

II. PSYCHOTHERAPY

(See Also Mental Hygiene and Psychiatry)

ALLEN, FREDERICK H.: *Psychotherapy with Children,* New York, W. W. Norton & Company, Inc., 1942.

ALLISON, D. RHODES, and RONALD G. GORDON: *Psychotherapy,* New York, Oxford University Press, 1948.

ARTHUR, GRACE: *Tutoring as Therapy,* New York, Commonwealth Fund, Division of Publication, 1946.

BARKER, LEWELLYS F.: *Psychotherapy,* New York, Appleton-Century-Crofts, Inc., 1944.

BECK, BERTRAM M.: *Short-term Therapy in an Authoritative Setting,* New York, Family Service Association of America, 1946.

BENEDEK, THERESE: *Insight and Personality Adjustment,* New York, The Ronald Press Company, 1946.

BROWN, WILLIAM: *Psychology and Psychotherapy,* 4th ed., Baltimore, The Williams & Wilkins Company, 1940.

CATTELL, RAYMOND B.: *Crooked Personalities in Childhood and After: An Introduction to Psychotherapy,* New York, Appleton-Century-Crofts, Inc., 1938.

DAVIES, J. TREVOR: *Sublimation,* London, George Allen & Unwin, Ltd., 1947.

FLETCHER, PETER: *Mastering Your Nerves,* New York, E. P. Dutton & Co., Inc., 1939.

FOULKES, S. H.: *Group-analytic Psychotherapy,* New York, Grune & Stratton, Inc., 1949. (Bibliography.)

FROHMAN, BERTRAND S., and EVELYN P. FROHMAN: *Dynamic Psychotherapy*, Philadelphia, Lea and Febiger, 1948.

GLUECK, BERNARD, ed.: *Current Therapies of Personality Disorders*, New York, Grune & Stratton, Inc., 1946.

HALLIDAY, JAMES L.: *Psychological Medicine*, New York, W. W. Norton & Company, Inc., 1948.

HAMILTON, GORDON: *Psychotherapy in Child Guidance*, New York, Columbia University Press, 1947.

HERZBERG, ALEXANDER: *Active Psychotherapy*, New York, Grune & Stratton, Inc., 1945.

HINSIE, LELAND E.: *Concepts and Problems of Psychotherapy*, New York, Columbia University Press, 1937.

KRAINES, SAMUEL H.: "Brief Psychotherapy," *Mental Hygiene*, 1943, 70–79.

———, and ELOISE S. THETFORD: *Managing Your Mind*, New York, The Macmillan Company, 1947.

LAPIERE, RICHARD T.: *Psychotherapy in Medical Practice*, New York, The Macmillan Company, 1942.

LEVINE, MAURICE: *Psychotherapy in Medical Practice*, New York, The Macmillan Company, 1946.

LIEBMAN, JOSHUA L.: *Peace of Mind*, New York, Simon & Schuster, Inc., 1946.

"Play Diagnosis and Play Therapy," *The Nervous Child*, July, 1948, 233–236. (Symposium.)

"Psychotherapy and Counseling," *Journal of Consulting Psychology*, March–April, 1948, 65–110. (Symposium.)

RAY, MARIE B.: *How to Conquer Your Handicaps*, Indianapolis, Bobbs-Merrill Company, 1948.

ROSS, THOMAS A.: *The Common Neuroses, Their Treatment by Psychotherapy, An Introduction to Psychological Treatment for Students and Practitioners*, 2d ed., Baltimore, William Wood & Company, 1937.

SCHILDER, PAUL: *Psychotherapy*, New York, W. W. Norton & Company, Inc., 1938.

SCHULLIAN, DOROTHY M., and MAX SCHOEN: *Music and Medicine*, New York, Henry Schuman, 1948.

SLAVSON, SAMUEL R.: *Recreation and the Total Personality*, New York, Association Press, 1946.

SMITH, GEDDES: *Psychotherapy in General Medicine*, New York, Commonwealth Fund, Division of Publication, 1946.

SOIBELMAN, DORIS: *Therapeutic and Industrial Uses of Music*, New York, Columbia University Press, 1948.

STEKEL, WILHELM: *Technique of Analytical Psychotherapy*, New York, W. W. Norton & Company, Inc., 1940.

TAFT, JESSIE: *The Dynamics of Therapy in a Controlled Relationship*, New York, The Macmillan Company, 1937.

WITMER, HELEN L., ed.: *Psychiatric Interviewing with Children*, New York, Commonwealth Fund, Division of Publication, 1946.

———: *Teaching Psychotherapeutic Medicine*, New York, Commonwealth Fund, Division of Publication, 1947.

III. PSYCHOANALYSIS AND INDIVIDUAL PSYCHOLOGY

ADLER, ALFRED: *The Neurotic Constitution*, New York, Moffat, Yard & Co., 1917.

———: *Study of Organ Inferiority and Its Physical Compensation*, New York, Nervous and Mental Disease Publishing Company, 1917.

ADLER, ALFRED: *Education of Children,* New York, Greenberg: Publisher, Inc., 1930. (Translated by Eleanore and Friedrich Jensen.)

————: *Guiding the Child in the Principles of Individual Psychology,* New York, Greenberg: Publisher, Inc., 1930. (Translated by Benjamin Ginzburg.)

ALEXANDER, FRANZ: *Fundamentals of Psychoanalysis,* W. W. Norton & Company, Inc., 1948.

————: *Medical Value of Psychoanalysis,* New York, W. W. Norton & Company, Inc., 1946.

BLITZSTEN, DOROTHY R.: *Psychoanalysis Explained,* New York, Coward-McCann, Inc., 1936.

BRILL, ABRAHAM A.: *Lectures on Psychoanalytic Psychiatry,* New York, Alfred A. Knopf, Inc., 1946.

DEUTSCH, FELIX: *Applied Psychoanalysis,* Grune & Stratton, Inc., 1949.

ENGLISH, OLIVER S., and GERALD H. J. PEARSON: *Emotional Problems of Living,* New York, W. W. Norton & Company, Inc., 1945.

FENICHEL, OTTO: *The Psychoanalytic Theory of Neuroses,* New York, W. W. Norton & Company, Inc., 1945.

FLIESS, ROBERT, and HENRY A. BUNKER: *A Psychoanalytic Reader,* New York, International Universities Press, Inc., 1946.

FRANZ, ALEXANDER, and THOMAS M. FRENCH: *Psychoanalytic Therapy,* New York, The Ronald Press Company, 1946.

FREUD, ANNA: *Introduction to the Technique of Child Analysis,* Mental Disease Monograph, Series 48, New York, Nervous and Mental Disease Publishing Company, 1928.

————: *The Ego and the Mechanisms of Defense,* London, Hogarth Press and The Institute of Psycho-analysis, 1937.

FREUD, SIGMUND: *Psychopathology of Everyday Life,* New York, The Macmillan Company, 1914. (Translated by A. A. Brill.)

————: *New Introductory Lectures in Psycho-analysis,* New York, W. W. Norton & Company, Inc., 1933. (Translated by W. J. H. Spratt.)

————: *The Interpretation of Dreams,* New York, The Macmillan Company, 1933. (Translated by A. A. Brill.)

————: *The Ego and the Id,* London, Hogarth Press, 1935.

————: *A General Introduction to Psycho-analysis,* New York, Liveright Publishing Corp., 1935.

————: *The Problem of Anxiety,* New York, W. W. Norton & Company, Inc., 1936. (Translated by Henry A. Bunker.)

————: *A General Selection from the Works of Sigmund Freud* (John Rickman, ed.), London, Hogarth Press and The Institute of Psycho analysis, 1937.

————: *The Basic Writings of Sigmund Freud* (A. A. Brill, ed.), New York, Modern Library, Inc., 1938.

GLOVER, EDWARD, and MARJORIE F. BRIERLEY: *The Investigation of the Technique of Psycho-analysis,* Baltimore, The Williams & Wilkins Company, 1940.

GUTHEIL, EMIL A.: *The Language of the Dream,* New York, The Macmillan Company, 1939.

HARRINGTON, MILTON: *Wish-hunting in the Unconscious: An Analysis of Psychoanalysis,* New York, The Macmillan Company, 1934.

HENDRICK, IVES: *Facts and Theories of Psychoanalysis,* New York, Alfred A. Knopf, Inc., 1939.

HORNEY, KAREN: *The Neurotic Personality of Our Time,* New York, W. W. Norton & Company, Inc., 1937.

HORNEY, KAREN: *Self-analysis,* New York, W. W. Norton & Company, Inc., 1942.

————: *Our Inner Conflicts,* New York, W. W. Norton & Company, Inc., 1945.

————, ed.: *Are You Considering an Analysis?* New York, W. W. Norton & Company, Inc., 1946.

JACOBI, JOLAN: *The Psychology of Jung,* New Haven, Yale University Press, 1945. (Translated by K. W. Bash, bibliography.)

JASTROW, JOSEPH: *The House That Freud Built,* New York, Greenberg: Publisher, Inc., 1933.

JONES, ERNEST: *What Is Psychoanalysis?* New York, International Universities Press, Inc., 1948.

KUBIE, LAWRENCE S.: *Practical Aspects of Psychoanalysis,* New York, W. W. Norton & Company, Inc., 1936.

LORAND, ALEXANDER S.: *Psycho-analysis Today,* New York, International Universities Press, Inc., 1944.

————: *Technique of Psychoanalytic Therapy,* New York, International Universities Press, Inc., 1946.

————, et al., eds.: *The Yearbook of Psychoanalysis,* New York, International Universities Press, Inc., Vol. I, 1945; Vol. II, 1946; Vol. III, 1947; Vol. IV, 1948.

LUDWIG, EMIL: *Doctor Freud: An Analysis and Warning,* New York, Hellman, Williams & Co., 1947.

McDOUGALL, WILLIAM: *Psychoanalysis and Social Psychology,* London, Methuen & Co., Ltd., 1936.

MEGROZ, RODOLPHE L.: *The Dream World,* New York, E. P. Dutton & Co., Inc., 1939.

OBENDORF, CLARENCE P.: *The Psychiatric Novels of Oliver Holmes,* New York, Columbia University Press, 1943. (Holmes is portrayed as a precursor of Freud.)

The Psychoanalytic Study of the Child, New York, International Universities Press, Inc., Vol. I, 1945; Vol. II, 1946. (An annual.)

REIK, THEODORE: *From Thirty Years with Freud,* New York, Rinehart & Company, Inc., 1942.

RÓHEIM, GÉZA, ed.: *Psychoanalysis and the Social Sciences,* New York, International Universities Press, Vol. I, 1947. (An annual.)

SACHS, HANNS: *Freud, Master and Friend,* Cambridge, Mass., Harvard University Press, 1944.

SEARS, ROBERT R.: *Survey of Objective Studies of Psychoanalytic Concepts,* Washington, D.C., Social Science Research Council, Committee on Public Administration, 1943.

SHARPE, ELLA F.: *Dream Analysis: A Practical Handbook in Psychoanalysis,* New York, W. W. Norton & Company, Inc., 1938.

SYMONDS, PERCIVAL M.: *The Dynamics of Human Adjustment,* New York, Appleton-Century-Crofts, Inc., 1946. (A bibliography of 883 annotated references.)

IV. TEXTS AND TREATISES IN PSYCHIATRY, PSYCHOPATHOLOGY, AND NEUROLOGY

ALEXANDER, FRANZ, and THOMAS M. FRENCH: *Studies in Psychosomatic Medicine,* New York, The Ronald Press Company, 1948.

BEERS, CLIFFORD: *A Mind That Found Itself: An Autobiography,* New York, Doubleday & Company, Inc., 1939.

BENTLEY, MADISON, and EDMUND V. COWDRY: *The Problem of Mental Disorder,* New York, McGraw-Hill Book Company, Inc., 1935.

BIDDLE, W. EARL, and MILDRED VAN SICKEL: *Introduction to Psychiatry,* Philadelphia, W. B. Saunders Company, 1948. (Written especially for nurses.)

BILLINGS, EDWARD G.: *Handbook of Psychobiology and Psychiatry,* New York, The Macmillan Company, 1947.

BLUEMEL, CHARLES S.: *The Troubled Mind,* Baltimore, The Williams & Wilkins Company, 1938.

BRADLEY, CHARLES: *Schizophrenia in Childhood,* New York, The Macmillan Company, 1941.

BROMBERG, WALTER: *The Mind of Man; The Story of Man's Conquest of Mental Illness,* New York, Harper & Brothers, 1937.

BURCHARD, EDWARD M. L.: *Physique in Psychosis,* Baltimore, Johns Hopkins Press, 1936.

CAMERON, DONALD E.: *Objective and Experimental Psychiatry,* New York, The Macmillan Company, 1941.

CAMERON, NORMAN: *The Psychology of Behavior Disorders,* Boston, Houghton Mifflin Company, 1947.

CAMPBELL, JOHN D.: *Everyday Psychiatry,* Philadelphia, J. B. Lippincott Company, 1945.

COBB, STANLEY: *Foundations of Neuropsychiatry,* Baltimore, The Williams & Wilkins Company, 1941.

DESPERT, J. LOUISE, *et al.:* "Psychosomatics in Childhood," *The Nervous Child,* Vol. V, 4, 1946.

DEUTSCH, ALBERT: *The Mentally Ill in America: A History of Their Care and Treatment from Colonial Times,* rev. ed., New York, Columbia University Press, 1946.

DRINKER, C. K., *et al.:* *Psychiatric Research,* Cambridge, Mass., Harvard University Press, 1947.

DUMAS, ALEXANDER, and GRACE KEEN: *A Psychiatric Primer for Veteran's Family and Friends,* Minneapolis, University of Minnesota Press, 1946.

DUNBAR, FLANDERS: *Synopsis of Psychosomatic Diagnosis and Treatment,* St. Louis, C. V. Mosby Company, 1948.

DUNBAR, HELEN F.: *Psychosomatic Diagnosis,* New York, Paul B. Hoeber, Inc., Medical Book Department of Harper & Brothers, 1943.

EBAUGH, FRANKLIN G., and CHARLES A. RYMER: *Psychiatry in Medical Education,* New York, Commonwealth Fund, Division of Publication, 1942.

ENGLISH, OLIVER S., and GERALD H. J. PEARSON: *Common Neuroses of Children and Adults,* New York, W. W. Norton & Company, 1937.

FARIS, ROBERT E. L., and HENRY W. DUNHAM: *Mental Disorders in Urban Areas,* Chicago, University of Chicago Press, 1938.

FISHER, VIVIAN E.: *Auto-correctivism: The Psychology of Nervousness,* Caldwell, Idaho, Caxton Printers, Ltd., 1937.

FRIEDLANDER, DOROTHIE: "Personality Development of Twenty-seven Children Who Later Became Psychotic," *The Journal of Abnormal and Social Psychology,* 1945, 330–335.

FROHMAN, BERTRAND S.: *Brief Psychobiology,* Philadelphia, Lea & Febiger, 1948.

GANTT, WILLIAM A. H.: *Experimental Bases for Neurotic Behavior,* New York, Harper & Brothers, 1944.

GOLDSTEIN, KURT: *Human Nature in the Light of Psychopathology,* Cambridge, Mass., Harvard University Press, 1940.

GORDON, RONALD G.: *A Survey of Child Psychiatry,* New York, Oxford University Press, 1939.

HALL, JAMES K., gen. ed.: *One Hundred Years of American Psychiatry,* New York, Columbia University Press, 1944.

HENDERSON, DAVID K., and ROBERT D. GILLESPIE: *A Textbook of Psychiatry, for Students and Practitioners,* New York, Oxford University Press, 1944.

HEWITT, LESTER E., and RICHARD L. JENKINS: *Fundamental Patterns of Maladjustment: The Dynamics of Their Origin,* State of Illinois, Institute for Child Guidance, 1945.

HINSIE, LELAND E.: *The Person in the Body; An Introduction to Psychosomatic Medicine,* New York, W. W. Norton & Company, Inc., 1945.

————: *Understandable Psychiatry,* New York, The Macmillan Company, 1948.

HUNT, J. McVICKER: *Personality and the Behavior Disorders: A Handbook Based on Experimental and Clinical Research,* New York, The Ronald Press Company, 1944. (2 vols.)

JUNG, CARL G.: *The Psychology of Dementia Praecox,* New York, Nervous and Mental Disease Publication Company, 1936.

KANNER, LEO: *Child Psychiatry,* 2d ed., Springfield, Ill., Charles C Thomas, Publisher, 1949.

KAPLAN, OSCAR J., ed.: *Mental Disorders in Later Life,* Stanford University, Calif., Stanford University Press, 1945.

KARDINER, ABRAM: *The Traumatic Neuroses of War,* New York, Paul B. Hoeber, Inc., Medical Book Department of Harper & Brothers, 1941.

KARNOSH, LOUIS J., and EDWARD M. ZUKER: *A Handbook of Psychiatry,* St. Louis, The C. V. Mosby Company, Medical Publishers, 1945.

KRAINES, SAMUEL H.: *The Therapy of the Neuroses and Psychoses: A Socio-Psychobiologic Analysis and Resynthesis,* Philadelphia, Lea & Febiger, 1941.

LANDIS, CARNEY, and JAMES D. PAGE: *Modern Society and Mental Disease,* New York, Rinehart & Company, Inc., 1938.

LEVY, DAVID M.: *New Fields in Psychiatry,* New York, W. W. Norton & Company, Inc., 1947.

LEWIS, NOLAN D. C., and BERNARD L. PACELLA: *Modern Trends in Child Psychiatry,* New York, International Universities Press, Inc., 1945.

LICHTENSTEIN, PERRY M., and SAUL M. SMALL: *A Handbook of Psychiatry,* New York, W. W. Norton & Company, Inc., 1943.

LIEF, ALFRED, ed.: *The Commonsense Psychiatry of Dr. Adolf Meyer,* McGraw-Hill Book Company, Inc., 1948.

LORAND, ALEXANDER S.: *The Morbid Personality,* New York, International Universities Press, Inc., 1945.

LOWREY, LAWSON G.: *Psychiatry for Social Workers,* New York, Columbia University Press, 1946.

MALZBERG, BENJAMIN: *Social and Biological Aspects of Mental Disease,* Utica, N.Y., The State Hospitals Press, 1940.

MASSERMANN, JULES H.: *Principles of Dynamic Psychiatry,* Philadelphia, W. B. Saunders Company, 1946.

————, and OTHO S. A. SPRAGUE: *Behavior and Neurosis,* Chicago, University of Chicago Press, 1943.

MENNINGER, WILLIAM C.: *Psychiatry in a Troubled World: Yesterday's War and Today's Challenge,* New York, The Macmillan Company, 1948.

MILLER, EMANUEL: *The Neuroses in War,* New York, The Macmillan Company, 1940.

MIRA Y LOPEZ, EMILIO: *Psychiatry in War,* New York, W. W. Norton & Company, Inc., 1943.

MOORE, THOMAS V.: *The Nature and Treatment of Mental Disorders,* New York, Grune & Stratton, Inc., 1944.

MUNCIE, WENDELL: *Psychobiology and Psychiatry: A Textbook of Normal and Abnormal Human Behavior,* 2d ed., St. Louis, The C. V. Mosby Company, Medical Publishers, 1948.

MYERS, CHARLES S.. *Shell Shock in France,* New York, The Macmillan Company, 1940.

NIELSON, JOHANNES M.: *Agnosia, Apraxia, Aphasia: Their Value in Cerebral Localization,* New York, Paul H. Hoeber, Inc., Medical Book Department of Harper & Brothers, 1946.

NOYES, ARTHUR P.: *Modern Clinical Psychiatry,* 3d ed., Philadelphia, W. B. Saunders Company, 1948.

ORGEL, SAMUEL Z.: *Psychiatry Today and Tomorrow,* New York, International Universities Press, Inc., 1946.

OVERHOLZER, WINFRED, and WINIFRED V. RICHMOND: *Handbook of Psychiatry,* Philadelphia, J. B. Lippincott Company, 1947.

PAVLOV, IVAN P.: *Conditioned Reflexes and Psychiatry,* New York, International Publishers Co., 1941. (Translated by W. H. Gantt.)

PRESTON, GEORGE H.: *Psychiatry for the Curious,* New York, Rinehart & Company, Inc., 1940.

REES, JOHN R.: *The Shaping of Psychiatry by War,* New York, W. W. Norton & Company, Inc., 1945.

RICHARDS, ESTHER E.: *Introduction to Psychobiology and Psychiatry,* St. Louis, The C. V. Mosby Company, Medical Publishers, 1941.

ROE, ANNE, and DAVID SHAKOW: *Intelligence in Mental Disorder,* New York, Annals of the New York Academy of Sciences, 1942, Vol. XLII.

ROSANOFF, AARON J.: *Manual of Psychiatry and Mental Hygiene,* 7th ed., New York, John Wiley & Sons, Inc., 1938.

SADLER, WILLIAM S.: *Modern Psychiatry,* St. Louis, The C. V. Mosby Company, Medical Publishers, 1945.

———: *Mental Mischief and Emotional Conflicts,* St. Louis, The C. V. Mosby Company, Medical Publishers, 1947.

SARGANT, WILLIAM, and ELIOT SLATER: *An Introduction to Somatic Methods of Treatment in Psychiatry,* Baltimore, The Williams & Wilkins Company, 1945.

SEABROOK, WILLIAM B.: *Asylum,* New York, Harcourt, Brace and Company, Inc., 1935. (Autobiographical.)

SHIRLEY, HALE F.: *Psychiatry for the Pediatrician,* New York, Commonwealth Fund, Division of Publication, 1948.

SMALL, VICTOR R.: *I Knew 3,000 Lunatics,* New York, Rinehart & Company, Inc., 1935.

SPIEGEL, ERNEST A., ed.: *Progress in Neurology and Psychiatry,* New York, Grune & Stratton, Inc., Vol. I, 1946; Vol. II, 1947; Vol. III, 1948; Vol. IV, 1949.

STERN, EDITH M., with the collaboration of SAMUEL W. HAMILTON: *Mental Illness: A Guide for the Family,* New York, Commonwealth Fund, Division of Publication, 1942.

STRECKER, EDWARD A., and KENNETH E. APPEL: *Psychiatry in Modern Warfare,* New York, The Macmillan Company, 1945.

———, FRANKLIN EBAUGH, and JACK R. EWALT: *Practical Clinical Psychiatry,* 6th ed., Philadelphia, The Blakiston Company, 1947.

The Mental Hospital, A Guide for the Citizen, New York, The National Committee for Mental Hygiene.

WECHSLER, ISRAEL S.: *Textbook of Clinical Neurology,* 6th ed., Philadelphia, W. B. Saunders Company, 1947.

WEIL, ARTHUR: *Textbook of Neuropathology,* 2d ed., New York, Grune & Stratton, Inc., 1945.

WEISS, EDWARD, and O. SPURGEON ENGLISH: *Psychosomatic Medicine: The Clinical Application of Psychopathology to General Medical Problems,* Philadelphia, W. B. Saunders Company, 1943.

ZILBOORG, GREGORY, and GEORGE W. HENRY: *A History of Medical Psychology,* New York, W. W. Norton & Company, Inc., 1941.

V. PERSONALITY STUDIES

ALLPORT, GORDON W.: *Personality: A Psychological Interpretation,* New York, Henry Holt and Company, Inc., 1941.

ANGYAL, ANDRAS: *Foundations for a Science of Personality,* New York, Commonwealth Fund, Division of Publication, 1941.

BARKER, ROGER G., BEATRICE A. WRIGHT, and MOLLIE R. GONICK: *Adjustment to Physical Handicap: A Survey of the Social Psychology of Physique and Disability,* Bulletin 55, New York, Social Science Research Council, 1946.

BENNETT, MARGARET E.: *Designs for Personality,* New York, McGraw-Hill Book Company, Inc., 1938.

BLOS, PETER: *The Adolescent Personality, A Study of Individual Behavior,* New York, Appleton-Century-Crofts, Inc., 1941.

BONNEY, MERL E.: "Personality Traits of Socially Successful and Socially Unsuccessful Children," *Journal of Educational Psychology,* 1943, 449.

BOWLBY, JOHN: *Personality and Mental Illness,* New York, Emerson Books, Inc., 1942.

BRUNSCHWIG, LILY: *A Study of Some Personality Aspects of Deaf Children,* Teachers College, Columbia University Press, 1936.

CASE, VIRGINIA: *Your Personality—Introvert or Extrovert,* New York, The Macmillan Company, 1941.

CATTELL, RAYMOND B.: "Interpretation of the Twelve Primary Personality Factors," *Character and Personality,* 1944, 55–91.

————: "The Principal Trait Clusters for Describing Personality," *Psychological Bulletin,* 1945, 129–161.

————: *Description and Measurement of Personality,* Yonkers, New York, World Book Company, 1946.

CHAREN, SOL, and LUIS PERELMAN: "Personality Studies of Marihuana Addicts," *American Journal of Psychiatry,* 1946, 674–682.

COFFIN, JOSEPH H.: *Visual Outline of the Psychology of Personality,* Student's Outline Series, New York, Longmans, Green & Co., Inc., 1940.

CRILE, GEORGE: *Intelligence, Power and Personality,* New York, McGraw-Hill Book Company, Inc., 1941.

ELLIS, ALBERT: "The Validity of Personality Questionnaires," *Psychological Bulletin,* September, 1946, 385–440. (Review of the literature.)

HABBE, STEPHEN: *Personality Adjustments of Adolescent Boys with Impaired Hearing,* New York, Teachers College, Columbia University, Contributions to Education, 1936.

HAGGARD, HOWARD W., and CLEMENTS C. FRY: *The Anatomy of Personality,* New York, Harper & Brothers, 1936.

HEALY, WILLIAM: *Personality in Formation and Action,* New York, W. W. Norton & Company, Inc., 1938.

JENNINGS, HELEN H.: *Leadership and Isolation: A Study of Personality in Interpersonal Relations,* New York, Longmans, Green & Co., Inc., 1943.

JUNG, CARL G.: *The Integration of Personality,* New York, Rinehart & Company, Inc., 1940.

KLUCKHOHN, CLYDE, and HENRY A. MURRAY, eds.: *Personality, in Nature, Society, and Culture,* New York, Alfred A. Knopf, Inc., 1948.

LEEPER, ROBERT: *Psychology of Personality,* Ann Arbor, Mich., Edwards Bros., Inc., 1946.

LINTON, RALPH: *The Cultural Background of Personality*, New York, Appleton-Century-Crofts, Inc., 1945.

McCALL, WILLIAM A., and JOHN P. HERRING: "Measuring and Promoting Growth in Personality," *Teachers College Record*, 1941, 612–618.

MACHOVER, KAREN: *Personality Projection in the Drawing of the Human Figure*, Springfield, Ill., Charles C Thomas, 1948.

McNEMAR, QUINN, and MAUD A. MERRILL, eds.: *Studies in Personality*, New York, McGraw-Hill Book Company, Inc., 1942.

MAGOUN, F. ALEXANDER: *Balanced Personality*, New York, Harper & Brothers, 1943.

MURPHY, GARDNER: *Personality, A Biosocial Approach to Origins and Structures*, New York, Harper & Brothers, 1947.

MURRAY, HENRY A.: *Explorations in Personality*, New York, Oxford University Press, 1938.

MYERS, GARRY C.: *Building Personality in Children*, New York, Greenberg: Publisher, Inc., 1938.

NAPOLI, PETER J.: *Finger-painting and Personality Diagnosis*, Genetic Psychology Monographs, Vol. 34, Second half, November, 1946.

NEWTON, ROY: *How to Improve Your Personality*, New York, McGraw-Hill Book Company, Inc., 1942.

PLANT, JAMES S.: *Personality and the Cultural Pattern*, New York, Commonwealth Fund, Division of Publication, 1937.

PRINCE, MORTON: *Clinical and Experimental Studies in Personality*, 2d rev. ed., edited by A. A. Roback, Cambridge, Mass., Sci-Art Publishers, 1938.

PULLIAS, EARL V.: "Notes on Personality Development," *Mental Hygiene*, April, 1948, 261–270.

RICHMOND, WINIFRED V.: *Making the Most of Your Personality*, New York, Rinehart & Company, Inc., 1942.

ROBACK, ABRAHAM A., ed.: *Personality, the Crux of Social Intercourse*, Cambridge, Mass., Sci-Art Publishers, 1931.

SOROKIN, PITIRIM A.: *Society, Culture and Personality: Their Structure and Dynamics*, New York, Harper & Brothers, 1947.

STAGNER, ROSS: *Psychology of Personality*, 2d ed., New York, McGraw-Hill Book Company, Inc., 1948.

STOGDILL, EMILY L., and AUDELL HERNDON: *Objective Personality Study: A Workbook in Applied Mental Hygiene*, New York, Longmans, Green & Co., Inc., 1939.

TERMAN, LEWIS M., and CATHERINE G. MILES: *Sex and Personality*, New York, McGraw-Hill Book Company, Inc., 1936.

THORNTON, GEORGE R.: "The Effect of Wearing Glasses upon Judgments of Personality Traits of Persons Seen Briefly," *Journal of Applied Psychology*, 1944, 203–207.

THORPE, LOUIS P.: *Psychological Foundations of Personality*, New York, McGraw-Hill Book Company, Inc., 1938.

VAUGHN, GWENYTH R., and CHARLES B. ROTH: *Effective Personality Building*, New York, McGraw-Hill Book Company, Inc., 1947.

WOLFF, WERNER: *The Personality of the Pre-school Child*, New York, Grune & Stratton, Inc., 1946.

———: *The Expression of Personality: Experimental Depth Psychology*, New York, Harper & Brothers, 1943.

WYATT, GERTRUDE L.: "Voice Disorders and Personality Conflicts," *Mental Hygiene*, 1941, 237–250.

YOUNG, KIMBALL: *Personality and Problems of Adjustment*, New York, Appleton-Century-Crofts, Inc., 1940.

VI. MISCELLANEOUS TOPICS

ALLPORT, GORDON W.: *The Use of Personal Documents in Psychological Science*, Washington, D.C., Social Science Research Council, Committee on Public Administration, 1942.

ANDERSON, JOHN E.: *The Psychology of Development and Personal Adjustment*, New York, Henry Holt and Company, Inc., 1949.

BARKER, ROGER G., TAMARA DEMBO, and KURT LEWIN: *Frustration and Regression: An Experiment with Young Children*, Iowa City, University of Iowa Child Welfare Research Station, 1941.

BARTLEY, S. HOWARD, and ELOISE CHUTE: *Fatigue and Impairment in Man*, New York, McGraw-Hill Book Company, Inc., 1947.

BARUCH, DOROTHY W.: *You, Your Children, and War*, New York, Appleton-Century-Crofts, Inc., 1942.

BAYLEY, NANCY: "Growth and Development," *Review of Educational Research*, American Educational Research Association, December, 1947, 301–379.

BEHANAN, KOVOOR T.: *Yoga, a Scientific Evaluation*, New York, The Macmillan Company, 1937.

BELL, JOHN E.: *Projection Techniques*, New York, Longmans, Green & Co., 1948.

BERG, CHARLES: *The Case Book of a Medical Psychologist*, 2d ed., W. W. Norton & Company, Inc., 1948.

BERRIEN, FREDERICK K.: *Practical Psychology*, New York, The Macmillan Company, 1944. (Especially Parts 2, 5, and 6.)

BEVERLY, BERT I.: *A Psychology of Growth*, New York, McGraw-Hill Book Company, Inc., 1947.

BICKNELL, FRANKLIN, and FREDERICK PRESCOTT: *The Vitamins in Medicine*, New York, Grune & Stratton, Inc., 1946.

BILLS, ARTHUR G.: *The Psychology of Efficiency: A Discussion of the Hygiene of Mental Work*, New York, Harper & Brothers, 1943.

BLISS, M.: "Neuro-endocrine Relationships," *Journal of Mental Science*, 1944, 90, 109–126. (120-item bibliography.)

BOSSARD, JAMES S.: *The Sociology of Child Development*, New York, Harper & Brothers, 1948.

BRECKENRIDGE, MARIAN E., and VINCENT E. LEE: *Child Development*, 2d ed., Philadelphia, W. B. Saunders Company, 1949.

BRIDGES, JAMES W.: *Psychology: Normal and Abnormal*, Toronto, Sir Isaac Pitman & Sons (Canada), Ltd., 1946.

BRITT, STEWART H.: *Social Psychology and Modern Life*, New York, Rinehart & Company, Inc., 1941.

BROWN, J. F.: *The Psychodynamics of Abnormal Behavior*, New York, McGraw-Hill Book Company, Inc., 1940.

BUHLER, CHARLOTTE, and LEFEVER D. WELTY: *A Rorschach Study of the Psychological Characteristics of Alcoholics*, New Haven, Yale University, Hillhouse Press, 1948.

BULLIS, H. EDMUND: *Human Relations in the Classroom*, Course II, Wilmington, Del., The Delaware State Society for Mental Hygiene, 1948.

BUROS, OSCAR K.: *The Third Mental Measurement Yearbook*, New Brunswick, N.J., Rutgers University Press, 1949.

BURROW, TRIGANT: *The Biology of Human Conflict,* New York, The Macmillan Company, 1937.

BURTON, ARTHUR, and ROBERT E. HARRIS: *Case Histories in Clinical and Abnormal Psychology,* New York, Harper & Brothers, 1947.

BURTT, HAROLD E.: *Applied Psychology,* New York, Prentice-Hall, Inc., 1948.

BYCHOWSKI, GUSTAV: *Dictators and Disciples,* New York, International Universities Press, Inc., 1948.

CARROLL, ROBERT S.: *What Price Alcohol?* New York, The Macmillan Company, 1941.

CHATTO, CLARENCE I., and ALICE L. HALLIGAN: *The Story of the Springfield Plan* (for overcoming racial prejudice), New York, Barnes & Noble, Inc., 1945.

COLE, LOUELLA: *Attaining Maturity,* New York, Rinehart & Company, Inc., 1944.

———, and JOHN B. MORGAN: *Psychology of Childhood and Adolescence,* New York, Rinehart & Company, Inc., 1947.

COWLES, EDWARD S.: *Don't Be Afraid!* New York, McGraw-Hill Book Company, Inc., 1941.

CRANE, GEORGE W.: *Psychology Applied,* rev. ed., Chicago, Hopkins Syndicate, Inc., 1948. (Especially Chaps. V, VI, X, and XV.)

CROLLMAN, ARTHUR: *Essentials of Endocrinology,* Philadelphia, J. B. Lippincott Company, 1948.

DENNIS, WAYNE: *Current Trends in Psychology,* Pittsburgh, University of Pittsburgh Press, 1947.

DOLLARD, JOHN: *Victory over Fear,* New York, Reynal & Hitchcock, Inc., 1942.

———, et al.: *Frustration and Aggression,* New Haven, Yale University Press, 1944.

DORSEY, JOHN M.: *The Foundations of Human Nature: The Study of the Person,* New York, Longmans, Green & Co., Inc., 1935.

DUNBAR, H. FLANDERS: *Emotions and Bodily Changes: A Survey of Literature on Psychosomatic Interrelationships, 1910–1933,* 2d ed., New York, Columbia University Press, 1938.

DURFEE, CHARLES H.: *To Drink or Not to Drink,* New York, Longmans, Green & Co., Inc., 1937.

ENGLISH, HORACE B., and VICTOR RAIMY: *Studying the Individual School Child,* New York, Henry Holt and Company, Inc., 1941.

FENLASON, ANNE F., and HELEN R. HERTZ: "The College Student and Feelings of Inferiority," *Mental Hygiene,* 1938, 389–399.

FLEMING, ALEXANDER: *Chemotherapy: Yesterday, Today, and Tomorrow,* New York, The Macmillan Company, 1948.

FRENCH, LOIS M.: *Psychiatric Social Work,* New York, Commonwealth Fund, Division of Publication, 1940.

FREUD, ANNA, and DOROTHY T. BURLINGHAM: *War and Children,* New York, Medical War Books, 1943.

FROLOV, IURII P.: *Pavlov and His School; the Theory of the Conditioned Reflexes,* New York, Oxford University Press, 1937. (Translated by Clemens P. Dutt.)

FRY, CLEMENTS C.: *Mental Health in College,* New York, Commonwealth Fund, Division of Publication, 1942.

GARRISON, KARL C.: *Psychology of Adolescence,* 3d ed., Prentice-Hall, Inc., 1946.

GATES, MARY F.: "A Comparative Study of Some Problems of Social and Educational Adjustment of Crippled and Non-crippled Girls and Boys," *The Journal of Genetic Psychology,* 1946, 219–244.

GESELL, ARNOLD L.: *Guidance of Mental Growth in Infant and Child,* New York, The Macmillan Company, 1931.

GESELL, ARNOLD L., and FRANCES L. ILG: *The Child from Five to Ten,* New York, Harper & Brothers, 1946.

———, and ———: *Infant and Child in the Culture of Today,* New York, Harper & Brothers, 1943.

———, et al.: *The First Five Years of Life,* New York, Harper & Brothers, 1940.

———, and CATHERINE S. AMATRUDA: *Developmental Diagnosis,* 2d ed., New York, Paul B. Hoeber, Inc., Medical Book Department of Harper & Brothers, 1947.

GIBBS, FREDERICK A., and ERNA L. GIBBS: *Atlas of Electroencephalography,* Cambridge, Mass., Lew A. Cummings Printing Company, 1941.

GILBERT, GUSTAVE M.: *Nuremberg Diary,* New York, Farrar, Straus & Co., Inc., 1947. (The psychology of some Nazi leaders.)

GOODENOUGH, FLORENCE L.: *Anger in Young Children,* Minneapolis, University of Minnesota Press, 1931.

———: *Developmental Psychology, An Introduction to the Study of Human Behavior,* 2d ed., New York, Appleton-Century-Crofts, Inc., 1945.

GORDON, RONALD G.: *Abnormal Behavior,* London, Medical Publications(/), 1946.

GRIFFITH, COLEMAN R.: *An Introduction to Applied Psychology,* New York, Rinehart & Company, Inc., 1944. (Parts 1 and 4.)

"Growth and Development," *Review of Educational Research,* December, 1947, 305–379. (A review of studies by means of tests of intellectual, personality, social, motor, and physical development.)

GUTHRIE, EDWIN R.: *The Psychology of Human Conflict, The Clash of Motives within the Individual,* New York, Harper & Brothers, 1938.

HAGGARD, HOWARD W., and ELVIN M. JELLINEK: *Alcohol Explored,* New York, Doubleday & Company, Inc., 1942.

HALL, CALVIN S.: "Temperament; A Survey of Animal Studies," *Psychological Bulletin,* 1941, 909–943. (References.)

HAMBLEN, EDWIN C.: *Endocrinology of Women,* Springfield, Ill., Charles C Thomas, Publisher, 1945.

HAMPTON, PETER J.: "A Descriptive Portrait of the Drinker," *The Journal of Social Psychology,* February, 1947, 69–132. (The normal, symptomatic, psychotic, and stupid drinkers; references.)

HART, HORNELL: *Chart for Happiness,* New York, The Macmillan Company, 1940.

HARTLEY, EUGENE: *Problems in Prejudice,* New York, Columbia University Press, 1946.

HEPNER, HARRY W.: *Psychology Applied to Life and Work,* New York, Prentice-Hall, Inc., 1941. (Especially Part 2.)

HESSE, ERICH: *Narcotics and Drug Addiction,* New York, Philosophical Library, Inc., 1946. (Translated by Frank Gaynor.)

HILGARD, ERNEST R., and DONALD G. MARQUIS: *Conditioning and Learning,* New York, Appleton-Century-Crofts, Inc., 1940.

HOGUE, HELEN G.: *Bringing Up Ourselves,* New York, Charles Scribner's Sons, 1943.

HOOTON, ERNEST A.: *Young Men, Are You Normal?* New York, G. P. Putnam's Sons, 1945.

HOSKINS, ROY G.: *Endocrinology; the Glands and Their Functions,* New York, W. W. Norton & Company, Inc., 1941.

HOYLAND, JOHN S.: *That Inferiority Feeling,* London, George Allen and Unwin, Ltd., 1937.

HUSBAND, RICHARD W.: *Applied Psychology,* rev. ed., New York, Harper & Brothers, 1949 (especially Parts II, V, and VI).

JASTROW, JOSEPH: *Wish and Wisdom; Episodes in the Vagaries of Belief,* New York, Appleton-Century-Crofts, Inc., 1935.

JELLINEK, ELVIN M.: *Alcohol Addiction and Chronic Alcoholism,* New Haven, Yale University Press, 1942.

———: *Recent Trends in Alcoholism and in Alcohol Consumption,* New Haven, Yale University, Hillhouse Press, 1947.

JERSILD, ARTHUR T.: *Child Psychology,* 3d ed., New York, Prentice-Hall, Inc., 1947.

———, and FRANCIS B. HOLMES: *Children's Fears,* New York, Teachers College, Columbia University Press, 1935.

JONES, HAROLD E.: *Development in Adolescence: Approaches to the Study of the Individual,* New York, Appleton-Century-Crofts, Inc., 1943.

KANTROW, RUTH W.: *Studies in Infant Behavior, IV: An Investigation of Conditioned Feeding Responses and Concomitant Adaptive Behavior in Infants,* Iowa City, University of Iowa Studies in Child Welfare, 1937, Vol. 13, No. 3.

KELIHER, ALICE V.: *Life and Growth,* New York, Appleton-Century-Crofts, Inc., 1938.

KENDIG, ISABELLE, and WINIFRED V. RICHMOND: *Psychological Studies in Dementia Praecox,* Ann Arbor, Mich., Edwards Bros., Inc., 1940.

KEYS, NOEL, and MARGARET S. GUILFORD: "The Validity of Certain Adjustment Inventories in Predicting Problem Behavior," *Journal of Educational Psychology,* 1937, 641–655.

KIERKEGAARD, SOREN A.: *The Concept of Dread,* Princeton, N.J., Princeton University Press, 1944. (Translated by Walter Lowrie.)

KNOTT, JOHN F.: "Electroencephalography, and Physiological Psychology: Evaluation and Statement of Problem," *Psychological Bulletin,* 1941, 944–975. (Bibliography.)

LAIRD, DONALD A.: *Increasing Personal Efficiency,* 3d rev., New York, Harper & Brothers, 1937.

———: *Why We Don't Like People,* 2d ed., New York, A. L. Glaser & Company, 1935.

LENTZ, BEATRICE: *Some Dynamic Aspects of Success and Failure,* Psychological Monographs, 1945, Vol. 59, No. 1.

LINK, HENRY C.: *The Rediscovery of Man,* New York, The Macmillan Company, 1938.

LOUTTIT, CHAUNCEY M.: *Clinical Psychology of Children's Behavior Problems,* rev. ed., New York, Harper & Brothers, 1947. (Especially Chap. XIII, Personality Problems.)

LUND, FREDERICK H.: *Emotions, Their Psychological, Physiological and Educative Implications,* New York, The Ronald Press Company, 1939.

MACKINTOSH, JAMES M.: *The War and Mental Health in England,* New York, Commonwealth Fund, Division of Publication, 1944.

MAIER, NORMAN R. F.: *Studies of Abnormal Behavior in the Rat,* New York, Harper & Brothers, 1939.

MALTZ, MAXWELL: *New Faces, New Futures; Rebuilding Character with Plastic Surgery,* New York, Richard R. Smith, 1936.

———: *Evolution of Plastic Surgery,* New York, Froben Press, Inc., 1946.

The Marihuana Problem in the City of New York, The Mayor's Committee on Marihuana, Lancaster, Pa., Jaques Cattell Press, 1944.

MARQUIT, SYVIL: *Understanding and Dispelling Fears,* New York, Philosophical Library, Inc., 1942.

MARSHALL, HELEN: "Alcohol: A Critical Review of the Literature, 1929–1940," *Psychological Bulletin,* 1941, 193–217.

MASLOW, ABRAHAM H., and BALA MITTLEMAN: *Principles of Abnormal Psychology,* New York, Harper & Brothers, 1941.

MEEK, LOIS R., *et al.: The Personal-Social Development of Boys and Girls with Implication for Secondary Education,* New York, Progressive Education Association, 1940.

MENNINGER, KARL A.: *Man against Himself,* New York, Harcourt, Brace and Company, Inc., 1938.

————: *Love against Hate,* New York, Harcourt, Brace and Company, 1942.

MILLER, JAMES G.: *Unconsciousness,* New York, John Wiley & Sons, Inc., 1942.

MONS, WALTER: *Principles and Practice of the Rorschach Personality Test,* London, Faber & Faber, Ltd., 1948.

MOODIE, WILLIAM: *The Doctor and the Difficult Child,* New York, Commonwealth Fund, Division of Publication, 1940.

MORGAN, JOHN J. B.: *The Psychology of the Unadjusted School Child,* New York, The Macmillan Company, 1936.

————, and GEORGE D. LOVELL: *The Psychology of Abnormal People,* rev., Longmans, Green & Co., Inc., 1948.

MURPHY, GARDNER: *General Psychology,* New York, Harper & Brothers, 1933. (Especially dreams, memory, and personality.)

MURPHY, LOIS B.: *Social Behavior and Child Personality: An Exploratory Study of Some Roots of Sympathy,* New York, Columbia University Press, 1937.

OLIVER, JOHN R.: *The Ordinary Difficulties of Everyday People,* Garden City, New York, Blue Ribbon Books, Inc., 1938.

————: *Fear: The Autobiography of James Edwards,* New York, The Macmillan Company, 1935.

OLSON, WILLARD C.: *The Measurement of Nervous Habits in Normal Children,* Minneapolis, University of Minnesota Press, 1929.

Personality Adjustment of the Elementary School Child, Fifteenth Yearbook, Department of Elementary School Principals, Washington, D.C., National Education Association, 1936.

PINTNER, RUDOLF, JON EISENSON, and MILDRED B. STANTON: *The Psychology of the Physically Handicapped,* New York, Appleton-Century-Crofts, Inc., 1941.

PITKIN, WALTER B.: *Escape from Fear,* New York, Doubleday & Company, Inc., 1940.

POWERS, FRANCIS F., THOMAS R. McCONNELL, WILLIAM C. TROW, BRUCE V. MOORE, and CHARLES E. SKINNER: *Psychology in Everyday Living,* Boston, D. C. Heath and Company, 1938.

PRATT, GEORGE K.: *Soldier to Civilian,* New York, McGraw-Hill Book Company, Inc., 1944.

RAY, MARIE B.: *Doctors of the Mind,* Boston, Little, Brown & Company, 1942.

ROBACK, ABRAHAM A.: "Pioneers of the Inferiority Complex," *Character and Personality,* 1934, 288–292.

ROBINSON, G. CANBY: *The Patient as a Person: A Study of the Social Aspects of Illness,* New York, Commonwealth Fund, Division of Publication, 1939.

ROGERS, CARL R.: *The Clinical Treatment of the Problem Child,* Boston, Houghton Mifflin Company, 1939.

RUCH, FLOYD L.: *Psychology and Life,* Chicago, Scott, Foresman & Company, 1940.

RUGGLES, ARTHUR H.: *Mental Health, Past, Present and Future,* Baltimore, The Williams & Wilkins Company, 1934.

SAUL, LEON J.: *Emotional Maturity,* Philadelphia, J. B. Lippincott Company, 1947.

SCHILDER, PAUL: *Goals and Desires of Man,* New York, Columbia University Press, 1942.

SEABURY, DAVID: *How to Worry Successfully,* Boston, Little, Brown & Company, 1936.

————: *Help Yourself to Happiness,* New York, McGraw-Hill Book Company, Inc., 1937.

SEASHORE, HAROLD: *All of Us Have Troubles,* New York, Association Press, 1947.

SEIDENFELD, MORTON A.: "Mental Hygiene in the Disabling Diseases," *Mental Hygiene,* April, 1947, 196–202.

SHAFER, ROY: *The Clinical Application of Psychological Tests,* New York, International Universities Press, Inc., 1948.

SHELDON, WILLIAM H., STANLEY S. STEVENS, and WILLIAM B. TUCKER: *The Varieties of Human Physique,* New York, Harper & Brothers, 1940.

——, and STANLEY S. STEVENS: *The Varieties of Temperament: A Psychology of Constitutional Differences,* New York, Harper & Brothers, 1942.

SHERMAN, MANDEL: *Basic Problems of Behavior,* New York, Longmans, Green & Co., Inc., 1941.

——: *Mental Conflicts and Personality,* New York, Longmans, Green & Co., Inc., 1938.

SILVERMAN, SYLVIA S.: *Clothing and Appearance: Their Psychological Implications for Teen-age Girls,* New York, Teachers College, Columbia University Press, 1945.

SKINNER, CHARLES E., ed.: *Educational Psychology,* rev. ed., New York, Prentice-Hall, Inc., 1945. (Especially Part IV.)

——: *Elementary Educational Psychology,* New York, Prentice-Hall, Inc., 1945 (Especially Parts II and V.)

SMITH, MADORAH E.: "A Study of the Causes of Feelings of Inferiority," *The Journal of Psychiatry,* 1938, 315–332.

SNYGG, DONALD, and ARTHUR W. COMBS: *Individual Behavior,* New York, Harper & Brothers, 1949.

STEIN, MORRIS I.: *The Thematic Apperception Test; An Introductory Manual for Its Clinical Use with Adult Males,* Cambridge, Mass., Addison-Wesley, 1948.

STRECKER, EDWARD A.: *Their Mothers' Sons,* Philadelphia, J. B. Lippincott Company, 1946.

——, and FRANCIS T. CHAMBERS, JR.: *Alcohol, One Man's Meat,* New York, The Macmillan Company, 1938.

——, KENNETH E. APPEL, and JOHN W. APPEL: *Discovering Ourselves,* 2d ed., New York, The Macmillan Company, 1943.

SYMONDS, PERCIVAL M.: *Psychological Diagnosis in Social Adjustment,* New York, American Book Company, 1934.

"Symposia on Difficulties of Adolescence," *The Nervous Child:* in the girl, October, 1944, 3–99; in the boy, January, 1945, 11–171.

TEAGARDEN, FLORENCE M.: *Child Psychology for Professional Workers,* rev. ed., New York, Prentice-Hall, Inc., 1946.

TERMAN, LEWIS M., and MELITA H. ODEN: *The Gifted Child Grows Up,* Stanford University, Calif., Stanford University Press, 1947. (Twenty-five years' follow-up.)

THORPE, LOUIS A., and BARNEY KATZ: *The Psychology of Abnormal Behavior,* New York, The Ronald Press Company, 1948.

TUTTLE, HAROLD S.: *Dynamic Psychology and Conduct,* New York, Harper & Brothers, 1949.

WALKER, CHARLOTTE F.: "Hysteria in Childhood; A Follow-up Study," *American Journal of Orthopsychiatry,* July, 1947, 468–476.

WALTON, ROBERT P.: *Marihuana: America's New Drug Problem,* Philadelphia, J. B. Lippincott Company, 1938.

WATSON, ROBERT I., ed.: *Readings in the Clinical Method in Psychology,* New York, Harper & Brothers, 1949.

WEXBERG, L. ERWIN: *Introduction to Medical Psychology,* New York, Grune & Stratton, Inc., 1948.

WHITE, ROBERT W.: *Abnormal Personality*, New York, The Ronald Press Company, 1948.

WHITE, WENDELL: *Psychology in Living*, New York, The Macmillan Company, 1947.

WILDE, REGINALD W.: *Health, Sickness, and Psychology*, New York, Oxford University Press, 1936.

WOLFE, WALTER B.: *Successful Living*, New York, Rinehart & Company, Inc., 1938.

YOUNG, PAUL T.: *Motivation of Behavior*, New York, John Wiley & Sons, Inc., 1936.

ZACHRY, CAROLINE B., and MARGARET LIGHTY: *Emotion and Conduct in Adolescence*, New York, Appleton-Century-Crofts, Inc., 1940.

ZILBOORG, GREGORY: *Mind, Medicine and Man*, New York, Harcourt, Brace and Company, Inc.. 1943.

VII. The School and Teacher-Pupil Phases and Factors

ADLERBLUM, EVELYN D.: "Mental Hygiene Begins at School," *Mental Hygiene*, October, 1947, 541–555.

ALILANAS, LEO J.: "Needed Research in Teacher Mental Hygiene," *Review of Educational Research*, 1945, 653–665.

ANDERSON, HAROLD H., and HELEN M. BREWER: *Studies of Teachers' Classroom Personalities, I, Dominance and Socially Integrative Behavior of Kindergarten Teachers*, Stanford University, Calif., Stanford University Press, 1945.

——, and JOSEPH E. BREWER: *Studies of Teachers' Classroom Personalities, II, Effects of Teachers' Dominance and Integrative Contacts on Children's Classroom Behavior*, Stanford University, Calif., Stanford University Press, 1946.

——, ——, and MARY REED: *Studies of Teachers' Classroom Personalities, III, Follow-up Studies of the Effects of Dominance and Integrative Contacts on Children's Behavior*, Stanford University, Calif., Stanford University Press, 1946.

AVERILL, LAWRENCE A.: *Mental Hygiene for Classroom Teachers*, New York, Pitman Publishing Corp., 1939.

BARUCH, DOROTHY W.: "Therapeutic Procedures as Part of the Educative Process," *The Journal of Consulting Psychology*, 1940, 165–172.

BRUMBAUGH, FLORENCE: "The Place of Humor in the Curriculum," *Journal of Experimental Education*, 1940, 403–409.

CHALLMAN, ROBERT C.: "Personality Maladjustments and Remedial Reading," *Journal of Exceptional Children*, 1939, 7–11, 35.

COX, GRACE B., and HAROLD H. ANDERSON: "A Study of Teachers' Responses to Problem Situations in School as Reported by Teachers and Students," *American Journal of Orthopsychiatry*, 1944, 528–544.

ELMOTT, CHARLOTTE: "The Development of a Mental Hygiene Program in the Santa Barbara City Schools," *Journal of Educational Research*, 1944, 493–499.

FERNALD, GRACE M.: *Remedial Techniques in Basic School Subjects*, New York, McGraw-Hill Book Company, Inc., 1943.

FRANK, LAWRENCE K.: "The Reorientation of Education to the Promotion of Mental Hygiene," *Mental Hygiene*, 1939, 529–543.

GANN, EDITH: *Reading Difficulty and Personality Organization*, New York, King's Crown Press, Columbia University, 1945.

Helping Teachers Understand Children, Washington, D.C., American Council on Education, Commission on Teacher Education, Division of Child Development and Teacher Personnel, 1945.

HILDREDTH, GERTRUDE: *Child Growth through Education,* New York, The Ronald Press Company, 1948.

JERSILD, ARTHUR T.: "Characteristics of Teachers Who Are 'Liked Best' and 'Disliked Most,' " *Journal of Experimental Education,* 1940, 139–151.

LAYCOCK, SAMUEL R.: "Mental Health Qualifications for Special Class Teachers," *Journal of Exceptional Children,* October, 1940, 4–8, 23.

———: "Helping Teachers Maintain Mental Health," *Understanding the Child,* 1944, 5–9.

LESTER, ELIZABETH J.: "The Contents of a Course in Mental Hygiene for Teachers," *Journal of Educational Research,* 1944, 534–537.

LOUTTIT, CHAUNCEY M.: "The School as a Mental Hygiene Factor," *Mental Hygiene,* January, 1947, 50–65.

"Mental and Physical Health," *Review of Educational Research,* Washington, D.C., American Educational Research Association, 1946.

Mental Health in the Classroom, Thirteenth Yearbook, Department of Supervisors and Directors of Instruction of the National Education Association, Washington, D.C., 1940.

"Mental Hygiene and Adjustment," *Review of Educational Research,* Washington, D.C., American Educational Research Association, 1936

"Mental Hygiene and Health Education," *Review of Educational Research,* Washington, D.C., American Educational Research Association, 1940.

MONROE, MARION, and BERTIE BACKUS: *Remedial Reading,* Boston, Houghton Mifflin Company, 1937.

NEWLAND, T. ERNEST: "Teachers Need Good Mental Health," *Understanding the Child,* 1941, 12–16.

O'BRIEN, FRANK J.: "Educating for Mental Health," *American Journal of Orthopsychiatry,* 1939, 273–286.

OTTO, HENRY J., and ERNEST C. MELBY: "An Attempt to Evaluate the Threat of Failure as a Factor in Achievement," *The Elementary School Journal,* 1935, 588–596.

PATEY, HENRY C.: "The Teacher as a General Practitioner in Mental Hygiene," *Mental Hygiene,* 1940, 600–613.

PRESCOTT, DANIEL A.: *Emotion and the Educative Process,* Washington, D.C., American Council on Education, 1938.

———: "The Teacher of the Future," *Understanding the Child,* 1941, 3–11.

"Psychopathology and Education," *The Nervous Child,* 1944. (A symposium.)

RIVLIN, HARRY N.: "The Personality Problems of Teachers," *Mental Hygiene,* 1939, 12–24.

SANDIN, ADOLPH A.: *Social and Emotional Adjustments of Regularly Promoted and Nonpromoted Pupils,* New York, Teachers College, Columbia University Press, 1944.

SNYDER, WILLIAM U.: "Recent Investigations of Mental Hygiene in the Schools," *Educational Research Bulletin,* 1945, 178–185, 222–224, and 231–248. (Review.)

SYMONDS, PERCIVAL M.: "Suggestions for the Adjustment of Teachers," *Teachers College Record,* 1943, 417–432.

———: "The Needs of Teachers as Shown by Autobiographies, II," *Journal of Educational Research,* 1944, 641–655.

———: "How Teachers Solve Personal Problems," *Journal of Educational Research,* 1945, 641–652.

WICKMAN, E. KOSTER: *Teachers and Behavior Problems,* New York, Commonwealth Fund, Division of Publication, 1938.

WOLF, THETA H.: *The Effect of Praise and Competition on the Persisting Behavior of Kindergarten Children,* Minneapolis, University of Minnesota Press, Series XV, 1938.

VIII. The Home and Parent-Sibling Phases and Factors

Anderson, Harold H.: *Children in the Family,* New York, Appleton-Century-Crofts, Inc., 1937.

Bassett, Clara: *Mental Hygiene in the Community,* New York, The Macmillan Company, 1934.

Bolles, M. Marjorie, Harriet F. Metzger, and Marjorie W. Pitts: "Early Home Background and Personality Adjustment," *The American Journal of Orthopsychiatry,* 1941, 530–534.

Bossard, James H. S., and Eleanor S. Roll: *Family Situations: An Introduction to the Study of Child Behavior,* Philadelphia, University of Pennsylvania Press, 1943.

Buhler, Charlotte: *The Child and His Family,* New York, Harper & Brothers, 1939.

Cunningham, Bess V.: *Family Behavior—A Study of Human Relations,* Philadelphia, W. B. Saunders Company, 1936.

Dreikurs, Rudolph: *The Challenge of Parenthood,* New York, Duell, Sloan & Pearce, Inc., 1948.

Fitzsimmons, Marian J.: *Some Parent-Child Relationships, As Shown in Clinical Case Studies,* New York, Bureau of Publications, Teachers College, Columbia University, 1935.

Folsom, Joseph K.: *Youth, Family, and Education,* Washington, D.C., American Council on Education, 1941.

Frank, Lawrence K.: "Facing Reality in Family Life," *Mental Hygiene,* 1937, 224–230.

Groves, Ernest R., and Gladys H. Groves: *Wholesome Parenthood,* Boston, Houghton Mifflin Company, 1929.

Hart, Hornell H., and Ella B. Hart: *Personality and the Family,* Boston, D. C. Heath and Company, 1935.

Kanner, Leo: *In Defense of Mothers,* New York, Dodd, Mead & Company, Inc., 1941.

Lafore, Gertrude G.: *Practices of Parents in Dealing with Pre-school Children,* New York, Teachers College, Columbia University Press, 1945.

Laycock, Samuel R.: "How Parents Hinder Adolescents' Adjustments to the Opposite Sex," *Understanding the Child,* 1945, 35–40.

Levy, David M.: *Maternal Overprotection,* New York, Columbia University Press, 1943.

————: *Studies in Sibling Rivalry,* New York, American Orthopsychiatric Association, Monograph Series No. 2, 1937.

Levy, John, and Ruth Munroe: *The Happy Family,* New York, Alfred A. Knopf, Inc., 1938.

Lowrey, Lawson: "The Family as a Builder of Personality," *American Journal of Orthopsychiatry,* 1936, 117–124.

Mowrer, Harriet R.: *Personality Adjustment and Domestic Discord,* New York, American Book Company, 1935.

Myers, Garry C.: *The Modern Parent: A Practical Guide to Everyday Problems,* New York, Greenberg: Publisher, Inc., 1937.

"Orphanhood," *The Nervous Child,* 1943, 8–58. (Symposium.)

Parents' Questions, rev. ed., New York, Harper & Brothers, 1947 (Study Association of America).

Radke, Marian J.: *The Relation of Parental Authority to Children's Behavior and Attitudes,* Minneapolis, University of Minnesota Press, 1946.

Read, Grantly D.: *Childbirth without Fear,* New York, Harper & Brothers, 1944. (Condensation in *Reader's Digest,* May, 1947, 89–95.)

Richardson, Henry B.: *Patients Have Families,* New York, Commonwealth Fund, Division of Publication, 1945.

SOMMERS, VITA S.: *The Influence of Parental Attitudes and Social Environment on the Personality Development of the Adolescent Blind,* New York, American Foundation for the Blind, 1944.

SYMONDS, PERCIVAL M.: *Psychology of Parent-Child Relationships,* New York, Appleton-Century-Crofts, Inc., 1939.

"The Unwanted and Rejected Child," *The Nervous Child,* 1944, 73–144. (Symposium.)

WALLENSTEIN, NEHEMIAH: *Character and Personality of Children from Broken Homes,* New York, Columbia University Press, 1937.

WALLIN, J. E. WALLACE: "The Child—His Morale Development, A Function of the Home and School," *The Crippled Child,* 1936, 64–67, 103–105; 1937, 125–127 and 157–158.

IX. MARRIAGE, DIVORCE, AND SEX

APPLEHOF, GILBERT, JR.: *You Can Be Happily Married,* New York, The Macmillan Company, 1941.

BABER, RAY E.: *Marriage and the Family,* New York, McGraw-Hill Book Company, Inc., 1939.

BECKER, HOWARD, and REUBEN HILL: *Family, Marriage, and Parenthood,* Boston, D. C. Heath and Company, 1948.

BERGLER, EDMUND: *Unhappy Marriage and Divorce,* New York, International Universities Press, Inc., 1946.

BIBBY, CYRIL: *Sex Education: A Guide for Parents, Teachers, and Youth Leaders,* New York, Emerson Books, Inc., 1946.

BIGELOW, MAURICE A.: *Sex Education,* rev. ed., New York, American Social Hygiene Association, 1936.

BOWLEY, AGATHA H.: *The Psychology of the Unwanted Child,* Edinburgh, Scotland, E. & S. Livingstone, 1947.

BOWMAN, HENRY: *Marriage for Moderns,* New York, McGraw-Hill Book Company, Inc., 1948.

———: "Marriage Preparation Must Be Modernized," *Mental Hygiene,* January, 1946, 74–82.

BURGESS, ERNEST W., and HARVEY J. LOCKE: *The Family, from Institution to Companionship,* New York, American Book Company, 1945.

CHESSER, EUSTACE, and ZOE DAIVE: *The Practice of Sex Education: A Plain Guide for Parents and Teachers,* New York, Roy Publishers, 1946.

CLARK, LeMON: *Emotional Adjustment in Marriage,* St. Louis, The C. V. Mosby Company, Medical Publishers, 1937.

CUBER, JOHN F., and ROLAND LESLIE: *Marriage Counseling Practice,* New York, Appleton-Century-Crofts, Inc., 1948.

DUVALL, EVELYN R., and REUBEN HILL: *When You Marry,* Boston, D. C. Heath and Company, 1945.

FISHBEIN, MORRIS, and ERNEST W. BURGESS: *Successful Marriage,* New York, Doubleday & Company, Inc., 1947.

FOLSOM, JOSEPH K., *et al.: Plan for Marriage,* New York, Harper & Brothers, 1938.

FOREST, ILSE: "The Libido Concept," *American Journal of Orthopsychiatry,* October, 1947, 700–706.

GOLDSTEIN, SIDNEY E.: *Marriage and Family Counseling,* New York, McGraw-Hill Book Company, Inc., 1945.

GROVES, ERNEST R.: *Conserving Marriage and the Family,* New York, The Macmillan Company, 1945.

GROVES, ERNEST R., GLADYS H. GROVES, and CATHERINE GROVES: *Sex Fulfillment in Marriage,* New York, Emerson Books, Inc., 1942.

GROVES, GLADYS H., and ROBERT A. ROSS: *The Married Woman,* New York, Greenberg: Publisher, Inc., 1936.

KIRKENDALL, LESTER A.: *Understanding Sex,* Chicago, Science Research Associates, 1947.

LANDIS, CARNEY, and M. MARJORIE BOLLES: *Personality and Sexuality of the Physically Handicapped Woman,* New York, Harper & Brothers, 1942.

——, *et al.: Sex in Development,* New York, Paul B. Hoeber, Inc., Medical Book Department of Harper & Brothers, 1943.

LANDIS, JUDSON T.: *The Marriage Handbook,* Prentice-Hall, Inc., 1949.

MADOW, LEO, and SHERMAN HARDY: "Incidence and Analysis of the Broken Family in the Background of Neuroses," *American Journal of Orthopsychiatry,* July, 1947, 521–528.

MOONEY, BELLE S.: *How Shall I Tell My Child?* New York, Cadillac Publishing Company, 1944.

MOORE, THOMAS V.: "The Pathogenesis and Treatment of Homosexual Disorders: A Digest of Some Pertinent Evidence," *Journal of Personality,* 1945, 47–83.

PALMER, GRETTA: "Marriage Control: A New Answer to Divorce," *Reader's Digest,* August, 1947, 51–54.

POPENOE, PAUL: *Modern Marriage,* New York, The Macmillan Company, 1940.

REIK, THEODORE: *The Psychology of Sex Relations,* New York, Rinehart & Company, Inc., 1945.

RICHMOND, WINIFRED V.: *An Introduction to Sex Education,* New York, Rinehart & Company, Inc., 1934.

SBARBARO, JOHN A.: *Marriage on Trial,* New York, The Macmillan Company, 1947.

SHULTZ, GLADYS D.: *Letters to Jane,* Philadelphia, J. B. Lippincott Company, 1949.

STRAIN, FRANCIS B.: *Sex Guidance in Family Life Education,* New York, The Macmillan Company, 1942.

SWIFT, EDITH H.: *Step by Step in Sex Education,* New York, The Macmillan Company, 1938.

TERMAN, LEWIS M.: *Psychological Factors in Marital Happiness,* New York, McGraw-Hill Book Company, Inc., 1938.

THORMAN, GEORGE: *Broken Homes,* New York, Public Affairs Committee, 1947, Pamphlet 135.

THORNTON, HENRY, and FREDA H. THORNTON: *How to Achieve Sex Happiness in Marriage,* New York, Vanguard Press, 1939.

TYRER, ALFRED H.: *Sex Satisfaction and Happy Marriage,* New York, Emerson Books, Inc., 1938.

WESSEL, MORRIS A.: "Venereal-disease Anxiety," *Mental Hygiene,* October, 1947, 636–646.

WORTIS, S. B., *et al.: Physiological and Psychological Factors in Sex Behavior,* Annals of the New York Academy of Sciences, 1947, 603–664.

X. RELIGIOUS PHASES

ADAMS, THEODORE F.: "The Clergyman Cooperates with the Psychiatrist," *Mental Hygiene,* April, 1948, 286–288.

BONNELL, JOHN S.: *Pastoral Psychiatry,* New York, Harper & Brothers, 1938.

CABOT, RICHARD C.: "Ministers and Spiritual Maladies," *Survey Graphic,* 1937, 330–331.

CLARK, ROBERT A., and ALBERT H. BALDINGER: "A Seminar in Psychiatry for Theological Students," *Mental Hygiene,* 1946, 110–113.

DICKS, RUSSELL: *Pastoral Work and Personal Counseling,* New York, The Macmillan Company, 1944.

FAIRBANKS, ROLLIN J.: "The Washington Conference of Clergymen and Psychiatrists," *Mental Hygiene*, April, 1948, 289–295.

FOSDICK, HARRY E.: *On Being A Real Person*, New York, Harper & Brothers, 1943.

FOX, EMMET: *Make Your Life Worth While*, New York, Harper & Brothers, 1946.

GILKEY, JAMES G.: *Getting Help from Religion*, New York, The Macmillan Company, 1937.

GREGORY, W. EDGAR: "The Chaplain and Mental Hygiene," *The American Journal of Sociology*, March, 1947, 420–423.

HILTNER, SEWARD: "The Contributions of Religion to Mental Health," *Mental Hygiene*, 1940, 366–377.

———: *Clinical Pastoral Training*, New York, Commission on Religion and Health, Federal Council of the Churches of Christ, 1945.

JACOBY, GEORGE W.: *Physician, Pastor, and Patient*, New York, Paul B. Hoeber, Inc., Medical Book Department of Harper & Brothers, 1936.

JOHNSON, ELEANOR H.: "Personality and Religious Work," *American Journal of Orthopsychiatry*, 1942, 317–323.

JOHNSON, PAUL E.: "Religious Psychology and Health," *Mental Hygiene*, October, 1947, 556–566.

JUNG, CARL G.: *Psychology and Religion*, New Haven, Yale University Press, 1938.

KEMP, CHARLES F.: *Physicians of the Soul*, New York, The Macmillan Company, 1947.

———: "The Minister and Mental Hygiene: His Opportunity and Responsibility," *Mental Hygiene*, January, 1948, 72–79.

KIRKPATRICK, MILTON E.: "Mental Hygiene and Religion," *Mental Hygiene*, 1940, 378–389.

LINK, HENRY C.: *The Return to Religion*, New York, The Macmillan Company, 1936.

McKENZIE, JOHN G.: *Nervous Disorders and Character: A Study in Pastoral Psychology and Psychotherapy*, New York, Harper & Brothers, 1947.

WIEMAN, REGINA W.: *The Family Lives Its Religion*, New York, Harper & Brothers, 1942.

WISE, CARROLL A.: *Religion in Illness and Health*, New York, Harper & Brothers, 1942.

ZAHNISER, CHARLES R.: *Techniques of Counseling in Christian Service*, Pittsburgh, Gibson Press, 1946.

XI. HEREDITY AND EUGENICS

BURLINGAME, L. L.: *Heredity and Social Problems*, New York, McGraw-Hill Book Company, Inc., 1940.

COLIN, EDWARD C.: *Elements of Genetics*, 2d ed., Philadelphia, The Blakiston Company, 1944.

DOBZHANSKY, TH., and M. E. ASHLEY MONTAGUE: "Natural Selection and the Mental Capacities of Mankind," *Science*, June 6, 1947, 587–590.

FRETS, GERRITT P.: *Alcohol and Other Germ Poisons*, The Hague, Martinus Nijhoff, 1931.

GATES, E. RUGGLES: *Human Genetics*, New York, The Macmillan Company, 1946. (2 vols.)

SEN. GUPTA, NARENDRA N.: *Heredity in Mental Traits*, London, Macmillan & Co., Ltd., 1942.

GUYER, MICHAEL E.: *Being Wellborn*, Indianapolis, Bobbs-Merrill Company, 1927.

HALDANE, JOHN B. S.: *New Paths in Genetics*, New York, Harper & Brothers, 1942.

JENNINGS, HERBERT S.: *Genetics*, New York, W. W. Norton & Company, Inc., 1935.

MYERSON, ABRAHAM, ed.: *Eugenical Sterilization—a Reorientation of the Problem*, New York, The Macmillan Company, 1936.

OSBORN, FREDERICK: *Preface to Eugenics*, New York, Harper & Brothers, 1940.

RILEY, HERBERT P.: *Introduction to Genetics and Cytogenesis,* New York, John Wiley & Sons, Inc., 1948.

SCHWESINGER, GLADYS C.: *Heredity and Environment,* New York, The Macmillan Company, 1934.

SNYDER, LAURENCE H.: *Principles of Heredity,* 2d ed., Boston, D. C. Heath and Company, 1940.

———: *Medical Genetics,* Durham, N.C., Duke University Press, 1941.

XII. GUIDANCE AND COUNSELING

ADLER, ALEXANDER: *Guiding Human Misfits,* New York, The Macmillan Company, 1938.

BAXTER, EDNA D.: *An Approach to Guidance,* New York, Appleton-Century-Crofts, Inc., 1946.

BELL, HUGH M.: "Counseling, Guidance and Personnel Work," *Review of Educational Research,* American Educational Research Association, 1948, 121–213.

BURNHAM, PAUL S.: *Counseling in Personnel Work, 1940–1944,* Chicago, Public Administration Service, 1944. (Bibliography.)

COX, PHILIP W. L., and JOHN C. DUFF: *Guidance by the Classroom Teacher,* New York, Prentice-Hall, Inc., 1938.

CURRAN, CHARLES A.: *Personality Factors in Counseling,* New York, Grune & Stratton, Inc., 1945.

ERICKSON, CLIFFORD E., ed.: *A Basic Text for Guidance Workers,* New York, Prentice-Hall, Inc., 1947.

FORRESTER, GERTRUDE: *Occupations: A Selected List of Pamphlets,* New York, The H. W. Wilson Company, 1946. (References.)

GARRETT, ANNETTE: *Interviewing, Its Principles and Methods,* New York, Family Welfare Association of America, 1942.

HARMS, ERNEST, ed.: *Handbook of Child Guidance,* New York, Child Care Publications, 1947.

HILTON, M. EUNICE: *Guide to Guidance,* Syracuse, N.Y., Syracuse University Press, 1945, also 1947. (Selected bibliographies.)

HUTSON, PERCIVAL W.: "Selected References on Guidance," *School Review,* 1944, 431–436.

KAHN, SAMUEL: *Practical Child Guidance,* Boston, Meador Publishing Company, 1947.

KAPLAN, OSCAR J.: *Encyclopedia of Vocational Guidance,* New York, Philosophical Library, Inc., Vols. I and II, 1947.

KITSON, HARRY D.: *I Find My Vocation,* McGraw-Hill Book Company, Inc., 1947.

LLOYD-JONES, ESTHER, and MARGARET R. SMITH: *A Student Personnel Program for Higher Education,* New York, McGraw-Hill Book Company, Inc., 1938.

McKINNEY, FRED: "Four Years of a College Adjustment Clinic," *Journal of Consulting Psychology,* 1945, 203–217. (References.)

MEEK, LOIS H.: *Your Child's Development and Guidance,* Philadelphia, J. B. Lippincott Company, 1940.

MUELLER, KATE H., Chairman: *Counseling for Mental Health, Student Personnel Work,* Washington, D.C., American Council on Education, Series VI, No. 8, 1947.

OLDFIELD, RICHARD C.: *The Psychology of the Interview,* London, Methuen & Co., Ltd., 1941.

Pupil Personnel, Guidance, and Counseling, Washington, D.C., Review of Educational Research, XII, American Education Research Association, A Department of the National Education Association, 1942.

REED, ANNA Y.: *Occupational Placement,* Ithaca, N.Y., Cornell University Press, 1946.

SMITH, CHARLES M., and MARY M. ROOS: *A Guide to Guidance,* New York, Prentice-Hall, Inc., 1941.

STRANG, RUTH M.: *Educational Guidance,* New York, The Macmillan Company, 1947.

————: *Pupil Personnel and Guidance,* New York, The Macmillan Company, 1940.

————: *The Role of the Teacher in Personnel Work,* rev. ed., New York, Teachers College, Columbia University, 1946.

TRAXLER, ARTHUR E.: *Techniques of Guidance,* New York, Harper & Brothers, 1945.

WARTERS, JANE: *High School Personnel Work Today,* New York, McGraw-Hill Book Company, Inc., 1946.

WILLIAMSON, EDMUND G.: *How to Counsel Students,* New York, McGraw-Hill Book Company, Inc., 1939.

————, and JOHN G. DARLEY: *Student Personnel Work,* New York, McGraw-Hill Book Company, Inc., 1937.

————, and MILTON E. HAHN: *Introduction to High School Counseling,* New York, McGraw-Hill Book Company, Inc., 1940.

WINN, RALPH B.: *Encyclopedia of Child Guidance,* New York, Philosophical Library, Inc., 1943.

XIII. DELINQUENCY AND CRIME

ABRAHAMSEN, DAVID: *Crime and the Human Mind,* New York, Columbia University Press, 1944.

ALEXANDER, FRANZ, and WILLIAM HEALY: *Roots of Crime,* New York, Alfred A. Knopf, Inc., 1935.

BAKER, HARRY J., and VIRGINIA TRAPHAGEN: *The Diagnosis and Treatment of Behavior-problem Children,* New York, The Macmillan Company, 1935.

BELL, MARJORIE, ed.: *Delinquency and the Community in Wartime,* New York, National Probation Association, 1943. (1943 yearbook.)

BRANHAM, VERNON C., and SAMUEL B. KUTASH: *Encyclopedia of Criminology,* New York, Philosophical Library, Inc., 1949.

CABOT, P. S. DE Q.: *Juvenile Delinquency,* New York, The H. W. Wilson Company, 1946. (927 annotations.)

CANTOR, NATHANIEL F.: *Crime and Society: An Introduction to Criminology,* New York, Henry Holt and Company, Inc., 1939.

CARR-SAUNDERS, ALEXANDER M., HERMANN MANNHEIM, and E. C. RHODES: *Young Offenders: An Inquiry into Juvenile Delinquency,* New York, The Macmillan Company, 1944.

DOSHAY, LEWIS J.: *The Boy Sex Offender and His Later Career,* New York, Grune & Stratton, Inc., 1943.

FRIEDLANDER, KATE: *The Psychoanalytic Approach to Juvenile Delinquency,* New York, International Universities Press, Inc., 1947.

GOLDBERG, HARRIET: *Child Offenders,* New York, Grune & Stratton, Inc., 1948.

HARRISON, LEONARD V., and PRYOR McN. GRANT: *Youth in the Toils,* New York, The Macmillan Company, 1938.

HOOTON, ERNEST A.: *Crime and the Man,* Cambridge, Mass., Harvard University Press, 1939.

KARPMAN, BEN: *The Individual Delinquent,* New York, Nervous and Mental Disease Publishing Company, 1939.

KVARACEUS, WILLIAM C.: *Juvenile Delinquency and the School,* Yonkers, New York, World Book Company, 1945.

MERRILL, MAUD A.: *Problems of Child Delinquency,* Boston, Houghton Mifflin Company, 1947.

NAUMBURG, MARGARET: *Studies of the "Free" Art Expression of Behavior Problem Children and Adolescents as a Means of Diagnosis and Therapy,* Nervous Disease Monographs, New York, Coolidge Foundation, 1947.

REIK, THEODORE: *The Unknown Murderer,* New York, Prentice-Hall, Inc., 1945. (Translated by Katherine Jones.)

ROBISON, SOPHIA M.: *Can Delinquency be Measured?* New York, Columbia University Press, 1936.

STRANG, RUTH, Chairman: *Juvenile Delinquency and the Schools,* Chicago, University of Chicago Press, 1948.

SULLENGER, THOMAS A.: *Social Determinants in Juvenile Delinquency,* New York, John Wiley & Sons, Inc., 1936.

TAFT, DONALD R.: *Criminology; An Attempt at a Synthetic Interpretation with a Cultured Emphasis,* New York, The Macmillan Company, 1942.

TANNENBAUM, FRANK: *Crime and the Community,* Boston, Ginn & Company, 1938.

TULCHIN, SIMON: *Intelligence and Crime,* Chicago, University of Chicago Press, 1939.

WALLACK, WALTER M., GLENN M. KENDALL, and HOWARD L. BRIGGS: *Education within Prison Walls,* New York, Teachers College, Columbia University Press, 1939.

YOUNG, PAULINE V.: *Social Treatment in Probation and Delinquency,* New York, McGraw-Hill Book Company, Inc., 1937.

XIV. TECHNICAL DICTIONARIES AND ENCYCLOPEDIAS

(In Psychology, Psychiatry, Education, and Medicine)

DORLAND, W. A. NEWMAN: *The American Illustrated Medical Dictionary,* 21st ed., Philadelphia, W. B. Saunders Company, 1947.

ENGLISH, HORACE B.: *Student's Dictionary of Psychological Terms,* New York, Harper & Brothers, 1934.

GOOD, CARTER V., ed.: *Dictionary of Education,* New York, McGraw-Hill Book Company, Inc., 1945.

HARRIMAN, PHILIP L., ed.: *Encyclopedia of Psychology,* New York, Philosophical Library, Inc., 1946.

————: *The New Dictionary of Psychology,* New York, Philosophical Library, Inc., 1947.

HINSIE, LELAND E., and JACOB SHATZKY: *Psychiatric Dictionary,* New York, Oxford University Press, 1940.

HUTCHINGS, RICHARD H.: *A Psychiatric Work Book,* Utica, N.Y., The State Hospital Press, 1943. (An abridged dictionary.)

MONROE, WALTER S., ed.: *Encyclopedia of Educational Research,* New York, The Macmillan Company, 1941.

"Revised Psychiatric Nomenclature Adopted by the Army," *Mental Hygiene,* July, 1946, 456–476.

RIVLIN, HARRY N., and HERBERT SCHUELER, eds.: *Encyclopedia of Modern Education,* New York, Philosophical Library, Inc., 1943.

STONE, CALVIN P.: *Glossary of Technical Terms,* Stanford University, Calif., Stanford University Press, 1944.

WARREN, HOWARD C., ed.: *Dictionary of Psychology,* Boston, Houghton Mifflin Company, 1934.

WINN, RALPH B., ed.: *Encyclopedia of Child Guidance,* New York, Philosophical Library, Inc., 1943.

AUTHOR INDEX

This index does not include the names of writers listed in the bibliography, pages 531 to 556, already arranged alphabetically under 14 topics.

SUBJECT INDEX